WATERLOO: THE TRUTH AT LAST

WHY NAPOLEON LOST THE GREAT BATTLE

PAUL L DAWSON

FRONTLINE
BOOKS

WATERLOO: THE TRUTH AT LAST
Why Napoleon Lost the Great Battle

This edition published in 2018 by Frontline Books,
an imprint of Pen & Sword Books Ltd,
47 Church Street, Barnsley, S. Yorkshire, S70 2AS

ISBN: 978-1-52670-245-6

CIP data records for this title are available from the British Library

For more information on our books, please visit
www.frontline-books.com,
email info@frontline-books.com
or write to us at the above address.

Printed and bound in the UK by TJ International Ltd, Padstow, Cornwall
Typeset in 10.5/13 point Palatino

To Martin Lancaster. Thank you for your support, friendship and many hours of discussion over the last twenty years.

Contents

Acknowledgements

In the preparation of this book I would like to thank all those who have offered advice and support, and all those who have helped me with my research. I am indebted to Mr John Franklin for his guidance, advice and provision of some research materials. Furthermore, I must also thank my excellent research team, M. Yves Martin, Ian J. Smith, John Lubomski and Sally Fairweather, for their generous assistance with, and photographing of, archival material at the Archives Nationales and Service Historique de la Défence Armée du Tére, in Paris. Without their help, the research for the book could not have been completed in two years, or the data analysed to the same degree.

Alasdair White has been of great assistance in our numerous discussions of the action at Hougoumont, for which I am grateful.

I need to also thank Martin Lancaster for our discussions on the empire, the emperor and Waterloo, as well for our more than twenty years of friendship and adding critical comment and much-needed analysis of the events of 18 June 1815.

Lieutenant Colonel Timmermans must be thanked for providing some illustrations. I heartily encourage visitors to his excellent website: http://Napoléon-monuments.eu/

Rachel Cresswell BA (Hons) PGCE and Sally Fairweather must be thanked for proofreading this text.

Introduction

La Haye Sainte, as many authors try to make clear, was the key to the Battle of Waterloo. This is only true if we ignore the Prussians. Holding or taking La Haye Sainte, as with Hougoumont, was of a very differing level of importance to the French than holding the line between Papelotte and Plancenoit. Despite a plethora of books on the subject, the hard strategic reality is that Hougoumont and La Haye Sainte were sideshows compared to the French and Prussian combats at Plancenoit and Papelotte. In traditional Anglo-phonic histories which ignore the Prussians the most, Hougoumont is presented as a brave bastion of plucky British soldiers holding out against an entire French army corps against all the odds, which is simply not the case. It is best remembered because the participants were mostly British. La Haye Sainte, held by British and Hanoverian troops, is again presented in the same manner. Indeed, the actions of Wellington's right flank are seen as vital tipping points of the battle for three reasons alone: the combatants on the whole spoke English; William Siborne's model agrees with Wellington's own version of events; and it over-emphasises the role of the British army at the cost to other Allied troops. Siborne not only underplayed the Dutch-Belgians, he totally ignored the Prussians and at least half of the French army. Lastly, the attack of the Old Guard is seen as a vital tipping point, as it was the British Foot Guards that a) defeated their French equivalents, and b) therefore won the battle. Not so. Anglo-centric or Anglo-phonic descriptions of the campaign ignore half of the Battle of Waterloo, and three-quarters of all military actions between 15 June and 3 July 1815!

Waterloo was a battle of two halves. The first half was fought between the French and the troops of Lord Wellington, and the second between French and the Prussian troops under Blücher. Since 17 June, Napoléon had been over-confident that he had destroyed the Prussian war machine at Ligny; so confident that he did not order an immediate pursuit of the Prussians on 16 June, but instead issued no orders until after midday on the 17th. The Prussians, therefore, had had a twelve hour head start to withdraw and regroup. News of the Prussians reached Napoléon from Marshal Grouchy around 10.00 on 18 June, who dispatched an order at 6.00 that morning. In this dispatch, Grouchy informed Napoléon that the Prussians were in three columns, and that he had found at least one column. A second letter dispatched from Grouchy at perhaps 11.00 told Napoléon that he was attacking one of the three Prussian columns.

The Prussians first appeared, we are told, around 13.00. Indeed, Napoléon, in an order to Marshal Davout dated 18 June 1815 at 14.30, is clear that he needed more troops and more ammunition if the war was to continue, and that, vitally, the Prussians had joined the left of the Allied army and had started to impact against the French right. It was then horribly clear to Napoléon that he faced a battle on two fronts. He was then certain that one, if not two, Prussian columns were marching to Waterloo. He also knew that Grouchy could not move to Waterloo.

With this book, I aim to describe the battle from the French army's point of view, and explore for the first time, what really happened at Hougoumont, La Haye Sainte and on the French right wing as the Prussians closed in. The actions between Papelotte and Frischermont were critical in the story of the battle, but have so far been seldom studied. Because no red-coated soldiers fought there, and the Waterloo myth says the redcoats won the battle, the study of half of the battle has, to a large extent, been ignored.

Our study is based on two forms of evidence; personal testimony and empirical hard data. What follows is a discussion of these sources to enable the reader to understand the strengths and weaknesses of the material used in the creation of a narrative about Napoléon's last army. The material used had undergone a variety of processes before it was read by the author. Not all the archival paperwork prepared in 1815 has survived to the current day. Not all written memoirs of participants have survived. Those cited here are just those the author could identify—many more may exist in private collections, museums and libraries, and they may well tell a different narrative from that presented here. The narrative has been constructed from the sources available to the author.

In creating our narrative, we have endeavoured to let the primary sources speak for themselves without having to fit what they say into a superficial construct, created by other authors. We must be aware, however, of the limitations and failings of these memoirs as a source of empirical data. The memoir, as Paul Fussell has established, occupies a place between fiction and autobiography.[1]

Since Fussell's work, recent research and developments in the fields of clinical and behavioural psychology, memory and the response to stress has called into question the value of memoirs and so-called eyewitness reports written by participants. Neuroscientist John Coates conducted research into memory; his study undertaken between 2004 and 2012 found that what is recalled from memory is what the mind believes happened rather than what actually happened. This effect is often referred to as 'false memory'.[2]

False memory is created by the eyewitness in two ways. Firstly, having read material since the event described took place, and has overwritten their own memories, they then write down and recall what they have read since the event rather than what they witnessed happen. Secondly, false memory can be created by the mind recording memories of what it thinks ought to have happened. This occurs even if the subject is not contaminated by other sources of data about the event, which we discuss below.

This fits neatly with the post-processual framework for under-standing the past as espoused by Michael Shanks and Christopher Tilley. A memoir, letter or other material used to help create a narrative of events is of limited value in terms of historical interpretation without context. This is defined as hermeneutics. Hermeneutics addresses the relationship between the interpreter and the interpreted; i.e. what does it mean? What were the author's intentions? Is the source authentic?

Therefore, the historian's primary aim is decoding the language of the source used, to understand the ideological intentions of the author, and to locate it within the general cultural context to which the source material belongs.[3] The letters cited in this narrative were written down by combatants or by family members long after the events had

---

1 Paul Fussell, *The Great War and Modern Memory*, Oxford University Press, Oxford, 1975, p. 311.

2 John Coates, *The Hour Between Dog and Wolf*, Fourth Estate, London, 2012.

3 Aron Guverich, *The French Historical Revolution: The Annales School*, in Hodder et al, *Interpreting Archaeology*, Routledge, London, 1995, pp. 158-61. This short paper offers a good introduction to the notion and concept of the Annales School for those unfamiliar with that theory of history.

taken place, and are not necessarily an accurate reflection of events that happened. Each of the writers of the letters included in this work had a personal and unique view of Waterloo—what they experienced will be different from participant to participant. The letters left by the participants recorded what was important to them. However, the time elapsed between the written narrative and the events that took place will affect what is recorded.[4] This is the reason why the police take statements immediately from as many eyewitnesses as possible without allowing them to hear what others are saying. They then tease out the facts from this jumble of data.

Who the writer is corresponding with, will also impact on what they say. Writing to parents, the writer will subconsciously edit out a lot of the detail. Writing to a brother, then the content may be more graphic. In both cases, the writer will concentrate on their regiment's achievements above others. A diary entry will be more candid and honest in what took place. When an author writes about events they cannot have seen or experienced, then we must question the whole content of the text. If the writer has constructed a narrative of events they did not take part in, clearly this is based on what they have been told or read, which may include all of what they have written.

The further the written narrative shifts away from a diary or the events, the closer the written narrative becomes to a figurative fiction. The recollection of crucial events will be re-evaluated and re-contextualised throughout the life of the author to the point of creating the written record—personal memoirs become influenced by the socio-political and socio-economic environment, and the experiences of the author will have an impact on how they recall an event.[5] As time passes between the event and the recollection of it by participants who were there, the degree of cognitive processing distorts the memories even further and various biases creep in, the main one being that people come to believe that the version of events that they recall is actually correct because they recall it. This becomes self-reinforcing until they are unable to accept that their original recall was incorrect. But, the biggest issue with memory recall after time is almost always that the person recalling the event has been influenced by other memories (their

---

4 Fussell, p. 311.
5 Anna Green, Kathleen Troup, *The Houses of History*, Manchester University Press, 1999, p. 231.

own and from other people), which have combined to create a new version of the event.

As critical evaluative historians, we must also take into consideration that observers do not always understand what they saw or thought they saw. The audience to which the author of the narrative is addressed is also important, and this again is a reflection of the social-political background and time of the author.[6]

Similar issues arise with personal letters. Soldiers writing home are doing so with self-imposed censorship, and the stories told differ according to the recipient of the letter; they include what the writer deems important, and also what the writer thinks the reader will think is important, and how the writer understands those events/facts. They are more objective and more reliable than memoirs, because they are a 'snapshot' and are immediate, but have already passed through one level of perception filter: the writer. It is only by collating data from various accounts that something approaching a balanced view of an event can be created. One must also bear in mind that what might be reported as 'fact' by the writer is in all actuality 'perception'.

Part way between memoirs and data come orders written in 1815 concerning troop movements and operation. Consulting the various archive boxes at the Service Historique Armée du Terre, at Vincennes in Paris, quickly reveals that a lot of accepted fact on the battle cannot be verified. As noted earlier, some writers like to present their side of the story, their version of events, and in doing so write biased versions of events, or in some cases are written to prove a point by the son of a senior officer. In the case of Marshal Ney and General Pajol, both their sons set out to rehabilitate their dead fathers' reputations. In doing so they presented dossiers of material relating to 1815 and their actions in the campaign.

To complicate the matter further, all the orders purporting to be from Waterloo are actually from a handwritten manuscript compiled between 1863 and 1865 taken from the collection of the Marquis du Casses. We do not know if the material is a word-for-word copy of the original.

---

6 Paul L. Dawson, *Memoires: Fact or Fiction? The Campaign of 1814*, The Napoleon Series, December 2013, available at http://www. napoleon-series.org/research/eyewitness/c_memoires.html [accessed 28 February 2017]

Therefore, a lot of what we think we know about the French army's movements, and the battles of Quatre-Bras, Ligny, Waterloo and Wavre is based on assuming the copies of documents made by Ney's son, Grouchy, Pajol's son and General Gérard are word-for-word copies and not edited, and that the manuscript and published editions have not redacted orders, reports and similar that present Ney, Grouchy, etc. in a bad light. We must, therefore, dismiss all these books, as they are secondary sources and not primary, empirical data written the day they claim they were.

Thankfully, the order books of Generals Pelet, Reille and Vandamme exist, and are the originals. These allow a careful re-examination of the works of Soult, Grouchy, Pajol and Gérard. In the case of the order book of Reille, it verifies only about 50 per cent of the documents published by Marshal Ney's son, so we have to still treat Ney's orders for the campaign as suspect. Reille's book gives us his first-hand accounts of the campaign that are not found elsewhere, and are written within hours of the end of the battles he writes about. Reille's material, therefore, has much to offer us in understanding the operations of 2nd Corps. The debate over the viability of the personal testimony leaves it impossible to discuss the battle impartially, as the sources are biased and, in most cases, worthless.

In some cases, the firsthand accounts are fabrications by men who were not at Waterloo, yet their account of the battle is accepted with no question. This point has been discussed at some length simply because historians routinely use eyewitness memoirs as though they were a categorical truth rather than a 'version of the truth'; to build a theory of what happened based on one, or even a few, stated sources often results in an incorrect narrative. Other examples abound and it is essential that to fully understand the events it is necessary to cross-reference the memoirs, and to re-interpret rather than to accept their rather romanticised and editorialised content as being correct. This is not to say that the memoirs are valueless or wrong, but a more careful analysis needs to be undertaken. To stress the point again, memoirs written immediately after the battle by participants are more likely to be accurate than those written fifteen or more years after the event. The material gathered by Siborne, de Mauduit and Pelet in the 1830s and 1840s is, in most cases, a decade after the events, yet has been used as the authorised standard version of events, with no critical judgement on the source. In the case of Pelet and de Mauduit, the original documents no longer exist, so we cannot tell if they have been edited for publication.

In order to quantify what memoirs say, we need to look for facts and data. For the Armée du Nord there are several options of obtaining the data open to us.

A vast resource, as yet untapped by the vast majority of researchers and historians for understanding the Battle of Waterloo (as well as the Napoléonic era in general), are the regimental muster lists preserved in the French Army Archives. These are called *Contrôle Nominatif Troupe*. Every officer and man who joined the army had their personal details recorded in a *contrôle* book. Every member of the Legion of Honour had a dossier of their military service, as well as baptismal certificates and other relevant material such as medical notes and date of death. These sources provide bias-free empirical data from which we can reconstruct the life story of the Battle of Waterloo from the French combatants. Empirical data, as defined by the Annales School, is obtained from records concerned with data capturing in a quantifiable way, which in this study comprise:

- Daily strength returns giving the number of men and horses under arms;
- Personal service records; and
- Equipment and uniform purchase and issue ledgers, receipts of purchase and similar documents.

The personal service record is primarily obtained from the relevant *Contrôle Nominatif Troupe* and *Contrôle Nominatif Officier* held in the Service Historique Armée du Terre. These volumes record information relating to every officer and man that was enlisted into a regiment. The information usually comprises, age, height, place of birth, physical appearance, service history, dates of promotion and if the individual was wounded, captured or deserted. If men were killed, deserted or were made prisoner was important, so the regiment could stop the man's pay and also request new recruits. Therefore, the data on the whole is largely bias-free. However, the fate of men in a battle was only recorded by the company adjutant into the register at muster parades after the battle, and relied on the remaining men informing the adjutant of their fate. The source, therefore, is fallible, which is why, as we will note later, we undertook a secondary study to check the viability of these records. These muster lists are the largest single source of empirical data for the Armée du Nord and form the core of the resulting study of the campaign.

These volumes were printed with pro-forma pages so that, in theory, every man enlisted in the army had the same information recorded about them. In order to conduct a data gathering exercise from these volumes, a team of Napoléonic-era researchers was put together, to search the *Registre Contrôle Troupe* as well as officers' muster lists and service papers for members of the Legion of Honour.

The date of entry of every man in a regiment is recorded, as is the fate of the men; for example if they retired, passed to new regiments, or, of importance to this study, if they were killed, wounded, made prisoner of war or deserted. In this way when the data is entered onto a spreadsheet, we can search our data to identify if any correlation exists between men who had been prisoners of war and if they became prisoners at Waterloo or they deserted. The data shows that the bulk of former prisoners of war deserted at Waterloo. We can hypothesise that the treatment of prisoners was so prejudicial to soldiers that the men would rather desert and face the threat of a firing squad than become a prisoner again. What the data also shows is that length of service and rank was no barrier to desertion. Veteran NCOs with ten or more years of service were just as likely to desert as a private with less than a year of service. In this manner we have collected data for all the Imperial Guard, line and light infantry regiments and what books exists for the cavalry, artillery, engineers and train troops. In 1944 the archives at Vincennes were badly damaged when the chateau was partially destroyed by the Gestapo. The chateau had been the headquarters for the Gestapo, and when the Allies were closing in on the city the plan, it seems, was to destroy the place and any incriminating documents. This means that several documents are not available for use by researchers due to water damage, notably for the 5th Légère, 7th Hussars, 12th Chasseurs, 1st and 12th Cuirassiers, 2nd to 6th Chevau-Légère-Lanciers, as well as the 6th and 8th Artillerie à Pied. Overall, my research colleagues and I, despite this lack of access to material, have collected approximately seventy thousand points of data. In addition, almost 5,000 data points have been recorded from the register of prisoners of war retuned to France, as well as 6,000 data points for members of the Legion of Honour, making a data sample of well over 80,000 with, in some cases, triple references for many officers and men.

For men awarded the Legion of Honour we can double check the man's entry in the *Contrôle Nominatif Troupe* by cross-referencing with the archives of the Legion of Honour. By comparing these two documents, we can see that men who were at Waterloo often don't mention this in their *etat de service*, or official service papers. A number of men are listed as wounded in the *Contrôle Nominatif Troupe* and not the *etat de service*, and vice versa. It must be remembered that the *etat de service* was compiled when the man left the army, whereas the *Contrôle Nominatif Troupe* was written in the days immediately after the battle. Despite the often conflicting nature of these two sets of records, comparison of the two has been a valuable check to both sets of archives.

The *etat de service* also provided a wealth of detail on the battle. Many officers and men proudly write about their military achievements. A lot of officers and men left the army soon after Waterloo, and are thus writing about their experience of the battle while still fresh in their heads, and before their memories have become contaminated by what they have read about the battle. As legal documents, which had to be signed by the officer or regimental colonel and a review inspector, who would no doubt question the events the individual wrote about, these records have more value than memoirs and letters home, and have more validity as they are, in essence, sworn statements which would easily be questioned by comrades and senior officers. This untapped source of first-hand accounts for the battle, and campaign as a whole, has provided over 200 new accounts of Waterloo.

The dossiers for legionnaires also hold medical records. These records report the injuries sustained during the empire period, or the injuries sustained at Waterloo, which caused the person to be invalided out from the army. These data points help us to start to understand what happened to a regiment and the type of fighting it endured. For example, a high proportion of men wounded with sabre cuts compared to gunshots suggest a cavalry attack, while a high proportion (or exclusively) gunshot wounds indicate a fire fight between infantry. This data can also be recorded on the various regimental muster lists. By compiling the data from the two sources, not only can we give total casualties to company level for around 80 per cent of the French army at Waterloo, we can also look at the type of injuries, which tells us more about the military operations a unit was involved in.

The 80,000 data points have given us new insights to the battle. By looking at which companies of a battalion took the most casualties, we can start to say on which flank a regiment was mostly affected.

One of the great problems concerning archive material is that it is often incomplete, either from the vagaries of preservation or the loss of documents in more recent times. Housed at the French Army Archives is a dossier of all surviving correspondence for the Armée du

Nord in the Hundred Days. The archive catalogue tells us that the box containing correspondence for the Waterloo period covers the dates 11 to 26 June. However, upon analysis, since the catalogue was created in the 1890s, the material relating to the period 25 June to 3 July is completely missing. No copies of this lost resource exist. Therefore, we are totally ignorant of what material existed.

Adding to the material from the Legion of Honour records and regimental lists come the records of prisoners of war. Two data sets exist, one in London and one in Paris. Neither list is complete, with approximately 75 per cent of the 4,200 or so French records not being found on the British lists. Nor can many of the men actually be found in the relevant muster lists—either they gave false names to the British, or the names were written down phonetically and are thus unintelligible. Therefore, we have to combine the two data sets to create a single entity. However, where men are recorded in a muster list as shipped to England and returned to France from imprisonment, we can chart the individual after Waterloo. These records mean that we can test the muster lists to ascertain if a man recorded as prisoner really was made a prisoner. By cross-referencing the muster lists with the prison lists we can confirm the number of men made prisoner and taken to England, and confirm the number of men per regiment who really were made prisoner. Thus, as we shall see, this new data set has a very major impact on our understanding of the battle.

Finally, we must also stress the role of the writer in the creation of the narrative. We all have preconceived ideas and personal biases about historical events based on what we have read about the subject and our own political, economic, sociological and ideological grounds; these will impact on the way the historian interprets the source material. No historian is free from bias. I am pro-Napoléon and anti-Britain at the start of the nineteenth century. I endeavour, though, to be even-handed, and offer critique against Napoleon and his commanders where it is justified.

I also need to make it clear that the narrative of events of the Battle of Waterloo, and others of the 1815 campaign, can only be based on remembrances of participants. We have no hard empirical fact for what actually occurred and when. The casualty data does not say when men were killed or wounded, merely on 18 June 1815. The hard data has to be contextualised by the field of battle, i.e. physical evidence (how did the landscape affect the battle? How did buildings affect the battle?) and also written testimonies from participants, many of who wrote down their own narration of events many decades later. The resulting narrative is a compromise, a best fit of all the evidence to try and create a coherent and logical narration of that day over 200 years ago.

What I present in the narrative of the events of Waterloo is an interpretation of the differing sources of data. It should be seen as *a* version of events and not *the* version of events. My underlying theoretical background is as a post-processual archaeologist, and an empirical historian. The post-processual framework as espoused by Shanks and Hodder states:[7]

- Creation of the historical narrative is an ongoing process, there is no final and definitive account of the past as it was;
- Interpretation is multi-vocal: different interpretations of the same source material are quite possible;
- Therefore we can expect a plurality of interpretations; and
- Interpretation of source material to construct a narrative is thereby affected by the response, desire and needs of different interpreters.

History is multi-vocal, and therefore the French narrative is equally as valid an interpretation of the events of Waterloo as the British. This is Waterloo as I understand it to be from the data I have amassed. Others may—and will—draw differing conclusions to the same material.

---

7 Michael Shanks, Ian Hodder, *Processual, postprocessual and interpretive archaeologies* in Hodder et al, *Interpreting Archaeology*, Routledge, London, 1995, p. 4.

Chapter 1

1815

Paris, in spring 1815, was restless. Unemployment and financial hardships, despite the longed-for peace, had not endeared the people to the king. With peace, thousands had been made unemployed with the closure of clothing and equipment factories that had been established to supply the army. In addition, the Napoléonic state had required a huge bureaucracy to function and with the change of government many hundreds of pen-pushers were without work, and what jobs had existed for the men who had served the state (in many cases for over a decade) were being given to returning royalists. Economic hardships were not helped by the new government levying heavy taxation to put money back into the government's coffers. France was virtually bankrupt and to save money the army, now on a peace footing, had jettisoned thousands of men who now flooded onto the labour market. The Duke of Wellington, the British ambassador, reported on the mood in Paris to the British government. Thankfully for the new government the large number of malcontents had no unified voice of opposition, nor could it agree on what it opposed. The opposition lacked a figurehead around whom they could rally. Rebellion and war was in the air in the spring of 1815.

The Congress of Vienna was busy endeavouring to re-draw the map of Europe; the process was not going smoothly at all. France, backed by her allies (Austria and Great Britain), seemed on the brink of declaring war over the fate of Saxony, one of Napoléonic France's allies, against the expansionist aims of Prussia. To face this crisis the French army needed to be brought up to a war footing. One of the last acts of the monarchy on 9 March 1815 was to call up 12,000 half-pay officers and 30,000 half-pay men, of which it seems some 8,952 men returned to the army.[8] We need to note that an amicable agreement was made on 24 October 1815 to solve the Saxony problem, the former Napoléonic Duchy of Warsaw was divided among the allied powers. Russia received most of the territory, the district of Poznań was handed to Prussia and Kraków became a free city. In addition, Prussia received 40 per cent of Saxony—later known as the Province of Saxony, with the remainder returned to King Frederick Augustus I. Prussia would later gobble up Bavaria, Westphalia, Württemberg and what remained of Saxony in expansionist wars in the middle years of the decade. Into this political milieu stepped Napoléon Bonaparte in March 1815.

When Napoléon returned to France in spring 1815, we forget that he was forced to do so as the treaty he had signed with the Allies on 13 April 1814 had not been upheld—Napoléon was out of sight and out of mind as the Allies debated a new vision for Europe in Vienna. Napoléon was denied his rights and income as agreed by the Congress of Vienna. Indeed, the British position was that the French nation had been in a state of rebellion since 1789 and that Napoléon Bonaparte was a usurper. Lord Castlereagh explained that he would not sign the Treaty of Chaumont, or any other treaty on behalf of the king, because to do so would recognise the legitimacy of Napoléon as emperor of the French. Given no treaty existed between Britain and Napoléon, the British Government had no grounds on which to declare war and, moreover, was bound by no treaty to pay the stipend to the former emperor. Clearly this was a case of 'one rule for one, one rule for the others'. The Allies failed to keep to their side of the treaty. In trying to explain to the British House of Commons as to why the treaty had not been acted upon, British Foreign Secretary Lord Castlereagh noted on 13 March 1815 that:[9]

> The French Government persevered in the opinion that the suspicious nature of some of Buonaparte's acts at Elba disentitled him from a conditional obligation, unless he previously tendered an explanation of certain acts which bore a dubious interpretation; but at my suggestion of the impolicy arising out of any complaint which he might want to create on his part, a person was dispatched by the French Government to Elba, to give him that quantum of aid which would prevent the possibility of his incurring that species

---

8 *Journal Militaire*, 2nd semester, 1814, p. 28.
9 Paul Lindsay Dawson, Benjamin Gaskell Lecture presented to mark the bicentenary of the Battle of Waterloo, 2015.

of privation, but not to give the entire stipend until a satisfactory explanation was given relative to certain points of his conduct, which lay open to suspicion. So, that it is evident there can be no ground for any argument in defence of his conduct, from the non-payment of a stipend which, as yet, has not become due.

We do note however, that there are no terms in the treaty that give payment dates. What suspicious acts Napoléon did on Elba to render the treaty null is not known. Clearly, the Allies had no intention of ever paying the stipend due to Napoléon. Furthermore, the treaty did not bar Napoléon from returning to France (it only barred him from taking government). So, until he returned to Paris and took control of France once more, he had not broken any treaty. Sir Francis Burdett MP spoke to the British House of Commons on this matter thus:[10]

> It was said that Buonaparte had entered France in contravention of the treaty concluded with him; but in that treaty, there was no mention of his not entering France, I cannot see how he has contravened the treaty.

He further added that:[11]

> [The] government would be blameable if they attempted to impose a governor on an independent nation against its will. Was it not plain that Buonaparte was the ruler of the French people's choice? The step he had taken had very absurdly been called the invasion of France. But whoever heard of a single man invading a nation of thirty million inhabitants, and gaining the sovereignty of that nation against its will? The fact was that the nation wished for him, and had in a great degree wished for him from their dislike of the government which he superseded. There was not a man in France who did not see a new order of things rising up under the Bourbons, and who did not fear that property was insecure. The government of Louis did not act up to the principles of that constitution which his brother had accepted for him before his return.

The treaty of Chaumont on 1 March 1814 bound the Allies to act only in defence if attacked. Despite France not having acted offensively or in breach of the treaty, the Allies declared war anyway on 13 March.

---

10 Dawson, Benjamin Gaskell. Lecture.
11 Dawson, Benjamin Gaskell. Lecture.

It was only on 20 March, legally speaking, that Napoléon broke the treaty with the Congress of Vienna. Given that the Allies had broken the treaty, the legality of any war based on a treaty the Allies failed to uphold is suspect. Indeed, in the House of Commons, George Tierney (1761-1830), the Whig MP, declared that parliament and the Congress of Vienna were blind, if not mad, for declaring war on France and Napoléon, stating that the French had chosen Napoléon rather than being forced to suffer under a tyrant that had been forced on them. He added that it was the right of all free men to choose their leaders. He declared that the Congress of Vienna was nothing short of a congress against France, and stated that the destruction of France was to destroy freedom.

Similar views were echoed by the Duke of Devonshire, the Duke of Bedford, Lord Holland, Earl Grey, Marquis of Tavistock, Samuel Romilly, Francis Horner and by the Duke of Wellington's nephew, Richard, Marquis Wellesley MP.

Regardless of the legal arguments about treaty violation, the Congress of Vienna declared war on Napoléon and not France or the French people, and sought to replace him with the Bourbon monarch. Clearly, it was assumed with Napoléon gone, the war would be over with no further ramifications in France. Little thought had been put into what happened when the war aims were over. The Allies pressed for regime change, much like wars of recent years, but thought little of the implications.

Myth tells us that Napoléon returned to France on a wave of hatred towards the Bourbons by the army, mainly officers and men on half-pay, a force that numbered perhaps 40,000 malcontents, most of which had been paid, but felt they had been badly treated by being placed on half-pay, and did not recognise the need to reduce the strength of the army to a peacetime footing. The call up of men to face the Saxony crisis returned many of these unemployed soldiers back to the army, diluting the opposition to the monarchy. But, we accept that the 'why me and not someone else should be on half-pay' was perhaps the primary grievance former soldiers had with the monarch, as opposed to being diehard Bonapartists. As we noted earlier, in 1814 and 1815 opposition to the monarch was not solely restricted to Bonapartists, many were republicans, diehard Jacobins, Orleanists and Liberalists, all of whom with their own agenda on how France should be governed. For Napoléon to succeed in rallying France behind him, he had to appeal to the disparate opposition groups, which led fundamentally to his own downfall as he had no single power base. Unlike 1799, he had to win over key sections of society to support his new government in a coalition, as opposed to the virtual dictatorship he had enjoyed previously.

At the Ecole Militaire in Paris on 1 June the army swore an oath of allegiance to Napoléon, and the people accepted the new constitution which had been voted for in a democratic referendum. An eyewitness was Colonel Noël, of the horse artillery, who reflects the mood of the army:[12]

> On 1 June, the ceremony took place on the Champ-de-Mars.
>
> Deputations from the military intermingled with the state bodies and authorities occupied a huge circular amphitheatre built against the front of the military academy, and rising to the level of the first floor. In front of this an altar was erected and beyond, arranged on both sides, were the troops of the National Guard stretching to the banks of the Seine.
>
> The emperor entered from the first floor of the military school, and took his place on a golden throne in the middle of the terraces. He wore a purple robe embroidered with gold and lined with ermine. He had on his head a black cap, surmounted with feathers held in place by a large diamond.
>
> Upon arrival, everyone stood up and he was acclaimed by all the spectators. His family was coldly received. They were not very popular and had cost France dearly.
>
> At the coronation, I was part of the deputation of the 1st Horse Artillery, the Champ-de-Mai, I had part of the 4th Regiment under my command, and I could see that on 1 June 1815 there were more cheers than on 2 December 1804. They seem less formal and sincerer. Many sympathies were returned to Napoléon.
>
> The Bourbons and their entourage had made themselves so unpopular that, although they had a thirst for peace, they still preferred the emperor, even with the prospect of war. We knew he had tried everything to keep the peace, and that the allied sovereigns had refused to receive his envoys; he was humiliated and angry. We sincerely believed that he had become open to more liberal ideas: the drafting of the Additional Act, entrusted to Benjamin Constant,

---

12 Jean-Nicolas-Auguste Noël, *Souvenirs Militaires d'un officier du Premier Empire*, Librairie des Deux Empires, 1999, p. 216.

the leader of the Constitutionalists; the choice of Carnot as Minister of the Interior; restored freedom of the press; his moderation; the absence of persecution against his enemies; pledges for the future; he was well aware, moreover, that the opinion had worked.

Finally, fate put us struggling with the whole of Europe, and it was felt that the genius of Napoléon alone in the terrible circumstances we were in gave us some chance of success. One could deplore his return, but France had again chosen him for sovereign; there was no alternative but to follow him.

The emperor sat on his throne, a Mass followed by a sung Te Deum; it was nothing like the imposing ceremonies of Catholic worship, accompanied by military pomp. There were 50,000 men under arms and one hundred pieces of cannon.

The show was great and severe. The faces of those present did not seem to be giving thanks to the heavens, but implored it for help. Everyone seemed to feel their help were needed.

The oath to the Constitution was sworn on the Gospel and was followed by the distribution of eagles to the National Guard and deputations from the regiments. The whole ceremony was beautiful.

Marshal Soult noted:[13]

An impressive ceremony has sanctified our institutions. The emperor received from the representatives of the people, deputations from the army, the expression and desire for the whole nation for the acceptance of the Additional Act to the Constitution of the Empire; a new oath has united France with the emperor; our destinies can be fulfilled, despite all the efforts of the impious league; they cannot separate the interests of a great people from our hero, whose brilliant triumphs are universally applauded.

It is when the national will shows itself with vigour that war cries are heard; it is when France is at peace with all Europe that foreign armies advance on our borders; what is the goal of this new coalition? Does it want to remove France from the existing nations? Does it plan to put twenty-eight million Frenchmen into servitude? How could they have forgotten the glory of our army? The impulse of a generous people no power can overcome and posterity will admire. To arms!

---

13 SHDDT: C3 *Dossier 1 Juin. Ordre du Jour 1 Juin 1815.*

> Soon the signal will be given, everyman shall do his duty, our
> phalanxes will be victorious and gain new splendour against our
> enemies. Soldiers! Napoléon will guide us, we will fight for the
> independence of our country; we are invincible!

Nominated as tribunes to the new government were several of Napoléon's marshals, who had sat in the Chamber of Peers during the previous Napoléonic administration, namely, Marshals Masséna, Lefebvre, Seurrier, Moncey and Kellermann.[14] Marshal Ney was also appointed as a tribune.[15] Napoléon was escorted by Marshals Soult, Grouchy, Oudinot and Jourdan. Myth implies very few marshals rallied in 1815, when in fact ten were present at the Champ de Mai. Indeed, Soult, Ney, Jourdan and Grouchy were mounted and rode alongside the emperor.[16] Mortier is noticeably missing, as is Brune, and for some reason Davout was not present either. Oudinot, we are told, rode as part of the emperor's cortege,[17] but his biographer makes it clear he was not involved in these events nor had rallied to the emperor.[18]

With the Allies ranged in opposition to him, Napoléon's hand was forced into taking military action. To prevent an invasion of France, he made plans to attack the mobilised Allied troops under Wellington and Blücher in the Netherlands. Despite being outnumbered, as in the 1814 campaign, Napoléon's modus operandi was to keep the two forces separate, over which he had a numerical advantage, and defeat each army in turn by rapid concentrations of the French army, just as he had so effectively done in 1814. While he would attack in the Netherlands with the Armée du Nord, the borders of France would be controlled by the Corps d'Observation:

- General Jean Rapp's Armée du Rhine was in position against the Austrians of Schwarzenberg;
- General Lecourbe's Armée du Jura faced 37,000 Swiss;
- Marshal Suchet's Armée des Alpes was placed to guard against the Austrio-Piedmontese army;
- Marshal Brune's Armée du Var was to contain the Neapolitan Army;

---

14 *Journal des débats politiques et littéraires*, 3 June 1815, p. 3.
15 ibid.
16 ibid.
17 ibid.
18 Gaston Steigler, *Le Maréchal Oudinot*, Plon, Paris, 1894, p. 371.

- In the department of the Vendée, General Lamarque was dispatched with 10,000 troops, including elements of the Young Guard;
- General Decean was at Toulouse with the Armée des Pyrenees Orientales;
- General Clausel with the Armée des Pyrenees Occidentales was at Bordeaux; and
- The minister of war, Marshal Davout, had 20,000 troops to protect Paris.

On 4 June, General Deriot issued orders for the Imperial Guard to move out. The artillery, matelots, engineers and train were ordered to move out on 5 June. The cavalry was to form two columns and was to take three days to arrive at Soissons, arriving there by 7 June. The 2nd Regiment of Grenadiers and the same of chasseurs were to move out on 7 June, along with the two regiments of voltigeurs and tirailleurs. They were to arrive at Soissons no later than 9 June. General Lefèbvre-Desnoëttes was placed in command of the two light cavalry regiments of the Guard, with Edouard de Colbert as his deputy and commanding officer of the lancers. The remainder of the Guard infantry moved out on 8 June. Each infantryman of the Guard was issued forty cartridges and four flints, each cavalryman twenty cartridges and two flints.[19]

A day behind schedule, in the early hours of 15 June 1815, the French army surged into the Netherlands. Capturing Brussels and defeating Wellington and Blücher would topple the British government and send shockwaves back to Vienna, and the hastily formed military coalition would have collapsed. Terms could then be dictated for peace between France and the Congress. Furthermore, the French-speaking population of the Netherlands would no doubt have risen in support of the emperor, further strengthening his position. The French-speaking population only rose up in 1830 to form modern day Belgium.

Winning early victories at Charleroi and Gilly, two battles were fought on 16 June; neither side ever gained the advantage over the other. After Ligny, the Prussians withdrew north-east and Wellington north. Marshal Grouchy was sent on the early afternoon on 17 June to chase the Prussians, and the emperor headed north with the left wing of the army towards Brussels. Wellington's rearguard was found at Genappe,

---

19 SHDDT: C15 39 *Décrets Cent-Jours 1815. Deriot Ordre du Jour, 4 Juin 1815.*

and a skirmish ensued during a torrential thunderstorm all the way to Waterloo. The *Journal de Rouen* of 21 June 1815 reported that:[20]

> We have received news from the army, dated the 17th, 11.00 in the evening. The emperor and his headquarters are at Plancenoit on the road to Brussels, which is five and a half leagues from this place. The Duke of Wellington is withdrawing to Brussels, Blücher on to the Meuse. Comte Lobau is marching to Namur, whose advanced guard is within half a league of this place.
>
> It is estimated that we have lost twelve thousand dead, killed by the enemy during the affair of the 16th.
>
> Among the French that have been wounded are General Girard, General Comte de Valmy and Prince Jérôme.

An unknown French officer writes in 1815:[21]

> It was a dreadful night. The rain fell in torrents and was most oppressive to the troops bivouacked as they were in the midst of mire and not having had time to construct any temporary shelter.
>
> Daylight having appeared, the French took their arms and were surprised to perceive that the English not only remained where they had been the night before, but appeared as if resolved to defend their positions.

The French took up what shelter they could. That night the Allied army drew up in its positions along the ridge to the north of La Haye Sainte. The night passed slowly for the men and horses devoid of warmth and dry clothing. Adjutant-Commandant Toussaint Jean Trefcon, an officer in the French 2nd Corps, commanded by General Reille, writes:[22]

> The rain had started to fall during the afternoon and at night it became a terrible storm; the rain had soaked the roads, filling them with a thick mud with which we were all covered from head to toe. The food convoy did not arrive until late at night, which meant

---

20 *Journal de Rouen*, 21 June 1815, p. 1.
21 The *Derby Mercury*, 16 November 1815. The similarity between this letter and that of Beraud are remarkable, suggesting either Beraud is the author of the 1815 letter or that he had access to this letter.
22 Toussaint-Jean Trefcon, *Carnet de la campagne du colonel Trefcon, 1793-1815*, E. Dubois, Paris, 1914.

that many soldiers slept without eating. I worked at length with General Bachelu in a barn, we received reports of colonels and generals, the actual situations and took our detailed provisions for the battle which was to deliver the next day. After dining on a very brief meal we divided a bundle of straw between the two of us. In the night, General Husson, who was unable to find a billet, soon joined us and I shared with him a little of the straw I had left. The soldiers were no less tired than us, they went to bed where they could, most simply slept in the mud.

On the day that the Battle of Waterloo was fought, the Chamber of Peers was discussing the situation in France. Joseph Fouché published a report into the political and economic state of the French Empire, and spoke out against Napoléon's mode of silencing his critics and stated that government had to govern according to public opinion— an argument for more democracy and legislative power for the two chambers. Fouché urged the chambers to 'put their minds to the laws that the current circumstances demanded of them'.[23] Fouché was beginning the process that would see him elected as president of France and overthrow Napoléon. As soon as Napoléon had left Paris it had become a hotbed of political dissent. There were ministers in his quickly assembled government itching for the chance to overthrow him, just as they had done in 1814. The Chamber of Deputies had many members willing to support their aims.

Morning of 18 June

Napoléon's headquarters were set up in the small farm at La Caillou. The little walled orchard that was on the northern side of the complex had been commandeered as a bivouac for the 'duty battalion', which comprised the 1st Battalion 1st Chasseurs under Duuring's command. The first room on entering the building was reserved for the duty officers, and in the rooms on the first floor were bales of straw for the staff officers. The well-known story of the battle states Jérôme Bonaparte and General Reille had found lodgings at the Hotel du Roi d'Espagne in Genappe. During the night, at around 2.00, Napoléon received a dispatch from Marshal Grouchy that the Prussians were withdrawing either to Wavre or Perwes. He never replied to this dispatch, and let Grouchy continue with his movements; ergo it seems Napoléon was in agreement with Grouchy's course of action.

---

23 *Journal de Paris*, 18 June 1815, p. 2.

The sun rose at 3.57. It was still raining and there was no prospect of the rain ceasing. Surgeon Renée Bourgeois, of the 12th Cuirassiers, writes:[24]

> The camp was much worse this night than the last, the rain having changed the earth into mud which was already soft. The rain also made the cold excessive, and we were not able to make many fires because the rain fell in torrents. It was not until dawn, the 18th, as time went on it became more serene and we could start maintaining fires. On all sides the musketry was soon to be heard by confused and irregular discharges, each preparing his weapons and awaiting the next battle.

Only some elements of the army were at Waterloo, with most troops strung out between Genappe and La Belle Alliance. Soon the many French regiments hit the road, arriving at Waterloo some time later. Adjutant-Commandant Toussaint Jean Trefcon, of 2nd Corps, writes:[25]

> The 18th. We were under arms at daybreak and ready to go. General Reille gave the order to start at five in the morning. En route we received an order from the major-general to stop, to clean their weapons, and to cook a meal. This news was received with joy, for many soldiers were dying of hunger…At eight o'clock we resumed our march forward. We stopped at the farm of La Caillou. The emperor was with a large staff. He had lunch. The emperor sent for General Reille, and he had a long conversation with him. At nine o'clock, the corps of Reille arrived at La Caillou. Reille and Jérôme entered it. The emperor asked about Reille's feelings of the British army, having often fought them in Spain.

Due to the army marching on a single road, many regiments had yet to join Napoléon as they had been caught up in the bottleneck of congestion trying to pass through Genappe. As dawn broke, 6th Corps was at Genappe still, with the Imperial Guard strung out between Genappe and Rossomme. It seems the infantry, due to the rain, could not march cross-country. Battalion Commander Joseph-Marcelin Rullieres, of the 95th Regiment of Line Infantry, notes in 1856:[26]

---

24 François-Thomas Delbare, *Relation circonstanciée de la dernière campagne de Buonaparte, terminée par le bataille de Mont-Saint-Jean, dite de Waterloo ou de la Belle-Alliance*, J. G. Dentu, Paris, 1816.

25 Trefcon.

26 SHDDT: GD 2 1135.

...the rain had started at two o'clock in the afternoon and soon drenched the ground and forced the army to march on the main road, in one column. The general movement was slowed considerably. It was almost dark when the 1st Corps, being formed in columns, arrived straddling the road, not far behind La Belle Alliance, where the headquarters of the emperor had been established. It was raining heavily and the soldiers had mud up to their knees, it was impossible to light a fire, even for soup. The night was so very bad for the French army. There we learned that the British army had taken position at some distance in front, leaning against the Soignes Forest where she had been sheltered by the trees and made fires.

Another eyewitness to the events writing very soon after the battle was General Drouot, who recalled:[27]

At daybreak, the enemy was perceived in the same position. The weather was horrible, which had ruined the roads.

The *Journal de Rouen* reported:[28]

The 18th. At this moment, 6.00 in the morning, the cannon can be heard; the army will force its entry into Brussels and Belgium will be in our hands.

About the start to the day, General d'Erlon writes with a good dose of hindsight that:[29]

An officer was sent in the morning from the emperor, who had realised that the enemy continued its retreat. I received orders to put myself on the road and to pursue them with vigour. Having considered the movement of the enemy more than any other officer, I sent my chief-of-staff to the emperor, telling him that I thought the enemy was preparing to receive battle.

The emperor came immediately to the outposts I had accompanied him to, having dismounted to get closer to enemy vedettes, and examine more closely the movements of the British army. He saw that I was right, and being satisfied that the army took position, he

---

27 *Journal de l'Empire*, 27 June 1815, pp. 1-2.
28 *Journal de Rouen*, 19 June 1815.
29 Jean-Baptiste Drouët, *Le maréchal Drouet, comte d'Erlon: Vie militaire écrit par lui même*, Guvatve, Paris, 1844.

said: 'order the troops to make the soup, to put their weapons into good condition, and we'll see about noon'.

That morning, the emperor ate, and in the pouring rain reconnoitred the battlefield, as Mameluck Ali noted:[30]

> The next day, the 18th, the emperor rose fairly early. He breakfasted with the grand marshal, the Duc de Dalmatie and some other persons, and then mounted his horse, followed by the major-general, the Duc de Dalmatie, the grand marshal, General Fouler, and all his suite. He went to the advanced posts to reconnoitre the positions occupied by the enemy and laid out the order of battle.

Napoléon had breakfasted at La Caillou about 7.00. He had eaten in company with his brother Jérôme, as well as with Bertrand, and Marshals Ney and Soult, Maret, Drouot and others. There is little doubt that the main subject discussed over breakfast was how he intended to fight the battle. The vexed subject of the time needed for the troops to arrive in the front line to take up their planned positions and the situation of the enemy were no doubt also topics of discussion. Based upon this viewing of the battlefield, the emperor issued his orders timed at 5.00:[31]

> The emperor orders the army to be ready to attack at nine o'clock in the morning. The commanders of the army corps will assemble their troops, see that the soldiers' weapons are in good order and allow the soldiers to prepare a meal and consume it. By nine o'clock in the morning precisely each army corps will be formed up in line of battle, along with their artillery and ambulances, in the same positions as indicated by the emperor in his orders of yesterday evening.

> The lieutenant-generals commanding the corps of the army of infantry and cavalry are to send field officers to the major-general to tell him of their positions and to carry orders.

---

30 Mameluck Ali, *Souvenirs sur l'empereur Napoléon,* Ed. Christophe Bourachot, Arléa, Paris, 2000.
31 No original copy of this order can be found in the boxes of documents at Vincennes nor in the order book of Marshal Soult at the Archives Nationales in Paris. The first order on 18 June is timed at 10.00 to Marshal Grouchy. However, the transcript we present was published in 1826 by Vaudoncourt. Vaudoncourt clearly had access to material now lost.

Despite the rain and mud Napoléon was preparing to fight, just as he had done at Dresden in 1813 or the campaign in France with mud on the shoes of his soldiers and wet greatcoats on their backs. One of the great tales of Waterloo is that mud delayed the start of the battle. This idea does not stand up to much scrutiny. The waterlogged ground, or at least the rain that was falling in the early hours of 18 June, was commented upon by the Duc de Bassano, Hugue-Bernard Maret, secretary of state and Peer of France as he sat at La Caillou that morning in a letter to the Minister of Foreign Affairs in Paris:[32]

> In the current situation of the army, communications are easy from one army corps to another, but this situation is likely soon to change…The campaign started with great success. The victory of Ligny and Fleurus is of very high importance. The right and centre of our army crushed the elite of the Prussian army. The morale of this army will be adversely affected for a long time to come. Our left has not obtained results as decisive, but they were also important. Lord Wellington commanded in person the struggle for the position of four roads between Sombreffe and Nivelles. The English, especially the Scots, were badly mauled. Their killed and wounded is estimated at four thousand men. Our army is as good as it was in our more prosperous times. Although the weather thwarts us. We will soon have more news for you…

At the time of the 5.00 order being written, there was no prospect of any improvement in the weather. The French and Allies had no idea when the rain would stop, we only know it did with hindsight. At the moment that the weather actually did improve, ironically about 9.00, there was no prospect for the fields to dry up to such an extent that troops could be moved with relative ease a few hours later. Napoléon made plans accordingly to attack, regardless of weather. The rain the previous day had not stopped operations at Genappe or Waterloo. As far as either army commander could tell, 18 June may have been one of continual rain based on the evidence they had to hand. Battles had been fought in torrential rain and deep snow, so rain would not have meant the battle would not have taken place. Even if it had not rained on the night of 17 June, the ground would still have been waterlogged after two major downpours on the 16th and 17th.

---

32 Jean-Phillipe Tondeur, Patrice Courcelle, Jean Jacques Patyn, Paul Megnak, *Carnets de la Campagne No. 10*—Editions de La Belle Alliance, 2007, p. 88.

To answer the question if mud prevented the deployment of artillery at Waterloo, the author and the living history group, Association Britannique de la Garde Impériale, instigated an experiment with the Royal Artillery at Topcliffe Barracks, North Yorkshire. Using a full size, full weight reconstructed 12-pounder field gun it was demonstrated that the design of the gun carriage was such that when the gun was dragged forward using *bricoles* (drag ropes), the trail end easily dragged through mud. The mud was generated by emptying two fire engines of water and driving a Challenger II tank across the saturated ground.[33] The experience clearly demonstrated that mud did not delay moving the guns. Soldiers have fought with muddy boots since Waterloo and it just became an excuse for eyewitnesses, and many officers fell into the trap of 'false memory'. Battalion Commander Jacques Bosse, of the 95th Regiment of Line Infantry, narrates (with hindsight) that moving cannon and cavalry:[34]

> ...was not practicable. I say this because I looked at myself in the morning of the 18th. Some officers deceived the emperor; they said that the artillery could manoeuvre. No, the infantry sank into the mud to the ankle and neither could the cavalry or artillery manoeuvre before eleven o'clock in the morning, or even by noon. I declare with sincerity, because it is the exact truth, because the terrain would not allow it before 11 a.m. or noon.

The battle's commencement was delayed by the fact that his army was not yet on the field. Indeed, the Imperial Guard at 9.00 had not yet even broken camp! Captain-Adjutant-Major Prax, of the 3rd Chasseurs, narrates the start of the day as follows:[35]

> On the 18th, at seven in the morning, we took up arms. They sent word that the emperor would need his guard during the day. This warning was received with enthusiasm, with gratitude the chasseurs went to clean their guns, and to put them in good condition to fire. We left our bivouac, however, about eight o'clock, and after crossing the main road and marching parallel to it for one hour, we took up a position behind a hill on which the Imperial Headquarters were established.

---

33 'Massacre at Waterloo', part of *Battlefield Detectives* series aired by Channel 5, 26 March 2005.
34 *La Souvenir Napoléonien No. 337*, September 1984.
35 D'Avout, *'L'infanterie de la garde a Waterloo'* in *Carnet de la Sabretache*, Vol. 13, 1905, p. 125.

At daybreak, the command of General Guyot was at Maransard, south of Plancenoit, where they had bivouacked the night, as General Guyot explains:[36]

> 18 June—Mont-Saint-Jean (two miles) In the morning at seven o'clock I received the order to go with my division, composed of the grenadier and dragoon guards, to headquarters of the emperor. I arrived there at 10.30. The army was concentrated at this point, since the reconnaissance of the avantgarde saw the English army position at Waterloo, his right resting on Braine-la-Leude, Ohain on his left.
>
> The emperor's army was formed up and moved forward. The general attack began around two o'clock; the enemy fired cannons at our centre without inhibiting the movement, due to the inequality of the land our army is obliged to manoeuvre and a large part of the enemy shots were unable to fall on them. Our right flank debouched and the enemy began a general engagement along the line, they are fighting on both sides fiercely. The terrain offers no obstacles; some lowland and hillocks only diversify the battlefield.
>
> The English army was stationed on a small rise in the shape of a half-circle, his seventy pieces of artillery were partly un-limbered and thirty paces to the rear in the extension of a valley where was placed all his infantry in masses and the cavalry: both arms are out to act as cover for the artillery while the batteries were forced to be abandoned through the effect of our various charges of cavalry. This tactic has prevailed on us because we have the courage to deliver it and we have discovered this. Towards three o'clock the enemy, seeing our movements on his left, began a general cavalry charge which had thrown our right wing into a little disorder. It was rejected immediately with large losses.

Clearly, it seems that as 18 June dawned, Napoléon's forces were not yet fully assembled until after midday, so an early start to the battle was, it seems, never going to happen. The state of the sodden ground as a point of delay diverted attention from the fact that the French army was not yet ready for action at 9.30 as Napoléon had wished.

The dispersed deployments of the French army, as opposed to well known myths regarding mud, delayed the Battle of Waterloo, and

---

36 Guyot, *Carnets de la Campagne du General Comte Guyot 1792-1815*, Tessedire, 1999.

perhaps robbed Napoléon of the time needed to defeat Wellington and then turn on Blücher.

As with Ney on 16 June, Napoléon was faced with the same situation. Napoléon criticised Ney on 16 June for not keeping his forces concentrated, yet on the morning of 18 June, his own forces were spread out up to ten miles from the battlefield. The French army was not concentrated. This mistake was a direct contributor to the loss of the battle. Napoléon knew the value of keeping his forces concentrated, yet had allowed the army corps under his command to separate. As we shall see, when Grouchy's daybreak dispatch arrived, Napoléon knew some of the Prussians from Ligny were heading to join Wellington; every hour of delay brought them closer. As with Ney at Quatre-Bras, he chose to wait for his forces to be concentrated. This, with hindsight, was a catastrophic mistake.

Around 9.00 the army began to take up its positions, as General of Division Marie Joseph Raymnd Delort, commander of the 14th Division of General Milhaud's 4th Cavalry Division, recalls:[37]

> The 18th at daybreak, the English army was ranged in battle, in front of Mont-Saint-Jean, and covered the main roads of Brussels and that to Nivelles. To the right was a ravine near Braine Leud and his left were the heights which were crowned with of hamlet of La Haye. Already the enemy line had been recognised by Engineer General Haxo, and it was not supported by fortifications, but the English occupied the castle of Hougoumont and the farm of La Haye Sainte with elite troops, to cover their centre right and centre left.

> Around nine o'clock the army divided into eleven columns and moved off. From all sides the trumpets sounded, the drums beat and the music played the cherished airs of victory. At ten o'clock this great movement was completed and the deepest silence reigned, the troops were all in admirable order and occupied the positions that had been assigned to them. Immediately, the emperor travelled across the lines and his presence roused in the soldiers what was for them the omen of victory. He placed himself on the heights of Rossomme, from where he could discover the movements of both armies. The reserve area was near the Imperial Headquarters and occupied a central position ready to go everywhere or give relief as necessary.

---

37 *Nouvelle Revue Retrospective*, Paris, January 1897, p. 374.

Marshal Soult sent this order to Grouchy at 10.00 on 18 June 1815 in the wake of Grouchy's own dispatch:[38]

> Mr marshal, the emperor has received your last report dated six o'clock in the morning at Gembloux.
>
> You speak to the emperor of only two columns of Prussians, which have passed at Sauvenieres and Sart-à-Walhain. Nevertheless, reports say a third column, which was a pretty strong one, had passed by Géry and Gentinnes, directed on Wavre, reported by Milhaud's cavalry before they left.
>
> The emperor instructs me to tell you that at this moment His Majesty has decided to attack the English army in its position at Waterloo in front of the Soignes Forest. Thus, His Majesty desires that you are to continue your movement to Wavre in order to approach us to put you in our sphere of operations and your communications with us, pushing before you those portions of the Prussian army which have taken this direction and which may have stopped at Wavre [where] you ought to arrive as soon as possible.
>
> You will follow the enemy columns which are on your right side with light troops in order to observe their movements and pick up their stragglers. Instruct me immediately as to your dispositions and your march, and also to the news which you have of the enemy; and do not neglect to keep your communications with us. The emperor desires to have news from you very often.

Of key note is the passage 'pushing before you those portions of the Prussian army which have taken this direction'. Clearly, Soult and Napoléon knew that only parts of the Prussian forces were going to be at Wavre. No reply is listed as being sent or received to this order by either Grouchy or Soult. Grouchy's operations are described at length in an accompanying volume to this series.

Battle is joined

As time went by during the early morning hours of 18 June it became clear to Napoléon that the situation was not developing the way he had accounted for in his mind. Jardine Aine, equerry to Napoléon, writes:[39]

---

38 AN: AFIV 1939 *Registre d'Ordres du Major General 13 Juin au 26 Juin 1815*, pp. 49-50.

39 Mackenzie MacBride, *With Napoleon at Waterloo*, J. B. Lippincott & Co, Philadelphia, 1911, pp. 181-5.

On the 18th, Napoléon, having left the bivouac, that is to say the village of Caillou, on horseback, at half-past nine in the morning came to take up his stand half a league in advance upon a hill where he could discern the movements of the British army.

There he dismounted, and with his field glass endeavoured to discover all the movements in the enemy's line. The chief-of-staff suggested that they should begin the attack; he replied that they must wait, but the enemy commenced his attack at eleven o'clock and the cannonading began on all sides; at two o'clock nothing was yet decided; the fighting was desperate. Napoléon rode through the lines and gave orders to make certain that every detail was executed with promptitude; he returned often to the spot where in the morning he had started, there he dismounted and, seating himself in a chair which was brought to him, he placed his head between his hands and rested his elbows on his knees. He remained thus absorbed sometimes for half an hour, and then rising up suddenly would peer through his glasses on all sides to see what was happening.

The planned confrontation had to be postponed, as the concentration of the army was taking much longer than expected and this did not permit the action to commence at 9.00. That morning Napoléon established his headquarters staff on a low mound close by La Belle Alliance, as Antoine Fee, pharmacist to General Marcogent's division of 1st Corps, explains:[40]

> ...I saw the emperor surrounded by generals and ADCs who went carrying orders to the various corps. Among them I recognised Marshal Soult.

> The emperor was standing a little in front of his staff, a small table was placed in front of him upon which was spread out a map, weighted down by two large stones; such was the tableau or sculpture set before us, who with his small hat, grey riding coat, under which one could see the simple green uniform of a senior officer. He held a large telescope in his right hand which he used often. Several of his officers carried rolls of paper under their arms which were no doubt maps and plans.

---

40 Antoine Fee, 'Un Temoignage inedt sur Waterloo: Souvenirs du pharmacien aide-major Fee' in Souvenier Napoléonienne, No. 251, March 1970, p. 4.

Despite the fact that the Old Guard and 6th Corps were not yet on the field of battle, at 11.00, Napoléon dictated the following order to Marshal Soult, addressed to Marshal Ney. The order reads:[41]

> Mont-Saint-Jean, 18th June, eleven o'clock.
>
> Once the army is arrayed in line of battle, and soon after one o'clock in the afternoon, the emperor will give the order to Marshal Ney and the attack will commence on the village of Mont-Saint-Jean in order to capture the intersection of the roads. To this end the 12-pounder batteries of the 2nd Corps, as well as those of the 6th Corps, will be united with those of the 1st Corps. These twenty-four guns will fire upon the troops holding Mont-Saint-Jean, and Comte d'Erlon will commence the attack first by launching his left-hand division and, when necessary, support it with the other divisions of the 1st Corps.
>
> The 2nd Corps will advance, keeping abreast of the 1st Corps.
>
> The company of engineers belonging to the 1st Corps are to hold themselves in readiness to barricade and fortify Mont-Saint-Jean as soon as it is captured.

Marshal Ney subsequently ordered that:[42]

> Comte d'Erlon is to understand that the attack is to begin on his left, instead of the right. Communicate this new provision to Commander-in-Chief Reille.

The order is ambiguous. Did it confirm that d'Erlon was to advance from his left, sending Quiot's division up the Brussels road first, and

---

41 SHDDT C15 Dossier 16 June 1815. This copy is dated September 1859, signed by General Rogniat as an exact copy of the original. For another exact copy, but annotated by Ney, see SHDDT: C15 5 Dossier 16 June *Documents Inedit XIX*, pp. 53-4. The document is signed 'Order dictated by the emperor on the field of battle of Mont-Saint-Jean 18th, at 11.00', written by Marshal Soult, Duc de Dalmatie, major-general. Paris 21 June 1829. It was also published in 1826 by Vaudoncourt. It is not impossible that Rogniat and Ney junior copied this text. The original is lost, but clearly as it existed in 1826 it is unlikely to be a fake.

42 SHDDT C15 5 Dossier 16 June. *Documens Inedit XIX*, pp. 53-4. Copy made in 1829. It was also published in 1826 by Vaudoncourt. It is not impossible that Rogniat and Ney junior copied this text.

then Donzelot, Marcognet and Durutte were to move off at intervals? Or did it mean Reille and 2nd Corps was to attack first? History tells us Reille did move off before d'Erlon. The attack on Hougoumont was to be a holding action and not, as a lot of history tells us, a diversionary attack to draw Wellington's strength from the centre and his right. The plan was for 1st and 2nd Corps to operate together; 1st Corps attacking first, and the 2nd Corps subsequently advancing in support. This means that the 2nd Corps was supposed to advance to the left-rear of the 1st Corps, with the division of Jérôme Bonaparte covering the left flank by occupying the low grounds around the complex of Hougoumont.

The action did indeed start on the left with Piré's light cavalry, and Jérôme did indeed move forward. For inexplicable reasons when d'Erlon advanced, Foy and Bachelu appear to have done nothing. Why? Why did Jérôme attack before any plans for the artillery bombardment of Wellington's centre had been completed?

The lack of clear source material, and sources that at times are contradictory, makes analysing what happened difficult. Jérôme is blamed by modern historians as the instigator of this fiasco on the French left. Another writer blames Guilleminot, while Reille himself says little and blames no one. Prince Jérôme's actions at Waterloo have often been described as reckless and that he needlessly destroyed his division and that of Foy. However, it seems on balance that the charges against Jérôme do not stand up to much scrutiny. Napoléon, who blames, Ney, Grouchy and Guyot for losing him the battle, blames no one for what occurred. Therefore, this means that the action was initiated in common consent. With this understanding, it makes sense of the way in which Reille describes the role of the division of Jérôme, i.e. as covering the left flank of the grand attack by occupying the low ground around the complex of Hougoumont. Until more archive source material can be found, the most logical explanation of the preliminary attack on Hougoumont is that close proximity of the complex in relation to the grand attack was to ensure the left flank of the attack was not threatened from the troops at Hougoumont. Thus, the decision was taken to neutralise this outpost and to attack immediately. Similarly, due to the lack of source material we may never know why Foy and Bachelu did not appear to advance in support of 1st Corps.

Perhaps d'Erlon, seeing the action unfolding at Hougoumont (and depending how one reads Ney's amendment to the 11.00 order), could have taken this as a signal for him to attack, pushing Quiot forward as planned and expecting Foy and Bachelu to move up, reading the order to mean that Reille and 2nd Corps would attack first. In reading the order this way why Reille did nothing is a mystery, or seeing he was not supported why did d'Erlon press on? Instead, Ney sent forward the cuirassiers, perhaps to fill the gap caused by Reille's inaction. Perhaps Reille's caution about Wellington's position[43] delayed his advance, and also perhaps his forward movement was blocked by the cuirassiers or the Allied cavalry attack, which occurred at the moment that Reille was to move off. We simply do not know why the attack did not go to plan.

---

43 Houssaye cites Reille as saying that Wellington 'was well deployed, as Wellington knows how to post it and attacked from the front, I consider English infantry to be impregnable, owing to its calm tenacity, and its superior aim in firing. Before attacking it with the bayonet, one may expect half the assailants to be brought to the ground. But the English army is less agile, less supple, and less expert at manoeuvring as our own. If we cannot defeat it by a direct attack, we may do so through manoeuvring.' The story may be apocryphal, but Reille had fought Wellington and may well have had misgivings about his master's plans. However, Reille was too good a soldier to disobey orders. He may have been cautious in his attack, but attack he would have done if ordered to do so, and when the opportunity arose. Perhaps Reille did not think until d'Erlon had reached the Allied lines did he need to move off. Wellington's cavalry was well hidden, and no French officer could conceive of the massive and sudden cavalry attack that descended on d'Erlon with the rapidity that it did.

Chapter 2

Hougoumont: Round One

As noted above, the first act in the great unfolding tragedy that was the Battle of Waterloo was the attack on the French left wing against the Hougoumont Wood. The farm complex of Hougoumont was the bastion at the southern end of Wellington's right wing and was defended by around 2,500 Allied troops; far less than the French. Numerically, the French should have easily defeated the Allied soldiers, but the Allies had the battlefield's terrain in their favour.

Unlike 2017, in 1815 the farm of Hougoumont was bounded on its south side by an orchard and a large wood. These are both highly visible on the Ferraris map of 1777. Siborne's map of 1830 shows a projected position of the orchard and also of the wooded area. The wooded area in 1777 was traversed by a north-south road. By 1830 a road running south-east, at roughly forty-five degrees to the north-south route, was in existence. An elaborate layout of trees in the form of a fashionable *par-terre* was in existence in 1777, but by the time of Siborne the area had been cleared and turned out to the plough. This *par-terre* may have been a decorative orchard. This latter route shown by Siborne may be the ghost of one of the diagonal paths through the ornamental *par-terre*.

The orchard, felled soon after Waterloo, was situated alongside the farm and comprised of apple trees planted at twelve metre intervals set out in a large square enclosure with internal pathways. The intervals were such that the tree canopy would not impede onto neighbouring trees. Traditionally, orchards and belt plantations like the Hougoumont Wood were bounded by a pale or similar barrier to prevent livestock eating young saplings, eating windfall crop, etc. as well as being of sufficient robustness to retain livestock. This pale, or boundary, was often a ditch and bank, the bank being topped by a hedge, often half a metre thick and over a metre and a half tall. In some cases this was set with a timber fence to the front or back. If we look at the Ferraris map, the boundary around the kitchen garden (comprising the belt plantation, fence, hedge and ditch) is also shown around the large *parterre* orchard and wooded enclosure to the south of the complex. The suggestion is, therefore, that the orchard, kitchen garden and southern enclosures were all bounded by a hedge and ditch. Such a feature was encountered at Quatre-Bras surrounding the Bossu Wood. de Jongh, of the 8th National Militia Battalion, writes about the initial troop positions and the action in the woods:[44]

> I had the company commanders move through a thick hedge in the wood and then had the men follow in order and on the other side of the hedge assemble the companies again.

The orchard and the southern enclosures at Hougoumont were, according to Allied and French sources, bounded by a ditch and hedge which formed a major barrier to French operations. Robert Batty, with the 1st Regiment of Foot Guards, describes the complex as follows in 1820:[45]

> About ten o'clock the enemy commenced moving down to the attack; the extreme left of his infantry line bearing obliquely towards the wood of Hougoumont, which was the most prominent angle of the Allied position and consequently exposed to the first efforts of the enemy; its possession being almost a necessary preliminary operation to any attack on the centre. The chateau of Hougoumont, with its enclosures, wood and orchard, form a large quadrangle, divided into four nearly equal parts by two hedgerows, which intersect it at right angles from the centre of its sides. The two divisions nearest to the Allied position consist of that on the right of the chateau, stables, and other outbuildings, to which is adjoined a garden, enclosed on its southern and eastern sides by a high wall; and that on the left of a large orchard, bounded on its western side by the eastern wall of the garden and on its three remaining sides by tall and compact hedges. The two divisions nearest to the French position consist of that on the right, which is immediately in front of the garden and chateau of thick coppice-wood; and that on the left

---

44 *Nieuwe Militaire Spectator*, No. 1 (Vol. 20), 1866. Erwin Muilwijk personal communication, 1 December 2012.

45 Robert Batty, *An Historical Account of the Campaign of Waterloo*, Rodwell and Martin and Co, London, 1820, pp. 89-90.

and in front of the orchard, of an open field, bounded on its western side by the wood, on its northern side by the orchard, and on the two remaining by the large hedgerow which forms the boundary of the whole enclosure.

Captain Büsgen, of the Grenadier Company 1st Battalion 2nd Nassau Regiment, writes about his troops which were initially deployed in the orchard:[46]

> Hardly had this disposition been completed when the enemy (of Jérôme's division) began their attack on the wood with a violent fire of shell and canister. Then, numerous skirmishers supported by closed columns of troops advanced, and, after encountering obstinate resistance, pushed the three companies back against the farm. The troops retreated partly to the right of the buildings and partly to the left of the garden and the hedge of the orchard, retiring into the latter, followed closely by the enemy. The English guards battalion then advanced into the orchard and threw the enemy back with great loss. However, we did not succeed in pushing the enemy out of the wood completely, as he was constantly supported by fresh troops. Thereafter, the English guards battalion went back to its former position. The Brunswick jäger company, having bravely helped to push the enemy back, had suffered severely, and re-joined its corps in the main positions.

Ferdinand von Uslar-Gleichen served in a composite rifle battalion formed from the rifle companies of the 1st, 2nd, 3rd and 4th Line Battalions of the King's German Legion, which formed part of the brigade commanded by Colonel G. K. du Plat, under the command of Captain Heise, of the 4th Line Battalion. He writes about the action in orchard thus:[47]

> Close to the farm were a group of three trees which marked the edge of the battlefield, and it was here that we had to repel several vigorous cavalry charges. Following these attacks, we were subjected to artillery fire from a battery of guns only 400 paces away, and then assailed by the fire from the enemy tirailleurs who were behind the hedges close to Hougoumont. We subsequently sustained very severe losses. Captain Holle, from the 1st, and Captain Diedel,

---

46 John Franklin personal communication, 20 August 2012.
47 John Franklin personal communication, 17 October 2012.

from the 3rd Line Battalions, were mortally wounded, along with the commander of the rifle battalion, Captain Heise, of the 4th Line Battalion, while many men fell. When the fourth captain, Beurmann, of the 2nd Line Battalion, received a grazing shot to the head which caused him to lose consciousness momentarily, it became necessary to avert the critical situation in which we were placed; Lieutenant Dehnel, of the 3rd Line Battalion, provided the impetus to do this, by stepping to the front a quarter distance, and with his sabre raised, he shouted: 'Forwards!'

Under his command, and that of the remaining officers, Ensign Heise, of the 1st, Lieutenants Dawson and Lowson, from the 2nd, as well as von Sode and Ensign von Rönne, of the 3rd, and von Lasperg and my humble self from, the 4th Line Battalion of the German Legion, we attacked the French tirailleurs behind the outmost hedge surrounding the orchard of the farm at Hougoumont. The attack was made with the bayonet, and was followed by our brave riflemen. We managed to drive the enemy back from their position, along with those who were situated behind a second hedge, lying farther to the rear. However, the French were reinforced and we subsequently retired to the first hedge. Thereafter, the combat swayed back and forth, until we finally regained the second hedge and were able to deploy in the position. During these attacks, I was on the extreme left wing of our line.

At the point where the hedge bordering the eastern edge of the orchard at Hougoumont met the second hedge at right angles, there was an opening leading into the field separating the two armies. I stepped through this opening in order to gain a better view of the action, and while doing so I met a French officer, who was riding very close to the hedge.

The French do not seem to have been aware of the farm's substantial garrison. The farm, its outbuildings and encircling woods were a major obstacle for the French and a strong bastion for the Nassau garrison which would be later bolstered by the British guards. The attack of the Hougoumont Wood by the 6th Infantry Division (commanded by Prince Jérôme) commenced about 12.30. The division comprised of the 1st Brigade (under Baron Bauduin) of the 1st Regiment of Light Infantry and 3rd Regiment of Line Infantry and the brigade of General Soye (the 1st and 2nd Regiments of Line Infantry). Prince Jérôme writes on 15 July 1815:[48]

---

48 *Memoires et Correspondence du roi Jérôme et la reine Catherine* (Vol. 7), E Dentu, Paris, p. 24.

18th in the morning, I passed the headquarters of the emperor, where I spent an hour with him. He received me with affection and much tenderness. He had assembled the senior general officers, and once the battle plan was given, everyone went to his post. At noon, the whole army was arrayed in line; I was on the far left, in front of a wood occupied by the British. We had 70,000 men and 280 pieces of cannon, and the enemy were 96,000; Marshal Grouchy, with 36,000 men, watched the Prussian army on our extreme right, but was not in communication with us.

At a quarter-past twelve, I received orders to begin the attack.

Piré attacks

The first French troops sent to the attack were elements of Piré's cavalry and Bauduin's infantry brigade. Bauduin's brigade comprised the 1st Regiment of Light Infantry and the 3rd Regiment of Line Infantry. The French infantry advanced along the road, protected by a screen of light cavalry from Piré's division. It seems that the 1st and 6th Chasseurs à Cheval advanced and skirmished against these dispersed light troops.

Henckens, of the 6th Chasseurs à Cheval under the orders of General Piré, notes:[49]

> The order was given that Piré's division was to be on the extreme left of the position at nine o'clock and that we should follow the orders of General Reille. We were not able to make a decent charge and we did nothing except to act as skirmishers so as to clear the infantry away from the 2nd Army Corps; in one of these skirmishes I lost my second horse. I had no other horse, but my peloton procured me one.

Comte Tallobre,[50] a captain in the 6th Chasseurs à Cheval, writes on 3 April 1815 confirming what Henckens says:[51]

---

49 J. L. Henckens, *Mémoires se rapportant à son service militaire au 6e régiment de chasseurs à cheval français de février 1803 à août 1816*, M. Nijhoff, La Haie, 1910.

50 Maurice Pierre Cyprien, Comte de Tallobre, was born on 19 November 1785 and admitted as a *velite* into the chasseurs à pied of the Imperial Guard on 10 March 1806. He was promoted to second-lieutenant in the 8th Regiment of Light Infantry on 25 March 1809, and thence to lieutenant on 17 December 1811. He was then appointed as aide-de-camp to General Savary on 24 August 1812 and named as a captain in the 6th Chasseurs on 14 September 1814.

51 Author's collection.

18 June, I, with a sub-lieutenant and fifty men, supported our sharpshooters in attacking the enemy sharpshooters. It was in this action that a spent musket ball hit my left leg, wounding myself and the horse.

It is very unlikely that the chasseurs deployed into the wood, and no doubt were, as Henckens says, on the extreme left of the French position. Both Henckens and Tallobre imply that the 6th Chasseurs à Cheval moved up the Chemins de la Maison du Roi, which runs along the ridge to the southwest of Hougoumont and behind the French line, and then turned onto this road in support of the voltigeurs from the 3rd Regiment of Line Infantry, which were spread out in front of the regiment as a skirmish screen. It is likely that here were the 1st Chasseurs à Cheval. Piré's men were spotted by Captain J. Ross, of the 51st Regiment of Foot, who notes the following about the advance of the French skirmishers to attack Hougoumont:[52]

> On the morning of the 18th, the brigade took up a position about ten o'clock in the rear of Hougoumont until the enemy made their appearance on the rising ground of La Belle Alliance, when on their columns advancing a company of the regiment was ordered to extend and cover the right of Hougoumont to meet the enemy's skirmishers, who were moving forward at the head of their columns.

> From the undulating nature of the ground and the high standing corn, this company, Captain Phelps's, did not come into contact with the enemy until about seventy paces of each other, when a firing commenced. The enemy's cavalry was supporting their advance, but our infantry at this time was not so supported. The enemy retired slowly towards the enclosures of Hougoumont; their columns were then halted upon the slope of the hill. At about this period of the affair, a small body of light cavalry came to support our skirmishers, and at the same time a staff officer arrived with a verbal order from Lord Hill to retire, and the company retired in the usual way.

Also deployed in this sector of the battlefield was the Allied 15th Hussars. Lieutenant-Colonel Thackwell, a captain who had been in the 15th Hussars at Waterloo, notes:[53]

---

52 William Siborne, *Waterloo Letters* ed. H. T. Siborne, Greenhill Books, 1993, No. 133.

53 ibid, No.62.

The enemy's cavalry and infantry moved in column in advance and retreat, the former being at about quarter-distance, and I understand when the British line advanced the three left troops of the 15th charged a body of infantry as well as some lancers.

The position of the regiment being in the rear of Hougoumont, the masses of infantry which would have closed on its post were intercepted by the troops defending that place, and none of the enemy's infantry, to the best of my recollection, passed its enclosures, and the first I saw of that force in the immediate front of the 15th Hussars was the column charged by my squadron; but I witnessed the advance of many heavy masses of infantry which attacked Hougoumont, although soon after the firing began the distant movements of the enemy's column were from this part of the position, but indistinctly seen, owing to the smoke which hung lazily on a surface saturated with rain.

Lieutenant H. Lane, of the same regiment, notes Piré's lancers were also here:[54]

I saw the first shot fired from our lines about eleven o'clock; it struck the column of the enemy advancing upon Hougoumont and caused some confusion and delay. The 15th Hussars was moved soon after to the ground on the right of the position, where I had marked a squadron as placed, and where the enemy showed a strong body of lancers, which we were preparing to attack.

So, it seems the 3rd Regiment of Line Infantry attacked with the support from all of Piré's cavalry division. Captain Walcott, of Webber-Smith's battery, writes on 18 January 1835:[55]

At 11 a.m. I re-joined my troop then under arms, close to the road leading Nivelles to Brussels and a little to the rear and left of Hougoumont. At half-past eleven o'clock the enemy showed himself in considerable force, and threatened the chateau of Hougoumont. Lieut-Colonel Webber-Smith's troop was ordered into position to protect the chateau and the enemy came on in force. We [the troop] continued to be hotly engaged and suffered severely from a battery in support of the attack, until the French troops arrived in the grounds of the chateau, the buildings

---

54 ibid, No.69
55 ibid, No.80

of which and the trees surrounding it prevented our longer annoying the enemy, in consequence of which the troop was withdrawn, and remained a short time in the rear of the right of the first line.

Alexander Dickson, of the Royal Artillery, who was in the same area recalls seeing both the French lancers, which must be Wathiez's men, as well as two artillery batteries. He also admits to a continued skirmish being kept up among the corn field which flanked either side of the Nivelles road.[56] The force seems to have been the 3rd Regiment of Line Infantry with Piré's cavalry and supported with either horse artillery or foot artillery.

During this action, or perhaps later in the day, wounded in the 1st Chasseurs à Cheval at Waterloo was Squadron Commander Vincent Jean Robert du Bourg at the head of the regiment's 1st Squadron.[57] Also wounded in 1st Squadron were Captain François Auguste Riquet (commanding the 1st Company) and Sub-Lieutenant Pierre Henry Raulet.[58] Captain François Auguste Riquet was wounded with a sabre cut.[59] In the 2nd Squadron, Lieutenant Bernard Berthe was wounded.[60] Squadron Commander Frederic Lanthonnet, who commanded the 3rd Squadron, had his horse killed under him.[61] Captain Daniel Girard and Sub-Lieutenant Niclasse, of 3rd Company, were wounded and Captain Jean-Baptiste Persy and Sub-Lieutenant Melchoir Brille, of 7th Company, were wounded.[62] The 4th Squadron was commanded by Claude Constant Marie Rambourgt, who would be killed under the walls of Paris on 1 July 1815. Captain Jean Baptiste Percy received his twelfth sabre cut and second gunshot wound at Waterloo.[63] Casualties for the 1st Chasseurs à Cheval at Waterloo were:[64]

---

56 ibid, No.89.
57 AN: LH 2351/17.
58 SHDDT: M291.
59 AN: LH 2337/21.
60 SHDDT: M291.
61 AN: LH 1474/9.
62 SHDDT: M291.
63 AN: LH 2117/35.
64 SHDDT: GR 24 YC 254.

Squadron	Killed	Died of Wounds	Wounded	Missing
1st	0	0	1	0
2nd	0	0	2	3
3rd	0	0	1	2
4th	0	0	2	7
Total	0	0	6	12

On 10 June, the regiment mustered 445 other ranks, and, it seems, took no part in the charges at Quatre-Bras, as no men are recorded dead or wounded. At Waterloo, eighteen men were lost, representing a mere 4 per cent of effective strength. In total, nine men and one officer were returned from prison in England in 1816. These nine men are all recorded missing at Waterloo, therefore the regiment's losses do not seem to have been very high, unless more men were taken prisoner than recorded in the regiment's muster list and more lists of returning prisoners with details of the men taken are found.[65]

The regiment was clearly in action, but was not overly exposed to Allied musketry and artillery fire. Compared to the other ranks, the high number of officer casualties implies that the officers were conspicuous targets, easily picked off by the Allied marksmen. However low the losses seem, we are not seeing horse losses in the data, which could treble the number. When we compare the losses to other light cavalry regiments at Waterloo, the regiment lost the least number of men overall, but not by a large margin. The 1st Lancers lost twenty-one men and the 11th Chasseurs twenty-two men. Losses in the action were far lower than popular myth and misconception would have us believe. Of the twelve men missing, nine were returned to France as former prisoners in February 1816.[66]

In total, the 6th Chasseurs at Waterloo lost sixty-two men, shown in the table below:[67]

---

65 SHDDT: Yj 11 *Etat nominatif des militaires prisonniers de Guerre français arrivés d'Angleterre*. See also: SHDDT: Yj 12 *Etat nominatif des militaires prisonniers de Guerre français arrivés d'Angleterre*. See also: SHDDT: Yj 13 *Etat nominatif des militaires prisonniers de Guerre français arrivés d'Angleterre*.
66 SHDDT: Yj 11.
67 SHDDT: GR 24 YC 282.

Squadron	Company	Killed	Died of Wounds	Wounded	Prisoner of War	Missing
1st	1st	0	0	1	0	9
	5th	1	0	2	0	7
2nd	2nd	1	0	2	0	4
	6th	0	0	1	0	2
3rd	3rd	0	0	0	0	4
	7th	1	0	1	0	6
4th	4th	0	0	1	0	9
	8th	2	0	0	0	8
Total		5	0	8	0	49

On 10 June, the regiment mustered 526 men. Fifteen men were lost at Quatre-Bras and two more at Genappe, giving 507 men present on the morning of 18 June. The loss of sixty-two men represents some 12 per cent of effective strength. Of the forty-nine men listed as missing, twenty-two of these returned from captivity in England in spring 1816.[68] The missing are very likely to be men who were dismounted.

Comment

The 6th Chasseurs à Cheval lost four times as many men at Waterloo than the 1st Chasseurs à Cheval. This implies that, as at Quatre-Bras, the bulk of the fighting of the brigade fell upon the 6th Chasseurs, which sustained far greater losses than any other cavalry regiment. The 9th Chasseurs lost the next highest number of men, with forty-six casualties. The losses for the 6th Chasseurs, being significantly higher than for the light cavalry, are in fact broadly similar to the losses of the heavy cavalry. The 2nd Carabiniers lost sixty-nine men for example, and the 9th Cuirassiers sustained sixty-one casualties. Therefore, it seems that the 6th Chasseurs were involved far more than any of the other light cavalry regiments. The 1st Chasseurs appear to have been kept from the fighting, given that the regiment had dubious loyalties.

de Mauduit, in his work on the campaign, notes one officer of the regiment went over to the Allies during the battle: Lieutenant Bachelet. This officer was actually Mat. No. 42 Lieutenant Gabrielle Antoine

---

68 SHDDT: Yj 11.

Labechelle.[69] Captain-Adjutant-Major Jean Debut (Matricule No. 14)[70] is recorded as endeavouring to prevent the desertion. Labechelle is recorded as deserted with Captain du Barail of the 2nd Carabiniers. Among the 5th Lancers, Squadron Commander Milet left his post and deserted to the Allies:[71]

> He took part in the 1815 campaign, and at the Battle of Waterloo quitted the army due to his deep attachment to the Bourbon family.

One can only imagine the effect this could have had on the officers and men of the regiment. Clearly, morale of officers, and no doubt men, was shaky during the campaign. Indeed, before the campaign began, Captain Andre Joseph de Brevedant is noted to have:[72]

> Refused to take part in the campaign of 1815 due to his attachment to the Bourbon family.

Myth suggests that only de Bourmont and du Barail had defected at Waterloo. The truth is that these two men were just the most famous of the officers who deserted the emperor's cause. The desertion of General Gordon and others on 16 June, officers from the 5th Lancers, 1st Chasseurs as well as five other officers from the carabineers makes it abundantly clear that the loyalty of the army to the cause of Napoléon was shaky among officers, which perhaps implies that the former Chasseurs du Roi, as with the 1st and 2nd Carabiniers, were held back from action on 16 June due to issues of morale, cohesion and loyalty. The fewer losses of the 1st Chasseurs compared to the 6th Chasseurs perhaps implies that the 1st were held back from more serious fighting in case the regiment galloped off and deserted to the Allies. Likewise, were the 5th Lancers held back from the fighting? Thus, of the division, only half were 'reliable' men, leaving the 6th Chasseurs and 6th Lancers to bear the brunt of the fighting.

Bauduin attacks

First blood at Hougoumont had gone to the cavalry. Behind the chasseurs came the 3rd Regiment of Line Infantry. To the right, the men

---

69 SHDDT: GR 24 YC 254.

70 ibid.

71 SHDDT: Xc 183 *5e et 6e Chevau-légers, pertes officiers depuis 18 Juin 1815*.

72 SHDDT: Xc 183 *pertes officiers depuis 18 Juin 185*.

of the 1st Regiment of Light Infantry darted forward into the wood. The 1st Regiment of Light Infantry being the senior regiment of the division would have occupied the right of the line, i.e. attacking the wood to the south of the farm complex. About the sequence of events, Jean Baptiste Jolyet, commanding 1st Battalion 1st Regiment of Light Infantry, narrates that:[73]

> My company of light infantry was sent to search the Hougoumont Wood on which rested the left of the army. I deployed the rest of my battalion to the left of the 61st, which was formed to the left of the 5th Division. A hollow concealed this division out of sight of the English, and also hid my battalion. A sunken road which followed the rise in the ground seemed to provide shelter to our 2nd Battalion, but as they were just moving back to our line, our brigadier (who was killed shortly after) ordered the 3rd Battalion to remain in place before the sunken road. This put him close to the enemy, scarcely had they arrived at this position where they were placed than the British batteries, established in advance, made a hot fire that lay on the ground about twenty men of the 3rd Battalion, and the shots succeeded each other with such rapidity that they were forced back down into the sunken road. These guns seemed to signal the main action and the fire was kindled along the line.

The battery that the 3rd Battalion came under fire from was in all likelihood Ramsey's or Bull's. The sunken road may be the Chemins du Goumont that runs through the ravine from Braine l'Alleud. Captain Bull writes on 24 June 1835:[74]

> We moved to the heights on the right of our first line, and immediately came into action with spherical case shot with the intention of dislodging the enemy's infantry from the left of a small wood and the garden with the farm called Hougoumont adjoining it, and at about 1,000 yards distance from our front, in which I have reason to believe we succeeded, for our infantry were able to enter the wood.

We are not aware of the location of the 2nd Battalion, but they presumably moved to the east towards the orchard in pursuit of the

---

73 Commandant Jolyet, '*Souvenirs du 1815*' in *Revue de Paris*, October 1903, pp. 545-55.

74 Siborne, *Waterloo Letters*, No. 78.

Nassau and Brunswick jägers. The former incurred heavy losses, especially among the officers. The wounds which the men sustained (bayonet stab wounds in a number of instances) show that the contest was both vicious and close-quarter. However, both the three companies of Nassau-Usingen troops and the Brunswick jägers were driven from the wood and orchard, and these five companies retired (the Brunswickers noted as doing so in good order) as far as Merbe Braine. The 1st Battalion under Jolyet's orders were deployed in the wood:[75]

> After various movements I was sent about one o'clock in the afternoon to support the skirmishers in the Hougoumont Wood. At the opening of the wood there was a house that the British had embattled. Many times our skirmishers, despite the order they had to merely contain the enemy on our left, wanted to take this house that bothered them. Each time they were repelled and had to retreat below the wood, so I had to support them and bring them back to their place, because I had been well warned that this was the place we had to pivot the army on and, therefore, that it was absolutely necessary to maintain our position. I spent a part of the day often with men wounded by English musket balls or shells.

Therefore, the entire regiment was deployed well away from the farm complex. Of importance to the story of Waterloo, Etienne Legros and his 3rd Battalion were deployed to the east of Hougoumont. Ferdinand von Uslar-Gleichen continues:[76]

> On the day of the Battle of Waterloo I was a very young ensign within the rifle company of the 4th Line Battalion. During the battle we left the position we had occupied in the second line on the right wing, which had been allocated to us within the order of battle, and advanced towards the farm of Hougoumont in order to support the troops there and in the immediate vicinity, who had been engaged for quite some time...I met a French officer, who was riding very close to the hedge. I felt great surprise, yet despite this, and the fact that I was little more than a boy, without any hesitation I grasped at the horse's reins with all my strength, attempting to prevent any resistance from the horseman, who was a powerful man, to ensure that the situation did not end badly for me. Fortunately, the

---

75 Jolyet, pp.545-55.
76 John Franklin personal communication, 17 October 2012.

corporal attached to the company's left wing passed through the opening at this moment and arrived in sufficient time to assist in the capture of the officer.

Once our captive had dismounted from his horse, he gave me his full purse, his watch and other precious belongings, all of which I handed to the corporal, but I ordered him to give half of the money back to the French officer. While I was considering what to do with the officer and his horse, Captain Beurmann, of our rifle battalion, who had recovered from the contusion he had received, approached me and stated: 'My dear little rifleman'—which was the affectionate manner in which my comrades used to describe me—'the horse is probably too big for you, leave the animal to me.'

It was affection towards this brave senior officer, and in a great part my naivety, that made me immediately agree to his suggestion. And so after the extraordinary capture of a mounted enemy officer, this 'small rifleman', with a certain sensation of victory, although somehow muted, was left with nothing but the modest part as the audience, as Captain Beurmann rode forward with the captive and his horse, while the corporal bagged the profits: the purse and the watch.

For the operations of the 1st Regiment of Light Infantry we have two forms of data: eyewitness accounts and the regiment's muster list. When we look at the casualty data for the regiment, we see that Jolyet's comments are backed up by this data. Total regimental losses at Waterloo are in the table below:[77]

1st Regiment of Light Infantry					
	Wounded	Wounded & Prisoner	Prisoner of War	Killed	Missing
1st Battalion	4	0	0	0	1
2nd Battalion	6	0	0	0	0
3rd Battalion	6	0	0	0	1
4th Battalion	26	0	3	7	5
Total	42	0	3	7	7

---

77 SHDDT: GR 21 YC 8 *1er régiment d'infanterie de ligne dit régiment du Roi, 1 mai 1814-6 décembre 1814 (matricules 1 à 3,000).*

On 27 May 1815, the regiment mustered seventy officers and 1,858 other ranks in three battalions. The 4th Battalion comprised eighty officers and 105 men.[78] The regiment's paperwork declares seven men were lost on 16 June and fifty-nine on 18 June. We do note that seventy-five men were returned as prisoners from England in 1816. We don't have the total number of prisoners taken, but clearly at some stage the regiment lost a lot of manpower not recorded in the regimental list.[79]

The cadre of the 4th Battalion was taken into the 3rd Battalion on 27 May 1815 and mustered 105 men.[80] The conjoined 3rd and 4th Battalions were involved in the heaviest fighting. Therefore, was it the conjoined 3rd Battalion that attacked Hougoumont? Perhaps so, considering the much smaller number of casualties sustained by the other two battalions. By 25 June the regiment mustered 572 men, representing a loss of 1,316 men.[81] A possible explanation of this can be found at the farm complex itself. The west side of the farm was not loopholed to any extent, although some defenders may have tried to loophole the roof. The first time that attackers would have been exposed to much in the way of fire is when they first turned around the south wall and, from all accounts, the British guard were so under pressure that they fell back very fast to the north gate. It is only at the north gate that any real exchange of fire would have been possible.

What is of note is that all three battalions had a high number of officer casualties compared to other regiments in 2nd Corps at Waterloo. In the attack, in the 1st Regiment of Light Infantry, at the head of the 1st Battalion, Battalion Commander Jolyet was wounded. Other officers wounded in 1st Battalion were Jean Louis Hagard, commanding the 1st Fusilier Company, with a gunshot to the left arm, as well as Lieutenant Vilcoq and Sub-Lieutenant Guillemin. The 2nd Company of Fusiliers also lost all its officers, with Captain Nanot being killed and Lieutenant Jean François Gouin and Sub-Lieutenant Gouvoine being wounded. The 3rd and 4th Fusilier Companies suffered no officers dead and wounded, and the voltigeur company commander, Captain Dogimont, was wounded.[82]

---

78 SHDDT: C15 34 *Situations Garde Impériale 1815. Situation Rapport 2e Corps 27 Mai 1815.*

79 SHDDT: Yj 11. See also: SHDDT: Yj 12. See also: SHDDT: Yj 13.

80 SHDDT: Xb 561 *1er régiment d'infanterie Legere 1814 a 1815.*

81 SHDDT: C15 34, *2e et 6e Corps recapitulation du 25 Juin 1815.*

82 SHDDT: 2Yb-641-05.

In the regiment's 2nd Battalion, Captain Louis Vibert (commanding the 1st Fusilier Company) was wounded. The 2nd Company of Fusiliers had Sub-Lieutenant Dumoulin wounded. Killed at the head of the 3rd Company of Fusiliers was Captain Poitaux. The company also suffered Sub-Lieutenant Sicard wounded.[83]

The battalion that suffered most that day appears to have been the 3rd Battalion, which undertook the audacious attack on the northern gates. Indeed, all the officers in the carabinier company were wounded. The carabineer-lieutenant, Pierre Auguste de Cussy, and Sub-Lieutenant Combescue were wounded. The company was, in theory, led by Captain de Brea[84] but he is listed as 'quit the army' on 1 June 1815,[85] which does rather contradict with his much later biographies which place him in the heart of the action at Quatre-Bras and Waterloo. In the 1st Company of Fusiliers, Captain Eugene Alexandre Husson was wounded and Sub-Lieutenant Legros was killed. Captain Prevost was wounded at the head of the 2nd Fusilier Company, and Sub-lieutenant Jacob, of the 4th Fusilier Company, was mortally wounded.[86] The lieutenant of the voltigeur company of the 3rd Battalion was Guillaume Armand Boutour de Flagny. He was born at Bayeaux on 13 September 1791 and was conscripted to the 3rd Regiment of Voltigeurs of the Imperial Guard on 29 March 1811. He was promoted to corporal-quartermaster on 20 May 1812, to sergeant-major on 26 March 1813 and was appointed sub-lieutenant in the 23rd Regiment of Light Infantry on 20 April 1813. He passed to the regiment on 22 June 1814 and was wounded at Waterloo with a gunshot to his right arm.[87] Conspicuous is the high ratio of killed or wounded officers.

This high ratio of officer casualties leads me to conclude that the officers were conspicuous in standing at the front of their companies leading their inexperienced troops into action. This shows the excellent quality of the officers in terms of leadership, but one wonders what the effect may have been as officer casualties began to mount and some of the shakier conscripts, who had joined the regiment in 1814 and had not been in action before, had to rely on sub-officers of the company. It is easy, therefore, to imagine that with the officers of a battalion either

---

83 ibid.

84 ibid.

85 SHDDT: Xb 561 *1er régiment d'infanterie Legere 1814 a 1815.*

86 SHDDT: 2Yb-641-05.

87 ibid.

being killed or wounded in the first attack on the farm, that the regiment would have had issues with command and control and may not have been able to partake in fighting later in the day due to the loss of key personnel. This high ratio of officer casualties compared to the loss of other ranks also fits in well with the regiment being deployed in the woods and orchard. Operating as a mass of sharpshooters deployed in the wood, officers would become very conspicuous targets. Given the nature of the terrain, the losses in such an action would be lower than a company attacking in line. Companies dispersed throughout the wood were smaller targets were harder to hit. The bulk of casualties may have been caused by Bull's artillery fire. We can also say that the 1st Regiment of Light Infantry never approached the garden wall, as when we look at other regiments that did, the casualty rates are far higher, as the men had to charge across a dead zone between the wall and the facing hedge, bank and ditch. Once through the hedge, the attackers would have been quickly cut down by Allied musketry. Clearly, the 1st Regiment of Light Infantry was not involved in any such attack given the very low number of dead and wounded.

Brigaded with the 1st Regiment of Light Infantry was the 3rd Regiment of Line Infantry. No eyewitness observations have survived to the present time from the latter. The regiment was on the left of the 1st Regiment of Light Infantry and seemingly operated to the west of the farm.

The 3rd Regiment of Line Infantry at Quatre-Bras had lost twenty-one officers and 292 men, and more officers and men would fall in the Hougoumont Wood. At Waterloo, Colonel Baron Vautrin had his left leg shattered by a cannon ball, which was amputated later the same day. Lieutenant Jean Adam Boot, who carried the regimental eagle, was also wounded. In the 1st Battalion, two of the officers of the grenadier company were wounded, namely Lieutenant Ambroise Brutus Le Roch and Sub-Lieutenant Dominique Botte. The company commander, Captain Laroche, was killed. The 1st Fusilier Company had their commander, Captain Jean Christophe Laurent, killed and Lieutenant Dominique Depeyre wounded. The 3rd Fusilier Company also lost its commander, Captain Jean Lavache, who was wounded and made prisoner of war, and Lieutenant Pierre Nicholas Lalore was wounded with a sabre cut during the retreat. Sub-Lieutenant Pierre Jean Baissac, of the 4th Fusilier Company, was wounded. In the voltigeur company of the battalion, Captain Joseph Grille was shot in the left buttock. At the head of the 3rd Fusilier Company, Lieutenant Antoine Joseph Laborie suffered a gunshot to the right arm, which was amputated that same day, and Sub-Lieutenant Gorget took command of the company.[88]

In the 2nd Battalion, Captain-Adjutant-Major Jean Baptiste Regard was wounded and lost his papers and personal effects in the retreat. Lieutenant-Adjutant-Major Denis Louis Legrand was wounded and made prisoner of war. Commanding the grenadier company of 2nd Battalion was Charles François Durousseau. He was wounded at Quatre-Bras with a bruise to the right shoulder and took a gunshot to the chest at Waterloo. The 1st Fusilier Company lost Lieutenant Alexander Lebrun, who was killed. The 2nd Fusilier Company lost its commander, Captain Dominique Lacadet-Merosiere, who was wounded, as well as Sub-Lieutenant François Celu. The 3rd Fusilier Company had Lieutenant Nicholas Prin and Sub-Lieutenant Etienne Cronnier wounded. Wounded at the head of the 4th Company of Fusiliers was Captain François Leydier, so too was Lieutenant Antoine Godard. Sub-Lieutenant Jean Baptiste Millet, of the voltigeur company, took a gunshot to the right thigh and another to the left of his groin which removed his right testicle.[89] It seems the 3rd Regiment of Line Infantry was eviscerated by the fighting against the farm, and on 24 June 1815 the regiment had barely 400 men.[90] Total regimental losses at Waterloo are in the table below:[91]

3rd Regiment of Line Infantry					
	Evacuated Wounded	Wounded & Prisoner	Prisoner of War	Killed	Missing
1st Battalion	82	1	75	18	1
2nd Battalion	71	1	76	25	0
3rd Battalion	102	0	118	23	2
Attached	12	0	7	4	1
Total	267	2	276	70	4

---

88 SHDDT: 2Yb-641-05.

89 ibid.

90 Hippolyte de Mauduit, 'Vieille Militaire. Charleroi, Fleurus et Waterloo' in La Sentinalle de l'armée, 1 June 1836.

91 SHDDT: GR 21 YC 31 3e régiment d'infanterie de ligne dit régiment du Dauphin, 16 Juillet 1814-17 Décembre 1814 (matricules 1 à 1,800). See also: SHDDT: GR 21 YC 32 3e régiment d'infanterie de ligne dit régiment du Dauphin, 17 décembre 1814-1 Juillet 1815 (matricules 1,801 à 2,135).

The regiment lost 619 other ranks on 18 June. On 1 May 1815, the regiment formed three battalions of forty-two officers and 1,430 other ranks: 453 men formed 1st Battalion, 441 men formed the 2nd Battalion and the 3rd Battalion mustered 536 men.[92] The regiment lost 43 per cent of effective strength at Waterloo.

The evacuated casualties sustained on the 18th presumably occurred in the first half of the battle, when it was more likely that they would be evacuated to the rear, rather than during the end of the battle when wounded men were more likely to be captured as prisoners of war. If this is the case, it is clear that the 3rd Regiment of Line Infantry, which sustained far heavier losses than the 1st Regiment of Light Infantry, was involved in a different scale of fighting. Assuming the 1st Regiment of Light Infantry was involved solely in clearing the southern woods and orchard, its men deployed *en tirailleur* in open order would have lost fewer men than a regiment attacking the farm complex itself. Therefore, using this analogy, it seems that it was the 3rd Regiment of Line Infantry, and not the 1st Regiment of Light Infantry, which attacked the farm of Hougoumont regardless of what the myth of the battle says.

---

92 SHDDT: Xb 348 *3e de Ligne 1808-1815. Dossier 1815. Rapport 1 Mai 1815.*

Chapter 3

Legros, Bouche or Bonnet?

One of the continuing unresolved questions about Waterloo is the issue of which French officer led the first attack that broke into the farm. The myth of Waterloo tells us a giant of a man called Legros, nicknamed *'l'Enforcer'* in popular histories of the battle, attacked the gates of Hougoumont with an axe, smashed the gates and entered the courtyard. However, the truth seems to be a little different.

The earliest reference to this episode was written in 1836, some twenty-one years after the battle. de Mauduit describes the scene and ascribes the command of the detachment from the 1st Regiment of Light Infantry to Lieutenant Legros. He also notes that the regiment attacked the British guards outside the farm, pushed them back through the main gate and endeavoured to follow up the attack by assaulting the gates:[93]

> A peloton of the 1st Light Infantry went forward with great audacity and pursued the English back to the principal point of entry to the farm, and penetrated into the farm and began a melee with the enemy. However, despite their best efforts the peloton had to renounce their conquest, despite their best efforts and courage.

> M. Legros, sub-lieutenant of the 1st Light Infantry, who served at Quatre-Bras where his brother was killed, led several men into the courtyard and found a glorious death.

Etienne Legros served as a second-lieutenant in the 1st Company 3rd Battalion,[94] which based on Jolyet's testimony, was in the sunken lane

---

93 Hippolyte de Mauduit, *'Vieille Militaire Charleroi, Fleurus et Waterloo'* in *La Sentinalle de l'armée*, 1 June 1836, pp. 1801-2.

94 SHDDT:2Yb-641-05.

to the north-east of the farm, i.e. a location away from the northern gates. Legros was killed at Waterloo, however how and where is the issue.[95] Colonel Cubières makes it clear that the officer involved was called Bonnet:[96]

> I formed a vanguard and gave the command of it to Second-Lieutenant Bonnet, a brave soldier from the army of Spain who had been made an officer by Marshal Suchet, the first man to enter the breach of Lerida. This detachment turned past the farm buildings and came to the carriage door and entered the yard. The 1st Light followed in his footsteps, Bonnet struck the carriage door with repeated blows, threw it down and penetrated into the courtyard, whence they shot at him and his men from a raised gallery.

If we check the officers' records for the 1st Regiment of Light Infantry no officer called Bonnet served in the regiment.[97] Bonnet could conceivably be Captain Theodore Nanot, commanding 2nd Company 1st Battalion, or Captain Prosper Nanot, commanding 2nd Company 2nd Battalion.[98]

In the third telling of the story, Auguste Pétiet, of the headquarters staff, says (based entirely on the letter Cubières had sent him) that the attack was led by an officer called Bouche.[99] Does this mean Cubières got the name wrong and corrected Pétiet in a now lost second letter? However, the name Pétiet gives, unlike Cubières, does tally with a known officer of the regiment which supports this theory. Antoine Bouche was a lieutenant in 3rd Company 3rd Battalion.[100] Bouche did not die until 13 January 1839, so clearly he could not have been killed as Pétiet makes out, and neither was he promoted to lieutenant by Marshal Suchet at Tarragone, as he was not promoted to sub-lieutenant until 18 February 1813 when his regiment was in Saxony. Therefore, *Pétiet's* narration and service details of Bouche are suspect, if not entirely fabricated. Colonel Cubières not recalling the name of the officer also seems a little odd.

---

95 SHDDT: Xb 561 *1er régiment d'infanterie Legere 1814 a 1815*.
96 Cubières to Auguste Pétiet. John Franklin personal communication, 24 February 2016.
97 SHDDT: 2Yb-641-05.
98 SHDDT: Xb 561 *1er régiment d'infanterie Legere 1814 a 1815*.
99 Auguste-Louis Pétiet, *Souvenirs militaires de l'histoire contemporaine*, Dumaine, Paris, 1844, pp. 221-2.
100 SHDDT: 2Yb-641-05.

How do we know de Mauduit's identification of Legros is correct, as neither Cubières nor Pétiet mention him, yet all describe a similar scene? What is more of a concern is that the 'received history' talks of thirty or so French getting through the north gate and all were killed, but that doesn't show up in the casualty report. More reliable perhaps is Captain George Evelyn's recollections. He writes that as the French skirmishers pressed closer to the farm:[101]

> They shut the gate and barricaded it with logs of wood on the inside. It was while he was assisting in doing this that George received his wound, through a hole in the old gate. He sunk upon his knees… the French were breaking in.

It is possible that the scene did not involve the 1st Regiment of Light Infantry at all. The regiment clearly had attacked the southern woods, the 1st Battalion, according to its commanding officer, with the 3rd deployed on the Chemins de Goumont from where it is not impossible some of the battalion headed west to the northern gates, but in this scenario Cubières, with 2nd Battalion, could not have witnessed the scene, nor did Pétiet or de Mauduit. If all the men involved were killed, who told these writers? The whole episode, when one starts to query the alleged facts starts to unravel. The uncomfortable truth is that it is very likely that the 1st Regiment of Light Infantry were not involved in this event.

Based on eyewitness accounts, the regiment was totally deployed to the east of the building complex, entirely within the southern wood, thus making the troops that Matthew Clay observed moving through the kitchen garden the 3rd Regiment of Line Infantry (which were deployed to the west of the 1st Regiment of Light Infantry). Thus in reality, it was the 3rd Regiment of Line Infantry that broke through the northern gates at Hougoumont.

Myth says that Sergeant Ralph Fraser attacked Colonel Cubières. Cubières himself says nothing of this other than stating that his horse was killed by a musket ball.[102] Therefore, the whole episode which often repeated that Fraser killed Cubières' horse simply does not tally at all. Either Fraser had something of an active imagination or he did not

---

101 John Franklin personal communication, 20 August 2012.
102 Cubières to Auguste Pétiet. John Franklin personal communication, 24 February 2016.

attack Cubières. Given the 1st Regiment of Light Infantry were to the east of the farm, it would have been members of the 3rd Regiment of Line Infantry that Fraser came across.

My own view is that Legros may well have been a composite figure, since three names are given by the French for the officers who led the attack and that the description of the north gate incident may well have been a composite description—that it took place is in little doubt, but was it really as simplistically depicted in the 'received history'? Legros was a real man, but it is very unlikely that he or the 1st Regiment of Light Infantry were involved in the attack on the farm buildings. Yet the myth of Legros being 'a giant of man' armed with an axe hacking his way through the gates of Hougoumont continues.[103] For interest, the 1st Regiment of Light Infantry had no *sapeurs* in 1815, and furthermore had no axes at all either in the regiment's depot or issued for Legros to take from a *sapeur*.[104] Therefore, Legros, Bouche or Bonnet/Nanot could not have taken an axe to the gates!

Soye's brigade attacks

With the 1st Regiment of Light Infantry and the brigaded 3rd Regiment of Line Infantry withdrawn from the attack of Hougoumont, the brigade of General Soye (comprising the 1st and 2nd Regiments of Line Infantry) were ordered to attack. In a letter thought to be written by Major Beaux, commanding the 1st Regiment of Line Infantry, is the following account:[105]

> Many of the regiments had to establish themselves on swampy ground, the mud coming up to the middle of their legs. The night was awful, the rain fell with such violence that it is impossible to describe it. About two o'clock in the morning I went to the rear of the farm of Plancenoit to see the emperor. He ordered us to clean our arms and prepare for combat, which was to begin at nine o'clock. He also said how the army was to be arrayed; the 2nd Corps was

---

103 Project Hougoumont, *Defence of Hougoumont*, Project Hougoumont, 2016, available at https://projecthougoumont.com/defence-of-hougoumont/ [accessed 11 February 2017].

104 SHDDT: Xb 565 *1e Légère*. Dossier 1815.

105 Letter dated 25 June 1815 published in the *Journal de Rouen*, 27 June 1815, pp. 3-4.

to be placed in two lines, so too was the 1st Corps on the right; the cavalry was to be in the rear, so too was 6th Corps and the Imperial Guard.

The enemy were deployed ready to fight; on their right was a fortified village [Hougoumont], masked by a small wood and filled with sharpshooters, their centre was placed on the reverse of the hill which masked both their infantry and cavalry; their artillery was not in any great number. (I am ignorant of our dispositions on our right flank). They fired the first shots, and soon after the cannonade began our artillery had a great superiority in number over the English; they perhaps had 130 caissons. Prince Jérôme attacked the right of the English, and after a hard-fought contest, was able to capture the wood and to become master of the village.

However, in the attempt to leave the cover aforded by the wood and hedge, and to endeavour to attack the garden wall, the 1st Regiment of Line Infantry were cut down by murderous volleys of musket fire, which Major Beaux makes clear in a second letter to Marshal Soult dated 16 April 1833:[106]

It was deemed imprudent to risk all three battalions that made up my regiment in view of the resistance put up by the defenders during the last attack, and so I ordered the 2nd and 3rd Battalions to remain in reserve, and by a normal movement, forgetting my wider responsibilities, I marched at the head of the 1st Battalion to attack the farm and capture it. However, we were repulsed with heavy losses, most noticeably from among the officers. I returned to the attack with the 2nd Battalion, which was combined with the debris of the 1st Battalion, but we had the same result despite our superhuman efforts and the fact that this effort was not as vigorous as the previous one. I observed and realised the cause of the destruction of my officers. By dividing the remnants of the two battalions and placing them as sharpshooters, and sending them onto the flanks of this farm from where the murderous fire came from, I marched on it with the 3rd Battalion; my last resource.

In the letter, Beaux describes the 1st Battalion being cut to pieces. He then returns to the attack with the 2nd Battalion, then when this too

---

106 SHDDT: IM 1962 *Correspondence au ministre de guerre-Infanterie*. Letter dated 16 April 1833.

was 'destroyed' he divides them into acting as sharpshooters on the flanks—to me, this strongly suggests that they were spread along the hedge opposite the orchard-cum-garden wall and facing towards the guards in the western garden. This is militarily the logical thing to have done, and confirms that they were not attempting to charge the wall itself. Beaux then goes back to the starting point and brings forward the 3rd Battalion. So, all in all, the entire regiment was used in a futile attempt to take the farm. As we shall see, the regiment's muster lists reports 336 men wounded with almost equal numbers from each battalion, but a surprisingly small number killed, with a ratio of one dead to six wounded. This suggests to me that the defenders raised firing positions and the cover provided by the wall, wood and the hedge were artificially reducing the kill rate. As Beaux writes, what is very significant is the loss of French officers in the action against Hougoumont. With command and control of companies falling on NCOs, some of whom had little or no combat experience, companies, if not entire battalions, would have had major issues controlling the men. Thus, it is hardly surprising that attacks faltered. According to Marshal Bugeaud, writing in 1831, Major Beaux's men broke into the farm of Hougoumont and scaled the walls:[107]

> Lieutenant-Colonel Lebeau [Beaux] commanded the 1st Line Regiment at Waterloo. He was at its head when he took the farm of La Belle Alliance [Hougoumont?], and in a manner that should be reported as a document of war. He established himself in the lee of the wall, the palisade being a heap of rubble. A sudden inspiration made him throw one of these stones over the wall. All his soldiers imitated him, and with this new fire quickly drove the defenders from the wall, which was immediately scaled with one man pushing another man over the wall.

This was presumably the south gate and wall that flanked the southern side of the garden. For the wall to be rubble clearly implies artillery had been in action, or the wall was partially collapsed before the battle. Other authors, like Mark Adkin, make it clear no French made it to the wall, and were all killed in the gap between the northern edge of the wood and the southern face of the garden wall. Clearly, some French

---

107 Eugene Tattet, *Lettres inédits du Maréchal Bugeaud, duc d'Isly (1808-1849) colligées et annotés par M. le Capitaine Tattet et publiées par Mademoiselle Féray-Bugeaud d'Isly*, Paris, Emile-Paul Freres, 1922, p. 157.

made it alive across this gap and scaled the walls. Confirming that the walls were scaled, the attack is noted by the Allied garrison captain, Büsgen, who writes:[108]

> Towards one o'clock the enemy renewed his attack with great haste against the buildings and garden and attempted to climb the garden wall, and gain a foothold behind the hedge of the orchard. However, he was chased away by the fire of the skirmishers from the garden wall, and was beaten back at all points. In this attack the enemy set fire to several stacks of hay and straw close to the farm, with the intention of spreading fire to the buildings, which was unsuccessful.

So, on balance it does seem that Major Beaux's men did at some stage get into the farm complex by climbing walls, as Marshal Bugeaud indicates, so the use of bricks as improvised missiles to bombard the defenders may be close to the truth. Total regimental losses for the 1st Regiment of Line Infantry at Waterloo are in the table below:[109]

1st Regiment of Line Infantry					
	Wounded	Wounded & Prisoner	Prisoner of War	Killed	Missing
1st Battalion	104	3	0	18	39
2nd Battalion	102	3	0	25	66
3rd Battalion	130	0	2	13	55
Total	336	6	2	56	160

Total losses at Waterloo were some 560 other ranks dead, wounded, missing or prisoner. A total of 842 men were lost from 16 to 18 June 1815. The 3rd Battalion had the highest number of men wounded, whereas the 2nd Battalion had the highest number of men killed. In total 1,454 were in ranks on the morning of 17 June, so the regiment lost 38.5 per cent of effective strength at Waterloo, and 703 men were under arms on 19 June. On the morning of 26 June 1815, the regiment had twenty-one officers and 535 other ranks—a loss of 168, or 24 per cent of effective

---

108 John Franklin personal communication, 20 August 2012.
109 SHDDT: GR 21 YC 8. See also: SHDDT: GR 21 YC 9 *1er régiment d'infanterie de ligne dit régiment du Roi, 6 décembre 1814-3 juillet 1815 (matricules 3,001 à 4,386).*

strength in the days after Waterloo. As with the 3rd Regiment of Line Infantry, these losses were sustained throughout 18 June.

Brigaded with the 1st Regiment of Line Infantry was the 2nd Regiment of Line Infantry, which does not seem to have attacked Hougoumont at all. The commander of the 1st Battalion 2nd Regiment of Line Infantry, François Michel de Brayer, writes:[110]

> It was perhaps between two or three o'clock and the enemy was routed, and we took the position in front of the telegraph that the English had established.
>
> On our left, the positions were held very well by the redoubtable English; we took up position in front of two woods that formed a triangle, where we had attempted to engage the enemy and dislodge them from this position; they were formed in a triangle with two artillery pieces which greatly incommoded our operations, and impeded our attempts to turn the English position; to do so we would need to capture the two pieces of artillery.
>
> We made numerous attempts to capture these artillery pieces, but with little success, and we suffered severely.
>
> However, Colonel Trippe sent to the attack Lieutenant Morfoise, a distinguished and intrepid officer, with fifty men, a force of grenadiers and voltigeurs; M. Morfoise succumbed to a gunshot wound to the thigh, M. Lecoq marched onwards in the footsteps of his officer, despite most of his comrades hitting the deck; his courage never left him, he never ordered his men to stop firing, and with his drawn sabre, attacked the two artillery pieces, captured them and killed the officer which commanded them. The two artillery pieces were taken away from the enemy, and conducted to the headquarters staff of the emperor, who personally decorated sub-officer Lecoq in the presence of Colonel Trippe.

Jean Thomas Lecoq served in 3rd Company 2nd Battalion 2nd Regiment of Line Infantry. He was born on 3 May 1793, the son of Maurice Lecoq and Keanne Oge. He was conscripted to the 21st Regiment of Line Infantry on 7 September 1808 and promoted to corporal on 1 October 1813. He then passed to the 2nd Regiment of Line Infantry on 1 July 1814 and promoted to sergeant on 15 February 1815.[111] Of interest, perhaps verifying this episode in the battle, is that a number of officers

---

110 AN: LH 1537/27.
111 ibid.

were wounded by artillery projectiles. Lieutenant William Anderson, who served in Captain Bolton's battery Royal Artillery, comments on 10 June 1838 that some field guns had been abandoned and were either Belgian or Brunswick pieces.[112]

Captain Robinaux, commanding 5th Company 2nd Battalion 2nd Regiment of Line Infantry, narrates the events as he witness them unfold:[113]

> Comte Reille, who commanded the 2nd Corps, came to give orders to take the position occupied by the English and make a firm attack. This kept us in this position during the battle without losing or gaining ground. Once the charge was ordered we went en masse with fixed bayonets on the enemy, who made a firm resistance. The battle was obstinate on both sides and the deadliest shooting continued with equal ardour, in just half an hour the French had captured this formidable position.

What is clear from Robinaux is that no mention of Hougoumont is made. The main thrust of the attack was not against the farm, but against the Allied position to the west of the farm. To attack Hougoumont with fixed bayonets makes no sense, so the attack was, it seems, against formed Allied infantry. The 1st and 2nd Battalions attacked at the very western limit of the French line.

At some stage during this action, elements of the 2nd Battalion became involved in the attack on the farm complex, which make sense, given the regiment was to the west of the farm and all the French had to do was turn some companies to their right. Battalion commander of the 2nd Battalion, Jean Louis Sarrand, writes:[114]

> After having crossed the small wood that covered it, while in contact with the enemy, he advanced through rolling fire up to the loop-holed walls and broke open a small side door on the side of the buildings with the blows from musket butts. He gave the order to the intrepid Lieutenant Toulouse to enter with sixty men while he advanced further with his own men to attempt to find a second entry point.

---

112 British Library: ADD MS 34706 FO 480.

113 Pierre Robinaux, Gustave Léon Schlumberger, *Journal de route du Capitaine Robinaux 1803-1832*, Plon-Nourrit, Paris, 1908.

114 Molieres and Plainville, *Dictionnaire des Braves des Napoléon* (Vol. 2), Paris, Livre Chez Vous, 2004, p. 894.

Soon after, Sarrand, presumably heading for either of the main gates, was incapacitated by a broken left thigh. He was taken prisoner, sent to Brussels and thence deported to Britain, and was ultimately returned to France on 1 November 1816.[115] The door mentioned is likely to be the west door that opened into the southern courtyard of the farm through a stable. The door today is now blocked, but the building into which the French gained entry is little changed since Waterloo. Once in the stable, which stands virtually opposite the chapel, the detachment of sixty men would have been able to fire into the upper courtyard, and would have been caught in a crossfire from the men in the three-floor chateau firing from the northern aspect of the gatehouse and farmer's house, and from any troops in the courtyard. In this position the Allied garrison could turn their fire inwards from the southern gate and shoot down onto the French. The fate of the French attackers is not clear, but certainly one man, Toulouse, escaped with nothing more than a bruise. It is not impossible that most of the French attackers escaped, as barricading the stable door in the courtyard and escaping through the external door would have slowed their pursuers. What is telling from the regiment's muster list is that the 2nd Battalion had the highest number of casualties—was this number increased through the loss of these sixty men in the farm complex? It does seem to be the case.

The Lieutenant Toulouse mentioned by Sarrand was Lieutenant Sylvian Toulouse.[116] The Allied garrison recall this attack and that it was now, in this third attack, that the farm buildings were bombarded by howitzers and set ablaze. As well as bombarding the farm, the French

---

115 AN: LH 2460/50.

116 Sylvian Toulouse was born in Bordeaux on 7 July 1786. He was the son of Bertrand Toulouse, rope maker, and Jeanne Courtaux. He was conscripted into the 10th Regiment of Line Infantry on 8 November 1806 and was promoted to corporal on 16 October 1808, to corporal-quartermaster on 3 July 1810, to sergeant on 25 March 1813, to sergeant-major of a grenadier company on 2 April 1813 and was awarded the Legion of Honour on 22 June 1813. He then was promoted to adjutant-major on 9 July 1813, to sub-lieutenant on 29 September 1813 and to lieutenant on 8 November 1813. He passed to the 107th Regiment of Line Infantry on 1 January 1814 and joined the 2nd Regiment of Line Infantry on 28 June 1814. At Waterloo he served in the 3rd Fusilier Company of 2nd Battalion. In the attack on Hougoumont he was bruised on his left side, perhaps from a musket butt. He was discharged on 26 November 1815. AN: LH 2616/53.

moved up artillery to attack the farm. The detachment from the 2nd Regiment of Line Infantry attacked the Coldstream Guards, who were positioned in the kitchen garden. Sergeant Aston recounts:[117]

> The French came on very rapidly, and in consequence of having been the foremost in pursuit and last to retreat to the chateaux, Caldwallder and his section, together with about an equal number of the Coldstream, on arriving at the chateaux found the yard filled and the house surrounded by the French. They could not enter. The French still came on and scattered all of both regiments who were outside. All these went towards the rear in unavoidable confusion.

The British guards, faced with rampaging Frenchmen coming from the south round the wall, as well as other bodies of French troops coming from the south and west, were no doubt retreated in some haste and disorder and simply wouldn't have put up any resistance. We know from Clay that he was chased towards the Nivelles road before sneaking back in through the gate once the north gate incident was over.

Lieutenant-Colonel Saltourn, of the Allied 1st Foot Guards, notes a cannon was brought up to the hedge enclosing the orchard.[118] Captain Büsgen, of the Nassau troops in the farm, notes:[119]

> Thereafter, between two and three o'clock, he placed a battery on the right flank of the buildings and proceeded to shell them with cannon and howitzers. After a short time, all the buildings were burning. The enemy now made a desperate attack for the third time, which was aimed mainly at the buildings. With the help of the smoke and flames his grenadiers penetrated through a small door into the upper courtyard, and only by the fire from the windows of the residence and the advance of a detachment of the aforementioned English guards through the lower gate to the upper courtyard, were they thrown out again and part of the enemy taken prisoner, but the same happened to seven of our grenadiers. This attack, which ended about half-past three and was the last serious attempt the enemy waged on the post of Hougoumont, although the fire of the skirmishers lasted with few interruptions to the end of the battle.

---

117 John Franklin personal communication.
118 Siborne, *Waterloo Letters*, No. 106.
119 John Franklin personal communication, 20 August 2012.

It seems on balance that Büsgen's narration and that of Sarrand seem to relate to the same event. However, Matthew Clay notes that this final attack was made against the southern, or upper, gates:[120]

> The enemy's artillery having forced the upper gates, some of them rushed in and were as quickly repulsed, there being none being left inside but a drummer boy without his drum, whom I lodged in a stable or outhouse; many of the wounded of both armies were arranged by the side of each other, having no means of conveying them to a place of greater safety. The upper gates being made again secure, a man (killed in this action, by the name of Philpott) and myself were posted under the archway for its defence, the enemy's artillery continuing their fire, at length a round shot burst open the gates; stumps intended for firewood, laying within, were sent in all directions. The enemy not having made an entry, the gate was again secured, although very much shattered.

This could be part of the same attack, whereby the men led by Sarrand made entry into the complex through the shattered southern gates. The attack mentioned by Clay could also be a fifth incursion into the complex that the French have not recorded; we cannot be certain that the event described by Büsgen and Clay are one and the same. Even so, the French had exploited a weakness of the farm complex: an unguarded door and its vulnerability to artillery fire. Many British writers claim the French never deployed artillery against the farm, whereas according to eyewitnesses, artillery pieces were deployed against the orchard gate, southern gate and western range of buildings. Therefore, this was no mindless infantry assault with no artillery support as we are led to believe by popular histories of the battle. Jérôme does not seem to have simply tried to bludgeon Hougoumont into surrender with futile infantry assaults, but with artillery support he came close to capturing the farm. These guns were presumably the division artillery manned by the 2nd Regiment of Foot Artillery.

During the attack by the 2nd Regiment of Line Infantry, in the 1st Battalion Second-Captain Jean Bourdageau (commanding the 2nd Company of Fusiliers) was wounded.[121] Commanding the grenadier company was François Dubarry, who was wounded twice—once with a gunshot and then he had his right arm blown off by a discharge of

---

120 ibid.
121 SHDDT: 2Yb-641-05.

canister from an artillery piece. Clearly, at some stage the 2nd Regiment of Line Infantry had come under artillery bombardment during the day. Also, wounded by artillery fire were Lieutenant Joseph Gabriel Pierre Nicolas Pierre and Adjutant Louis Pierre Duhamel, who was unlucky enough for a howitzer shell to explode near to him and remove his left ear. In the 3rd Company of Fusiliers, Lieutenant Nicholas Simaire suffered a gunshot to the head. Killed in the grenadier company was Sub-Lieutenant Normand.[122]

Others wounded in the 2nd Battalion included Captain-Adjutant-Major Louis Charles Gallois, who had a musket ball pass through his upper body.[123] Captain Jean François Baron Poncet, who commanded the grenadier company of 2nd Battalion, was wounded in the attacks. At the head of the voltigeur company was Captain Mazaire Bordot, who took a gunshot to the right thigh. In the 2nd Fusilier Company, Sub-Lieutenant Moulin was wounded. In the 4th Fusilier Company, Lieutenant Jean Pierre Deshu was shot in the right side of the chest and made prisoner of war. Those killed in the 2nd Battalion included Captain Lacomme at the head of the 3rd Fusilier Company, Sub-Lieutenant Detchemendy in the 4th Fusilier Company, and Sub-Lieutenants Dupuy and Salmon.[124]

In the 3rd Battalion, Captain-Adjutant-Major Nicolas Gallimardet was shot in the right leg[125] and Captain Maurice Guillaume, commanding the voltigeur company, had a musket ball pass through his left arm.[126] In the 2nd Company of Fusiliers, Captain Laignoux was wounded by a gunshot, so too was Lieutenant Mouginot. In the 3rd Company of Fusiliers, Lieutenant Toussaint Augustin Morfouasse was wounded with a gunshot to the right thigh. In the 4th Company of Fusiliers, Sub-Lieutenants Begagnon and Claude Charton were wounded.[127] Sergeant-Major Patrice Joseph Edouard Carlier had his left knee shattered by a musket ball.[128] Killed in the 3rd Battalion, in the 2nd Company of Fusiliers, was Sub-Lieutenant Le Senecal.[129]

---

122 SHDDT: 2Yb-641-05.
123 AN: LH 1063/05.
124 SHDDT: 2Yb-641-05.
125 AN: LH 1062/20.
126 AN: LH 1053/29.
127 SHDDT: 2Yb-641-05.
128 AN: LH 429/26.
129 SHDDT: 2Yb-641-05.

Total regimental losses for the 2nd Regiment of Line Infantry at Waterloo are in the table below:[130]

2nd Regiment of Line Infantry					
	Wounded	Wounded & Prisoner	Prisoner of War	Killed	Missing
1st Battalion	82	9	8	8	10
2nd Battalion	109	9	0	24	12
3rd Battalion	70	31	4	17	18
Total	261	49	12	49	40

On the morning of 18 June, the regiment had 1,556 men under arms. At Waterloo, a total of 411 men were lost. This represents a loss of 26.4 per cent of effective strength, leaving, on 19 June, 1,145 men under arms. On 26 June 1815 the regiment mustered twenty-nine officers and 585 men. This represented a loss of 560 men after Waterloo, or 49 per cent of effective strength. For the regiment, far more men were lost through desertion after Waterloo than during the fighting of 15 to 18 June. Of note, the losses sustained by the 1st Regiment of Line Infantry were far higher, thus supporting the comment by Major Beaux that it was the 1st Regiment of Line Infantry at the head of the column in the later attacks that lost the most men in the brigade, if not the division. Again, we cannot tell when the losses were sustained, so we have to be cautious in ascribing losses to the action against Hougoumont. However, the total losses are similar to the number of men evacuated from the regiment, suggesting these losses, given a similarity in number, occurred at the start of the action rather than at the close of the action.

Given the space available for the French to deploy at Hougoumont, it seems the 1st Regiment of Line Infantry deployed to the right, and thus operated primarily in the wood and fields to the south of the farm complex, and the 2nd Regiment of Line Infantry formed the left and attacked, presumably, in the Nivelles road and also the farm road, from where they could threaten the batteries on the end of the ridge. The Allied garrison at Hougoumont had mustered 1,210 men, compared to Jérôme's 2,989 men. However, the French troops were committed by

---

130 SHDDT: GR 21 YC 19 *2e régiment d'infanterie de ligne dit régiment de la Reine, 20 mai 1814-21 août 1814 (matricules 1 à 2,997).* See also: SHDDT: GR 21 YC 20 *2e régiment d'infanterie de ligne dit régiment de la Reine, 9 septembre 1814-6 juin 1815 (matricules 3,000 à 4,723).*

brigade, roughly 1,500 men. When one factors in the fact that not all regiments committed all their men to the attack, we can easily see that the French were actually outnumbered in the attack on Hougoumont. Jérôme's men attacked in two waves, at no time was all the division involved in the attack due to the restricted space on the French left flank. This is very important in understanding the action here. The Allies held Hougoumont, but not through the fighting spirit of a few men against hordes of French. The French and Allies had about the same number of men deployed at any one time, but the Allied garrison had the advantage over the French in that they had prepared positions to fire from. Any attacking force against a defensive outpost like Hougoumont was always going to be disadvantaged. The terrain to the south of Hougoumont also acted in the favour of the Allies. The French could not launch a direct assault; they had to pass through a number of very thick hedges in order to assault the southern range of buildings. Only by skirting the orchard and attacking from the east through the garden and orchard, or by skirting to the west of the southern wood and attacking the farm from the Nivelles road, could the French gain any advantage. In the first attack, the 1st Regiment of Light Infantry attacked the wood and orchard and skirted north-east around the farm, leaving the 3rd Regiment of Line Infantry to attack the farm complex.

2nd Foot Artillery

The battery attached to Jérôme' division, the 2nd Company 2nd Foot Artillery, had lost two men on 16 June.[131] Regimental losses were as follows for Waterloo:[132]

Company	Army Corps	Killed	Died of Wounds	Wounded	Wounded & Missing	Prisoner of War	Missing
2nd	2nd Corps, 6th Division	1	1	1	0	0	1

The battery lost four men at Waterloo. During the route, one gun was lost on the 18th, a 6-pounder.[133] Commanding the battery was Captain

---

131 SHDDT: GR 25 YC 21 *2e Artillerie à Pied 1814–1815.*
132 SHDDT: GR 25 YC 21.
133 SHDDT C15 34. *Situation Artillerie 26 Juin 1815.*

Antoine Gabriel Louis Meunier. He was born in 1770 and joined the army in 1786, before being commissioned as a second-lieutenant on 29 March 1794 in the 2nd Foot Artillery. Promotion to captain came on 14 August 1802 and he was placed in 7th Company. In July 1809, he was passed to the 21st Company and in August 1814 he was placed in command of 2nd Company. He was killed at Quatre-Bras.[134]

The battery sergeant-major was Jean Giroud, who was born at Touvet on 13 July 1772. He enlisted in the 4th Foot Artillery in 1794, made corporal in 1801, sergeant in 1803 and named sergeant-major in the 82nd Cohort of the National Guard on 21 June 1812. He was then named as a sergeant-major in the 2nd Foot Artillery on 19 December 1813. He had been wounded at Aboukir in Egypt in 1800.[135]

Comment

In the fighting in and around the farm complex, the division was in action for three hours, or at most four. Total losses for the division at Waterloo were as follows:

6th Infantry Division							
	Wounded	Evacuated Wounded	Wounded & Prisoner	Prisoner of War	Killed	Missing	Total
1st Regiment of Light Infantry	42	0	0	3	7	7	59
3rd Regiment of Line Infantry	0	267	2	276	106	4	655
1st Regiment of Line Infantry	336	0	6	2	56	160	560
2nd Regiment of Line Infantry	261	0	50	12	49	30	402
Total	639	267	58	293	218	201	1,676

---

134 État militaire du Corps royal d'artillerie de France, 1815, pp. 118 and 338.
135 AN: LH 1152/41.

The highest losses in the division were sustained by the 1st and 3rd Regiments of Line Infantry. The highest number of killed was in the 3rd, the only regiment that seems to have been totally committed to the attack on the farm complex. The 1st Regiment of Light Infantry, it seems, took no further action in the fighting once it had attacked the wood and orchard, perhaps due to a lack of officers. From the data, what is striking are the incredibly low losses for the 1st Regiment of Light Infantry—the data clearly shows that the regiment at no stage assaulted the farm complex, given its significantly lower losses than the other regiments in the division. In reality, only two French regiments from the division were deployed directly against the farm complex, which have significantly higher losses than the 2nd Regiment of Line Infantry. Waterloo myth says the entire 2nd Corps was destroyed against the walls of Hougoumont. The idea does not stand up to any scrutiny, and the contest here has been over-inflated by British historians to make the action here far more important than it was in reality.

Jérôme, therefore, seems to have been overly maligned by British and French writers and, furthermore, most British writers over-exaggerate the French forces actually deployed, as the majority of the fighting for Hougoumont was undertaken by Jérôme's division. This was no repeat of Thermopolis or precursor to Rourke's Drift, as the French attacking force deployed at any one time was equal to, or less than, the Allied garrison. These unfortunate facts, however, get in the way of the story of Waterloo that has come down to us since 1815.

Prince Jérôme's actions at Waterloo have often been described as reckless and that he needlessly destroyed his division, and that of Foy. On assessment based on cold, hard facts, the charges against Jérôme are unjustified.

The French artillery

In accordance to the emperor's 11.00 order, as the precursor to d'Erlon's attack, the French drew up a battery of guns on their right flank to bombard the Allied lines. General Baron de Salle, commanding the artillery of 1st Corps, writes:[136]

---

136 *'Des extraits des Souvenirs du général Dessales, ou de Salle'* in *la Revue de Paris*, 15 January 1896.

About ten o'clock, the emperor made the 1st Corps and the 2nd Corps advance, which occupied the left of the road to Brussels. We occupied the right of this road, and cashed in on this point. Two divisions of the 6th Corps and the guard formed the reserve. I was with Comte d'Erlon when M. La Bédoyère, general aide-de-camp of the emperor, came to tell me that he had given me command of a battery of eighty guns, which consisted all my 6-pounder batteries, the 12-pounders of my reserve and also the reserve batteries of 2nd and 6th Corps, which actually formed only fifty-four guns, twenty-four of them being 12-pounders. I had to order all the guns placed into battery in the position we occupied, halfway up the slope, on one line, and begin firing all at once to astonish and shake the morale of the enemy.

Colonel Bro, of the 4th Lancers (attached to 1st Corps), narrates that:[137]

The 18th, we were given the objective of Mont-Saint-Jean. Napoléon, after an inspection at the farm of Caillou, stopped and dictated at eleven o'clock the order, once the army is arranged in order of battle, about one o'clock in the afternoon, (when the emperor give the order to Marshal Ney), the attack will begin to seize the village of Mont-Saint-Jean, where there was an intersection of roads.

To this end, the 12-pounder batteries of the 2nd Corps and those of the 6th were convened with those of the 1st Corps. These fifty-four guns fired at the troops of Mont-Saint-Jean and Comte d'Erlon began the attack by bringing forward his left division and, according to circumstances, brought up in support the remaining divisions of the 1st Corps. The 2nd Corps was able to advance to guard the flank of Comte d'Erlon.

Napoléon claims in his report of the battle that the battery mustered eighty guns, almost double the number given by de la Salle and Bro. de Mauduit states in 1848 that the battery had ten guns. Pontécoulant, of the Guard Horse Artillery, states the battery had sixty guns, of which thirty-six were 12-pounders manned by the Imperial Guard.[138] This myth of a vast battery of eighty guns has been perpetuated to modern times with a high complement of gunners from the Imperial Guard.

---

137 General Bro, *Mémoires, 1796-1844*, Librairie des deux Empires, 2001, p. 148.

138 Gustave de Pontécoulant, *Mémoires*, Paris, 1866, p. 266.

According to Colonel Louis Bro, the battery was formed into three elements and was placed on the ridge of high ground running perpendicular to the Brussels road, with the flank resting against La Belle Alliance. The first battery was against the right of a French battalion, which stood to the east of La Belle Alliance. The second battery was on the crest of the 'French' ridge, protected in front by a hedge and small trees, with the bulk of 1st Corps drawn up on the slopes below the battery. The third battery was on a small hill, towards Papelotte. As discussed later, the battery against La Belle Alliance were the 6-pounders of Quiot's division, the central battery were the 12-pounders and horse artillery and the third battery were the divisional artillery of Durutte, which would be joined later by the 12-pounders from 6th Corps. The central battery was supported on either flank by the light cavalry of the Guard, and by three infantry battalions, presumably from 6th Corps.[139] The disposition shown by Bro correlates with that noted by de la Salle. Colonel Bro also shows a battery to the west of the Brussels road being flanked by infantry battalions and supported by cavalry.[140] In reality, the battery was composed of:

- One 12-pounder battery from 2nd Corps (twelve guns)
- One 12-pounder battery from 6th Corps (twelve guns)
- One 12-pounder battery from 1st Corps (twelve guns)
- Four 6-pounder batteries from 1st Corps (thirty-two guns)
- One 6-pounder horse artillery battery from 1st Corps (six guns)
- Total: sixty-two guns

However, it seems that the 6-pounder foot artillery battery from Durutte's division was not part of the grand battery, giving a battery strength of fifty-four guns, just as de la Salle and Bro state. The guns were not drawn up in a single line. Each infantry division retained its own artillery, with only the reserve guns being placed in a single battery. Quiot's artillery, which was thirty-six guns strong, seems to also have been forward of the main line—hardly the grand battery of the Waterloo myth.

---

139 AN: 82 AP 5 *Fonds Bro de Commerce*, Dossier 2. 1814-1819.
140 ibid.

The movement of guns was observed by the Allies. Lieutenant-Colonel Jonathan Leach, of the 95th Rifles, notes some years after the battle:[141]

> We perceived our adversaries bringing into position, on the heights opposite, gun after gun; and here much time had elapsed, there were, at a moderate computation, fifty pieces of artillery in the battery, staring us in the face, and intended particularly to salute our division, the farm of La Haye Sainte, and the left of Baron Alten's division. The enemy's columns were not as yet visible, being covered by some undulations of ground near the summit of their position. In an instant this numerous and powerful artillery opened on us, battering at the same moment the farmhouse of La Haye Sainte. Under cover of this cannonade several large columns of infantry, supported by heavy bodies of cavalry, and preceded by a multitude of light infantry, descended at a trot into the plain, with shouts and cries of *'Vive l'Empereur!'* some of them throwing up their caps in the air, and advancing to the attack with such confidence and impetuosity, as if the bare possibility of our being able to withstand the shock was out of the question, fighting as they were under the immediate eye of their emperor. But, Napoléon was destined, in a few minutes after the commencement of this hubbub, to see his imperial legions recoil in the greatest confusion, with a dreadful carnage, and with a great loss in prisoners.

About the effect of the grand battery on the French right firing blindly over the Allied ridge, Colonel Ffiennes Miller, of the Inniskilling Dragoons, notes:[142]

> You may remember that when we advanced, and the men began to fall from the fire of the artillery, we dismounted and marched up the hill on foot, and on reaching the top we mounted, and then I perceived the enemy's close columns advancing near the hedge.

Tomkinson, of the 16th Light Dragoons, notes:[143]

---

141 Jonathan Leach, *Rough Sketches of the life of an Old Soldier*, London, Brown and Green, London, 1831, pp. 386-8.

142 Siborne, *Waterloo Letters*, No. 46. Letter dated 18 June 1839.

143 William Tomkinson, James Tomkinson, *The Diary of a Cavalry Officer in the Peninsular and Waterloo Campaigns 1809-1815*, S. Sonnenschein, London, 1894, p. 300.

We moved to the ground assigned for our brigade, and, all being quiet on our front, dismounted. We had not been long on our ground before the cannonade opened and became general along the whole line. Colonel Ponsonby, myself, and some others (my brother Henry was of this party) rode out in front to see what was going on, and standing together near a hedge, attracted a few of the enemy's round shot.

Captain Eberhard von Brandis, of the 5th Line Battalion King's German Legion, served as the aide-de-camp to Colonel Baron Christian von Ompteda during the Waterloo campaign, and he described the French artillery thus:[144]

During the contest on our right wing the French also attacked the left of our line, where the Hanoverian brigade, commanded by Colonel Best, was situated, but this attack was repulsed. Towards two o'clock it became our turn to be exposed to the cannonade which had spread along the whole of the front line, because Napoléon wished to accomplish his general plan and break through the British centre. For this purpose, he had positioned eighty cannon opposite our line, and these cannon raged with their full power against the two central divisions, those of Alten and Picton. At this time, Colonel von Hacke, whose regiment, the Cumberland Hussars, was just behind us, rode towards Colonel von Ompteda and requested permission to move his regiment out of range of the cannon fire, which they could no longer endure. Ompteda directed him to Lord Uxbridge, the commander of the cavalry. Besides the regiment of Cumberland Hussars there were several English and Dutch cavalry regiments immediately behind us that were suffering greatly from the cannon fire, like ourselves, but which maintained their designated position with the utmost courage and calm.

Quite clearly, some of the shots from the battery were finding targets and inflicting losses on the Allied troops on the reverse slope. The effects of artillery fire on human and horse alike could be terrifying. Artillery round shot, canister shot or shell fragments were virtually guaranteed to cause casualties ranging from a slight flesh wound to the removal of heads and limbs, as well as items of equipment, in all directions.

---

144 John Franklin personal communication, 19 October 2012.

d'Erlon's attack

The third move made by Napoléon's army that day was the massed assault by the fresh troops of 1st Corps, headed by General d'Erlon. Following the bombardment of the Allied lines, the infantry was ordered to the attack. However, it seems Napoléon's original point of attack was at Papelotte and La Haye Sainte, to out flank the Allied lines and not engage with a full-frontal assault. The arrival of the Prussians at Saint-Lambert appears to have changed Napoléon's original plans. With the Prussians advancing, time was of the essence, so he planned to use 1st Corps, the 'grand battery' and part of the cavalry reserve as a crude battering ram to break the Allied lines in a single stroke.

For the attack, d'Erlon formed his corps into vast attacking columns, termed *colonne de division par bataillon*, in essence being a column formed from an entire infantry division. de Mauduit, based on the narratives of Generals Brue and Pégot, as well as Battalion Commander Rulliers, notes that four columns were formed of deployed battalions, with closed intervals, each column being 500 to 600 paces apart.[145]

On the left of the line, by the Brussels road, General Quiot's division formed up, comprising of the aforementioned 54th and 55th Regiments of Line Infantry (under Charlet) and the 2nd Brigade (under Bourgeois), comprising the 28th and 105th Regiments of Line Infantry. The 2nd Brigade, according to Duthlitt (who served with Bourgeois), attacked first and was later supported by Charlet's men, which may have moved up from La Haye Sainte. Therefore, each brigade formed separate columns.

To the right of Quiot's 1st Division was Donzelot's 2nd Division, comprising of two battalions of the 13th Regiment of Light Infantry (the third was detached with the 7th Hussars towards Saint-Lambert) and 17th Regiment of Line Infantry in the 1st Brigade (commanded by Schmitz), and the 19th and 51st Regiments of Line Infantry in the 2nd Brigade (commanded by Baron Aulard). The division was formed in *colonne de division par bataillon*, with the 2nd Brigade at the head of the column. In this formation, each battalion was formed in line some 150 files wide. Each battalion was twenty-four paces apart and would be, in Durutte's division of six battalions, eighteen ranks deep. This would give an approximate size of one hundred metres wide and 125 metres deep,

---

145 Hippolyte de Mauduit, *'Vieille Militaire. Charleroi, Fleurus et Waterloo'* in *La Sentinalle de l'armée*, 24 June 1836.

with twenty-four-pace intervals used for an eight battalion frontage. This formation was neither new nor unusual, and had been used by the French before. The five-pace interval, often cited as the cause of failure of the French attack, is as far as can be ascertained an invention by the strategist Jomini, later verified by writers such as Battalion Commander Rulliers, of the 95th Regiment of Line Infantry, and Adjutant Gastineau, of the 13th Regiment of Light Infantry. Marching such a concentration of troops with this interval across the difficult terrain would result in the battalions becoming mixed up, and there would be no way to restore order. If this had been the case, then when the columns attacked the success that they achieved would, in theory, have not been possible. Furthermore, with such intervals the time taken to actually form the columns would have been both lengthy and very difficult to align. Based on the French 1813 infantry manual, it would be a much faster and a more obvious way to form these columns with the twenty-four-pace interval by forming columns by section.[146]

To the right of Donzelot was Marcognet's 3rd Division, formed in the same manner, and comprised of the 21st and 46th Regiments of Line Infantry in the 1st Brigade (commanded by Noguès) and the 2nd Brigade of Grenier, comprising the 25th and 45th Regiments of Line Infantry.

On the far right came Durutte's division which comprised of the 1st Brigade of General Pégot (the 8th and 29th Regiments of Line Infantry) and the 2nd Brigade of General Brue (the 85th and 95th Regiments of Line Infantry). Durutte's column comprised the 1st Brigade and the 95th Regiment of Line Infantry (totalling six battalions), making the column 150 files wide and eighteen deep, less the sub-officers.[147]

The cuirassiers attack

Elsewhere on the field, as the 3rd Regiment of Light Infantry were passing through the kitchen garden of Hougoumont, and de la Salle was getting his guns into position, Marshal Ney began to assemble the heavy cavalry. General Gaspard Gourgaud, of the Imperial Staff, writes of the same event from his viewpoint with Milhaud's cuirassiers:[148]

---

146 Jakub Samek personal communication, 18 July 2012.
147 Hippolyte de Mauduit, op. cit.
148 'Bataille de Waterloo 18 Juin 1815: relation d'un Officier General Francaise' in *Nouvel Revue Retrospective*, January 1896.

At midday, the emperor ordered me to carry the order to Marshal Ney, who commanded the right wing, to attack the enemy with energy, which was to be proceeded by an artillery barrage. This battery was formed in front of the corps of d'Erlon and had sixty-four guns, of which thirty were 12-pounders, and began a vigorous cannonade. The enemy greatly suffered from this. Our sharpshooters advanced to Mont-Saint-Jean. Marshal Ney ordered the line to advance; the artillery quit their good position to support the advance. Ney ordered four squadrons of cuirassiers to charge along the left side of the road. Three or four hundred Brunswickers were ambushed on Mont-Saint-Jean and were captured.

Aide-de-camp to Marshal Ney, Octave Levavasseur, notes that he was on a reconnaissance mission for the marshal:[149]

Shortly before noon, the emperor dictated the orders that Soult was writing in his notebook, the major-general then ripped the sheet off and gave it to Marshal Ney, who, before handing it to me to communicate with the commanders-in-chief, wrote in the margin in pencil: 'Comte d'Erlon is to understand that it is he who must begin the attack.' I went galloping off to the left, and I arrived firstly with Prince Jérôme, whose troops are occupying a valley en masse, behind a small wood. I continued, but, before reaching General d'Erlon, my horse fell and the paper, covered in mud becomes almost indecipherable, so that I am obliged to help his reading of the order. I returned to Marshal Ney, who I found behind La Haye Sainte. Already, Comte d'Erlon had started to commence his attack, the battle was joined.

The marshal summoned all the colonels of cavalry and ordered them each to send a squadron. These squadrons moved up from the rear and he told one of his oldest aides, Crabbe, a retired brigadier-general who had only been a few days with us, to take command of the cavalry, and added: 'you will follow the left and sweep all that lies between the artillery and infantry, passing over the land occupied by the enemy behind La Haye Sainte'.

Meanwhile, Comte d'Erlon advanced amid the shrapnel on the slope of the plateau, but he failed to take the position. General Crabbe advanced and penetrated into the valley; the marshal turned and addressed me: 'Levavasseur,' he said, 'go with that charge.

---

149 Octave Levavasseur, *Souvenirs militaires 1800-1815*, Librairie des Deux Empirés, 2001, pp. 303-5.

I'm leaving and you go join Crabbe at the front.' After passing the lines of enemy artillery, Crabbe formed in column by squadron and continued the charge. We start pushing them back with the cries of '*Vive l'Empereur*! Forward!'

With the fight for La Haye Sainte spilling out onto the slopes of the plateau, the Lüneburg Battalion presented an irresistible target for the cuirassiers. Michel Ordener was commanding the 1st Regiment of Cuirassiers and recounts the charge as follows:[150]

> Ney gave me orders to take an English battery placed near the farm of Mont-Saint-Jean, whose fire was causing great havoc in our lines. I made my regiment advance at the trot, putting my regiment into column by squadron at large intervals. The Hanoverian Battalion of Lünenburg and the 2nd Light Infantry of the King's German Legion were placed in our way, and we fell on them with the corps. I killed with my own hand three officers, their flag came into our possession; we addressed in the same breath the English battery, and we captured the twenty-four guns and limbers that composed the battery and had the guns spiked, and I continued the charge that carried us to the edge of the Soignes Forest. Here, I am ten feet away from a square, when one face opened a murderous fire on us. My horse was killed, struck by a bullet to the neck. Protected by my armour I freed myself, I leave my horse and returned with my men to our lines, where, after some quickly conducted first aid, I mounted a fresh horse and resumed my command.

The cuirassiers attacked the King's German Legion of Ompteda. With the Allied infantry broken up and dispersed, the British Household Brigade of heavy cavalry was launched against the intrepid cuirassiers. Carl Jacobi narrates:[151]

> The 5th and 8th Line Battalions advanced against the enemy infantry which had attacked La Haye Sainte. The battalion closed ranks and advanced to attack the enemy. But, while advancing the enemy cavalry, which had been involved in the earlier attacks against the squares of the 1st Hanoverian Brigade on the heights,

---

150 Henri Lot, *Les deux généraux Ordener*, R. Roger et F. Chernoviz, Paris, 1910.

151 John Franklin, *Waterloo Hanoverian Correspondence* (Vol. 1), 1815 Limited, 2010, pp. 26-7.

fell upon them. The 5th Line Battalion was supported just in time by the English cavalry, which was falling back, and they suffered small losses. However, the 8th Line Battalion was completely destroyed as they endured the surprise attack which was eventually driven off by the English cavalry. The officer who bore the colour received three severe wounds and the colour was lost.

Under the swords of the cuirassiers, Ompteda's command was decimated. The brigade on the morning of 18 June mustered 1,527 officers and men. Of these, some 787 were killed or wounded and 207 were listed as missing, a total loss of 994 officers and men, or 65 per cent of effective strength being lost in the attack by the cuirassiers.[152]

---

152 Deleveot, 'Cowards at Waterloo?' in Napoléon, No. 16, Summer 2000, p. 31.

Chapter 4

La Haye Sainte: Round One

The farm of La Haye Sainte, with its Allied garrison, was on the extreme left wing of the envisioned attack by 1st Corps. It had to be controlled, if not captured, to prevent an Allied flanking movement against 1st Corps. The attack on La Haye Sainte was supported by the French heavy cavalry and is detailed in the companion volume by the same author. Colonel Bro, of the 4th Lancers (attached to 1st Corps), narrates that:[153]

> The companies of sappers were ready to barricade themselves on the spot in Mont-Saint-Jean, and at noon all arrangements were made.

Aide-de-camp to Marshal Ney, Octave Lavavasseur, notes that French engineers attacked the farm:[154]

> I galloped to Marshal Ney, who had just given General [name omitted from the original source] an order to seize the farm of La Haye Sainte with about three thousand men. This march was conducted in close column to the farm, but arrived a short distance off; they swerved to the right as they came under fire from this small house. The marshal, indignant at the hesitation of the general, sent me to tell him to carry the position at the charge. I went down to the road where I found two companies of sappers, which were formed up by the road. The captain came towards me and handed me his card: 'Monsieur l'aide de camp', and he cried, 'look, here is my name'. Then he beat the charge, and his engineers ran to the

---

153 Bro, p. 148.
154 Levavasseur, pp. 303-5.

farm with cries of 'Forward!' As I departed to carry the marshal's order to the general, the firing began and we seized the gardens and hedges, and had pushed back the enemy...La Haye Sainte was occupied by our troops, but the English came in superior force and soon re-captured it.

Sergeant de Mauduit, of the 2nd Battalion 1st Regiment of Grenadiers à Pied of the Imperial Guard, notes that:[155]

> M. Vieux, in 1815 at the Battle of Waterloo was attached to the 1st Corps as officer of engineers, was dismounted when a ball killed his horse. He remained with his battalion of sappers which were attacking La Haye Sainte. In stature, he was remarkable, standing over six feet tall, and he with an axe, along with those of 1st Corps, attacked the gates. A ball wounded him in the left hand and he was forced to abandon the field of battle. As he went to escape from his assailants, a second ball passed through his shoulder.

Pierre Vieux was born at Sainte-Menehould in the Marne Valley on 21 February 1791 and was killed in action in 1837. He graduated from the engineering school and was promoted as second-lieutenant in the 6th Company of the 1st Engineer Battalion on 5 July 1813. This story may be apocryphal, as it is hard to imagine how de Mauduit observed this event firsthand and clearly must be ghost writing this, based on stories he was told after the battle, perhaps in his capacity as a newspaper editor. This attack by the 1st Engineers was led by Battalion Commander Jean Antoine Marie Borrel Vivier. He writes:[156]

> In 1815 at the Battle of Waterloo I had my horse killed under me at the capture of the farm of La Haye Sainte, when I was at the head of 400 soldiers from the engineers.

In the attack, the barricade across the Brussels road was attacked and captured. This action was led by Edme Paul Boutaul, who was a:[157]

> second-lieutenant of the 1st Regiment of the Arm [engineers] on 15 May 1815, which was attached to the 1st Corps of the Armée du

---

155 Hippolyte de Mauduit, *Les derniers jours de la Grande Armée* (Vol. 2), Paris, 1848, p. 334.
156 AN: LH 299/20.
157 *Le Montieur de l'Armee*, 16 November 1854.

Nord. He took part in the affair of 16 June at Quatre-Bras, and that of 18 June at the Battle of Waterloo. This was an imposing debut for a young officer beginning his military life.

At Waterloo he inaugurated his career with an action of great daring: at the head of his company, in the middle of a hail of balls that rained down, he captured and removed the barricade that was behind the crenulated farm of La Haye Sainte.

It was perhaps in this attack that Sergeant-Major Claude Boron, of the 1st Regiment of Engineers, was wounded with a gunshot to the lower abdomen.[158] Among the 3rd Company of the 2nd Battalion of the 1st Regiment of Engineers, attached to the 3rd Infantry Division, wounded in this assault was Captain Watrin and Second-Lieutenant Buquet. At the head of 4th Company 2nd Battalion 1st Regiment of Engineers (attached to the 4th Infantry Division of Durutte), Captain Perpete Joseph Louis Urbain had a leg pulverised by a cannon ball.[159] Corporal Jean Pierre Delorme was wounded with a gunshot to the right ear and made prisoner of war at the close of the battle.[160] Just as Marshal Ney's aide-de-camp noted (and as the emperor's written order instructed), the first assault to capture the farm appears to have been conducted by engineers and not infantry. However, it does appear to have been supported by infantry. Battalion Commander Joseph-Marcelin Rullieres, of the 95th Regiment of Line Infantry, notes (albeit in 1856) that:[161]

The division on the left of 1st Corps crossed to the left side of the road and marched on La Haye Sainte, and the other divisions of the army corps onto the English troops, which were to their front.

This movement has been said by French historians like Charras, Quinet, Thiers and Houssaye to be the brigade of Charlet from Quiot's division. Alas, they do not give a source for this statement. Colonel Louis Bro in 1822 states no troops from 1st Corps crossed the Brussels road to attack La Haye Sainte. It seems likely that the attack was by engineers and not, if we believe the accounts left to us by Fleuret and Duthlitt, by the 54th and 55th Regiments of Line Infantry.

---

158 AN: LH 299/37.
159 Jean Marc Boisnard personal communication, 3 June 2012.
160 *Medalle de Sainte Helene*, No. 26662.
161 SHDDT: GD 2 1135.

The command of Ompteda, with the 2nd King's German Legion Brigade, had opposed the engineers, and presumably another body of French troops as well, since Crabbe's cuirassiers lost 65 per cent of their strength during the day; some 787 men dead or wounded and 207 missing, a total of 994 men lost out of the 1,527 who were in ranks at the start of 18 June.[162]

d'Erlon's attack commences

With the cuirassiers controlling the left flank, 1st Corps now advanced to the attack. About the attack, Drouet d'Erlon writes:[163]

> Precisely at noon, the first shots of the great battery were heard. It was the signal to attack, all the troops engaged and the 2nd Corps sought to seize the farm of Hougoumont, and the 1st Corps had become master of La Haye Sainte, placed on the road to Brussels. These two positions, which were at the bottom of the position of the British army, had been barricaded and were defended by a large body of infantry hidden behind the hedges. Much loss was experienced on both sides; we became masters of these places, as they were forced to abandon them.

Captain Pierre Charles Duthlitt, aide-de-camp to General Bourgeois (commanding 2nd Brigade, part of 1st Division of 1st Corps), narrates about the movements of the 28th and 105th Regiments of Line Infantry:[164]

> The 2nd Brigade of the 1st Division of 1st Corps, commanded by General Bourgeois, were ordered to seize the position of Mont-Saint-Jean, which had become the centre of operations...In front of Mont-Saint-Jean, in relation to us, we had a farm which was occupied by the infantry, its approaches were blocked by carts and ploughs and tree branches, their slender branches being intertwined, and further in front was a *chevaux de fries*, which made the attack difficult, the surrounding hedges were also lined with Scottish sharpshooters and supported by several other regiments placed in ambush. There was also a body of cavalry protected by

---

162 Delevept, op. cit.
163 Drouët.
164 Pierre Duthlit, *Les Mémoires du Capitaine Duthlit*, Lille, 1909.

71

a formidable battery, which was placed on a concealed height and made this position an excessively fortified one.

The 2nd Brigade was placed in a hollow, having been formed in column of attack by battalion, and began marching at the *pas-des-charge* preceded by skirmishers, and shouts of joy; but this precipitation and enthusiasm would become fatal in that the soldiers had yet to do a long march to reach the enemy. They were soon tired by the difficulty of moving on land that was greasy and soggy and which broke the straps of their gaiters, and some even lost their shoes burdened by the amount of mud attached to them and by the fact that the mud stuck the soles of the shoes to the ground, and because the commands could not be heard as they were covered by thousands of repeated shouts and noise from the drums.

Soon there was some confusion in the ranks, especially when the head of the column had reached within range of the enemy's fire. Between the column head and the enemy was a deep ravine that we had not seen before, and it was impassable [the sunken road east of La Haye Sainte]. The column was forced to make a move to the left to skirt the ravine and the embankment by distance of some hundred metres; but the command had not been well understood throughout the column, some battalions made a move to the left while others made a move to the right, which resulted in confusion and wasted time.

During this confusion, the enemy made use of every means, a terrible fire burst out upon the column; bullets, cannonballs and grapeshot killed in an instant a third of the men of this brigade. However, we were not weakening, and when we finally closed and assailed their position, the charge was beaten, and the pace was not rushed; repeated a thousand times over were cries of 'long live the emperor', we then rushed onto the batteries.

For the actions of the 28th Regiment of Line Infantry at Waterloo we are lucky that we have the memoirs of Pierre Louis Canler.[165] About Waterloo, he writes:[166]

> Around noon we went to take a position on the plateau of La Belle Alliance, on which had been established a battery of eighty guns, then we were sent down into the ravine of the same name, and we were assailed by a formidable battery that the English had established during the night in front of ours, and continually fired on us.
>
> Soon it was a dreadful duet performed by two batteries composed of nearly 200 guns; balls, bombs and shells passed whistling over our heads. After half an hour wait, Marshal Ney ordered the attack and to take by storm the English battery; three rolls of the drum to get the corps ready to march; we were formed up in close column by battalion, I noticed that Adjutant Hubaut, who formed the divisions, an old soldier who made all the campaigns of the empire, was concerned and extremely pale. Finally, the columns were formed and General Drouet d'Erlon, in the middle of his corps, pronounced with a strong clear voice: 'It is today that we must conquer or die!'
>
> The cry of 'long live the emperor!' came from every mouth to answer this short speech, and with shouldered arms, the sound of drums beating the charge, the columns moved against the English guns without firing a single shot. Then the enemy's batteries, which until then had only sent well-aimed ball and shell onto our columns, now decimated them by firing grapeshot. Hardly had we gone a hundred steps than the commander of our 2nd Battalion, M. Marine,[167] was mortally wounded; the captain of my company,

---

165 MAT No. 132 Pierre Louis Canler was the son of Joseph Louis and Anne Sophie Genève Bram, born on 3 April 1797. He was admitted to the regiment on 20 December 1811 and promoted to corporal on 21 August 1813. He was discharged on 29 September 1815. SHDDT: GR 21 YC 264 *28e régiment d'infanterie de ligne, 6 juillet 1808-23 juin 1815 (matricules 1 à 1,762)*.

166 Louis Canler, *Mémoires de Canler* (Vol. 1), Roy, Paris, 1882, p. 21.

167 Marens had served as battalion-commander in the 123rd Regiment of Line Infantry during the 1812 campaign and was admitted to the 28th Regiment of Line Infantry in 1814. He was killed at Waterloo. SHDDT: 2 Yb 208 *Contrôle Nominatif Officier 28e regiment d'infanterie de ligne 18 Octobre 1808 a 23 Juin 1815*.

M. Duzit,[168] was struck by two bullets and Adjutant M. Hubaut and the eagle-bearer, M. Crosse, were killed.

Amidst all this the calm and serious voices of our commanders called the only command: 'close the ranks!' At the second discharge of the English battery, the grenadier's drummer, Lecointre, had his right arm carried off by a round shot, but this courageous man continued to march at our head beating the charge with the left hand, until the loss of blood made him faint. (In 1828 I saw him in Paris, where he entered the Invalides.) The third discharge reduced the leading company of our battalion; the terrible cry of 'close the ranks!' was heard again. This cry warded away the terror and despair in our hearts, it produced a completely different effect, inspiring us with courage and the determination to overcome and avenge our dead brothers-in-arms, who were killed before our eyes.

Due to poor reconnaissance, the sunken road and hedges had slowed the advance of the French. Despite these setbacks, at least two of the columns had crossed the road and surged into vicious hand-to-hand fighting with the Allied troops. Due to the French onslaught, some Allied regiments pulled back from the front line. With the Allied front line pushed back, the 28th Regiment of Line Infantry fell on to the British 32nd Regiment of Foot. In this melee, Edward Cotton notes:[169]

During this same attack, a French officer, who's horse had been shot under him, seized the regimental colour of the 32nd, which was carried at the moment by Lieutenant Belcher: a struggle ensued; the Frenchman was in the act of drawing his sword when he received a thrust in the breast from a sergeant's halberd, and instantly after, notwithstanding the major (Toole) called out, (alas! too late,) 'Save

---

168 No officer called Duzit served in 1815. However, Duzit is likely to be Louis Marc Gilbert Dulcis, who was born on 15 February 1772 and was admitted to the regiment on 28 August 1799 with the rank of sergeant-major. He was promoted to second-lieutenant in 1805, to lieutenant in 1807 and then appointed as pay officer in 1808. Promotion to captain came on 20 January 1810 and he was made quartermaster-treasurer on 15 June 1812. He had served in Spain from 1808 to 1813 and was discharged on 30 September 1815. AN: LH 840/35.
169 Edward Cotton, *A Voice from Waterloo*, Mont-St-Jean, Belgium, 1877, p. 56.

the brave fellow!' he was shot by a man named Lacey, and fell dead at Lieutenant Belcher's feet.

For this episode to have taken place, the 28th Regiment of Line Infantry must have broken into the 32nd Regiment of Foot. Lieutenant Belcher notes:[170]

> In the second attack of the French infantry on the left centre of the line, the brigade advanced in line to charge. Immediately on passing the narrow road which ran along our front, the ensign carrying the regimental colours was severely wounded. I took the colour from him until another ensign could be called. Almost instantly after, the brigade still advancing, and the French infantry getting into disorder and beginning to retreat, a mounted officer had his horse shot under him. When he extricated himself, we were close to him. I had the colour on my left arm and was slightly in advance of the division. He suddenly fronted me and seized the staff, I still retaining a grasp of the silk; the colours were nearly new. At the same moment, he attempted to draw his sabre, but he had not accomplished it when the covering colour-sergeant, named Switzer, thrust his pike into his breast and the right rank and file of the division, named Lacy, fired into him. He fell dead at my feet.

Major F. Calvert, of the 32nd Regiment of Foot, omits this incident, however:[171]

> The 32nd was in line on the crest of the hill behind the hedge, which was at right angles from the road leading from Brussels to Charleroi, nearly opposite the farmhouse of La Haye Sainte...from about half-past twelve p.m. the brigade had to sustain repeated attacks.

Another British officer writes with some more detail of this event:[172]

> After having tried the right and found it strong, Buonaparte manoeuvred until he got forty pieces of artillery to play on the left, where the 5th Division, a brigade of heavy dragoons and two companies of artillery were posted. Our lines were formed behind a hedge, with two companies of the 95th extended in front, to annoy

---

170 Siborne, *Waterloo Letters*, No. 154.
171 ibid, No.152.
172 John Booth, *The Battle of Waterloo*, Booth, Egerton, London, 1816, pp. xlvii-xlvv.

the enemy's approach. For some time we saw that Buonaparte intended to attack us; yet as nothing but cavalry were visible, no one could imagine what were his plans. It was generally supposed that he would endeavour to turn our flank. But all of a sudden, his cavalry turned to the right and left, and showed large masses of infantry, who advanced up in the most gallant style, to the cries of 'vive l'Empereur!' while a most tremendous cannonade was opened to cover their approach. They had arrived at the very hedge behind which we were the muskets were almost muzzle-to-muzzle, and a French mounted officer had seized the colours of the 32nd Regiment, when poor Picton ordered the charge of our brigade, commanded by Sir James Kempt. When the French saw us rushing through the hedge, and heard the tremendous huzza which we gave, they turned; but instead of running, they walked off in close columns with the greatest steadiness, and allowed themselves to be butchered without any material resistance.

However, the 32nd Regiment of Foot had lost a colour to the 28th Regiment of Line Infantry. The French mounted officer is likely to have been Battalion Commander Marens. He had served as battalion-commander in the 123rd Regiment of Line Infantry in the 1812 campaign and he was admitted to the 28th Regiment of Line Infantry in 1814. He was killed at Waterloo.[173]

As the 28th Regiment of Line Infantry surged forward, officers and men were wounded. Sergeant-Major Jean Louis Lafontaine suffered howitzer shell splinters hitting the left side of his chest. The wound does not seem to have caused him serious injury and he remained with his regiment as it advanced up the slope. At some stage in this attack he took a bayonet wound to the right leg. For his conduct and bravery he was nominated by Bourgeois for the Legion of Honour. He was captured at the field dressing station at the end of the battle.[174] The medal was not awarded, however, until 23 December 1876. Sergeant Jean Baptiste Pierre Millet was born at Beauvais on 3 November 1785 and was conscripted to the regiment on 25 October 1808. He was promoted to corporal on 6 July 1813 and to sergeant on 1 May 1814, and was wounded at Waterloo with a gunshot while a member of a grenadier company. Corporal Rene Deffay, born on 26 December 1793,

---

173 SHDDT: 2yb 208.
174 AN: LH 1437/16.

was conscripted to the regiment on 13 December 1813 and was wounded with a gunshot and captured at Waterloo.[175]

As the 28th Regiment of Line Infantry attacked the British 32nd Regiment of Foot, behind them came the 105th Regiment of Line Infantry. As the regiment moved forward it came under Allied musket fire. Colonel Jean Genty, commanding the 105th Regiment of Line Infantry, suffered a gunshot wound to the right side of his chest. When the regiment retreated, he was left for dead, and was among those captured by the Allied cavalry and made prisoner. He was returned to France on 7 January 1816.[176] In the attack, Battalion Commanders Louis Bonnet (commanding the 1st Battalion) and Jean Pierre François Impériale (commanding the 2nd Battalion) were both killed. As the brigade had advanced, the 105th Regiment of Line Infantry lost officers and men to the Allied artillery barrage. Captain-Adjutant-Major Philippe Magdeleine Riboud, of the 2nd Battalion, aged just twenty-three, was unlucky enough to be close to a howitzer shell which exploded among the regiment. A fragment of the iron shell passed through his left shoulder. He then suffered a gunshot wound to the abdomen. These injuries, serious as they were, did not kill him and he died on 9 April 1859 having been evacuated to a field dressing station.[177]

Others wounded by the exchange of musket fire were Captain Jean Pierre Barthelemy Castan (commanding the voltigeur company of 1st Battalion) who suffered a gunshot to the left knee;[178] Captain Jean Jacques Joannis (commanding the 4th Fusilier Company of 1st Battalion) who was wounded by a musket ball and captured by the Allied cavalry;[179] Captain Jean Etienne Lepin (commanding the 3rd Fusilier Company of 2nd Battalion) who was shot in the face by a musket ball;[180] and Captain Jacques Antoine Philippeaux (commanding the grenadier company of 1st Battalion, which formed the very front line of the attacking column) who was shot in the right hand, perhaps when brandishing his sabre urging his men forward.[181] Similarly wounded was Sub-Lieutenant Anselme Felix Paul Normand, of the voltigeur

---

175 SHDDT: GR 21 YC 264.
176 AN: LH 1113/34. See also: SHDDT: Yj 11.
177 AN: LH 2316/60.
178 AN: LH 444/25.
179 AN: LH 1367/9.
180 AN: LH 1593/74.
181 AN: LH 2138/62.

company of 1st Battalion, who took a musket ball to the right side of his chest.[182] Sergeant Mathieu Larue, serving in a grenadier company took a musket ball to a leg, and he was captured later by the Allied cavalry. The 105th Regiment of Line Infantry at some stage made contact with Allied infantry at the point of their bayonets. It was in this close quarter fighting that Lieutenant Raymond Druhle, of the 2nd Fusilier Company 2nd Battalion, was bayoneted, the tip of the bayonet passing through the right side of his chest. He was left for dead as the regiment retreated and made prisoner by the Allied cavalry.[183] Perhaps, the regiment had crested the ridge and were involved in a melee with the enemy either to their front or flank during the general attack of 1st Corps. Brevet-Major Leach, commanding the 95th Rifles in the sandpit location, notes:[184]

> The fierce onset of the French with overwhelming numbers forced back my two companies on the main body of the 95th Regiment, and this hillock was also instantly assailed in such a manner as to render it impossible for one weak battalion, consisting only of six companies, to stem the torrent for any length of time. We were consequently constrained to fall back on the 32nd Regiment, which was in line near the thorn hedge which runs from the Genappe road to the left, and along the front of Picton's division. We were closely pressed and hotly engaged during the retrograde movement, and very soon after reaching the spot where the 32nd was in position, a volley and a charge of bayonets caused the French to recoil in disorder and with heavy loss.

This was clearly the 28th and 105th Regiments of Line Infantry that had inflicted heavy losses on the 95th and 32nd Regiments of Foot. In this action, Kempt's brigade suffered large casualties. On 16 June, the 8th British Brigade had mustered 2,471 officers and men, of which 638 men were killed or wounded at Quatre-Bras, some 26 per cent of effective strength. At Waterloo, 663 men were killed or wounded, a loss of 36 per cent of effective strength, which was down to 1,833 men on the morning of 18 June.[185]

To the right of Quiot's division came Marcognet. Donzelot's command appears to have halted. Marshal-du-Camp Baron Schmitz,

---

182 AN: LH/ 2002/42.
183 AN: LH 8058/43.
184 Siborne, *Waterloo Letters*, No. 159.
185 Deleveot, op. cit.

commanding 1st Brigade 2nd Infantry Division, writes as follows in his after-action report dated 25 June 1815:[186]

> The division took up arms at eleven o'clock in the morning and was formed in columns by battalion in echelon behind the 3rd Division. At noon, when the signal was given for the attack, the division followed, in the order above, the movement of the 3rd and 4th Divisions. The enemy cavalry charged, and having routed these two divisions, the 2nd Division remained in the position where it stood, formed square by means of filling in the gap between battalions by the platoons from the flank, and in this position repulsed the cavalry with considerable loss to them. The division had stopped and rendered null the impetuosity of the enemy, and saved the life of an infinite number of soldiers of the 3rd and 4th Divisions, which had been cut to pieces.

Attacking in column by battalions was not a new tactic, but it required well-trained soldiers. In order to keep each company in perfect alignment with the other, the company markers (the guides) and the NCOs would have had to constantly keep checking the dressing of their company, to ensure the frontage of the battalion was as near perfect a straight line as possible; easily done on a parade ground, but rather more difficult on a muddy field under enemy fire, knocking out key personnel, as well as blasting holes in the ranks. It seems that as the 3rd Division attacked the formation began to drift apart laterally. The companies on the left flank, i.e. numbers 4 and 3 Companies, assuming the voltigeurs were detached as sharpshooters, had moved sufficiently far over to their left to impede on Donzelot's movement. Donzelot's command had no option but to halt. Therefore, it seems as Schmitz states, Donzelot's column had to halt to avoid chaos. This robbed the attack of 25 per cent of its firepower. This gave the division time to form square and defend itself against the Allied cavalry.

Jacques Martin, of the 45th Regiment of Line Infantry, the rear-most regiment of Marcognet's column, notes:[187]

> At last we arrived at the summit. We were about to receive the prize for such bravery, already the English had started to bolt for it; already their guns were retiring at the gallop. A sunken road,

---

186 *Revue Etudes Napoléoniennes*, 1932, pp. 360-5.
187 Jacques François Martin, *Souvenirs d'un ex-officier 1812-1815*, Paris, 1867, pp. 275-6.

lined with hedges, was now the only obstacle separating us from them. Our soldiers did not wait for the order to jump across; they charged, leaping over the hedges, leaving their ranks disordered to chase after their enemies.

As the 46th Regiment of Line Infantry advanced, Battalion Commander Pierre Louis Poujade was wounded by a musket ball.[188] A similar fate befell Jean Baptiste Couturad, who commanded the 2nd Battalion, and was taken prisoner in the cavalry attack.[189] Captain Louis Granger, aged thirty-one at Waterloo, took a gunshot to the right leg.[190]

Among the 25th Regiment of Line Infantry, Battalion Commander François Guilay was shot, and Captain-Adjutant-Major Armand Louis Doutrelaine was shot in the left foot.[191] Captain Pierre Marquille was also shot in the right foot.[192] Sub-Lieutenants Petit and Villa each suffered a gunshot wound, as did Sub-Lieutenant Lhéritier, who was invalided out of the regiment. Also wounded was Sub-Lieutenant Joseph Marie Marmagnant, who was wounded with a gunshot to his right arm. He was captured during the melee with the Allied cavalry, and was returned on 15 September 1815.[193]

Behind the 25th Regiment of Line Infantry came the 45th Regiment of Line Infantry. At the head of his 1st Battalion, Louis Probace Sivan was wounded with a gunshot wound during an exchange of musket fire.[194] In the same firefight, François Gruard, commanding the 2nd Battalion, fell when a ball passed through the left side of his chest.[195] Lieutenant Le Bon took a gunshot wound,[196] as did Captain Jacques Paul Desire Lecoq.[197] Marcognet's troops, unperturbed by the hedges and almost point-blank volleys, surged through the hedge and over the road. The 7th and 8th Dutch-Belgian Militia Battalions recoiled in horror. The 7th retreated some one hundred paces, supported by the 5th Militia Battalion. The rest of Bijlandt's brigade retreated. About

---

188 AN: LH 2210/28.
189 AN: LH 622/12.
190 AN: LH 1190/22.
191 AN: LH 799/70.
192 AN: LH 1750/51.
193 AN: LH 1746/67.
194 AN: LH 2529/28.
195 AN: LH 1211/54.
196 AN: LH 1517/6.
197 AN: LH 1537/181.

the attack, a senior officer in the Dutch-Belgian Militia, Colonel Nyvelt reports:[198]

> The enemy now succeeded in passing our first line and had arrived on the plain. The second line made ready to advance against him, while a cavalry regiment of the English guards came to harass them and were forced to retreat.

Bijlandt lost 351 dead and wounded and 349 missing; in total 700 men, or 27 per cent of men who had been in ranks at the start of the day. Bijlandt had lost 39 per cent of his starting strength at Quatre-Bras already, while Kempt had lost 26 per cent. Standing alongside Bijlandt was the 9th British Brigade of General Pack. The brigade began the campaign with 2,173 men. At Quatre-Bras, a staggering 957 men were killed or wounded, a loss of 44 per cent of effective strength. On the morning of 18 June, the brigade had 1,216 officers and men under arms, of which 374 men (31 per cent) were killed or wounded.[199] With losses of 39 per cent of Bijlandt's command, 26 per cent of Kempt's and 31 per cent of Pack's, we can see that the assault of 1st Corps was very effective indeed. Little wonder Kempt and Bijlandt's troops had to be replaced in line of battle.

The Allied left had almost been punched through. The French needed to exploit this success. On the left, La Haye Sainte was pinned down by Charlet's brigade from Quiot's division and the cuirassiers of Colonel Crabbe had silenced two batteries of guns and forced the Allied infantry to the north of La Haye Sainte to fall back. Everything was set for a French breakthrough in the centre and right. With the Prussians arriving on the French right, Napoléon needed a quick breakthrough, to separate the two Allied forces and defeat the troops under Wellington before turning his attention onto Blücher. The French had inflicted 2,732 casualties in this attack, and had almost smashed the Allied lines.[200]

With no time to spare, gone was the chance for a flanking movement. A sudden quick stroke was what was needed. Myth of the battle implies that Bijlandt's men ran away as cowards, and the musketry and artillery of the British smashed the columns before they opened fire.

---

198 Deleveot, p.34.
199 ibid, p.31
200 ibid.

This understanding is totally at odds to French eyewitnesses and also, crucially, English and Dutch-Belgian accounts.

The Allied cavalry charge

A major crisis point in the battle had been reached: if Wellington did not react quickly enough the battle was lost. Captain von Bronkhorst, a Dutch-Belgian officer, recounts what happened next:[201]

> It was impossible to absorb the shock. We received orders to retreat behind the English troops who were in the second line. In those moments were suffered considerable losses. The French had reached the edge of the heights we occupied. Scottish troops were determinedly waiting for them. The English cavalry, which was positioned behind them, saw the moment for the charge had arrived and crossed the space which separated the masses of troops, hurled itself upon the French and sabered down every resistance.

An officer of 1st Corps, who alas remains anonymous, notes the following about the 1st Infantry Division, nominally commanded by General Quiot:[202]

> Comte d'Erlon attacked the village of Mont-Saint-Jean and supported his attack with eighty pieces of cannon, which must have occasioned great loss to the English army. All the efforts were upon the plateau. A brigade from the 1st Division of Comte d'Erlon took the village of Mont-Saint-Jean. The 2nd Brigade was charged by a corps of English cavalry which occasioned it much loss. At the same moment, a division of English cavalry charged the battery of Comte of d'Erlon by its right and disorganised several pieces; but the cuirassiers of General Milhaud charged that division, three regiments of which were broken and cut up.

---

201 ibid, p.33.
202 *Leeds Mercury*, 1 July 1815.

Chapter 5

Quiot's Division

Colonel Bellina Kupieski, attached to the Imperial Headquarters, notes in a report dated 23 June 1815 that:[203]

> The brigade of Marshal-du-Camp Quillot [sic], of the 1st Army Corps, was entirely dispersed by the enemy cavalry and the terror spread to the troops in other army corps. At the moment when victory would be decided in our favour this brigade, being in line and not having formed battalion squares, was charged by four squadrons of cavalry and was cut up; other corps seeing this fled shouting 'everyman for himself, we have been betrayed'.

For the fate of the 1st Division at Waterloo, Dominique Fleuret notes:[204]

> The 18th, at seven o'clock in the morning all the army was in line and the bands of each regiment were at their heads. The signal was given. We formed the 1st Division of the 1st Army Corps on the right wing. We were engaged against English light infantry sharpshooters and sixteen pieces of cannon formed in battery fired at us. In under a quarter of an hour the infantry had been pushed back and the cannons were captured at the point of the bayonet without firing a single shot. It was our voltigeurs who burnt their cartridges.

---

203 SHDDT: C15 5 *Correspondance Armée du Nord 11 Juin au 21 Juin 1815. Rapport 23 Juin 1815.*

204 Fernand Fleuret, *Description des passages de Dominique Fleuret*, Firmin-Didot et Cie, Paris, 1929, pp. 148-57.

After our assault had captured the battery, a mass of cavalry charged us and we jumped into the ditches. We did not have time to rally many. They were cut down by their sabres, and some others were made prisoners. The cavalry continued its charge, and we were then driven back by infantry. But as we stood in a depression, to our left, two regiments of French lancers came to our aid and saved us…With the cavalry passed, we crawled on our stomachs to join our squares, which fired from their four faces into the English dragoons. The drums of the regiment beat the rally. We were re-united. The regiment was reduced to about four hundred men, and were formed into a single battalion. We then deployed as sharpshooters along with the Young Guard. We marched against the Prussians, who moved against our right wing to cut off the army's line of retreat. We repulsed them twice, but the Prussian army arrived in force and made us retreat.

I stayed with our light cavalry, the hussars and chasseurs, with fifty men of the regiment to support the retreat to Charleroi. The bridges were barricaded. We waded through the river.

So, it does seem that some regiments of the division formed squares. Officers killed or wounded in the 54th Regiment of Line Infantry included the following men:[205]

- Captain-Adjutant-Major Augustin Emile Charlon (born 26 September 1795) was admitted to the military school at Saint-Cyr on 12 June 1812 and admitted as second-lieutenant to the regiment on 30 January 1813 before promotion to lieutenant on 8 July 1813, to lieutenant-adjutant-major on 8 November 1813 and to captain-adjutant-major on 8 March 1814. He was wounded at Waterloo.
- Captain Jacques Etienne Bellissent (born 20 February 1781) was admitted to the regiment on 21 July 1814 from the 25th Regiment of Line Infantry. He was wounded at Waterloo.
- Captain Augustin Emile Charlon, aged just twenty at Waterloo, took a musket ball to his left shoulder.[206]
- Captain Jacques Etienne Bellissent suffered a gunshot wound.[207]
- Captain Michel Hager suffered a gunshot wound.[208]
- Lieutenant Jean Etienne Segondy (born 1 July 1787) was killed at Waterloo.

---

205 SHDDT: Xb 453 *54e de Ligne 1813-1815*. Dossier 1815. *Situation Rapport 1 Mai 1815*.
206 AN: LH 491/91.
207 AN: LH 172/56.
208 AN: LH 1257/65.

- Sub-Lieutenant Jean Claude Xavier LeRoy (born 16 August 1785) was conscripted into the regiment on 11 April 1802 and was promoted to corporal on 28 September 1803, to corporal-quartermaster on 28 July 1804, to sergeant on 11 July 1807, to sergeant-major on 1 January 1808, to second-lieutenant on 20 July 1811, and to lieutenant on 21 April 1813. He was wounded at Waterloo.
- Sub-Lieutenant Jean Baptiste Peres (born on 1 July 1780) was conscripted into the regiment in 1803 and promoted to corporal-quartermaster in 1804, to sergeant on 15 February 1809, to sergeant-major on 15 April 1809, to second-lieutenant on 10 August 1813, to lieutenant on 17 February 1814, and to captain on 7 April 1814. He was demoted to second-lieutenant on 21 July 1814 and was wounded at Waterloo with a gunshot to the left foot.[209]

In total, the 54th Regiment of Line Infantry lost the following number of men at Waterloo:[210]

54th Regiment of Line Infantry					
	Wounded	Wounded & Prisoner	Prisoner of War	Killed	Missing
1st Battalion	0	0	158	10	0
2nd Battalion	2	0	154	1	0
3rd Battalion	1	0	140	2	0
Total	3	0	452	13	0

The regiment lost 468 other ranks at Waterloo. On 10 June 1815, the regiment had mustered 921 other ranks, so lost 51 per cent of effective strength at Waterloo. It seems that the regiment was attacked in the front and on its left flank. The frontal attack makes sense, as the regiment formed the head of the column of the brigade; therefore it seems very likely that the regiment was attacked by the Household Cavalry Brigade, namely the 1st and 2nd Life Guards, the Royal Horse Guards and the King's Dragoon Guards. In the same exchange of musketry Sergeant François Corneloup took a gunshot wound to the right knee, as did Sergeant Gilbert Rouger Corneloup, of the 54th Regiment of Line Infantry, who received a sabre cut to his left shoulder.[211]

---

209 AN: LH 2096/76.
210 GR 21 YC 456 *50e régiment d'infanterie de ligne (ex 54e régiment d'infanterie de ligne), 21 juillet 1814-10 mai 1815 (matricules 1 à 1,660).*
211 SHDDT: GR 21 YC 456.

Among the 55th Regiment of Line Infantry, officers wounded in the 1st Battalion were:[212]

- Battalion Commanders: Joseph Delamoussaye.
- In the grenadier company: Captain Gaspard Genty, who had served with the Imperial Guard from 1806 to 1814, had his jaw broken by a musket butt;[213] and Lieutenant Hippolyte Andre was made prisoner of war.
- In the 1st Fusilier Company: Captain Jacques Coutelle suffered from a gunshot wound to the right arm;[214] Lieutenant Pierre Chaumet was made prisoner of war; and Sub-Lieutenant Degueus de Saint-Hilaire was wounded.
- In the 2nd Fusilier Company: Captain Eli Degoy and Lieutenant Jean Vary were wounded; and Sub-Lieutenant Labeyre was missing.
- In the voltigeur company: Captain Simon Dupuy, Lieutenant Antoine Frachisse and Sub-Lieutenant Pierre were all wounded.

The 2nd Battalion lost the following officers:[215]

- In the 1st Fusilier Company: Sub-Lieutenant Louis Bouche was wounded.
- In the 2nd Fusilier Company: Captain Jean-Baptiste Coroz was wounded; Lieutenant Dumonceau Louvray was made prisoner of war; and Sub-Lieutenant Pierre Buffele was not seen again after 18 June 1815.
- In the 3rd Fusilier Company: Lieutenant Jean Champeau was wounded.
- In the 4th Fusilier Company: Lieutenant Nicolas Birard was made prisoner of war; and Sub-Lieutenant François Fitu was wounded.
- In the voltigeur company: Captain Pierre Ricome and Lieutenant Nicolas Louvet were both made prisoners of war.

From this list of names we see that the majority of company officers were either wounded or made prisoners of war. This major loss of

---

212 SHDDT: Xb 455 *55e de Ligne 1791-1815*. Dossier 1815. *Etat Nominatif 1 Aout 1815*.
213 AN: LH 1113/30.
214 AN: LH 621/26. See also: SHDDT: Xb 455. Dossier 1815. *Etat Nominatif 1 Aout 1815*.
215 SHDDT Xb 455. Dossier 1815. *Etat Nominatif 1 Aout 1815*.

officers would have impacted on the regiment's command and control, and its effectiveness on the field.

Found among the vast amounts of archival paperwork in Vincennes for the infantry of the line are the muster rolls of the 55th Regiment of Line Infantry in 1815. From these we find the casualty reports from the campaign, from which the table below is generated:[216]

55th Regiment of Line Infantry					
	Wounded	Wounded & Prisoner	Prisoner of War	Killed	Missing (presumed Prisoner)
1st Battalion	58	0	109	7	39
2nd Battalion	57	0	132	7	37
3rd Battalion	14	0	40	0	12
Total	129	0	281	14	88

The regiment lost a recorded 512 men at Waterloo. On 16 June, one man was wounded and three deserted, along with one officer wounded, making a total loss of 516 men. Nominally, the 1st Battalion mustered twenty-four officers and 556 men, and 2nd Battalion had twenty-one officers and 547 men. The 3rd Battalion was merged with the 2nd to bring it up to strength on 30 May 1815. The regiment totalled 1,103 men on 10 June. Between 16 and 18 June, 46 per cent of the regiment's effective strength was lost. Some 587 men remained in ranks on 20 June, but by 26 June the regiment only mustered 426 men; 161 men (or 27 per cent) of the remaining effective strength had left the regiment since 18 June.

About the 2nd Brigade, Louis Canler, of the 28th Regiment of Line Infantry, further notes:[217]

> No sooner had we reached the plateau than we are received by the Queen's Dragoons who fell on us, uttering wild cries. The 1st Division did not have time to form square; it could not sustain this charge and was pressed back, then started veritable carnage. Each man found himself separated from his comrades and fought only for himself. The sabres and the bayonet opened a passage through the quivering masses, because we were too close to each other to make use of our firearms.

---

216 SHDDT: GR 21 YC 463 *51e régiment d'infanterie de ligne (ex 55e régiment d'infanterie de ligne), 1 août 1814-3 août 1815 (matricules 1 à 2,049).*

217 Canler, p. 21.

But, the position was untenable for infantry fighting alone and, surrounded by horsemen, I soon found myself an isolated, unarmed prisoner.

During the melee of cavalry and infantry, the 28th Regiment of Line Infantry lost the following officers dead or wounded:[218]

- Battalion Commanders: Marens was killed at Waterloo;[219] and Louis Monck d'Uzer was wounded.[220]
- Captain-adjutant-majors: Hubault was wounded at Waterloo.
- Captains: Louis Frederick Courmaceul was wounded with a musket ball to his right arm;[221] Jean Joseph Faure was wounded with a gunshot to the left arm;[222] Charles Guinaudeau was wounded;[223]

---

218 SHDDT: 2 Yb 208.

219 Marens had served as battalion-commander in the 123rd Regiment of Line Infantry in the 1812 campaign and was admitted to the 28th Regiment of Line Infantry in 1814. He was killed at Waterloo.

220 Louis Monck d'Uzer was born on 30 September 1778 and served as an aide-de-camp, and promoted to battalion-commander of the 28th Regiment of Line Infantry in 1813, when he made an Officer of the Legion of Honour. He was wounded at Waterloo and promoted to colonel of the 64th Regiment of Line Infantry after the battle. He retired from the army on 27 December 1830 with the rank of marshal-du-camp and Grand Officer of the Legion of Honour.

221 Louis Frederick Courmaceul, born at Flers on 10 September 1783, was admitted to the regiment in 1803 and promoted to second-lieutenant on 20 January 1810, to lieutenant on 14 June 1813, to adjutant-major on 6 July 1813 and to captain on 14 October 1810. He was wounded at Waterloo with a musket ball to his right arm.

222 Jean Joseph Faure was born at Chatillon on 9 December 1780 and admitted to the Velite-Grenadiers of the Imperial Guard in 1803, before being promoted to corporal-quartermaster in 1805. He passed as a sergeant to the Fusilier Grenadiers of the Imperial Guard on 17 March 1809 and was promoted to second-lieutenant in the 63rd Regiment of Line Infantry on 13 July 1807, thence promoted to lieutenant on 11 July 1809 and to captain on 2 March 1813. He was admitted to the 12th Voltigeurs of the Imperial Guard on 8 April 1814 and passed to the 28th Regiment of Line Infantry on 6 July 1814. He was wounded with a gunshot to the left arm at Waterloo.

223 Charles Guinaudeau was born at La-Roch-Sur-Yon on 14 June 1788 and was conscripted into the 22nd Regiment of Light Infantry on 3 July 1799.

Philippe Jérôme Ledoulx de Sainte-Croix was wounded;[224] Amand Vicherat (born 10 June 1774) was mortally wounded; and Vimont was wounded.

- Lieutenants: Boussard was wounded at Waterloo; Benjamin Thomas Hubert Klein was wounded with a sabre cut to his jaw in the charge of the Union Brigade against the attack of 1st Corps;[225] Laforest was wounded; Bernard Louis Richard was wounded;[226] and Thevenet was wounded.
- 2nd Lieutenants: Lemmens, Miedan and Wannault were all wounded at Waterloo.

Among the other ranks, Sergeant-Major Jean Baptist Crucifix, who had served with the 28th Regiment of Line Infantry since 18 October 1808, was wounded by a gunshot and was later wounded with a sabre cut to the left arm. As a result, he was captured. Sergeant-Major Pierre Joseph Mollinier (born at Toulon 28 February 1792) was wounded by a sabre

---

He was successively promoted to captain-adjutant-major on 12 August 1813 and passed to the 133rd Regiment of Line Infantry on 11 December 1813. He was then admitted to the 28th Regiment of Line Infantry on 6 July 1814 and was wounded at Waterloo.

224 Philippe Jérôme Ledoulx de Sainte-Croix was born at Tartas on 2 September 1791 and volunteered into the 16th Regiment of Light Infantry on 1 September 1809, being rapidly promoted to sergeant on 17 October 1810. He then passed as a second-lieutenant into the 28th Regiment of Line Infantry on 21 June 1811, and was promoted to first-lieutenant on 14 June 1813 and to captain on 15 December 1813. He was wounded at Waterloo.

225 Benjamin Thomas Hubert Klein was born at Strasbourg on 31 August 1793 and admitted to the military school of Saint-Cyr on 9 November 1811. He graduated as a second-lieutenant into the 123rd Regiment of Line Infantry on 9 November 1812 and was promoted to lieutenant on 22 May 1813 before being admitted to the 28th Regiment of Line Infantry on 5 July 1814. He was wounded with a sabre cut to his jaw in the charge of the Union Brigade.

226 Bernard Louis Richard was born on 14 March 1790 and admitted to the military school in Paris on 12 January 1810. He was promoted as a second-lieutenant into the 20th Regiment of Line Infantry on 22 June 1811, and then promoted to lieutenant on 28 January 1813. He was admitted to the 28th Regiment of Line Infantry on 6 July 1814 and was wounded at Waterloo.

cut and was captured. Sergeant Jean Paul Foelle was wounded with a sabre cut, and in consequence was made prisoner of war. Sergeant Jean Baptiste Pierre Millet, serving in the grenadier company of 1st Battalion was shot in the left arm, which upon being evacuated to the field hospital had to be amputated.[227] As well as using their sabres, the cavalry also used their pistols to great advantage. Captain Louis Frederick de Courmaceul took a pistol shot to the right arm.[228] Similarly wounded was Captain Jean Joseph Faure, who took a pistol shot to the left arm.[229]

In total, the 28th Regiment of Line Infantry lost the following number of men at Waterloo:[230]

28th Regiment of Line Infantry					
	Wounded	Wounded & Prisoner	Prisoner of War	Killed	Missing
1st Battalion	9	23	267	0	0
2nd Battalion	4	69	227	0	0
3rd Battalion	4	21	78	0	0
Total	17	113	572	0	0

The regiment lost 702 other ranks at Waterloo. On 10 June 1815, the regiment had mustered 856 other ranks. The 3rd Battalion had been taken into the 2nd Battalion on 30 May 1815. The regiment lost a staggering 82 per cent of its strength at Waterloo. It seems the regiment was attacked on its left flank; therefore it seems very likely that it was attacked by the Household Cavalry Brigade, namely the 1st and 2nd Life Guards, the Royal Horse Guards and the King's Dragoon Guards. The 105th Regiment of Line Infantry, it seems, lost men primarily from the right flank companies and also the left flank, suggesting a primary cavalry attack from the right flank (likely to be the 1st Royal Dragoons), as well as from the left. In both regiments the voltigeurs seem to have been detached.

Behind the 28th Regiment of Line Infantry was the 105th Regiment of Line Infantry. As the cavalry surged in among the 105th Regiment of Line Infantry, officers and men were sabred. Captain Jean Jacques

---

227 SHDDT: 2 Yb 208.
228 AN: LH 611/45.
229 AN: LH 941/34.
230 SHDDT: GR 21 YC 264.

Raphael Mang, commanding the elite, or grenadier, company of the 2nd Battalion (who had been appointed to this post of honour on 5 May 1815) suffered from six sabre cuts and was taken prisoner by the cavalry. He returned to France on 7 September 1815.[231] Lieutenant Emile Victorie Cardon, aged twenty-one at Waterloo, was wounded and taken prisoner by the cavalry also.[232] Lieutenant Xavier Louis Hillenweck took a sabre cut to the left arm, a defensive injury perhaps, and took two further sabre cuts, both of which were to his head. None of these three wounds appear to have been serious, as he was able to retreat with his regiment and continued to serve with the French army until 1838. He died in 1860.[233] Sergeant Louis Charles Marais had his face slashed open by a sabre.[234]

In the attack by the cavalry, the eagle of the 105th Regiment of Line Infantry was taken by Corporal Stiles, of the Royal Dragoons. An account of this is given in the following letter:[235]

> The Royals on the right appeared not to be outdone by the Greys, and amidst the loud and hearty cheers of the Highlanders, two squadrons under Lieut-Col. Clifton and Major Dorville, rushed into the second column of the enemy, consisting of about four thousand men, which had been kept in reserve, when, after the most desperate individual exertion, the eagle of the 105th Regiment was seized by a serjeant of the name of Styles. The best part of this column threw down their arms and was immediately swept off to the rear by the Inniskillings. The greater part of the Royals fell in this attack.

Lieutenant George Gunning, of the 1st Royal Dragoons, notes:[236]

> In the night at intervals it rained in torrents, and continued very dark at the proper time of daybreak at this season of the year. The heavy black clouds cleared away at 7 a.m., and at 8 a.m. on Sunday morning, 18 June, about three hours before the battle began in earnest, I was sent by Sir W. Ponsonby with a pass order for the

---

231 AN: LH 1715/56.

232 AN: LH 424/79.

233 AN: LH 1301/5.

234 AN: LH 1722/27.

235 Author's collection.

236 'Correspondence: To the Editor of the *Hereford Times*. Death of General Ponsonby at Waterloo', *Hereford Times*, 23 August 1845, p. 7.

cavalry and horse artillery to feed; the opportunity of seeing (what few officers of the army did see) nearly the whole of our line and the extreme left of the enemy. At (say) 11 a.m. the battle raged with fury on the British right. The cannonade at midday was general throughout the line; at 1 p.m. the enemy moved large bodies of cavalry against our left centre (General Picton's division) without effect; British bayonets could not be forced.

At 2 p.m. the battle raged on the right centre, near the Wellington tree, but British bayonets were invulnerable. At 3 p.m. the grand effort of Napoléon was made. Suddenly, General Comte Drouet's division showed themselves on our extreme left; cavalry skirmishers supported by strong bodies of light infantry drove in the advanced posts of the foreign auxiliaries, on the left of the British line of infantry, and those regiments came through the intervals of our squadrons in great confusion, all order being quite destroyed among them. This corps of the French army was said to amount to 9,000 men, some of the oldest and best soldiers of Napoléon's army at Waterloo. They advanced steadily, as if at a review, covered by guns on their left that kept up a continued fire on our brigade. This splendid corps of the enemy moved in one compact body ready to wheel up into solid square against cavalry, with light troops in each flank ready as skirmishers, or to form stars or bastions in the square; these flank troops covered the front of their advance as sharpshooters, and came within a hundred yards of our brigade before we charged the main body. Had this division of the French army succeeded in obtaining permanent possession of this part of the field of Waterloo, I would have left it to His Grace, the Duke of Wellington, to explain the consequences. Be that as it may, the Union Brigade of heavy cavalry did not disappoint their leaders. The charge was made; in proof of our victory the Royals have the honour to say that the eagle of the 105th Regiment of French infantry was captured in that charge by Corporal Styles, belonging to the troop of the regiment that day under my command, for which Mr Styles was promoted to an ensigncy in the army.

The Greys have the honour to say that the eagle of the 45th Regiment of French infantry was captured in that charge by Sergeant Ewart, for which he was also promoted to an ensigncy in the army.

The Union Brigade was in line, but by bringing up our left shoulders in the attack, we came into contact with the French nearly in a column of squadron in echelon, so that the right squadron of the Royals came in contact with the left corner of the square of the enemy, and suffered most severely in officers and men. The centre and left squadrons of the Royals did great execution against the middle of the enemy's square. I commanded the left half of the centre squadron. As a matter of course the Enniskillen's [*sic*] did not receive so much fire from the square as first fell on the Royals; the Greys came in contact with the right corner of the square, and also received a severe volley of musketry from the light infantry of the enemy on the extreme right of their attack; this body of troops retreated in excellent order. It is impossible to say too much in praise of the steadiness of this body, and the broken regiment formed on them. After our charge the enemy were running in every direction for their own lines. I saw an eagle among a small body, I told Corporal Styles to secure it, and led the men on to the attack. At this moment, I saw no officer near me. I killed the French officer who commanded the party, whose sword passed between my arm and my body at the moment my sword passed through his left breast. He was a fine looking elegant man; his last words were *'vive Napoléon!'* The prisoners said he was the commanding officer of the 105th Regiment. It was for the work of a moment, I saw the eagle in the hands of Corporal Styles and I ordered him to leave the field, and not to give up the eagle till he had a proper receipt for it at headquarters from one of the Duke of Wellington's personal staff…

At the moment, Corporal Styles left me, going to the rear with the eagle, General Ponsonby rode up to me by himself and said 'for God's sake, sir, collect your men and retire on the brigade'. At this moment, the French infantry on our left advanced rapidly and fired a volley of musketry among the scattered cavalry. By this volley, General Ponsonby was killed within twenty yards of me. I saw him fall from his horse at the bottom of the hollow way to the left of General Picton's division. The ridiculous story about the general's horse being unmanageable was all a farce to please the lovers of the marvellous. I was severely wounded by the same volley of musketry and a few seconds afterwards my horse had his near fore leg hit by a cannon ball. I then made my way into the square of the 28th Regiment of Foot (General Picton's division) with several other dismounted men, and remained there till evening before I could get a horse and go to the rear. I arrived in Brussels late that night.

Corporal Francis Stiles writes:[237]

---

237 Ian Smith personal communication, 24 June 2012.

Ipswich Barracks, 31 Jan. 1816
To Lt Gunning, 1st Dragoons,
Cheltenham, Glostershire [sic]

Sir,

This day Co. Clifton sent for me about the taking the eagle and colours. He asked me if I had any person that sees me take the eagle; I told him that you see me, I believe, as the officer of the French was making away with it. I belonged to your troop at that time, and you gave me orders to charge him, which I did, and took it from him.

When I stated it to him this day he wants to know the particulars about it, and me rite [sic] to you for you to state to him how it was.

I would thank you to rite [sic] to the colonel, as you was the nearest officer to me that day. Sir, by so doing you will much oblige.

Your most obedient humble servant,
Francis Stiles, Sergt, 1st Royal Drag.

Stiles was twice promoted as a result of his claim, whereas Clark did not receive anything directly for his claimed actions, suggesting that the powers that be recognised Stiles' claim, which was further supported by Gunning himself when he wrote to Major-General Sir H. Torrens on 22 February 1816:[238]

> Sir, it being believed that some military honour may be conferred in consequence of the eagles taken at the ever-memorable Battle of Waterloo, induces me to state, for the consideration of his Royal Highness the commander-in-chief, that it was by my orders that Sergeant Stiles secured the eagle of the 105th Regiment of French infantry. I am enabled to prove this fact by Sergeant Stiles' letter to me of the 31st ult. a copy of which I have the honour to enclose. I should have made this statement before, but my extreme ill state of health, in consequence of my wounds received at the Battle of Waterloo, has caused me to be absent from my regiment, and I did not consider it consistent to write to a sergeant for the particulars which he has now unsolicited sent to me. I have heard that other claims are about to be made relative to the eagle taken by Sergeant Stiles; his letter proves most clearly it was by my orders he did secure the eagle, and as no other officer was near me at the time, I gave the order. I hope his Royal Highness the commander-in-chief

---

238 ibid.

will consider that it was owing to my orders the eagle was captured from the enemy; as had I acted differently to what I did at that critical moment, I think the eagle would not have been taken from the enemy, which, by a personal interview, I think I could explain fully to the satisfaction of his Royal Highness.

Francis Stiles, of the 1st Royal Dragoons, unquestionably took the eagle of the 105th Regiment of Line Infantry, and not many paces away Sir William Ponsonby was shot dead. He was not killed by lancers.

The eagle of the 105th Regiment of Line Infantry that day was carried by Lieutenant Jean Chantelet. He was born in Bourges on 20 October 1769 and had served with the regiment since 15 April 1794, being progressively promoted through the various ranks of sub-officers until he was promoted to lieutenant on 7 July 1813, and had carried the eagle since 19 November 1813. In this melee, the eagle and colour were wrestled from his hands as he had been incapacitated by a pistol shot to the left leg. This somewhat contradicts Captain Clarke Kennedy, who claims to have sabred the porte-aigle.[239] It is possible that with Chantelet wounded the eagle was carried by another officer who was later killed. However, given an inquiry was launched in the Royals about who captured the eagle, either Clarke Kennedy or Stiles, we cannot rule out the suspicion that Kennedy's account is entirely fictitious. We note, however, that Chantelet was not captured and was discharged from the regiment on 1 September 1815.[240] The eagle was guarded by the second and third porte-aigle, armed with halberds and a pair of pistols, and wore distinctive helmets with a red transverse crest; the second porte-aigle was MAT No. 25 Jean Jacques Lecomte, born on 20 October 1778. He had been admitted to the regiment in 1795 and had been made second porte-aigle on 3 December 1808. He was struck off the regimental list on 1 September 1815. The 3rd porte-aigle was MAT No. 66 Gabriel Lamy, born on 13 January 1780. He was admitted to the regiment in 1803 and promoted to corporal on 1 October 1811, becoming third porte-aigle on 18 December 1813 and discharged on 30 September 1815.[241] In total, the

239 de Ainslie, Historical *record of the First or the Royal Regiment of Dragoons*, London, Chapman and Hall, 1887, p. 156.
240 AN: LH 481/29.
241 SHDDT: GR 21 YC 771 *86e régiment d'infanterie de ligne (ex 105e régiment d'infanterie de ligne), 13 août 1814-21 février 1815 (matricules 1 à 1,800)*. See

105th Regiment of Line Infantry lost the following number of men at Waterloo:[242]

105th Regiment of Line Infantry					
	Wounded	Wounded & Prisoner	Prisoner of War	Killed	Missing
1st Battalion	0	0	164	12	3
2nd Battalion	1	0	155	7	4
3rd Battalion	0	0	97	6	1
Total	1	0	416	25	8

The regiment, on the morning of 18 June, mustered forty-two officers and 941 men. At Waterloo, 450 men were lost, or 48 per cent of the regiment's effective strength. The vast majority of the men were recorded as prisoners of war, but this number is also likely to include dead and wounded.

Summary

Losses for the 1st Infantry Division are as below:

1st Infantry Division						
Regiment	Wounded	Wounded & Prisoner	Prisoner of War	Killed	Missing	Total
54th Line Infantry[243]	3	0	452	13	0	468
55th Line Infantry[244]	129	0	281	14	88	512
28th Line Infantry[245]	17	113	572	0	0	702
105th Line Infantry[246]	1	0	416	25	8	450
Total	150	113	1,721	52	96	2,132

The division had mustered 6,063 men at the start of the campaign, and lost 2,132 men at Waterloo, or 35 per cent of effective strength.

---

also: SHDDT: GR 21 YC 772 *86e régiment d'infanterie de ligne (ex 105e régiment d'infanterie de ligne), 24 février 1815-10 août 1815 (matricules 1,801 à 1,881).*

242 SHDDT: GR 21 YC 771. See also: SHDDT: GR 21 YC 772.
243 SHDDT: GR 21 YC 456.
244 SHDDT: GR 21 YC 463.
245 SHDDT: GR 21 YC 264.
246 SHDDT: GR 21 YC 771. See also: SHDDT: GR 21 YC 772.

Turning to the 28th Regiment of Line Infantry, it formed the head of column of the brigade. The regiment came into hand-to-hand combat with the 32nd Regiment of Foot, which is likely when the men who were bayoneted received their wounds. Looking at the casualty data, the 28th Regiment of Line Infantry suffered the highest losses of the division, being attacked primarily on the left flank, and suffered proportionately more losses to the right than the centre companies. The 28th Regiment of Line Infantry seems to have borne the brunt of any Allied counter-attack. The 105th Regiment of Line Infantry lost the least men. Neither unit is reported as taking part in later offensives, so it seems the losses of the 28th Regiment of Line Infantry occurred in this episode.

Traditional histories have the 105th Regiment of Line Infantry being decimated by the Allied cavalry. Clearly this is not the case. The 105th Regiment of Line Infantry, based on recorded wounds, charged with the bayonet or got in a melee with the Allied infantry. From its position on the field, this could have been elements of the 95th Rifles and/or elements of the King's German Legion in the area of La Haye Sainte, assuming these losses happened at this point. Given the 105th Regiment of Line Infantry lost the least in the brigade, it makes sense that some of the regiment, seeing what was happening in front, had chance to form square.

Given, however, that the 54th and 55th Regiments of Line Infantry were in action at Plancenoit later in the day, we cannot be sure when all the casualties were sustained.

Marcognet's division

General Antoine Noguès, a general commanding the 21st Regiment of Line Infantry and the 46th Regiment of Line Infantry, narrates the day's events (in 1840) as he saw them unfold:[247]

> We advanced towards the enemy line with supported arms, without deploying sharpshooters or responding with a single shot to those of the enemy, when a body of cavalry at full gallop fell on us, passed us without threatening us, and turned on the battalions formed behind, one after the other. These battalions, they were not able to open fire and formed into circles, holding their bayonets over their

---

247 Antoine Noguès, André Maricourt, *Mémoires du général Noguès (1777-1853) sur les guerres de l'Empire*, A. Lemerre, Paris, 1922, pp. 273-6.

heads to ward off sabre blows. The cavalry, having disunited the troops who had fallen under their first blows, continued to chase them to the tail of our column.

In the 21st Regiment of Line Infantry, Captain Claude Marguerite Constant, commanding the grenadier company of 1st Battalion, was wounded with two sabre cuts to the left arm, and one to the right arm; from this we supposed that he was wounded while fighting with the Allied cavalry.[248] Captain Joseph Philippe Bourgogne took a sabre cut to the right shoulder, right upper arm and head.[249] Captain Antoine Joseph Delcourt, commanding the grenadier company of 2nd Battalion, was wounded with a sabre cut and made a prisoner.[250] Lieutenant Pierre Pacaud, who had been conscripted into the 21st Regiment of Line Infantry on 10 February 1807 and had progressed through the ranks to become lieutenant on 20 November 1813, was wounded with a sabre cut.[251] Total regimental losses at Waterloo were as follows:[252]

21st Regiment of Line Infantry				
	Wounded	Missing	Prisoner of War	Killed
1st Battalion	65	144	74	3
2nd Battalion	21	111	167	2
3rd Battalion	8	38	37	0
Total	94	293	278	5

At Waterloo, the regiment lost 670 men. Our only strength report for the regiment is dated 10 June 1815, and gives the regiment two battalions (996 men). From this, it is clear the regiment lost 67 per cent of effective strength at Waterloo. Theoretically, on 19 June the regiment had 189 other ranks and, by 23 June, it mustered twelve officers and 158 men.

Behind the 21st Regiment of Line Infantry came the 46th Regiment of Line Infantry. With the cavalry attacking the division, Battalion Commander Louis Joseph Innocent Bonnefoi, commanding the 1st

---

248 AN: LH 582/26.
249 AN: LH 329/82.
250 AN: LH 708/24.
251 AN: LH 2060/34.
252 SHDDT: GR 21 YC 197 *21e régiment d'infanterie de ligne, 18-20 mai 1815 (matricules 1 à 1,800)*. See also: SHDDT: GR 21 YC 198 *21e régiment d'infanterie de ligne, 29 avril 1815-16 juin 1815 (matricules 1,801 à 1,817)*.

Battalion 46th Regiment of Line Infantry, was hit by a sabre across the eyebrows. As the shako peak was designed to stop wounds to the face, it seems he had lost his shako by this stage. Presumably he would be blinded by the blood running into his eyes, he fell to the ground and was trampled by his assailant's horse. He, however, managed to drag himself out of the melee and get to a field dressing station.[253] Captain Pierre Florimand Bizet was wounded by a sabre cut down his face, perhaps splitting his shako in two, the blade then dragging down his face.[254] Captain Jean François Gérard was wounded by a blow from a sabre and captured in the melee.[255] Lieutenant Louis Joseph Firon took a sabre cut and was also made prisoner.[256] Lieutenant Antoine Andre Hippolyte Peyrollon had his abdomen cut open by a sabre cut and was taken prisoner in the melee. He did not return to France until 29 December 1816, when he was well enough to be returned home. He had spent over a year convalescing from his wound.[257] Sub-Lieutenant Jean Baptiste Barre was wounded and taken prisoner.[258] In total, the 46th Regiment of Line Infantry lost the following number of men at Waterloo:[259]

46th Regiment of Line Infantry					
	Wounded	Wounded & Prisoner	Prisoner of War	Killed	Missing
1st Battalion	4	0	75	7	58
2nd Battalion	2	0	66	4	49
3rd Battalion	4	0	57	1	18
Total	10	0	198	12	125

The regiment lost 345 other ranks at Waterloo. On 10 June 1815, the regiment had mustered 845 other ranks, therefore losing 41 per cent of its men at Waterloo. It seems the regiment was attacked on its right

---

253 *Bulletin des Lois*, 1823, p. 355.
254 AN: LH 246/42.
255 AN: LH 1118/72.
256 AN: LH 976/29.
257 AN: LH 2135/8.
258 AN: LH 120/86.
259 SHDDT: GR 21 YC 400 *43e régiment d'infanterie de ligne (ex 46e régiment d'infanterie de ligne), 1 août 1814-31 mai 1815 (matricules 1 à 1,800)*. See also: SHDDT: GR 21 YC 401 *43e régiment d'infanterie de ligne (ex 46e régiment d'infanterie de ligne), 31 mai 1815-30 juillet 1815 (matricules 1,801 à 2,075)*.

flank, so it seems very likely that it was attacked by the Union Cavalry Brigade. The voltigeurs seem to have been detached.

As the cavalry surged through the 2nd Brigade, at the head of his 1st Battalion (of the 25th Regiment of Line Infantry), Battalion Commander Joseph Vincent Paquet took a sabre cut to his left arm, a defensive injury, in trying to ward off blows from the Allied cavalry.[260] Captain Pierre Laurent Paradis was wounded in this melee. He writes:[261]

> I was wounded with two blows of the sabre to the head on 18 June 1815 at the Battle of Mont-Saint-Jean (Brabant) at the moment when I and my company were charged by a mass of English.

Members of the 25th Regiment of Line Infantry appear, as in other regiments in 1st Corps, to have given themselves up in the aftermath of the cavalry charge. Captain-Adjutant-Major Bonin and Captain Charles Emmanuel Houriet gave themselves up to the Allied cavalry, as both were captured at Waterloo without being wounded.[262] Also captured, it seems without being seriously wounded, was Captain Barnabe Bernard Dupeyre. In the attack, his horse was killed and he became separated from it. He was unable to retrieve his portmanteaux, which contained not only his personal effects, but also his papers, among which was the paper brevet nominating him a member of the Legion of Honour which was dated 17 March 1815. The medal was finally awarded to him on 29 May 1819.[263] The 25th Regiment of Line Infantry lost the following number of men at Waterloo:[264]

25th Regiment of Line Infantry					
	Wounded	Wounded & Prisoner	Prisoner of War	Killed	Missing
1st Battalion	5	0	263	0	0
2nd Battalion	3	0	260	0	0
3rd Battalion	1	0	210	0	0
Total	9	0	733	0	0

---

260 AN: LH 2046/70.

261 AN: LH 2048/6.

262 AN: LH 1312/45.

263 AN: LH 851/64.

264 SHDDT: GR 21 YC 238 *25e régiment d'infanterie de ligne, 1er août 1814-20 janvier 1815 (matricules 1 à 1 800).*

The regiment lost 742 other ranks at Waterloo. On 10 June 1815, the regiment had mustered 934 other ranks, thus losing 79 per cent of effective strength at Waterloo. It seems the regiment was attacked in front and on its left flank, therefore it seems very likely that it was attacked by the Union Brigade.

The rear-most regiment was the 45th Regiment of Line Infantry. Jacques Martin places his regiment at the east-west hedge line when attacked by the Allied cavalry. This means that the hedge had already been crossed by the 21st, 45th and 25th Regiments of Line Infantry, meaning Bijlandt and Pack had been pushed back a long distance by the points of the French bayonets. About the attack, Jacques Martin notes:[265]

> Death flew from all around; entire ranks disappeared under the hail, but nothing could stop our march. It carried on with the same order, the same precision. Dead men were replaced on the field by those who survived; the ranks although thinner, were no less formed.

> At last we arrived at the summit. We were about to receive the prize for such bravery. Already the English had started to bolt for it; already their guns were retiring at the gallop. A sunken road, lined with hedges, was now the only obstacle separating us from them. Our soldiers did not wait for the order to jump across; they charged, leaping over the hedges and leaving their ranks disordered to chase after their enemies. Fatal mistake! We had to enforce good order. We halted them to rally...Just as I was pushing one man into his rank, I saw him fall at my feet from a sabre blow. The English cavalry charged at us from all directions and cut us to pieces. I just had time to throw myself into the middle of the crowd to avoid the same fate. The noise, the smoke, the confusion, all happening together, we could hardly see that on our right several squadrons of English dragoons, having come down through a sort of ravine, had extended and formed behind us and charged us in the rear.

In the melee, Captain Claude Gurault, of the 45th Regiment of Line Infantry, took a sabre cut to the head.[266] Claude Cyprien Jamonet, also of the 45th Regiment of Line Infantry, took sabre cuts to the shoulders and was captured by the Allied cavalry.[267] Lieutenant Jules Hercule

---

265 Martin, pp. 275-6.
266 AN: LH 1150/28.
267 AN: LH 1351/35.

Marie Farrat took a gunshot to the left leg at some stage in the action, perhaps by a cavalry pistol, and was also unlucky enough to take a sabre cut to the palm of his right hand. Clearly, he had lost his sabre by this time in the melee and was trying to ward off blows with his arms, as this wound is a classic defence wound. Perhaps he was prone on the ground and doing all that he could to fend off his opponent's sword. He, however, escaped this chaos and died in 1844 aged seventy-three.[268] Sub-Lieutenant Jacques Louis Levacher suffered a sharp blow to his left knee.[269] Sub-Lieutenant Jean Louis Mayeux took a sabre wound and was captured by the Allied cavalry. He was returned to France on 17 January 1816.[270] Adjutant-Sub-Officer Guillaume Rene Rolland, who was born on 11 March 1787 and had joined the 45th Regiment of Line Infantry on 7 March 1807, suffered a pistol shot to the left leg.[271] Captain-Adjutant-Major Jean Baptiste Poree was wounded in this melee. He had joined the Imperial Guard in 1811, serving in the 2nd Battalion 1st Regiment of Grenadiers à Pied, and was promoted to first-lieutenant on 6 December 1811. Following the Russian campaign, he was admitted as an adjutant-major of the 10th Tirailleur Grenadiers on 8 April 1813. With the First Restoration he was placed on half-pay and was recalled to the army, joining the 45th Regiment of Line Infantry on 25 April 1815. Other officers wounded that day were Captains Dreptin, Drollet and Sergent, First-Lieutenants Bernon and Perrard, and Second-Lieutenants Augeau, Augette, Destres, Gardet, Gauthier, Jacques, La Guerre, and La Pierre. Killed were Captains Guibert and Vallat.

In the midst of the melee with the column of Marcognet, the 45th Regiment of Line Infantry lost their eagle, by tradition to Sergeant Ewart. Ewart himself writes:[272]

> The enemy began forming their line of battle about nine in the morning of the 18th; we did not commence till ten. I think it was about eleven when we were ready to receive them. They began upon our right with the most tremendous firing that ever was heard, and I can assure you they got it as hot as they gave it; then it came down to the left, where they were received by our brave Highlanders. No

---

268 AN: LH 934/30.
269 AN: LH 1623/35.
270 AN: LH 1809/18.
271 AN: LH 2372/17.
272 National Library of Scotland: *Caledonian Mercury*, 18 July 1815.

men could ever behave better: our brigade of cavalry covered them. Owing to a column of foreign troops giving way, our brigade was forced to advance to the support of our brave fellows, and which we certainly did in style; we charged through two of their columns, each about five thousand; it was in the first charge I took the eagle from the enemy: he and I had a hard contest for it; he thrust for my groin—I carried it off, and cut him through the head; after which I was attacked by one of their lancers, who threw his lance at me, but missed the mark, by my throwing it off with my sword by my right side: then I cut him from the chin upwards, which went through his teeth;[273] next I was attacked by a foot soldier, who, after firing at me, charged me with his bayonet—but he very soon lost the combat, for I parried it, and cut him down through the head; so that finished the contest for the eagle. After which I presumed to follow my comrades, eagle and all, but was stopped by the general saying to me, 'you brave fellow, take that to the rear: you have done enough until you get quit of it' which I was obliged to do, but with great reluctance. I retired to a height and stood there for upwards of an hour, which gave a general view of the field; but I cannot express the horrors I beheld: the bodies of my brave comrades were lying so thick upon the field that it was scarcely possible to pass, and horses innumerable. I took the eagle into Brussels amidst the acclamations of thousands of the spectators who saw it.

However, Corporal John Dickson writes that it was a small troop of the regiment that took the eagle. All the men associated with the capture of the eagle served under Captain Verner, namely Sergeant Charles Ewart, Corporal John Dickson and Sergeant William Clarke.[274] Dickson writes:[275]

We now came to an open space covered with bushes, and then I saw Ewart, with five or six infantry men about him, slashing right and left at him. Armour and I dashed up to these half-dozen Frenchmen, who were trying to escape with one of their standards. I cried to Armour to 'come on!' and we rode at them. Ewart had finished two

---

273 This lancer is said to be Sergeant Orban, of the 4th Lancers. de Mauduit, Vol. 2, p. 300. Ewart claimed he killed the lancer, but Orban did not die until 1848, so the killed lancer, if the event happened, cannot have been Orban. It is likely that Orban invented this story.
274 Charles Dalton, *The Waterloo Roll Call*, Eyre and Spottiswood, London, 1904, p. 253.
275 MacBride, pp. 138-48.

of them, and was in the act of striking a third man who held the eagle; next moment I saw Ewart cut him down, and he fell dead. I was just in time to thwart a bayonet thrust that was aimed at the gallant sergeant's neck. Armour finished another of them.

However, we should note that James Armour, in his account of Waterloo, makes no mention of this event at all, and places himself elsewhere on the field, so we cannot verify what Dickson claims.[276] Another eyewitness says that another man captured the eagle:[277]

I, Peter Swan, late sergeant of the Scots Greys, do hereby declare, on the honour of a soldier, that I was present at the Battle of Waterloo when the standard of the 45th French Regiment was taken by my corps, and I declare the following to be true:

I belonged to the centre squadron and charged with the corps. The flag in question, and the largest of the two hanging in Chelsea Hospital, was taken in the first instance, in the first charge, by a trumpeter named Hutchinson, who, with his horse, was immediately killed; whereupon Ewart, then a corporal, seized the colour, and having fought hard for it, kept it.

I did not see him take the standard, nor fight for it (and he had tough work to keep it), as I had enough to do to mind myself, but on coming out of action after the first charge, Captain Cheeney, the senior officer living of the Scots Greys, ordered Captain Fenton, of my troop, to take four good men and true with him and carry the standard to Brussels, which I saw them do at about twelve or one o'clock in the day, and the standard was never again in the hands of the French.

Peter Swan, D Troop, Scots Greys.

At Waterloo, Peter Swan was a trooper in Captain Fenton's troop, and is listed as wounded at Waterloo.[278]

It is not impossible to reconcile both accounts. Trumpeter Hugh Hutchinson was a trumpeter in Vener's troop, in which Ewart served. So, it seems likely that Ewart came to the aid of his troop trumpeter and carried off the eagle that Hutchinson had captured already. When we look at Ewart's account from the French archive sources, his

---

276 *Nottinghamshire Guardian*, 30 May 1873, p. 3.
277 *The Times*, 2 September 1862, p. 10.
278 Dalton, p. 254.

account does start to unravel badly. The eagle of the 45th Regiment of Line Infantry was carried by Pierre Guillot. He was born the son of Pierre Guillot and Cecile Mege on 2 December 1771 at Saint Remy. He enlisted in the 45th Regiment of Line Infantry on 3 October 1792 and was promoted to corporal-quartermaster on 11 April 1793, to sergeant on 1 November 1798, to sergeant-major on 27 May 1800, to adjutant-sub-officer on 1 June 1808 and to second-lieutenant on 4 March 1810. Following service in Spain, he was made lieutenant on 20 May 1813, appointed a member of the Legion of Honour on 17 March 1815 and was honoured with the position of lieutenant-porte-aigle a few weeks later on 20 May 1815. During the melee with the Scots Greys, he was seriously wounded in the hard-fought contest for the eagle, taking two close-range gunshots, which incapacitated him. Yet, Ewart claimed to have killed him with a sword cut! Due to his injuries, Guillot was placed on half-pay from 25 July 1815, as he could no longer fulfil his duties. The surgeon-major of the Departmental Legion of the Bouches du Rhone, a M. Vernet, writes:[279]

> I, surgeon-major of the Legion of the Department of the Bouches des Rhone, do hereby certify that M. Guillot, Pierre, lieutenant received two gunshot wounds, one to the chest, passing from front to back and another to the inside of the right thigh, which has resulted in a large [illegible] some three *pouces* long [roughly three inches], he has lost his means of subsistence and he can only walk with great difficulty as a result of this injury, which has reduced the use of his leg and thigh.
>
> Marseille 1 May 1816. Signed, Vernet.

Baron General Noguès confirms that Lieutenant Pierre Guillot was discharged from the army, as he had lost the use of his right leg from a wound at Waterloo, implying the gunshot wound to the chest had occurred in the years before the battle was fought.[280] Ewart claims he cut the porte-aigle down through the head.[281] Either Ewart is mistaken, or he did not kill the porte-aigle, and in reality the eagle was taken in the first instance by someone other than Ewart, who

---

279 Ian Smith personal communication, 26 October 2012. Citing material in his private collection.

280 ibid.

281 National Library of Scotland: *Caledonian Mercury*, 18 July 1815.

temporarily lost the eagle, which Ewart then re-captured with the help of Dickson and Armour, and took it off the field, exactly as Peter Swann says. The third porte-aigle, one of the two sergeants detailed to guard the eagle (and armed with a pair of pistols and a long spontoon, as opposed to a musket) was Jean Pierre Allivons. He was born at Baudument in the department of Basse Alpes on 15 April 1775. He entered the army on 13 April 1797 into what was to become the 45th Regiment of Line Infantry. He was promoted to corporal on 1 May 1808 and passed to the voltigeur company of the 2nd Battalion on 9 July 1809. On 6 June 1815 he was named third porte-aigle. He was wounded and made prisoner of war in this attack, no doubt in defence of the eagle.[282] Also captured was Sergeant Jacques Dugrais, who had served with the regiment since 1795.[283] Corporal Rene Pecantine, who had joined the regiment on 29 March 1809, was also captured.

Concerning the wounding of Lieutenant Guillot, it is likely that Hutchinson shot Lieutenant Guillot using one or more pistols in the right leg. Certainly, Lieutenant Guillot cannot have been the man attacked by Ewart, given the major discrepancies between the wounds Ewart claims he inflicted and the actual wounds received by Lieutenant Guillot. Therefore, on balance, it seems that Hutchinson shot and wounded Lieutenant Guillot, and snatched the eagle away. Hutchinson was then killed moments later and in the ensuing melee Ewart took the eagle from Hutchinson's body as a French officer endeavoured to retrieve it. Ewart then took the eagle from the field. This scenario neatly fits all the evidence we have for the episode; Hutchinson's involvement in the capture of the eagle being overlooked since the day he died.

Of note, the battalion marker flag (*fanion*) of the 2nd Battalion 45th Regiment of Line Infantry appears to have been captured by Private Wheeler, of the 1st Battalion 28th (Gloucestershire) Regiment of Foot.

In total, the 45th Regiment of Line Infantry lost the following number of men at Waterloo:[284]

---

282 AN: LH 24/25.

283 AN: LH 837/30.

284 SHDDT: GR 21 YC 391 *42e régiment d'infanterie de ligne (ex 45e régiment d'infanterie de ligne), 1 août 1814-4 juin 1815 (matricules 1 à 1,800)*. Research undertaken by Mr I. J. Smith.

45th Regiment of Line Infantry					
	Wounded	Wounded & Prisoner	Prisoner of War	Killed	Missing (presumed Prisoner)
1st Battalion	22	0	0	0	357
2nd Battalion	23	0	0	2	365
Total	45	0	0	2	722

The regiment, on the morning of 18 June, mustered forty-three officers and 980 men. At Waterloo, 769 men were lost, or 78 per cent of the regiment. It is likely that these losses were sustained during the attack by the Union Brigade.

Summary

In the 3rd Division, losses were as follows:

3rd Infantry Division						
Regiment	Wounded	Wounded & Prisoner	Prisoner of War	Killed	Missing	Total
21st Line Infantry [285]	94	0	278	5	293	670
25th Line Infantry [286]	9	0	733	0	0	742
45th Line Infantry [287]	45	0	0	2	722	769
46th Line Infantry [288]	10	0	198	12	125	345
Total	158	0	1,209	19	1,140	2,526

Marcognet's command had mustered 3,905 men at the start of the campaign, with 2,526 men being lost at Waterloo, equating to a staggering loss of 65 per cent of effective strength.

Of note, the 45th Regiment of Line Infantry lost the most men. If Jacques Martin is correct, this was when the regiment was disorganised and crossed the east-west hedge line in front of the Allied positions on

---

285 SHDDT: GR 21 YC 197. See also: SHDDT: GR 21 YC 198.
286 SHDDT: GR 21 YC 238.
287 SHDDT: GR 21 YC 391.
288 SHDDT: GR 21 YC 400. See also: SHDDT: GR 21 YC 401.

the left flank. Clearly the 46th Regiment of Line Infantry did something different to the other regiments in the division. The highest losses are men made prisoner or listed as missing, which may well be a mix of the both, as well as including dead and wounded. These losses are very likely to have occurred during the attack of the Union Brigade.

Chapter 6

Durutte's First Attack

By the time that d'Erlon had set off to the attack with the 1st, 2nd and 3rd Divisions of his corps, the 4th Division had just taken its place in line of battle. The 4th Division had become detached on 16 June and only re-joined the 1st Corps once the battle had started.

The 1st Brigade was commanded by General Pégot and comprised the 8th and 29th Regiments of Line Infantry; a force of some 1,800 men. The 2nd Brigade was commanded by General Brue and comprised the 85th and 95th Regiments of Line Infantry, and we are told had the same effective strength as the 1st Brigade.[289]

The aide-de-camp to General Durutte, Camille Durutte (his son), notes:[290]

> During the night, General Durutte was ordered to reach Villers-Perwin on the morning of 17 June. He arrived early in this village. After a few hours of rest he was ordered to re-join 1st Corps, which was on the march to Genappe. Following the road to Brussels, General Durutte marched until evening without being able to unite with 1st Corps; he only stopped when it became dark, half a league beyond Genappe. These troops were assailed in their camp by a terrible rain that lasted until dawn. They then began marching and joined the other divisions of 1st Corps on the Brussels road, which was parallel with the wood of Hougoumont; they took a stand on this height, which was crowned by a wood. It was on this height that the English had built a structure to establish a telegraph.

---

289 Hippolyte de Mauduit, 'Vieille Militaire. Charleroi, Fleurus et Waterloo' in La Sentinalle de l'armée, 24 June 1836.

290 La Sentinelle de l'Armée, 4th year, No. 134, 8 March 1838.

After about two hours of rest, the 4th Division of the 1st Corps was ordered to place itself on the right of the main road to Brussels. This important order came an hour too late from the major-general, because the staff officer who was responsible, not knowing where the division was, had been running in all directions without finding it. Due to this, when the division came into line, the position was already occupied and artillery was firing all along the line of battle.

Battalion-Commander Joseph-Marcelin Rulliers, of the 95th Regiment of Line Infantry, notes (in 1856) the following:[291]

> The rain ceased to fall at four o'clock in the morning, but on our side, the rain had so soaked the ground it would have been impossible for artillery, the cavalry and even the infantry to operate immediately, it was really only practicable at eleven o'clock.
>
> At six o'clock, Durutte's division was ordered to go and establish itself on a hill to the left of the highway where the British had established for a while a telegraph. It arrived about eight o'clock and immediately set about making soup and setting fires to dry clothing and equipment. From this height, which dominated all those around it, we could distinguish the French and British lines. The British had their front crowned with formidable artillery. Their main strengths of infantry and cavalry were slightly right of the centre, in front of the forest, which was masked by elevations in the terrain. They occupied the strong point of Hougoumont, as well as the gardens and a small wood. Their left extended until Papelotte, in front of the woods.

About the attack, Captain Camille Durutte notes that as soon as his father's command arrived with 1st Corps:[292]

> It was immediately announced that it was necessary that all divisions should form in columns by battalion, and we had to attack the enemy main force, starting with the left.
>
> General Durutte, perceiving that his right could be overwhelmed, and that a village which was at the end of our line, was occupied by enemy troops, he observed that it was appropriate that he should deal with these troops. However, he was told that nothing could

---

291 SHDDT: GD 2 1135.

292 *La Sentinelle de l'Armée*, 4th year, No. 134, 8 March 1838.

change the provisions of the emperor, and he executed his orders as given when he saw the divisions of the left begin their movement.

The artillery of the Guard was placed on the heights behind this division, and was bombarding the enemy, who were replying with a roughly equal number of guns. Some cavalry regiments were established behind the guns. General Durutte began his movement and the cavalry placed on his right also followed this movement, but it did nothing. Persistence by the emperor to keep each arm separate, and not to make the cavalry subordinate to the generals who commanded the divisions of infantry, was fatal and made this day very hard for us. The 4th Division was to have on its left Donzelot's 3rd Division [*sic*], but we could not find them, they were probably further behind.

Durutte was sent to attack the Hanoverian troops under Best. The column does not seem to have made contact with the Allied lines.

Of the Grey's and guns

What happened next is one of the most celebrated episodes of the Battle of Waterloo, immortalised by Lady Butler and the film, *Waterloo*, is the charge of the Scots Greys against the French artillery. Trooper James Armour, of Captain Fenton's troop Scots Greys,[293] writes as follows about this episode:[294]

When we got clear through the Highlanders, we were soon on the charge, and a short one it was. A crossroad being in our way, we leaped the first hedge gallantly, traversed the road, and had to leap over another hedge. At this time the smoke from the firing on both sides made it so dark that we could not see distinctly. We had not charged many yards till we came to a column. As yet we had stuck pretty well together, although a great number had fallen about the crossroads. In a very short time we were down upon the column making pretty clean work of them. Numbers by this time had dropped off; still we pushed forward, and very soon came upon another column, who cried out 'prisoners!', threw down their arms, stripped themselves of their belts, in accordance with French discipline, and ran like hares towards the rear. We pushed on still and soon came up to another column, some of whom went down on their knees, called

293 Dalton, p. 254.
294 *Nottinghamshire Guardian*, 30 May 1873, p. 3.

out 'quarter!' in tone of supplication. Now, then, we got among the guns, which had so terribly annoyed us and paid back the annoyance in slaughter such as never before was witnessed; artillerymen were cut down and run through, horses were houghed, harness was cut and all rendered useless. Some who were good judges of such work reckoned we had made a very good job of it. I was engaged among six or seven guns, all brass, where almost all the artillerymen were cut down, and most, if not all the horses were houghed.

While at work among these guns, no thought had we but that we should have nothing to do when we were done but to retrace our steps. I admit I was much surprised when we began to return whence we came to behold great numbers of the cuirassiers and lancers pushing across betwixt us and our own forces. They were the first troops of this kind I had ever beheld in my life, and now they were cutting off our retreat. Nothing daunted, we faced them manfully. We had none to command us now. Lieutenant-Colonel Hamilton had been killed, and many of the officers killed and wounded. But, every man did what he could. 'Conquer or die!' was the word. When the regiment returned from this charge, the troop to which I belonged did not muster above one or two sound men, unwounded, belonging to the front rank. Indeed, the whole troop did not muster above a dozen; there were upwards of twenty of the front rank killed and others wounded.

The Scots Greys charged into Durutte's 4th Infantry Division. Durutte's division was partially overrun by the Allied cavalry charge. About the movement of the 4th Division, Captain Camille Durutte writes:[295]

Upon reaching the heights, General Durutte saw a column of cavalry was advancing on the 2nd Division, commanded by General Marcognet; the cavalry charged with great vigour entirely on that division. General Durutte advanced quickly towards this division with his column, but was soon forced to stop to receive the cavalry, which was heading towards him. When the cavalry was within musket range, a discharge of musketry from the leading battalions stopped them, and he even believed that some leaders of this column were wounded; 150 riders not knowing how to restrain their horses came up to his positions.

General Durutte had ordered the artillery of his division to be established on a hill in front of the Guard, while they were

---

295 *La Sentinelle de l'Armée*, 4th year, No. 134, 8 March 1838.

performing this movement, these horsemen arrived on them, sabred some of the gunners, and others took flight. The drivers cut the traces of their horses and fled. The result was that the artillery of the division remained on the battlefield without horses.

After this event, General Durutte formed his division into two columns by brigade: one commanded by General Pégot and the other by General Brue.

The division of General Marcognet was forced to go to rally behind our line.

We are told that Pégot's brigade lost 300 killed or wounded and 200 captured. The prisoners were placed in the rear of the Allied lines in a wood which covered the extreme left of the Allied position.[296] It was perhaps now that Augustin Joseph Duquesnoy, commanding the 2nd Battalion 29th Regiment of Line Infantry, was wounded. He took a sabre cut to the inner thigh close to his groin.[297] In the melee, Sergeant-Major Jean Boijout, of the 29th Regiment of Line Infantry, was lightly wounded and captured.[298] The same fate befell Sergeant-Major Pierre Simon Joseph Laigle.[299]

Pégot's brigade, and the two battalions of the 95th Regiment of Line Infantry, were caught in the open and did not, or could not, form square. Battalion-Commander Jacques Bosse, of the 95th Regiment of Line Infantry, narrates:[300]

If we had formed square I could have saved my entire battalion while deployed in this fatal journey. I lost forty men killed or captured. The other battalions of the division and corps lost far more. If the attack had been well-led and supported by the heavy cavalry, it would have given victory to the French army.

Battalion-Commander Joseph-Marcelin Rulliers, also of the 95th Regiment of Line Infantry, notes, in 1856, that:[301]

---

296 Hippolyte de Mauduit, 'Vieille Militaire. Charleroi, Fleurus et Waterloo' in *La Sentinalle de l'armée*, 24 June 1836.
297 AN: LH 864/38.
298 AN: LH 268/41.
299 AN: LH 1445/40.
300 *La Souvenir Napoléonien*, No. 337, September 1984.
301 SHDDT: GD 2 1135.

General Durutte had left behind his division a regiment with no more than 800 men to serve as support if necessary. This regiment formed in square and successfully repelled the charges of the English cavalry.

The regiment involved was the 85th Regiment of Line Infantry. Captain François-Claude Chapuis, of the 85th Regiment of Line Infantry (part of 12th Brigade commanded by General Brue), notes that his was regiment was:[302]

> Established near the battery with grounded arms, the 85th, for several hours, experienced losses so sensitive that my grenadier company had twenty-two killed or wounded. Seeing these men fall horribly mutilated by the bullets, one might think that the morale of those left standing would be disrupted, but no one is wavering. Beautifully ordered, our soldiers were still at the height of courage and our general and our colonel gave us fine examples. Also, in this time of sorrow, there were acts of such firmness one would hardly believe such heroism and such abnegation.

He further reports that:[303]

> Following their success, they arrived at the front face of our square, where a lively fire, well aimed, entirely paralysed the élan of the cavalry, which had appeared so great that it was incapable of being stopped. The ground was littered with red coats and grey horses, and our cries of *'vive l'Empereur'* proved to them that it would not be easy to beat us. They whirled around us, and everything that our fire spared was soon destroyed by a regiment of our lancers and a regiment of chasseurs à cheval that had formed a short distance behind the 85th.

In the centre, the charge carried on through the intervals between the French divisions and attacked the forward lines of the grand battery, and began sabreing the gunners and horses. The reserves, the 12-pounders, do not seem to have been attacked, only the more advanced 6-pounder batteries. General Baron de Salle, commanding the artillery of 1st Corps, writes:[304]

---

302 Chapuis, 'Waterloo' in *Sentinalle de l'armée*, 24 February 1838.
303 ibid.
304 *'Des extraits des Souvenirs du général Dessales, ou de Salle'* in *de la Revue de Paris*, 15 January 1896.

Squadron Leader Waudré, who commanded my horse artillery, came to warn me that on the far left of the enemy a considerable body of cavalry was formed, he wondered if he should report to the emperor. I replied back to him that the emperor is not a man not to prepare for something to be expected: he is armed with an excellent telescope and probably sees this cavalry. I sent him back to his post.

By the time the fire had been resumed from my reserve, I did not wish to leave a huge gap between them and my six guns. I sent my aide to tell the officers who commanded them to join the left of the battery. It was too late! The infantry, pushed backwards by a great mass of cavalry, was broken. They arrived pell-mell with the enemy on the reserve artillery that could not fire, because they were paralysed by the fear of killing our own men. I only had time to order a change of front, and to bring the right wing back upon the guns placed on the left. I managed to open fire with my reserve of my own corps, which was commanded by Battalion-Commander Saint-Michel; a brave officer full of sang-froid: but the others were meek and are driven along by the general disorder. The rest of the battery was in the middle of this cavalry, and were forced to flee. I mounted my horse, I pushed him to a gallop in the middle of the fray, to try and rally this alarmed multitude at my side, that is to say near the sunken road along which I had managed to arrange my reserve of 12-pounders. But vain efforts! No one listened to me! Moreover, the leaders and soldiers of the artillery and the train fled. I recommenced my fire from Saint-Michel's battery with a new energy: my officers that I had sent to the rear failed to rally a single battery, although the charge had been repulsed and that men of honour would have had returned to their position, since no guns and no ammunition caissons had been taken by the enemy: there were only men and horses killed. This failure was serious.

The emperor sent to ask who ordered the movement. I replied to him that I was too experienced for having ordered it and was very sorry that I could not have prevented it. He sent the artillery of the Guard, commanded by Colonel Duchant, to supplement the losses that I had suffered. The battle continued after this bloody episode, as if it had not taken place. The French cavalry charged in a beautiful attack.

de Salle notes the following about this incident:[305]

---

305 ibid.

I said in the course of this narration that Lieutenant-Colonel X—
who, without my orders, had inopportunely precipitated the
movement of my large battery, and had been the cause not only of
the loss, but of the dispersion of these useful forces. What I must still
add makes my heart sorry in writing. This officer, full of honour,
came to be made lieutenant-colonel with the passage of Napoléon
through Grenoble (4th Regiment of Foot). He had followed part of
the battery in its escape. He had made vain efforts to bring back
some guns to the combat, but having not succeeded he came to find
me to return an account to me and acknowledge his mistake. I was
so furious, I was not able to contain my feelings; I received him with
these exact words: 'sir! When one has committed a similar military
fault, one does not reappear any more, one simply dies'. The poor
young man! He left by the gallop. I never again heard of him.

This officer was apparently Major Chandon/Chaudon. According to
Achille Vaulabelle, writing in 1845, Marcognet and Donzelot's divisions
of infantry were pushing back the Dutch-Belgian troops and the troops
of General Picton, and in order to exploit the situation, Marshal Ney:[306]

> Ordered Colonel Chandon to move his guns to the plateau of Mont-
> Saint-Jean. The colonel obeyed, and the fire from these twelve guns
> ceased; these guns were hitched up to their horses, and moving
> at the gallop descended the slopes of La Belle Alliance to climb
> the opposite side. But, when Wellington glanced at the bottom of
> the ravine, seeing that the horses of the battery were stopped, as
> they had sunk up to their knees, the carriages up to their axles,
> despite the efforts of the gunners, the guns and teams remained
> motionless. The duke sent on the spot two regiments of dragoons
> from their position at the end of the valley, they were sent at full
> speed on the bogged down batteries, they cut the traces, killed the
> horses, slashed the men, and meleed around the guns. Most of the
> men in the ranks had consumed d'eau de vie [brandy, or other such
> alcohol], and the curb chains had been taken off the bits. In front of
> the dragoons everything had to yield to the shock of these furious
> horses, which the half-drunk riders could no longer control, who
> stiff and motionless, passed with the swiftness of an arrow through
> the batteries on the fronts of our squares. When they were passing,
> the battery was broken and many guns were out of action. Colonel
> Chandon was killed.

---

306 Achille de Vaulabelle, *Campagne et bataille de Waterloo*, Perrotin, Paris,
1845, p. 122.

In this narrative it seems that rather than a myth that the Allied cavalry sabred gunners standing at their guns, the cavalry exploited a situation of a battery, or batteries, moving forward, slowed by mud and the cavalry killing horses, drivers and men as they tried to get the guns free from the mud. Colonel Chandon was actually Battalion-Commander Antoine-Victor-Barthelemy Chaudon, born in 1784 and killed at Waterloo. He was chief-of-staff of the artillery of 6th Corps.[307]

Another writer who confirms that the 12-pounder battery of 6th Corps was cut up by the Scots Greys is Sergeant de Mauduit, of the 1st Regiment of Grenadiers à Pied of the Imperial Guard, who notes that:[308]

> The 6th Corps, commanded by Comte Lobau, and with the deduction of the division of General Teste, which was sent on 17 June to Marshal Grouchy, perhaps counted no more than 6,000 combatants. After standing in closed-columns by division to the left of the Brussels road, many paces behind La Belle Alliance, they received, around one o'clock, the order to change direction and to place themselves in line behind the 1st Corps, in order to support the attack against the centre and left of the enemy army. They had not long been in this new position when disaster struck: the battery of 12-pounders belonging to the corps was captured and the gunners sabred. The pieces were no longer able to be served after this charge by the English dragoons.

So clearly, one of the attacked batteries was the 12-pounder battery from 6th Corps. This is supported by Winand Aerts,[309] as well as the archives for the Imperial Guard artillery, which state that the 12-pounder battery of 6th Corps and another battery from 1st Corps was 'culbutee' by the Scots Greys, which had begun its movement to advance in support of the infantry. The Scots Greys were then attacked by the lancers of Jacquinot, which were on the French extreme right on reconnaissance.[310]

The 12-pounder reserve battery of 6th Corps was commanded by Captain Alphonse Louis Joseph Colle, of the 8th Regiment of Foot

---

307 SHDDT: Xd 360 *Artillerie Armée du Nord 1815. Rapport 10 Aout 1815.*

308 Hippolyte de Mauduit, *'Veillee Militaire Charleroi, Fleurus et Waterloo'* in *Sentinale de l'armée*, 16 June 1836.

309 Winand Aerts, *Waterloo, opérations de l'armée prussienne du Bas-Rhin pendant la campagne de Belgique en 1815, depuis, la bataille de Ligny jusqu'a l'entrée en France des troupes prussiennes*, Spineux, Brussels, 1908, p. 237.

310 SHDDT: Xab 74 *Artillerie à Pied (formation de 1815).*

Artillery of the Line. He was born at Lille on 7 May 1784.[311] Lieutenant Armand Fromentin was mortally wounded, perhaps in this action.[312]

The other battery which was attacked belonged to 4th Division, as Captain Camille Durutte writes:[313]

> General Durutte commanded the artillery of his division to stand on a hill in front of the Guard, while he performed this movement, these horsemen arrived on him, sabred several gunners, and others fled and the drivers who cut the traces of their horses meant that the artillery of the division remained without horses on the battlefield.

These two batteries, contrary to de Salle, at least fired some rounds before being knocked out of action. Major General Vinke, of the 5th Hanoverian Infantry Brigade, notes:[314]

> About noon, two enemy batteries moved up to less than 2,000 paces from the 5th Brigade. They had very heavy guns, and the balls fell so far to the rear of us that the dressing station had to be moved further back.

It is of course eminently possible that the Scots Greys caught the batteries preparing to advance after opening fire. Perhaps we shall not know the exact circumstances when the two batteries were attacked. The Household Brigade (and no doubt part of the Royals when they charged against Quiot's division) encountered Quiot's artillery. This rather supposes that the battery was not in the main gun line commanded by de Salle, but was still retained by Quiot to support his infantry. This matches comments made by Colonel Bro in 1817 about the battle, and the non-existence of the 'grand battery'.[315] In the ensuing melee, the French fought back. Sub-Lieutenant Kopp, of the 1st Squadron of Artillery Train, writes:[316]

---

311 AN: LH 566/35.

312 Jean Marc Boisnard personal communication, 3 June 2012.

313 *La Sentinelle de l'Armée*, 4th year, No. 134, 8 March 1838.

314 Julius von Pflugk-Harttung, *Vorgeschichte der Schlacht bei Belle-Alliance, Wellington*, R. Schröder, Berlin, 1903, p. 60.

315 AN: 82 AP 5 *Fonds Bro de Commerce*. Letter and map of Waterloo dated 1817.

316 Author's collection.

18 June, at the affair of Mont-Saint-Jean, the English cavalry charged my battery. I killed three English and wounded two others. I prevented with my action the enemy taking into their hands a howitzer and a 6-pounder.

Kopp served in the 5th Company 1st Squadron of Artillery Train. The company was attached to the 1st Infantry Division.[317] Captain Pierre Charles Duthlitt, aide-de-camp to General Bourgeois (who commanded a brigade in the 1st Division), recalls the guns being attacked:[318]

> The brigade began its retreat surrounded and attacked from all sides by the cavalry and the earth was strewn with dead and wounded. That's when the two regiments of lancers commanded by General Gobrecht came and stopped this charge, which had cleared away some 1,000 soldiers and a battery of six guns and their draught horses, which were attached to the column.

The artillery mentioned by Duthlitt may have been the 20th Company 6th Regiment of Foot Artillery of the Line, which served a battery of six 6-pounders and two 24-pounder howitzers. In this cavalry attack, Second-Lieutenant Corrard was wounded with a sabre cut.[319] This could have occurred at this juncture, or later in the day; alas we will never know. By this stage, the grand battery would have been a gun line of thirty-eight guns, far less than the one hundred or eighty guns the Waterloo myths state were in action when the Allied cavalry attacked. It makes perfect sense for the 6-pounder divisional artillery to move up in support of the artillery. As we have seen, the guns would have been very much operating beyond what was classed as maximum effective range. Close artillery support to the attacking artillery would have been essential if d'Erlon was to exploit the developing situation of his columns breaking through the Allied lines.

Clearly, the French were no easy push over, as some officers like Kopp did all they could to save their guns and gunners.

Therefore, it seems that the Royals or the Household Brigade got in among Quiot's divisional artillery, and only two batteries were attacked by the Scots Greys, as opposed to the entire battery. Durutte's battery appears to have become entangled by the Scots Greys, but only a small

---

317 SHDDT: Xd 360. *Situation Rapport 1 Juin 1815.*
318 Duthlit.
319 Ian Smith personal communication, 26 June 2012.

element of the regiment, contrary to myth. Sergeant Clarke, of the Scots Greys, confirms a small detachment of the Scots Greys attacked some artillery which General Durutte, General Brue, Colonel Bro and Captain Chapuis identify as being the divisional artillery of Durutte's division and not the grand battery itself, which kept firing.

Due to water damage of the regimental muster lists for the 6th and 8th Foot Artillery we cannot generate losses for the bulk of the battery. However, we do have losses for the 12-pounder battery from 2nd Corps, which were as follows for Waterloo:[320]

Company	Killed	Died of Wounds	Wounded	Wounded & Missing	Prisoner of War	Missing
7th	3	1	4	1	0	24
8th	1	0	1	0	0	0
16th	0	0	0	1	0	5
Total	4	1	5	2	0	29

Due to a shortage of manpower, the 7th Company was bolstered with men from the 8th and 16th Companies. The killed and wounded are likely to have been victims of either the Prussians or the Union Brigade. The missing are likely to have been lost during the route. 7th Company, which was the reserve 12-pounder battery of 2nd Corps, was commanded by Michel Valnet. He was born at Rougermont-les-Cendrey on 22 December 1770 and enlisted in the 2nd Foot Artillery on 11 October 1790. He was promoted to fourrier on 1 June 1792, to sergeant on 24 November 1792 and to sergeant-major on 1 March 1798. Promotion to second-lieutenant came on 22 February 1801, to second-captain on 13 July 1807 and to captain on 12 October 1811. He was placed in command of 7th Company in August 1814.[321]

During the campaign, 7th Company (comprising of six 12-pounder and two 6.4-pounder howitzers) lost far more men. At Quatre-Bras, one gunner was killed and three wounded. On the 17th, four men were lost. At Waterloo, three gunners were killed, six wounded and nineteen missing. The 7th Company was posted to join the artillery of 1st Corps on the right flank at Waterloo. It seems possible that the much higher losses from the battery can be partially explained by the fact that the battery was charged by the Union Brigade in the first half of the battle,

---

320 SHDDT: GR 25 YC 21.
321 AN: LH: 2670/44.

and then around 19.00 was deployed with the troops of General Pégot in supporting the attack of the Imperial Guard. Given that General de Salle, who commanded the reserve 12-pounder batteries of 1st Corps, tells us the reserves were not attacked, but fired into the Allied cavalry. The losses, therefore, seem to be primarily from the closing stages of the battle, when the Allied cavalry charged the guns.[322]

The horse artillery of Jacquinot's 1st Cavalry Division was the 2nd Company 1st Horse Artillery. The company lost two men as prisoners and one missing at Waterloo,[323] far fewer losses than the 12-pounder reserve. Clearly, the battery was not heavily involved in the charge by the Union Brigade, nor, it seems, came under fire from the Prussians later in the day.

---

322 SHDDT: GR 25 YC 21.
323 SHDDT: GR 25 YC 14 1e Artillerie à Cheval.

Chapter 7

Jacquinot's Lancers

Napoléon's line had been brutally weakened by the Union and Household Brigades. This was the point at which the British cavalry ought to have stopped, regrouped and returned to their starting position. For many, however, this was their first experience of combat and instead, exhilarated by their success over the massed ranks of d'Erlon's hapless infantry, the Scots Greys, and no doubt elements from other regiments, charged disastrously onwards. Despite some success in cutting down some French gunners, Ponsonby's Union Brigade carried on the charge further into the French lines. Ponsonby and his staff's efforts were useless in endeavouring to rally their troops. It was said that one officer was heard to cry out 'to Paris!' as he charged by. The Allied charge had disrupted Napoléon's plans and bought Wellington time to wait for more Prussians to arrive to tip the balance in the Allies' favour.

French retribution was swift and merciless; spotting their opportunity, Jacquinot's lancers and chasseurs attacked and exacted a terrible toll on the British cavalry, killing or wounding one-third of their number. In this melee of cavalry and artillery, intermingled with infantry soldiers, it appears that General Desvaux de Saint Maurice, commanding the Guard artillery, was killed. Sergeant-Major Chevalier, of the chasseurs à cheval of the Imperial Guard, notes:[324]

> A strong enemy force executed a vigorous cavalry charge, pushed back our infantry and took sixteen guns. Napoléon then advanced with his Guard cavalry and cuirassiers. We charged headlong, we fell onto the English cavalry, it was now our turn, slashing at

---

324 Lieutenant Chevalier, *Souvenirs des Guerres Napoleoniennes* ed. Jean Mistler and Helene Michaud, Hachette, Paris, 1970, p. 323.

everything that blocked our way, we captured back our artillery pieces as well taking in addition two flags and seven guns from the enemy, despite the terrible fire of their artillery. The melee became horrible, the carnage was appalling, the earth became littered with dead or dying men and horses.

Colonel Bro, of the 4th Lancers, explains what happened to his regiment:[325]

Our infantry was cut up and dispersed; Drouet d'Erlon ordered the cavalry to charge. A boggy field did not allow us to operate at ease. I advanced my 4th Lancers.

On the right was a little wood, we could see the English cavalry, who promptly reformed, they threatened to outflank the 3rd Chasseurs. I was at the head of the squadrons, crying 'come, children, we must reverse this rabble!' The soldiers replied 'forward! Long live the emperor!'

Two minutes later, the attack takes place. Three enemy ranks were pushed in. We savagely attacked the others! The scrummage became frightful. Our horses crushed the bodies of corpses and the cries of the injured arose from all sides. I found myself for a moment to be lost in the gun smoke. When the smoke thinned, I saw British officers around Lt Verrand,[326] with our eagle. Rallying a few riders, I came to his aid. Fourrier Orban[327] killed General Ponsonby with a

---

325 Bro.

326 Sub-Lieutenant Jeanne Marie Verrand was appointed on 21 May 1813. He received the regiment's eagle on 1 June 1815. SHDDT: Xc 182 *3e et 4e Chevau-légers. Dossier 4e Lanciers. Folio 1815.*

327 MAT No. 6 François Orban was a sergeant in the 1st Company of 1st Squadron 4th Lancers. He was born in the Saint-Denis department of the Ain on 12 January 1778 and was admitted to the regiment on 17 December 1798 before being promoted to corporal on 1 October 1813 and to sergeant on 1 March 1815. He was discharged from the regiment on 16 September 1815 and died on 8 April 1848. His discharge papers make no mention at all of him killing Ponsonby. AN: LH 2020/22. Given in other regiments, officers and men recorded their deeds of valour and glory in the immediate aftermath, for instance Isaac Palaa (of the 9th Cuirassiers) taking a colour at Waterloo, it seems unlikely that Orban would not have commented upon this. Orban, I have no doubt, was involved in a melee with the Scots Greys, but I doubt he killed Ponsonby, as neither he nor his commanding officer could have recognised Sir William Ponsonby on the field of battle.

lance.[328] My sword mowed down three of his captains. Two others escaped.

> I returned to the front to save my adjutant. I emptied my second pistol when I suddenly felt my right arm paralysed...Stunned, I was forced to take hold of the mane of my horse. I had the strength to say to Major Perrot[329] 'take command of the regiment!' General Jacquinot concurred when he saw the blood flood my clothes, supported me and said, 'withdraw' and he went to lead the charge. Major Motet[330] cut my jacket and applied a bandage and lint on my wound, pronouncing: 'this is not fatal, but do not stay here'. The rage in having to leave my squadrons brought tears to my eyes.

In the melee, it is very likely that Sergeant Orban killed Colonel Hamilton. We know the Scots Greys and 45th Regiment of Line Infantry were towards the centre of the French right wing, and somewhere close by La Haye Sainte was the 1st Royal Dragoons, attacking the 105th Regiment of Line Infantry. According to George Gunning, here was Sir William Ponsonby, who was shot dead by French infantry. The Scots Greys were attacked by lancers, arguably the 3rd and 4th Lancers. Given that Sir William Ponsonby was nowhere near the 4th Lancers, and that Orban, as we shall see, saved the eagle of the 21st Regiment of Line Infantry and claims to have killed a British senior officer, the only other such high-ranking officer killed from the brigade was Colonel Hamilton. Even in undress, the colonel's heavy bullion epaulettes

---

328 How did Bro know this? I have no doubt that the 4th Lancers were involved in a melee with the Scots Greys, but Bro could only have known after the fact that General Sir William Ponsonby was killed by lancers. Given that Ponsonby was shot dead while with the Royal Dragoons at the moment Corporal Stiles (of that regiment) took the eagle of the 105th Regiment of Line Infantry, Orban cannot have killed Ponsonby. It is highly likely that Bro was claiming the credit for the death of Ponsonby for his regiment, and to provide some degree of authenticity, added a name of a member of the regiment, and claimed he killed three officers from the Scots Greys. This seems very unlikely that of the eleven recorded officer casualties Bro killed three. Beyond Colonel Bro, there is no historical evidence that Orban killed Ponsonby.

329 Major Perrot joined the regiment on 12 June 1815. SHDDT: Xc 182. *Dossier 4e Lanciers*.

330 Assistant Surgeon Motet joined the regiment on 10 June 1815. SHDDT: Xc 182. *Dossier 4e Lanciers*.

would have marked him out as a superior officer. Bro and Orban say Orban killed an officer of senior rank. Thus, as Ponsonby was shot dead 500 metres or more to the west of where the 4th Lancers were, the man killed by Orban was Hamilton.

In his own recollections of Waterloo, Orban states he saved an eagle. Clearly, this cannot be that of the 45th Regiment of Line Infantry, as that is housed in Edinburgh. So, what eagle did he save? It must have been an eagle from Marcognet's command, so this narrows down the possibilities. In this melee, the 21st Regiment of Line Infantry were, we are told by its major, 'destroyed'.[331] When we look at the casualty records for the 21st Regiment of Line Infantry, we see that standing out from the mass of data is that the porte-aigle, Sub-Lieutenant Jean Fleury, was made prisoner of war, and the third porte-aigle was also made prisoner.[332] So, what happened to the eagle? Well, it seems to have been captured by the Inniskilling Dragoons, as Trooper Penfold relates:[333]

> After we charged, I saw an eagle which I rode up to, and seized hold of it. The man who bore it would not give it up, and I dragged him along by it for a considerable distance. Then the pole broke about the middle, and I carried off the eagle. Immediately after that I saw a comrade, Hassard, in difficulties, and, giving the eagle to a young soldier of the Inniskillings, I went to his aid. The eagle got dropped and lost.

Colonel Miller, commanding the regiment, notes:[334]

> When we took [up] our position on the 18th, the Royals were formed on the right, the Inniskillings on the left, the Greys in reserve, and so formed we charged. I commanded the left squadron, Madox the right, and Browne the centre. My squadron was composed of Holbeck's and Douglas's troops. In charging the French column, I was bayoneted in two places slightly, and lost my horse. In returning to the rear I met Sergeant Small, who had lost his own horse and was leading one which had belonged to a French officer of lancers, and on that I rode, with the lancer's appointments, for the rest of

---

331 SHDDT: C15 5. Dossier 21 June 1815. Letter from the major of the 21st Regiment of Line Infantry to Soult.

332 SHDDT: Yj 12.

333 Ian Smith personal communication, 24 June 2012.

334 Siborne, *Waterloo Letters*, No. 45.

the day. I then found out Rickatts got some sticking-plaster put on my bayonet wounds, and re-joined the brigade—then reduced to three squadrons, some having been from thence, after some time, we were ordered to the right of the Genappe road, moved up to the front, and there I was again wounded, and left them under the command of Madox, with you commanding the brigade. As to time I cannot pretend to any accuracy whatever. I should guess we charged about twelve—Ponsonby was killed at that time—that we moved towards the right about four, and that I left the field about five. I was wounded shortly before you, and, I believe, also before Lord Anglesey—but of that I am not certain. As to Penfold taking an eagle, I only know what I heard at the time, that he took an eagle which was by some means dropped or lost, and brought off by a man of the Greys or Royals. But, Penn says that Penfold told him that after we charged he saw an eagle—which he rode up and seized hold of; that the person who held it would not give it up, and that he dragged him by it for a considerable distance; that the pole broke about the middle and Penfold carried it off; that immediately afterwards he saw Hassard engaged by himself, and went to his assistance, giving the eagle to a young soldier of the Inniskillings, whose name Penn now forgets.

So, the Inniskillings captured and lost an eagle. Where the regiment was on the field of Waterloo places it in the same location as the 21st Regiment of Line Infantry. Seemingly the regiment lost its eagle to the Inniskillings.

However, Sergeant Orban, of the 4th Lancers, records that he was escorting a senior officer who had been made prisoner, and as he looked around he observed English dragoons coming to the officer's rescue. Before they reached him, Orban observed an eagle under attack, in an instant he says he killed the officer and rode forward to save the eagle. Orban states that he killed the horse of the dragoon taking the eagle away with a lance thrust to the left shoulder, and then killed the dismounted trooper. He then picked up the eagle and rode to the rear to present it to Colonel Bro.[335] Was it the young trooper that Orban killed? Perhaps so, though Miller believes Corporal Stiles, from the Royal Dragoons, took the eagle from the trooper, which is highly unlikely. Thus, it seems the Inniskillings for a moment had taken an eagle, and it had been saved by the French.

---

335 de Mauduit, Vol. 2, p. 300.

The rumour about the loss of the eagle prompted the regiment's major to write on 21 June that the regiment, despite being destroyed, did save the eagle. Clearly, for him to have to say this in writing to Marshal Soult means that rumours must have been rife that the regiment lost its eagle.[336] Trooper Jean Armand Flotard, of the 4th Lancers, relates that:[337]

> One of our soldiers said to our captain, pointing to a regiment of English dragoons against which we would charge: 'upon my word, captain, these j… f… they have the nerve to wait for us!' 'Comrades,' says Colonel Bro before we conducted our first charge of the day: 'at this hour I have been at your head for only one month and I shall know it's an honour, and you will know in a moment whether I am worthy of it'. This kind of challenge delivered to our regiment was enough to exalt in us fury, the desire to fight. At seven o'clock, at the time of the decisive attack of Blücher, we had three officers; two killed or wounded.

Trooper James Smithies, of the 1st Royal Dragoons (brigaded with the Greys), writes about the tactics of the French lancers as follows:[338]

> We were next ordered to charge a whole regiment of French lancers, who looked if possible a still uglier enemy than their coated brethren. The lance was fastened to their boot and when we neared them, they sent it out with all their might; and if the man at whom they aimed did not manage to parry the blow, it was all over with him.

This was a tactic the French used elsewhere in the battle. Captain Fortune de Brack, of the light horse lancers of the Imperial Guard, notes that:[339]

> At Waterloo, when we charged the English squares, one of our lancers, not being able to break down the rampart of bayonets which opposed us, stood up in his stirrups and hurled his lance like a dart; it passed through an infantry soldier, whose death would

---

336 SHDDT: C15 5. Dossier 21 June 1815. Letter from the major of the 21st Regiment of Line Infantry to Soult.
337 Jacques-Antoine Dulaure, *1814-1830 Historie des Cent-jours*, Paris, 1834, p. 205 citing Armand Jean Flotard, of the 4th Lancers.
338 British Library: *Middleton Albion*, 15 February 1868, p. 4.
339 Ian Smith personal communication, 2 June 2015.

have opened a passage for us, if the gap had not been quickly closed. That was another lance well lost.

In this action, the 3rd and 4th Lancers lost men and horses. In the 3rd Lancers, commanded by Colonel Martigue, Captain Denis Gros suffered a gunshot wound to the left leg.[340] Captain Martial Lepage, who had joined the regiment in 1814, suffered a gunshot wound to the left shoulder, as well as a sabre cut to the left thigh and one to the right arm.[341] Lieutenant François Aubert was unlucky enough to be bruised by a cannon ball.[342] Squadron-Commander Jean Theodore Dudouit was seriously wounded in the battle and was placed on half-pay due to his infirmity resulting from his wounds.[343] Sub-Lieutenant Guillaume Dessaux was slightly wounded when his horse was killed under him.[344] Sub-Lieutenant Jean François de Saint Romain suffered the same fate.[345]

In terms of casualty data and demographics of the men we can say nothing. The archive for both regiments was damaged in 1944 and until it is conserved, it is not accessible by researchers. This means that we rely upon our two eyewitnesses for the operations of the brigade, and sadly we can say very little about the men of the two regiments. The 3rd Lancers, on 10 June, mustered twenty-seven officers and 379 other ranks. On 23 June 1815, Jacquinot informed Marshal Soult that the 3rd Lancers had twelve officers and 180 other ranks.[346] This represents a loss of 199 men, or 52.5 per cent of the regiment's effective strength. The 4th Lancers had twenty-two officers and 274 other ranks on 10 June. On 23 June, Jacquinot informed Marshal Soult that they had just six officers and eighty-four other ranks.[347] This represents a loss of 190 men, or 69 per cent of the regiment's effective strength strength. Flotard states the regiment was reduced to 250 men from 600.[348] This figure of 600 is totally at odds with all other sources for the strength of the 4th Lancers.

---

340 AN: LH 1206/63.
341 AN: LH 1593/39.
342 AN: LH 64/3.
343 AN: LH 829/70.
344 AN: LH 758/71.
345 *Carnet de la Sabretache*, 1909.
346 SHDDT: C15 34. *2e Division de Cavalerie Situation au 25 Juin 1815*.
347 SHDDT: C15 34. *2e Division de Cavalerie Situation au 25 Juin 1815*.
348 Dulaure, p. 205 citing Armand Jean Flotard, of the 4th Lancers.

Therefore, the figures he cites cannot be accurate. Prisoner of war records list the following men:[349]

Constant Virellau;
Louis Charles Andrien;
Contant Brunel;
Jean BaptisteTourvenot;
Joseph Louch;
Antoine Charlo;
Aimeau Laborde;
Jean Charles Andrieaux;
Louis Brunel;
Jean Loret; and
Herbine Babin.

For the 3rd Lancers, Chief-of-Staff Vialla, of 1st Corps, reports the regiment mustered nineteen officers and 211 men, a gain of thirty-one men since 23 June, and the 4th Lancers had twelve officers and 110 men on 1 July, a gain of thirty-four men.[350] Prisoners in England were the following members of the 3rd Lancers:[351]

Lieutenant Louis Noiret;
Sous-Lieutenant Marguerite Amedu;
Sous-Lieutenant Alphonse Magaurite—placed on parole on 29 August 1815 in Ashburton, Derbyshire;
Sergeant-Major Amedee Masaurice;
Corporal Jean Soulier Cointin;
Aime Gentun;
Jean Baptiste Martinet;
Claude Dufourd;
François Treille;
Gille Privet;
Antoine Bourroutte;
Alexander Giraideau;
Antoine Grampteille;
François Dupain;
Pierre Gilleaux;
François Detrick;
Gilbert Bouillain;

349 SHDDT: Yj 11. See also: SHDDT: Yj 12. See also: SHDDT: Yj 13.
350 SHDDT: C15 35 *Situations Armée du Nord 1815. Rapport Vialla 1 Juillet 1815.*
351 SHDDT: Yj 11. See also: SHDDT: Yj 12. See also: SHDDT: Yj 13.

Louis Schneider;
Paul Fevrard;
Pascal Benoit;
Pierre Fonvielle;
Jean Sanon;
Antoine Borot;
Frederick Dupain;
Paul Ferrart;
François Monthue; and
Daniel Michel.

The 3rd Chasseurs

Also moving up with the lancers were the brigaded 3rd Chasseurs. General Bruno states the following:[352]

> I had the honour to serve under the orders of General-of-Division Jacquinot, commanding the 1st Brigade of cavalry, comprising the 3rd Chasseurs à Cheval of Colonel de La Woëstine and the 7th Hussars of Marbot.
>
> I had in the morning detached the 7th Hussars to keep in communication with General Domont, and I was placed on the extreme right of 1st Corps with the 3rd Chasseurs, which consisted of three squadrons. The enemy artillery fired at us and we lost an officer and some chasseurs, some distance behind us was an undulation in the terrain that would protect us from the enemy's fire, into which we moved.
>
> The artillery stopped and there was a great silence. Our attention was quickly drawn to our left where there was a great cloud of dust [what happened to the mud? Or does the term refer to the clods of grass and earth kicked up by the horses' hooves?], I judged that though still some distance away, it was a charge of enemy cavalry against our infantry. Shortly after the column of cavalry composed of English Dragoon Guards and Belgian lancers [sic] attacked the squares, being unable to break the squares they headed directly towards us.

---

352 Bruno, 'Le 3e Chasseurs à Cheval à Waterloo' in Sentinalle de l'armée, 1 March 1838.

Squadron-Commander Pozac,[353] commanding the 1st Squadron of the regiment, I ordered to charge the flank, and at the same time Colonel La Woëstine, with the remaining two squadrons, charged the English front.

The charge was executed with the great energy and was entirely successful. The English column was shattered, and to avoid utter destruction, made a turn to the left and retired in great disorder.

The 3rd Chasseurs à Cheval had saved Durutte's division from destruction. It was only when that they had already retreated a good distance that I saw a new charge conducted by the cuirassiers, under the orders of General Milhaud.

The Belgian cavalry mentioned were in fact the Dutch-Belgian cavalry brigade of General de Ghingy. de Ghingy's brigade was moved up along with the English light cavalry brigade of Vandaleur at the request of Prince Sachsen-Weimar, who was defending La Haye Sainte, Papelotte and Smohain. Losses for the 3rd Chasseurs were as follows:[354]

3rd Chasseurs à Cheval				
Squadron	Killed	Died of Wounds	Wounded	Missing
1st	1	0	2	12
2nd	3	0	2	8
3rd	0	0	2	11
4th	1	0	0	1
Total	5	0	6	32

353 Joseph Pozac was born on 31 July 1781. He volunteered to the 12th Hussars on 25 May 1798 and was promoted to corporal on 20 April 1799, by which time the hussars had become the 30th Dragoons. He was made a fourrier on 22 March 1800, a sergeant-major on 26 February 1801, a sub-lieutenant on 28 June 1803 and a lieutenant on 18 September 1806. He was named aide-de-camp to General Fournier on 12 November 1807 and named aide-de-camp to General Dalton on 9 July 1809. He was then made a captain in the newly formed 12th Hussars on 8 November 1809 and promoted to squadron-commander on 21 March 1813 in the 23rd Chasseurs. He then passed as a squadron-commander to the 3rd Chasseurs on 16 August 1814. AN: LH 2218/13.
354 SHDDT: GR 24 YC 264.

The regiment began the campaign with twenty-nine officers and 336 other ranks, but forty-three men were lost at Waterloo, representing 13 per cent of effective strength.

While the 3rd Chasseurs were attacking the Allied cavalry, Chapuis (of the 85th Regiment of Line Infantry) notes that if it was not for the proven courage of Colonel Masson and General Brue, the regiment would have been easily crushed. As Pégot's men fell back in disorder, the 85th and 95th Regiments of Line Infantry began an offensive movement, and the rump of Pégot's brigade rallied behind the division of General Brue, which formed a 'living redoubt as at Marengo', with reference to the baptism of fire of the 1st Regiment of Grenadiers à Pied of the Imperial Guard. Pégot's division, we are told by Chapuis, was out of action for the remainder of the day.[355] However, Pégot's men were, according to Durutte, in action later in the day.

The cuirassiers intervene

As Gobrecht's lancers surged forward, Milhaud ordered forward one of his cuirassier brigades. A member of the Scots Greys, David Regent, writes as follows about the cuirassiers falling on to the Union Brigade:[356]

> The cuirassiers and Polish lancers came to the rescue of the infantry; we attacked them right and left, and there was no such thing as mastering them but by downright strength. After some hard fighting they broke up and fled. However, we, the Greys, followed the French too far, and Sir William Ponsonby, in trying to bring us back, was killed in a ploughed field to our left by a troop of Polish lancers, his horse having become fast in the clay. It was thus following the enemy that we lost our brave Colonel Hamilton: he was a brave man. The Enniskilillens [sic] did all they could to save General Ponsonby, and sixteen of the brave fellows lost their lives in the attempt. I saw Shaw, of the Lifeguardsmen, the day after the battle: he was frightfully mangled, but had not a mortal wound about him: he died from loss of blood. I came off with three slight sabre wounds. My comrade, Wilson, parried a blow made at me and saved my life, but lost his own.

---

355 J. L. Brue, *'Lettre Addresse au Colonel Chapuis'* in *La Sentinalle de l'armée,* 1 March 1838.

356 *Nottinghamshire Guardian,* 3 August 1854, p. 4.

Moving up after the light cavalry were the 7th and 12th Cuirassiers, as Sergeant-Major Dickson writes:[357]

> you can imagine my astonishment when drawn below, on the very ground we had crossed, appeared at full gallop, a couple of regiments of cuirassiers on the right, and away to the left a regiment of lancers. I shall never forget the sight. The cuirassiers in their sparkling steel breastplates and helmets, mounted on strong black horses, with great blue rugs across the croups, were galloping towards me, tearing up the earth as they went, the trumpets blowing wild notes in the midst of discharges of grape and canister shots from the heights. Around me there was one continuous noise of clashing arms, shouting men, neighing and moaning of horses.

In General Milhaud's after-action report to Marshal Soult, the major-general notes:[358]

> At the battle of the 18th, the 4th Cavalry Corps saved the right wing of Comte d'Erlon, and saved many thousands of our infantry and twenty guns from the hands of the English cavalry, which left more than 800 dragoons dead on the field of battle and more than 150 horses in the hands of our brave cuirassiers.

Both brigades of Dubois and Travers had been in action already that memorable day, but were not dispirited at returning to the charge once more. The four regiments surged up the slope and Colonel Michel Ordener, at the head of his 1st Cuirassiers, writes:[359]

> Our first shock was irresistible. Despite a rain of iron which fell on our helmets and our armour, sent by the English batteries which were established behind a ravine, I rode with our front rank. We crowned the crest of the heights, and we went like lightning through the guns, and addressed the English infantry, which fell back in disorder on the squares that were formed hastily behind them by the Duke of Wellington. These squares were formidable, but in their turn were attacked and decimated.

---

357 MacBride, pp. 144-5.
358 Delort, 'Notice sur la batailles de Fleurus et de Mont Saint Jean' in *Revue Hebdomadaire*, June 1896, pp. 379-80.
359 Lot.

Moving up in echelon with Wattier's division was the as yet uncommitted division of General Delort. About the operations of his division, Delort writes:[360]

> The intrepid cuirassiers of the divisions of Vathier and Delort continued their success, charged and broke a square of the English guards and covered the ground with dead, but they could not, because of the terrain, enjoy all the benefits of these brilliant charges.

The disorganised Allied cavalry were no match for the cuirassiers. The charge of the Union Brigade and Household Cavalry Brigade had achieved two things. Firstly, it had disrupted Napoléon's first, and potentially successful, attack. More importantly, it had bought Wellington time, as it meant that with every minute of delay, Blücher's Prussians were closer to arriving at Waterloo, enabling the Allied armies to crush Napoléon with overwhelming numbers.

A lot has been written commentating about the French cavalry's inabilities to carry off artillery, and that it was needlessly sacrificed. The British cavalry in a single charge suffered large losses of six regiments of heavy cavalry for the temporary gain of twelve artillery pieces—little different to the French cavalry's charges against the Allied guns. In both cases, the gains of the cavalry were not exploited. The heavy cavalry had disrupted the French first attack, but with huge losses. The French lost around 1,500 dead and wounded; 500 or so more than the English cavalry lost.

The 1st Royal Dragoons had eighty-six killed out of 400 men, another 107 wounded and 238 horses killed or wounded, representing losses of 48 per cent. The Scots Greys lost eight officers, four sergeants, seven corporals, one trumpeter and ninety-five privates killed, and seven officers, seven sergeants, nine corporals, one trumpeter and seventy-four privates wounded out of 444 all ranks. Furthermore, 183 horses were killed and sixty-seven wounded.

Of the men in the two Allied brigades that charged, approximately 41 per cent were killed, wounded or missing at Waterloo (991 out of 2,407).

Approximately 54 per cent of the horses were killed, wounded or missing from the Union Brigade and supporting squadrons. Since a cavalryman without a horse was out of action, the horse loss figures are

---

360 *Nouvelle revue Retrospective*, Paris, January 1897, p. 374.

the minimum number of men out of action, that is 1,305 men out of 2,407 no longer in the ranks. This leaves, at most, 900 men available. In total, the Household Brigade lost 45 per cent of their effective strength and the Union Brigade 46 per cent. With a further 400 escorting prisoners, this left 500 men.

By 15.00, 1st Corps was operational once more and the grand battery was quickly augmented with two batteries from the Imperial Guard. Elements of the battery had not stopped firing. Overall, the Union Brigade had checked Napoléon's advance and bought time, but the losses to the French were far from crippling. As we note later, Marcognet's division suffered the most in the charge of the Allied cavalry, and only took a partial role in the rest of the day's actions. Donzelot's division was relatively intact, Quiot had a brigade not yet committed and Durutte had a regiment which had not yet seen any major fighting. d'Erlon still had seven regiments (or just under half of 1st Corps) that were still relatively fresh. Durutte's command and that of Donzelot would soon be in action against the Allied centre and left flank. The charge had disrupted the French plans, but it was not a knockout blow to either 1st Corps or the French artillery, in direct contradiction of the Waterloo myth and the film of the same name, which has perhaps done the most in suggesting the battery and 1st Corps was totally destroyed by the Scots Greys; a notion that does not stand up to close scrutiny of original source material.

The Allied light cavalry had disrupted the French attack. Bourgeois's column of two regiments and Marcognet's column of four regiments were cut up and retreated in disorder. Donzelot and Durutte's columns held fast against the tide of cavalry and repelled them with crisp volley fire. The grand battery kept firing into the mass of cavalry, before and during the charge.

Marbot is sent on reconnaissance

The Prussian army had been badly bloodied at Ligny two days earlier, and Napoléon felt that the Prussians were a spent force and could not take to the field. Since the arrival of Grouchy's report of 17 June, the headquarters staff knew Prussians were at Wavre and that Grouchy had made contact with the Prussian army, which was seemingly headed north-east. Additional news had reached headquarters around 9.30 to 10.00 in Grouchy's 6.00 dispatch.

To establish the nature of the Prussian threat, on the night of 17 June a reconnaissance patrol had been sent to Wavre:[361]

> Since Quatre-Bras, the division of Domon was detached to scout along the left bank of the Dyle, along to the Brussels road; the 4th Regiment of Chasseurs passed the bridge at Moustier, where his skirmishers opened fire with their carbines at the Prussian cavalry. With the onset of night, the division returned and bivouacked to the right of headquarters.

Headquarters now had intelligence of the Prussians still being on the right bank of the Dyle at Moustier. Early on 18 June, a second patrol was sent out towards Wavre and Moustier. It comprised the 7th Hussars and the 3rd Battalion 13th Regiment of Light Infantry. About the operations of his regiment on the French right wing:[362]

> The 7th Hussars, of which I was colonel, was part of the light cavalry division attached to the 1st Corps, forming, 18 June, the right wing of the army that the emperor commanded in person.
>
> At the beginning of the action, about eleven o'clock, my regiment was detached from the division along with a light infantry battalion, which was placed under my command. These troops were established as a reserve at the far right, behind Frischermont facing the Dyle.
>
> Specific instructions were given to me from the emperor by his aide-de-camp, General La Bédoyère, and an aide, that I cannot remember the name of, specified that I was to leave most of my troops always in view of the battlefield, and I was to take 200 infantry into the woods of Frischermont, and establish a squadron in Lasne, moving towards the positions at Saint-Lambert with another squadron, place half at Couture, and half at Beaumont, which were to send out reconnaissance patrols along the Dyle, and towards Moustiers Ottignies. The commanders of various detachments had to leave quarter of a mile between each outpost, forming a contiguous string along on the battlefield, so that by means of hussars, galloping from one post to the other, the officers on reconnaissance might inform me quickly before they met the vanguard troops of Marshal Grouchy, who were to arrive on the side of the Dyle. I was finally ordered to send directly to the emperor all the reconnaissance reports.

---

361 Berton, pp. 49-50.
362 Grouchy, Vol 4.

I executed the order that I was given; it would be impossible after a period of fifteen years to determine which you ask for, the time at which the detachment arrived at Moustiers. Especially as captain Eloy,[363] who commanded, had been instructed by me to proceed in his march with the utmost caution, but noting that he started at eleven o'clock from the battlefield, and had not more than two miles to go, one must assume that he did so in two hours. Which would set his arrival in Moustiers at one o'clock.

A note from Captain Eloy that I was promptly handed from the intermediate stations, told me that he found no troops in Moustiers, nor at Ottignies, and the inhabitants assured him that the French left on the right bank of the Dyle, were crossing the river in Limalette and Wavre.

I sent this letter to the emperor with Captain Kounkn,[364] acting as adjutant-major, he returned accompanied by an aide, who said to me, from the emperor, to keep the line at Moustiers, and to send an officer and detachment along the defile of Saint-Lambert, and to dispatch the various parties in the directions of Limale, Limalette and Wavre.

I sent this order, and even sent a copy with my detachment chief at Lasnel Saint-Lambert (his name is no longer in my memory, but I think it was Lieutenant Municheffer).[365]

One of our platoons having advanced to a quarter of a mile beyond Saint-Lambert encountered a picket of Prussian hussars, of which we took several men including an officer! I informed the emperor of this strange capture, and sent him the prisoners.

Marbot's times are impossible to reconcile with Prussian sources. We are sure that Marbot was sent on such a mission and reached Chapelle-Saint-Lambert and Moustier, but much earlier in the day. Marbot, I feel, set off at first light and got to Lasne and Moustier before the Prussians, and that in reality, the Prussians he found were in fact the advance guard of Bülow's 4th Corps. If he encountered the Prussians heading to Saint-Lambert as he states, he must have been there before 10.30. Given the

---

363 Captain Eloy was appointed to the 7th Company of 3rd Squadron on 15 December 1814. SHDDT: Xc 249 *7e Hussard 1791-1815*. Dossier 1815.
364 No officer of this name is listed in the regiment. SHDDT: Xc 249. Dossier 1815.
365 Lieutenant of the elite company. SHDDT: Xc 249. Dossier 1815.

prisoner had arrived at headquarters by 13.00, the prisoner must have left Saint-Lambert say an hour or more earlier. It is very likely, given the place names he gives, that Eloy went via the rue d'Anogrune and thence to the rue de Lasne, passing through Couture, Lasne, Chapelle-Saint-Lambert and then swung south-east along the rue des Ottignies, a journey of ten miles. Marbot infers it took two hours to get to Moustier. Chapelle-Saint-Lambert is midway, so for the prisoner to get back to Waterloo for say 12.30, he must have been on his way to headquarters an hour or more earlier. It is very possible that Marbot was at Chapelle-Saint-Lambert as the Prussians arrived, and it was these Prussians he found at 10.30, from which he took a prisoner. If so, this places Marbot leaving Waterloo by 9.00 to get to Chapelle-Saint-Lambert before the Prussians. If Domon had been at Moustier on 17 June and had spotted Prussians, it made sense for another patrol to be sent out, backed up with infantry to double check what Domon reported to confirm the Prussian threat on the right wing. The arrival of the prisoner now made headquarters realise that some of the Prussians had evaded Grouchy.

The elite gendarmes of the Imperial Guard are said to have brought in the Prussian prisoner, from the 2nd Silesian Hussars, to the French headquarters, who was questioned by the staff. He revealed that he was carrying a dispatch from Bülow (commanding the Prussian 4th Corps) to Wellington, saying his command had just arrived at Chapelle-Saint-Lambert.

This intercepted letter is reported in an order Napoléon sent to Grouchy sometime between 13.00 and 13.30:[366]

> A letter which has just been intercepted, which says General Bülow is about to attack our right flank, we believe that we see his corps on the height of Saint-Lambert. Lose not an instant in moving towards us to join us, in order to crush Bülow, whom you will crush in the very act.

Therefore, it does seem credible that Marbot is correct that such a document was captured. The Prussian 4th Corps was the strongest of

---

366 SHDDT: C15 *Registre d'Ordres et de correspondance du major-general à partir du 13 Juin jusqu'au 26 Juin au Maréchal Grouchy*, p. 30. SHDDT: C15 5. Dossier 18 June 1815. Soult to Grouchy 13.00. Copy of the original order made by Comte du Casses in June 1863. du Casses either copied Grouchy's version of the letter or had access to a duplicate set of material. This order is missing from the correspondence register of Marshal Soult.

the Prussian corps, as it had not been involved in the Battle of Ligny. Napoléon probably incorrectly assumed that the rearguard Grouchy had at Wavre were the rear-most men from Bülow's corps, and that Grouchy would be moving up behind.

The 7th Hussars mustered, on 15 June, thirty-seven officers and 415 other ranks, with 500 horses. Only one man was killed in the days leading up to Waterloo: Fourrier Chanalm, who was killed on 17 June at Genappe.[367] Thus, the regiment, on the 18th, was one of the strongest and freshest light cavalry regiments available to Napoléon. The regiment does not appear to have suffered greatly in the campaign, as on the 1 July it mustered thirty-two officers and 348 men.[368] Among the wounded was Sergeant Nicolas Joseph Celestin with a sabre cut to the left arm. Sergeant Louis Ogi was wounded with a sabre cut at Waterloo in action against Prussian cavalry. Sergeant-Major Léger Lespinasse was wounded with a gunshot to the left side of his chest and another to the left arm. Trumpeter MAT No. 102 Charles Him had his horse killed under him and became separated from his regiment. However, he enlisted into the 2nd Hussars on 6 April 1816.[369]

The infantry detachment came from the 13th Regiment of Light Infantry. It seems the 3rd Battalion was detached for this purpose.

Durutte's second attack

With Marbot's command dispatched to try and link with Grouchy following the Allied cavalry attack against 1st Corps, General Durutte now directed his men against La Haye Sainte, Papelotte and Frischermont. If the Prussians were coming, the French needed to control their vulnerable right flank—this meant containing or capturing the numerous farms in this sector. While there is any amount of information available about Hougoumont and La Haye Sainte, the attack against the numerous farm buildings that secured Wellington's left flank is less well understood. The Anglo-phonic nature of the history of the battle has also resulted in the actions of non-English speaking troops at Waterloo not being written about in any great detail—because German

---

367 SHDDT: GR 29 YC 422 *Contrôle Nominatif Troupe 7e Hussards 9 Septembre 1814 à 12 Aout 1815.*

368 Edmund Charles Constant Louvat, *Historique du 7e Hussards*, Pirault, Paris, 1889.

369 SHDDT: GR 29 YC 422.

and Dutch-Belgian troops held Papelotte and Frischermont, most of the major Waterloo historians have ignored them.

Part of the problem is that for most histories of the battle the Prussians are often ignored, and the action at Hougoumont is played out as the tipping point of the battle. The truth is that the action at Hougoumont was of less tactical significance than the other two farms of Papelotte and Frischermont. The defence of Papelotte and Frischermont mattered tactically and strategically: the very fact that Wellington had far fewer troops on his left flank than on the right meant that the farms had to be held. Wellington knew the Prussians were coming, and a link-up with Blücher would be hard, if not impossible, if the French had captured Papelotte, La Haye Sainte and Frischermont, and had succeeded in out-flanking Wellington.

Controlling the vulnerable right flank is what Durutte set out to achieve, by sending one body of troops to Papelotte and La Haye Sainte, and the second towards Smohain and Frischermont and its adjacent houses and enclosures. These farms had been occupied by a portion of the 2nd Brigade of Perponcher's division of the troops of the Netherlands since the night before.

The Orange-Nassau Regiment, consisting of two battalions, held Smohain and La Haye Sainte, while the farm of Papelotte was occupied by the light company of the 3rd Battalion 2nd Nassau Regiment, which, together with the 2nd Battalion of this regiment and four guns of Captain Bijleveld's Dutch-Belgian battery of horse artillery, were posted upon the rear slope immediately under the brow of the main ridge, and a little to the west of the lane leading directly up the slope from the farm of Papelotte.

The 2nd Nassau Regiment, along with the Orange-Nassau Regiment (28th Netherlands Line) and a volunteer jäger company, formed Prince Bernhard of Sachsen-Weimar's 2nd Brigade of the 2nd Netherlands Division. Having fought the French at Quatre-Bras, the entire brigade (except for the 1st Battalion 2nd Nassau Regiment) took position on the morning of 18 June in the Papelotte area. The 1st Battalion had marched off to Hougoumont about 9.00, in order to reinforce its garrison of British guards and Hanoverians. An advanced squadron of General Vivian's 10th Hussars had been stationed at Smohain village earlier in the day.

About the deployment of the Nassau troops in this area, Captain Carl Rettburg, commanding the light company of the 2nd Battalion 3rd Nassau Regiment, notes:[370]

---

370 Pflugk-Harttung, p. 206.

The 2nd Regiment formed a brigade together with the Orange-Nassau Regiment, under the command of Prince Bernhard von Sachsen-Weimar. During the evening of 17 June, the brigade took its position on the extreme left wing of the line in front of the farms of Papelotte, La Haye and the village of Smohain. The 3rd Battalion, commanded by Major Hegmann, had the 2nd Battalion of the 2nd Regiment on its right and on its left, slightly farther away, the 1st Battalion of the Orange-Nassau Regiment.

Carl Jacobi, who served at Waterloo in the Lüneburg Light Infantry Battalion, describes the terrain thus:[371]

There were hedges along the edge of the road on the slope of the height on the left wing that was standing, leading towards Papelotte, which constituted the extreme point of this wing; these hedges could be partly used as cover for the troops in line and partly for cover by the aforementioned tirailleurs. Beside the thicket hedge ran a path leading from the road to Smohain, which formed a hollow way for quite a distance.

Captain (Hauptmann) Friedrich von Jeckeln, of the Flanqueur Company of 2nd Battalion 28th Orange-Nassau Regiment, writes:[372]

On the 17th, in the evening towards five o'clock, there was a short cannon engagement, and the day ended with a tremendous downpour which lasted the whole night from the 17th to the 18th. It was the worst night of my life. Without shelter, up to my knees in mud, without food, and the ever-continuous rain. So, it was that the morning of the 18th began. At nine o'clock the operations of the two armies commenced, and each took up their position and prepared for the forthcoming battle. Soaked to the core and suffering from hunger, as we had had nothing to eat for two days, we moved to the position which had been assigned to us. Our division stood with its right flank close to the road leading to Brussels, and with the left flank close to a village, which was of the utmost importance to both armies, as it served as the point of communication with Blücher's army. Towards midday on the 18th, the bloody battle began, and

---

371 John Franklin personal communication, citing Niedersachishes Hauptstaatarchive, Hannover: Hann 41XX1 156.

372 John Franklin personal communication, 7 September 2016, citing Hessisches Hauptstaatsarchiv, Wiesbaden: Abt.1041, Nr.1. Letter, dated 14 July 1815.

according to the statements of those present, it was even worse than the Battle of Leipzig.

It was vital that these three bastions were held. If the French took the position, any communication between Blücher and Wellington could be compromised. Furthermore, with the French established on the Allied left, with as yet three relatively fresh cavalry brigades and all of 6th Corps, Napoléon could roll up Wellington's flank, or at least draw off troops from other sectors, to weaken the centre. A major French presence across the Prussian line of advance would also delay the arrival of the Prussians, by which time Wellington may have been defeated.

The action began when the vedettes of the British 10th Hussars were withdrawn due to the advance of the 7th Hussars as they moved off east. Behind came the 13th Regiment of Light Infantry and elements of Durutte's infantry. The 13th Regiment of Light Infantry seemingly pushed back the two Nassau battalions of the 2nd Regiment, which were lining the valley road and began threatening the second line of defences—the Hanoverians of Vincke and Best. Colonel Carl Best, in the 4th Hanoverian Brigade, observed the first attacks against the Allied left:[373]

> A detachment of enemy infantry, composed mostly of light troops (probably from Lieutenant-General Durutte's division) attacked our extreme left flank, and attempted to gain possession of Smohain and the farms of Papelotte and La Haye, and also the chateau of Frischermont; each of these were defended obstinately by the brave Nassau troops. The attack by this detachment was executed by several columns formed into line and was supported by artillery, with the tirailleurs at the head. I cannot state if it was the enemy's intention to overthrow our left wing, because even though the enemy attacked furiously the division did not appear to be strong enough to achieve this task, despite being vastly superior in number to the Nassau troops.

This suggests that the first attack was towards Smohain rather than head due north to attack the Allied line proper, and was conducted by the 3rd Battalion 13th Regiment of Light Infantry. By looking at the regimental

---

373 John Franklin, *Waterloo Hanoverian Correspondence*, 1815 Limited, 2010, pp. 164-7.

muster list we see that the battalion had been bulked out with men from the 4th Battalion to bring it up to strength. Total losses were:[374]

13th Regiment of Light Infantry					
	Wounded	Wounded & Prisoner	Prisoner of War	Killed	Missing
3rd Battalion	4	0	3	3	17
4th Battalion	24	0	23	3	189
Total	28	0	26	6	206

Overall, some 266 men were lost from the composite battalion. Very few were fatalities; the vast majority being listed as missing. This means the men had not been seen since the battle when the muster roll was called, thus were dead, wounded or prisoner of war, or possibly deserted. Colonel Crabbe, of the Imperial Headquarters, comments:[375]

At the right extremity of the plateau, the fighting was fierce around the farms of La Haye and Papelotte and the chateau of Frischermont by the 6th Corps of General Mouton, Comte Lobau, who contained the Prussians of Bülow.

About the operations on the French right following the repulse of the Union Brigade and Allied cavalry, Captain Camille Durutte writes:[376]

The corps commanded by General Lobau placed itself behind the division of General Durutte, who was forced to send sharpshooters out and face the enemy troops which threatened to outflank his right flank. He soon felt the need to send one or two battalions to Frischermont.

374 SHDDT: GR 22 YC 116 *13er régiment d'infanterie Légère 1806 à 1815.*
375 Crabbe, pp. 16-17.
376 *La Sentinelle de l'Armée,* 4th year, No. 134, 8 March 1838.

Chapter 8

Frischermont

Historian Pierre de Witt notes that the first time the chateau is mentioned is in 1250 when a donation of nearly two hectares of land at Frischermont to the Abbey of Aywiers was agreed to. In 1440, a reference is made to a *'courtil à Feceraimont'*. The chateau, as it stood in 1815, probably dated from the mid-sixteenth century. The buildings, comprising the chateau and a farm, formed an irregular rectangle around a large courtyard. In its south-west corner was a huge barn.[377] The complex was dominated by a massive square tower, which based on contemporary engravings had no windows, only narrow lancet type windows, which no doubt made idea loopholes to fire from. This tower was situated in the north-east corner of the complex. The dilapidated state of the upper part of the tower forced the owner to demolish it in 1830. The remaining farm complex was demolished in 1859 and the ruins can still be found today, although heavily overgrown. On its north side the complex was bordered by a garden and a park. The whole complex was surrounded by tall trees which formed a small, triangular wood. The chateau was garrisoned by the 28th Orange-Nassau Regiment. A member of the regiment, Sergeant Johann Heinrich Doring, writes:[378]

> Our battalion was posted for several hours on the left wing of the plateau, at the farm of Frischermont, which was surrounded by a wall three to four feet high. We were able to defend this fairly important position for quite some time against the attacks of a regiment of voltigeurs. They attempted several times to force the wall, each time with no success, until they were reinforced by the

---

377   Pierre de Witt personal communication.
378   *Historiche Beilage*, Vol. 56, No. 11, Herbon, 1988.

arrival of a corps of some 4,000 men. We then had to retire from this position in great haste and we continued our defence further back at the hamlet…for us this was the day's most critical and dangerous moment, as the French moved against us with ever more powerful columns. We were separated from the enemy by no more than half musket-shot range. Due to the huge clouds of powder smoke which was blown into our faces by the wind, we could only discern the enemy from the flashes of his muskets. The turmoil became more general by the minute, and there could be no thought of some form of order. Without interruption, we loaded and fired into the enemy's ranks: there was no use in aiming at a particular target. As the enemy was forcefully pushing forward, gaining reinforcements all the time, we could have hardly withstood his attack much longer. Wellington, moreover, had pulled many regiments to his faltering centre. It was at this critical and decisive moment that the vanguard of Bülow's corps descended.

The fighting for the chateau of Frischermont was, we assume, bitter and conducted at close range. The sunken lanes, numerous hedges and wooded terrain was ideal cover for the attacking and defending forces, especially for voltigeurs to operate detached from their parent regiment in the hollows and thickets. The voltigeurs were either the men Durutte ordered forward as sharpshooters, or more likely the 13th Regiment of Light Infantry, and it is Durutte's troops that are the corps mentioned by Doring, with the ever-larger columns he comments on being Lobau and 6th Corps. Captain Eberhard, of the Orange-Nassau regiment, recalls that:[379]

During the night of the 17th to 18th, one of our companies occupied a village [Smohain] located in front of the battalion. Defending the village and maintaining contact with the localities left and right was the battalion's objective.

Our lack of ammunition was barely alleviated by cartridges being obtained from the Duchy of Nassau regiments. But, before these supplies arrived, the battalion was already facing the enemy and his tirailleurs were engaged with our skirmishers. At first, holding the village seemed not to be overly difficult. But, when in the afternoon the French right wing started to press hard on our left wing, in support of his operations in the centre, our lone company was not able to withstand his attacks. It had to be reinforced first

---

379   John Franklin personal communication.

with the grenadier company, and then with No. 1 and eventually with part of No. 2 Company. The battalion nevertheless held onto the village.

The lack of ammunition led to an improvised means of obtaining more cartridges. Friedrich May, a former drummer with the 1st Battalion 28th Orange-Nassau Regiment, writes:[380]

> As early as three o'clock we realised that the ammunition was in very short supply, and we could not use the ammunition from the 2nd Battalion, because they have had French rifles and were using a different calibre. Therefore, I removed all of my leather accoutrements and ran back through the line of fire to the British troops from whom I received sufficient cartridges to fill my haversack. Having returned to the battalion and distributed the cartridges, I ran back a second time, but on the way back I was struck just beneath the right hip by a spent musket ball (which I later found in my underwear). But this did not prevent me from returning a third time. However, when I returned on this occasion with my haversack full of cartridges I met Prince Sachsen-Weimar, and he asked me how many times I had been to collect ammunition in this manner, and then asked how many cartridges a haversack can hold. My having answered, he then told me that I would not have to return for more, because the men had enough cartridges, but that he would remember me. I put my leather accoutrements back on and picked up my drum. Now we were face-to-face with the French Guards, who received us with the utmost calm, which forced us to retire a short distance. The prince arrived along with Lieutenant Rath, and he ordered us not to retire a single step further. When I heard this I went to the front, and without having received any orders I beat the *pas de charge*, whereupon my comrades cried: 'follow the little one, do not to leave him alone!' Under the heaviest fire imaginable, we advanced. The reserves followed and the French subsequently retired. During this attack, I received a ball in the neck and collapsed. From this moment on I was unconscious for almost half an hour, and recall nothing which transpired.

Ammunition and the lack of it was also a concern for Emil Bergmann. A report dated 3 January 1816 from Captain (Hauptmann) Bergmann,

---

380   John Franklin personal communication, 7 September 2016, citing *Das Leben des Herzog, Bernhard von Sachsen-Weimar: königlich niederländischer General der Infanterie*, Gotha, 1865.

officer commanding the Nassau jäger volunteers, describes his role in the defence of the chateau and the major problems he had with ammunition supply:[381]

> On the 17th we stood close to Quatre-Bras, and I believed that after the events of the 16th, almost all of the jägers had exhausted their powder and ammunition. Unfortunately, this was confirmed during an inspection of the troops. On this day, we retreated to Waterloo and towards evening our brigade was ordered to deploy in the battle line. I believed that we would be engaged with the enemy's advance guard, and so I gave the order to those jägers with ammunition to advance, while those jägers without ammunition retired with First-Lieutenant von Bierbrauer. I had been placed in an awkward position; I understood perfectly well that this decision was not entirely acceptable, but I moved with Second-Lieutenant Schnabelius and between ten and twelve jägers to a position close to Frischermont, not far from the company commanded by Captain Bartmann, of our regiment. Because of all I had witnessed I wanted to participate, but I was concerned that the fact I had ordered the jägers to retire due to lack of ammunition would be doubted by those in authority. It was in this position, close to Frischermont, that I took part in the battle on the 18th, as skirmishers under the command of Lieutenant-Colonel von Dressel, and because of this behaviour, which was observed by the senior commanders, I received the Military Order of King Wilhelm.

Johann Jost Holighausen, a former private with the 1st Battalion 28th Orange-Nassau Regiment, writes:[382]

> It must have been towards four o'clock when we arrived at Waterloo; that same evening there was a terrible thunderstorm and the ground was turned to quagmire; we remained in our camp until the early morning of 18 June, when the enemy came so close that I thought—like so many of my comrades—that God needed to be with me and with us all. Fortunately, this happened. That morning Prince von Sachsen-Weimar came to us and told us to form square; it was thus ordered how we should fight. Shortly thereafter I once again became afraid. An advance guard was to be formed from the 3rd Company. Volunteers were called for, but no men stepped

---

381   John Franklin personal communication, 7 September 2016, citing Hessisches Hauptstaatsarchiv, Wiesbaden: Abt. 202, Nr 1163.
382   John Franklin personal communication, 7 September 2016.

forward. Therefore, ten sub-divisions were separated from the right wing, including myself. The cannonade shocked me. I thought 'my God, what will become of me'; we were then led into battle. I thought to myself, 'Lord, God, give me strength, help me to fight, so that I might receive the crown someday'; and this happened, thank God, for when the battle was over we had been victorious with the help of the Lord Almighty. It was towards four o'clock in the afternoon when we heard Dutch music, the Lord's music.

Johann Philipp Pinstock, of the Flanqueur Company of 1st Battalion 28th Orange-Nassau Regiment, writes to his parents, brothers and sisters in Eisemroth on 22 July 1815 recalling the events of Waterloo:[383]

We held firm against the French from the 15th until ten o'clock on the morning of the 17th, whereupon we had to retreat for two hours to Waterloo, because we had not received any assistance. In the evening, we had a position in front of the enemy once more. At nine o'clock on the morning of the 18th our army had assembled. Then began a battle which was terrible, and the cannon fire and musketry lasted until the evening.

Papelotte and La Haye Sainte

Pierre de Witt, an excellent modern-day historian of the battle, tells us that the Walloon word *'papelotte'* corresponds to the French word *'papilotte'*, which means of a strip of leather or textile. In 1673 it had eighteen hectares and was owned by Alexandre de Baillancourt Courcol. The farm complex was purchased by Pierre François Xavier de Bienne in 1807. In 1815 it was inhabited by Melchior Mathieu, who—according to the local tradition—didn't leave the farm during the battle. As the farm was for a part damaged by fire it was being restored not long after the battle. The farm was, and is, built around the sides of a rectangular enclosure. The north side of the farm was formed by the huge barn. Stables formed its east part, as well as a part on the south side. Here, the house of the farm could be found. Near the house was a well like the one which could be found at Le Caillou and the inn of La Belle Alliance. Apart from the fact that the old buildings have been reconstructed, some have been added after 1815. The wall on the west side has been

383 ibid.

expanded with stables and a large, vaulted main entrance gate. Later, probably in 1860, this main gate was crowned with a small lantern-style tower.[384] From the south side of the complex, the ground slopes steeply away to a narrow road. The network of roads present in 2017 is virtually unchanged since 1815, as are the sunken lanes bordered by thick hedges. However, the approach to the farm is concealed by a low ridge which separates the farm complex, La Haye Sainte and Marache from the valley that slopes towards Plancenoit. It means that the French could use this ridge line as an excellent defensive position in case of Prussian troops emerging from the direction of Lasne. It also meant the French could move up troops without being immediately spotted by the Allied garrison here.

Less than 200 metres due east of Papelotte is the farm of La Haye Sainte. Pierre de Witt notes that the farm of La Haye Sainte dated from 1744. The buildings formed a rectangle, with a garden on the north side and one on the south, surrounded by a low wall which was covered in bushes. A gateway led into a barn, from which access to the inner courtyard could be gained. There was also a small door leading from one of the gardens to the courtyard.[385] The farms were garrisoned by the 2nd and 3rd Battalions 2nd Nassau Regiment. Captain Inglby, of the Royal Horse Artillery, writes:[386]

> Some Nassau troops were a little in advance, occupying the hedgerows in our front, and near the village of Papelotte, supported by the first of three or four guns.

General Baron August von Kruse writes as follows about the Nassau troops at Papelotte and La Haye Sainte:[387]

> Towards eleven o'clock in the morning, the 2nd and 3rd Battalions of the regiment moved into the line of battle. On their right stood Hanoverians, and on their left the 1st Battalion of the Orange-Nassau regiment. Behind them was a column of light cavalry of the King's German Legion. The Flanqueur Company from the 3rd Battalion of the 2nd Nassau Regiment occupied Papelotte. Between

---

384 Pierre de Witt personal communication.
385 ibid.
386 Siborne, *Waterloo Letters*, No. 82.
387 John Franklin personal communication, 7 September 2016, citing Hessisches Hauptstaatsarchiv, Wiesbaden: Abt. 202, Nr 1372.

midday and one o'clock an overwhelming mass of tirailleurs forced this company to retire, and so Captain Rettburg, the company commander, was reinforced by a further four companies. With these he was able to recapture Papelotte, and to hold it until the end of the battle, despite several attacks by the enemy tirailleurs. To attack the enemy in their position was not possible from Papelotte, as they were supported by artillery, whereas the Nassau troops were unsupported.

These guns could well be the 12-pounders that General d'Erlon sent over to General Durutte in the early afternoon. Durutte's divisional artillery had been caught by the Scots Greys earlier in the day, robbing the division of much needed artillery support. Captain Reichenau, of the 2nd Battalion 2nd Nassau Regiment, writes:[388]

> The 2nd and 3rd Battalions of our regiment were stationed of the left wing of the English army under orders to occupy a small village, called La Haie Sainte [sic] if I am not mistaken. Towards evening our entire battalion was posted there as skirmishers.

About the fighting in this sector, Captain Carl Rettburg, commanding the light company of the 2nd Battalion 3rd Nassau Regiment, notes:[389]

> Between eleven and twelve o'clock in the morning the enemy artillery batteries deployed opposite our position, along with their ammunition wagons. One of the first cannon shots injured Major Hegmann, and Captain Frensdorf succeeded to the command.
>
> Between twelve and one o'clock the line of enemy artillery advanced towards Papelotte. Prince von Sachsen-Weimar sent me and my company, the 3rd Flanker, to confront them. Shortly thereafter, a detachment from the Orange-Nassau Regiment occupied the villages of Smohain and La Haye, and I established communication with this detachment. The farm of Papelotte formed a square (quadrangle) built of stone and was surrounded by hollow ways and hedges; it was very well suited to a successful defence. I succeeded in driving the enemy artillery back to the furthest hedge at the end of the grass valley, which separated our position from the enemy's, and I was able to occupy several small houses there.

---

388 Pflugk-Harttung, p. 76.
389 ibid, p.206.

In this account, Rettburg implies the French attacked in open order in waves of skirmishers. He also alludes to the fact he withdrew from Papelotte, as he had to move his line forward to reach Papelotte. The implication is he was either towards the Ohain road or La Haye Sainte. He also comments that Smohain and La Haye Sainte had fallen into French hands, leaving, we assume, only Frischermont in Nassau hands. Perhaps Papelotte was still garrisoned, but with the outbuildings being occupied by the French. A number of French writers, like Durutte, who were eyewitnesses to the event that day, state that La Haye Sainte and Smohain had indeed been taken by the French. Major Pierre François Tissot, officer commanding the 92nd Regiment of Line Infantry (part of General Foy's 9th Infantry Brigade), notes that 'Comte d'Erlon had seized the farms of La Haye and Papelotte'.[390]

This appears to corroborate what Rettburg says. Captain Carl Friedrich Frensdorf, in a report dated Bussey 10 August 1815, concerning the part played by the 3rd Battalion 2nd Nassau Regiment during 16, 17 and 18 June 1815, says:[391]

> On the 18th, towards half-past eleven in the morning, enemy infantry columns, supported by numerous artillery that fired at the 3rd Battalion, which at this moment was formed in line, showed themselves opposite the village. The second shot killed Major Hegmann, and I, the undersigned, took command. I was ordered to form square because of an approaching cavalry column, which, however, was repulsed by our artillery fire. This is why their attack was unsuccessful; the enemy now tried to take possession of the village. I ordered the flank company, under command of Capt. von Rettburg, to the hedges and sunken lanes leading to the village, because of the growing numbers of enemy tirailleurs, and due to the heavy losses sustained by his company I had to send the 12th, 11th and 10th Companies forward, one at a time, to augment this force, while at the same time the 9th Company of grenadiers maintained their ground under a continuous and heavy artillery fire, in a manner equal to that of skirmishing comrades under Capt. von Rettberg's command. The repeated efforts of the enemy to occupy the village were in vain, despite their endeavours, and

---

390 Pierre François Tissot, *Histoire de Napoléon, rédigée d'après les papiers d'État, les documents officiels, les mémoires et les notes secrètes de ses contemporains, suivie d'un précis sur la famille Bonaparte* (Vol. 2), Delange-Taffin, Paris, 1833, pp. 277-8.

391 John Franklin personal communication, 7 September 2016.

they were thrown back each time with heavy losses. However, the various attacks resulted in the loss of our colours.

With the arrival of evening, the Prussians approached on our left wing. Some of the skirmishers from our battalion, not being informed of this arrival, considered them hostile, and rounds were exchanged. This, however, was stopped immediately when the error had been noticed.

A few more details on the action can be found in a letter by Colonel (Oberst) Johann Friedrich Sattler, a former major with the 1st Battalion 2nd Nassau Regiment:[392]

On 18 June at nine o'clock a staff officer from the Duke of Wellington ordered the 1st Battalion of the regiment to move to the farm of Hougoumont, which was situated on the extreme right wing of the army. The battalion, under the command of Captain Büsgen, immediately marched to this new destination and defended the farmstead during the course of the battle, despite the fact that the buildings were totally destroyed by the enemy artillery fire. I advanced with the 2nd and 3rd Battalions some one hundred paces, and at eleven o'clock, I moved from the position we had held during the night, opposite to the two farms of La Haye and Papelotte, and when I saw that an enemy infantry column had started to march to this side, I occupied the two with detachments of tirailleurs, and strong reserves from both battalions. All of the attacks which the enemy made against these two farms during the day were steadfastly repulsed. The remainder of the two battalions, which had stayed in the line, were continuously shot at by the enemy artillery.

Captain Carl Rettburg, commanding the light company of the 2nd Battalion 3rd Nassau Regiment, notes:[393]

Between three and four o'clock in the afternoon the reinforced enemy artillery line moved forward again, and it was supported by a significant formation of infantry. I was forced to leave my position and withdrew to Papelotte, which I had prepared in this very short time as well as possible to serve as a point of retreat.

---

392 John Franklin personal communication, 7 September 2016, citing Hessisches Hauptstaatsarchiv, Wiesbaden: Abt. 202, Nr 1372.

393 Pflugk-Harttung, p. 206.

I requested reinforcements and Captain Frensdorf sent the 10th, 11th and 12th Companies, accompanied by the Flanqueur Company from the 2nd Battalion of our regiment, with orders to obey my command. The enemy formation was stopped by the fire from Papelotte and from the detachment in the small houses, where the units bravely resisted, and was thrown back and pursued to the previously mentioned furthest hedge. Here we were welcomed by an enemy battery and their muskets only 500 paces away. Our loss was great, the 3rd Flanqueur Company lost two officers in its position and was reduced to half of its number by the end of the battle, but the enemy did not attempt another serious attack and contented itself by shooting heavily from a hedge beyond the grass valley at the foot of its position. This attack was delivered by a part of the division commanded by Durutte; I cannot tell exactly the force of this formation, but it was composed of many more men than I had at my disposal.

Towards six o'clock in the evening the enemy appeared on my left wing. I had lost contact with the 1st Battalion Orange-Nassau. The enemy had taken Smohain and La Haye Sainte and moved the line of artillery forward to Papelotte. Even though this attack was very lively, it was not supported by the infantry columns, so it was not very difficult as we were in an advantageous position to push the enemy back. After seven o'clock in the evening, the enemy retired without being forced to do so. This event was as inexplicable to me as the heavy cannon and musket fire, which seemed to be coming from Smohain and Plancenoit; shortly afterwards my line, which I had pushed forward towards La Haye Sainte, was forced back to the road which separated La Haye Sainte from Papelotte, and was forced back by artillery fire followed by a great many infantry units, which were also in my rear. Having driven these back I realised that we were engaged with the Prussians. They also realised the error, which had lasted for no more than ten minutes, but had cost both of us several killed and wounded.

I left Papelotte, which I had defended the whole time, but it was now that it was set on fire and this made it too difficult to defend any longer, and I joined the Prussians advancing towards Plancenoit.

The attacking force in this second attack mentioned by Rettburg was undoubtedly the 95th and 85th Regiments of Line Infantry. Around 19.00, a voltigeur company and two fusilier companies of the 95th Regiment of Line Infantry were detached, under the orders of Battalion-Commander Rulliers, to attack the enemy troops which were firing against the French artillery to the left of General Brue's brigade and held off the enemy for an hour and a half.[394] Battalion-Commander Rulliers, of the 95th Regiment of Line Infantry, notes:[395]

> Sometime between three or four o'clock we began to perceive movements of the Prussians on the right of our army. Shortly after we received musket fire from their scouts. My battalion was ordered to stop them—we succeeded—a vigorous exchange of musketry began and reigned for a half hour.

Chapuis, of the 85th Regiment of Line Infantry, notes that:[396]

> The English sharpshooters, and then the Prussian sharpshooters, had advanced close enough to worry us, the companies of our regiment were sent against them, in succession, one after another. The turn of the grenadier company that I commanded eventually arrived. We marched on the enemy with enthusiasm to half-range. There we employed all the willingness and energy to fulfil this worthy mission that had been asked of us. I believe we were not lacking either, and that if success did not crown our efforts it was due to a lack of something other than courage, as we had done everything that was humanly possible to do, and the grenadier company had performed as well as sharpshooters as it had done under artillery fire. Charged at the end of the day by the cavalry, we succumbed almost completely, and those that the ball or the shot had spared was slashed and trampled under the horses' feet.

Lieutenant Jacqmin, of the 85th Regiment of Line Infantry, recalls the retreat as follows:[397]

> I was at Waterloo with the two battalions of the regiment. At one hour after the commencement of the battle, following the wounding of Captain Chapuis and the death of Lieutenant Monsieur Legay, I took command of the company. At six o'clock in the evening, we perceived that we had been outflanked and part of the army began to beat the retreat. I was then reunited with the rest of the company and numerous other soldiers of the battalion, perhaps 150 men,

---

394 Hippolyte de Mauduit, *'Vieille Militaire. Charleroi, Fleurus et Waterloo'* in *La Sentinalle de l'armée*, 24 June 1836.

395 SHDDT: GD 2 1135.

396 Chapuis, 'Waterloo' in *Sentinalle de l'armée*, 24 February 1838.

397 Jean-Marc Largeaud personal communication, 10 August 2012.

who had marched forward as sharpshooters against the Scottish soldiers which we had pressed back.

A short time after this, our brave Colonel Masson, who commanded the regiment, saved our eagle; I assisted in taking hold of the shaft upon which was the eagle. This struggle lasted for ten minutes and was very heavy. The two battalions both suffered badly and we retained perhaps a dozen officers.

General Brue's brigade held the Papelotte-Frischermont line until the end of the battle, with 6th Corps holding the line between Frischermont and Plancenoit. Eventually the brigade was overwhelmed by the Prussians, as Jacqmin notes. The collapse of the French defence here allowed the Prussians to sweep along the French right flank and threaten La Haye Sainte at the very moment the Old Guard attacked.

4th Infantry Division

In total, the 8th Regiment of Line Infantry lost the following number of men at Waterloo:[398]

8th Regiment of Line Infantry					
	Wounded	Wounded & Prisoner	Prisoner of War	Killed	Missing
1st Battalion	3	6	105	0	0
2nd Battalion	0	20	89	0	0
3rd Battalion	0	12	103	0	0
Total	3	38	297	0	0

The regiment lost 338 other ranks at Waterloo. On 10 June 1815, the regiment had mustered 943 other ranks, so had lost 36 per cent at Waterloo.

The 29th Regiment of Line Infantry lost the following number of men at Waterloo:[399]

---

398 SHDDT: GR 21 YC 74 *8e régiment d'infanterie de Ligne dit régiment de Condé, 30 août 1814-11 mai 1815 (matricules 1 à 1,800).* See also: SHDDT: GR 21 YC 75 *8e régiment d'infanterie de ligne dit régiment de Condé, 14 mai 1815-10 juillet 1815 (matricules 1,801 à 2,379).*

399 SHDDT: GR 21 YC 271 *29e régiment d'infanterie de ligne, 21 juillet 1814-24 décembre 1814 (matricules 1 à 1,800).* See also: SHDDT: GR 21 YC 272 *29e*

29th Regiment of Line Infantry					
	Wounded	Wounded & Prisoner	Prisoner of War	Killed	Missing
1st Battalion	20	1	120	5	0
2nd Battalion	14	1	132	6	0
3rd Battalion	20	1	119	5	0
Total	54	3	371	16	0

The regiment lost 444 other ranks at Waterloo. On 10 June 1815, the regiment had mustered 1,106 other ranks and so had lost 40 per cent strength in the battle. The brigade had lost 38 per cent of its effective strength at Waterloo.

The table below gives the losses for the 85th Regiment of Line Infantry:[400]

85th Regiment of Line Infantry					
	Wounded	Wounded & Prisoner	Prisoner of War	Killed	Missing
1st Battalion	8	0	85	12	0
2nd Battalion	16	0	78	6	0
3rd Battalion	9	0	91	6	0
Total	33	0	254	24	0

At Waterloo, the regiment lost 311 other ranks out of 591 men total, representing a loss of 53 per cent of effective strength. The regiment, on 20 June 1815, mustered 280 men with twenty-five officers. On 26 June, it mustered 180 men, or 64 per cent of its remaining strength after Waterloo. Oddly, the regiment appears to have fielded three battalions, in contradiction to Chapuis, who states two.

The table below gives the losses for the 95th Regiment of Line Infantry:[401]

---

régiment d'infanterie de ligne, 24 décembre 1814-21 juillet 1815 (matricules 1,801 à 2,226).

400   SHDDT: GR 21 YC 655 *72e régiment d'infanterie de ligne (ex 84e régiment d'infanterie de ligne), 20 janvier 1815-24 juillet 1815 (matricules 1,801 à 2,756).*

401   SHDDT: GR 21 YC 717 *79e régiment d'infanterie de ligne (ex 95e régiment d'infanterie de ligne), 26 août 1814-25 mai 1815 (matricules 1 à 1,800).*

95th Regiment of Line Infantry					
	Wounded	Wounded & Prisoner	Prisoner of War	Killed	Missing
1st Battalion	1	0	1	0	359
2nd Battalion	2	0	0	0	362
Total	3	0	1	0	721

At Waterloo, the 95th Regiment of Line Infantry lost 725 men from an effective strength of 1,060; a staggering 68 per cent of the regiment's effective strength. At Ligny, on 16 June, seven men were lost, making a total loss of 732 men. Some 328 men remained in ranks on 20 June 1815. On 26 June, the regiment mustered twenty-four officers and 239 men, a loss of eighty-nine men, representing 37 per cent loss of effective strength. Nearly all men were listed as missing. Does this mean they surrendered? Or perhaps deserted? The nature of the returns made by the regiment in 1815 relied upon men seeing what happened to their comrades. Therefore, we can only be certain of the fate of four men of the battalion. It is possible that with the Allied cavalry surging down the field towards the squares, the square dissolved and entire companies were rounded up and made prisoner. This is possible, but it is more likely that the missing includes dead and wounded men whose fate was not known, as no one remained in the regiment to say what happened to them.

Summary

Combined, the division lost 1,818 men as shown below:

4th Infantry Division					
Regiment	Wounded	Wounded & Prisoner	Prisoner of War	Killed	Missing
8th Line	3	38	297	0	0
29th Line	54	3	371	16	0
85th Line	33	0	254	24	0
95th Line	3	0	1	0	721
Total	93	41	923	40	721

On the morning of 18 June, the division had mustered 3,700 men. Of this number, 49 per cent were lost at Waterloo, the vast majority being prisoners of war or deserters. Presumably, the missing and prisoners also included dead and wounded men. Clearly what happened to the 1st Brigade when it moved to the centre of the French positions, compared to the 2nd Brigade which deployed against the Prussians, was different. The data for the 95th Regiment of Line Infantry is meaningless and no comment on the losses can be made, whereas the losses of the 85th Regiment of Line Infantry are lower than those for either the 8th or 29th Regiments of Line Infantry. The lack of any clear data for the 95th Regiment of Line Infantry hinders any comparison between the brigades. We do note that the losses are far lower than in the 3rd Division.

Chapter 9

The Prussians Emerge

Not having been in action on 16 June, the Prussian 4th Corps, commanded by General Bülow, was the strongest of the four Prussian corps in the field. Due to this, it was the first Prussian force sent to Waterloo. However, getting to Waterloo was not straightforward. No major road went from Wavre to Mont-Saint-Jean, and because of the heavy rain from the previous two nights, the roads towards the battlefield were in poor condition; in essence they were little more than a morass of ankle-deep, cloying mud. Making matters worse, the men of Bülow's command had had to pass through the congested and narrow streets of Wavre together, which took time. Indeed, the last elements of the corps did not leave Wavre until around 10.00. It had taken a full six hours for the corps to cross through Wavre. Behind 4th Corps came the Prussian 1st and 2nd Corps under Pirch and Zieten. Sensibly enough, the Prussians left a strong rearguard at Wavre to hold back the French pursuit conducted by Marshal Grouchy.

Bülow's objective was Plancenoit, which the Prussians intended to use as a springboard into the rear of the French positions.

Since Marbot had brought in his prisoner, Napoléon had been aware that a body of Prussians was marching to Waterloo. He knew from Grouchy's dispatches that the Prussians were in three columns, and that Grouchy was in action with at least one. Therefore, Napoléon now knew that at least one, if not two, Prussian columns were heading his way. Grouchy's operations are described at length in an accompanying book, but we need to record that Marshal Soult sent the following order to Grouchy at 13.00 on 18 June 1815:[402]

---

402 SHDDT: C15 *Registre d'Ordres et de correspondance du major-general à partir du 13 Juin jusqu'au 26 Juin au Maréchal Grouchy*, p. 30.

Monsieur marshal, you wrote to the emperor this morning at six o'clock, saying that you were marching on Sart à Walhain, and that you planned then to move to Corbaix and to Wavre. This movement conforms with the dispositions of the emperor which have been communicated to you.

However, the emperor orders me that you should manoeuvre in our direction and try to get closer to the army, so that you can link with us before another corps can come between us. I do not indicate a direction of movement. It is for you to see the place where we are, to govern yourself accordingly and link with our communications, and to always be prepared to fall upon any of the enemy's troops who seek to annoy our right and crush them.

At this moment, the battle is won on the line of Waterloo, in front of the Soignes Forest; the centre of the enemy is at Mont-Saint-Jean, and manoeuvre to reach our right.

The marshal, Duc de Dalmatie

P.S.: A letter which has just been intercepted which says General Bülow is about to attack our right flank, we believe that we see his corps on the height of Saint-Lambert. Lose not an instant in moving towards us to join us, in order to crush Bulow, whom you will crush in the very act.

Marshal Soult sent the following letter to Marshal Davout at 14.30 on 18 June:[403]

The bivouac in front of La Caillou, 18 June at 1.15

Monsieur marshal, the fighting has begun at this moment; the enemy are in position in front of the Soignes Forest, their centre placed on Waterloo. We are consuming a lot of ammunition; a great quantity of munitions was used in the battle of Ligny.

The emperor orders that you send munitions from the citadels in the north to Avesnes with all speed in the midst of the battalions which I had ordered to be established there to escort the prisoners. From there, they will be directed to Beaumont via Charleroi to join the army.

You must, M. marshal, carry out these important orders of the emperor and ensure that they are promptly executed and that will prevent the worst from happening in this regard.

403 AN: AFIV 1939, pp. 50-1.

160

P.S.: It is half-past two, the cannonade is joined all along the line. The English are in the centre, the Dutch and Belgians are on the right, the Germans and the Prussians are on the left. The general battle has begun, 400 cannon have opened fire at this moment.

These letters are of huge importance in our understanding of Waterloo. Clearly, Napoléon was concerned that his ammunition was running low and needed to be urgently replenished, and that he also felt he needed an additional ten battalions of infantry with him in the field as soon as was practicable. With the arrival of Grouchy's 10.00 dispatch with Soult, and from the observations made by the headquarters staff at Waterloo cited earlier, clearly Napoléon, by 14.30, knew that some of the Prussian army had eluded Grouchy and had made contact with Wellington.

Either Napoléon believed that only a small portion of the Prussian army had eluded Grouchy (hardly surprising given the twelve to sixteen hour lead they had over the marshal) or Napoléon was over-confident in his chances of success against Wellington and the Prussians. As we shall see, his judgement on both scenarios was horribly wrong. When Napoléon announced the arrival of Grouchy late in the afternoon of the 18th it was a cynical ploy to rally his army, as he had known since the start of the battle that the Prussians would arrive to aid Wellington, and had already made an appearance on the field. He also knew that Grouchy would not arrive, as he had ordered him to move with all speed to Wavre to keep pressing to the east.[404]

For fact, Napoléon knew he faced both Wellington and Blücher, and that Grouchy was not marching to his aid regardless of what later French and Anglo-phone writers have stated. Napoléon knew by 14.30, if not sooner, that at least one column of Prussians had managed to link with Wellington. This left two columns heading either to Waterloo or Wavre. He had also known with Grouchy's dispatch timed at 10.00 that Grouchy was fighting, or was about to engage, the Prussians in accordance with his own order of 10.00.

Did Napoléon honestly believe that Grouchy, once committed to action, could quickly break the action off and move to Wavre without having to leave a rearguard against what we now know to be Thielemann's forces and get to Waterloo? Napoléon now seems to have set in motion, in his own mind and the minds of his subordinates, that

---

404 AN: AFIV 1939, p. 50.

Grouchy would respond to the summons and indeed even announced Grouchy had arrived several hours later to bolster the flagging French army. He was failing to acknowledge his own failings, as it must have been clear to him once the 10.00 dispatch arrived that Grouchy could not get to Waterloo. About the appearance of the Prussians, Baudus (aide-de-camp to Marshal Soult) recounts:[405]

> I cannot find words to make the impression that I felt when, returning from carrying orders to our right wing, where I had seen the balls and bullets of Bülow's corps beyond the 6th Corps, which had just been placed in line parallel to the road to oppose the attack on this part of the Prussian army.

Renee Bourgeois, of the 12th Cuirassiers, commented in 1816 that:[406]

> At the moment in which all his enterprises had completely miscarried, he received the intelligence of the advance of the Prussian columns against our right flank, and of their menacing our rear; but he would attribute no faith to these reports, and repeatedly answered that they had been deceived in their observations, and that these pretended Prussians were nothing more than the corps of Grouchy. He even abused and angrily dismissed several aide-de-camps who successively brought him this information. 'Be gone,' he said to them, 'you have become afraid; approach these columns with confidence, and you will soon be satisfied that they are those of Grouchy'.

> After so positive an answer, several of them, indignant at such treatment, approached the Prussian sharpshooters, and in spite of a hot fire by which they were assailed, advanced near enough to be either slain or made prisoners—it was, however, necessary to yield to evidence. It was indeed impossible to disparage any longer the truth of this intelligence, when at length these columns, which severally on their coming up had formed themselves in line, actively attacked our right. One detachment of the 6th Corps was sent to sustain this new shock, in expectation of the arrival of the divisions under Marshal Grouchy, on whom we always reckoned. The report even prevailed that his troops were already in line...It is evident that this operation had been concerted between the two

---

405 Marie Élli Guillaume de Baudus, *Études sur Napoléon*, Debecourt, Paris, 1841.

406 Delbare, pp. 69-72.

generals-in-chief, and that the English only defended their position with so invincible a tenacity in order to allow time for the Prussians to effectuate this combined movement on which depended the whole success of the battle, and of which the first demonstrations were every moment expected.

Buonaparte, who in spite of all that happened, seemed to harbour no doubt of the speedy arrival of Marshal Grouchy, and who, without doubt, persuaded himself that he would immediately hold the Prussians in check.

The Prussians attacked the French hard; Napoléon was forced to commit more troops over the course of the afternoon. In response to the Prussian arrival, the cavalry of Generals Domon and Subervie were detached to defend the Paris Wood. Perhaps at the same time, 6th Corps was ordered to take up new positions. The division of Durutte was placed in an L-shaped formation in front of the chateau of Frischermont and Hannotelet Farm. Sir Hussey Vivian observed the Prussian arrival and the immediate French response:[407]

> The first Prussians that came into action, I should say, were the advanced guard of a corps not exceeding two regiments and supported by another; they passed the hedge of Papelotte, drew up across the valley in line almost at right angles to us. They were directly under where I stood and I saw the operation as plainly as if at a field day.
>
> The French at once advanced against them [their flank rather] and drove them back. They then occupied the village of Smohain or Papelotte, I forget exactly the name. This must have been somewhere between five and six o'clock. I should say nearer five. It was a considerable time after this that the Prussians arrived in force.

We must note that despite arriving on the field of battle, the men were not fresh. They had marched through thick mud and across arduous terrain since just after daybreak. These men were hungry, thirsty and tired, and with no rest were flung straight into action. The Young Guard and 6th Corps, by comparison, were fresh troops who had to 'yomp' to battle, to use a Royal Marine Commando terminology. The Prussians may have arrived on the field of battle, but until field commanders had

---

407 Siborne, *Waterloo Letters*, No. 73.

assessed the ground and state of play, and given some of the men a much-needed rest, and more troops had arrived, the Prussians were initially not a major threat to the French.

Domon and Subervie move to the attack

General-of-Division Marie Joseph Raymond Delort, commander of the 14th Division of General Milhaud's 4th Cavalry Division, recalls that:[408]

> At eleven o'clock in the morning were perceived, in the direction of Saint-Lambert, troops who were moving towards the left flank of the English army. Our spirits were raised in hope. Were these troops emerging those of the detachment of Marshal Grouchy, or were they the rearguard of the Prussian army? However, we remained uncertain, a Prussian hussar carrying a dispatch to the English was made prisoner by the light cavalry that was posted between Wavre and Plancenoit, and said that the corps of Bülow, a force of 30,000 men, was coming. This corps was intact and redoubtable, as it had not taken part in their defeat at Ligny. Their advance was later confirmed by Generals Domon and Subervie, and their divisions of light cavalry moved forward immediately to their right. Having been informed of the presence of the Prussian army, our patrols could not discover the movements of Marshal Grouchy. The emperor detached the corps of Comte Lobau, along with the light cavalry of General Domon, to contain the Prussians. Our spirits filled with confidence, with 10,000 French troops advantageously placed, filled with ardour and guided by their chief to whom they were devoted, we could resist at this point the troops of Bülow. They were to be joined by the corps of Marshal Grouchy, while the centre of the English army would be pressed back by our irresistible impetuosity. But, the fortified English army resisted us strongly and many were killed during the attack and we must remark on the advantage of their position against our immensely superior forces.

General Jean-Simon Baron Domon (1774-1830) was a French cavalry commander who served throughout the Revolutionary and Napoléonic Wars, and whose career survived the Bourbon Restoration. General Gourgaud notes:[409]

---

408 *Nouvelle revue Retrospective*, Paris, January 1897, p. 374.
409 Gaspard Gourgaud, *La campagne de 1815*, P. Mongie, Paris, 1818, p. 94.

Great advantages were anticipated from the marshals coming upon the rear of Bülow's corps. But, as that corps appeared to be not more than two short leagues from the field of battle, it became necessary to send off a force to oppose it. Marshal Grouchy might delay passing the Dyle, or might be prevented by unforeseen obstacles. Lieutenant General Domont [sic] was therefore sent forward with his light cavalry, and Subervick's [sic] division of Pajol's corps of cavalry, making altogether a force of nearly 3,000 cavalry, to meet Bülow's advance guard; his instructions were to occupy all the passes, to prevent the enemy's hussars from attacking our flanks, and to send off couriers to meet Marshal Grouchy. Comte de Lobau, with both divisions of his corps [7,000 men], proceeded to reconnoitre his field of battle, in the rear of General Domont's cavalry, so that, in case General Bülow's movement should not be stopped by Marshal Grouchy, he might advance against the Prussians, and protect our flanks. Thus, the destination of this corps was changed.

de Mauduit goes on to note that:[410]

Comte Lobau advanced his infantry and replaced his 1st Line with the cavalry of General Domon. General Bülow emerged to his right on the heights and wood of Smohain, the left of which descended into a valley of the brook of Lasne, and thence the wood of Virer. The cavalry of the reserve made a movement in two columns and debouched to the left, where Prince William of Prussia commenced the battle.

Domon and Subervie's cavalry had succeeded in delaying the Prussian advance, but they could not stop the combined arms of their opponents. Their delay of the Prussians allowed Lobau's troops to set up a strong line of skirmishers. As the Prussian skirmish line engaged they were charged and driven back by the French cavalry, these were classic and successful delaying tactics. On the slope from the wood of Frischermont there was little cover and both sides suffered, the artillery fire was especially telling. Colonel Pétiet, of the imperial staff, notes:[411]

However, we had no news of the corps of Marshal Grouchy, while Bülow's troops arrived in front of our lines, extending into the right

---

410 Hippolyte de Mauduit, 'Veillee Militaire Charleroi, Fleurus et Waterloo' in *Sentinale de l'armée*, 16 June 1836.

411 Pétiet, pp. 445-6.

hand of Comte Lobau, at the height of La Belle Alliance. The 6th Corps was immediately reinforced by the division of the Young Guard, commanded by Duhesme, supported with two batteries. Bülow attempted to destroy the French cavalry with his artillery, because it had caused him such trouble. General Jacquinot displayed sang-froid and stoicism in the face of a situation that could have been so unfortunate for him. This general officer commanded two divisions of cavalry. A cannon ball came in from the flank of the 1st Lancers and took off the head of Chef d'Escadron Dumanoir, passed through the body of Colonel Jacquinot's [the general's brother] horse and cut off two legs of Chef d'Escadron Trentignant's horse. The three superior officers fell as one. Confusion spread through the ranks, Jacquinot, sword in hand, reordered the line himself with a firm voice and it was only after re-establishing order that he bent down to check if his brother was dead, but who was happily unhurt. Taking the hamlet of La Haye stopped the movement of Bülow.

We know very little about the operations of Domon and Subervie in the battle beyond the limited comments of the Prussians. However, General Domon prepared a review of his division on 6 July 1815, outlining the officers and men deserving of promotion or decoration. From this report, we learn a great deal about episodes of the battle on the French right flank.[412]

Squadron-Commander Robert, of the 4th Chasseurs, was recommended to be made Officer of the Legion of Honour for his acts of bravery in the battle. Sous-Lieutenant Mommot was recommended to be awarded the Legion of Honour for acts of bravery at Waterloo, as was Sous-Lieutenant Robinot. Adjutant-Sub-Officer Richard was also recommended for the Legion of Honour for his conduct and bravery in the battle. Sergeant Veyrems, Domon noted, a veteran who had returned from Moscow, was wounded in the battle and dismounted, but still fought bravely for which he too was recommended for the Legion of Honour. Sergeant Philippe was also likewise recommended for the Legion of Honour, having been wounded in the action, having his horse killed under him and returning to fight with his company on a captured horse in spite of his wounds. A similar recommendation was made for Sergeants Collin and Batty, as was Sergeant-Major Bidault. Sergeant-Major Andre was also recommended for the Legion of Honour, as

---

412 SHDDT: Xc 192 *4e Chasseurs à Cheval. Dossier 1815. Rapport 6 Juillet 1815.*

General Domon states that Bidault killed or wounded three Prussians in the space of four minutes.[413]

Among the 9th Chasseurs, Squadron-Commander Petit was recommended for the decoration of Officer of the Legion of Honour for the capture of 300 prisoners on 15 June. Also for his bravery on 15 June, Chasseur Parecellier, of 6th Company, was recommended for the Legion of Honour. Sergeant-Major Pierre Perrin, General Domon records, killed two Prussian hussars during the retreat, when he was searching for a line of retreat which the Prussians endeavoured to block.[414] Were the hussars encountered by the 9th Chasseurs the same body as that encountered by the 4th Chasseurs? Possibly.

In the 12th Chasseurs, Chasseurs Ferrant and Schneiblin were recommended for the Cross of the Legion of Honour for saving the life of Lieutenant-General Gérard and his chief-of-staff at the Battle of Ligny. Likewise, Sergeant-Majors Nicolas Rhis and Rhomer were recommended for the Cross of the Legion of Honour for capturing an enemy artillery piece at Ligny. At Waterloo, Adjutant-Sub-Officers Devina and Degennes, as well as Corporal Collard, were recommended for the Legion of Honour for their distinguished conduct.[415]

However, we need to state that the colonel of the 11th Chasseurs reported un-nerving news. Two officers are listed as 'quitting the regiment without orders' on 18 June: Major Alexander Rigny and Captain Mathey. Neither man had been seen by 6 December 1815 when the regiment was disbanded.[416]

Alexander Rigny was born on 19 March 1790. He studied at the Ecole Militaire and graduated on 16 January 1807 before passing to the 26th Regiment of Light Infantry as a sous-lieutenant. He was wounded on 10 June 1807 and again on 21 May 1809. Promotion to lieutenant came on 31 May 1809 and he was named aide-de-camp to General (later Marshal) Suchet on 15 July 1809. Rigny became a prisoner of war at Leipzig in 1813 while serving on Berthier's staff, and returned to France in summer 1814. He was named major of the 11th Chasseurs then deserted on 18 June 1815. He held no military post until he served in Spain in 1823 and was named colonel of the 2nd Hussars in 1830 before being promoted to marshal-du-camp on 25 October 1830. He served

---

413 SHDDT: Xc 192. *Dossier 1815. Rapport 6 Juillet 1815.*
414 ibid.
415 ibid.
416 SHDDT: Xc 206 *11e Chasseurs à Cheval*. Dossier 1815.

with distinction in Algeria and died in 1873.[417] His biography glosses over his desertion at Waterloo.

Eugene Mathey was born on 4 May 1777 and was a career soldier. He had enlisted as a gunner in 1794 and left the army in 1798. He enlisted once more, this time in the prestigious Gendarmes d'Ordonnance of the Imperial Guard on 1 January 1807. In the regiment at the same time was Charles du Barail, who also deserted at Waterloo—perhaps both men shared the same pro-Bourbon sympathies? Mathey was promoted to corporal on 8 January 1807 and to sergeant on 10 August the same year. He was then admitted as sous-lieutenant in the 5th Chasseurs à Cheval on 19 February 1808 before passing to the 11th Chasseurs à Cheval. He was made a captain on 10 June 1809 and made prisoner of war on 15 July 1812, returning to the regiment on 11 September 1814.[418] He is recorded as having deserted at Waterloo.

These officers were not the only deserters that day, as the carabiniers lost four officers, among who was Captain Vincenot, of the 1st Carabiniers,[419] and from the 2nd Carabiniers were:[420]

Captain du Barail;[421]

Lieutenant Hedouville;[422] and

Lieutenant Charles Desire Prudhomme.[423]

---

417 Charles Mullié, *Biographie des célébrités militaires des armées de terre et de mer de 1789 à 1850*, 1852.

418 AN: LH 1788/9.

419 AN: LH 2724/27.

420 SHDDT: 18 YC 9 *2e Regiment de Carabiniers (Monsieur) officiers 1814-1815*.

421 The entry in the *controle* reads: 'du Barail Charles Né à Nomeny (Meurthe) 10 juin 1785 Entré aux gendarmes d'ordonnance 14 novembre 1806 Brigadier 20 décembre 1806 Maréchal des logis 15 janvier 1807 Sous-lieutenant au 9e régiment de Dragons 16 juillet 1807 Lieutenant au 2e régiment de Carabiniers 2 mars 1809 Légionnaire 12 août 1809 Adjudant major par décret 11 juillet 1810 Capitaine 31 juillet 1811 Nommé Chevalier de l'ordre Royal militaire de St-Louis par son Altesse Royale Monsieur, comte d'Artois 1er novembre 1814'.

422 The entry in the *controle* reads: 'Hedouville Joseph Hubert Né à Sommairemont (Haute-Marne) 25 mai 1781 Carabinier 10 mars 1802 Brigadier 31 décembre 1803 Maréchal des logis honoraire 27 juin 1804 Maréchal des logis en pied 30 octobre 1806 Sous-lieutenant par décret 14 mai 1809 Légionnaire 12 août 1809 Lieutenant 1812 Rayé de l'effectif ayant quitté le corps le 19 juin 1815 et n'ayant point reparu depuis'.

423 The entry in the *controle* reads: 'Prudhomme Charles Désiré Né à Salins Jura 22 novembre 1784 Carabiniers 12 avril 1802 Brigadier honoraire 24 janvier

In the 5th Lancers, Squadron-Commander Milet left his post and deserted to the Allies:[424]

> He took part in the 1815 campaign, and at the Battle of Waterloo quitted the army due to his deep attachment to the Bourbon family.

One can only imagine the effect this could have had on the officers and men of the regiment. de Mauduit, in his work on the campaign, notes one officer of the 1st Regiment of Chasseurs à Cheval went over to the Allies during the battle: Lieutenant Bachelet. This officer was MAT No. 42 Lieutenant Gabrielle Antoine Labechelle.[425] Captain-Adjutant-Major Jean Debut (Matricule No. 14)[426] is recorded as endeavouring to prevent the desertion. Labechelle, it is recorded, deserted with Captain du Barail, of the 2nd Carabiniers, and also likely Squadron-Commander Philippe Auguste Milet, of the 5th Lancers, went over to the Allies at the same time.[427] This implies that with the desertion of General Bourmont on 15 June and the desertion of General Gordon and others on 16 June, the loyalty of the army to the cause of Napoléon was shaky among officers. Historian Ian James Smith, who has undertaken groundbreaking research into the two regiments of carabiniers during the First Empire, argues that due to issue of loyalty, the former 1st Chasseurs du Roi (as with the 1st and 2nd Carabiniers) were held back from action on the 16th due to issues of morale, cohesion and loyalty. Does the fewer losses of the 1st Chasseurs compared to the 6th Chasseurs imply the former were held back from more serious fighting in case the regiment galloped off and deserted to the Allies?

The loyalty of the army was, it seems, shaky and wavering. With officers of dubious loyalty, it is little wonder that when the great lie of Waterloo unfolded, many thousands of men quit their colours.

1803 Maréchal des logis honoraire 1er janvier 1804 Maréchal des logis en pied 1er décembre 1806 Sous-lieutenant par décision 14 mai 1809 Lieutenant 5 novembre 1811 A fait les campagnes des années 13-14 vendémiaire an 14, 1806, 1807 et 1809. Prisonnier de guerre en Russie le 13 octobre 1812 Rayé de l'effectif le 29 novembre ayant quitté le corps le 19 juin 1815 et n'ayant point reparu depuis'.

424 SHDDT: Xc 183.
425 SHDDT: GR 24 YC 254.
426 ibid.
427 SHDDT: Xc 183.

3rd Cavalry Division

Losses in the division are given regiment-by-regiment below:

4th Chasseurs à Cheval

In the 4th Chasseurs à Cheval, Lieutenant Hugues Pepin Claviere was shot with a musket ball to the right foot.[428] Sub-Lieutenant Jean Pierre Moutard took a gunshot wound to the left shoulder. He had served in the famed 7th Hussars from 30 October 1804, before entering the Lancers of Berg Regiment on 1 September 1807.[429] Sub-Lieutenant Charles Benjamin Robinot had his horse killed under him and he was wounded at the same time.[430]

Casualties for the 4th Chasseurs à Cheval at Waterloo were as follows:[431]

4th Chasseurs à Cheval					
Squadron	Killed	Died of Wounds	Wounded	Prisoner of War	Missing
1st	1	0	0	12	6
2nd	1	0	0	0	5
3rd	3	0	2	1	5
4th	0	0	0	1	8
Total	5	0	2	14	24

On 10 June, the regiment mustered 306 other ranks. General Domon records six chasseurs were wounded and seven troop horses killed at Ligny, and one officer's mount.[432]

At Waterloo, forty-five men were lost, representing, a mere 15 per cent of effective strength. However, 161 horses were dead or wounded, giving a strength of 144 men and 138 horses. This represents a loss of 52 per cent of effective strength; far higher losses in horses than men.[433]

---

428 AN: LH 547/37.
429 AN: LH 1958/37.
430 AN: LH 2356/28.
431 SHDDT: GR 24 YC 274.
432 SHDDT: C15 5. Dossier 16 June, Domon to Soult.
433 SHDDT: C15 6 *Correspondance Armée du Nord 22 Juin au 3 Juillet 1815*. Dossier 23 June, Domon to Soult.

9th Chasseurs à Cheval

Casualties for the 9th Chasseurs à Cheval at Waterloo are in the table below:[434]

9th Chasseurs à Cheval						
Squadron	Company	Killed	Died of Wounds	Wounded	Prisoner of War	Missing
1st	1st	1	0	2	0	4
	5th	0	0	2	2	0
2nd	2nd	2	0	0	0	1
	6th	1	0	0	0	1
3rd	3rd	0	0	2	0	3
	7th	1	0	2	0	8
4th	4th	0	0	1	0	3
	8th	4	0	2	1	2
Total		9	0	11	3	22

In total at Waterloo, forty-five men were lost. On 10 June, the regiment mustered 327 men. Six men were lost at Ligny, giving 321 men present on the 18th. This represents a loss of 14 per cent of effective strength. On 23 June, General Domon records 102 men with ninety-five horses and seventeen officers with thirty-nine horses,[435] thus between 18 and 23 June some 174 men were lost, nearly four times the number as lost on 18 June. It seems these men were absent without leave and had fled the army, or had become dismounted, separated from the regiment and were made prisoner or deserted.

12th Chasseurs à Cheval

On 10 June, the regiment mustered twenty-three officers with sixty-five horses and 273 men with 263 horses, along with six draught horses. In total, sixteen men and five officers were lost before Waterloo: killed was Sub-Lieutenant Menzo. Wounded were Captain Aubrey and Sub-Lieutenant Remy. Corporal Bruguiere was killed.

In terms of losses of other ranks, the regiment lost 5 per cent of its strength at Ligny. In terms of horses, 9.6 per cent were lost (twenty-five horses); a ratio of almost two horses lost for every man.

---

434 SHDDT: GR 24 YC 299.
435 SHDDT: C15 6. Dossier 23 June, Domon to Soult.

On the morning of 18 June, the regiment had 238 horses and 258 men. General Domon reports that 198 men were lost on and after 18 June, along with 182 horses, leaving sixty men with fifty-six horses and seven officers with fifteen horses. At Waterloo, 76 per cent of the regiment's manpower was lost, and 76 per cent of the regiment's horses. Of the twenty-three officers present at the start of the campaign, sixteen were dead or wounded.[436]

Martinien records that at Waterloo Lieutenant Richard was killed. Furthermore, he states that wounded were Colonel Grouchy, Captain Joseph Laurent Constantin Huck, Captain Onesime Stanislas Dumont, Lieutenant Renard, Lieutenant Dolemans and Sub-Lieutenant Lusignan. Sub-Lieutenant Augustin Louis Pierre Perardel was born in Paris on 7 January 1788 and served in the 12th Chasseurs à Cheval since 1807. He was promoted to sub-lieutenant on 8 January 1814.[437] Sub-Lieutenant Antoine Faustin Renaud was born on 15 February 1791 at Cagliari in Sardinia. He was admitted to the 12th Chasseurs à Cheval on 16 July 1814 and was wounded at Waterloo with a gunshot to the abdomen, and another to the right arm.[438] Other ranks wounded included:

- Sergeant-Major François Hinout, born 1793 at Rouen. He was admitted to the 12th Chasseurs à Cheval on 9 July 1811 with the matricule number 2762. He was promoted to corporal on 15 July 1812, to fourrier on 16 July 1812, to sergeant on 9 July 1813 and to sergeant-major on 21 September 1813. He had his horse killed under him at Waterloo and was discharged on 21 December 1815. He died in 1881.[439]

- Sergeant Valentin Lapp was born on 13 March 1787 at Gimbrett and was admitted to the 12th Chasseurs à Cheval on 12 March 1807. He was promoted to corporal on 1 February 1813 and to sergeant on 11 December 1813. He was wounded with a gunshot that passed through the right side of his chest at Waterloo.[440]

Divisional losses

The table below gives the losses for the division as a whole:

---

436 SHDDT: C15 6. Dossier 23 June, Domon to Soult.
437 AN: LH 2094/42.
438 AN: LH 2296/12.
439 MSH 148375.
440 AN: LH 1480/20.

3rd Cavalry Division						
	Killed	Died of Wounds	Wounded	Prisoners of War	Missing	Total
4th Chasseurs à Cheval	5	0	2	14	24	45
9th Chasseurs à Cheval	9	0	11	3	22	45
12th Chasseurs à Cheval	No data available					198[441]
Total						140 to 298[442]

5th Cavalry Division

1st Lancers

Officers killed or wounded in the action included:

- Squadron-Commander Guillaume Felix Comte le Chanoine de Manoir de Juaye had his head carried away by a cannon ball. He was born at Troyes on 7 July 1783 and had served in the 1st Lancers since 1812.
- Captain-Adjutant-Major Pierre François Haxo was born at Luneville on 21 February 1780 and was wounded and had his horse killed under him. He had joined the regiment on 16 August 1814.[443]

Losses of the regiment were as follows:[444]

1st Lancers					
Squadron	Killed	Died of Wounds	Wounded	Prisoner of War	Missing
1st	0	0	0	0	3
2nd	1	0	0	3	2
3rd	0	1	0	1	1
4th	3	0	0	0	5
A la suite	0	0	0	0	2
Total	4	1	0	4	13

---

441 For the period 18 to 23 June and therefore lists losses of men after Waterloo. It is likely that the losses are, as with the other regiments in the division, under fifty.

442 The data for the 12th Chasseurs à Cheval includes figures post-Waterloo. The lower figure here (140) assumes that the regiment had losses no higher than fifty men on 18 June 1815. The upper figure (298) includes the full 198 casualties in the row above.

443 AN: LH 1273/73.

444 SHDDT: GR 24 YC 96.

The regiment lost one man at Ligny and thirteen at Genappe. Furthermore, another source states thirty men were dismounted at Ligny and fifteen at Genappe.[445] This makes a loss of forty-five other ranks. A further twenty-two men were lost at Waterloo. On 10 June, the regiment mustered forty officers and 375 other ranks. In total, thirty-five men were lost. The regiment theoretically mustered 348 men on 19 June, so if we include the forty-five men dismounted and therefore no longer on the effective list, the total increases to eighty.

Despite only recording four men as prisoners, the following six men were held in prison in England:[446]

Jean Baptiste Tatel;
Germain Buipet;
Louis Chanteau;
Joseph Choquet;
François Rousseau; and
François Visceron.

Clearly, the tally of the missing also included men made prisoners. Including these losses, the regiment lost 20 per cent effective strength in the campaign. On 26 June 1815, it fielded 299 men, suggesting the losses of the regiment overall were low.

2nd Lancers

On 10 June, the regiment mustered forty-one officers and 379 men. At Genappe on 17 June, the regiment lost 46 per cent of its effective strength. Indeed, 28 per cent of the regiment's officers were wounded on the 17th. However, as we have seen with the 12th Chasseurs à Cheval, the loss of horses on average seems to be a ratio of one man to every two horses wounded, reducing the regiment to a mere 115 men in the field on 18 June; little more than a squadron strong. Given the high losses on the 17th, it is not impossible to imagine the regiment was badly shaken. Since the brigaded 1st Lancers lost a mere twenty-one men at Waterloo, it seems the brigade was not involved in heavy fighting, and may well have been pulled back earlier in the day from fighting the Prussians on the French right flank. In this scenario, the shaky morale of the 2nd Regiment may have influenced the operation of the brigade, and thus was not committed to any serious fighting.

---

445 Jérôme Croyet, *'Le 1e Chevau-Leger-Lancier'* in *Traditions Magazine*, Vol. 3, August 2015, pp. 26-32.
446 SHDDT: Yj 11. See also: SHDDT: Yj 12.

Among the wounded officers was Sub-Lieutenant Henry Joseph Mathieu, born at Mons on 21 December 1786. He volunteered into the 3rd Dragoons in 1803 and was named as porte-etendard on 2 November 1814. He was wounded on 17 June 1815 and dismissed from the regiment on 16 October 1815.[447] One wonders if he was wounded in defence of the eagle during the action at Genappe.

The muster list of the regiment for the period 1814 to disbandment in 1815 exists at the French Army Archives at Vincennes. However, the document was damaged in the 1940s and is not available for researchers to consult until it has been conserved sometime close to 2020. Therefore, we are not able to obtain losses for the regiment at Waterloo. One man who was at Waterloo was Jacques Louis Aimee Cahagne. He was born on 1 October 1787 and had served with the 3rd Dragoons since 1807. He was promoted to corporal on 11 September 1810, to fourrier on 5 February 1812, to sergeant on 16 July 1813 and to sergeant-major on 1 February 1814. He was admitted to the regiment on 18 August 1814 and wounded with a cannon ball to the kidneys at Waterloo.[448] Prisoners of war from the regiment were:[449]

Sergeant Jacques Druet. Held in Plymouth;
Corporal Yves Deuit;
Corporal Jean Tise;
Noel Berry;
Auguste Chenu;
Alexandre Girardeau;
Hycanithe Soreau;
Joseph Soule; and
Jean Thullie.

11th Chasseurs à Cheval

The 11th Chasseurs à Cheval lost Squadron-Commander Brucelles wounded. Lieutenant Anheiser was also wounded, so too were Captain Larcohe, Captain Mathey (who was wounded and disappeared) and Sub-Lieutenants Billordeaux, François Lacombe, Grenier, Malval, Menu (who carried the regiment's eagle) and Periola. Also wounded were Captain-Adjutant Major Rosselange and Adjutant-Major Guichert.

---

447 AN: LH 1690/12.
448 AN: LH 404/17.
449 SHDDT: Yj 11. See also: SHDDT: Yj 12.

Trooper Jean Louis Deprez, who joined the regiment in 1813, was also wounded. Trooper Antoine Morreton, born 21 April 1794 and who had joined the regiment in December 1812, was made prisoner of war.

Casualties for the 11th Chasseurs à Cheval at Waterloo are as below:[450]

11th Chasseurs à Cheval					
Squadron	Killed	Died of Wounds	Wounded	Prisoner of War	Missing
1st	3	0	0	0	1
2nd	5	0	3	3	0
3rd	2	0	2	3	3
4th	3	0	0	0	1
Total	13	0	5	6	5

On 10 June, the regiment mustered 458 other ranks. At Waterloo, twenty-nine men were lost. In addition, five men were lost at Ligny; a mere 6 per cent of effective strength was lost at Waterloo. In comparison, the 1st Lancers in the 1st Brigade of the division lost twenty-one men at Waterloo, a mere 4.6 per cent of effective strength, comparable figures to the 11th Chasseurs à Cheval and the 1st Chasseurs à Cheval in Piré's division. It seems that Subervie's cavalry was in action on the 18th, but took no part in any major fighting.

Observations

The losses of the 3rd and 5th Cavalry Divisions are presented below:

	Killed	Died of Wounds	Wounded	Prisoner of War	Missing
3rd Division	14	0	13	17	46
5th Division	17	1	5	10	19
Total	31	1	18	27	65

From the table, it is clear that the 3rd Cavalry Division lost far more men than the 5th. Due to a lack of data, we cannot present any further details of losses for the light cavalry at Waterloo. However, it does seem that the 5th Division were not as heavily engaged as the 3rd, though they had more men killed outright.

---

450 SHDDT: GR 24 YC 309.

Chapter 10

Hougoumont: Round Two

Meanwhile, over a mile to the west of where General Domon's cavalry stood, at Hougoumont sometime between 15.30 and 16.00, the troops of Prince Jérôme were exhausted and were pulled back from the fray. Towards 16.30 Reille sent forward the 9th Infantry Division of General Foy.

Foy's men do not seem to have endeavoured to assault the farm complex, but instead pressed forward to the orchard and gardens, perhaps hoping to attack the farm on its eastern side through the garden gates, rather than attempt to storm the southern gate which acted like a bastion upon which two attacks had floundered. Once Jérôme's men were withdrawn, the notion of trying to capture Hougoumont through direct attacks, supported with artillery, seems to have been dropped by the French, who opted instead to out-flank the farm and control the Allied troops in the orchard.

We have no eyewitness reports for the operations of the 92nd Regiment of Line Infantry. It is possible it attacked Hougoumont in conjunction with the brigaded 93rd Regiment of Line Infantry. Total regimental losses at Waterloo are in the table below:[451]

---

451 SHDDT: GR 21 YC 690 *76e régiment d'infanterie de ligne (ex 92e régiment d'infanterie de ligne), 4 septembre 1814-28 mars 1815 (matricules 1 à 1 512).* See also: SHDDT: GR 21 YC 691 *76e régiment d'infanterie de ligne (ex 92e régiment d'infanterie de ligne), 25 avril 1815-27 juin 1815 (matricules 1 513 à 1 728).*

92nd Regiment of Line Infantry					
	Evacuated Wounded	Wounded & Prisoner	Prisoner of War	Killed	Missing
1st Battalion	36	0	3	4	43
2nd Battalion	61	0	4	5	33
3rd Battalion	81	0	2	4	41
Total	178	0	9	13	117

On the morning of 18 June, the regiment mustered 850 other ranks. At Waterloo 317 men were lost, representing some 37 per cent of effective strength. The losses are significantly lower than the losses in the 6th Infantry Division.

Lieutenant Puvis, of the 93rd Regiment of Line Infantry (part of the same brigade as the 92nd Regiment of Line Infantry), narrates how the fighting developed as he witnessed it:[452]

> On the morning of the 18th, drenched by the rain of the night, we were informed of the proclamation of the emperor, 'the British army is before us and we will attack it'. The whole army was massed in front of Genappe; the rain did not cease. At six o'clock we left the position that we had occupied on the right side of the road to Brussels and marched into line of battle. The rye, in the midst of which we were marching, was so high that our bayonets were just taller than it and we could see nothing around us! The terrain that we were marching over was very undulating, and on the elevated points the enemy bullets began to reach us. To our right, we saw a mound on which the emperor stood, surrounded by his staff.
>
> As we advanced the cannonade around us became livelier. Arriving in a hollow, deeper than elsewhere, we stopped behind a hedge. General Reille, who commanded the 2nd Corps under the orders of Marshal Ney, remained with us during the time in which we remained in this position. The cannon fire increased, our senior officers came to tell us that we were going to attack the English lines with the bayonet, and we had to warn everyone. It was two o'clock in the afternoon when we marched forward, the enemy seemed to be no longer in front of us.

---

452 *Extrait des Souvenirs historiques de Théobald Puvis, paru dans la Revue historique des Armées*, 1997, No. 3, pp. 101-29.

We deployed in skirmish order into a tall wood that was to our left, we approached a large building that was fortified on all points and was protected by very high hedges and deep ditches. We crossed the ditches where they were less wide, and arrived at a hedge which was vigorously protected by the enemy. We tried in vain to pass through the hedge. We suffered enormous losses; the lieutenant of my company was killed close to me. A ball struck the peak of my shako and tumbled me on to my back. The shock was so great I thought I had been wounded, but there was no blood. I quickly recovered my senses. At this time, I was to the right of my company; the captain followed the movement to the left. Marshal Ney rushed up to us on horseback, bareheaded and with no escort. As I was the closest officer to him, he sent me with the order for the 100th Regiment of Line, which was about one hundred paces behind us, to advance and support us. Throughout this movement Marshal Ney remained with us. The orderly officers to the marshal said we needed cannon to take the position.

Sergeant-Major Silvain Larreguy, also of the 93rd Regiment of Line Infantry, narrates the same events as he witnessed them:[453]

The division of the former king of Westphalia had disappeared under the fire of the enemy; Foy's division was sent to replace the batteries in Hougoumont. Around this farm were piled thousands of dead, injured and dying, which we soon doubled in number, as we were broke in turn by shrapnel of the English and Scottish entrenched in their formidable positions. Before reaching this awful slaughter, the order came to leave behind the eagles in the custody of the sergeant-majors. My friends and I had refused to obey this provision, but by this act of disobedience we won the cheers from our regiment. Here I might describe the terrible scenes of carnage. Soon we had our feet bathed in blood; in less than half an hour our ranks were thinned by more than half. Everyone waited stoically for death or horrific injury. We were covered with bloody splashes, but our courage was at the highest pitch of excitement. No one wounded left the battlefield, not a dying man breathed his last without giving a thought of devotion to the emperor. My captain, pierced by two bullets and losing all his blood, never ceased to excite us with his faltering voice, until he fell amid the carnage to everlasting slumber.

---

453 Silvain Larreguy de Civrieux, *Souvenirs d'un cadet, 1813-1823*, Hachette, Paris, 1912.

After the most stubborn fighting, we remained masters of the woods and orchards. It took a superhuman effort to seize Mont-Saint-Jean and La Haye Sainte, which was taken and retaken many times by us and the enemy. Everywhere we were finally victorious.

Private Triquenot, of the 93rd Regiment of Line Infantry, narrates how he was promoted to sergeant at the start of the campaign and saved the life of his battalion-commander, who had promoted him when he was badly wounded. He writes in the third person:[454]

> At the Battle of Waterloo, the 93rd was one of the first regiments ordered to attack the corps commanded by Wellington. In the midst of the fray, Battalion-Commander Lugnot received two bullets which fractured his left leg; one to the lower leg, the other to the left thigh. M. Triquenot, who never took his eyes from his benefactor, hastened to fly to his rescue, and, with two friends, they carried him on their shoulders and took him a half-mile from the battlefield. Here they chanced to find him a horse. The saddle and bridle were checked and their precious burden was placed on the horse; the work of a moment. But, soon they realised that they could go no further. The commander could not endure the horrible pain he felt in his left leg which was hanging down. M. Triquenot quickly placed himself beside the horse and with both hands supported the affected leg, and in silence marched the two miles to reach the nearest ambulance. Upon his arrival, he gave his commander all the necessary help, and when he saw he was safe, he ran to join his battalion.

Battalion-Commander Joseph Lugnot[455] commanded the 2nd Battalion 93rd Regiment of Line Infantry. At Waterloo, despite the best efforts of M. Triquenot, when the French field hospital was overrun, he was left

---

454 Jarry de Mancy, *Portraits et Histoire des Hommes Utiles*, Imprime Chez Paul Renouard, Paris, 1833, p. 30.

455 Joseph Lugnot was born on 12 December 1780 at Charentenay. His father, Michel Lugnot, was a captain in the French army in 1791, and his son became an *enfant de troupe* at the age of fourteen in 1794. During the Peninsular War, he was seriously wounded at the Siege of Girone on 19 September 1809, which mutilated his lower jaw. He served during the Russian campaign and was wounded again at Polosken on 18 August 1812. He was made Battalion-Commander of the 93rd Regiment of Line Infantry in 1813, and served in the garrison of Magdebourg.

for dead on the field of battle and only on 20 June 1815 was his body found. He was taken to England as a prisoner of war and was returned in 1816. He was named major of the 14th Regiment of Light Infantry in 1821 and fought in Spain in 1823. He served in the campaign in Algeria in 1830 and died on 13 February 1857.[456]

Also wounded was Captain Toussaint Dellier, of the 93rd Regiment of Line Infantry, who was born on 3 June 1788 and was wounded and left for dead. He notes that he suffered:[457]

> Total loss of the right eye by a shot received from the enemy and whose ball came in through the orbit of the right side and passed out through the temporal region in front of the ear canal; that ball had destroyed the entire eye, broken the cheekbone and injured the inner ear; this resulted in total deafness on that side.

Regimental losses on 18 June were as follows:[458]

93rd Regiment of Line Infantry					
	Wounded	Wounded & Prisoner	Prisoner of War	Killed	Missing
1st Battalion	42	0	16	7	37
2nd Battalion	46	0	10	21	21
3rd Battalion	99	0	13	6	85
4th Battalion	18	0	7	12	59
Total	205	0	46	46	202

On the morning of 18 June, the regiment had 1,744 men in ranks. At Waterloo, 499 men were lost, representing 29 per cent of the regiment. Looking at the data, the 3rd Battalion had the highest number of wounded, but the 2nd Battalion recorded the highest number of dead, followed by the 4th Battalion. This left 1,245 men in ranks on 20 June. The regiment lost significantly more men than the brigaded 92nd

---

456 AN: LH 1675/22.

457 AN: LH 714/58.

458 SHDDT: GR 21 YC 701 *77e régiment d'infanterie de ligne (ex 93e régiment d'infanterie de ligne), 13 août 1814-22 décembre 1814 (matricules 1 à 1 800).* See also: SHDDT: GR 21 YC 702 *77e régiment d'infanterie de ligne (ex 93e régiment d'infanterie de ligne), 22 décembre 1814-8 août 1815 (matricules 1 801 à 3 108).*

Regiment of Line Infantry, suggesting the fighting by the former was of a different magnitude to that experienced by the latter.

We cannot say when at Waterloo these losses were incurred. What we can say is that all four battalions were in action. On 26 June, the regiment mustered 442 men. This is a loss of 803 men after Waterloo, or 64 per cent of the remaining effective strength.

The 92nd and 93rd Regiments of Line Infantry were withdrawn from the action and replaced by the 4th Regiment of Light Infantry and the 100th Regiment of Line Infantry, which, it seems, took no part in the fighting for the farm. The brigade, in conjunction with the 92nd and 93rd Regiments of Line Infantry, attacked the Allied left near the sunken road and orchard of Hougoumont around 18.00.

Not until late in the day did Foy's men get committed to an attack on the orchard and gardens. The action at Hougoumont has been used to demonstrate the prowess of the plucky little garrison against overwhelming odds, a diversionary attack by Napoléon that destroyed his left wing. This is clearly not the case. Foy's men were ordered to attack during an interval in the massed French cavalry charges, and Bachelu was ordered to attack in a likewise manner. Prince Jérôme's actions at Waterloo have often been described as reckless and that he needlessly destroyed his division and that of Foy. In all actuality, the charges against Jérôme do not stand up to much scrutiny. Jérôme was inexperienced, but he did have appointed as chief-of-staff Lieutenant-General Armand Charles Guilleminot, one of the best staff officers in the French army. Upon a closer examination of the French and Allied material, Jérôme's troops broke into Hougoumont four, or possibly five, times, and rather than being fritted away in an hour, his troops appear to have been fed in over a period of four or five hours.

Ney charges with Milhaud's cavalry

As Foy's men were beginning to get entangled with the wood and garden at Hougoumont, elsewhere on the field the French artillery continued pounding the Anglo-Allied lines. The barrage was, if anything, harder than before, so much so that Wellington ordered his infantry to lie down to make less conspicuous targets. Despite this precaution, the artillery barrage caused heavy losses in the ranks. Under the hail of shell and round shot came a massive cavalry attack on the Anglo-Allied centre.

Various historians since 1815 have put forward a number of explanations for why the main French cavalry charges commenced.

Firstly, did Ney misjudge through his telescope the sight of the light infantry companies (that had moved to the western side of La Haye Sainte) moving back up the slope as a major retreat on the part of Wellington? Or secondly, was it the ridge seemingly becoming vacant, with Wellington ordering his men to lie down, that from Ney's vantage point seemed to be a major retreat that caused him to launch the cavalry forward without infantry support? If Wellington's men were retreating, then a sudden cavalry attack would crush the retreating troops with no recourse for infantry support. Thirdly, some writers comment that the charges happened spontaneously with no orders. It seems very unlikely that this happened, but it neatly shifts the blame from Ney and Napoléon on to subordinate commanders. The propagator of the myth is Captain de Brack, of the Red Lancers, who some writers have believed to be a true statement of fact. For the charges to have 'simply occurred' it means Milhaud and his cavalry corps would have had to leave his position on the right wing, cross the battlefield with no orders and then charge. In doing so they would have had to avoid the gaze of Ney and Napoléon. This is very unlikely, and on balance the charges were deliberately ordered. This spontaneous charge is a way of French senior officers blaming no one for the charges, which only after the fact were considered to have been a failure. If no one ordered the charge, therefore no one was to blame.

On balance, it does seem more likely that Wellington's order to some regiments to withdraw a few paces was misinterpreted by the French. When the British had retreated to the reverse slope, the British infantry could no longer be seen from the French position. This was mistaken as a general retreat. About the operations of the light infantry screen, Lieutenant John Pratt, of the 30th Regiment of Foot, notes:[459]

> This force consisted to the best of my recollection in the following details: four British light companies formed into a battalion under Lieutenant-Colonel Vigoureux, of the 30th Regiment; 1st and 2nd Battalions KGL. They occupied the farmhouse and garden of La Haye Sainte a light Hanoverian battalion and the jägers von Kilmansegge (Rifles).

> The orders delivered to me upon that occasion as adjutant of the light battalion by Major-General Sir C. Halkett were to the following effect: 'to cover and protect our batteries. To establish at

459 Siborne, *Waterloo Letters*, No. 138.

all times as much in advance as might be compatible with prudence. To preserve considerable intervals from the fire of the enemy's batteries. To show obstinate resistance against infantry of the same description, but to attempt no formation or offer useless opposition to charges of cavalry, but to retire in time upon the squares in our rear, moving in a direct line without any reference to regiments or nations. When the charge was repulsed, to resume our ground'.

About midday, rather before twelve, the first shot was fired, it was the first report that reached my ears that morning and was directed against masses of infantry moving on Hougoumont. The enemy's artillery did not reply for some time, but we could see them distinctly taking up their position immediately in our front.

The enemy's artillery had now opened a tremendous fire along the entire extent of the left centre of the position, but chiefly directed against our batteries. Several large shells also fell with precision in the midst of us, but the ground being very soft they generally buried themselves deep and did not do as much mischief as under other circumstances might have been the case.

The light troops crept down the hill nearly to its foot. At first, they did not encounter any infantry, but were driven back by a charge of cavalry. They took refuge in the squares when the charge was repulsed and immediately occupied their former position.

The fire of the enemy's artillery became now very galling, exposed as we were to it, and almost all the artillery horses had already fallen to it.

In the interval we experienced more than one charge of cavalry and the light infantry, in their occasional advances, now we encountered the same description of force, usually engaging and sustaining desultory fire near the foot of the respective positions.

For the French seeing this battalion and the three other accompanying battalions operating on the slope by La Haye Sainte, and which retreated in front of the advancing cavalry, the ordered retreat seems to have been mistaken for a rout of the British army. When the British had retreated to the reverse slope, the infantry could no longer be seen from the French position.

Having ridden over the ground, it becomes clearly apparent that the steepness of the slope and boggy nature of the ground on the day would have slowed the French advance to a trot. It was not until the

French cavalry crested the slope that the cavalry could see where to attack. The charges could not be directed against specific targets—the cavalry was attacking blindly. A charge is best executed by cavalry when the target of the charge can be clearly seen, and the squadrons of the attacking force can attack the target in line in successive waves. Not being able to see the target greatly reduces the effect of the charge, as a result the attacks were haphazard and piecemeal. Rather than hitting squares in solid waves of horsemen, the attacks faltered as the cavalry crested the hill to be met by close-range volley fire from the infantry squares.

The first wave of attacking cavalry was Milhaud's 4th Cavalry Corps. Before Milhaud could attack, his division had to re-deploy from the French extreme right wing towards Hougoumont. Clearly therefore, the cavalry charges cannot have been spontaneous, as Milhaud had to be ordered to re-locate on the field of battle. However, we do not know when Milhaud moved to the French left, conceivably it could have occurred after the counter-attack against the Union and Household Brigades. This would seem logical, as it would unite all of Milhaud's corps in the centre of the French positions, as opposed to having a division detached to the French right. In General Milhaud's after-action report to Marshal Soult, the major-general notes that after his charge on the French right:[460]

> The 4th Corps, supported by the 3rd Cavalry Corps, the cavalry brigade of the Guard, charged with fearlessness on to the plateau, crushed five or six English squares and a line of cavalry three times greater in number, and, having slashed thousands of English infantrymen, captured forty pieces of artillery and sabred the gunners who did not have time to jump into squares.

> The second line of enemy batteries established behind the ravine [the sunken road] and supported by large reserves of infantry and, as well as other inaccessible batteries which fired on our exposed flank. This fire did not permit us to keep the forty pieces of artillery, but the 4th and the 3rd Cavalry Corps and the cavalry of the Guard rallied and held with heroic constancy the rear of the plateau for three hours, under the hail of shrapnel and musket fire, but were unfortunately supported too late by some battalions of the French line and the Guard.

---

460 Delort, 'Notice sur la batailles de Fleurus et de Mont Saint Jean' in Revue Hebdomadaire, June 1896, pp. 379-80.

Wattier's 13th Cavalry Division

Michel Ordener, commanding the 1st Regiment of Cuirassiers, recounts the charge as below. We should note that he is writing to exonerate his own actions, and those of Guyot and Kellermann. Both these two generals were blamed for wasting the cavalry reserve of the Imperial Guard heavy cavalry and the famed carabinier brigade. Here, Ordener shifts the blame to Ney for ordering the charges and for not supporting the attacks with infantry. Despite its bias, the source gives a good graphic account of the charge undertaken by Wattier's division that day:[461]

> Observing how well I executed the command of Ney, General Milhaud confided to me the command of one of his brigades, composed of my regiment and the one I had directed more than once in the campaigns of Austria and Russia: the 7th Cuirassiers.
>
> We had yet to seize at all costs Mont-Saint-Jean, the position on which depended the fate of the battle. The corps of d'Erlon, half destroyed and disorganised, could not do anything more. Napoléon understood, he passed through our ranks, his smile was electric. The enthusiasm was general. Our four beautiful lines were still almost all fresh; they all shook at the same moment to the cry of 'long live the emperor!' I do not know if we find in the history of armies of another example of such a mass of riders rushing to combat. To me, who had taken part in the famous charges of Austerlitz, Jena, Eylau, Friedland and Wagram, I never saw such a scrimmage. We were nearly five thousand horses. Marshal Ney had placed himself at our head. It was now two o'clock.
>
> Our first charge was irresistible. Despite a rain of iron which fell on our helmets and our armour, which was sent by the English batteries which were established behind a ravine, I rode with our front rank. We crowned the crest of the heights, and we went like lightning through the guns, and addressed the English infantry, which fell back in disorder on the squares that were formed in a hurry behind them by the Duke of Wellington.

Colonel Ordener was wounded in the charge. Also wounded that day in the regiment was Squadron-Commander Etienne Patzius, who was shot in the right leg by a musket ball.[462] Squadron-Commander Frederic

---

461 Lot.
462 AN: LH 2068/38.

Pierre Felicite Zephrin Salm-Kirbourg de Renneberg was wounded and made a prisoner of war, being released on 25 November 1815.[463] Lieutenant Antoine Claude Joseph Bernard was wounded four times in the charges he undertook that day. He suffered a gunshot wound to the left hand, and another to the left hip, as well as two sabre cuts to his right arm; the latter no doubt inflicted during a melee with the Allied cavalry.[464] Sub-Lieutenant Joseph Louis Andre Bon, aged just twenty-two at Waterloo, was shot in the right shoulder by a musket ball. He had previously been wounded at the Battle of Hanau on 30 October 1813.[465]

Due to the vagaries of history, principally the semi-destruction of the French Army Archives in 1944 by Nazi soldiers, the regimental muster roll for the regiment is not available to be consulted. However, we have three sources at our disposal regarding losses of the regiment, Firstly, the regimental history of the 1st Cuirassiers lost in total four officers killed, thirteen wounded and 117 men killed, wounded or disappeared. The regiment began the campaign with eighty-one officers and 423 other ranks, and lost 27 per cent of its effective strength at Waterloo. Even so, the regiment still had a theoretical strength of 300 on 19 June. For the men made prisoner of war we have two lists: one partial list of men in England,[466] and as prisoners returned to France.[467] Combined, the records list forty-eight NCOs and men and six officers as prisoners, which means of the 130 men wounded or disappeared, we know the fate of forty-eight, leaving eighty-two unaccounted for as either dead, died from wounds or went missing. The men made prisoners were:

1. Sergeant Antoine Caylo
2. Sergeant Etienne Marat, 6th Company of 2nd Squadron
3. Corporal Charles Grard

---

463 AN: LH 2300/55.

464 AN: LH 194/21.

465 AN: LH 276/60.

466 National Archives, Kew: ADM 103/102 Dartmoor. French prisoners of war, 1815. See also: ADM 103/513 Alphabetical List of prisoners of war, Dartmoor, 1755-1831; ADM 103/99 Dartmoor. French prisoners of war, 1815; ADM 103/311 Plymouth. French prisoners of war, 1815; ADM 103/595 Register of French POWs Released on parole, Okehampton and Oswestry, 1815.

467 SHDDT: Yj 11. See also: SHDDT: Yj 12.

4. Corporal François Michel Massonnet
5. Corporal Jean Fisher[468]
6. Toussaint
7. Joseph Liquet
8. Jean Bordier
9. Alexis Namur
10. François Vincent
11. Jean Clabry
12. Joseph Derick
13. Frederick Dujardin
14. Antoine Deriau
15. Pierre Seliere
16. Joseph Cordin
17. Jean Charles Godard
18. Georges Gaipa
19. Jean Barres
20. Jacques Mouchy
21. Michel Sandino
22. Louise Dreve
23. Barthelemy Aram
24. Florentine Thierry, hospitalised in the 3rd Company of 3rd Squadron
25. Pierre Finance
26. Louis Fordier
27. Jean Guile
28. Etienne Marin
29. Jean Gill
30. David Weille
31. Benjamin Azam
32. Etienne Brun
33. Jean Louis Bordic
34. Antoine Dore
35. Jean Baptiste Dupuis
36. François Danlais

---

468 His Legion of Honour dossier records 'Admitted to service of 2nd Regiment of Cuirassiers, 2 January 1804. Corporal 14 May 1813. Legionnaire 14 May 1813. Passed to 1st Regiment of Cuirassiers 14 March 1814. Made prisoner of war by the English at Mont-Saint-Jean. Discharged 7 February 1817'. Ian Smith personal communication.

37. Napoléon Drouet
38. Jean Guerre
39. Auguste Gauthier
40. Jean Jourdon
41. Jean Julien
42. Pierre Lalovre
43. Jean Mouche
44. François Marie Massonais
45. François Marian
46. François Simon
47. Pierre Vincent
48. Trumpeter Charles Germeyer

Brigaded with the 1st Cuirassiers were the 4th Cuirassiers. Killed in the action were Captain-Adjutant-Major Marchand, Captain Goupil de Prefelin, Captain Lebrun, Sub-Lieutenant Desereinnes and Lieutenant Macrez, who was mortally wounded. Wounded was Squadron-Commander Baron Charles Robert de Morell, who took a gunshot wound to the head.[469] In a melee with the Allied cavalry the following officers were wounded:[470]

- Captains: Pierre François Bailly was wounded with two sabre cuts to the head and one to his face.[471] A similar fate befell Ambroise Ferdinand Versigny, who suffered a sabre cut to the left arm and one to the head.[472] Pierre François Viard, who joined the regiment on 1 July 1814, was wounded as the regiment charged up the slope against the Allied infantry squares.[473]
- Lieutenants: Brousse was wounded with numerous sabre cuts. Joseph Angelloz[474] and Joseph Ridray were slightly wounded when their horses were killed under them, the latter having four horses killed under him during the battle.[475]

---

469 AN: LH 1935/17.
470 Moulins de Rochefort, *Histoire de 4e regiment de Cuirassiers*, Paris, A Lahure, 1897, p. 346.
471 AN: LH 95/50.
472 AN: LH 2696/68.
473 AN: LH 2704/91.
474 AN: LH 38/37.
475 AN: LH 232/74.

- Second-lieutenants: Charles Herbulot suffered a gunshot wound to his right leg.[476] Jean Eloi Horreaux suffered a gunshot to an arm.[477] Amable Ferdinand Joseph Robidet suffered a gunshot to a leg and a sabre cut to the wrist.[478] Roux, Zeppenfeld and Auraux were also all wounded. Reveillon was lightly wounded when his horse was killed under him. One of the officers to escape the campaign with no wounds was Lieutenant Raulet.

In addition, nine other ranks were killed and twenty-nine wounded. Sergeant-Major Memmie Sebastian Brisson, who had joined the regiment on 1 July 1814, suffered a sabre cut to the head. He had served in the 1st Carabiniers from 2 March 1809 and passed to the 13th Cuirassiers in Dresden on 9 February 1814.[479] Sergeant-Major François Honore Hippolyte Reynier, who had served with the regiment since 16 March 1809, was wounded. He suffered five sabre cuts: two to his right arm, one to his left arm, one to his head and a sabre thrust to the right side of his chest.[480]

Corporal-Trumpeter Martin Schmidt, who had served in the regiment since 1803, suffered a sabre cut to the head. Corporal Bernard Gairdt, who had been with the regiment since 12 April 1809, was wounded and made prisoner, as were Trooper Benoit Mortellette, Corporal Amable Joseph Mortellette and Trooper Rio, who had joined the regiment on 9 April 1813. Trumpeter Joseph Guinchier, who served in the 4th Company of 4th Squadron, was wounded and made prisoner along with Trooper Jean Louis Monnel, of the same company, who suffered a sabre cut to the arms.[481] Furthermore, 106 men disappeared—probably captured or killed when their horses were shot under them.[482] By far and away the loss of horses was more crippling to the regiment than the loss of men. Losses of other ranks were as follows:[483]

---

476 AN: LH 1291/25.
477 AN: LH 1308/67.
478 ibid.
479 AN: LH 368/77.
480 AN: LH 2312/270.
481 SHDDT: GR 24 YC 24.
482 de Rochefort, p. 347.
483 SHDDT: GR 24 YC 24.

Squadron	Company	Killed	Died of Wounds	Wounded	Wounded & Missing	Prisoner of War	Missing
1st	1st	0	0	0	7	0	5
	5th	0	2	0	1	0	11
2nd	2nd	3	0	1	0	0	12
	6th	1	0	1	2	0	6
3rd	3rd	0	1	0	4	0	6
	7th	0	0	0	3	0	8
4th	4th	0	0	0	4	0	20
	8th	1	1	1	2	0	17
Total		5	4	3	23	0	85

The regiment began the campaign with fifty-two officers and 286 other ranks, losing 120 other ranks at Waterloo. This represents a loss of 42 per cent of effective strength. The regimental history gives nine men killed, twenty-nine wounded and 106 missing, totalling 144.[484]

Of the men deserted, only one man (Mat No. 188 Pierre Adrien Macron, who had served in the regiment since 22 February 1813 and was a corporal in 8th Company) disappeared with his horse. This suggests that the disappeared men were likely to be prisoners of war, as they were dismounted and not able to keep pace with the regiment during the retreat.[485]

At the head of the 2nd Brigade of the division came the 7th Cuirassiers. Among the officers killed were Lieutenant Forceville and Sub-Lieutenant Thervais. Squadron-Commander Jean Antoine Loup suffered a gunshot to the lower abdomen and had his horse killed under him.[486] Sub-Lieutenant Gervais Hanin suffered a sabre cut to a shoulder.[487] One of the regiment's officers who came away from the field of battle was Major Desmot.[488]

---

484 ibid.

485 ibid.

486 AN: LH 1666/5.

487 AN: LH 1263/65.

488 Jacques Desmot was born at Meuville, on the Department of Calvados, on 2 April 1770. He was admitted into the 12th Chasseurs on 27 January 1789 and promoted to corporal on 1 July 1793, to sergeant later the same year, to sergeant-major in 1799 and to sub-lieutenant later the same year. He was admitted into the chasseurs à cheval of the Consular Guard in 1800,

Among the ranks of 4th Company in 4th Squadron, Sergeant MAT No. 77 Jean Baptitse Gabrielle Cuenier suffered a sabre cut in the Allied counter-attack and Adjutant-Sub-Officer MAT No. 431 Jean Pierre Leblonde had his horse killed under him, as did Trumpeter MAT No. 429 Joseph Erich.[489] Trooper Simon Barbe, who had joined the regiment in 1811 and served in 6th Company, had his horse killed under him and was made prisoner.[490] Casualties for the other ranks were as follows:[491]

Squadron	Company	Killed	Died of Wounds	Wounded	Wounded & Missing	Prisoner of War	Missing
1st	1st	0	0	0	0	0	7
	5th	1	0	0	0	0	3
2nd	2nd	0	0	0	0	0	4
	6th	1	0	0	0	0	10
3rd	3rd	0	0	0	0	0	12
	7th	0	0	0	0	4	4
4th	4th	0	0	1	0	0	14
	8th	1	0	0	0	0	8
Total		3	0	1	0	4	62

The regiment began the campaign with twenty-two officers and 158 other ranks, and lost seventy other ranks at Waterloo. This represents a loss of 44 per cent of effective strength.[492] Of the wounded men, MAT No. 72 Jean Baptiste Gabrielle Cuenier, who had joined the regiment on 18 March 1807, was wounded with a sabre cut to the right buttock. MAT

---

passed to the grenadiers à cheval in 1803 and was promoted to second-lieutenant, being promoted to first-lieutenant in the following year. Following the Battle of Eylau, he was appointed captain on 18 February 1807 before transferring as major of the recently activated 13th Cuirassier regiment then serving in Spain on 16 October 1811. He then passed as major of the 4th Cuirassiers on 16 November 1812 and thence to the 7th Cuirassiers on 16 January 1815. He was awarded the Legion of Honour in 1804 and was made a Knight of the Legion on 14 May 1806. He was discharged from the 7th Cuirassiers on 27 November 1815.

489 SHDDT: GR 24 YC 46 Contrôle Nominatif Troupe 7e Cuirassiers 9 Aout 1814-6 Aout 1815.
490 SHDDT: Yj 11.
491 SHDDT: GR 24 YC 46.
492 ibid.

No. 481 Jean Pierre Leblond, who had joined the regiment on 17 May 1809 and was on the regiment's staff as adjutant-sous-officer, had his horse killed under him.[493]

At the head of the brigaded 12th Cuirassiers was Colonel Thurot, under the orders of General Travers. About Thurot's actions that day, General Milhaud writes in 1815:[494]

> I had the honour to request the rank of marshal-du-camp for M. Colonel Thurot, who after the wounding of Marshal-du-Camp Baron Travers, took command of the brigade composing the 4th and 12th Cuirassiers, who at the head of these brave regiments completely crushed three English squares on the plateau of Waterloo and captured twelve pieces of English artillery at the same moment that the 4th Cavalry Corps took a battery of forty guns and quickly sabred the gunners at their pieces.

In a second letter, General Milhaud adds more details in a letter of 30 November 1831:[495]

> General Thurot had his horse killed under him from three bayonet wounds delivered while charging the front of an English square, which was behind the English artillery pieces that he had captured. General Thurot had not received his promotion demanded by myself and Marshal Ney to the emperor.

During the attack of the 12th Cuirassiers, eighty-five other ranks were killed, wounded, made prisoner or deserted. An additional 150 had been killed, wounded or dismounted at Ligny.[496] The regiment had mustered 234 men and the regimental history lists all men who were wounded, disappeared or killed between 16 and 18 June. However, we cannot check these facts, as the relevant book in the Army Archives at Vincennes which lists the 12th Cuirassiers muster list for 1815 is, at the time of writing in 2017, undergoing conservation and will not be available for consultation until 2020. Prisoners in England were the following men:[497]

---

493 SHDDT: GR 24 YC 46.

494 SHDDT: Dossier Charles Nicolas Thurot. Document 176.

495 SHDDT: Dossier Charles Nicolas Thurot. Document 149.

496 Ruby and de Labeau (*Historique du 12ème Cuirassiers*).

497 National Archives, Kew: ADM 103/102. See also: ADM 103/513; ADM 103/99; ADM 103/311; ADM 103/595. See also: SHDDT: Yj 11; SHDDT:

1. Veterinarian Julien Sigmore
2. Sergeant Nicolas Mathieux
3. Corporal François Seiseigue
4. Corporal Jean Baptiste Tavernier
5. Corporal Marc Matiere
6. Corporal Nicolas Moitheaux
7. Corporal Etienne Charlemagne Gate
8. Jean Pierre Gelinel
9. Pierre Magnien
10. Leonard Goumbin
11. Pierre Boulogne
12. François Vainqueur (*nom de geurre*)
13. François Dermusier
14. Leonard Goubin
15. François Lourc
16. Jean Baptiste Jeavahnier
17. Pierre Boulogne
18. Pierre Beune
19. François Baingeurs
20. François Demoulle
21. Louis Guieux
22. Theodore Draise
23. François Julien
24. Jean Moitieux
25. Claude François Moselle
26. Jean Schalder
27. Jean Baptiste Teavaguir
28. Jean Louis L'hostis

This leaves the whereabouts of fifty-six men not accounted for at Waterloo, which presumably includes the dead, mortally wounded and deserted.

Officers killed included Captain Meneret and the Second-Lieutenants Marechaux and Desavoye. Wounded were Captain François Joseph Pfister,[498] and Lieutenants Gérard and Morin.[499] Furthermore, Second-Lieutenant Paulin Nicolas Regnonval de Courcelle was wounded. He

---

Yj 12; SHDDT: Yj 13.

498 AN: LH 21.38/25.

499 Rene Louis Gustave de Place, *Historique de 12e Cuirassiers (1688 to 1888)*, Paris, A. Lahure, 1889, p. 127.

had served in the Empress Dragoons of the Imperial Guard from 8 June 1808 until joining the regiment on 8 February 1813.[500] Thurot, despite having a horse killed under him, managed to make it back to the French lines, where he was presented by Ney to the emperor for promotion, but this rank was not awarded until 1831.

---

500 AN: LH 228/72.

Chapter 11

Delort's 14th Cavalry Division

General-of-Division Marie Joseph Raymond Delort, commander of the 14th Division of General Milhaud's 4th Cavalry Division, recalls that:[501]

> The intrepid cuirassiers of the divisions of Vattier and Delort continued their success, charged and broke a square of the English guards and covered the ground with dead, but they could not, because of the terrain, enjoy all the benefits of these brilliant charges in which fourrier Isaac Pallan, of the 9th Cuirassiers, and Sergeant Aubert, of the 10th Cuirassiers, each carried off a flag.

> They were forced to fall back a few paces by the two divisions of English cavalry which wheeled about, and which were forced to seek their salvation under the protection of their infantry. But, placed at the end of the great plateau where they were exposed to the fire of the whole English army, there became an urgent need to strengthen the body of cuirassiers of Lieutenant-General Kellermann with the divisions of Roussel d'Hurbal and the division of the cavalry of the Imperial Guard commanded by General Lefèbvre-Desnoëttes. This cavalry reunited after having attacked several squares, sabred thousands of foot soldiers and repeatedly rejected all charges of the English cavalry, supported by only a few battalions and all the repeated efforts of the English army. General Lhéritier fell severely wounded by a shot through the body; the chief-of-staff of General Milhaud was killed. Lieutenant-General Milhaud and Delort had several horses killed under them, their clothes and hats were riddled with bullets. The latter again injured by a shot and several sabre cuts. Almost all the senior officers were knocked out, the dead litter the ground on which the cavalry is placed, but his heroic constancy cannot be shaken by the multiple charges of the English cavalry or by the

---

501 *Nouvelle Revue Retrospective*, Paris, January 1897, p. 374.

terrible fire of artillery and musketry that faced them. In consequence of the backward movement they had to make, it compromised the French army, and 10,000 elite cavaliers surged forward, and for three hours when death was all around them, they maintained themselves in the face of the English on the ground they endeavoured to conquer. Arguably our military annals perhaps do not record such devotion in the midst of such memorable prodigies of courage by French soldiers.

At the head of the 1st Brigade were the 5th Cuirassiers. The 5th Cuirassiers lost a total of two officers killed, one died of wounds and twelve wounded; twenty other ranks were also killed. Colonel Gobert was wounded. He died of his injuries on 1 February 1816. Also wounded was Captain-Adjutant-Major Jean de Brouville, who suffered a gunshot wound to the left leg.[502] The paperwork for the 5th Cuirassiers is preserved in the Army Archives at Vincennes; however its state of conservation at the time of writing is such that it won't be available for consultation until the year 2020. Therefore, the loss of twenty men recorded in the regiment's history is all we can suggest as losses for Waterloo. If this figure is accurate it is a lot higher than the losses of the 10th Cuirassiers, which is perhaps not unexpected, as the regiment was at the head of the brigade when it charged. Prisoners in England from the regiment were:[503]

1. Sous-Lieutenant Duchambon
2. Pierre Chareau
3. Charles Hoeshe
4. François Claude Serva
5. Andre Sabellion
6. Jean Stansilas Vaillant
7. Charles Maconosky
8. Vincent Cudile
9. Rene LeCoq
10. Jean Michel Merrieux
11. Nicolas Arnout
12. Charles Hache
13. Vincent Houdel
14. Bernard Picarre

---

502 AN: LH 376/26.
503 National Archives, Kew: ADM 103/102. See also: ADM 103/513; ADM 103/99; ADM 103/311; ADM 103/595; SHDDT: Yj 11; SHDDT: Yj 12; SHDDT: Yj 13.

15. Nicolas Marie Suvrou
16. Andre Tabillion

Behind came the 10th Cuirassiers. Officers killed in this regiment at Waterloo were Squadron-Commander Dijon and Lieutenant Collin. Furthermore, ten officers were wounded:[504]

- Captains: François Louis Guinet (with a gunshot to the right leg)[505] and Magnien.
- Captain-adjutant-majors: Jean Ferdinand Fere had a gunshot to the kidneys, having passed through his cuirass. He had joined the regiment on 6 August 1814 and had served in the grenadiers à cheval of the Imperial Guard from 6 July 1806 to 17 February 1811.[506]
- Lieutenants: Amand Antoine Scherb had joined the regiment in 1804 and took two gunshot wounds: one to the chest, one to the left shoulder. He retired from the army with the rank of general.[507] Chandebois and Pierre François Aubert were wounded, the latter with a sabre cut to the head.
- Second-lieutenants: Seguin, Hiacynthe Adnet (who was shot in the neck by a musket ball), Collas and Rousseau were all wounded.

Casualties for the 10th Cuirassiers at Waterloo were as follows:[508]

10th Cuirassiers						
Squadron	Company	Killed	Died of Wounds	Wounded	Prisoner of War	Missing
1st	1st	1	0	1	2	6
	5th	2	0	0	2	6
2nd	2nd	1	0	0	1	3
	6th	0	0	0	2	1
3rd	3rd	1	0	0	3	7
	7th	1	0	0	1	5
4th	4th	0	0	0	0	6
	8th	0	0	0	0	2
Total		6	0	1	11	36

---

504 Georges Guimet de Juzancourt, *Historique de 10e regiment de Cuirassiers (1643-1891)*, Paris, Berger-Levrault, 1893, p. 88.
505 AN: LH 1245/18.
506 AN: LH 1034/42.
507 AN: LH 2476/74.
508 SHDDT: GR 24 YC 60 *Contrôle Nominatif Troupe 10e Cuirassiers 15 Avril 1815 a 27 Juillet 1815 organisation 1814.*

On the morning of 10 June 1815, the regiment had thirty-six officers and 327 other ranks. The regiment lost fifty-four men at Waterloo, representing 16 per cent of effective strength. It is likely three times this number of horses were killed or wounded. Even so, the regiment still had over 300 men on the morning of 19 June.[509]

At one stage in the attack, the regiment clearly got very close to breaking into a square, as General Delort records that Sergeant Aubert took a colour from an Allied square.[510] Alas, we do not know which colour was taken.

Vial's 2nd Brigade had the 6th Cuirassiers at its head. Charging at the front of the 6th Cuirassiers was Colonel Jean Baptiste Isidore Martin, who suffered a gunshot wound to the right arm. The wound was so serious that he had to have the arm amputated the same day in the field hospital.[511] Squadron-Commander Philippe Pierre Kelh, who had joined the regiment on 1 August 1814, having previously served in the 1st and 3rd Hussars since 1792, had two horses killed under him.[512] Squadron-Commander Tilly was also wounded.[513] Company officers who were wounded in the campaign were:[514]

- Captain-Adjutant-Major Denis Pierre Alexis Arbey had a horse shot from under him at Ligny and Waterloo;[515]
- Captain Jacques Christophe Maurlaz was shot in the lower left arm;[516]
- Captain Leopold Yung[517] had a horse killed under him at Waterloo;[518]

---

509 SHDDT: GR24 YC 60.
510 *Nouvelle Revue Retrospective*, Paris, January 1897, p. 374.
511 *Carnet de la Sabretache*, 1908, p. 185. See also: *Carnet de la Sabretache*, 1908, pp. 65 and 181.
512 AN: LH 1395/52.
513 P. Brye, *Historique du 6e regiment de Cuirassiers*, 1893, p. 251.
514 Brye, p. 251.
515 AN: LH 45/36.
516 AN: LH 1772/3.
517 Leopold Yung was born at Forbach in the Moselle on 12 January 1778. He entered the service of the 1st Chasseurs à Cheval on 28 September 1796, was admitted to the grenadiers à cheval on 13 October 1801 and promoted thence to corporal on 17 April 1813, to sergeant on 22 December 1805 and then to second-lieutenant on 25 June 1809. Following the Russian campaign, he was made captain in the 6th Cuirassiers on 9 February 1813. He left the army on 21 November 1815. He had a horse killed under him at Waterloo.
518 SHDDT: GR 30 YC 61.

- Lieutenant Vernet;
- Sub-Lieutenant Corneille Joseph Frankard was wounded when his horse was killed under him; and
- Sub-Lieutenant Louis Bignault was wounded when his horse was shot under him.

Other ranks killed were:[519]

- Sergeants: Boulanger and Durand.
- Corporals: Bardy.
- Troopers: Lavergue, Neuilles, Samper, Crosnier, Payen, Godard, Poncet, Jeammes, Rambaud, Favre, Keunts, Midy, Breban, Derab, Wagner, Muller, Hess, Heurion, Debout, Guerpel, Defaut, Boouvet, Klain, Gay, Faure, Petitand Grandjean.

Other ranks wounded were:[520] Sergeant-Major Legrand, Sergeant-Major Jean Louis Solable (with a gunshot)[521] and Corporal Dutertre.

The regiment's muster list presents the following losses, albeit at odds with the regimental history which lists thirty killed and three wounded:[522]

6th Cuirassiers				
Squadron	Killed	Died of Wounds	Wounded	Missing
1st	2	2	3	12
2nd	2	0	0	7
3rd	1	1	1	10
4th	0	0	2	5
Total	5	3	6	34

On the morning of 10 June 1815, the regiment fielded twenty-two officers and 263 men. At Ligny, twelve men had been lost. At Waterloo of the 251 other ranks under arms, 19 per cent of the effective strength was lost, some forty-eight men.[523]

Behind the 6th came the 9th Cuirassiers. Trooper Pilloy, who served in 2nd Company, writes on 24 June 1815 about his experiences at Waterloo:[524]

---

519 Brye, p. 311.
520 Brye, p. 311.
521 AN: LH 2531/70.
522 SHDDT: GR 24 YC 41. Research undertaken by Miss S. Fairweather.
523 SHDDT: GR 24 YC 41.
524 *Carnet de la Sabretache*, 1907, pp. 513-15.

On 17 June, I was one of twenty men ordered to escort General Delort. In a moment, on the 18th, he left us off at full gallop and I have not seen him since. At the time, I found myself greatly embarrassed, not knowing where to find my regiment. The 5th Regiment was, in my view, ready to charge on a battalion square of the English. Unwisely, I put myself in their ranks, we charged three times and it was only during the third charge that we were able to enter the square. You can believe that a great number of cuirassiers and horses remained on the field. I retired; and shortly after, I saw that our regiment was about to charge the English dragoons, so I am yet to find my party. We charged three times and we put them to flight. You can believe me that my poor horse was exhausted. It is also good to tell you that due to the heavy rain which had fallen during the night of 16th to 17th our horses were continually in the mud up to their bellies.

In the charges, Captain Jean Baptiste Guillaume Marie Bourdon took a gunshot wound to the left thigh and was captured when his horse was killed under him.[525] The 9th Cuirassiers at some stage in the day's fighting were counter-charged by Allied cavalry. In this melee Lieutenant Jean Antoine Victor Marcelin Julia suffered two sabre cuts to the head.[526] The numbers of other ranks lost at Waterloo were as follows:[527]

9th Cuirassiers						
Squadron	Company	Killed	Died of Wounds	Wounded	Prisoner of War	Missing
1st	1st	1	0	0	2	11
	5th	0	0	0	0	10
2nd	2nd	3	0	0	0	7
	6th	1	0	0	1	6
3rd	3rd	0	0	0	0	8
	7th	2	0	0	5	2
4th	4th	1	0	0	0	4
	8th	0	0	0	0	2
Total		8	0	0	8	50

---

525 AN: LH 325/44.

526 AN: LH 1387/57.

527 SHDDT: GR 24 YC 55.

On 10 June 1815, the regiment had thirty-four officers and 378 other ranks. It lost sixty-six men at Waterloo, representing 17 per cent of effective strength. The regiment, however, at the time of its disbandment records that a total of 363 men had left the regiment without authorisation since 18 June for as yet 'unknown reasons'. This number no doubts includes losses from Waterloo and men lost in the rout, retreat and who had quit the army with the return of the king.[528]

Captured colours

As an unknown officer comments, the 9th Cuirassiers took an Allied colour at Waterloo. General Delort tells us the colour was taken by Fourrier Isaac Palaa.[529] General Milhaud writes on 11 July 1815 that Fourrier Isaac Palaa 'with great valour he captured a flag from inside an English square on the battle of the 18th'. The regiment's muster list records the following details about Palaa:[530]

> MAT No. 193 Isaac Palaa. Son of Andre and Marie Sauvier, born 23 October 1788 at Orthez in the department of the Bass Pyrenees. He stood 1.76 metres tall. Admitted to the army 10 July 1807, passed to the 2nd Carabiniers 10 July 1807, and was taken into the 13th Cuirassiers on 21 October 1808. Promoted corporal 10 July 1813, fourrier 1 March 1814. He had been wounded on 23 November 1808. Passed to the 9th Cuirassiers 9 August 1814. Struck off from the regiment 26 November 1815. He served in 1st Company, 1st Squadron.

The discharge papers for Isaac Palaa tell us he was made sergeant-major on 21 July 1815. Colonel Bigarne, commanding the 9th Cuirassiers, writes on 22 October 1815 that Palaa was:[531]

> Wounded with a gunshot to the head and a lance thrust to the left arm at the Battle of Tudella in Spain, October 1809. He also had a horse killed under him at the same affair, and another on 18 June 1815.

> Monsieur Palaa is a soldier of great zeal, courage and bravery, and I had proposed him to be [promoted to] officer and made Knight of the Legion of Honour for his conduct on the battlefield.

---

528 SHDDT: Xc 110 9e Cuirassiers.
529 *Nouvelle Revue Retrospective*, Paris, January 1897, p. 374.
530 SHDDT: GR 24 YC 55.
531 Ian Smith personal communication, 18 October 2016.

It seems that Palaa broke into an Allied square at Waterloo, captured a colour and had had his horse killed under him. It seems the unknown officer who writes about this episode provided Palaa with a horse, so he could retreat with the rest of the regiment with the colour. The colour was handed to Marshal Grouchy on 26 June 1815.[532]

Allied response

Captain Batty, of the 1st Regiment of Foot Guards, narrates that:[533]

> The enemy, having gained the orchard, commenced their desperate charges of cavalry under cover of the smoke which the burning houses, etc. had caused; the whole of which the wind drifted towards us, and thus prevented our observing their approach. At this period the battle assumed a character beyond description... Buonaparte was about to use against us an arm, which he had never yet wielded but with success. Confidently relying upon the issue of this attack, he charged our artillery and infantry, hoping to capture the one, and break the other, and, by instantly establishing his own infantry on the heights, to carry the Brussels road, and throw our line into confusion. These cavalry, selected for their tried gallantry and skill (not their height or mustachios), who were the terror of Northern Europe, and had never yet been foiled, were first brought up by the 3rd Battalion of the 1st Regiment. Never was British valour and discipline so pre-eminent as on this occasion; the steady appearance of this battalion caused the famous cuirassiers to pull up; and a few of them, with a courage worthy of a better cause, rode out of the ranks and fired at our people and mounted officers with their pistols, hoping to make the face of the square throw its fire upon them, and thus become an easy prey: but our men, with a steadiness no language can do justice to, defied their efforts, and did not pull a single trigger. The French then made a sudden rush, but were received in such a manner, and with a volley so well directed, as at once to turn them; they then made an attempt on the 2nd Battalion, and the Brunswickers, with similar success; and, astonished at their own failure, the cool intrepidity of their opponents, and the British cheers, they faced about. This same game was played in succession by the Imperial Horse Guards, and Polish Lancers, none of whom could at all succeed in breaking

---

532 SHDDT: C15 5. Letter dated 26 June 1815.
533 Booth, pp. lvi-lvii.

our squares, or making the least impression upon them whatever. During their attacks, our cavalry rushed out from between the squares, and carried havoc through the enemy's ranks, which were nearly all destroyed. I cannot here resist relating an anecdote of Major Lloyd, of the artillery, who, with another officer, (whose name I could not learn) was obliged to take refuge in our square at the time these charges were made, being unable to continue longer at their posts. There was a gun between our battalion and the Brunswickers, which had been drawn back; this, Major Lloyd with his friend discharged five or six times at the French cavalry, alternately loading it and retiring to the square, as circumstances required. We could see the French knocked off their horses as fast as they came up, and one cannot refuse to call them men of singular gallantry; one of them, indeed, an officer of Imperial Guards, seeing a gun about to be discharged at his companions, rode at it and never suffered its fire to be repeated while he lived. He was at length killed by a Brunswick rifleman, and certainly saved a large part of his regiment by this act of self-devotion.

Macready, of the 30th Regiment of Foot, recalls:[534]

In a few minutes after, the enemy's cavalry galloped up and crowned the crest of our position. Our guns were abandoned, and they formed between the two brigades, about a hundred paces in our front. Their first charge was magnificent. As soon as they quickened their trot into a gallop, the cuirassiers bent their heads, so that the peaks of their helmets looked like visors, and they seemed cased in armour from the plume to the saddle. Not a shot was fired till they were within thirty yards, when the word was given, and our men fired away at them. The effect was magical. Through the smoke, we could see helmets falling, cavaliers starting from their seats with convulsive springs as they received our balls, horses plunging and rearing in the agonies of fright and pain, and crowds of the soldiery dismounted, part of the squadron in retreat, but the more daring remainder backing their horses to force them on our bayonets. Our fire soon disposed of these gentlemen. The main body re-formed in our front and rapidly and gallantly repeated their attacks. In fact, from this time (about four o'clock) till near six, we had a constant repetition of these brave, but unavailing, charges. There was no difficulty in repulsing them, but our ammunition decreased alarmingly. At length, an artillery wagon galloped up,

---

534 *United Service Magazine*, 1852.

emptied two or three casks of cartridges into the square, and we were all comfortable.

An anonymous officer writes to his parents on 22 June about the battle thus:[535]

> At noon on the 18th the French made the most desperate attack with artillery, cavalry and tirailleurs ever witnessed. Our defence was equally terrible. The whole line was formed in squares and battalions; not one man fell back; the whole stood firm. The French cavalry repeatedly attacked echelon of squares after echelon, and were repulsed ten or eleven times with immense loss. Our squares stood in the face of shot, shells, and everything else; which caused great destruction, without our being able to return a shot.

Against the French cuirassiers of Milhaud's 4th Cavalry Corps came the Allied cavalry. Its charge is brought to life by Edward Cotton, who narrates over twenty years later that:[536]

> The fire of the enemy's artillery had been continued with great vigour; it was now increased upon that part of our position which was between the two high-roads. Our squares, which were lying down behind the crest of the ridge and could not be seen by the enemy, were protected in a great degree from the round and grape-shot, but not from the shells, which were bestowed upon them most liberally. They sometimes fell among us with great effect. Those missiles may be both seen and heard as they approach; so that by keeping a look-out many lives were saved; the ground too was so saturated with rain that the shells in some instances sunk beneath the surface, and bursting threw up mud and sand, which were comparatively harmless. The oldest soldier, however, had never witnessed so furious a cannonade. The duke, writing to Lord Beresford, says, 'I never saw such a pounding match'. The havoc was dreadful in the extreme, for some considerable time before the impetuous Ney came on with his grand cavalry attack, made by forty squadrons. On their right, close to La Haye Sainte, were the cuirassiers; then the lancers and chasseurs à cheval of the Imperial Guard. They advanced in lines, *en echelons*, their left reaching nearly to the east hedge of Hougoumont.

---

535 Booth, p. 49.
536 Cotton, pp. 74-6.

As those on the right neared the ridge, their artillery discontinued firing; and ours opened with grape, canister and shrapnel shells, which rattled like hail on the steel-clad warriors; but they still pressed on, regardless of our fire, towards the guns, the horses— which had been sent to the rear. Every discharge (the load was usually double) threw them into great disorder; but excited by the trumpets sounding the charge, they rode up to the cannons' mouths, shouting, 'vive l'Empereur!'

Our gunners fled to the squares, which were all ranged in chequer; the front ones had advanced again nearly close to the guns. The French, not perceiving the advantage which the squares afforded the gunners, and imagining that they had captured the guns, shouted out in triumph, and then crossed over the ridge; here they were assailed by a rolling fire from our squares, which were all prepared, the front ranks on the right knee, the next rank at the charge.

When the cuirassiers had passed over the ridge, they were out of sight of the lancers and chasseurs, who immediately pressed on to share in the contest. Our artillery received them in a similar manner; some of the men rushing back to their guns, and after discharging them at the foe, taking shelter again within the squares, or under the guns. The firing produced a much greater effect upon such of the enemy's cavalry as were not protected by the cuirass and casque; consequently their ranks were much more disordered than were the cuirassiers'; still they pursued their onward course, passed the guns, raised a shout and swept round the squares. Some halted and fired their pistols at the officers in the squares; others would ride close up, and either cut at the bayonet or try to lance the outside files. No sooner had the broken squadrons passed the guns, than the gunners were again at their post, and the grape rattled upon the retiring hosts; but frequently, before a succeeding round could be discharged, the hostile cavalry were again upon them, and compelled them to seek shelter.

During the cavalry attacks, those of the enemy were at one time on the Allied position, riding about among our squares for three-quarters of an hour; all cannonading having ceased between the two high-roads.

When the enemy's squadrons became broken and disordered, our cavalry, who were kept in hand till the favourable moment, again attacked them and drove them down the slope, often following too far, by which they burned their fingers, and likewise prevented our gunners from keeping up a constant fire.

Our position was scarcely free from the enemy's cavalry, before their numerous artillery began to ply us again with shells and round-shot. After the first cavalry charges, our infantry squares, finding the odds in their favour, gained confidence, and it was soon evident they considered the enemy's cavalry attacks as a relief, and far more agreeable than their furious cannonade, which was invariably suspended on their attacking force crowning our ridge. I am confident, from what I saw and heard; as during as well as after the battle, that most of our British infantry would rather, when in squares, have the enemy's cavalry among them than remain exposed to the fire of artillery. The 1st Foot-Guards had the enemy's cavalry on every side of their squares several times, and beat them off. Our squares often wheeled up into line, to make their fire more destructive: on this, the cuirassiers would suddenly wheel round to charge; but our infantry were instantly in square, and literally indulged in laughter at the disappointment and discomfiture of their gallant opponents. Throughout the day our squares presented a serried line of bristling bayonets, through which our enemy's cavalry could not break. Had the enemy made their attacks throughout with infantry and cavalry combined, the result must have been much more destructive; for, although squares are the best possible formation against cavalry, there can be nothing worse to oppose infantry. I am not aware of any parallel to the extraordinary scene of warfare now going forward: most of our infantry were in squares, and the enemy's cavalry of every description riding about among them as if they had been our own, for which, but for their armour and uniforms, they might have been mistaken.

The Guard light cavalry

At some stage, the light cavalry of the Imperial Guard was sucked into Ney's charges. de Brack, of the Regiment of Light Horse Lancers of the Imperial Guard, narrates the charge of his regiment as he recalled it in the 1830s, no doubt with the benefit of hindsight:[537]

From that moment, lining up to the left, we crossed the road diagonally so as to have the whole Guard cavalry on the left of

---

537 Digby Smith personal communication, 2010.

this road. We crossed the flat ground, climbed up the slope of the plateau upon which the English army was drawn up, and attacked together.

The order in which that army was drawn up, or the part exposed to our view was as follows: to its right were the Scots Foot, close to the undergrowth which extended to the bottom of the slope. This infantry delivered heavy and well directed fire. Then came the squares of the infantry, offered in a chequer board pattern, then similar squares of Hanoverian light infantry; then a fortified farm. Between the squares were uncoupled batteries, whose gunners were firing and then hiding under their guns, behind them some infantry and some cavalry.

We were nearly level with this farm, between which and us, our cuirassiers were charging. We rode through the batteries which we were unable to drag back with us. We turned back and threatened the squares, which put a most honourable resistance. Some of them had such coolness that they were still firing ordered volleys by rank.

It has been said that the dragoons and grenadiers à cheval to our left broke several squares; personally, I did not see it—and I can state that we lancers did not have the same luck, and that we crossed our lances with the English bayonets in vain. Many of our troopers threw their weapons like spears into the front ranks to try and open the squares. The expenditure of ammunition by the English front line and the compact pattern of the squares which composed it meant that the firing was at point blank range, but it was the harm which the artillery and squares in the second line were doing to us, in the absence of infantry and artillery to support our attack, which determined our retreat. We moved slowly and faced front again in our position at the bottom of the slope, so that we could just make out the first English line.

It was then that Marshal Ney, alone, without a single member of staff accompanying him, rode along our front and harangued us, calling out to the officers he knew by their names. His face was distracted, and he cried out again and again: 'Frenchmen, let us stand firm! It is here that the key to our freedom is lying!' I quote him word-for-word.

Five times we repeated the charge; but since the conditions remained unchanged, we returned to our position at the rear five times. There at 150 paces from the enemy infantry, we were exposed to the most murderous fire. Our men began to lose heart. They were being hit at the same time by bullets from the front and by cannon balls from the flank, and by new projectiles, which exploded over their heads and fell. These were shrapnel shells and we had not come against them before.

At last a battery of the Guard was sent over to support us, but instead of light artillery, it belonged to the foot artillery of the reserve of 12-pounders. It had the utmost difficulty in moving forward through the mud and only took up position behind us after endless delay. Its first shots were so badly aimed, that they blew away a complete troop of our own regiment.

A movement to the rear was ordered. We carried this out at ordinary pace and formed up again behind the battery. The chasseurs à cheval, dragoons and grenadiers à cheval extended their movement further and took up position in echelon a short distance behind and to the left of us.

The English cavalry advanced on and off to follow us, but as soon as they came up to our line they stopped, respecting our lances above all—the long lances intimidated them. They were limited to firing their pistols at us before retiring behind their infantry line, which made no move. Then a voluntary truce was reached between the combatants due to the complete exhaustion of the troops. Half our squadrons dismounted in musket range.

Sergeant-Major Chevalier,[538] of the chasseurs à cheval of the Imperial Guard, notes:[539]

It was only four o'clock in the evening and the victory seemed decidedly won, the English army was sabred by our cavalry, and fled in all directions in an appalling rout, throwing themselves in disorder on the road to Brussels. Caissons, artillery, baggage, cavalry, infantry, wounded, etc. everything tumbling pell-mell.

---

538 Chevalier was born on 23 June 1780 at Versailles. He enlisted into the 7th Battalion of Marine Artillery on 22 March 1795 and passed to the 9th Chasseurs à Cheval on 10 February 1801 before being promoted to corporal on 10 September 1802, to sergeant on 21 January 1806 and then admitted to the chasseurs à cheval of the Imperial Guard on 3 November 1808. He was then promoted to corporal on 15 June 1810, to quartermaster-corporal on 25 November 1811 and to sergeant-major on 27 January 1813. He remained with the regiment in 1814 and was discharged on 1 November 1815.

539 Chevalier, p. 323.

Officers and soldiers alike all fled, the English army appeared entirely lost...General Lefèbvre-Desnoëttes, who commanded our regiment and the lancers, led us forward. We sabred the English squares and removed several pieces of cannon. In an instant, everything was tumbling back and we were masters of the plateau of Mont-Saint-Jean and the enemy fled on all points in a rout. It was six o'clock, we had triumphed over all obstacles and we sang victory, but Napoléon did not think so.

'Here is a premature movement which could be costly to us, it is too early by an hour, but we must support what is started.'

The emperor sent Kellermann's cuirassiers to support us, they moved at a gallop to shouts of 'vive l'Empereur'.

By mid-afternoon the only intact heavy cavalry force Wellington had to face down the scores of French cuirassiers were the Dutch carabiniers. The regiments had been formed for a year, and this was to be their first combat. Many of the men had served previously in Napoléon's armies, often as cuirassiers, so they knew well enough how to handle their sabres. Lieutenant-Colonel Baron van Heerdt, who was on the staff of the 1st Cavalry Brigade, notes that the brigade of de Ghigny was moved to the centre of the Allied position. He writes as follows about the French charge and the Allied counter-charge:[540]

Towards three o'clock in the afternoon General Ghigny received the order from a British adjutant to move his brigade to the centre of the position, where at that moment the battle raged furiously; a destructive fire, and each moment cavalry charges succeeded each other, which had the most devastating effect; despite the strong defence, the position seemed about to be overwhelmed. The brigade placed itself in two lines, the 4th Light Dragoons in the first and the 8th Hussars with one squadron from the 4th Dragoons in the second between squares of British and Nassau troops, who had already driven back several French cavalry charges.

Opposite the brigade was an imposing mass of cavalry, composed of cuirassiers, lancers and chasseurs of the Imperial Guard; the cannonade and musketry was continuous and well nourished. HRH the Prince of Orange galloped along our front and he exclaimed towards General de Ghigny: 'General Ghigny, fîtes charger' and then he put himself at the head of the Nassau regiments. As a result of the

---

540 Franklin, Vol. 1, p. 159.

orders issued, the brigade advanced at a trot up to the ridge of the plateau, the French cavalry (if I am not mistaken) consisting of the 5th and 12th Cuirassiers commanded by General Travers, fell back, probably to incite the brigade to charge, which would have led into disaster as its flanks were threatened by chasseurs and lancers of the Imperial Guard. It was at this moment that the brave and honourable Lieutenant-Colonel Renno was obliged to leave the field due to a wound in his leg and the command of the 4th Light Dragoon Regiment devolved upon Major von Staedel.

Doherty, of the 13th Light Dragoons, writes thus about the lancers:[541]

From this time until I suppose about one or two o'clock they remained under a heavy fire of artillery, when the 13th were again ordered across the road, and remained in the hollow for about an hour. They were then for the first time called upon to act, and re-crossing the road moved up to the crest of the position, and formed in line, opposed to a line of French heavy dragoons, which were immediately charged and routed. On returning after the charge, the regiment re-formed in rear of the columns of infantry, and again moved halfway up towards the top of the position, when a large column of French cavalry appeared in front of our left squadron, which they immediately charged in the most gallant manner, commanded by Captain Gregory, and checked their advance, and [they] were subsequently obliged to retire, I suppose from seeing the force of cavalry ready at hand to support the left squadron. On arriving at the crest of the position the 13th were again opposed to the enemy's cavalry, and forced them back, and afterwards retired under the brow of the position, where they remained for a short time. The 13th again moved and retook a brigade of guns that had been momentarily taken by the enemy, and after driving back the enemy's cavalry the regiment again retired to their former position. It was at this period that Lieutenant-Colonel Dalrymple, of the 15th Hussars, lost his leg, and the same cannon shot that struck him also passed through the body of Sir C. Grant's horse. The officers of the 13th and 15th were almost all assembled together and talking to Sir C. Grant, when the ball bounded from the top of the hill and came into the midst of them. Not long after this the 13th were again called upon, and on advancing in line up the position, Lord Anglesey and Lord Hill were observed by the regiment, the latter with his hat off, cheering them forward, and on reaching the crest of the position, the centre squadron of the 13th, commanded by the late Major Doherty,

541 Siborne, *Waterloo Letters*, No. 66.

found itself opposed to a strong column or square of infantry. The cheering cry of their old general, Lord Hill, 'at them, my old friends, the 13th,' was quite sufficient, and instantly the centre squadron dashed into them, and completely upset them, dispersed them, and with the assistance of the rest of the regiment nearly annihilated them. This slaughter continued until a regiment of Polish lancers on our left, and a regiment of cuirassiers in our front came to their assistance, which obliged the 13th to retire, and which they only did at the last moment, and then retreated in rear of two squares of infantry, one of which was composed of the German Legion, and as Sir C. Grant's horse was wounded, he was obliged to enter the square for safety. The cuirassiers and lancers suffered severely from the fire of the infantry, and as soon as the 13th Dragoons were again reformed, and finding the enemy's cavalry so much broken from the fire of the infantry, they again advanced and pursued and cut down the enemy's cavalry as far as they could prudently follow, when they again retired under cover of the position.

In the attacks, the chasseurs à cheval came against the 1st Brigade of the King's German Legion, part of which was deployed as skirmishers. As the chasseurs à cheval advanced, the Lüneburg Light Battalion was brought up in support. The Hanoverians were thrown into confusion and a colour was captured by Captain Klein.[542] Leopold von Rettberg, of the 1st Line Battalion King's German Legion, notes:[543]

Towards three o'clock the brigade received the order to advance to the left and, after we marched forward some hundred paces, to form battalion squares. In this formation we advanced towards the masses of the enemy cavalry which had pushed our own cavalry back. The enemy appeared ready to charge, but as we advanced calmly, they turned around and retired without waiting to be fired upon. After this we attacked the height immediately in front (being the original position of the centre of the right flank), where the enemy's troops had taken possession of our cannon [the attack by the 100th Regiment of Line Infantry?]; the guns were quickly recovered. It was now that several strong enemy infantry columns, supported by cavalry, violently attacked the position occupied by our cannon. The enemy infantry advanced to within thirty or forty paces of our square, beneath the fire of our artillery. Colonel

542 Ronald Pawly, *Napoléon's Mounted Chasseurs of the Imperial Guard*, Osprey, Oxford, 2008, p. 44.

543 John Franklin personal communication, 30 June 2012.

Robertson, our commander, fell severely wounded from his horse at this moment, because the enemy's fire was most efficient. Fortunately we received the order to attack; we charged in square, drove the enemy back in complete disorder and repelled an attack by lancers [the famed Red Lancers of the Imperial Guard], who themselves sustained severe losses. The enemy infantry retired into the wood at Hougoumont, where it took position along the edge of a ditch and with a deadly musket fire inflicted heavy losses upon us. The enemy lancers and dragoons threatened us incessantly and did not retire until they had suffered significant losses. The 2nd Line Battalion, along with a number of other troops, entered the wood at this time and saved us from incurring any further losses from the enemy.

While our front and right flank, which had been exposed to the fire from the enemy's infantry, was almost completely disordered, new masses of enemy cavalry appeared; the 3rd Line Battalion, which had initially been beside us, was ordered to join with us and together we formed a single square. This movement had hardly been accomplished when the carabiniers of the Imperial Guard [sic] (as we later discovered from the wounded prisoners) formed on our left, which fortunately was our strongest flank, at a distance of 150 to 200 paces and rode at the trot, galloped and then charged in our direction, however this was received by our men in the calmest and most cold-blooded manner possible, at a distance of between thirty and thirty-five paces the cavalry was subjected to two volleys of emphatic musket fire, which rendered a great number of these beautiful troops either killed or wounded, while the rest passed hastily in front of us and reformed out of range of our fire, only to be repulsed further by the well maintained cannon fire, mostly of canister from the battery commander, by Sympher.

At some stage in the action, the chasseurs à cheval were fired upon by artillery. Trooper Jean Louis Quartier, who was born in 1771 and joined the regiment in 1801, graphically relates:[544]

At the Battle of Waterloo, 18 June 1815, I charged with my regiment onto the plateau of Mont-Saint-Jean under a hail of cannon balls and shot. My horse's head was pulped by a cannon ball. The remains of my horse's head smashed into my face, and as a result I lost my left eye.

---

544 Collection of Ian Smith.

Trooper Jean Philippe Jouanne, who was born on 6 February 1785 at Beaumont and had joined the chasseurs à cheval of the Imperial Guard on 2 May 1812, writes:[545]

> I was made a member of the Legion of Honour on 30 April 1815, and I wore the medal during the Hundred Days. I lost both the medal and the brevet on the field of Waterloo when my horse was killed. I was not able to retrieve my portmanteaux which remained attached to my horse where it fell. I was lucky to escape from being trapped by the horse and being trampled by the hooves of the cavalry.

Among the ranks of the chasseurs was Sergeant Henry Dayet. He was one of the few black soldiers involved in the fighting that day. He was born at Port-au-Prince in Saint Dominica on 6 January 1785. He arrived from the colonies with his father, Jean Claude Dayet, in 1791 and entered the 21st Chasseurs à Cheval in 1805. He was promoted to corporal on 12 July 1808, to sergeant on 20 March 1810, to sergeant-major on 21 January 1813, admitted to the chasseurs à cheval of the Imperial Guard on 2 February 1814, promoted to corporal on 24 April 1815, and to sergeant in 10th Company on 1 May 1815. At Waterloo, he suffered a gunshot wound to the left side of his chest. He was discharged from the regiment on 26 October 1815.[546]

In total, the chasseurs à cheval of the Imperial Guard, according to the regimental muster list, had seven officers and thirty-two sub-officers and troopers killed, sixteen officers and seventeen sub-officers and troopers wounded and four sub-officers and troopers deserted, in total seventy-six officers and other ranks dead or wounded. The recorded wounded were:[547]

1. Corporal Feval
2. Trooper Choix
3. Trooper Pizeaux
4. Trooper Buquet
5. Trooper Jean Louis Quartier
6. Trooper Ignace Benoit Coemelck

---

545 Author's collection.
546 SHDDT: GR 20 YC 143. See also: SHDDT: GR 20 YC 144.
547 ibid.

However, the following men were recorded wounded according to records for the Legion of Honour:[548]

1. Sergeant-Major Jean Baptiste Rue. Born 22 September 1790 at Lyon. Served in the 4th Chasseurs à Cheval from 1809. Wounded at Waterloo, when his horse was killed under him.

2. Sergeant Henry Dayet. Born at Port-au-Prince in Saint Dominica on 6 January 1785. At Waterloo he suffered a gunshot wound to the left side of his chest. He was discharged from the regiment on 26 October 1815.

3. Sergeant Edme Louis Marchand.[549] Wounded at Waterloo with a bayonet wound to his right arm and numerous smaller cuts.

4. Corporal Rene Morin.[550]

5. Trooper François Cabut.[551] At Waterloo he suffered a musket ball lodging into his left arm.

6. Trooper Ignace Benoit Coemelck[552] suffered a gunshot wound to the right arm at Waterloo.

---

548 Ian Smith personal communication, 2 January 2013.

549 Sergeant Edme Louis Marchand was born at Labrot on 3 April 1772, the son of Jacques Marchand and Angelique Collot. He enlisted into the 2nd Battalion of Volunteers of the Aube on 21 April 1793, passed to the chasseurs à cheval of the Imperial Guard with the rank of sergeant on 2 February 1814 and was wounded at waterloo with a bayonet wound to his right arm and numerous smaller cuts.

550 Corporal Rene Morin was born on 27 November 1774 at Outremcourt. He enlisted into the 25th Regiment of Chasseurs à Cheval in 1793, but deserted a year later. He then re-enlisted into the 25th Chasseurs à Cheval on 3 July 1801 and passed to the chasseurs à cheval of the Imperial Guard on 8 March 1812. Following the Russian campaign, he was promoted to corporal on 27 February 1813 and served in the Royal Corps of Chasseurs à Cheval of France in 1814, passing to the 1st Regiment of Grenadiers à Cheval of the Royal Guard on 5 November 1815.

551 François Cabut was born at Cuse on 31 October 1781, the son of Jean François Cabut and Claude Françoise Ducray. He entered the service of the 20th Regiment of Dragoons on 22 December 1800, passed to the 12th Cuirassiers on 28 October 1814 and was admitted to the chasseurs à cheval of the Imperial Guard on 7 April 1815. At Waterloo he suffered a musket ball lodging into his left arm. He passed to the 2nd Dragoons on 7 July 1817 and served until 7 July 1831.

552 Ignace Benoit Coemelck was born at Poperingue in Belgium on 3 January 1772, the son of Louis Coemelck and Cecile Alwine. He entered the

7. Trooper Antoine Faverot[553] took a bayonet wound to his back at Waterloo. He was discharged on 30 August 1815.

8. Trooper Front Perier[554] was wounded at Waterloo with a sabre cut to his head, two sabre cuts to his body and a gunshot wound to his left leg. He was discharged due to his wounds on 31 August 1815.

9. Trooper Jean Baptiste Pieron was born in 1784. He had four horses killed under him and was wounded at Waterloo.

10. Trooper Jean Louis Gendarme[555] was wounded in the head at Waterloo, and was captured when the ambulance he was in was overrun by the British.

11. Trooper Jean Louis Quartier was born in 1771 and joined the regiment in 1801. Blinded in one eye at Waterloo.

This makes a total of seventeen other ranks wounded. The regiment records the following men missing or prisoner:[556]

---

service of the 5th Chasseurs à Cheval on 18 October 1793, was promoted to corporal on 12 January 1806, admitted to the Royal Corps of Chasseurs à Cheval of France on 1 July 1814, passed to the chasseurs à cheval of the Imperial Guard on 1 April 1815 and suffered a gunshot wound to the right arm at Waterloo. He returned to Paris on 5 July 1815 and entered the military hospital in the city from the ambulance at Chareloi before being discharged on 30 September 1815.

553 Antoine Faverot entered the service of the 29th Chasseurs à Cheval on 29 May 1806, passed to a regiment of line lancers in 1812, to the 7th Chasseurs à Cheval in 1814, admitted to the chasseurs à cheval of the Imperial Guard on 7 May 1815 and served in 6th Company, which was part of 2nd Squadron. He took a bayonet wound to his back at Waterloo and was discharged on 30 August 1815.

554 Front Perier was born on 17 May 1775 and admitted to the 2nd Hussars on 23 April 1799 and to the chasseurs à cheval of the Imperial Guard on 28 July 1806. He was wounded at Waterloo with a sabre cut to his head, two sabre cuts to his body and a gunshot wound to his left leg. He was discharged due to his wounds on 31 August 1815.

555 Jean Louis Gendarme was born on 20 February 1777 at Briey, the son of Jean Gendarme and Anne Renauld. He was admitted to the 20th Chasseurs in 1797, entered the chasseurs à cheval of the Imperial Guard on 8 July 1807, was wounded in the head at Waterloo and was captured when the ambulance he was in was overrun by the British.

556 SHDDT: GR 20 YC 143. See also: SHDDT: GR 20 YC 144.

1. Trooper Gendarme
2. Trooper Guillian
3. Trooper Rativeau
4. Trooper Voillereaux

Legion of Honour records add the following men as missing:[557]

1. Trooper Jean Gabriel Dodinot de la Boissiere.[558] Deserted with arms and baggage in the chaos following Waterloo.
2. Corporal Charles Alexis Boubert.[559] Deserted with horse, arms and baggage on 5 July 1815.

For the men made prisoner of war, we have two lists, one partial list of men in England,[560] and as prisoners returned to France:[561]

1. Fourrier François Michel Pleignier, of the Mameluks. Not recorded as missing in the *controle*.
2. Corporal Louis Augustin Poertevin. Not recorded as missing in the *controle*.
3. Trooper Jean Louis Gendarme. Recorded as missing at Waterloo.

---

557 Ian Smith personal communication, 2 January 2013.
558 Jean Gabriel Dodinot de la Boissiere was born at Egletons on 17 February 1790, the son of Joseph de la Boissiere and Toinette Chavebec d'Anglard. He entered the service of the 24th Chasseurs à Cheval on 23 February 1807, promoted to corporal on 1 September 1810 and to sergeant on 17 June 1812. He was captured at Wilna on 12 December 1812 and released from prison by the Russians on 21 November 1814 before then being admitted to the chasseurs à cheval of the Imperial Guard on 21 May 1815. He deserted with arms and baggage in the chaos following Waterloo. Afterwards, he was admitted to the Military Police of the Correze on 21 February 1816, being promoted to second-lieutenant on 6 April 1840. He died on 19 August 1849.
559 Charles Alexis Boubert was born on 9 October 1784 at Andamille, the son of Alexis Boubert and Marie François Calippe. He entered the Mameluks on 25 January 1814, promoted corporal on 17 February 1814 and deserted with arms and baggage on 23 April 1814. He then re-entered the chasseurs à cheval of the Imperial Guard on 9 April 1815 and deserted with horse, arms and baggage on 5 July 1815.
560 National Archives, Kew: ADM 103/102. See also: ADM 103/513; ADM 103/99; ADM 103/311; ADM 103/595.
561 SHDDT: Yj 11. See also: SHDDT: Yj 12.

4. Trooper François Bernauld. Not recorded as missing in the *controle*.
5. Trooper Aime Berttraux. Recorded as Aime Bertaux, and as killed in the *controle*.
6. Trooper Charles Louis Saumont. Not recorded as missing in the *controle*.
7. Trooper Jean Godfroi Borthel. Not recorded as missing in the *controle*.
8. Trooper Jean Baptiste Maltaire. Not recorded as missing in the *controle*.
9. Trooper Louis Lemaire. Recorded as killed in the *controle*.
10. Trooper Julien Voilleau. Listed in the *controle* as Julien Voillereaux, recorded as missing.
11. Trooper Georges Contes, of the Mameluks. Not recorded as missing in the *controle*.
12. Trooper Jean Lambert. Not recorded as missing in the *controle*.

This makes twenty other ranks wounded, and a minimum of nine missing. The regiment's muster list records the following as dead:[562]

- Sergeant-majors: Foux.
- Sergeants: Rancilha and Bartin.
- Corporals: Jamme and Berne.
- Trumpeters: Grigny.
- Troopers: Harault, Trecourt, Lolagnier, Launay, Bertaux, Schnell, Weber, Gaillard, Lemaire, Lergeuly, Daguet, Fillker, Charpentier, Lebas, Frainay, Rotmann, Rose, Graindorge, Mick, Boulon, Bourdennet, Miron, Merry, Leguen, Guyon and Malavergne.

As seen earlier, Bertaux and Lemaire were prisoners, and Legion of Honour records resurrect from the dead:

1. Trooper Hubert Trecourt. Born 1 February 1772. Admitted to 12th Chasseurs on 12 April 1789. Admitted to the chasseurs à cheval of the Imperial Guard on 19 January 1803. Passed as sergeant to the hussars of the Royal Guard on 1 November 1815.[563]

This makes twenty-nine dead as opposed to thirty-two. By 19 June 1815, nearly 60 per cent of the regiment were lying dead on the field of battle, lying in a field hospital having their wounds attended to, or

---

562 SHDDT: GR 20 YC 143. See also: SHDDT: GR 20 YC 144.
563 AN: LH 2625/62.

milling about with no horses. Officers killed in the battle or died of wounds were:[564]

1. Captain François Rocourt
2. Captain Louis Seve
3. First-Lieutenant Louis Durand
4. First-Lieutenant Faures
5. Second-Lieutenant Blaise de Sey
6. Second-Lieutenant Antoine Kapfer
7. Second-Lieutenant Jean Leqaurte

Officers wounded in the battle were:[565]

1. General François Antoine Lallemand
2. Squadron-Commander Marc Antoine Agnes Blanquefort[566]
3. Squadron-Commander François Antoine Kirmann
4. Squadron-Commander Eitenne Lafitte[567]

---

564 Jean Michel Achille personal communication.
565 Christian Granger personal communication.
566 Marc Antoine Agnes Blanquefort was born at Barran on 4 September 1778. He was admitted to the 24th Regiment of Chasseurs à Cheval in 1798, promoted to corporal in 1800, to sergeant in 1801, to adjutant-sub-officer in 1804 to lieutenant on 26 May 1809, to adjutant-major on 27 July 1809 and to captain on 11 September 1809. He was admitted to the chasseurs à cheval of the Imperial Guard with the rank of lieutenant on 26 November 1811. Following the Russian campaign, he was promoted to squadron-commander with the brevet rank of major. He was awarded the Legion of Honour on 1 October 1807, made an Officer of the Legion of Honour on 16 August 1813 and a Knight of the Order of the Reunion on 28 November 1813. He had a horse killed under him at Waterloo and was wounded in the fall when he was hit by a musket ball in the chest.
567 Eitenne Lafitte was born at Tizac on 23 June 1774. He volunteered in the Battalion of the Gironde on 18 September 1791, was promoted to corporal on 20 October 1792, passed to the 30th Half-Brigade in 1796, promoted to sergeant-major then to second-lieutenant in 1799, to captain on 3 January 1807 (serving with General Durosnel), passed to the 26th Dragoons on 19 June 1808, promoted to squadron-commander on 28 August 1808, to major on 7 September 1811 (at the head of the 20th Dragoons), passed to the chasseurs à cheval of the Imperial Guard as squadron-commander on 9 December 1811, placed as major of the 1st Hussars on 20 November 1814, passed back to the chasseurs à cheval of the Imperial Guard on 14 April 1815 and was seriously wounded at Waterloo, assumed killed.

5. Captain Louis Gay. Born at Lyon on 23 August 1772
6. Captain Christophe Ladroitte
7. Captain David Joseph Leblanc. Gunshot wound to the neck, left for dead on the field of battle
8. Captain Jean Georges Louis Massa[568]
9. First-Lieutenant Arnoux
10. First-Lieutenant Charles Bayard[569]
11. First-Lieutenant Brunet
12. First-Lieutenant Caprentier
13. First-Lieutenant Antoine d'Armagnac[570]

He then entered the 8th Dragoons as lieutenant-colonel in 1816 and retired on 7 November 1821. He died on 1 July 1836.

568 Jean Georges Louis Massa was born at Strasburg on 25 August 1775, the son of Joseph Guillame Massa and Claudine Barbe Winckelmann. He entered the service of the 1st Battalion of the Bas-Rhon on 1 April 1792 and was then taken into the 1st Regiment of Foot Artillery of the Line in 1794. He passed to the 8th Hussars in 1798, was promoted to corporal in 1800, to sergeant in 1801, to sergeant-major in 1804, to adjutant-sub-officer on 1 March 1807, to second-lieutenant on 3 April 1807, to first-lieutenant on 21 July 1809 and to captain on 25 October 1812. With the reduction of the army in 1814 by the royalist authorities, he was taken into the new 3rd Hussars Regiment, formed from the 8th and 10th Hussars on 2 August 1814. He was then admitted to the chasseurs à cheval of the Imperial Guard on 11 April 1815 and was wounded when his horse was killed under him at Waterloo.

569 Charles Bayard was born on 12 January 1774 at Saint-Bel in the Rhone Valley. He was the son of Benoit Bayard and Cecile Decrussily. He entered the service of the Battalion of the Rhone on 18 August 1791 and then was admitted as a grenadier in the 1st Battalion of the Villefranche on 15 October 1793, admitted thence to the 8th Dragoons on 19 July 1794, the Guides of General Bonaparte in 1796, to the chasseurs à cheval of the Guards of the Consul on 3 January 1800, quickly promoted to sergeant by 1803 and to second-lieutenant standard bearer on 28 October 1808. Following the Russian campaign he was promoted to first-lieutenant on 27 February 1813. At Waterloo, he took a gunshot wound to left foot and was discharged from the regiment on 26 October 1815.

570 Antoine d'Armagnac was born at Condom on 18 December 1776. He entered the 5th Regiment of Light Infantry on 4 October 1792, passed to the 24th Half-Brigade of Light Infantry in 1797, admitted to the 3rd Chasseurs à Cheval in 1799, to the chasseurs à cheval of the Guard of the

14. First-Lieutenant Etienne Foullon
15. First-Lieutenant Martin Speriere
16. Second-Lieutenant Pierre Honore Dackweiller[571]
17. Second-Lieutenant Jacques Antoine Morel[572]
18. Second-Lieutenant Jean Pierre Pellion

On 8 April 1815, the regiment comprised fifty-four officers and 569 sub-officers and men. Of the theoretical 930 sub-officers and troopers by 1 June 1815, only 426 were available for service, along with thirty officers and 691 horses. This represented a loss of twenty-four officers and 143 sub-officers and men; being equipped in the depot were a further twenty-five officers, 609 sub-officers and troopers and 261 horses. In total, the regiment had some 1,035 sub-officers and men by 10 June 1815. Of these, 609 were new entrants. The regiment was organised on a war footing of four squadrons. Looking at a sample of 200 men who joined the regiment between 1 and 26 April 1815, the

---

Consuls on 3 January 1800, promoted to corporal in 1802, to corporal-quartermaster in 1803, to second-lieutenant on 16 February 1807 and to first-lieutenant on 29 February 1813. At Waterloo, he was wounded with a gunshot wound to his right hand, received a sabre cut and was taken prisoner.

571 Pierre Honore Dackweiller was born in Paris on 9 June 1787. He entered the 39th Regiment of Line Infantry in 1801, passed to the 2nd Regiment of Light Infantry in 1805, admitted to the chasseurs à cheval of the Imperial Guard on 10 July 1806, promoted to corporal on 5 June 1810 and to sergeant on 26 December 1811. Following the Russian campaign he was named as second-lieutenant-adjutant-major on 27 February 1813, placed on half-pay in August 1814 and was admitted back to the regiment on 8 April 1815 with the rank of second-lieutenant. He was wounded at Waterloo and placed on half-pay from 1 November 1815.

572 Jacques Antoine Morel was born on 28 February 1785 in Paris. He was admitted to the 9th Hussars on 20 June 1803, promoted to corporal on 1 March 1808, to sergeant on 10 December 1811, to sergeant-major on 24 March 1812, passed to the 1st Regiment of Hussars on 1 May 1814, promoted to second-lieutenant on 8 June 1814 and admitted to the chasseurs à cheval of the Imperial Guard on 19 April 1815. At Waterloo, he suffered a shrapnel wound to the left side of his head, removing the left ear and inflicting puncture wounds to left temple, as well as a lance wound to right arm. Clearly at some stage the regiment, or elements of the Guard cavalry, engaged Prussian uhlans during a rearguard action.

average age of a chasseur upon entry was twenty-seven. The youngest man who joined was twenty-one years old and the oldest man was thirty-seven years of age. The average length of service prior to joining the regiment was four years five months. Some men in this sample had served for only three years. Some men of this sample had served as long as eleven years before enlistment. The men came from across the cavalry force of France. The men entering the regiment came from twenty-three different backgrounds, which included infantry of both the line and Guard, artillery train of the line and Guard, as well as from the National Guard. Of the men taken into the lancers, only 8.3 per cent were drawn from the line lancer regiments. The line chasseurs à cheval provided 18 per cent of the manpower. Sixty-one men, or 8.9 per cent, came from the cavalry of the Guard. Twelve men, representing 1 per cent, came from the Guard artillery, and the remaining 64 per cent of the manpower came from the line cavalry, infantry, and artillery. Clearly, those taken into the regiment in 1815 had, on the whole, never carried a lance, and more importantly had little in common with the regiment. These 680 men needed to be clothed, equipped and trained before the campaign opened. Clearly therefore, the lancers were far from cohesive or well-disciplined during the Hundred Days campaign.[573]

6 June saw a detachment of nine officers and 239 sub-officers and troopers join the regiment in the field, bringing the strength of the four service squadrons up to forty-seven officers and 823 sub-officers and men. On the morning of 10 June 1815, the regiment had eleven officers and sixty-nine sub-officers and troopers in Paris available for service, ten officers and 437 men in the depot, but not available for service, and the troops with the army mustered forty-one officers and 732 men.[574] By 16 June, the number of officers with the army had risen to forty-seven, and the number of sub-officers and troopers to 833, organised into four nearly full-strength squadrons. The problems of cohesiveness, training and equipment encountered in the summer of 1814, it seems, were ongoing as the regiment readied itself to march to war for the last time.[575] Losses were as follows:[576]

---

573 SHDDT: GR 20 YC 166 *Régiment de chevau-légers lanciers, crée par décret du 8 avril 1815 et formé de l'ex-corps royal des lanciers de France, 8 avril 1815-22 décembre 1815 (matricules: 1 à 1,608).*

574 AN: AFIV 1940, folio 200.

575 ibid.

576 SHDDT: GR 20 YC 166.

Lanciers de la Garde					
Squadron	Wounded	Wounded & Prisoner	Prisoner of War	Killed	Missing
1st	21	0	0	3	8
2nd	20	0	0	3	14
3rd	29	0	1	1	7
4th	15	0	0	3	25
Total	85	0	1	10	54

Working with the muster list we see that the lancers lost ten men killed and eighty-five wounded at Waterloo. One man was captured, leaving a total of 150 men lost. One officer was killed and twelve were wounded.[577] Twenty-three men were wounded on the 16th and three killed, making total casualties of thirteen sub-officers and men killed and 108 wounded.

A second record of losses was prepared on 23 June for the entire campaign. It lists the losses as follows:[578]

Lanciers de la Garde					
Squadron	Wounded	Wounded & Prisoner	Prisoner of War	Killed	Missing
1st	21	0	0	3	51
2nd	20	0	0	1	32
3rd	29	0	0	4	45
4th	18	0	0	0	50
Total	88	0	0	8	178

This report gives 274 losses, an increase of 124 men from the muster list returns. This list however, does contain losses between 19 and 23 June, which is recorded as one officer and 178 men. A third report states the losses of the regiment as one officer, twenty-eight men and fifty-five horses killed and seven officers, seventy-nine men and forty-seven horses wounded. In addition, one officer, 146 men and 206 horses were listed as lost, and thirty-two men were noted as prisoner of war between 19 and 20 June. Between this return dated 23 June and the regiment's

---

577 SHDDT: GR 2 YB 87 *2e regiment de chevau-legers lancers de la Garde Impériale.*

578 SHDDT: Xab 73 *Dragons et Chevau-léger (formation de 1815).*

muster roll, we must assume the men listed as missing on the 18th were dead or wounded. A final reckoning of losses is given as fourteen officers, 256 men and 289 horses. Clearly, for losses to decrease, missing men must have returned to the ranks.[579] These four reports demonstrate the complexities of the researcher in endeavouring to reconcile the archival paperwork generated in 1815. In total, one officer was killed and twelve were wounded. Twenty-three men were wounded on the 16th and three killed, making total casualties of thirteen sub-officers and men killed and 115 wounded. Furthermore, 202 horses had been killed.

Kellermann's 3rd Cavalry Corps

By now, Milhaud's cuirassiers were exhausted and the light cavalry of the Guard had done as much as they could. All that Ney could call on now was Kellermann's 3rd Cavalry Corps. About the charge, General Gourgaud writes with hindsight in 1818 that:[580]

> The emperor directed Kellermann's cuirassiers to support our cavalry on the height, lest it should be repulsed by the enemy's cavalry, which, in the present state of affairs would have occasioned the loss of the battle: for it was one of those critical moments in which a very trivial incident may give rise to the most important result. This movement of the cavalry, who galloped forward exclaiming 'vive l'Empereur!' overawed the enemy, encouraged our troops, and prevented them from being alarmed by the Prussians continuing their fire on our rear.

General Kellermann, commanding the 3rd Cavalry Corps, recalls that:[581]

> The cavalry division of General Milhaud was launched first, then that of the Imperial Guard, and finally the right wing of the 3rd Cavalry Corps was ordered forward imprudently by the imbecilic General Lhéritier, who had not waited for the orders of Comte de Valmy, the commander-in-chief, and they arrived pell-mell, in disorder, on blown horses on the plateau occupied by a line of English artillery. The guns were at that moment abandoned, but we had no horses with which to draw them off.

579 SHDDT: Xab 73.
580 Bourgaud, p. 102.
581 SHDDT: MR 7178 *Observations sur la Campagne du 1815.*

Elsewhere, to the rear was a double line of infantry formed into squares. The cavalry had to somehow stop and get back into order, while under fire from the enemy, but it was no longer possible for the cavalry, as excellent as it was, to carry out new charges, as they found themselves in the cruellest position, without infantry and artillery support.

The enemy squares reserved their fire, and were covered by a cloud of sharpshooters from which every shot counted. It was in this awful position that our cavalry remained for several hours between the wood of Hougoumont and La Haye Sainte...The charge was neither skilfully nor fortunately executed. The masses of cavalry did not advance using their imposing order, which inspires confidence and promises success. Instead of reserving this for the critical moment.

Chapter 12

Lhéritier's 11th Cavalry Division

With the French first wave of attack checked, the Allied cavalry withdrew from the mayhem. The respite was short-lived, as a second wave of French cavalry moved up the churned morass of the slope to the Allied positions. By now the slope was boggy, covered in dead and dying men and horses. If at the start of the day the cavalry could barely canter in the charge, by late afternoon most charges were done at the trot or walk. No dash and swagger, but tired men and horses dragging themselves through the mud and dead and wounded to return to the combat once more. So far only half of Kellermann's cavalry corps had not been in action during the campaign. Lhéritier's men had fought at Quatre-Bras and had captured at least one British colour. Lhéritier was itching to fight, as he explains:[582]

> We had been placed in a position so exposed, and had been so dreadfully galled by the fire of their infantry and guns, that the impetuosity of the French character would no longer be restrained within bounds, especially as the suddenness of their reorganisation after Napoléon's return had of necessity somewhat upset their discipline; and there arose such a dangerous clamour in the ranks, and such earnest demands to be led forward, and in their own words, that the officers were compelled to lay aside their better discretion, and at once bring them into action at all hazards.

About the operations of the 2nd Dragoons, their corps commander, General Lhéritier, writes:[583]

---

582 *United Services Magazine*, 1831, Part 2, p. 526.
583 Pierre Bruyere, *Historique du 2e regiment des Dragons*, de Garnier, Chartres, 1885, pp. 123-5.

The 2nd Regiment of Dragoons formed the head of the corps of heavy cavalry under the command of Major General Kellermann. This regiment covered itself with immortal glory in the midst of the enemy's squares throughout the day of the 18th.

It is impossible to name the prodigies of valour and the excesses of extraordinary bravery, if not heroism, with which the 2nd Dragoons exhibited when under the fearful fire of musketry and of a huge number of cannon…This regiment distinguished itself in 1815 by its bold charges against the masses of enemy cavalry. They had consistently maintained the front line, rushing headlong into the thick of the fray and competing with the Imperial Guard, with which they shared the glory.

The losses sustained by the 2nd Dragoons are immense, but they retreated in good order, keeping their eagle. Lieutenants Henry and Dineur, Sub-Lieutenants Letaudy and Graffin were killed, Lieutenants Mottiée and Libault injured. Captain Rivaud and Lieutenant Fournier were taken prisoner.

Squadron-Commander Dieudonne Rigau, of the 2nd Dragoons, writes about his actions in the charge:[584]

About eleven o'clock the battle began, we were on the front lines, General Lhéritier arrived, but at the same time, in addressing me, he received a bullet which passed through his shoulder and he had to retire, it is in this moment that we lost our sappers.

Then came the 7th Regiment, commanded by Colonel Leopold,[585] who stood back to the left of 1st Regiment. Two pieces of small-calibre guns, led by a sergeant, were placed away from our squadrons. They barely had time to fire when the British cavalry charged them. This is when, with no command and no order, the two squadrons closest to me, which I commanded, marched in front of the guns to meet the enemy cavalry with the general cry of 'open ranks'.

This movement was followed by the other squadrons, and then by the regiment of Leopold. We stood on the heights of Mont-Saint-

---

584 Rigau, *Souvenirs des Guerres de l'Empire*, Garniere Freres, Paris, 1846, pp. 108-17.
585 Charles Philippe Leopold was born in Kallstadt, Germany, on 10 January 1775 and died on 5 November 1816. He was confirmed as the colonel of the 7th Dragoons on 25 April 1815. AN: LH 1592/47.

Jean, the location of the Lion all day, until the retreat. We had to continually charge the enemy's squadrons, who advanced to make us retreat. Never was there a longer and more compact cavalry melee, because there was no intermission, and our squadrons were held in check by the English squares standing on the roadway and backed to the village, which dared not thin out their fire all day. Our troops were so tired from always going to the attack that every moment we heard the warning from officers that men collapsed and fell from their horses with fatigue. We have been falsely accused of having Ney order this premature movement, but, as I said, it was made instantaneously.

Our misfortunes prevented then to make known the glorious details of the regiments. Thus, in the 2nd Dragoons:

An officer named Graffin was nearly killed, after having two horses killed under him, and was remounted, for the third time, on horse from the artillery train;[586]

The adjutant, Libault,[587] who retired to Pau, did not hesitate in the middle of the melee, jumping from his horse to give to it to the colonel, who had been dismounted;

Captain Henry was cut to pieces;[588]

Perreau, who bears traces of the battle and serving in the gendarmerie;[589]

Hurtaut, retired captain, now mayor of his village in the department of Allier;

---

586 Martinien lists an officer called Graffin, belonging to the 2nd Dragoons, as killed at Waterloo.

587 Nicolas Libault, born 27 January 1785, was admitted to the regiment with the rank of second-lieutenant on 20 March 1809, was promoted to lieutenant on 22 May 1813 and was named lieutenant-adjutant-major on 22 May 1814.

588 Martinien lists an officer called Henry, belonging to the 2nd Dragoons, as killed at Waterloo.

589 Jean François Perreau, born 2 September 1772, was admitted to the regiment on 7 January 1808 as lieutenant-quartermaster, becoming captain-quartermaster on 13 February 1812.

Suchel,[590] captain, who was to become an object of curiosity for the people we passed, as he had been covered with sabre wounds head to foot.

Take praise for all these braves; almost all the officers and sub-officers were wounded: many remained on the battlefield, though gloriously for themselves and their families. I had the honour to lead this day (my friends will remember) twelve times the squadrons to the charge, which were addressed thoroughly. Major Collet,[591] retired to Saint-Germain, was among these good numbers. I feel regret at not being able to name all those that I saw to be heroes, but I witnessed their dangers and their actions, unable to remember the names of all.

As the 2nd Dragoons surged up the slope by La Haye Sainte, officers, men and horses fell dead or wounded. The regiment was commanded that day by Colonel François Joseph Planzeaux. He had commanded the regiment since 29 May 1815, having previously served in the 8th Chasseurs à Cheval, and thence the 15th Chasseurs from 8 October 1814. Planzeaux is reported to have charged at the head of a single squadron of his regiment to extricate the 8th Regiment of Cuirassiers from an encounter with the Allied cavalry and was, we are told, one of the last men to leave the field of battle.[592] Captain Hippolyte François Gabriel Dubois, of the 2nd Dragoons, was wounded.[593] Fellow captain, Jean Rivaud, was wounded and made prisoner of war.[594] Lieutenant Jean Jacques Moittie had his right thigh fractured by a gunshot. He is recorded as being in the military hospital at Philippeville on 1 July 1815 and was discharged from the army on 1 September 1815.[595] Sub-Lieutenant Fleury Brossette had his horse killed under him in one of the

---

590 Served under Squadron-Commander Rigau.

591 Amand Honore Collet, born 16 May 1785, was admitted to the 4th Dragoons in 1804, and was promoted to corporal on 24 March 1806, to fourrier on 28 July 1807, to sergeant on 1 April 1811, to sergeant-major the same year on 1 October, to adjutant-sub-officer on 1 April 1813 and to sub-lieutenant-adjutant-major on 24 July 1814. He was admitted to the regiment on 8 May 1814. Following Waterloo, he passed to the Garde du Corps of the Ling on 26 December 1815.

592 *Le Moniteur de l'Armée*, 26 June 1856.

593 AN: LH 812/42.

594 AN: LH 2339/9.

595 AN: LH 1897/8.

charges.[596] Sub-Lieutenant Victorice Quentin Fournier was wounded with a gunshot to the right side of his chest, and had, it seems, his horse killed under him, and was made prisoner of war.[597] Friedrich von Arentschildt, who commanded the 7th British Cavalry Brigade, observed the dragoons attack:[598]

> The battle commenced with a heavy cannonade which inflicted severe suffering upon our regiment in this first position. Several men and as many as twenty horses were lost within the first thirty minutes. Subsequently, several movements were made, both to the left and to the right, and each in perfect calmness and with precision, in order to protect the regiment from the artillery fire. Nevertheless, the regiment suffered severely from the intense artillery fire from the enemy cannon; it also lost its brave commander, Lieutenant-Colonel Meyer, who was struck on one of his legs by a cannonball and was taken to the rear.

> Between two and three o'clock in the afternoon the regiment moved to the head of the column, as the leading cavalry had been posted to, and was engaged at, different points, as stated. Three companies, under the command of Captain von Kerssenbruch, now made a successful charge against two squadrons of cuirassiers, which they repulsed and vigorously pursued for quite some distance.

> But, before these three companies had returned, the two remaining squadrons of the regiment were ordered by Major-General von Arentschildt to engage the enemy cavalry regiments, one of cuirassiers and the other of dragoons, which had advanced towards the English line. This attack was executed most vigorously, and the sections of enemy cavalry that were charged by the aforementioned squadrons were forced to yield and were repelled. However, as the enemy had a much wider frontage than our own, our squadrons were quickly surrounded on both sides and sustained considerable losses among the officers, men, and of course horses. Captain Janssens, Lieutenant and Adjutant Bruggermann, and Cornet Deichmann were killed, while Lieutenants Oehlkers, True and Cornet von Dassel were severely wounded and forced to leave the field of battle.

The muster list of the 2nd Dragoon Regiment for the period 1814 to disbandment in 1815 exists at the French Army Archives at Vincennes.

---

596 AN: LH 373/38.
597 AN: LH 1018/38.
598 John Franklin personal communication, 18 November 2012.

However, the document was damaged in the 1940s and is not available for researchers to consult until it has been conserved sometime close to 2020. Therefore, we are not able to obtain losses for the regiment at Waterloo. At the time of disbandment on 5 December 1815, the regiment admitted to the loss of the following men:[599]

2nd Dragoons			
Squadron	Company	Wounded in Hospital	Missing since 18 June
1st	1st	4	32
	5th	4	33
2nd	2nd	3	30
	6th	2	40
3rd	3rd	4	29
	7th	0	25
4th	4th	0	37
	8th	0	38
Total		17	264
5th	Depot	2	98

From 18 June onwards, the regiment lost a recorded seventeen men wounded and 264 men missing, either prisoners, deserted, or killed. The men in the depot are likely to be deserters. In comparison, we can use records of 10 June and 24 June to give total losses for the regiment in the intervening fourteen days. On 10 June, the regiment mustered forty-three officers and 543 other ranks. Kellermann informed Marshal Soult on 24 June that the regiment mustered twenty-four officers with thirty-five horses and 301 other ranks with 299 horses.[600] This represents a loss of 242 other ranks, or 44 per cent of effective strength being lost between 10 and 24 June 1815. Officers and men in prison in England were:[601]

1. Sous-Lieutenant Auguste Gremont
2. Sergeant Auguste Grimon
3. Jean Beaufsan
4. Joseph Georges Ankerman

---

599 SHDDT: Xc 135 *2e Dragons*. Dossier 1815.
600 SHDDT: C15 34. *Situations du 24e Juin 1815*.
601 National Archives, Kew: ADM 103/102. See also: ADM 103/513; ADM 103/99; ADM 103/311; ADM 103/595; SHDDT: Yj 11; SHDDT: Yj 12; SHDDT: Yj 13.

5. Jacques Bpussion
6. Jean Conygham
7. Trumpeter Raphael Cramer
8. Jean Plantade
9. Gilles Morel
10. Jean Schmidt
11. Jean Baptiste Ackerman
12. Jean Lacharre
13. Jean Lacroix
14. Guillaume Rabot
15. Antoine Main

Brigaded with the 2nd Dragoons were the 7th Dragoons. Squadron-Commander Georges Marc Nicolas l'Etang, of the accompanying 7th Dragoons, narrates his experience of riding against the Allied infantry squares:[602]

> The farm of Hougoumont was attacked and was defended by the English. The French infantry was placed entirely at this farm and at La Saint Alliance [La Haye Sainte], and renewed their attacks. The heavy cavalry division of Lhéritier, formed in closed columns with the men dismounted, stood behind the infantry. They charged the English who evacuated their positions. At the same time, the English artillery sent some round shot which fell on our infantry and on the division of Lhéritier, causing confusion among the men and horses. It was decided to charge the line with the cavalry. The English had time to prepare their dispositions for the attack, we moved to the offensive in front of our infantry, which then formed a line between the farms, with no other dispositions, this was a great fault.

> The squadron formed the head of column of Lhéritier's division and advanced against the infantry, followed by the other squadrons, due to the distance separating us from the English, it permitted to perform the movement to form square to receive the charge. The squares resolutely awaited the cavalry, and were determined to hold their fire until point-blank range. The infantry's fire had a powerful impact on the cavalry's morale, which was greater than its physical impact on the cavalry, which was never better demonstrated. The coolness of the British infantry was all the more remarkable for the absence of the fusillade which we were

---

602 SHDDT: MR 717 *letter du Chef d'Escadron l'Etang.*

expecting, and that to our great surprise we did not receive, which disconcerted our men. They were then seized with the thought that they were going to be received by a fire that would be much more murderous from being at point-blank range, and probably to escape such a fire, the 1st Squadron wheeled to the right, and thus decided a similar movement by all the following squadrons. The charge failed and none of the squadrons rallied till they reached the embattled farm of Saint-Alliance [La Haye Sainte], which being still occupied by the British, fired upon us, wounded and killing many in an instant. Among those who were wounded were General Lhéritier, who commanded the division, General Picquet, who commanded the brigade, Colonel Leopold, who commanded the 7th Regiment of Dragoons, and two squadron-commanders of the same regiment. The command of the 7th Regiment of Dragoons passed to Squadron-Commander Letang at the moment they rallied behind Saint-Alliance.

Following this event, the emperor, informed of the danger to our position, ordered that the farm of Saint-Alliance was to be attacked and taken. Ney was placed at the head of the infantry and marched to this post and captured it. From thence, the division of Lhéritier ceased to run the gauntlet of murderous fire which it was long exposed to.

Forced to move from their entrenchments, the English moved in disorder from this farm and turned back to the bulk of their army. They then placed the flank of our cavalry against the farm, from which they could charge with success. The fact did not escape the sagacity of Squadron-Commander Letang, commanding the 7th Dragoons. He went in person to the head of the 1st Dragoons [actually the 2nd Regiment, which had become the 1st Regiment in 1814], which preceded his regiment, and remarked to the commandant of the 1st Dragoons on the opportunity to charge that presented itself and gave orders to commence this movement, which if carried out vigorously with the 7th Dragoons placed in echelons to the right of the 1st Dragoons at the bottom of the slope, they would take the plateaux. But, the commander of the 1st Dragoons said he had no orders and did not accept the advice of the commander of the 7th Dragoons. In vain, Commandant Letang objected, saying that since the generals were absent and wounded and that there would be no orders, he was determined not to wait. Unmoved, the commander of the 1st Dragoons remained in his place of battle. The commander of the 7th Dragoons declared he would charge...Quick as lightning, Commandant Letang re-joined his regiment and advanced at the trot so as not to tire the horses moving uphill and to then push the charge home with vigour. But, time was lost and the English infantry fleeing a few moments before was reformed and was supported by fresh troops which had hastened to meet the charge. Despite this, the charge of the 7th Dragoons succeeded and the English squares were barely formed when troops marching to their aid were cut down by the sabres. An inconceivable fatality resulting from this annulled the fine exploit. The 1st Dragoons, at the same time as the regiment began its charge, made a retrograde movement to occupy the place the 7th Dragoons had just left.

About the motive of this movement it was certainly not appropriate, because the 7th Dragoons being engaged with the English, seeing the 1st Dragoons turn around instead of supporting them, believed that our line was turned, and gave up the attack on the infantry and had to follow the 1st Dragoons. They then had to rally near where they ceased their retrograde movement. Thus, this unfortunate movement stopped the brilliant success of the charge commanded by Squadron-Commander Letang, who has afterward loudly and energetically denounced the precipitated retreat which turned his regiment back from the front. The English infantry had received reinforcements and had reformed in good order, while the 7th Dragoons were weakened, because after breaking ranks of the infantry, many men of this regiment had been able to rally with the 1st Dragoons and were left in the middle of the squares. He could not usefully attempt another charge.

Shortly after, an artillery battery of the Imperial Guard came and stood in front of the 7th Dragoons and burned in a few minutes all the ammunition they had left. They then began a retrograde movement, when Squadron-Command Letang ordered them to remain in position where they had come to a halt, telling its commander that by remaining they could make the enemy believe they still had ammunition…he did not let them withdraw…

At Waterloo, Colonel Charles Philippe Leopold was seriously wounded in the attack, so much so he was retired from the army.[603] Squadron-Commander Lerminier was wounded, and Squadron-Commander Joseph François Marlinge had a horse killed under him, as did Sub-Lieutenant Jean Pierre Perlet.[604] Adjutant-Sub-Officer Simon Joseph Colmant suffered a gunshot to the right thigh and was made a

603 AN: LH 1592/47.
604 AN: LH 2101/33.

prisoner of war.[605] Other wounded officers included Captains Sarcus and Billancourt, Lieutenant Costard de Saint-Legere, Sub-Lieutenants Bouchard and Duvergier, and thirty other ranks were wounded.[606] Killed in the action was Lieutenant Marc Houry, along with Troopers Ohenois, Jean Commerson, Louis Labiche, Jean François, Jean Legal, Louis Dehault, Jacques Rey, Jean Maitrejean, Jean Prost, Pierre Fouquet Jean Boucher, Benoit Belin, Joseph Sousse, Pierre Gauvin, Claude Boissot, Jean Babin, Jean Blanchard, Pierre Vigeur, Laurent Demailly, Nicolas Meuthe, Philippe Fournier, Jean Renaud, Jean Jacquier, Jean Sauledubois, Claude Bernard, Pierre Rose, Pierre Fleury, Dominique Jacques and Joseph Michel.[607]

The regiment began the campaign with forty-one officers and 476 other ranks. The regiment's archive lists two men lost on 16 June at Quatre-Bras. In total seventy-four men were lost at Waterloo, representing 16 per cent of effective strength, shown in the table below:[608]

7th Dragoons						
Squadron	Company	Killed	Died of Wounds	Wounded	Prisoner of War	Missing
1st	1st	2	0	3	0	0
	5th	1	0	3	1	0
2nd	2nd	4	0		5	0
	6th	1	0	0	4	1
3rd	3rd	6	0	2	0	1
	7th	5	0	1	3	3
4th	4th	2	0	1	10	0
	8th	4	0	1	9	1
Total		25	0	11	32	6

Of the thirty-two men made prisoners, officers and men held in England were:[609]

---

605 AN: LH 571/69.

606 Rene Marie Timoleon de Cosse-Brissac, *Historique du 7e regiment de dragons*. Lerory, Paris, 1909, pp. 74-5.

607 de Cosse-Brissac, pp. 178-9.

608 SHDDT: GR 24 YC 158.

609 National Archives, Kew: ADM 103/102. See also: ADM 103/513; ADM 103/99; ADM 103/311; ADM 103/595; SHDDT: Yj 11; SHDDT: Yj 12; SHDDT: Yj 13.

- Held in Dartmoor:

  1. Jacques Pocard
  2. Bernard Dupuis
  3. Sergeant-Major Joseph Souvley
  4. Jacques Boar
  5. Joseph Jolyet
  6. Jean Jgoas
  7. Sergeant Edme Riou
  8. Joseph Pocare
  9. Corporal Joseph Sens
  10. Pierre François Barbeau

- Parole in Ashburton:

  1. Sous-Lieutenant Alphonse Lermine
  2. Sous-Lieutenant Simon Colmant
  3. Sergeant-Major Jacques Dominique
  4. Benjamin Dupuis

Alongside the dragoon brigade came Guiton's cuirassiers, which may still have been badly shaken after the events of 16 June. At the head of the 8th Cuirassiers, Colonel Antoine Laurent Marie Garavque was wounded, as was Squadron-Commander Jean Baptiste Ceyrat. He had been wounded at Ligny and was wounded again at Waterloo when a howitzer shell exploded close to him, as his regiment charged up the slope to the Allied infantry.[610] As well as loosing men to wounds and a lack of horses, men also deserted. The losses for Waterloo are shown in the table below:[611]

8th Cuirassiers							
Squadron	Killed	Died of Wounds	Wounded	Wounded & Prisoner	Prisoner of War	Deserted	Missing
Total	3	0	1	31	50	5	15

The 8th Cuirassiers, with Colonel Garavque at their head, mustered thirty-one officers and 438 men on 10 June. Fifteen men had been lost

---

610 AN: LH 462/81.
611 SHDDT: GR 24 YC 50.

at Quatre-Bras. At Waterloo, 105 men were lost. Of the 423 men at Waterloo, 25 per cent were lost.

Colonel Baron Eleonore Ambroise Courtier, of the brigaded 11th Cuirassiers, was wounded. Also wounded were Squadron-Commanders François Grandeau and Antoine Raimond Delville, who was bayoneted by the Allied infantry after his horse was killed under him close to an infantry square. The attached horse artillery, the 3rd Company 2nd Regiment of Horse Artillery, lost its company commander, Louis François Marie Gaston De Cruzy de Marcillac, who was left dead on the field of battle. Wounded were Lieutenants Gérard and Vignot. The losses for Waterloo are shown in the table below:[612]

11th Cuirassiers						
Squadron	Company	Killed	Died of Wounds	Wounded	Prisoner of War	Missing
1st	1st	2	0	0	0	10
	5th	0	0	0	0	2
2nd	2nd	1	0	0	0	6
	6th	3	0	0	0	5
3rd	3rd	1	0	0	0	5
	7th	1	0	0	0	3
4th	4th	1	0	0	0	4
	8th	0	0	0	0	3
Total		9	0	0	0	38

In total, the regiment lost forty-seven men. On 10 June, it mustered twenty-four officers and 308 men. At Quatre-Bras thirty-four men had been lost, giving 274 men present on 18 June. At Waterloo, 17 per cent of effective strength had been lost.

Piré's lancers

Seemingly sucked into the action came the 5th and 6th Lancers. No French accounts exist of this episode, but the Allies do mention it. J. B. Doren, of the 5th Dutch Light Dragoons, writes:[613]

---

612 SHDDT: GR 24 YC 64.

613 J. B. J. van Doren, *Strategisch verhaal van de veldslagen tusschen het Fransche leger en dat der Geallieerden op 15, 16, 17 en 18 Junij 1815, Mont-Saint-Jean,*

The cheveaux-legers regiment had excelled themselves on 16 June at Quatre-Bras and again distinguished themselves on 18 June, but with the loss of many men. No less brave had been the division of heavy cavalry composed of the 1st and 3rd Regiment Cuirassiers [*sic*] (Dutch), as well as the 2nd Regiment of Carabiniers, which was composed of Belgians and had been raised in 1814 in Brussels. These regiments, which were posted on a plateau in front of the farm of La Belle Alliance (a position Napoléon wanted to conquer, because it benefited the entire line and commanded the roads to Namur and Nivelles), had to its left a battalion of Hanoverians, which were formed in square, and to the right a battalion of English, also formed in square. Three regiments of French cuirassiers, together with a regiment of lancers, made several charges on these squares to enter them, but these were fruitless.

Major P. A. Lautour, of the 23rd Light Dragoons, recalled seeing lancers attacking with cuirassiers:[614]

The German light dragoon regiments formed our immediate left, and the other a little to our left-rear; and in rear of our brigade was formed a regiment of Belgian heavy cavalry, where the regiment remained dismounted until the French lancers and cuirassiers advanced to attack our guns and the position we occupied, when the brigade mounted and led by our gallant General Dorneberg (who was severely wounded in that charge) repulsed the enemy with great loss, and when the 23rd Light Dragoons animated and borne away by this success, pursued its advantage a little too far, crossed a very wide and deep ravine into which several of our rear rank horses fell, driving back the cuirassiers and lancers on their own guns, and throwing the French gunners into the greatest confusion.

After reforming (Lieutenant-Colonel Cutcliffe having been severely wounded), I moved it up in advance of its first position, and to the support of the 33rd Regiment, commanded by Colonel William Elphinstone.

Lieutenant William Turner of the 13th Light Dragoons also remembered the Lancers:[615]

Amsterdam, 1865.

614 Siborne, *Waterloo Letters*, No. 49.

615 C. R. B. Barrett, *The History of the XIIIth Hussars*, London, 1911, p. 277.

…before two o'clock we had three officers and several men killed by cannon balls and shells, we were then put close to some Belgian artillery to keep them to their guns and there we suffered from musketry and round shot; we then moved to the right of the line to charge the French lancers, but they retired. We then came back to our place close to the artillery, which the French Imperial Guard à Cheval and cuirassiers had taken, we immediately formed up in line with the 15th, gave three cheers, and went at them full speed, they retired immediately and we charged after them all down their position up to their infantry, when we were ordered to retire, which we did, but in confusion, we formed and told off again having lost a good many men; I shot one Frenchman with my pistol, but did not use my sword, (I had the misfortune to break the double barrelled one in marching up the country or else I should have shot two).

The lancers seemed to have engaged in support of Picquet's dragoons. Captain Quintus von Goeben, of the 3rd Hussar Regiment King's German Legion, narrates that following the charge of the Dutch-Belgian carabiniers:[616]

The Dutch heavy cavalry fell back *en debandade* towards the two squadrons on the right wing of the regiment, so that the two squadrons had great difficulty in maintaining their position and not being swept along by this movement; and because they were followed by large squadrons of enemy cuirassiers. The three squadrons on the left wing of the regiment, which had avoided any entanglement with the Dutch heavy cavalry as they retired, were assembled under the command of Captain von Kerssenbruch, who now commanded the regiment, and launched a counter-attack against the enemy squadrons, which were thrown back in great disorder.

During this time the squadrons at the front of the regiment which had become free, advanced to the brow of the height and immediately received personal orders from General, the Earl of Uxbridge, who commanded the entire cavalry, to attack the line of enemy cavalry 200 to 250 paces from the regiment, which consisted of one regiment of cuirassiers on the right wing and one regiment of dragoons and some lancers [Piré's lancers?]. But the superiority of the enemy, being at least three or four times stronger, or the lack of a proper commander, because Captain von Kerssenbruch was

---

616 Franklin, Vol. 1, p. 183.

absent having executed the counter-attack moments before, the two squadrons did not start the attack immediately and there was a slight hesitation; Lord Uxbridge encouraged the two squadrons to advance at a brisk trot and to attack the enemy line, which was advancing slowly without fear. The right squadron of the regiment met the right squadron of the enemy dragoon regiment at the gallop, while the second squadron met the cuirassiers. The enemy's line was pierced at both points, but the two squadrons were so completely surrounded by the wings of the enemy, who attacked them from the rear, that only a few men escaped. The men were dispersed and the few remaining were pursued by the enemy back to the infantry squares, where they rejoined the rest of the regiment, which had gathered behind the same, and they ascertained the severe losses the regiment had sustained during the two attacks. The seven companies had been reduced to no more than sixty men, which were formed into one squadron under Captain von Kerssenbruch.

Sadly, we will never find out the real story behind these Allied observations until the regimental muster lists of the 5th and 6th Lancers are available for study at the French Army Archives sometime after 2020. For the men made prisoner of war from the 5th Lancers, we know the fate of only five men:[617]

1. Sergeant Andre Sibillat
2. Louis Chantreau
3. Jean Fenney
4. Charles Bacoffe
5. Jacques Lesseur

No men are listed as prisoner from the 6th Lancers.[618] It is the only Waterloo regiment to record no prisoners of war at all.

Roussel d'Hurbal's 11th Cavalry Division

Of the two brigades in the division, only Donop's cuirassier brigade went into action. The carabiniers were held back as a reserve.

The 2nd Cuirassiers was commanded by Colonel Louis Stanislas François Grandjean. The regiment, on 1 May 1815, was billeted at

---

617 SHDDT: Yj 11. See also: SHDDT: Yj 12.
618 ibid.

Montigny, Magny, and Augny. It mustered twenty-one officers with thirty-one horses and 214 men with 216 horses, formed into three squadrons. The regiment's depot housed a further 205 men, but they were neither clothed nor equipped. Due to the lack of horses, clothing and equipment the 3rd Squadron was disbanded on 26 May 1815 and the men distributed to the 1st and 2nd Squadrons, bringing the number of other ranks to 282.[619] On 10 June 1815, the regiment had twenty-one officers and 290 other ranks. Some 22 per cent of effective strength was lost on 18 June, a total of sixty-four men.

Of these, fifty-four were missing, including three presumed prisoners; these men are likely to have been dismounted in the action. Encumbered by the cuirass and stiff riding boots, these men would not have easily kept pace with the retreating army, and it seems were made prisoners or simply fell behind and were not seen again. Some five men are known to have been killed (witnessed and confirmed as such), one severely wounded in hospital, one died of wounds in hospital, one who fell behind two days after Waterloo, presumably wounded and dismounted, and two deserted.[620]

Charging against the Allied squares at Waterloo was Colonel Jean Guillaume Lacroix, colonel of the 3rd Cuirassiers, who was mortally wounded with a gunshot to the head. He died on 30 June 1815. Wounded in the regiment was Captain Pierre Alexandre Carel with a musket ball to the left shoulder. He had served as a velite in the grenadiers à cheval of the Imperial Guard from 27 January 1806. He had passed to the 3rd Cuirassiers with the rank of sub-lieutenant on 13 July 1807 and was promoted to lieutenant on 3 June 1809 and to captain on 12 August 1812.[621] Fellow captain, Jean Baptiste Moraine dit Morel, was slightly wounded when his horse was killed under him.[622] Lieutenant Louis Pierre François Chandru was wounded when a musket ball passed through his left hand.[623] Fellow lieutenant, Pierre Joudioux, who had joined the regiment on 14 November 1802 and had progressed through the ranks of sub-officers to be promoted to sub-lieutenant on 12 August

619 Antoine Ernest Rothwiller, *Histoire du deuxième régiment de cuirassiers, ancien Royal de cavalerie, 1635-1876, d'après les archives du corps, celles du dépôt de la guerre et autres documents originaux*, E. Plon, Paris, 1877, p. 621.
620 SHDDT: GR 24 YC 21 *Régiment de Reine organisation 1814-29 Juillet 1815*.
621 AN: LH 427/5.
622 AN: LH 1923/45.
623 AN: LH 480/8.

1812 and lieutenant on 8 July 1813, had his left elbow shattered by a musket ball; the same ball, after passing through his arm, also killed his horse.[624] Sub-Lieutenant Victor Baudinet de Courcelles was also wounded and had his horse killed in the charges.[625] In the charges, one officer was killed, one died of wounds, and twelve others were wounded. Other rank losses are shown below:[626]

3rd Cuirassiers	
Observations in the *Contrôle*	Number of Other Ranks
Killed on the field of battle, 18 June 1815	19
Dead or prisoner, 18 June 1815	24
Wounded, 18 June 1815	1
Missing	2

In addition, in October there were still eight men who were wounded and in hospital, but the date their wounds were received are not recorded.[627]

In total at Waterloo, forty-six men were lost. On 10 June, the regiment mustered thirty-eight officers with fifty-three horses and 427 other ranks with 415 horses; 11 per cent of effective strength was lost in the battle.

The regiment, however, at the time of its disbandment records that a total of 390 men had left the regiment without authorisation since 18 June for as yet 'unknown reasons'. This number no doubt includes losses from Waterloo and men lost in the rout, retreat and who had quit the army with the return of the king.[628]

---

624 AN: LH 1378/52.

625 SHDDT: 2 Yb 644.

626 SHDDT: GR 24 YC 26 *Régiment du Dauphin organisation 1814-Juin 1815.* Research undertaken by Mr Ian Smith.

627 SHDDT: GR 24 YC 26. Research undertaken by Mr Ian Smith.

628 SHDDT: Xc 99 *3e Cuirassiers.* Dossier 1814.

Chapter 13

Allied Reaction

The French cavalry repeatedly charged at, and were repelled by, the infantry squares, aided by the fire of British artillery and the counter-charges of the Allied light cavalry regiments, the Netherlands heavy cavalry and some of the few remaining effective units of the British heavy cavalry. After many heroic, but failed, assaults, the French cavalry gave up its attacks. The squares, though ravaged by French artillery fire, had started to break under the relenting pressure, as Macready, of the 30th Regiment of Foot, notes:[629]

> Though we constantly thrashed our steel-clad opponents, we found more troublesome customers in the round shot and grape, which all this time played on us with terrible effect, and fully avenged the cuirassiers. Often as the volleys created openings in our square would the cavalry dash on, but they were uniformly unsuccessful. A regiment on our right seemed sadly disconcerted, and at one moment was in considerable confusion. Halket rode out to them, and seizing their colour, waved it over his head, and restored them to something like order, though not before his horse was shot under him...The enemy's cavalry were by this time nearly disposed of, and as they had discovered the inutility of their charges, they commenced annoying us by a spirited and well-directed carbine fire. While we were employed in this manner it was impossible to see farther than the columns on our right and left, but I imagine most of the army was similarly situated: all the British and Germans were doing their duty.

---

629 *United Services Magazine*, 1852.

Clearly, Ney had seen sense in allowing the accompanying horse artillery to move up. Standing nearby was Thomas Pockocke, of the 71st Regiment of Foot, who narrates:[630]

> About two o'clock, a squadron of lancers came down, hurrying to charge the brigade of guns: they knew not what was in the rear. General Barnes gave the word, 'form square'. In a moment, the whole brigade was on their feet, ready to receive the enemy. The general said, 'Seventy-First, I have often heard of your bravery, I hope it will not be worse than it has been, today'. Down they came upon our square. We soon put them to the right-about. Shortly after we received orders to move to the heights. Onwards we marched, and stood, for a short time, in square; receiving cavalry every now and then. The noise and smoke were dreadful. At this time, I could see but a very little way from me; but, all around, the wounded and slain lay very thick. We then moved on, in column, for a considerable way, and formed line; gave three cheers, fired a few volleys, charged the enemy, and drove them back.
>
> At this moment, a squadron of cavalry rode furiously down upon our line. Scarce had we time to form. The square was only complete in front when they were upon the points of our bayonets. Many of our men were out of place. There was a good deal of jostling, for a minute or two, and a good deal of laughing. Our quartermaster lost his bonnet, in riding into the square; got it up, put it on, back foremost, and wore it thus all day. Not a moment had we to regard our dress. A French general lay dead in the square; he had a number of ornaments upon his breast. Our men fell to plucking them off, pushing each other as they passed, and snatching at them.
>
> We stood in square, for some time; while the 13th Dragoons and a squadron of French dragoons were engaged. The 18th Dragoons retiring to the rear of our column, we gave the French a volley, which put them to the right-about; then the 13th at them again. They did this, for some time; we cheering the 18th, and feeling every blow they received. When a Frenchman fell, we shouted; and when one of the 13th, we groaned. We wished to join them, but were forced to stand in square.

Ensign Grownow relates the following, clearly based upon what he was told by others and what he later read, as he states in a letter to his mother in June 1815 that he could observe nothing of the battle from where he stood:[631]

---

630 Thomas Pockoke, *Journal of a soldier of the 71st or Glasgow regiment, Highland Light Infantry 1806-1815*, William and Charles Taite, Edinburgh, 1819, p. 220.

631 Grownow, pp. 94-6.

About 4 p.m. the enemy's artillery in front of us ceased firing all of a sudden, and we saw large masses of cavalry advance: not a man present who survived could have forgotten in afterlife the awful grandeur of that charge. You perceived at a distance what appeared to be an overwhelming, long moving hue, which, ever advancing, glittered like a stormy wave of the sea when it catches the sunlight. On came the mounted host until they got near enough, while the very earth seemed to vibrate beneath their thundering tramp. One might suppose that nothing could have resisted the shock of this terrible moving mass. They were the famous cuirassiers, almost all old soldiers, who had distinguished themselves on most of the battlefields of Europe. In an almost incredibly short period they were within twenty yards of us, shouting 'vive l'Empereur!' The word of command, 'prepare to receive cavalry,' had been given, every man in the front ranks knelt, and a wall bristling with steel, held together by steady hands, presented itself to the infuriated cuirassiers.

Comment

Losses in the 3rd Cavalry Corps were as follows:

3rd Cavalry Corps							
Division	Regiment	Killed	Died of Wounds	Wounded	Wounded & Missing	Prisoner of War	Missing
11th Division	2nd Dragoons[632]	0	0	17	0	0	264
	7th Dragoons[633]	25	0	11	0	32	6
	8th Cuirassiers[634]	3	0	1	31	50	20
	11th Cuirassiers[635]	9	0	0	0	0	38
	3rd Company 2nd Horse Artillery	1	0	0	0	4	1
Division Total		38	0	29	31	86	329

---

632 SHDDT: Xc 135. Dossier 1815.
633 SHDDT: GR 24 YC 158.
634 SHDDT: GR 24 YC 50.
635 SHDDT: GR 24 YC 64.

12th Division	1st Carabiniers[636]	0	0	0	0	0	281
	2nd Carabiniers[637]	6	0	4	58	0	1
	2nd Cuirassiers[638]	5	0	2	0	3	56
	3rd Cuirassiers[639]	19	0	1	0	24	2
	2nd Company 2nd Horse Artillery	1	0	0	0	4	0
Division Total		31	0	7	58	31	340
Corps Total		69	0	36	89	117	669

Kellermann lost a recorded 980 men in the charges. The corps had mustered 3,245 cavalry and 309 artillery. Some thirty-eight men from the 8th and 11th Cuirassiers were lost on the 16th, and two men were men were wounded from 3rd Company 2nd Horse Artillery. Kellermann's corps lost 30 per cent of its men at Waterloo. Losses in the 4th Cavalry Corps were as follows:

4th Cavalry Corps							
Division	Regiment	Killed	Died of Wounds	Wounded	Wounded & Missing	Prisoner of War	Missing
13th Division	1st Cuirassiers[640]	0	0		0	0	117
	4th Cuirassiers[641]	9	0	29	0	0	0
	7th Cuirassiers[642]	3	0	1	0	4	62
	12th Cuirassiers	0	0	0	0	0	85

---

636 SHDDT: C15 34.
637 SHDDT: GR 24 YC 9 *Contrôle Nominatif, Troupe 1814-1815*. See also: SHDDT: Xc 93 *2e Carabiniers*.
638 SHDDT: GR 24 YC 21.
639 SHDDT: GR 24 YC 26.
640 Lot.
641 Moulins de Rochefort, p. 346.
642 SHDDT: GR 24 YC 46.

	5th Company 1st Horse Artillery[643]	0	0	0	0	6	0
Division Total		12	0	30	0	10	264
14th Division	5th Cuirassiers[644]	20	0	0	0	0	0
	10th Cuirassiers[645]	5	0	1	0	11	36
	6th Cuirassiers[646]	8	0	6	0	0	34
	9th Cuirassiers[647]	8	0	0	0	8	50
	4th Company 3rd Horse Artillery[648]	1	0	2	0	0	0
Division Total		42	0	9	0	19	120
Corps Total		54	0	39	0	29	384

Milhaud's command lost notably fewer men, some 506 individuals being killed, wounded or made prisoners; some 474 men less, or losses almost 50 per cent lower than the 3rd Cavalry Corps. It is very likely that the missing and prisoners were dismounted men who could not keep up with their regiment during the retreat. What we are not seeing is horse losses: a ratio of one man to every three horses. The two corps had lost 1,486 men at Waterloo out of 6,684 men, or 22 per cent of effective strength.

Six colours[649] had been captured and at least two squares had been broken into. This was of small comfort for the loss of hundreds of men

643 SHDDT: GR 25 YC 14.

644 SHDDT: Xc 103 *5e régiment de Cuirassiers*. Dossier 1814.

645 SHDDT: GR 24 YC 60.

646 SHDDT: GR 24 YC 41.

647 SHDDT: GR 24 YC 55.

648 SHDDT: GR 25 YC 40 *3e Artillerie à Cheval*.

649 1) A flag from the Lüneburg Battalion taken by the 1st Cuirassiers; 2) A flag from the 8th Battalion Kung's German Legion; 3) An English flag captured by Fourrier Isaac Palau, from the 9th Cuirassiers in Milhaud's Corps; 4) An English flag captured by Marshal de Logis Gauthier, of the 10th Cuirassiers; 5) A 'Belgian' flag captured by Captain Klein de Kleinenberg, of the chasseurs à cheval of the Imperial Guard. Klein's service record states: '*et un cheval tue sous lui dans un carré belge dont il à*

and horses. Both General Delort and Corporal Pilloy, of the cuirassiers, both state at least one British square, if not three, were broken. Certainly, the combined square of the 33rd and 69th Regiments of Foot broke at some stage in the cavalry charges. It also seems the 9th Cuirassiers broke a square and carried away the regiment's colours. So, with the massacre of the 5th and 8th Battalions King's German Legion and breaking of two squares at least, the cavalry had some impact on the Allied troops. Macready continues:[650]

> About six o'clock I perceived some artillery trotting up our hill, which I knew by their caps to belong to the Imperial Guard. I had hardly mentioned this to a brother officer when two guns unlimbered within seventy paces of us, and, by their first discharge of grape, blew seven men into the centre of the square. They immediately reloaded, and kept up a constant and destructive fire. It was noble to see our fellows fill up the gaps after every discharge. I was much distressed at this moment; having ordered up three of my light bobs, they had hardly taken their station when two of them fell horribly lacerated. One of them looked up in my face and uttered a sort of reproachful groan, and I involuntarily exclaimed, 'I couldn't help it.' We would willingly have charged these guns, but, had we deployed, the cavalry that flanked them would have made an example of us.

The square of the 30th and 73rd Regiments of Foot stood its ground well, but the square of the 33rd and 69th Regiments of Foot gave way under the cavalry attacks. Morris, of the 73rd Regiment of Foot, later wrote:[651]

> As the enemy's artillery was taking off a great many of our men, we were ordered to lie down, to avoid the shots as much as possible; and I took advantage of this circumstance to obtain an hour's sleep, as comfortably as ever I did in my life, though there were at that time upwards of 300 cannon in full play. But our services were now soon to be required. A considerable number of the French cuirassiers made their appearance, on the rising ground just in our front, took the artillery we had placed there, and came at a gallop down upon us. Their appearance, as an enemy, was certainly

---

enleve le drapeau le 18 juin 1815'; and 6) An unidentified flag captured by the chasseurs à cheval of the Imperial Guard.

650 *United Services Magazine*, 1852.
651 Thomas Morris, *Recollections of Military Service in 1813, 1814 and 1815*, James Madden & Co, London, 1845, pp. 218-9.

enough to inspire a feeling of dread—none of them under six feet; defended by steel helmets and breastplates, made pigeon-breasted to throw off the balls. Their appearance was of such a formidable nature that I thought we could not have the slightest chance with them. They came up rapidly, until within about ten or twelve paces of the square, when our rear ranks poured into them a well-directed fire, which put them into confusion, and they retired; the two front ranks, kneeling, then discharged their pieces at them. Some of the cuirassiers fell wounded, and several were killed; those of them that were dismounted by the death of their horses immediately unclasped their armour to facilitate their escape. The next square to us was charged at the same time, and were unfortunately broken into, and retired in confusion, followed by the cuirassiers; but the Life Guards coming up, the French in their turn, were obliged to retrograde, and the 33rd and 69th resumed their position in square, on our right, and maintained it during the rest of the day.

Perhaps the breaking of the combined square of the 33rd and 69th Regiments of Foot is that alluded to by Macready. Morris also notes that the cuirassiers were accompanied by horse artillery:[652]

The same body of the enemy, though baffled twice, seemed determined to force a passage through us; and on their next advance they brought some artillerymen, turned the cannon in our front upon us, and fired into us with grapeshot, which proved very destructive, making complete lanes through us; and then the horsemen came up to dash in at the openings. But, before they reached, we had closed our files, throwing the dead outside and taking the wounded inside the square, when they were again forced to retire. They did not, however, go further than the pieces of cannon—waiting there to try the effect of some more grapeshot. We saw the match applied, and again it came thick as hail upon us. On looking round, I saw my left-hand man falling backwards, the blood gushing from his left eye; my poor comrade on my right, by the same discharge, got a ball through his right thigh, of which he died a few days afterwards.

Our situation now was truly awful; our men were falling by dozens every fire. About this time a large shell fell just in front of us, and while the fuse was burning out, we were wondering how many of us it would destroy. When it burst, about seventeen men were

---

652 Morris, pp. 220-2.

either killed or wounded by it; the portion which came to my share was a piece of rough cast-iron, about the size of a horse-bean, which took up its lodging in my left cheek; the blood ran copiously down inside my clothes, and made me rather uncomfortable. Our poor old captain was horribly frightened, and several times came to me for a drop of something to keep his spirits up. Towards the close of the day he was cut in two by a cannon-shot.

6th Corps is sent to stop the Prussians

With the Prussians now arriving in numbers that Domon and Subervie's cavalry could contain, General Lobau, with his 6th Corps, were sent forward along the road to the Paris Wood, to take up positions at the eastern limit of the wood. If the Prussians were to be stopped, the village of Smohain, the chateaux of Frischermont and the farms of Papelotte and La Haye Sainte needed to be occupied, or the garrisons controlled, to protect the exposed left flank of 6th Corps. Bülow's command mustered around thirty thousand men against Lobau's 10,000-strong command. Since fighting on the Danube in 1809, Lobau had proved that he was a capable and resourceful general.

Lobau's command at Waterloo comprised the 19th and 20th Infantry Divisions. The 19th Infantry Brigade was commanded by General-of-Division Baron Simmer, who was wounded at Waterloo, and the 20th by General Jeanin. Antoine Nicolas Beraud, an officer in the 4th Regiment of Grenadiers à Pied of the Imperial Guard, was an eyewitness to the events as they developed on the French right wing:[653]

> The Prussians, which had shown themselves in the morning, gave rise to increasing concern, and the threat they posed had now to be taken seriously. Comte Lobau was charged with the 6th Corps and the Young Guard in repelling the attack which began on our right. This provision decreased all of a sudden the forces we could have against the English by 20,000 men. In this situation, the emperor merely desired to contain the English until he knew the result of the movements of the Prussians, those of Grouchy and Comte Lobau.

The Prussian assault on Plancenoit and La Haye Sainte was the vital turning point to the battle, as Adjutant-Commandant Janin (of 6th Corps) narrates:[654]

---

653 Beraud, pp. 279-80.
654 E. F. Janin, *Campagne de Waterloo*, Chaumerot Jeune, Paris, 1820, pp. 35-6.

The 6th Army Corps moved forward to support the attack on the centre: as it arrived on the crest of the ravine that separated the two armies, General Durrieux and his staff, who had led the advance, turned back wounded and announced that enemy sharpshooters had penetrated our right flank.

Comte de Lobau advanced with General Jacquinot and I to reconnoitre their positions, and soon we saw two columns on the march of about ten thousand men each: it was the Prussian army corps of Bülow. The destination of the 6th Army Corps was changed by this incident: it was no longer to continue the attack against the English, but instead was now to repel the Prussians.

de Mauduit, who served in the 1st Regiment of Grenadiers à Pied, notes that:[655]

The 6th Corps were ordered to move forward to support the attack against the centre, and it reached the crest of the ravine between the two armies, it was here where Chief-of-Staff General Durrieux had advanced to examine the terrain, became embroiled with sharpshooters and was seriously wounded with a musket ball to the thigh, which announced that enemy sharpshooters had extended along on our right flank. Comte Lobau advanced with General Jacquinot and Colonel Janin, the assistant chief-of-staff to reconnoitre whence he identified two columns were debouching, each of around ten thousand men: it was Bülow's Prussians... Comte Lobau advanced his infantry and replaced his 1st Line with the cavalry of General Domon. The men of General Bülow emerged to his right on the heights and wood of Smohain, the left of which descended into a valley of the Lasne Brook, and thence the Virer Wood. The cavalry of the reserve made a movement in two columns and debouched to the left, where Prince William of Prussia commanded the battle. The combat was violent. The Prussian Foot Battery No. 14 had three guns knocked out, thus the Prussian 12-pounder Battery No. 13 was placed in the centre of the Prussian 14th Brigade. The 6th Corps defended the position with great dedication, which is noted by Wagner [Prussian writer on the campaign], that they [the Prussians] were twice pushed back by an audacious bayonet charge, at the heads of which were Generals Janin and Durrieux. This charge caused the first Prussian battalions to retreat.

---

655 de Mauduit, 'Vieillee Militaire Charleroi, Fleurus et Waterloo' in Sentinale de l'armée, 16 June 1836.

Assistant chief-of-staff to 6th Corps was Colonel Jean Isaac Suzanne Combes-Brassard. He was born on 11 February 1772 at Montauban in the Tarn-et-Garonne, the son of Pierre Thomas Combes-Brassard and Anne Presque d'Ollier. He writes about Waterloo as follows:[656]

> The 6th Corps formed the reserve, I was chief-of-staff to the corps, and it marched to support the attack of the right. The corps was composed entirely of infantry.
>
> It was half-past three when an infernal fire extended all along the line of the two armies. The 6th Corps completed its deployment in reserve on the right of the army, when, returning to the extreme right, I recognised heads of columns emerging from the direction of Wavre, by Ohain and Saint-Lambert.
>
> These columns were Prussian. Their arrival occurred without the emperor issuing any orders. We were outflanked.
>
> Napoléon was the first to be aware of this danger. He ordered Lobau to cross the Brussels road and change direction to the right with his division, and move towards the chapel of Saint-Lambert, and was supported by the cavalry of Domon and Subervie, who were also employed to reconnoitre the Prussians.
>
> Still uncertain about the nature and the intentions of these troops, I approached them to reconnoitre their movements. I soon learned that this column was Prussian and manoeuvring to get on our flank and our rear, so as to cut the French army from retreating to Genappe and the bridge on the Dyle.
>
> I hastened to prevent this movement. There was still time, by taking the position where the army had bivouacked the night before, to prevent the danger we were in. We had not a moment to lose. To lose was to lose the army. The fates had thus been cast. The Prussians manoeuvred towards our rear.
>
> The emperor, who had been obstinately trying to force the centre of the enemy, took no account of the movement which were made on the flanks. The Prussians had already joined the left of the English and deployed on our rear, so that the right wing of our army and the 6th Corps were formed in an acute triangle where on two sides and the point were the English and Prussian army.

---

656 Combes-Brassard, *Notice sur la bataille de Mont-Saint-Jean* in *Souvenirs et Correspondance sur la bataille de Waterloo*, Librairie historique Teissèdre, Paris, 2000.

A terrible fire of artillery and musketry welcomed us. The English, French and Prussian regiments disappeared like ghosts into the smoke. The rear and flanks were engaged by the enemy. The 6th Corps opened a passage with their bayonets, we left the positions, the entire French army was in disorder and beginning to retreat, but it was not too late to stop an awful rout.

The Prussian official account of the start of their operations at Waterloo notes that:[657]

It was half-past four o'clock. The excessive difficulties of the passage by the defile of Saint-Lambert had considerably retarded the march of the Prussian columns, so that only two brigades of the 4th Corps had arrived at the covered position which was assigned to them. The decisive moment had come; there was not an instant to be lost. The generals did not suffer it to escape. They resolved immediately to begin the attack with the troops which they had at hand. General Bülow, therefore, with two brigades and a corps of cavalry, advanced rapidly upon the rear of the enemy's right wing. The enemy did not lose his presence of mind; he instantly turned his reserve against us, and a murderous conflict began on that side. The combat remained for a long time uncertain, while the battle with the English army still continued with the same violence.

An officer in the Prussian 18th Infantry Regiment writes about the opening stages of the attack at Frischermont and pushing back the French cavalry:[658]

When we reached Frischermont and found the farm buildings to the left of the village were occupied, we threw out sharpshooters under Captain von Pugwash and attacked the enemy positions. Their front line was taken by the first bayonet charge which was very determined. Captain von Pugwash's charge was a great contribution. Supported by the brigade artillery and the 2nd Silesian Hussar Regiment under Oberst von Eicke, he forced the enemy to abandon their positions. The hussars drove back the enemy skirmish screen which was posted to the left of Frischermont and forced a chasseur regiment to retire. However, a second enemy cavalry regiment attacked them in the flank, throwing them back. The 3rd

---

657 Booth.

658 Albert Burow, *Geschichte des Königlich Preussischen 18 Infanterie-Regiments von 1813 bis 1847* ed. Rudolph von Wedell, Posen, 1848, p. 166.

Silesian Landwehr cavalry under Rittmeister von Altenstein and a horse artillery battery soon restored the situation.

About the Prussian artillery, Georg Wilhelm Müller, 1st Hanoverian Foot Artillery Battery, in a letter dated 29 September 1837 writes:[659]

> I commanded the two guns attached to the division for the rest of the day, and these formed the extreme left wing of our artillery line. It was the express wish of General Picton that we were separated from Rettberg's battery by larger intervals than those found among the other artillery in our line. The battery had consumed half of its ammunition at Quatre-Bras, and the replacement ammunition only arrived when the wagons reached the battlefield during the night from the 18th to 19th, and so by six o'clock only a few canister rounds which we had saved were left to repel a possible attack by the enemy cavalry. At a quarter to seven the Prussian artillery, which was deployed some distance from our guns on the diagonal, opened fire on the French line, which was almost directly opposed to our own, and which forced the French guns on their extreme right wing to make a quarter turn in order to reply. The ammunition we had left was now sent to the guns on the flank. The battery was then limbered and moved to the rear in column.
>
> Shortly after the first two Prussian guns had arrived on our left, they wanted to advance with Rettberg's battery, and I was asked to lead them onto the field and to acquaint them with as much information as possible on the battlefield. This occurred at approximately the same time as the last French attack upon our centre. General Ziethen rode forward to our position in the twilight, as Rettberg's battery moved back to a position across the high road close to La Haye Sainte in order to bivouac there. I remember distinctly that General Ziethen has been very surprised by the terrible sight which the battlefield presented, and he could not compare it with any other he had experienced in his many years. He told us of the circumstances surrounding his withdrawal on the 15th and left us after he had enquired about the nearby villages, where supplies could be found for his troops.

The head of the French attack was formed by the 5th and 11th Regiments of Line Infantry under the orders of General Bélair, which was part of 6th Corps.

---

659 John Franklin personal communication, 18 October 2012.

The attack was spearheaded by the 19th Infantry Division. The 5th Regiment of Line Infantry, it seems, took the place of honour on the right to lead the attack. In the 4th Fusilier Company of 1st Battalion, Lieutenant Jules Michelin was mortally wounded. His thigh was shattered by a round shot, and the stump of the leg was amputated on 24 June 1815 in the military hospital in Brussels. He died of gangrene on 10 July 1815. He writes:[660]

> A cannonball shattered my thigh. In that moment, a boy and a *sapeur* carried me, but with great sorrow, to a house where there were already around fifty wounded. It was here that I realised our infallible cavalry had been crushed.

Corporal Wagre narrates Waterloo as he remembered it:[661]

> My regiment, the 11th, and 84th held the line on top of Mont-Saint-Jean, 18 June, from four o'clock until nine at night. The army was already defeated, and we were still at our posts when we saw that all was lost. We were then driven back, despite our best efforts, by the torrent of men retreating in the greatest disorder. I will not give any details on this unhappy day; many others have laid out this memorable occasion. We remember that I said that my captain was very strict and sometimes too severe. He was killed a moment after responding to a grenadier, wounded by a bullet which penetrated his stomach, who he ordered not to quit his rank. He told this soldier, 'stay, it's nothing'. However, despite the captain's orders, many men left their ranks.

Drawn up in the second line were the 27th and 84th Regiments of Line Infantry. They came under artillery bombardment and, it seems, were also attacked by the Prussian cavalry. Sub-Lieutenant Jean Laurent Martin Simon Litti, of the 27th Regiment of Line Infantry, writes:[662]

> I was made prisoner of war on 18 June 1815 at Waterloo, returned 2 January 1816. At the Battle of Waterloo on 18 June 1815 I suffered three sabre cuts to the head, a lance thrust, and a howitzer shell exploded near me which fractured the proximal end of the interior face of the tibia.

---

660 *Carnet de la Sabretache*, 1902, pp. 696-7.
661 Maurice Fleury, *Les prisonniers de Cabrera; souvenirs d'un caporal de grenadiers (1808-1809) publiés par le comte Fleury*, E. Paul, Paris, 1902.
662 AN: LH 1646/24.

Clearly, it seems the 27th Regiment of Line Infantry had suffered heavily from the Prussians in the defence of the French right wing on that fateful evening.

Sadly though, due to a lack of archive sources and eyewitness accounts, we know very little of the operations of the 19th Infantry Division from the men who were part of it. Indeed, Prussian sources do not add greatly to any discussion of what occurred here. From the few French accounts we have, which we have presented above, it is clear the division was under musket fire as well as artillery fire, and was attacked by Prussian cavalry.

To the left of the 19th Infantry Division was the 20th Infantry Division. The 20th Infantry Division was commanded by General Jeanin. It comprised the 10th and 107th Regiments of Line Infantry and the 5th Regiment of Light Infantry. The 47th Regiment of Line Infantry was still in the Vendée and had not joined the division by the time the Waterloo campaign began. Therefore, the 107th Regiment of Line Infantry was broken up so a battalion was attached to the 10th Regiment of Line Infantry, and the remainder to the 5th Regiment of Light Infantry. The adhoc brigade was commanded by General Trommelin. General Trommelin, commanding the 2nd Brigade of the 20th Infantry Division (part of 6th Corps), explains as follows about his deployments against the Prussians:[663]

> At three o'clock in the afternoon, Jeanin's division, followed by the 1st Division of Simmer, crossed the road 200 metres to the south of La Belle Alliance, moving behind Milhaud's cuirassiers, and with Plancenoit to their right, deployed to the rear of the 1st Division, on a ridge between two streams, a quarter of a league to the north of this village. The three regiments of the division were split into two groups, the 10th Regiment of Line Infantry and a battalion commanded by Cuppe, from the 107th Regiment of Line Infantry, were under my direct command, and were placed into a small wood. In front were two horse artillery batteries from the cavalry division, which were already firing against the Prussians.
>
> To our left the squadrons of Milhaud quaked. The Prussian attack started towards four o'clock in the evening. Our cavalry sabred the enemy squadrons. Then we formed square by brigade and remained under the fire of forty Prussian guns, which caused us great harm. We were unaware of what else was happening on the battlefield.

663 Henry Lachouque, *Le General Tommelin*, Tournai, n.d., pp. 227-9.

About half-past five o'clock, the enemy were reinforced by infantry and cavalry, and the artillery fire became terrible. We kept a bold front, but suffered greatly from the fire of the guns; the four squares of the corps retired slowly in echelon formation towards Plancenoit where we finally established ourselves. We were outflanked by the Prussian cavalry, and we occupied the gardens and orchards of the village.

The firing was prolonged on our right by the Young Guard, reinforced by my old chief, General Morand, at the head of the battalion of grenadiers [actually chasseurs]. The melee was terrible; the units became intermingled with each other, but had pushed back the Prussian assaults. Due to this, we were able to deploy a few hundred paces in front of Plancenoit.

We have an eye witness to the role of the 107th Regiment of Line Infantry at Waterloo: Sergeant-Major Marq. He was born on 13 December 1792, the son of Louis Marq and Mary Thérèse Briodar, in Eclaron in the canton of Saint Dizzier in the department of Haut-Marne. By trade he was a shop assistant. He was admitted to the 56th Cohort of the National Guard on 17 April 1812, promoted to corporal on 26 April 1812, transferred to the 153rd Regiment of Line Infantry on 22 February 1813, promoted to corporal on 22 February 1813, to sergeant-major on 26 March 1814. With the disbandment of the 153rd Regiment of Line Infantry, he passed to the 88th Regiment of Line Infantry, which had been the 107th Regiment of Line Infantry on 21 July 1814. The 88th Regiment of Line Infantry became the 107th Regiment of Line Infantry again on 1 April 1815. He was wounded on 18 June[664] and writes as follows about Waterloo:[665]

About ten o'clock in the morning (18 June 1815), the regiment left its camp and headed to Waterloo, where the battle was already animated. The regiments that were part of our corps (the 6th) were united. They marched in column to the battle. We were made to stand in this position until three o'clock in the afternoon, and having been exposed to a great number of cannonballs that were falling into our ranks; we marched in close column to the middle of the battlefield. Marching to this point, several men were killed

---

664 SHDDT: GR 21 YC 781 *88e régiment d'infanterie de ligne (ex 107e régiment d'infanterie de ligne), 21 juillet 1814-6 juillet 1815 (matricules 1 à 1,396).*
665 *Revue Napoléonienne*, 1901.

in the ranks, and having arrived, we were made to form square, because the British cavalry were near us and fought with the French cuirassiers. They came several times to press our square, but with no success. Bullets and shrapnel fell into our square like hail. We were there with orders not to fire a shot and to have fixed bayonets. Many men were killed in this position. After a few hours in square at this position, the battalion-commanders were ordered to send their voltigeur out as sharpshooters.

I was sergeant-major of the 3rd Company and immediately gave the order. We were led by our officers. Having arrived near the enemy we were positioned near a wood located on the road to Brussels. Being well emplaced and supported by columns of cavalry who were behind us, we forced the enemy to retreat, but soon our pursuit stopped, 40,000 enemies at once flushed us out of the woods and they opened fire on us.

The voltigeurs who were there were all killed and wounded. I was wounded by a bullet that went through my body through the left groin and came out after an incision in the bulk of the right buttock. This dropped me to the ground and was immediately picked up by two of my sergeants who were close to me. I was picked up and put on an artillery horse.

But, hardly had I gone twenty paces on the horse than I was obliged to get off of said horse, because I could not bear his movement. I stayed on the battlefield on 18, 19 and 20 June, when I was picked up by peasants and led away in Brussels. There I was dressed for the first time. I was part of a convoy of 1,500 men wounded.

The battle was terrible for the French. They had a complete rout; parks of artillery, ammunition wagons and food are left in enemy hands. The retreat was so hasty that there was hardly time to cut the traces of horses harnessed to pieces during the escape. Finally, I cannot describe the whole of this unfortunate retirement, since I was taken prisoner. But, having remained on the battlefield, I saw much of the enemy troops who marched in pursuit of the French.

Drawn up with the 107th Regiment of Line Infantry was the 5th Regiment of Light Infantry. At the head of the 1st Battalion, Battalion-Commander Louis Gaud was wounded.[666] Captain Jean Baptiste Anne Augustin Boullier was wounded twice, taking a gunshot to the right shoulder and a lance thrust to the head. From this, it seems the 5th

---

666 AN: LH 108/8/10.

Regiment of Light Infantry was attacked by Prussian lancers at some stage.[667] Also wounded by Prussian lancers was Lieutenant Field Marie Gabriel David de Belville, who suffered a lance wound also to the head.[668]

19th Infantry Division

The attack of 6th Corps was spearheaded by the 19th Infantry Division. Lieutenant General Simmer commanded the division, the larger of the two divisions in 6th Corps. At some stage in the battle, General François Martin Valentin Baron Simmer was wounded, and his chief-of-staff, Adjutant-Commandant Antoine Juchereau de Saint-Denys, was wounded with a contusion.

5th Regiment of Line Infantry

At the head of the 5th Regiment of Line Infantry, heading the 1st Brigade of General Bélair (part of Simmer's 19th Division), was Colonel Jean Isaac Roussille. He was seriously wounded.[669] Also wounded was Battalion-Commander Augustin Pierre Lefevre, at the head of the regiment's 1st Battalion.[670] Serving with the grenadier company was Lieutenant Jean Pierre Matter, who suffered a gunshot wound. Lieutenant Jean Antoine Ruffin, of the 1st Fusilier Company took a gunshot wound as did Sub-Lieutenant Jean Laurent. Wounded in the 2nd Fusilier Company was Lieutenant Jean Julien Vallette, who had been with the regiment since September 1813.[671] Marching at the head of the 3rd Fusilier Company, Captain Pierre Caillet took gunshot wounds to both legs which crippled him, and he was picked off the field of battle by the Allies and made prisoner of war.[672]

The captain-adjutant-major of 2nd Battalion, Louis Bleut, was killed. Commanding the grenadier company of 2nd Battalion was Captain Pierre Philibeaux, who took a gunshot wound. Also wounded from the same company was Sub-Lieutenant Leonard Giraud. The 1st Fusilier

---

667 AN: LH 319/12.
668 AN: LH 674/40.
669 AN: LH 2407/25.
670 AN: LH 1548/79.
671 Jean Marc Boisnard personal communication, 3 June 2012.
672 AN: LH 407/2.

Company had its sub-lieutenant, Jean Baptiste Gillet, wounded and the 2nd Fusilier Company had Sub-Lieutenant Jacques Griou killed. In the 3rd Fusilier Company, Lieutenant Pierre Paradis was wounded with a musket ball. At the head of the 4th Fusilier Company of the same battalion, Captain Nicolas Rimbault suffered a gunshot wound, as did Sub-Lieutenant Philippe Regnard. In the voltigeur company, Sub-Lieutenant Simon Andre was killed.[673] Other officers who were wounded attached to the regiment included Captain Descleves, Captain Honore Salomon Genibaud (who was also made a prisoner of war), Captain Thebault (who was also captured, transported to England, and died upon his return to France on 11 January 1816) and Sub-Lieutenant Delale was killed. Overall, according to Colonel Roussille, the regiment lost twenty-one officers and 1,200 men dead, wounded or captured out of 1,600.[674] Total regimental losses at Waterloo are in the table below:[675]

5th Regiment of Line Infantry				
	Wounded	Prisoner of War	Killed	Missing
1st Battalion	42	45	4	3
2nd Battalion	36	78	12	4
3rd Battalion	50	56	7	5
Total	128	179	23	12

On 18 June, the regiment mustered 1,541 men in three battalions.[676] The 3rd Battalion has so far never been listed in any order of battle for Waterloo, despite an order issued on 26 May 1815 ordering the battalion to join the Armée du Nord.[677] The regiment lost 342 men at Waterloo, or 22 per cent of effective strength. Colonel Roussille states the regiment lost 1,200 men out of 1,600; this is a gross exaggeration.[678] He also gives

---

673 Jean Marc Boisnard personal communication, 3 June 2012.
674 *Carnet de la Sabretache*, 1902, p. 691.
675 SHDDT: GR 21 YC 49 *5e régiment d'infanterie de ligne dit régiment d'Angoulême, 6 septembre 1814-23 décembre 1814 (matricules 1 à 1,800)*. See also: SHDDT: GR 21 YC 50 *5e régiment d'infanterie de ligne dit régiment d'Angoulême, 23 décembre 1814-25 août 1815 (matricules 1,800 à 2,208)*.
676 SHDDT: GR 21 YC 49. See also: SHDDT: GR 21 YC 50.
677 A. Chuquet, *Les inédits Napoléoniennes* (Vol. 2), p. 478.
678 Henri Martial Edmond Manceaux Demiau, *Historique du 5e régiment d'infanterie de ligne (1569-1890): rédigé conformément aux ordres de MM. les colonels Livet et Guasco*, E. Brulfert, Caen, 1890, p. 228.

twenty-one officers dead or wounded, when the figure is in fact twenty-four.

11th Regiment of Line Infantry

In the accompanying 11th Regiment of Line Infantry, Battalion-Commander Jean Haulon, formerly of the Flanqueur-Grenadiers of the Imperial Guard, took a gunshot wound to the right knee.[679] Étienne Maxent, a career soldier with the 11th Regiment of Line Infantry since volunteering to the regiment in 1800 as a private (and promoted to captain on 9 March 1815), had a musket ball pass through his left thigh.[680] Captain Guillaume Montegut, who served with the regiment since 1 December 1790, took a musket ball to the left arm.[681] Hachin de Courbeville was a career soldier, born on 2 April 1790, and joined the military school at Fontainebleau on 29 November 1806. He graduated as sub-lieutenant in the 11th Regiment of Line Infantry on 28 April 1807 and was promoted lieutenant on 20 June 1809 and to captain on 11 June 1813. Placed on the non-active list on 26 July 1814, he was recalled to the 11th Regiment of Line Infantry on 1 February 1815. Following Waterloo, he was named captain in the Legion of the Seine on 14 August 1816, named battalion-commander of the 20th Regiment of Line Infantry in 1835, as lieutenant-colonel in the 8th Regiment of Light Infantry in 1842, as colonel in the 25th Regiment of Light Infantry in 1843, and as colonel in the 54th Regiment of Line Infantry in 1848. He retired in 1850 and left the army on 3 June 1852. He had been wounded at Znaime on 11 July 1809 and took a musket ball to the left arm at Waterloo.[682]

The brigade lost 595 men at Waterloo, representing a loss of 22 per cent of effective strength from the brigade total strength of 2,676 men formed into six battalions.

In the 2nd Battalion, Battalion-Commander Antoine Bujon was wounded, having been wounded previously at Ligny. His aide, Captain-Adjutant-Major Jean Baptiste Delcombe, was wounded also. Commanding the grenadier company, Captain Etienne Marin was killed and Lieutenant Servais Delbrouck was wounded. Captain Jean Joseph Regnault, commanding the 1st Fusilier Company, was wounded. The

---

679 AN: LH 1271/67.
680 AN: LH 1806/47.
681 AN: LH 1919/71.
682 AN: LH 1256/59.

2nd Fusilier Company, at some stage (and perhaps the entire battalion) came under attack by presumably Prussian cavalry. In this attack, Lieutenant Dominique Ardussy was wounded with a sabre cut, as was Sub-Lieutenant Jean Laurent Martin Simon Litti. He suffered three sabre cuts to his head, and a lance wound. At some point before or after this attack his company had come under the fire of an artillery battery, and a howitzer shell exploded close to him, which fractured the head of his tibia. He was left for dead on the battlefield and made prisoner of war, being returned to France on 2 January 1816. The 3rd Fusilier Company had Lieutenant Edouard Barthelemy wounded, and the 4th Fusilier Company had Captain Louis Serravalle wounded.[683]

In the 3rd Battalion, at the head of the 3rd Fusilier Company, Captain Antoine Perrier was wounded. Also wounded from the battalion were Lieutenants Clerc and Estelle and Sub-Lieutenants Louis Masse and François Augustin Metzger, the latter serving in the voltigeur company.[684] Total losses for the 11th Regiment of Line Infantry are below:[685]

11th Regiment of Line Infantry					
	Wounded	Wounded & Prisoner	Prisoner of War	Killed	Missing
1st Battalion	70	0	11	26	1
2nd Battalion	65	0	44	19	3
3rd Battalion	Not at Waterloo				
4th Battalion	3	0	10	1	1
Total	138	0	65	46	5

In the fighting, the 11th Regiment of Line Infantry lost 254 men at Waterloo. Looking at the losses in detail, the 3rd Battalion lost one man wounded in 1st Company on 16 June. The 4th Battalion, hastily raised on 27 April 1815, dissolved rapidly after Waterloo.[686] Five men were lost at Charleroi in the 3rd Battalion on 18 June. In total, 22 per cent of

---

683 Jean Marc Boisnard, personal communication, 3 June 2012.
684 ibid.
685 SHDDT: GR 21 YC 100 *11e régiment d'infanterie de ligne, 9 septembre 1814-4 février 1815 (matricules 1 à 1,800)*. See also: SHDDT: GR 21 YC 101 *11e régiment d'infanterie de ligne, 4 février 1815-23 août 1815 (matricules 1,801 à 2,690)*.
686 SHDDT: GR 21 YC 100. See also: SHDDT: GR 21 YC 101.

the regiment's effective strength was lost at Waterloo. Despite this, the regiment still mustered 882 men by 20 June. By 26 June, the regiment mustered 575 other ranks, representing a loss of 307 men after Waterloo, or 35 per cent of effective strength. The 1st Battalion lost 108 men out of 402 at Waterloo, or 27 per cent; 2nd Battalion lost 131 out of 372, or 35 per cent; 3rd Battalion had mustered 361 other ranks, and following Waterloo formed the nucleus of the regiment. The 4th Battalion had a theoretical strength of 688 men. However, only 264 men seem to have served before 1 June 1815.[687] The battalion is absent from the 10 June muster list. Compared to other regiments in 1st or 2nd Corps, or indeed the Imperial Guard, these losses are on average 20 per cent lower. What does this tell us about the fighting that the brigade, and possibly 6th Corps in general, undertook? Clearly, the brigade either withdrew from the fighting on the French right wing earlier than we assume and thus was in action for a shorter period of time), was committed to the fighting later in the day, or the sector in which it stood did not experience heavy fighting.

27th Regiment of Line Infantry

The leading regiment of the 2nd Brigade of the 19th Infantry Division, under the orders of General Louis Marie Joseph Thevenet, who was mortally wounded at Waterloo, was the 27th Regiment of Line Infantry.

At the head of the grenadier company of 1st Battalion, Captain Jean Verdier was wounded,[688] as was Lieutenant Hartmann, of the same company. Commanding the 1st Fusilier Company was François Joseph Coliny, who suffered a gunshot to the right thigh.[689] In the 3rd Fusilier Company, Sub-Lieutenant Ambroise Sault was wounded.[690] Pierre Boudreaux, of the voltigeur company, was wounded. Commanding the 2nd Battalion was Antoine Bujon, who was wounded with a gunshot at Waterloo.[691] Killed at the head of the grenadier company was Captain Etienne Marin. Lieutenant Servais Delbrouck was also wounded, according to Martinien, but his service papers make no record of this.[692]

---

687 ibid.
688 AN: LH 2688/27.
689 AN: LH 565/14.
690 AN: LH 2464/38.
691 AN: LH 392/54.
692 AN: LH 707/79.

Jean Joseph Regnault, commanding the 1st Fusilier Company, was wounded. Total regimental losses are shown below:[693]

27th Regiment of Line Infantry					
	Wounded	Wounded & Prisoner	Prisoner of War	Killed	Missing
1st Battalion	17	0	43	4	21
2nd Battalion	20	0	28	8	3
3rd Battalion	11	0	10	3	4
Total	48	0	81	15	28

The regiment was commanded by Colonel Gaudin. Three battalions were present at Waterloo; the 3rd and 4th Battalions had been dispatched to the Loire under the orders of Battalion-Commander Desjoyaux,[694] but it is clear the 3rd Battalion was at Waterloo. We only know the strength of the 1st and 2nd Battalions, as the 3rd had not joined the army by 10 June, but clearly had done so by the 18th. It is likely that the 3rd Battalion mustered approximately the same strength as the 2nd Battalion, some 380 men, giving a theoretical regimental strength of 1,161 men. The 4th Battalion raised at the start of the Hundred Days never seems to have been recruited to full strength. One man is listed as wounded at Waterloo from the 4th Battalion, which may indicate that the 3rd and 4th Battalions were combined into a single battalion.[695] The regiment lost 171 men at Waterloo, thus around 15 per cent of effective strength. On 20 June, the regiment tentatively mustered 990 men. Compared to other regiments in 6th Corps, it did not suffer greatly at Waterloo. On 26 June 1815, the regiment mustered thirty-four officers and 437 men, representing a loss of 553 men since the Battle of Waterloo during the retreat. Some authors have used the 26 June muster list to equate this to losses at Waterloo, which in no way for the 27th Regiment of Line Infantry reflects losses on 18 June 1815, and shows just how destructive the retreat to Paris was. The regiment's returns were taken on 19 June, so we can be fairly certain of the losses sustained on the previous day.

---

693 SHDDT: GR 21 YC 255 *27e régiment d'infanterie de ligne, 1 août 1814 (matricules 1 à 1,800)*. See also: SHDDT: GR 21 YC 256 *27e régiment d'infanterie de ligne, 1 juillet 1814-19 juillet 1815 (matricules 1,801 à 2,778)*.
694 AN: LH 750/58.
695 SHDDT: GR 21 YC 255.

84th Regiment of Line Infantry

Total regimental losses are shown below:[696]

84th Regiment of Line Infantry					
	Wounded	Wounded & Prisoner	Prisoner of War	Killed	Missing
1st Battalion	83	5	0	14	11
2nd Battalion	28	1	10	11	57
3rd Battalion	26	1	5	1	20
4th Battalion	11	0	1	2	13
Total	148	7	16	28	101

In total, the regiment lost 300 men at Waterloo out of 1,527 men, equating to 20 per cent of effective strength. On the morning of 20 June 1815, the regiment mustered 1,228 men.

Comment

Divisional losses are shown in the table below:

19th Infantry Division						
Regiment	Wounded	Wounded & Prisoner	Prisoner of War	Killed	Missing	Total
5th Line	128	0	179	23	12	342
11th Line	138	0	65	46	5	254
27th Line	48	0	81	15	28	172
84th Line	148	7	16	28	101	300
Total	462	7	341	112	146	1,068

The 5th Regiment of Line Infantry bore the brunt of the fighting based on overall losses, followed by the 84th Regiment of Line Infantry. However, the highest number of dead was in the 11th Regiment of Line Infantry, which we are told by eyewitnesses stood alongside the 84th Regiment of Line Infantry. The 27th Regiment of Line Infantry has the lowest number of losses from any regiment in the division.

---

696 SHDDT: GR 21 YC 653 *72e régiment d'infanterie de ligne (ex 84e régiment d'infanterie de ligne), 1 août 1814-4 février 1815 (matricules 1 à 1,800).* See also: SHDDT: GR 21 YC 655.

One wonders if it was kept as a reserve, as the losses are significantly lower than the other regiments in the division.

20th Infantry Division

The division was commanded by General Jeanin. It was under-strength, and only comprised three regiments: the 10th and 107th Regiments of Line Infantry and the 5th Regiment of Light Infantry. The 47th Regiment of Line Infantry was still in the Vendée and had not joined the division by the time the Waterloo campaign began. Therefore, the 107th Regiment of Line Infantry was broken up so that a battalion was attached to the 10th Regiment of Line Infantry, and the remainder to the 5th Regiment of Light Infantry. The adhoc brigade was commanded by General Trommelin.

107th Regiment of Line Infantry

In the action, Battalion-Commander Jean Henri Cuppe, at the head of the 1st Battalion, took a gunshot to the stomach, which occasioned a hernia.[697] Colonel Druot, commanding the regiment, was wounded. Captain Vincent Frederick Delarue was grievously wounded to the left leg and was left for dead on the field of battle, becoming a prisoner of war.[698] The same fate befell Captain Alexandre Ducasse.[699] Sub-Lieutenant Jean Antoine Azaret Scevola Anthouard was shot in the right thigh. He was unable to keep pace with his retiring regiment and was left on the field of battle to be captured by the Allies. He was released from prison on 23 August 1815.[700]

In the closing stages of this fire fight, Lieutenant François Xavier Dericq was wounded. He was aged twenty-four at Waterloo. During this exchange of musketry, he was shot in the right hand. Later in the day with the Prussian cavalry flooding onto the battlefield, the rump of the 107th Regiment of Line Infantry was attacked by Prussian cavalry. In this melee, Lieutenant Dericq took a sabre cut to the right shoulder and

---

697 AN: LH 640/78.
698 AN: LH 703/88.
699 AN: LH 819/72.
700 AN: LH 41/109.

three wounds from a lance. He, however, survived this ordeal and died in 1860.[701] Total regimental losses at Waterloo are in the table below:[702]

107th Regiment of Line Infantry					
	Wounded	Wounded & Prisoner	Prisoner of War	Killed	Missing
1st Battalion	34	5	7	3	44
2nd Battalion	33	1	0	8	47
3rd Battalion	15	0	6	2	20
Total	82	6	13	13	111

The regiment lost 225 men on 18 June. It began the campaign with 691 other ranks and forty-four officers, forming three battalions. Overall 33 per cent of the regiment's effective strength was lost defending the French right flank.

5th Regiment of Light Infantry

At Waterloo, the regiment's archive admits to only six men being lost.[703] This figure is undoubtedly incorrect. Further archive research is needed to endeavour to discover the true casualties of the regiment at Waterloo. By 25 June, the regiment mustered twenty-seven officers and 371 men.[704] This represents a loss of 487 men in the period 10 to 25 June, or 57 per cent of effective strength.

10th Regiment of Line Infantry

Wounded at the head of the 1st Battalion was Battalion-Commander Jean François Elie Decos. Captain Jacques Henri Gabriel Drouas was also wounded. Captain Jean Baptiste Auguste Rey de Morande was shot by a musket ball that passed through his left thigh.[705] Captain Louis Auguste Lemaire was wounded, as was Captain Bertrand Cazenave, who commanded one of the regiment's grenadier companies.[706] The

---

701 AN: LH 738/25.

702 SHDDT: GR 21 YC 781.

703 SHDDT :GR 22 YC 48. See also: SHDDT: GR 22 YC 47.

704 SHDDT: C15 34.

705 AN: LH 2309/35.

706 AN: LH 458/41.

eagle of the regiment during the campaign was carried by Lieutenant Edmee Bouchu. He was born on 15 January 1776 at Tonnerre. Between 1809 and 1814 he had served in the Royal Guard of Spain and thence the Imperial Guard. At Waterloo, in defence of the eagle, he took a gunshot wound to the left leg.[707] Lieutenant Germain Beaufrère was born on 26 December 1785, had joined the regiment on 31 April 1814 having served in the Imperial Guard since 26 September 1806, and had progressed through the ranks from private to sub-lieutenant. He too was wounded at Waterloo.[708] At some stage Sergeant-Major Jean Pierre Casimir Husset was captured. He had served in the Imperial Guard since 8 October 1809 and was promoted as sergeant-major of the 10th Regiment of Line Infantry from the Flanqueur of the Guard on 1 September 1814.[709] Total regimental losses at Waterloo are below:[710]

10th Regiment of Line Infantry					
	Wounded	Wounded & Prisoner	Prisoner of War	Killed	Missing
1st Battalion	0	0	33	1	0
2nd Battalion	1	1	37	2	0
3rd Battalion	2	0	43	1	0
4th Battalion	0	0	15	1	0
Total	3	1	128	5	0

At Waterloo, the regiment lost 137 men; the overwhelming majority were prisoners of war. This number surely included wounded men. The regiment, it seems, was in action for a very short period, suffering five men killed and a recorded four men wounded. The data suggests that the regiment was possibly held in reserve. About the 10th Regiment of Line Infantry at Waterloo, we have the following account written in 1838, which suggests the regiment left the field in good order:[711]

---

707 AN: LH 307/70.

708 Jean Marc Boisnard personal communication.

709 AN: LH 1329/54.

710 SHDDT: GR 21 YC 92 *10e régiment d'infanterie de ligne dit régiment Colonel-Général, 1 septembre 1814-6 mai 1815 (matricules 1 à 1,800).* See also: SHDDT: GR 21 YC 93 *10e régiment d'infanterie de ligne dit régiment Colonel-Général, 6 mai 1815-22 juillet 1815 (matricules 1,801 à 1,943).*

711 Germain Sarrut, *Biographie des Hommes du Jour* (Vol. 4), Pluout, Paris, 1838, p. 217.

Major Laurent Hoffmayer commanded the Empress Dragoons at Waterloo.

Louis Harlet began his military career on 4 September 1791. After twenty-three years of distinguished service he was placed on the none-active list on 1 September 1814. He rallied to the Emperor on his return from Elba and was given command of the 4th Grenadiers of the Guard on 19 May 1815.

Louis Friant is best known for his service as an exceptional divisional commander under his brother-in-law, Marshal Davout. He began his career in 1781. During the Hundred Days, Napoleon placed General Friant in command of the 1st Brigade of Grenadiers, and he led the attack of the Old Guard.

FRIANT.

CAMBRONE

Pierre-Jacques-Etienne Cambronne is best known today for the 'mot de Cambronne' when ordered to surrender, which is reported to have been the French swear-word 'merde'. Cambronne was a Grand Officer of the Legion of Honour and was created Count of the Empire and a peer of France. On 8 April he was placed in commander of the 1st regiment of Chasseurs à Pied de la Garde Impérial.

General Drouot was admired as an honest man, known for always carrying a bible and for his exemplary discipline. In the Hundred Days he was nominal head of the Imperial Guard.

Maréchal de camp Pierre Francois Antoine Huber commanded the 1st Brigade of cavalry from Pire's 2nd Cavalry Division.

Mont. St Jean

Haie sainte (intérieur)

Mont. St Jean

Haie sainte (porte d'entrée)

Four views of the farm of la Haie Sainte, the key to the Allied position. These photographs were published in 1880. The farm was fought over throughout the day of the battle and was eventually captured by the French towards 16.00 hours.

Looking from the crossroads north of La Haie Sainte in this view of c.1816. La Haie
Sainte can be seen in the centre mid-ground. The depth of the banks either side of
the Brussels road here is clearly evident, as well as the depth of the sunken road that
heads off to join the Nivelles road to the right of the image. The 1st Life Guards had
to negotiate this major obstacle before they could charge. Many writers on the battle
forget the major obstacle presented by the abatis blocking the Brussels road by La Haie
Sainte, and the major obstacle caused by the sunken roads. It was no easy task for
cavalry to traverse this ground.

An image c.1816 of the view looking towards La Belle Alliance, in the middle
foreground, and, beyond, la Haie Sainte. This view from Wellington's right shows the
French positions taken up on the mid-morning of 18 June. The great chasm beyond La
Belle Alliance was again where the Brussels road sinks into the surrounding landscape.
This major obstacle caused problems for the retreating French on the night of 18 June.
One can also see the excellent field of view from Wellington's position, and how the
Allied troops had chance to prepare themselves before the onslaught of the French
cavalry charging up the slope. It was there too that the infantry of the Imperial Guard
made the last attack at Waterloo to try and tip the battle in favour of the French.

A view of the woods of Hougoumont c.1816. Up this slope, the severity of which is quite evident, the French cavalry charged for four hours. The scene today is greatly changed as the Allied ridge was dug away to make the Lion Mound, greatly altering the topography of the battlefield.

Looking towards Plancenoite and Papalotte. This is where the left wing of Wellington's army stood, and it was up the gentle slope that the French 1st Corps attacked. Here too was the charge of the Union Brigade in this view of c.1816.

General of Division Charles Claude Jacquinot commanded the 1st Cavalry Division, part of d'Erlons 1st Corps.

General of Division Pierre François Joseph Durutte commanded the 4th Division of d'Erlon's 1st Corps. His men held off the Prussian advance at Smohain until reinforced by 6th Corps and the Young Guard. The scars to his face and missing hand are the result of wounds received at Waterloo.

General Amable Guy Blancard was appointed commander of the Carabinier Brigade on 12 March 1815. He was wounded at Waterloo.

A rare photograph of the farm complex at Frischermont. All the buildings are now demolished. All these buildings were standing at Waterloo, and the complex was said to be demolished in 1859, if so, this image must date to just before this event.

A photograph of de Coster's house as it was 1875-1880. The house today bears no resemblance at all to this humble single-storey cottage.

A rare photograph of the farm of Papelotte taken between 1875 and 1880, and published in 1880. The tower over the entrance way was added after the battle.

Photographed sometime before 1880, we see the farm of La Caillou some sixty years after the battle, a scene no doubt little changed since 1815.

La Belle Alliance as it was some sixty years after the battle. The trees along the road side were not present in 1815 according to the 1777 map by Ferrari. They were cut down c.1900 to make way for a tram line, which too has been removed in the years after the Second World War.

It is incredibly rare to be able to put faces to the events of Waterloo. One eye-witness was Jean Bourg. MAT No. 4286 Jean Francois Bourg was admitted to the 1st Company, 1st Battalion of the 4th Grenadiers on 24 May 1815 from the 26th regiment of Line Infantry. At Waterloo he was wounded and made a prisoner of war. He returned to France in 1816. He was photographed in 1858.

An eye-witness to the events at Waterloo was Charles Picq. He was an officer serving under General Christiani. Admitted to Grenadiers à Pied of the Directory Guard on 15 November 1796, he rose through the ranks to 1st Lieutenant. Re-admitted to Imperial Guard in 1815, he served in the 2nd Battalion, 2nd Grenadiers à Pied. He was discharged on 17 July 1816.

Very rarely do portraits exist of private soldiers, especially one which has the name of the person depicted. Here, however, we have Jean Baptiste Chabrol, who served at Waterloo in the 3rd Company, 1st Battalion, 3rd regiment of Grenadiers à Pied. He deserted the army on 1 August 1815. (Private collection)

The southern, or upper, gates at Hougoumont, photographed c.1860. This view appears to have been unchanged since the time of the battle.

Hougomont

Maison du jardinier et ferme

The last remaining vestiges of the southern wood at Hougoumont partially obscure the garden wall in this photograph taken c.1860.

Hougomont

Mur du verger

Here were see the southern garden and orchard wall stretching eastwards towards the Brussels road. We also see remains of the thick hedge that ran in front of the wall that was a virtually impenetrable barrier to the attacking French troops.

Hougomont

Porte du nord (vue prise de l'extérieur)

The northern or lower gate as it appeared c.1880. The cross beam above the gates is not present in images made twenty years earlier, so cannot be the original. It was this gate that the 3rd regiment of Line Infantry attempted to break through at the start of the battle.

The western range of the farm complex at Hougoumont. Of note is the large archway in this range of buildings. It was through this gate that the 2nd regiment of Line Infantry broke into the southern or upper courtyard.

The chapel at Hougoumont dominates the scene, with the remains of the chateau still partially standing, in a photograph taken about 1860. Through the large gate at the centre of the image the 1st regiment of Line Infantry, led by Major Le Beaux, broke into the southern, or upper, courtyard.

Mont St Jean

La ferme

The Farm of Mont Saint Jean. Though not heavily involved in the action, it still stands as a testimony to that famous day in 1815.

At the Battle of Waterloo, the 10th of the Line formed part of 6th Corps and was one of the last to leave the field, and affected its retreat in good order until reaching Laon, which it reached drums playing and the band at its head. It took part in the retreat to Paris, and retired behind the Loire, where it was disbanded.

Clearly, this statement has some truth about it, as the regiment suffered the least casualties of any regiment of line at Waterloo. Did 6th Corps leave the battle early? Was this the cause of the collapse of the French right wing?

Comment

Divisional losses are in the table below:

20th Infantry Division						
Regiment	Wounded	Wounded & Prisoner	Prisoner of War	Killed	Missing	Total
5th Light	Data not available					
10th Line	3	1	128	5	0	137
107th Line	82	6	13	13	111	225
Total	85	7	141	18	111	362

We have no data for the 5th Regiment of Light Infantry, so we cannot offer any comment regarding divisional losses. The 107th Regiment of Line Infantry lost more men than the 10th Regiment of Line Infantry, as we commented earlier. The bulk of the 10th Regiment of Line Infantry were lost as prisoners of war, whereas the 107th Regiment of Line Infantry had far more men killed and wounded, suggesting the 10th Regiment of Line Infantry listed all its losses as prisoners of war (i.e. missing, or the regiment went into action and lost the bulk of its manpower during the rout).

Chapter 14

La Haye Sainte: Round Two

Meanwhile in the centre, the Allied garrison at La Haye Sainte was proving to be troublesome; the defenders were firing into the flank of the French cavalry attacking Wellington's right. Squadron-Commander Georges Marc Nicolas l'Etang, of the 7th Regiment of Dragoons, writes:[712]

> Following this event, the emperor informed of the danger to our position, ordered that the farm of Saint-Alliance [La Haye Sainte] was to be attacked and taken. Ney was placed at the head of the infantry and marched to this post and captured it. From thence, the division of Lhéritier ceased to run the gauntlet of murderous fire which it was long exposed to.
>
> Forced to move from their entrenchments, the English moved in disorder from this farm and turned back to the bulk of their army.

General Gourgaud notes that Napoléon:[713]

> Ordered Marshal Ney to establish himself at La Haye Sainte, to fortify it and to station several battalions there; but to make no movement till he saw the issue of the manoeuvres of the Prussians. Half an hour after, about five o'clock, at the moment when the Prussians were attacking us with the greatest vigour, the English attempted to retake La Haye Sainte. They were vigorously repulsed by the fire of our infantry, and by a charge of cavalry.

---

712 SHDDT: C16 Correspondence 1815 Folio 717.
713 Gourgaud, pp. 98-9.

General Drouet d'Erlon writes:[714]

> The fighting was restored, La Haye Sainte was taken about three
> o'clock, the battle seemed to decide in our favour. At that time,
> the Duke of Wellington would not have hesitated in ordering a
> retreat on Brussels where great confusion already reigned, if he had
> learned that the Prussian corps of Bülow, 40,000 men strong, would
> lead to our right. The Duke of Wellington then redoubled his efforts
> to maintain his position, and about half-past four the head of the
> Prussian columns effectively debouched.

Lieutenant-Colonel Jonathan Leach, of the 95th Rifles, notes some years
after the battle about the effect the French artillery was having to the
Allied lines, and how the attack against La Haye Sainte developed for
a second time:[715]

> Nothing could exceed the determined bravery with which the
> Germans defended the farmhouse of La Haye Sainte; but in the
> desperate attack which was now made on it, having expended
> the whole of their ammunition, and there being no means of supplying
> them with more, they were driven out, and the house was instantly
> filled with the enemy's infantry. For several hours afterwards they
> kept up a dreadful fire from loopholes and windows in the upper
> part of it, whereby they raked the hillock so as to render it untenable
> by our battalion. They were also enabled to establish on the knoll,
> and along the crest of the hill, a strong line of infantry, which knelt
> down, exposing only their heads and shoulders to our fire.

> Thus, the closest and most protracted contest with musketry perhaps
> on record was continued for several hours; during which we were
> several times supplied with fresh ammunition. The artillerymen
> were swept from the guns which were within reach of the house
> and the hillock. The possession of La Haye Sainte by the French
> occasioned a vast loss to our division, which was so diminished in
> numbers that all our reserves of infantry were brought up into our
> first, and now only line, as were also the 4th and 40th Regiments...
> Every kind of exertion was made by the French officers during this
> blaze of musketry to induce their men to advance from the crest
> of the ridge and from the hillock, to charge us; and although, by
> the daring and animating example shown by many of them, they
> at times prevailed on a certain portion of their men to advance a

---

714 Drouët.
715 Leach, pp. 388-92.

few yards, the fire which we sent among them was such that they were glad to get back under cover of the knoll; some of them, at least, were not disabled. In this manner continued the contest on our part of the line hour after hour, without any appearance of its being decided as long as anyone remained alive on either side.

Marshal-du-Camp Baron Schmitz, commanding the 1st Brigade of the 2nd Infantry Division (1st Corps), writes as follows in his after-action report dated 25 June 1815, explaining the sequence of events leading to the capture of the farm:[716]

The enemy, seeing the firm and unshakable countenance of the brave regiments that made up the division, employed every means which were in his power to push it back and he was not content to launch bullets and shells on its masses; he fired more than 200 Congreve rockets at it.

> The marshal-du-camp commanding the brigade, having observed that the enemy had positioned the machines that were used to launch these rockets behind a mound which covered them, he detached two voltigeur companies of the 13th Regiment who flushed out the machines and forced the withdrawl of the cavalry which protected them, and the enemy withdrew to its own lines. The division was formed in square by regiment.
>
> In this position, the 2nd Brigade received orders to stand on the highway and attack the embattled house that covered the centre of the hostile army, the brigade having been repulsed in the attack, the general commanding the 1st Brigade was ordered by Marshal Ney to attack again the crenelated house; the 17th Regiment crossed the highway to protect the left of the house from attack. We advanced to within pistol range, but the enemy stubbornly defended the battlements.

As the general commanding the brigade, I saw the impossibility of dislodging the enemy and I sent for two pieces of cannon to drive in the walls. The enemy then left the house and retreated behind the barricades that were erected on the plateau across the road.

The 1st Brigade maintained this position before the house until eight at night. Having no more ammunition, M. Marshal Ney had them relieved by a portion of the 8th Regiment of Line Infantry. George Baring, commanding the garrison, notes:[717]

---

716 *Revue Etudes Napoléoniennes*, 1932, pp. 360-5.
717 Pflugk-Harttung, p. 102.

The enemy renewed his efforts with his infantry in the same manner as before. Now our lack of ammunition could be felt already, but my repeated requests were in vain, except that 200 Nassau sharpshooters were sent to our assistance. Because the enemy could not impose himself, despite the cannon fire directed against the farm and the force of their weapons, they tried to set the farm on fire by throwing fire into the barn and which immediately set light to the straw inside; nevertheless, we managed to extinguish the fire without too much difficulty, thanks to the camp kettles carried by the Nassau troops. The enemy retired, exhausted by his efforts so as to form and advance for the fourth time, but with renewed strength, although in the same way as they had during the three previous attacks, only with the support of more artillery than before. Because of our lack of ammunition, there being only three or four cartridges per man, the result of this attack could be foreseen, which I announced in the most colourful way, but without any consequence. Once the enemy found their firing unanswered, they climbed up the walls and assailed the gateways and gates and pushed us—as we were unable to resist—out of the farm. We withdrew through the garden behind towards the main position, where the various detachments re-joined their respective corps, and I united with the 1st Light Battalion with the forty to fifty men who remained of my battalion.

Baring confirms Schmitz's statement that artillery was brought up against the farm. The 1st Brigade comprised the 13th Regiment of Light Infantry and 17th Regiment of Line Infantry.[718] About the attack of the division, Adjutant Gastineau[719] writes:[720]

We were placed to the right of the road from Charleroi to Brussels, at the centre of 1st Corps. Each division was formed in two lines, separated by 300 metres. At 2 p.m. we received the order to march against the English, who stood to our left, under the protection of eighty guns. A terrible fire was given by the English 95th which ambushed us from the Ohain road, the 13th Light pushed them back

---

718 SHDDT: GR 21 YC 116 *13er régiment d'infanterie Legere 1806 à 1815.*

719 MAT No. 2107 Jean Baptiste Gastineau, born 15 August 1789. He was conscripted to the regiment on 16 May 1808, promoted to corporal on 1 April 1809, to fourrier on 3 November 1809, to sergeant on 7 February 1811, to sergeant-major on 17 August 1811 and to adjutant-sub-officer on 1 September 1812. He retained his post in 1814. SHDDT: GR 21 YC 116.

720 B. Coppens personal communication.

with the bayonet and the 3rd Echelon rolled back the Hanoverians. We reached the second line of the English, who were carefully lying on the ground, who suddenly stood up and stopped us by the means of this unexpected fire. For a moment we were turned back by a charge by the brigades of Pack and Kempt, but we again went forward with the bayonet, led by Generals Bourgeois and Donzelot. A bloody melee began.

The rocket battery is stormed

As Quiot's men attacked the embattled farm, it seems that Donzelot detached the voltigeur companies of the 13th Regiment of Light Infantry to attack Allied artillery and rockets which were firing into the attacking French troops.

This attack was witnessed by Friedrich d'Huvele, a lieutenant with the 1st Hanoverian Foot Artillery. He notes that French troops did attack artillery and, importantly, the rocket battery:[721]

> The rocket battery remained for about an hour in its position, and it also suffered considerable losses during this time.

Comment

At Waterloo, the 3rd Battalion of the 13th Regiment of Light Infantry seems to have been detached to the French right flank, along with the 7th Hussars, to link up with Grouchy and to keep the lines of communication open. Total regimental losses at Waterloo are in the table below:[722]

13th Regiment of Light Infantry					
	Wounded	Wounded & Prisoner	Prisoner of War	Killed	Missing
1st Battalion	57	0	7	10	111
2nd Battalion	15	0	4	5	69
3rd Battalion	4	0	3	3	17
4th Battalion	24	0	23	3	189
Total	100	0	37	21	386

721 John Franklin personal communication, 3 July 2012,
722 SHDDT: GR 21 YC 116.

On the morning of 10 June, the regiment mustered sixty-one officers and 1,424 other ranks. On 16 June, ten men were wounded or deserted in the action at Quatre-Bras. On 17 June, at Genappe, two men were lost: one man killed and another wounded. Thus, on the morning of Waterloo, 18 June, the regiment mustered 1,412 men. The 4th Battalion mustered 413 men and lost 239 men at Waterloo, some 58 per cent of effective strength.

In total, 544 men were lost at Waterloo, representing 38 per cent of effective strength. When we look at the data, the 2nd and 3rd Battalions suffered the least, while the 1st and 4th Battalions suffered the most. This suggests that the latter two were fighting at Waterloo, with the 2nd and 3rd Battalions being detached to the right flank.

This final and successful attack was carried out by the 17th Regiment of Line Infantry. Adjutant Dieppedalle narrates in a letter of 29 January 1816:[723]

> At the Battle of Mont-Saint-Jean, on 18 June 1815, I was made prisoner of war during the rout. In my capacity as adjutant-sub-officer, I was the first to enter the farm of La Belle Alliance [La Haye Sainte] with a detachment of five men, and we made an officer and twenty Brunswick chasseurs [Hanoverian light infantry] lay down their arms and were made prisoners.

Henry Houssaye states that the farm was taken by the 13th Regiment of Light Infantry, which does not seem to have been the case. He cites Colonel Planzeaux, of the 2nd Regiment of Dragoons, as the source for this information. Other historians claim the 19th Regiment of Line Infantry was the regiment which captured the farm. As we have seen, the 17th Regiment of Line Infantry should take the honour. With the brigade of Schmitz taking losses, the 8th Regiment of Line Infantry were brought in to support Schmitz after his brigade ran out of ammunition. The regiment was part of General Durutte's division of 1st Corps. It was brigaded with the 29th Regiment of Line Infantry, under General Pégot. This movement of manpower to the centre is noted as follows by Captain Camille Durutte:[724]

---

723 Ian Smith personal communication, 7 July 2012 citing letter from Dieppedalle dated 29 January 1816.
724 *La Sentinelle de l'Armée*, 4th Year, No. 134, 8 March 1838.

The numbers of our troops so diminished in the centre near the main road, they were obliged to take troops from General Durutte, who sent a brigade to the left of this road, and a regiment was placed on the highway to support the troops who had taken position at the maison carré [La Haye Sainte].

Total regimental losses at Waterloo are in the table below for the 17 Regiment of Line Infantry:[725]

17th Regiment of Line Infantry					
	Evacuated Wounded	Wounded & Prisoner	Prisoner of War	Killed	Missing
1st Battalion	2	0	2	9	190
2nd Battalion	2	0	3	24	167
3rd and 4th Battalions	0	0	1	3	54
Total	4	0	6	36	411

The regiment lost 457 other ranks on 18 June. In addition, two men had been lost on 16 June, making a total loss of 459 men. On 10 June, the regiment mustered forty-two officers and 955 other ranks, thus 48 per cent of its effective strength was lost at Waterloo.

The 2nd Brigade was commanded by General Aulard and comprised the 19th and 51st Regiments of Line Infantry. In the attack of 1st Corps, the 19th Regiment of Line Infantry, which we assume formed the head of column of General Aulard's 2nd Brigade, came under fire. Perhaps it was now that Battalion-Commander Jean Thomas Maussion was wounded. Captain-Adjutant-Major Jean François Frelois was shot through the upper torso.[726] Captain Felix Balthazard Gresse took a musket ball to the shoulder.[727] Captain Bonaventure Ponsard received two gunshot wounds to each shoulder.[728] In the same fire fight, Sub-Lieutenant Vincent Millot had a musket ball pass through his chest.[729] Sub-Lieutenant Henri Fleurus Olivier, who was aged just twenty at Waterloo, had a musket ball hit him in the left of the chest and a second

---

725 SHDDT: GR 21 YC 158 *17e régiment d'infanterie de ligne, Octobre 1814-22 juin 1815 (matricules 1 à 2,593).*
726 AN: LH 1032/75.
727 AN: LH 1199/10.
728 AN: LH 219/79.
729 AN: LH 1881/58.

pass through the upper part of his left arm.[730] Adjutant Pierre Ballet was also wounded.[731]

As well as coming under fire from musketry, the 19th Regiment of Line Infantry also came under artillery fire. Sergeant-Major Simon Lemaire, aged just twenty-one at Waterloo, was wounded when a howitzer shell exploded near to him, the fragments hitting him in the face and head. He was left on the field of battle and was captured by the Allied cavalry. Taken to Brussels, he was taken to prison in England and was returned to France on 10 January 1816.[732] Total regimental losses for the 19th Regiment of Line Infantry at Waterloo are in the table below:[733]

19th Regiment of Line Infantry					
	Evacuated Wounded	Wounded & Prisoner	Prisoner of War	Killed	Missing
1st Battalion	1	85	0	10	130
2nd Battalion	1	79	0	17	121
3rd and 4th Battalions	1	33	0	3	42
Total	3	197	0	30	293

The regiment lost 523 other ranks on 18 June. In addition, one man was lost on 16 June, and three men were wounded and two reported as lost on 17 June. This makes a total loss of 529 men. On 10 June, the regiment formed two battalions, 989 men strong, and therefore lost 53 per cent at Waterloo.

In the fighting, the 51st Regiment of Line Infantry battalion-commander, Michel Prenet, was shot in the head, the musket ball entering the skull close to the temple and apparently passing through his skull. He was left for dead on the field of battle and was taken prisoner by the Allies. He returned from England on 2 March 1816 and was retired from the army. He died in 1842. Perhaps uniquely for a French officer of the line at Waterloo, he had been wounded at the Battle of Trafalgar while serving as ship's garrison.[734]

---

730 AN: LH 2014/56.

731 AN: LH 99/30.

732 AN: LH 1575/13.

733 SHDDT: GR 21 YC 178 *19e régiment d'infanterie de ligne, 18 août 1814-26 avril 1815 (matricules 1 à 1,800)*. See also: SHDDT: GR 21 YC 179 *19e régiment d'infanterie de ligne, 26 avril 1815-16 juillet 1815 (matricules 1,801 à 2,598)*.

734 AN: LH 2012/12.

Other officers wounded included Captain Cyr Billot, who suffered a gunshot wound to the left side of his chest in the battle.[735] Captain Jean Biot suffered a similar wound, but to the right side of his chest[736] and Captain Damien Exupre Dabadie suffered an identical wound.[737]

Captain Jean Cormilliot was wounded during the battle.[738] Sub-Lieutenant Pierre Felix Ansous was wounded by a gunshot at some stage during the day.[739] Killed in the attack were Colonel Rignon and Captains Penaud, Guillaume Escarguel (at the head of the grenadier company of 1st Battalion) and Harant. Furthermore, Lieutenant Denis Joron was mortally wounded and died later of wounds. Total regimental losses at Waterloo are shown below:[740]

51st Regiment of Line Infantry					
	Evacuated Wounded	Wounded & Prisoner	Prisoner of War	Killed	Missing
1st Battalion	3	102	0	6	126
2nd Battalion	1	81	0	5	141
3rd Battalion	3	57	0	6	109
Total	7	240	0	17	376

The regiment lost 640 other ranks on 18 June. In addition, one man was lost on 16 June and three men were wounded and two reported as lost on 17 June at Genappe. One officer was also wounded on 17 June. This makes a total loss of 646 men.[741] On 10 June, the regiment formed three battalions, 1,126 men strong, and lost 57 per cent of its troops at Waterloo. It is likely that the high number of casualties were suffered during the assault on La Haye Sainte, which General Schmitz (who commanded a brigade of Donzelot's 2nd Infantry Division) tells us

---

735 AN: LH 241/62.

736 AN: LH 243/78.

737 AN: LH 644/3.

738 AN: LH 590/78.

739 AN: LH 41/53.

740 SHDDT: GR 21 YC 433 *47e régiment d'infanterie de ligne (ex 51e régiment d'infanterie de ligne), 6 août 1814-15 mars 1815 (matricules 1 à 1 800).* See also: SHDDT: GR 21 YC 434 *47e régiment d'infanterie de ligne (ex 51e régiment d'infanterie de ligne), 20 mars 1815-13 septembre 1815 (matricules 1 801 à 2 627).*

741 SHDDT: GR 21 YC 433. See also: SHDDT: GR 21 YC 434.

eviscerated the division, so much so that elements from 4th Division were sent to bolster the troops in this position. Total divisional losses are as follows:

1st Infantry Division						
Regiment	Wounded	Wounded & Prisoner	Prisoner of War	Killed	Missing	Total
13th Light[742]	100	0	37	21	386	544
17th Line[743]	4	0	6	36	411	457
19th Line[744]	3	197	0	30	293	523
51st Line[745]	7	240	0	17	376	640
Total	114	437	43	104	1,466	2,164

The division had mustered 5,130 men and lost a total of 2,164 men (42 per cent) at Waterloo. In comparison, Quiot's 1st Division lost 35 per cent, and Marcognet's lost 64 per cent. The farm fell around 17.30 as Pontécoulant, of the Imperial Guard horse artillery, writes:[746]

> Two batteries of the Guard horse artillery were detached, which he [Napoléon] ordered to advance as far forward as was possible. It was half-past five o'clock. They deployed to the left of the farm of La Haye Sainte, which the enemy no longer disputed with us, on the slopes of the plateau of Mont-Saint-Jean, which had been occupied for some time by our cavalry, and soon swept the English line with balls and canister.

Donzelot's men had been flung at La Haye Sainte and had been replaced by the troops of General Pégot; elements of Quiot's command had been sent to Plancenoit, leaving whatever remained of Marcognet's division in the void. To bolster the line between La Haye Sainte and Papelotte, Napoléon ordered that a battery was to be established on the plateau of Mont-Saint-Jean. The two remaining uncommitted batteries of Imperial Guard horse artillery (the 1st and 2nd Companies) and the 5th and 6th Companies of the Old Guard Foot Artillery were ordered to take up positions. The Guard infantry that had not yet been deployed would

---

742 SHDDT: GR 21 YC 116.
743 SHDDT: GR 21 YC 158.
744 SHDDT: GR 21 YC 178. See also: SHDDT: GR 21 YC 179.
745 SHDDT: GR 21 YC 433. See also: SHDDT: GR 21 YC 434.
746 Pontécoulant, pp. 245-6.

be sent into action sometime between 19.30 and 20.00, in Napoléon's last attempt to break the British and Allied lines. The stage was now set for Napoléon's last gamble, as he ordered the Old Guard to make preparations to attack Plancenoit and the Allied centre, in a last attempt to snatch victory from the impending jaws of inevitable defeat. Ordered to attack once more, in conjunction with the Old Guard, was what was remaining of the 1st and 2nd Corps.

Chapter 15

Reille Goes on the Offensive

On the French right, 1st Corps had captured La Haye Sainte and had also overrun troublesome Allied artillery batteries. Ney now turned his attention back to the left wing. After two hours of cavalry charges, supported by artillery, the scene was set for the French infantry to return to the assault.

The advance of the 3rd Cavalry Reserve against the entire Allied line was a prelude to a French infantry assault. On the French left, 2nd Corps was being prepared to march forward to attack the Allied lines to the immediate north of the Hougoumont Wood, to cut it off from the Allies and, therefore, enable the place to be captured, as well as to punch a hole in the Allied lines for the yet as uncommitted carabiniers and the heavy cavalry of the Imperial Guard to surge through.

The fighting in the environs of Hougoumont lasted all day, with elements of the 2nd Corps being ordered to advance in support of the final attack of the Imperial Guard.

It was not until around 18.00, according to General Trefcon, that the divisions of Foy and Bachelu were fully committed to the attack in the wake of the cavalry. We cannot be sure of the exact time, as time was not yet standardised. Foy's division had been involved in the attack on Hougoumont earlier in the day, and so were already reduced in terms of manpower and stamina. Bachelu's command had seen comparatively little action and headed the French attack columns. Thus, some twenty French battalions, perhaps 6,000 men after the losses of Quatre-Bras and earlier in the day, marched forward to break the Allied line. Also involved was the 3rd Regiment of Line Infantry, which, according to Major Beaux (of the 1st Regiment of Line Infantry), were stationed on the right of the orchard of Hougoumont. Major Beaux hints his regiment was also involved in this action. These two regiments would add perhaps another 1,000 to 1,500 bayonets to the French infantry assault. This attack has been written out of the story of Waterloo. Perhaps because it was against primarily non-British troops, most British or Anglophone authors have been ignorant of the attack; perhaps because it has been often assumed 2nd Corps by this time had been bled dry at Hougoumont and could not mount an attack; and finally, that the myth created by the French that Ney demanded infantry and Napoléon replied that he had none to spare has been openly taken as hard fact. These two competing myths have irradiated the part played by the French infantry on the French left in mounting a large attack on the Allied right. Indeed, Siborne is ignorant of this attack, and even ascribes actions undertaken by the Imperial Guard or 2nd Corps to elements of 1st Corps, which by tradition was annihilated by the Union Brigade! The truth is that neither force was annihilated and were spent combat forces in the evening of 18 June. Napoléon was not yet running out of men. The failure of Ney's infantry assault was the last roll of the dice, which forced Napoléon to commit the Imperial Guard to action. The chief-of-staff to General Bachelu, Colonel Trefcon, narrates that:[747]

> At six, I remember looking at my watch as the day wore on, we were ordered out of the Hougoumont Wood to support the efforts of our cavalry. No sooner had we left the woods and formed up in columns by division that a rain of bullets and shrapnel fell on us like rain. I was standing next to General Bachelu, he was hit by several bullets and had his horse killed under him.
>
> The brigadier-general was wounded at the same time, so I took temporary command of the division. Take it by our élan and despite their fire we were about the English when there arrived an important reinforcement. No doubt they would have otherwise been forced to retreat. A violent fire greeted us when we came into contact with the English with our bayonets. Our soldiers fell in their hundreds; others had to beat a hasty retreat: the English would not be easily overcome. I received two severe contusions to the chest and I had my horse killed under me by grapeshot. In my fall, I landed on my left wrist. The violence of the shock and pain that I felt made me lose consciousness. Fortunately for me, my fainting was short lived and I was soon regained of all my senses. Housed behind the body of my horse, I saw go past me a charge of English dragoons pursuing our unhappy divisions.

---

747 Trefcon.

The 2nd Regiment of Light Infantry formed the head of column of Husson's brigade. An eyewitness from the 2nd Regiment of Light Infantry writes:[748]

> At seven o'clock the victory seemed to be crowned through our prodigious efforts. Marshal Ney arrived on foot, sword in hand, to the 2nd Light Infantry Regiment, which had fought under the marshal's order on all the preceding days, but there were no more than a small number of men. 'My comrades,' he cried 'victory depends on you, remember that it is the English who are ahead of you!' The ammunition of the regiment being exhausted, the officers of a regiment of cavalry, which was placed behind them and unable to make any movement, brought to them in their helmets, the pistol cartridges which they had remaining, which were used to load the muskets of the regiment.

Jean Baptiste Jolyet, commanding the 1st Battalion 1st Regiment of Light Infantry, narrates:[749]

> It was late and, despite our best efforts, we had not been able to seize the castle of Hougoumont. We lost more than two-thirds of our men, our brave colonel, Cubières, was seriously injured. General-of-Brigade Bauduin was killed. What was left of our regiment met in a hollow to re-form. Beside us was General Guilleminot,[750] who sent his aide-de-camp to Prince Jérôme to have new orders. It was about seven o'clock when his aide-de-camp came to tell us, from the prince, that Grouchy emerged into the left of the English and, therefore, the battle was won. Such triumphal joy. A deceptive general. We marched forward and placed ourselves in line of battle in front of the sunken road, next to a squadron of Red Lancers of the Guard.

> Soon the enemy's batteries, who initially retreated, regained their initial positions and we were covered with bullets, then all of a sudden we saw a battalion of the Guard retreating back onto the highway.

---

748 Raymond-Balthasard Maiseau, *Vie du Maréchal Ney*, Pillet, Paris, 1816, pp. 164-5.

749 Commandant Jolyet, *'Souvenirs du 1815'* in *Revue de Paris*, October 1903, pp. 545-55.

750 Lieutenant-General Armand Charles Guilleminot, second-in-command of 6th Division, under the orders of Prince Jérôme Bonaparte.

Prior to the advance of 2nd Corps, the French artillery had been at work once again bombarding the Allied lines, as Conrad Fuhring, of the Osnabrück Landwehr Battalion, notes:[751]

> Once the brigade of cuirassiers had withdrawn, we were warmly welcomed by the enemy's cannon, which was placed *vis a vis* on the opposite height; this is why we received the order to lie down on the reverse slope of the aforementioned height. At this time First-Lieutenant Uffel was decapitated while three sergeants and several soldiers were killed, along with Major Count von Munster's horse. My comrades were resting at this time, because I was ordered to release the horses from their torment, and several of them were awakened by the enemy's shells and cannonballs, while others among them found eternal sleep.

Just prior to this advance, the troops of Colonel du Plat's brigade of the King's German Legion had advanced from their position in the second line, crossed the brow of the height, and started to descend into the valley beyond. The 1st Horse Artillery Battery, under Augustus Sympher, supported this movement and then moved further forward. The four battalions of du Plat's Brigade, which were preceded by the four rifle companies—which had been formed into a battalion under the command of Captain Heise—moved to counter the French advance. The 2nd Line Battalion King's German Legion on the extreme right wing was advancing in square. The 1st Line Battalion also advanced in square, with the 3rd and 4th Line Battalions advancing in square together. Georg von Müller, of the 2nd Line Battalion King's German Legion, adds some more detail about the French infantry attack, but suggests that the French were easily pushed back, contrary to Rettburg:[752]

> After we had advanced about one thousand paces in square, enemy infantry, formed in line, which I judged to have been between 1,000 and 1,200 men, showed itself on one of the undulating heights about four hundred to six hundred paces on our immediate left. The brigade then made a movement so that the 2nd Battalion became the right wing and then halted. A short musket exchange ensued. However, Colonel du Plat gave the order to advance and to attack the enemy with the bayonet, which they were not expecting, and as we advanced they retreated into an old oak coppice which

---

751 John Franklin personal communication, 30 June 2012.
752 ibid.

was surrounded by a deep ditch and banks of earth. I believe this is where Colonel du Plat was killed, for I did not see him thereafter.

When we arrived on the brow of the height, we saw on our right, some 800 to 1,000 paces in front of us, a rather extended line of infantry, in front of which was a line of French cuirassiers; 600 to 800 men which, if I remember correctly, halted and were attacked by the 2nd Dragoon Regiment of the King's German Legion, who were in turn thrown back by the fire of the infantry, which had retired into the coppice, and overthrown by the enemy cuirassiers as far as our square; these on their part were stopped by the fire from our square. Our dragoons turned around and pursued the fleeing enemy; this series of events were replayed two or three times.

The enemy infantry which had retired into the aforementioned coppice, and which now due to the advance of our line was lying on our right flank only a short musket-shot away, inflicted considerable losses on the brigade with a sustained fire. Subsequently, General Clinton sent his adjutant to order the 2nd Line Battalion to enter the coppice and to secure it, which after the battalion had deployed from square, was achieved with very little resistance. The oak coppice was one of two in our front in which we heard the violent musket fire at the commencement of the battle, for we found various dead Frenchmen dressed in blue and red, as well as light infantry soldiers belonging to the English guards and some dead men of the Brunswick corps. The remaining battalions of the brigade remained in square.

After about half an hour the enemy manoeuvred around the outside of the coppice, the rear of which must have been unoccupied, and fell with a few hundred men as far as I could judge on our right flank and started an attack in front *en debandade*. As a result, the coppice was relinquished, but as the rest of our battalions out of the coppice were standing in the same position, the battalion reformed and attacked once again. The coppice was happily retaken and we remained the master of it throughout the remainder of the fight.

Adolphe Hess, of the 2nd Line Battalion, adds more to the attack of the wood:[753]

We arrived in a position in front of the garden of Hougoumont. But here our square was exposed to very heavy fire, because the French tirailleurs were only forty paces from us, having taken a position

---

753 John Franklin personal communication, 30 June 2012.

behind the hedges. Due to the close proximity of the enemy's cavalry we could neither deploy nor become fully engaged within the contest; our brigadier and the brigade-major had already been shot, and no one knew if we should advance farther. It was not advisable to stay exposed to the enemy's fire in such a closed mass. Therefore, a decision was taken: the battalion rushed into the hollow, which was located next to the garden. The great predominance of the enemy infantry which occupied the ditches along the edge of the garden meant that is was impossible for us to act without being reinforced, and so a battalion of Brunswick troops arrived to support us. The garden was gradually taken step-by-step.

The two forces closed to within thirty yards of one another, but the repeated fire from the artillery and the supporting fire from the King's German Legion troops forced the French to move to the left and break, seeking shelter along the edge of the wood and orchard at Hougoumont. General Foy, as we have seen, describes this and his seeking shelter having been wounded. The troops in the orchard at Hougoumont were forced to retire, as the French troops streamed into it. Indeed, those in the orchard thought it was an attack, rather than a retreat. The remaining French troops lined the edge of the wood and orchard, taking shelter in the large ditch which ran parallel with the wood, and fired into the squares of the King's German Legion, inflicting heavy casualties. du Plat was killed, along with several other senior officers. The troops of the King's German Legion advanced. The four rifle companies, which had been joined in a single battalion under Captain Heise, entered the rear of the orchard and advanced, attacking the French. Captain Heise was killed, and the sheer number of French held the position, so the 2nd Line Battalion King's German Legion, under Major Georg von Müller, also entered the orchard and advanced. With the support of the remaining Allied troops in the orchard (mainly the 3rd Foot Guards and some Nassau troops), they managed to force the French to retire slowly.

The Allied troops only secured the orchard later, when they were joined by two battalions of Brunswickers, and at this point they advanced. The French reformed as best they could to the south of Hougoumont, and were engaged only when the attack was begun by the Imperial Guard. The division of Foy had almost cut off Hougoumont from the Allied lines and prevented the vital flow of munitions to the garrison. The French were only pushed back by a similarly large Allied counter-attack. It was then that Adams's brigade was moved up to fill the gap in the Allied lines.

In the fighting, Sub-Lieutenant Antoine Florentin Moutardier was struck by a canister round in the left knee.[754] Battalion-Commander Pierre François Basset took a gunshot to the left thigh.[755] Also wounded in a fire fight was Captain Jean Mathurin Deleschelle, who had served with the regiment for just under a year, having previously served in the Imperial Guard,[756] as was Captain Louis Norbert Lussignol.[757] Lieutenant Jean Nepomucene Simon Carvoe was wounded and captured by the Allies.[758] Sub-Lieutenant Charles Louis Urbain Acier was shot in the right leg,[759] as was Sub-Lieutenant Achille Carimantrand, with a musket ball to the right foot.[760] A similar fate befell Sub-Lieutenant Louis Joseph Osman, aged twenty-eight. A musket ball struck him in the left knee and a second ball penetrated his right hip, causing the total paralysis of the leg. He died in 1863 aged seventy-six, so the lack of a leg does not seem to have hindered him.[761] In this fire fight, Adjutant François Gabriel Bourdon suffered a gunshot wound to the right leg,[762] as did Adjutant François Mocquard.[763] Sergeant-Major Pierre Moules, of a carabinier company, was unlucky enough to be wounded at both Quatre-Bras and Waterloo, taking a gunshot to the left arm at Quatre-Bras and a contusion to the left knee at Waterloo. He had served with the Imperial Guard from 1808 to 1814, when he was admitted to the regiment upon disbandment of the Young Guard.[764] A similar fate befell Sergeant Charles Nicolas Darras, of a carabinier company, who had also served in the Imperial Guard from 7 May 1811 to 1 June 1814. At Quatre-Bras, he suffered a gunshot to the left arm and at Waterloo a gunshot to the right foot.[765] Sergeant-Porte-Agile Simon Dubrec was captured in the closing stages of the battle due to the wound he sustained: a gunshot

---

754 AN: LH 1958/46.

755 AN: LH 131/17.

756 AN: LH 710/13.

757 AN: LH 1677/23.

758 AN: LH 432/6.

759 AN: LH 5/65.

760 SHDDT: Xb 567 *2e Légère*. Dossier 1815.

761 AN: LH 2024/35.

762 AN: LH 325/27.

763 AN: LH 1891/29.

764 AN: LH 1949/72.

765 AN: LH 663/5.

to the right leg at Quatre-Bras.[766] Clearly, some men coped better with their wounds than others, but all three men were classed able enough, despite their injuries, to fight again after Quatre-Bras. Sergeant Jean Claude Frey was shot in the left leg.[767] Sergeant François Lacour was shot in the lower left arm.[768] Total regimental losses at Waterloo are in the table below:[769]

2nd Regiment of Light Infantry					
	Wounded	Wounded & Prisoner	Prisoner of War	Killed	Missing
1st Battalion	0	0	7	0	0
2nd Battalion	63	0	0	12	2
3rd Battalion	1	0	19	6	3
4th Battalion	17	0	31	5	3
Total	81	0	57	23	8

On 27 May 1815, the regiment mustered four battalions, comprising ninety-eight officers and 2,468 men.[770] On the morning of 18 June, it mustered 2,435 other ranks. At Waterloo, 169 men were lost, representing just 7 per cent of effective strength. It is clear that the 2nd Battalion was the most heavily engaged in the action for the farm of Hougoumont. By 25 June, the regiment mustered 634 men,[771] a loss of 1,632 men since 18 June. These men no doubt were lost in the rout as the Armée du Nord disintegrated from the early hours of 19 June. The retreat for the 2nd Regiment of Light Infantry was far costlier in manpower than either of the two battles it fought in during the campaign.

Along with the 2nd Regiment of Light Infantry, the 61st Regiment of Line Infantry was a spectator to the bulk of the battle. When Husson's brigade attacked around 18.00, it was then, perhaps, that Sub-Lieutenant Pierre Cambdessedes was wounded and made prisoner of war. He had volunteered to the 61st Regiment of Line Infantry on 1 January 1802, and had been promoted through the ranks from private, being made a

---

766 AN: LH 871/25.
767 AN: LH 1031/41.
768 AN: LH 1426/83.
769 SHDDT: GR 21 YC 19.
770 SHDDT: C15 34. *Situation Rapport 2e Corps 27 Mai 1815.*
771 SHDDT: C15 34. *2e et 6e Corps Situation du 25 Juin 1815.*

sub-lieutenant on 10 April 1813. He was discharged from the regiment on 3 November 1815.[772] Total losses for the regiment are shown below:[773]

61st Regiment of Line Infantry					
	Wounded	Wounded & Prisoner	Prisoner of War	Killed	Missing
1st Battalion	41	0	93	21	3
2nd Battalion	41	0	82	10	6
3rd Battalion	32	0	110	11	8
Total	114	0	285	42	17

On the morning of 18 June, the regiment had 1,058 men in ranks. Some 458 men were lost at Waterloo, or 43 per cent of effective strength. On 20 June, it mustered 617 men and on 26 June just 206 men, a loss of 394 after Waterloo. Thus 66 per cent of the regiment's effective strength was lost during the retreat. Wounded that day was Captain-Adjutant-Major Jean Fourgeaud, who took a gunshot to the right leg.[774] Captain Jacques Chaucheprat also took a gunshot to the leg,[775] as did Captain Antoine Destor, who had also been wounded at Quatre-Bras.[776]

Of note on 16 June is that 106 men were wounded, a figure comparable to the losses at Waterloo. The dead on the 16th were eight men, compared to forty-two on 18 June. Can we assume the fighting on both days was of comparable intensity? Perhaps. The prisoner of war figures perhaps also represent deserted men and wounded or dead men left on the field of battle. We will not know the ratio of true prisoners of war to those actually wounded. On balance, the fighting at Waterloo resulted in more men killed than at Quatre-Bras. We know at Waterloo the losses were sustained in two attacks, the first around 18.30 and the second about an hour later in support of the Imperial Guard.

In the action, north of the Hougoumont Wood, the 72nd Regiment of Line Infantry came under artillery fire. Captain Thomas Dupuy was unlucky enough to be wounded when a howitzer shell exploded close

---

772 AN: LH 412/35.

773 SHDDT: GR 21 YC 516 *57e régiment d'infanterie de ligne (ex 61e régiment d'infanterie de ligne), 1 août 1814-14 juin 1815 (matricules 1 à 1,800).*

774 AN: LH 1012/42.

775 AN: LH 504/70.

776 AN: LH 760/47.

to him, shell fragments entering his left thigh.[777] Commanding the 1st Battalion was Jacques Joseph Touré, who was rendered *hors de combat* in this attack.[778] Captain-Adjutant-Major Bazile François Legrain suffered a gunshot to the left knee,[779] Captain Antoine Joseph Leloup, also of 1st Battalion, was wounded, as were Sub-Lieutenants Boisson, Guybert, Grilliere, Roy and Tomberly. Total regimental losses at Waterloo are shown below:[780]

72nd Regiment of Line Infantry					
	Evacuated Wounded	Wounded & Prisoner	Prisoner of War	Killed	Missing
1st Battalion	24	0	39	3	84
2nd Battalion	22	1	32	1	92
Total	46	1	71	4	176

On the morning of 18 June, the regiment mustered 737 other ranks. At Waterloo, 298 men were lost, representing some 40 per cent of effective strength. At Quatre-Bras the regiment suffered 162 men wounded, over three times as many as on the 18th, and thirteen men killed, again more than three times as many. The missing was, however, eleven times greater. Clearly, the fighting at Waterloo was less intense than at Quatre-Bras. It also seems the companies that suffered the most at Quatre-Bras had the highest number of men reported missing or deserted. Clearly, therefore, the fighting spirit, cohesion and morale of the companies had been tested to breaking point. The grenadier company of 1st Battalion suffered no casualties, but reported the highest number of men missing on 18 June, but only had listed two men on 16 June. Clearly, at some stage in the battle this company, along with the 3rd Company of the same battalion, and the 3rd Company and grenadier company of the 2nd Battalion, panicked and the men fled, whereas in the remaining companies of both battalions, the men were noted as prisoners and not as missing.

---

777 AN: LH 863/74.

778 AN: LH 2617/76.

779 AN: LH 1559/50.

780 SHDDT: GR 21 YC 599 *66e régiment d'infanterie de ligne (ex 72e régiment d'infanterie de ligne), 11 août 1814-27 février 1815 (matricules 1 à 1,800).*
See also: SHDDT: GR 21 YC 600 *66e régiment d'infanterie de ligne (ex 72e régiment d'infanterie de ligne), 21 février 1815-4 août 1815 (matricules 1,801 à 2,092).*

In the attack at Waterloo, Sergeant Auguste Mamelin, of the grenadier company of 1st Battalion 108th Regiment of Line Infantry, had a leg pulverised by a cannonball and suffered numerous lesser wounds. He was taken to a field dressing station by comrades, where Surgeon Larrey removed the shattered leg. However, it appears with the French rout that not all the wounded were evacuated, if any, and he was captured by the Allies. Mamelin tells us he spent six full days on the field of battle with little food or drink before being evacuated to Brussels. From there he was shipped to Anvers and thence to prison in England.[781] At the head of the 3rd Battalion, Battalion-Commander François Marie Lefranc took a musket ball to the lower right arm, breaking his wrist.[782] Captain Germain Claude took a musket ball also. Captain Jean Michel Remy was one of the oldest officers in the regiment, being aged fifty when Waterloo was fought. In this attack, he took a musket ball to the stomach and was left for dead on the battlefield when the regiment retreated. However, he may have been taken from the field of battle, had his wounds dressed and sent into captivity in England, during which his personal effects were stolen from him. He writes:[783]

> I attest and declare that during the Battle of Waterloo, I was commanding the rank of captain, I lost my portmanteaux, which contained my own personal items, as well as my portfolio of the papers, among which was the brevet nominating me a member of the Legion of Honour.

Sub-Lieutenant Jean Bezian was also wounded in the action with a gunshot wound to his right arm.[784] Also, falling dead or wounded in the attack were Battalion-Commander Mery, Captains Arnault, Claude and Simon, Lieutenants Basprey, Bonnet, Tabard, Michel, Lesassier, Girardin, Gossin, Gérard, Rhinck, Paquiez and Salsez. Adjutant Remi Laurent Constant Lavaur was hit by a musket ball that passed through the right side of his chest.[785] Sergeant-Major Pierre Victor Fayet took two musket balls and was captured by the Allies as they pushed back the retreating French. Sergeant Charles Firmin Douin took a musket

---

781 AN: LH 1712/37.
782 AN: LH 1552/76.
783 AN: LH 2293/60.
784 AN: LH 231/27.
785 AN: LH 1505/43.

ball to the left shoulder and fellow sergeant, Mathurin Le Guilloux, was shot and captured by the Allies,[786] as was Sergeant Marie Pierre Augustin Legay, who suffered a gunshot wound.[787] Sergeant Jean Nicolas Melinon was unlucky enough to be shot by a musket ball in the groin.[788] Corporal François Julien Avril took a gunshot wound to the left side of his chest.

It seems the 108th Regiment of Line Infantry came into contact with Allied troops at the point of the bayonet. In this attack, or indeed defence from an Allied bayonet charge, Colonel Philippe Higonet, a baron of the empire commanding the regiment, suffered two puncture wounds in addition to the two contusions he suffered leading his regiment at Quatre-Bras.[789] Sub-Lieutenant Herbillon, of the 108th Regiment of Line Infantry, notes that the retreat began about 20.00 and that the regiment marched all night of the 18th, the roads being encumbered with artillery caissons and wagons. The regiment, we are told, reached Saulx-le-Chateau on 19 June and Laon on 21 June, arriving at Soissons on 23 June. He notes that the retreat ended at Laon, where a great number of the troops returned to their corps.[790] Total regimental losses at Waterloo are in the table below:[791]

108th Regiment of Line Infantry					
	Evacuated Wounded	Wounded & Prisoner	Prisoner of War	Killed	Missing
1st Battalion	0	0	175	10	2
2nd Battalion	0	2	189	2	3
3rd Battalion	0	3	199	8	2
Total	0	5	563	20	7

On 10 June, the regiment mustered sixty-one officers and 1,046 other ranks in three battalions. We only know the fate of twenty-four men

---

786 AN: LH 1565/75.

787 AN: LH 1556/18.

788 AN: LH 1820/13.

789 AN: LH 1300/58.

790 Émile Herbillon, *Quelques pages d'un vieux cahier: souvenirs du Général Herbillon (1794-1866)*, Berger-Levrault, Paris, 1928, pp. 11-12.

791 SHDDT: GR 21 YC 790 *89e régiment d'infanterie de ligne (ex 108e régiment d'infanterie de ligne), 9 septembre 1814-7 juin 1815 (matricules 1 à 1,800).*

on 16 June. At Waterloo, 595 men were lost, on both days a total of 619 men, which represents 59 per cent of effective strength.

Of interest, Sub-Lieutenant Herbillon tells us the 3rd Battalion was virtually destroyed. On 10 June, it had eighteen officers and 233 men, losing 212 men in total. Therefore, Herbillon's comments are verified by the data recorded in the regiment's archive. Herbillon states the losses on 16 June caused the disbandment of the battalion. It is not impossible that the losses of 18 June also include those of 16 June as well.

Also moving up came Jamin's brigade from Foy's division. General Foy, general officer commanding the 9th Division, writing on 23 June 1815 concurs, noted that:[792]

> While the French cavalry was undertaking this long and terrible charge, the fire of our artillery was already lessoning and our infantry did not move. When the cavalry had returned and the English artillery, which had stopped firing for half an hour, had started to fire again, we were ordered with the divisions of Bachelu and Foy to ascend the plateau in squares. To the right advanced our cavalry, who had not been recalled. The attack was formed in column by regiment in echelons; Bachelu forming the most advanced post. I stood by the hedge to my left and I had deployed to my front a battalion as skirmishers. We almost reached the English when we received a rapid fire of grapeshot and musketry. It was a hail of death.
>
> The enemy square had the front rank kneeling on the ground and had a hedge of bayonets. The columns of the 1st Division fled first: their movement led to one of my columns advancing half-heartedly.

In this attack against the Allied right wing, General Jamin's brigade of Foy's division came into contact with the Allied artillery. Battalion-Commander Honore Leblanc, commanding the 3rd Battalion of the 100th Regiment of Line Infantry, narrates that:[793]

> At Waterloo, I was noted for my distinguished conduct when I mounted an attack with my battalion on a battery of seven enemy cannon. We carried it with the bayonet and captured the pieces.

---

792 Maurice Girod de l'Ain, *Vie militaire du Géneral* Foy, E. Plon, Nourrit et Cie, Paris, 1900, p. 282.
793 AN: LH 1515/9.

The 100th Regiment of Line Infantry became involved in a fire fight, as we shall see in the Allied observations cited later, perhaps when Lieutenant Nicolas Jallet was shot in the right leg with a musket ball.[794] In a melee with the Allied cavalry, Lieutenant Luise Narcisse Armand Despret, of the 100th Regiment of Line Infantry, was wounded, who notes he was:[795]

> Wounded many times with sabre cuts, one of which was very serious, to my left shoulder on 18 June 1815 at the affair of Mont-Saint-Jean.

Sub-Lieutenant Michel Augustin Doublet, also of the 100th Regiment of Line Infantry, concurs, writing in 1816 that he 'was wounded with three sabre cuts at the Battle of Waterloo'.[796] Sergeant Mansuy Godard, who had served with the 100th Regiment of Line Infantry since 31 May 1799, was wounded with three sabre cuts to the groin. Presumably for this to happen he was lying prone on the battlefield and stabbed from the rear as the cavalry surged through his company. Fellow sergeant in the 100th Regiment of Line Infantry, Antoine Nicolas Joseph Lejeune, was running away as fast as he could from the Allied cavalry when he received a puncture wound to the back of his right knee and a defensive injury to his left hand. Clearly, the 100th Regiment of Line Infantry seems to have been broken by the Allied cavalry at some stage at the close of the battle. Total regimental losses at Waterloo are below:[797]

100th Regiment of Line Infantry					
	Evacuated Wounded	Wounded & Prisoner	Prisoner of War	Killed	Missing
1st Battalion	47	0	1	3	62
2nd Battalion	30	0	0	5	131
3rd Battalion	38	0	0	6	168
Total	115	0	1	14	361

---

794 AN: LH 1349/68.

795 AN: LH 757/1.

796 AN: LH 795/75.

797 SHDDT: GR 21 YC 734 *81e régiment d'infanterie de ligne (ex 100e régiment d'infanterie de ligne), 24 septembre 1814-1er mai 1815 (matricules 1 à 1,800).* See also: SHDDT: GR 21 YC 735 *100e régiment d'infanterie de ligne, 1 mai 1815-16 août 1815 (matricules 1,801 à 2,248).*

On 10 June, the regiment had mustered fifty-one officers and 1,070 other ranks. At Quatre-Bras, 233 men were lost, representing 22 per cent of effective strength. The heaviest losses were in the grenadier and voltigeur companies of 1st Battalion and in 4th Company of 3rd Battalion. These losses impacted upon battlefield performance on 18 June. On the morning of the 18th, the regiment mustered 837 other ranks. At Waterloo, 491 men were lost, representing some 59 per cent of effective strength. The fate of the 2nd and 3rd Battalions at Waterloo is noticeably different to the 1st Battalion. It seems 1st Battalion managed to retain cohesion at the close of the battle, whereas 2nd and 3rd Battalions broke and fled, perhaps during the Allied cavalry charge at the close of the battle. Major Lebeaux, of the 1st Regiment of Line Infantry, tells us that the infantry attack to the immediate east of Hougoumont failed and had it not been for the French cavalry not one man would have escaped, which it seems is graphically borne out. The evacuated wounded were perhaps lost in the first half of the battle, when it was far easier to evacuate wounded to the field dressing stations and then further to the rear to the hospital at Charleroi. The high number of missing may well include dead and wounded.

Brigaded with the 100th Regiment of Line Infantry was the 4th Regiment of Light Infantry. As the French troops advanced they came under fire from the Allied artillery, killing and wounding many French soldiers. In the attack on the Allied lines, it seems that the 1st Battalion 4th Regiment of Light Infantry, led by Battalion-Commander de Hennault de Bertancourt, came under artillery fire; a howitzer shell exploded near to him, a splinter from the resulting explosion passed through the middle of his right leg. A discharge of canister by the battery also found its mark on the battalion, and one of its many small balls passed through Sergeant Leroy's left shoulder. He served in the carabinier company of the 1st Battalion.

Following the artillery bombardment, at some stage the 4th Regiment of Light Infantry was overrun by Allied cavalry. It was perhaps now that the wounded and rather unlucky Sergeant Louis Leroy received a puncture wound caused by either a sabre or bayonet to the abdomen. He was left for dead by his comrades on the field of battle and captured by the Allies. Remarkably, he survived these injuries and returned to France on 29 February 1816, and died in Paris in 1842 aged fifty-four. It was perhaps now that Adjutant-Major Eleonor Clouet was wounded, along with Battalion-Commander Jean Pierre Louis de Hennault de Bertancourt. Serving in 3rd Company 3rd Battalion was Colin Nicolas

Lepelu, who was wounded, but unlike his comrades, was not left on the field of battle and was taken to a military hospital.[798] Sergeant Antoine Ducrot, of the 4th Regiment of Light Infantry, was wounded with numerous sabre cuts, left for dead on the battlefield and was captured by the Allies. He was returned from captivity in England on 20 June 1815.[799] Total regimental losses at Waterloo are in the table below:[800]

4th Regiment of Light Infantry					
	Wounded	Wounded & Prisoner	Prisoner of War	Killed	Missing
1st Battalion	4	1	2	0	0
2nd Battalion	21	0	1	4	0
3rd Battalion	27	0	4	0	0
4th Battalion	102	0	69	2	1
Suite	14	0	5	0	0
Total	168	1	81	6	1

On 10 June 1815, the regiment mustered four battalions, comprising of ninety-four officers and 1,848 men. The regiment's paperwork admits to the loss of 208 men on the 16th, or a loss of 11 per cent of effective strength. On the morning of 18 June 1815, the regiment mustered 1,640 men. The 4th Battalion suffered the most losses and appears to have borne the brunt of the fighting on the 18th. The regiment lost 257 men at Waterloo, representing 16 per cent of effective strength. The bulk of the losses came from the 4th Battalion, as on 16 June. Was the battalion more exposed to enemy fire? We don't know, other than to state that the battalion bore the brunt of the losses in the campaign.

Comment

Losses were as follows in the French forces involved in the infantry assault in support of the massed cavalry charges, which the myths of Waterloo say never took place:

---

798 SHDDT: GR 22 YC 40 4er régiment d'infanterie Légère 1814 à 1815.
799 An: LH 892/2. See also: SHDDT: GR 22 YC 40.
800 SHDDT: GR 22 YC 40.

2nd Corps							
Division	Regiment	Wounded	Evacuated Wounded	Wounded & Prisoner	Prisoner of War	Killed	Missing
9th	4th Light[801]	168	0	1	81	6	1
	100th Line[802]	0	115	0	1	14	361
5th	2nd Light[803]	81	0	0	57	23	8
	61st Line[804]	114	0	0	285	42	17
	72nd Line[805]	46	0	1	71	4	176
	108th Line[806]	0	0	5	563	20	7
Total		409	115	7	1,058	109	570

When we look at the losses of the attacking French forces, 2,268 men were lost in the action. Some 1,503 men were lost by Bachelu's division during the attack. Of worthy comment, during the fighting at Hougoumont some 1,676 men were lost, 176 more than were lost in the attack on the Allied right. Clearly, the fighting in this sector of the battlefield was of a different degree of intensity. The 6th Division lost men wounded, killed and made prisoner over the course of four hours, whereas the men lost in the attack on the Allied right cut down 2,268 men in under an hour, but we do acknowledge that the 5th Division did attack again an hour or so later to support the Imperial Guard, so we cannot be certain that all the losses took place now.

The evacuated wounded from the 100th Regiment of Line Infantry were wounded when the regiment relieved the brigade of General Tissot, comprising the 92nd and 93rd Regiments of Line Infantry. The fewer losses in the 2nd Regiment of Light Infantry imply that the regiment was deployed in front of the attacking waves of infantry in skirmish order, along with the 4th Regiment of Light Infantry. Of the attacking force, the 108th Regiment of Line Infantry lost the most.

---

801 SHDDT: GR 22 YC 40.
802 SHDDT: GR 21 YC 734. See also: SHDDT: GR 21 YC 735.
803 SHDDT: GR 22 YC 19 2er régiment d'infanterie Légère 1814 à 1815.
804 SHDDT: GR 21 YC 516.
805 SHDDT: GR 21 YC 599. See also: SHDDT: GR 21 YC 600.
806 SHDDT: GR 21 YC 790.

Chapter 16

Guyot Charges
with the Cavalry Reserve

Moving up in support of 2nd Corps was the carabinier brigade and
Guard heavy cavalry. With the 1st Division of the corps having dashed
headlong up the slope to the Allied infantry earlier in the day, General
Roussel d'Hurbal was left with the 2nd Division, which comprised
both regiments of carabiniers as well as the 2nd and 3rd Regiments of
Cuirassiers, under General-of-Brigade Donop. The famed carabinier
brigade was commanded by General-of-Brigade Baron Amable Guy
Blanchard, who was wounded at Waterloo.

Guyot recounts on his service papers the following details about
Waterloo and the involvement of his division in the battle. It is dated
13 December 1816:[807]

> At six o'clock I received the order to charge twenty pieces of artillery
> placed in the front of several English squares. I executed relentlessly
> three charges that had no success, because I had neither infantry
> nor artillery to support me; whatever the case I lost a lot of men
> and horses. I had my horse killed from a shell splinter at the head
> of the second charge. I had a few minutes to overpower the enemy.
> I received several sabre cuts on the head running through my hat
> in two places. But, soon I was saved by my division who obtained
> me a troop horse. As I prepared to execute at a third charge I receive
> a shot in the chest and a shell splinter to the left elbow, the horse
> I rode was killed at the same instant. I then gave my command to
> General Jamin, major of the regiment.

---

807 Guyot, op. cit.

In a letter addressed to General Pelet, dated 27 April 1835, General Guyot (commanding the heavy cavalry of the Guard) says the following about the charge he and the carabiniers were ordered to undertake:[808]

> At six o'clock the emperor, wanting to force the centre of the enemy line, gave the order to the Duc de Valmy to charge. This division was brought up to my left. I received the order at the same time to bring my division forward and act under the orders of Marshal Ney. He made me immediately execute a charge on a few squadrons which masked the artillery and our approach to the squares behind. The retrograde movement made by the cavalry exposed me to artillery fire and to the fire from the squares that protected it and made us suffer great losses.

> Our two divisions alternately charged on this line of artillery and failed every time to capture it and we were always obliged to retire precipitately because we only had our swords to use against the volley fire from the squares and the grapeshot from the artillery, which greeted us as we arrived on the plateau.

> The enemy cavalry took advantage of each disorder, the bullets and grapeshot was fired into our ranks to pursue our dishevelled squadrons, but since we did not allow him long term success, as we had earlier repulsed his major means of defence.

Guyot says the following about the next charge he and the carabiniers were ordered to undertake:[809]

> It was in the second charge that I was dismounted and obliged to retire on foot. I did not have time to retire for I had not gone ten steps to the rear when I was thrown over and trampled under the feet of the cavalry, and I was wounded by a sabre passing through my body. I could not withdraw from the fray and they could not, however, capture me, for I was immediately saved by the third charge executed by my division. They had procured me a troop horse from the regiment's reserve.

> I met the enemy again, but I was not long in the saddle when I was shot in the chest and took a shell splinter to my left elbow. I then passed command to General Jamin, who then led a new charge, but he was killed by a gunshot. It was then about half-past seven o'clock at night.

---

808 Guyot.
809 Guyot.

I made my way to the point where the emperor was. During the first part of battle I learned that a Prussian corps of 30,000 men commanded by Bülow, after being spotted at four o'clock in the afternoon, had eventually deployed into the village of Plancenoit and was close to getting their hands on the general headquarters. This news placed our army's rear area into great alarm.

In this attack, Sergeant-Major Antoine-Sylvian Cantillon, a veteran of the regiment since 1813, led a number of grenadiers in an attack against English artillery. Cantillon noted he charged against a hail of canister shot and musket balls, overcame the defenders of the English battery and sabred the gunners where they stood around their guns.[810]

Cantillon was born on 26 November 1789, the son of Antoine Joseph Cantillon and Marie Louise Prot. He entered the 4th Dragoons on 31 May 1806, and was promoted to corporal on 13 June 1806 and soon after to quartermaster-corporal on 12 July 1806. Clearly, he was a man of some ability and could read and write. He was promoted to sergeant on 1 April 1809. He entered the 1st Regiment of Grenadiers à Cheval of the Imperial Guard on 1 April 1813 and was promoted to quartermaster-corporal on 1 August 1813. During the Battle of Hanau, his company commander, Captain Franquin, was surrounded and captured by two Bavarian cuirassiers. This so enraged Sergeant Cantillon, who charged at the Bavarians, put them to flight and rescued his commanding officer. In recognition he was awarded the Legion of Honour. He served in the 1814 campaign and was promoted to sergeant-major on 1 April 1814. He was then admitted to the Royal Corps of Cuirassiers of France on 22 July 1814 and was passed back to the grenadiers à cheval of the Imperial Guard as sergeant-major in April 1815. At Waterloo, he overran a British artillery piece and sabred the gunners. Following Waterloo, he was arrested for attempting to assassinate the Duke of Wellington. His deeds were rewarded by his exiled emperor. In an amendment to Napoléon's will, dated 24 April 1821, Napoléon stipulated that:[811]

> Likewise leave 100,000 francs to sub-officer Cantillon, who was tried for having sought the murder of the Duke of Wellington and found not guilty. Cantillon had as much right to kill that oligarch as the latter had to send me to St. Helena. Wellington, who conceived

---

810 AN: LH 419/92.

811 Jean-Pierre Babelon and Suzanne d'Huart, *Napoléon's Last Will and Testament*, Paddington Press, New York, 1977, p. 78.

this murderous plot, sought to justify it as being in the interests of Great Britain. Cantillon, had he really assassinated the duke, would have been similarly justified by France's need to dispose of a general who had, moreover, violated the Peace of Paris and thereby rendered himself responsible for the blood of the martyrs Ney, La Bédoyère, etc, and for the crime of pillaging museums, contrary to the spirit of the treaties.

This accusation, however, does not seem to have damaged his military career and he does not seem to have been a diehard Bonapartist. He was appointed as adjutant-sub-officer in the 1st Regiment of Cuirassiers of the Royal Guard on 1 November 1815 and was promoted to second-lieutenant on 15 July 1817.

It was in this same attack, perhaps, that Grenadier Brachot single-handedly attacked one of the British guns. He killed two gunners and forced the rest to abandon the gun. However, the captured gun was not able to be removed from the field, but was rendered inoperable. For his action, General Guyot personally awarded Brachot with the Legion of Honour in front of the regiment for his act of bravery. The regiment was withdrawn behind a ridge towards Hougoumont, where it was re-formed for its next charge out of danger from the British artillery. Brachot tells us that General Guyot personally placed the ribbon from his own Legion of Honour through the jacket button hole of Brachot, who had won his decoration with the point of the sabre. During Waterloo, trooper Brachot had had two horses killed under him and was wounded later in the day.

The decoration was, however, not granted until 1853. The royalist authorities, it seems, were reluctant to grant the decoration, as they could not be seen to congratulate a member of the former Imperial Guard who won the decoration in the Hundred Days campaign. Following the Waterloo campaign, Brachot passed to the Gendarmes of the Department of Doubs and retired from the army on 22 March 1816.[812]

The grenadiers' second charge was, in theory, to be repulsed by an attack of the Dutch- Belgian cavalry division of van Merlen, consisting of the 6th Hussars and 5th Light Dragoons, as Carl Theodore Fischer explains:[813]

---

812 Author's collection.
813 From Karl Theodore Fischer's campaign diary of 1815 in *Braunschweig Magazin*, January 1912, Edition 1. Translated by the author.

The hill was taken by the French; part of the English withdrew in the direction of Brussels through the woods, especially the King's Dragoon Guards. The woods were packed. Decision to our advantage was achieved at 5 p.m. Our Rgt charged four times the French cuirassiers and grenadiers of the Guard.

The 6th Hussars were particularly mauled by their encounter with the grenadiers. In their various contests with the grenadiers that day, the 6th Hussars lost 205 men dead, wounded or missing and 302 horses, about two-thirds of the regiment's strength, while the 5th Light Dragoons lost 155 men and 123 horses.[814] Lieutenant Henry Lane, of the 15th Hussars, notes about the charge that:[815]

> We were no sooner on our ground than we advanced in line and charged the grenadiers à cheval, who fled from us. Our next attack (in line without reserve) was a square of French infantry, and our horses were within a few feet of the square. We did not succeed in breaking it, and, of course, suffered most severely. In short, during the day we were constantly on the move, attacking and retreating to our lines, so that, at the close of the battle, the two squadrons were dreadfully cut up. When the cuirassiers made their first attack, they passed through the squares considerably in rear of our lines, and in retiring a body of them followed the high road to Nivelles.

The Empress Dragoons, it seems, came against the 8th Dutch-Belgian Militia Battalion, as Lieutenant-Colonel Wijbrandus de Jongh narrates:[816]

> During the first attack made by the enemy, I unhorsed a corporal serving with the dragoons of the Imperial Guard, by parrying his blows and thrusting my sabre into his side. Captain Sijbers immediately mounted this horse.

The 3rd Hussar Regiment of King's German Legion seems to have been involved in the fight back against the Guard heavy cavalry. von Goeben,

---

814 Deleveot, p. 193.

815 15th or King's Light Dragoons (Hussars) Historial Re-enactment Group, *Battle of Waterloo 1815*, XVLD, 2014, available at http://www.xvld.org/waterloo-1815.html [accessed 1 November 2011].

816 Franklin, Vol. 2, p. 104.

major of the regiment, narrates that following an attack by French cavalry between 16.00 and 17.00:[817]

> At this time, several squadrons of enemy cavalry drew up in line about three hundred to four hundred paces away. The officers sported tall bearskin hats [the grenadiers à cheval or elite gendarmes] and several of them rode up, challenging our officers to single combat. As they were much stronger, the regiment could not accept this honour, and the enemy cavalry did nothing else other than offer these big bearskin hats as targets to the sharpshooters of the Hanoverian Field Battalion.

Carl Jacobi notes about the 1st Hussars of the King's German Legion:[818]

> In the evening the brigade moved to the right wing and charged the enemy cavalry as the whole line advanced. The brigade advanced in columns of squadrons against the enemy and engaged the cavalry of the Imperial Guard and threw them entirely back, causing the utmost disarray within the enemy forces.

At some stage, the remains of the Household Brigade were brought forward and thrown against the French columns, perhaps against Foy and Bachelu's columns, as opposed to later in the day against the retreating French army, as trooper Joseph Lord, of the Lifeguards, explains:[819]

> We reached the enemy line, which received us with the greatest firmness, now we were able to move them, they being so many more in number. We cut away a long time, but two columns more coming to their assistance. We were obliged to retreat, which we did for half a mile and formed again, and again charged them without stopping a moment. This time they fled and we followed till another body three times the strength of ours came to their assistance. Here we should all have been prisoners had they been as daring as the English, for we were two miles [exaggeration on Lord's part] in the French lines and had all their army to pass, every column of which fired a volley into our 1st Brigade, which was now reduced to about a squadron, which at first was about ten.

---

817 John Franklin personal communication.
818 Franklin, Vol. 1, p. 31.
819 Oldham Local Studies and Archives: 2006-046.

About the charge of the four regiments comprising the reserve cavalry, General Kellermann says that the order for the charge came not from Napoléon, but from Ney. It seems perfectly reasonable that the order would have come from Napoléon. Here, we see Kellermann blaming Ney for the loss of the carabiniers and the Imperial Guard heavy cavalry, and not his actions or the orders of Napoléon. Kellermann was writing a version of history that exonerated both his own actions and Napoléon's, and as Ney would be dead by the time Kellermann wrote his own view, Ney was easily made the villain of the piece and could not defend his reputation:[820]

> Napoléon promptly recognised that it was unwise to charge all the cavalry without infantry, such a movement would succeed or compromise us; if it failed and then there was no hope of victory. The evil destiny of France seemed to preside over all these false moments. The carabinier brigade, a force of a thousand horses, was preserved from these fatal advances. They were placed near to a battery of artillery from the Imperial Guard for their defence, and expressly ordered that they were not to move without the direct orders of Comte de Valmy. The carabinier brigade was, therefore, in the plain. Marshal Ney saw them, ran to them, harangued them that they were unworthy for its inaction, and ordered them to rush the 7,000 or 8,000 English placed on the slope of the hill near the Hougoumont Wood, flanked by numerous artillery batteries. The carabiniers were forced to obey. Either through impotence or clumsiness, their charge had no successes; in a moment half the brigade was lying on the ground.

Here, Kellermann seems to deliberately ignore the fact that his men went to the attack following Reille's infantry attack. In a second letter, Kellermann notes that the carabinier brigade:[821]

> Advanced in line where the foolish General Lhéritier had so foolishly led his division. He wanted to withdraw the cavalry from this unstable situation, but fearing that any movement to the rear would occasion a stampede, the general resigned himself to maintain their presence with the troops who were constantly falling and condemned to death the men and horses with no defence.

---

820 SHDDT: MR 718 *Observations sur la campagne de 1815.*
821 SHDDT: MR 718 *Observations sur la bataille de Waterloo, en réponse à un ouvrage intitulé Campagne de 1815 et publié sous le nom du général Gourgaud.*

Suddenly he saw in the distance the red helmets of the carabiniers in motion. The Comte de Valmy, sensing misfortune, ran to stop it. He could not arrive in time. This superb body, in a few minutes, was half destroyed.

This time, Kellermann blames General Samuel-François Lhéritier de Chézelles for the loss of the carabiniers as opposed to Marshal Ney. Clearly, Kellermann was seeking to pass the blame to exonerate his own actions. His statement that the brigade advanced with no orders contradicts his own statement that Marshal Ney ordered the brigade to attack. On balance, given that the carabiniers moved up to support the attack of 2nd Corps against the Allied right, the charge must have been deliberately planned by Napoléon. Historian Ian James Smith, who has undertaken groundbreaking research into the two regiments of carabiniers during the First Empire, comments that:[822]

the carabiniers had been held back from action on 16 June due to issue of loyalty, and the brigade no doubt had been placed out of harm's way at Waterloo. Ney ordered them to attack. Kellermann, rather than desiring to leave a reserve of heavy cavalry, kept the brigade out of action due to issues of loyalty and the fact that many men of the regiment were barely trained. Carabinier Antoine Favau, whose mutilated cuirass is on display in the Musee de l'Armee, had joined the regiment days before it left for the campaign, along with many dozens of new entrants. These men could barely sit on their horses and not fall off, and in no way were well trained or experienced soldiers. Favau perhaps had at most six or seven days of training before he went to war. Little wonder, given the two regiments had been bulked out with johnny raw recruits, who could barely ride, let alone wield a sabre. The carabiniers were not elite soldiers at Waterloo. They lacked the combat experience and cohesion of the 2nd and 7th Dragoons, which were the two elite regiments of the division.

Colonel Arnaud Rogé, of the 1st Regiment of Carabiniers, writes:[823]

In the first charge of the carabiniers executed on the Scottish infantry, where I lost thirteen officers, I had my horse killed by gunfire at close

---

822 Ian Smith personal communication, 20 December 2016.

823 Anon, *Biographie du Gal Rogé* Impr, De Julien, Lanier et Cie, Le Mans, 1849, pp. 4-5.

range, and found myself embarrassed and hooked up by a stirrup leather to my saddle, and I could not pull myself free. Many brave men surrounded me amidst the deadliest fire to keep me safe and defend me. Saberjeon, who was one of them, dismounted to help me free myself, and told me after having done so 'colonel, get on my horse, we need you here with us, I will get out of this as best as I can'.

In that same moment, another carabineer, who was wounded in the thigh, shouted for help. Saberjeon, who was devoted to his comrades in the midst of danger, took him on his shoulders and carried him off, but no sooner had he done so for a few hundred paces that his burden was carried away by a cannonball...

Saberjeon had earned the Cross of the Legion of Honour, and it is very painful to me not to have the time to ask for him before our dissolution, etc.

In witness, whereof I have delivered to him, etc.

Marshal-de-camp, Rogé

Rogé also notes that the crest of his helmet was damaged by two musket balls and the red comb had come away. The only Scottish troops on the Allied right were the 71st Regiment of Highland Light Infantry, brigaded with the 95th and 51st, also light infantry regiments. The former did not wear kilts, so we assume that the attribution to Scots by the French is in error. The French writers habitually describe that they were defeated by the Scottish troops, as the French saw these 'exotic' troops as elite and special, when compared to the bulk of the Allied army, which genuinely seemed to have fascinated the French. In the same manner, the English and other Allied writers attribute their regiments to attacking and defeating the Imperial Guard, to enhance the prestige of their regiment.

So serious was this attack by the heavy cavalry of the Imperial Guard and the carabiniers to the Allied lines that the Prince of Orange ordered a counter-attack from the Dutch-Belgian 1st Light Cavalry Division, led by Major-General de Ghigny. It comprised the 4th Light Dragoons and the 8th Hussars. The 8th Hussars were led by Baron Ignance Duvivier, former officer of the grenadiers à cheval. The brigade advanced through the Allied infantry squares and rode directly into the horse artillery accompanying the Guard heavy cavalry. There followed a series of charges and counter-charges, the final charge being followed up around 19.30 by the last roll of the dice: Napoléon had to commit the Old Guard to the attack.

Guyot charged three times alongside the carabiniers. Total losses of the grenadiers à cheval at Waterloo are given in the table below:[824]

Grenadiers à Cheval					
	Wounded	Wounded & Prisoner	Prisoner of War	Killed	Missing
1st Squadron	11	0	0	3	18
2nd Squadron	10	0	0	3	20
3rd Squadron	9	0	0	6	15
4th Squadron	8	0	0	6	25
Total	38	0	0	18	78

On the morning of 18 June, the regiment mustered 719 sub-officers and men, with 532 present on 19 June and some 462 in ranks on 26 June 1815. At Waterloo, 134 other ranks were lost and 187 horses.

The Empress Dragoons mustered 749 other ranks on 18 June. Losses by squadron for the battle are shown below:[825]

Empress Dragoons					
	Wounded	Wounded & Prisoner	Prisoner of War	Killed	Missing
1st Squadron	6	0	0	10	23
2nd Squadron	5	0	0	1	26
3rd Squadron	10	0	2	2	21
4th Squadron	3	0	0	4	26
Total	24	0	2	17	96

On the morning of 10 June 1815, the 1st Carabiniers mustered thirty-two officers and 402 other ranks. The regiment's paperwork housed in the French Army Archives at Vincennes for 1815 cannot be located. Therefore, we have to rely upon Kellermann's after-action report to give us total losses between 10 and 24 June 1815. He notes the regiment had fifteen officers with thirty-two horses and 121 other ranks with 178 horses. This represents a loss of 281 men over fifteen days.[826] Given the regiment was not in action until 18 June, the losses were incurred at

---

824 SHDDT: GR 20 YC 137.
825 SHDDT: GR 20 YC 154 *registre matricule Dragons Garde Impériale.*
826 SHDDT: C15 34. *3 Corps de Cavalerie Situation au 24e Juin 1815.*

Waterloo and the immediate aftermath of the battle. We cannot say how many of the 281 men were lost at Waterloo specifically.

At Waterloo, the 2nd Carabiniers are memorialised by the cuirass of Trooper Favau, of 4th Company 4th Squadron, and the treason of Captain du Barail and other officers. The 2nd Carabiniers lost some sixty-nine killed or mortally wounded men at Waterloo, as shown in the table below:[827]

2nd Carabiniers					
	Wounded	Wounded & Prisoner	Presumed Killed	Killed	Missing
1st Squadron	2	0	18	1	1
2nd Squadron	0	0	21	1	0
3rd Squadron	2	0	19	4	0
Total	4	0	58	6	1

On the morning of 10 June 1815, the regiment mustered thirty officers and 383 other ranks. An officer was killed and eleven wounded at Waterloo. On 26 June, the regiment had 180 other ranks, a loss of 129 since 18 June, or 41 per cent of the regiment after Waterloo.

The Young Guard at Smohain

As Reille was taking the offensive on the French left, on the French right the Young Guard was ordered into action. Lobau was losing his grip on the right flank. Napoléon had no option but to turn to his reserve troops. The entire division was ordered up from its positions on the Brussels road and directed to the right flank. At the fiery furnace of the centre of the battlefield, sometime between 18.00 and 18.30, the French at last took control of La Haye Sainte, which was captured by men from the 17th Regiment of Line Infantry.

The Young Guard was commanded by General Duhesme, who began his military career by joining the National Guard in 1789. Two years later he was elected a captain in the 2nd Battalion of Volunteers of Saône-et-Loire and in October 1793, Duhesme was promoted to general-of-brigade by the representatives of the people with the Armée du Nord. After Napoléon's abdication, Duhesme was made inspector

---

827 SHDDT: GR 24 YC 9 *Contrôle Nominatif, Troupe 1814-1815*. See also: SHDDT: Xc 93 *2e Carabiniers*.

general of infantry and a Knight of Saint Louis. When Napoléon returned to power in 1815, Duhesme rallied to him and was named a Peer of France.

Deputy to Duhesme was General Barrois. Pierre Barrois first joined the French army in August 1793 when he enlisted in the Battalion of Scouts of the Meuse, and in barely a month was made lieutenant. He served with distinction at Marengo, was promoted to battalion-commander in October 1800 and then was made colonel of the 96th Regiment of Line Infantry in 1803. He was promoted to general-of-brigade in 1811 and was given command of a division of the Young Guard for the campaigns in Germany of 1813. General Barrois' 1st Division was then ordered to assault the buildings at Smohain.

As more Prussian troops arrived on the battlefield, Napoléon was faced with either withdrawing or committing his last reserves to try and snatch victory. Most of 2nd Corps was committed to the attack of Hougoumont and 6th Corps, under Lobau, was deployed against the Prussians at Papelotte and La Haye Sainte. The Young Guard were committed to Plancenoit. General Drouot notes:[828]

> Meantime the Prussian corps, which had joined the left of the English, placed itself *en potence* upon our right flank, and began to attack about half-past five in the afternoon. The 6th Corps, which had taken no part in the battle of the 16th, was placed to oppose them, and was supported by a division of the Young Guard and some batteries of the Guard. Towards seven o'clock we perceived in the distance towards our right a fire of artillery and musketry.

The Prussian assault on La Haye Sainte was the vital turning point to the battle, as Adjutant-Commandant Janin, of 6th Corps, narrates:[829]

> Despite the inferiority of our artillery, we stopped the march of the leading Prussian corps. However, they began to extend beyond our right flank, and necessitated the intervention of the Guard.

> The commander-in-chief of the Young Guard was Lieutenant-General Duhesme, his chief-of-staff being Adjutant-Commandant Mellinet. The 1st Brigade, comprising the 1st Regiments of Tirailleurs and Voltigeurs, was led by Jean Hyacinthe Sébastien Chartrand, and the 2nd Brigade, comprising the 3rd Regiments

---

828 Author's collection.
829 Janin, pp. 35-6.

of Tirailleurs and Voltigeurs, by General Nicolas Philippe Guye, Marquis de Rios-Molanos.

By 18.30 with ever increasing numbers of Prussian troops flooding onto the battlefield around Plancenoit, the remaining two Auxiliary Guard artillery batteries were ordered to support the beleaguered 6th Corps. In total, some forty-four guns of the Imperial Guard artillery were deployed to endeavour to push back the Prussians, under the command of Bülow. Pontécoulant narrates:[830]

> He ordered General Duhesme, who commanded the Young Guard, to stand to the right of Comte Lobau with his two brigades of infantry and twenty-four pieces of artillery of the Guard. Fifteen minutes later, the battery opened fire, and soon gained a marked superiority over the Prussian batteries. As soon as the Young Guard was in line, the offensive movement of the Prussians appeared arrested, but yet they still continued to extend their left, obviously with the intention to turn and enter onto the rear of our line.

The Young Guard held their position for an hour or more. General Barrois tells us that:[831]

> 18 June at Waterloo, I was charged to defend the right of the line, at the village of Smohain, where a Prussian corps attacked. He maintained this position till seven o'clock in the evening, and only retired when he was wounded.

Clearly, the Young Guard were not deployed directly into Plancenoit, as many historians of the battle claim, but had headed east to support Lobau and 6th Corps. Lobau and Duhesme had succeeded in holding off the Prussians, as Napoléon comments:[832]

> The Prussian division, whose movement had been foreseen, then engaged with the light troops of Comte Lobau, spreading its fire upon our whole right flank. It was expedient, before undertaking anything elsewhere, to wait for the event of this attack. Hence, all the means in reserve were ready to succour Comte Lobau, and overwhelm the Prussian corps when it should have advanced...

---

830 Pontécoulant, p. 305.
831 *Revue de l'Empire, fondée en 1842*, Paris, 1845, pp. 260-1.
832 *Journal des débats politiques et littéraires*, 26 June 1815, pp. 2-3.

It was impossible to deploy our reserves of infantry until we had repulsed the flank attack of the Prussian corps. This attack always prolonged itself perpendicularly upon our right flank. The emperor sent thither General Duhesme with the Young Guard, and several batteries of reserve. The enemy was kept in check, repulsed, and fell back—he had exhausted his forces and we had nothing more to fear. This was the moment that indicated for an attack upon the centre of the enemy.

General Gourgaud, on the French headquarters staff, offers a similar view to these events:[833]

About six o'clock we found that the Prussians had engaged their whole force: they ceased to act on the offensive, and their fire became stationary. Half an hour after they began to fall back our troops advanced. The balls of the Prussians no longer reached the high road, or even the first position which the troops of Duhesme and Comte de Lobau had occupied: these troops had now advanced. The extreme left of the Prussians wheeled round on the rear, and proceeded to replace itself in line with the 1st Brigade.

From the initial deployment beyond the Frischermont Wood, Lobau, with the 6th Corps, had been pushed back over the course of perhaps two hours, due to ever mounting pressure from the Prussians. Lobau formed up a new defensive line between Frischermont and Plancenoit. He was bolstered by the timely arrival of four regiments of the Young Guard. The Young Guard's actions here are recalled by Major Ludwig Wirths, a former captain (hauptmann) in the 2nd Battalion 2nd Nassau Regiment, and writes as follows:[834]

The 2nd Battalion of the 2nd Nassau Regiment was ordered to take its position behind the farm of La Haye, fronting this farm on the small height leading gently down towards it; forming from there the extreme left wing of the army, in close columns. Just a little in the rear of this position an English light dragoon regiment arrived. The 3rd Battalion was sent forward towards the farm of Papelotte. In this position, obliquely opposite to the enemy's right wing battery, the 2nd Battalion received, after the battle had begun, an assault

---

833 Gourgaud, pp. 101-2.
834 John Franklin personal communication, 7 September 2016, citing Hessisches Hauptstaatsarchiv, Wiesbaden: Abt. 1049.

from several 8-pounders from the same battery, which injured and killed some of the men. Just at the beginning of the affair, the 2nd Flanqueur Company, which was under the command of First-Lieutenant Fuchs, was sent forward to the farm of La Haye to operate against the artillery on the enemy's right wing and to prevent it from moving onto our left wing. After several hours, around three o'clock in the afternoon, Sergeant Lind, from this company, let us know that all three of the lieutenants (Captain Joseph Müller had already been injured on the 16th), First-Lieutenant Fuchs and Second-Lieutenant Cramer were wounded and unable to continue in the battle, and that the junior second-lieutenant, von Trott, was dead; so, I was ordered by the commander of the battalion, von Normann, to go and to support the flanker company with my own, the 8th. I met the rest of that company, which had suffered a great deal, in the farm of La Haye, with some of the men in the gardens surrounding the farm, they being occupied in combating the enemy artillery. As a result of the reinforcement from my company, our combined and stronger fire made the enemy retire towards its right wing and I subsequently passed the farm with my company and moved down the grass valley leading to Smohain, and having passed this deep, but narrow, valley, I arrived on the open field, and at one side of the enemy's army, by turning a little to the right, I was faced by a line of artillery, which was covered by two batteries ready to open fire and a battalion of the Moyenne Guard. I operated here, half advancing, half driven back again, until I could place myself into a hollow way which protected my front and from where I advanced to drive the enemy back with a heavy fire, and I did not have to leave this position until the end. During this combat the company lost many men, although I cannot state the exact number. Leiter and Wagner, two of the second-lieutenants were wounded, the first on his leg, the second by a shot in his head, and I myself was also slightly wounded, being heavily bruised by a shot in the lower leg which, however, did not force me to leave my position. Towards six o'clock in the evening, the Prussians arrived in the rear of my position, coming from Smohain with their artillery, and so it happened that they fired upon my company for a short time, thinking that we were French; however, this error was soon discovered.

The comment regarding the Moyenne Guard may of course be perfectly true, but rather it was the Young Guard. The Young Guard was deployed in this sector, but we have no evidence of it being deployed at Papelotte, but it seems that Wirths was engaging the Young Guard

312

closer to Plancenoit than to Papelotte. Captain Pontécoulant, of the Imperial Guard horse artillery, notes from his position close to La Belle Alliance that:[835]

> Blücher, whose column heads we had seen for an hour in the village of Ohain, whose infantry had finally managed to reach the defiles of Saint-Lambert. He then brought the head of two brigades to the hamlet of La Haye and farm of Papelotte to get in communication with the left wing of the English army. These points were occupied by two battalions of the Young Guard, which Napoléon had sent to relieve the troops of Comte d'Erlon, who had gloriously stood, but were worn out with fatigue...Seeing themselves assailed by fresh troops, and very superior numbers at the end of a day so deadly, the two battalions were taken with a panic, and, without attempting a useless resistance, they retired in the greatest disorder. It is even asserted that in this hasty retreat we heard the cry of 'every man for himself!'...our men became demoralised.

General Baron August von Kruse writes as follows about the 2nd Nassau Regiment based at Papelotte and La Haye Sainte:[836]

> Shortly after seven o'clock the enemy suddenly retired and numerous skirmishers from the Royal Prussian Army, followed by columns, appeared. They advanced from Smohain and Plancenoit and fired on the Nassau troops, who returned the fire at the beginning, as they had not been informed of the arrival of the Prussians. The fire lasted for about ten minutes. There were dead and wounded on either side. However, the mistake was soon realised and the firing was stopped. Now Papelotte was left and the Prussians and Nassau advanced together. This movement was followed by the 2nd Battalion, which had maintained its position throughout the battle, but had been under artillery fire the whole time. This movement is marked on the map in yellow. The losses of the 2nd Regiment on 18 June 1815: four officers and sixty-nine non-commissioned officers and soldiers killed; twenty officers and 153 non-commissioned officers and soldiers wounded. It should also be noted that two officers serving on my staff were wounded. With the expression of my most perfect esteem, I have the honour to remain your most obedient Kruse.

---

835 Pontécoulant, pp. 327-8.
836 John Franklin personal communication, 7 September 2016, citing Hessisches Hauptstaatsarchiv, Wiesbaden: Abt. 202, Nr. 1372.

Comment

Napoléon had been aware of the Prussian 4th Corps since 13.00. Based on Grouchy's intelligence contained in his 10.00 dispatch, Napoléon knew that the Prussian 1st, 2nd and 3rd Corps were heading to Louvain to gain the Brussels road, and a rearguard was at Wavre. Therefore, he no doubt reasoned that the 4th Corps was the only body of Prussian troops likely to arrive at Waterloo. To make matters worse, Napoléon probably incorrectly assumed that the rearguard Grouchy had at Wavre were the rear-most men from Bülow's corps, and that Grouchy would be moving up behind as ordered to do so, ergo the next troops to arrive at Waterloo would be Grouchy. The tragedy for the French was that when Ziethen arrived, his entire 1st Corps and Pirch's 2nd Corps had evaded Grouchy and Napoléon's forces on 17 June, long before Grouchy had been sent off in pursuit. At daybreak on 17 June, the Prussian 1st and 2nd Corps had headed north from Ligny, while the 3rd and 4th Corps had headed east and then north-east. Grouchy had been sent south-east and then north-east, being ordered to move in a sphere of operations that made it impossible for Grouchy to find half of the Prussian forces: the 3rd and 4th Corps. Thus 40,000 Prussians had marched to Waterloo virtually unopposed. Generals Milhaud and Domon had found the columns on 17 June, and Marbot had been sent out to confirm their reports that the Prussians were at Moustier. His report told the French staff that the Prussians had headed to Wavre and had not crossed the River Dyle at Moustier. Moustier was the most obvious place to cross the Dyle for the Prussians to march to Wellington. Given that the Prussians had headed to Wavre, seemingly to gain the Namur to Louvain road, Napoléon assumed they were not going to Waterloo.

Napoléon, no doubt felt confident that no other Prussians would arrive, as Grouchy, as far as Napoléon was concerned, was attacking the Prussian 1st, 2nd and 3rd Corps. Both men were wrong. Grouchy only ever found the Prussian 3rd and 4th Corps. Even then, the Prussian 4th Corps had largely evaded him. Napoléon no doubt had bargained that the next troops to arrive at Waterloo would not be Prussian, but elements of Grouchy's command. Grouchy is not to blame for his intelligence report concerning the Prussian corps. He never observed them, so assumed he had all the Prussian army from Ligny in front of him. He had received no news about any other Prussian body of troops other than at Namur, so he felt confident in what he reported back. Napoléon only told Grouchy about Milhaud and Domon's news on 18 June, when it was far too late for him to act upon it. The French had found all the Prussians from Ligny, but only ever pursued part of it. The Prussian 1st and 2nd Corps getting past Napoléon's forces on 17 June was a game changer. Failure of French commanders to act upon Milhaud and Domon's intelligence reports about large Prussian columns heading north from Sombreffe, and as distinct columns separate from those heading north-east, which Grouchy was chasing, lost the emperor the campaign. The French, on the morning of 17 June, had found all the Prussian army columns, but had come to the wrong conclusions about them. Headquarters, it seems, assumed that the columns Grouchy had in front of him and the columns Milhaud found were the same body of men. This was totally wrong. It was a miscalculation that lost the emperor the campaign, as we assess in our companion volume on Grouchy in the Waterloo campaign.

Chapter 17

Plancenoit

Against Lobau and Duhesme, Bülow had been making little headway as he advanced out of the Paris Wood. By the time Ziethen's command began to reach Waterloo, the fighting at Papelotte and Frischermont had reached another crisis point. So serious was the situation that when General Ziethen approached the battlefield, he was so concerned at the sight of stragglers and casualties coming from Wellington's left that he stopped his advance. No doubt, from Ziethen's point of view, these troops heading to the rear appeared to be withdrawing. Fearing that his own troops could be caught up in a general panic, after assessing the situation, he started to head away from Wellington's left flank. A major crisis point in the battle had been reached. The French were close to neutralising the Prussian 4th Corps and preventing the Prussians joining Wellington's threatened left flank.

It was crucial that immediate and decisive action be taken to prevent a French breakout. About the same time, General Thielemann was in desperate need of reinforcements to fend off Grouchy. If Ziethen fell back to aid Thielemann, as seemed possible, for the Allies the battle was lost.

The Prussian army liaison officer to Wellington, General Muffling, seeing Ziethen's command and its subsequent about-face, galloped over to find the general and persuaded him to support Wellington's left flank.[837] The outcome of the battle, thanks to Muffling, was now in the favour of the Allies.

With Ziethen's men now arriving on the battlefield, by 20.00 Lobau and Duhesme's position was increasingly untenable. He had to pull

---

837 John Franklin personal communication.

back. At Plancenoit, the Prussians were making their first tentative moves. This left the 6th Corps and the Young Guard deployed in front of the Paris Wood, in a very vulnerable position. That Lobau and Duhesme had clung tenaciously to this position for perhaps four hours is of great credit to these generals, but they had no choice but to fall back to Plancenoit to stop their command being surrounded on both flanks. This retrenchment to Plancenoit now left Napoléon's right flank dangerously exposed.

Flanqueur Pinstock, of 1st Battalion 28th Orange-Nassau Regiment, writes to his parents, brothers and sisters in Eisemroth on 22 July 1815 recalling the events of Waterloo:[838]

> At six o'clock the Prussians came to our assistance, and then the French had to run for five days and nights until they had reached Paris. We followed them to Paris, and there we had to lie in our camp for ten days, but on 17 July we were billeted in the city. From 15 to 17 June we had to lie in the fields at night, drenched in water and covered in mud, my knapsack was the pillow under my head, my coat was my blanket and the sky my hat.

These Prussian troops were Ziethen's men. From now on the battle only had one outcome. Senior aide-de-camp to Marshal Ney, Colonel Pierre Heymès, admits that:[839]

> Between seven and eight o'clock, the right of the Prussian corps, together with the left of the English, forced our extreme right and drove back toward the centre, in the same time threatening the rear of 6th Corps.

Due to this threat, Lobau retreated. Marshal Ney writes:[840]

> The Prussians continued their offensive movements, and our right sensibly retired, the English advanced in their turn.

General Trommelin recounts this final episode of the battle as follows:[841]

---

838 John Franklin personal communication, 7 September 2016.
839 Colonel Heymès, *Relation de la campagne de 1815, dite de Waterloo*, Gaultier-Laguionie, Paris, 1829, pp. 26-7.
840 *The Times*, 13 July 1815.
841 Trommelin, pp. 227-8.

At about eight o'clock in the evening, decimated by the Prussian attacks, which had been constantly reinforced, turned our right wing and the cavalry of Blücher pushed to the left with the English cavalry and began the pursuit of the army which fell into disorder, I had to order my battalions to abandon Plancenoit, which was in flames, and return to the main road.

At that moment when the last brigade of the 1st Division passed mine, I started my own retreat; my square was pressed from all directions, and broke in disorder. Remaining alone, I had a great trouble to remount, and went to rally my men in a wood to the rear of my position. I found it occupied by the Prussians, who forced me onto the main road, with those men that remained to me. I rallied some men to the left of the square of grenadiers of the Imperial Guard, but noticing that they were unsteady, I decided to reach the main road where I found the divisional command.

Sergeant-Major François Marq, in the 107th Regiment of Line Infantry, narrates his treatment by the Allies after being wounded at Waterloo, as well as detailing improvised methods of evacuating the wounded:[842]

I had remained on the field swimming in my blood and despite this cruel position, I had still the precaution, before the enemy did it to us, to undo my trousers and my underpants, and put myself on my belly my nose to the ground to make them think that I was killed and robbed. Despite this precaution, there was a cavalryman who wanted me to meet my fate: he launched a thrust of the sword on the back of my neck, but I still had enough strength to not move from my position. Had I made any movement, it is to believe that I would be killed. I was in my plight quite happy to keep the little money I had taken the precaution of hiding in my mouth.

Corporal Wagre, of the 11th Regiment of Line Infantry, narrates that he was thirsty and also terrified of being made a prisoner of war again:[843]

We had to flee before the enemy, and despite the kind of despair that we felt in our own country, to those we had so often vanquished, we had to flee, and the only road that remained to be taken to retreat on was that of Mont-Saint-Jean in Fleurus. The whole army occupied

---

842 *Revue Napoléonienne*, 1901.
843 Fleury, *Les prisonniers de Cabrera*.

it, and complete disorder seemed to add to the sad picture of our defeat: the roads were covered with debris of the army, and the debris made them impassable. I will never forget it.

Lieutenant Pontécoulant, of the Guard artillery, summarises the situation on the French right:[844]

> Comte Lobau, fearing being cut off, carried out his retreat towards our centre. The consequences of this movement was to allow the Prussian batteries, who had been substantially reinforced and which counted more than sixty guns, to gain ground so that their balls and even their case shot fell as far as the Charleroi road, which served as the main line of communications for our army, around the farm of La Belle Alliance, and even the high ground around Rossome, where the emperor was in the middle of his Guard. The trees lining the road were riddled, and often men, horses or caissons, moving from the reserve to the line of battle, were struck.

Lobau and Duhesme combined still lacked the men to be able to check the Prussian advance; some 14,000 against 30,000 Prussians. That these two commanders held out as long as they did is admirable. The French forces were strung out from Frischermont to Plancenoit; the left being held by Durutte. Durutte's men were, however, ordered to move towards the Brussels road, thinning out even more the French defensive line. This fatally weakened the French resistance. From 1st Corps, only Donzelot's division, with what remained of Quiot and Marcognet's divisions, now held the line between the Brussels road and Frischermont. Camille Durutte writes:[845]

> The number of our troops so diminished in the centre near the main road they were obliged to take troops from General Durutte, who sent a brigade to the left of this road and a regiment was placed on the highway to support the troops who had taken position at the Maison Carree. Around seven o'clock, we realised that our two wings faltered. That's when the emperor decided to make an effort on the centre, with part of his Guard he had held until then in reserve.

---

844 Pontécoulant, pp. 323-7.
845 *La Sentinelle de l'Armée*, 4th year, No. 134, 8 March 1838.

To replace General Pégot's men who moved to the centre, troops from 1st Division were moved to the right flank, as Lieutenant Domonique Fleuret,[846] of the 55th Regiment of Line Infantry, notes:[847]

> The regiment was reduced to about four hundred men, and they were formed into a single battalion. We were used as sharpshooters along with the Young Guard. We marched against the Prussians, who moved against our right wing to cut off the army's line of retreat.

This move of manpower undermined the already weak left flank of Lobau's line. Marshal Ney, in ordering this movement to the centre, fatally compromised the French right wing and its capability to hold off the Prussians.

Meanwhile, despite being initially checked by the French, Bülow did what all competent generals do: extend the line and search for a flank. He found it at Plancenoit. The village was the largest populated centre in the area, with the impressive church rising from its northern side.

As Bülow advanced, he immediately sent part of the 15th Brigade out on his right to secure Frischermont and its neighbouring wood, to prevent any flank attack from Durutte's troops. This was achieved with relative ease and the Prussians linked up with Sachsen-Weimar's Nassau troops, but not without a number of 'friendly fire' incidents. The rest of the 15th Brigade then moved on to engage Lobau's main force on the ridge north of Plancenoit, while the 13th Brigade followed them in reserve. The 16th Brigade marched forward with their artillery and the cavalry protecting their flanks, determined to take the village of Plancenoit. Possession of the village would leave Napoléon's rear completely unprotected, making his army very vulnerable; for the French, it was vital that the village was held.

Bülow, therefore, directed his precious reserves to Plancenoit and forced Lobau to retire or risk being outflanked. The French redeployed

---

846 MAT No. 231 Dominique Fleuret was born on 30 April 1787 at Bouthenville in the department of the Meuse, the son of Domonique Fleuret and Ann Folly. He was conscripted into the 55th Regiment of Line Infantry on 12 May 1807, promoted to corporal on 9 March 1809 and to adjutant on 1 July 1813. He was discharged on 1 September 1815. SHDDT: GR 21 YC 463.

847 Fleuret, pp. 149-54.

quickly and in good order, and moved into position behind Plancenoit, placing a strong garrison in the village. The depleted elements of Durutte's division continued to engage the hamlets around Smohain, having more or less gained supremacy at Frischermont, supported by Domon and Subervie. Hiller's 16th Brigade formed line and the six battalions marched directly on Plancenoit, determined to oust the French defenders; with the 14th Brigade moving up in their rear to form a reserve. The Prussian assault was initially successful, pushing the French defenders back as far as the open space around the church, which sat on a small hillock and was surrounded by a defensive wall. Here, they met a furious resistance and the advance was halted. Bloody hand-to-hand fighting spread through the village without either side truly gaining the upper hand, although the Prussians did capture some cannon and a few hundred prisoners. Fighting in built up areas was always some of the bloodiest fighting in the Napoléonic wars; Plancenoit would be no exception. It was hard to keep any kind of cohesion, units broke down into small groups of men either assaulting or defending, individual buildings became fortresses. Given the amount of hatred between the French and the Prussians, quarter was neither asked for nor given.

Two battalions of the 15th (3rd Reserve) Infantry Regiment pushed into the village and then on the high walls of the cemetery and church. The Prussians found themselves under fire from French snipers stationed in the houses. A murderous exchange of shots erupted from a distance of no more than twenty paces.

By now, information had been passed back to Napoléon and the headquarters staff about what was happening on the right flank. The news was dire and there was no doubt a great deal of unease in the staff. The high morale of the French at the start of the battle was wavering. The Prussian intervention was having a telling and damaging effect on the French, the battle against the Allies on Mont-Saint-Jean was also not yielding morale-boosting results, and now the Prussians were threatening to overwhelm the rear. The Prussian artillery's effectiveness is documented by Sergeant Hippolyte de Mauduit, who writes:[848]

> We were very surprised to see from these batteries, which we believed to be French [Grouchy], simultaneously appear twenty or so white clouds and a few seconds after to hear around us, or

---

848 de Mauduit, Vol 2, pp. 445-6.

above our heads, the whistling of balls! Nearly all of the balls of the second discharge landed either in our square, or in that of the *sapeurs* and marines of the Guard, placed on the same line as us, but next to the road.

A third discharge of the same batteries struck accurately, and killed several of our brave grenadiers, we served as the target for nearly an hour, without moving, we thus received death with ordered muskets and arms crossed.

For some time, we did not have a single gun to reply to these uncomfortable neighbours; our own battery had been sent over to 6th Corps to replace theirs that had been lost while on loan to d'Erlon. The emperor was immediately informed and a 12-pounder battery of the Guard reserve was sent to replace it and it deployed a hundred paces above us. From there, it fired on the Prussian columns beyond the village of Plancenoit. Its fire, well directed, quickly reduced the effectiveness of the Prussian fire, which, nevertheless, had caused us about fifty casualties in our square. The shells in particular caused us the most damage.

Each discharge thus knocked down several grenadiers, but our post was there, and neither the balls, nor shells would force us to abandon it.

One French officer writing on 24 June commented:[849]

The Young Guard fought valiantly, so much so that they should be nominated for the Middle Guard. However, in an instant a Prussian column, whose march we were ignorant of, commenced to attack them in the flank, the terrible cry of 'save yourselves!' did not cease to be heard. In result, the soldiers were dispersed in the greater part into the forests. At Avesnes, and also at Marle, the villagers were so frightened that they abandoned their houses and retired into the woods with their livestock.

Jardine Aine, equerry to Napoléon, writes:[850]

The fighting was desperate. Napoléon rode through the lines and gave orders to make certain that every detail was executed with promptitude; he returned often to the spot where in the morning he had started, there he dismounted and, seating himself in a chair

---

849 *Journal de Rouen*, 30 June 1815, p. 2.
850 MacBride, pp. 181-5.

which was brought to him, he placed his head between his hands and rested his elbows on his knees. He remained thus absorbed sometimes for half-an-hour, and then rising up suddenly would peer through his glasses on all sides to see what was happening. At three o'clock an aide-de-camp from the right wing came to tell him that they were repulsed and that the artillery was insufficient. Napoléon immediately called General Drouot in order to direct him to hasten to reinforce this army corps, which was suffering so heavily, but one saw on Napoléon's face a look of disquietude instead of the joy which it had shown on the great day of Fleurus. The whole morning, he showed extreme depression; however, everything was going on as well as could be expected with the French, in spite of the uncertainty of the battle.

The fighting on the French right flank now switched to Plancenoit, as Lobau and Duhesme pulled back. Prussian General Gneisenau narrates:[851]

Towards six o'clock in the evening, we received the news that General Thelma, with the 3rd Corps, were attacked near Wavre by a very considerable corps of the enemy, and that they were already disputing the possession of the town. The field-marshal, however, did not suffer himself to be disturbed by this news: it was on the spot where he was, and nowhere else, that the affair was to be decided. A conflict, continually supported by the same obstinacy, and kept up by fresh troops, could alone ensure the victory, and if it were obtained here, any reverse sustained near Wavre was of little consequence. The columns, therefore, continued their movements. It was half an hour past seven, and the issue of the battle was still uncertain. The whole of the 4th Corps, and a part of the 2nd, under General Pvich [Pirch] had successively come up. The French troops fought with desperate fury: however, some uncertainty was perceived in their movements, and it was observed that some pieces of cannon were retreating. At this moment, the first columns of the corps of General Ziethen arrived on the points of attack, near the village of Smouhen [Smohain], on the enemy's right flank, and instantly charged. This moment decided the defeat of the enemy. His right wing was broken in three places; he abandoned his positions. Our troops rushed forward at the *pas de charge*, and attacked him on all sides, while, at the same time, the whole English line advanced.

---

851 John Franklin personal communication.

Circumstances were extremely favourable to the attack formed by the Prussian army; the ground rose in an amphitheatre, so that our artillery could freely open its fire from the summit of a great many heights which rose gradually above each other, and, in the intervals of which the troops descended into the plain, formed into brigades, and in the greatest order; while fresh corps continually unfolded themselves, issuing from the forest on the height behind us. The enemy, however, still preserved means to retreat, till the village of Plancenoit, which he had on his rear, and which was defended by the Guard, was, after several sanguinary attacks, carried by storm.

Plancenoit was now the scene of bitter fighting. The Young Guard had managed to fall back into the village and used the churchyard as a defensive bastion, much as the Prussians had done at the church of Saint-Amand at Ligny only two days before. General Hiller recalls that with support from the 1st Battalions of the 1st and 2nd Pomeranian Landwehr Regiments:[852]

> Overcoming all difficulties and with heavy losses from canister and musketry, the troops of the 15th Infantry and 1st Silesian Landwehr penetrated to the high wall around the churchyard held by the French Young Guard. These two columns succeeded in capturing a howitzer, two cannon, several ammunition wagons, two staff officers and several hundred men. The open square around the churchyard was surrounded by houses, from which the enemy could not be dislodged in spite of our brave attempt. A fire fight continued at fifteen to thirty paces, which ultimately decimated the Prussian battalions. Had I at this moment the support of only one fresh battalion at hand, this attack would have indeed been successful.

The 3rd Voltigeurs capture Prussian artillery

With Plancenoit forming the defensive bastion on the French right, the Prussians renewed their attack:[853]

---

852 Ollech, *Geschichte des Feldzuges von 1815 nach archivalischen quellen Berlin,* 1876, pp. 248-9.

853 August Wagner, *Plane der Schlachten und Treffen, welche von der Preussischen Armee in den Feldzügen der Jahre 1813, 14 und 15 geliefert worden* (Vol. 4), Reimer, Berlin, 1825, p. 89.

The general ordered Colonel Hiller to the third attack: two battalions of the 15th Regt, under Major Wittig, moved to the right of action against the village, two battalions from the 1st Silesian Landwehr Regiment, under the command of Major von Fischer in the middle, and Lieutenant-Colonel Blandowski with two battalions of the 2nd Silesian Landwehr Regiment on the left. The 14th Brigade followed as a reserve, and sent the 1st Battalions from the 1st and 2nd Pomeranian Landwehr Regiments to support this attack. The troops on the right forced their way into the middle by enfilade fire to the village, captured two guns and a howitzer, and took possession of the churchyard.

But, the enemy held its own in the surrounding houses and gardens, and there was now at thirty paces a murderous small-arms fire, in consequence of which the Prussians were obliged to retreat, especially as another enemy column appeared to them in the rear. The French cavalry pursued, and attacked the Foot Artillery Battery No. 2. The troops rallied again, the 2nd Battalion of the 11th Line and 1st Pomeranian Landwehr Regiment suffered by the action united with 1st Battalion, and were advancing with the 15th Regiment following them. This second attack succeeded, and the French were driven from the village.

The French counter-attacked, and managed to re-take at least one of the captured guns before being repulsed from the burning charnel house of the churchyard and village. Involved in this attack was the brigade of General Guye, comprising the 3rd Regiments of Tirailleurs and Voltigeurs. As Wagner notes, the French captured two field guns and a howitzer.

These appear to have been taken by the 3rd Voltigeurs. Indeed, the officer leading a detachment which captured the howitzer was Lieutenant Benoite Presle. Presle was born in Saint-Leger on 27 March 1771, the son of Benoit Presle and Marguerite Duperray. Admitted to the 2nd Battalion of the Rhine on 15 March 1793, he was quickly promoted to corporal, thence to sergeant in 1795 in what was to become the 44th Regiment of Line Infantry. He was promoted to sub-lieutenant in 1796 and to lieutenant on 24 February 1806 before being admitted to the 3rd Voltigeurs on 15 May 1815, and discharged on 15 September 1815. Between 3 July 1803 and 3 July 1814, he had been a prisoner of war in England. About Waterloo, Lieutenant Presle writes:[854]

---

854 AN: LH 2222/55.

> At the affair of Mont-Saint-Jean, through my bravery, I succeeded in capturing from the enemy a howitzer which the enemy had taken from us.

At some stage in the battle at Plancenoit, the 3rd Tirailleurs became involved in an action that resulted in two officers and an NCO being promoted or awarded decorations for distinguished conduct. Battalion-Commander Claude Jacquot, of the 2nd Battalion 3rd Regiment of Tirailleurs, writing about his career in the third person, notes that:[855]

> He continued in the service with the 3rd Regiment of Tirailleurs of the Imperial Guard on 15 April 1815, fought valiantly at Mont-Saint-Jean and went at the head of the grenadiers of the Old Guard three times against the village of Plancenoit, which was defended by the Prussians. He had his horse killed under him by shrapnel and had by so many miracles escaped from the field of Waterloo. The emperor, who witnessed himself of these deeds of valour, felt obliged to re-compensate for one last time by naming him baron on the battlefield. But, the times changed quickly, and instead of getting the confirmation of this title justly deserved, he was reformed without treatment with royal decision of 8 November next, and restored to his rank of lieutenant-colonel on 15 October 1817, while he was put into retirement.

3rd Tirailleurs distinguish themselves

Captain Demonte, of the 3rd Tirailleurs, says:[856]

> I was named Officer of the Legion of Honour on the field of battle by the captain-general of the Imperial Guard, in the name of the emperor. I was wounded during the battle, I was made prisoner of war.

We assume the captain-general was General Drouot. Jean François Demonte was born in 1775 and enlisted into the army in 1792. At Waterloo, he was wounded with canister shot to the left leg. He spent the night on the field, and was made prisoner of war.

At some stage in the action, presumably the same episode as Demonte, Sergeant Cuisset was of such meritorious conduct that

---

855 E. de Stein, *Notice biographique sur M. le chevalier Jacquot (Claude),*
     lieutenant-colonel, Panthéon Universel, Paris, 1856.
856 Author's collection.

he was proposed for the Legion of Honour, as Colonel Pailhes, who commanded the 3rd Tirailleurs, tells us:[857]

> I, marshal-du-camp, commanding the Department de Aveyron, formerly colonel of the 3rd Regiment of Tirailleurs of the Imperial Guard, certify, that I proposed to be awarded the Cross of the Legion of Honour on Monsieur Nicolas Celestin Cuissel, sergeant of the corps, for his distinguished conduct at the Battle of Waterloo.

Nicolas Celestin Cuisset had been born on 16 December 1787 and had been admitted to the 1st Regiment of the Garde de Paris on 10 February 1807. Promotion to corporal came on 12 August 1807 and to sergeant on 1 July 1808. He was made prisoner of war on 19 July 1808 at Baylen, where he was wounded, and was returned to France on 17 May 1814. He was placed on leave from 2 June 1814 and recalled to the army on 28 March 1815, where he was named sergeant in the 3rd Tirailleurs on 6 May 1815. He passed to the 2nd Infantry Regiment of the Royal Guard on 3 February 1817 and left the regiment on 3 February 1823. Found among the vast amounts of archive paperwork in Vincennes is the muster rolls of the Imperial Guard in 1815.

The 1st Tirailleurs

In the fighting in Plancenoit, the 1st Tirailleurs lost the following other ranks dead, wounded or prisoner of war:[858]

1st Tirailleurs					
	Wounded	Wounded & Prisoner	Prisoner of War	Killed	Missing
1st Battalion	5	0	1	6	203
2nd Battalion	8	0	0	8	137
Total	13	0	1	14	340

The regiment lost 368 men, although sustained very few men killed or wounded, but suffered a high proportion of men that were sent to the rear or never seen again. It seems, therefore, that the regiment was involved in a fire fight with the Prussians and then retreated, haemorrhaging men as it

---

857 Author's collection.
858 Compiled from SHDDT: GR 20 YC 18. See also: SHDDT: GR 20 YC 19.

did. The regiment lost 33 per cent effective strength in the battle. Between 20 and 26 June, a further 736 men were lost; representing 89 per cent of the regiment's remaining effective strength. Some authors on Waterloo have used the muster strength of 26 June to demonstrate that the Young Guard was eviscerated at Waterloo. This is wrong. It is quite clear that the Young Guard lost more men during the retreat than at Waterloo.

At the head of the 1st Battalion was Jérôme Etienne Cogne.[859] In the fighting at Plancenoit, he was seriously wounded when a musket ball broke the second and third false ribs on his left side, and suffered a howitzer shell splinter to the sacrum. He was made prisoner of war. Despite his injures he did not die until 20 July 1836.[860] Also wounded was Louis Jean Baptiste Delaunay, at the head of the 2nd Battalion, who was wounded and left for dead and made prisoner of war at some point when the French evacuated Plancenoit.[861]

Among the company officers wounded was Captain Charles Antoine Trappier,[862] at the head of the 1st Company of 1st Battalion, who had a musket ball pass through his body and he was left behind in the retreat and made prisoner.[863] Lieutenant Antoine Jean Henry Verdie, a native of Tours, had served with the regiment since 13 April 1815 and was shot with a musket ball that entered above the hip, passed through his scrotum, and lodged itself in his right thigh.[864] Also wounded was Second-Lieutenant Jean Pierre Huteau.[865]

---

859 He was born at Lens-l'Etang on 30 September 1774 and had enlisted in 1791, was promoted to second-lieutenant in the 2nd Regiment of the Grenadiers à Pied of the Imperial Guard on 1 May 1806, to first-lieutenant in the fusilier-grenadiers on 5 April 1809, to captain in the 3rd Tirailleurs on 17 March 1811, returned to the fusilier-grenadiers as captain-adjutant-major on 25 April 1812 and to major of the 13th Regiment of Line Infantry on 10 April 1813. He was made prisoner of war on 19 October 1813, and recalled on 19 May 1815. AN: LH 560/22.

860 AN: LH 560/22.

861 Ian Smith personal communication, 1 July 2013.

862 He was born at Grozannes on 18 August 1785. He had been conscripted to the 76th Regiment of Line Infantry on 6 February 1806, and progressed through the ranks being promoted to captain on 1 March 1813. Placed on half-pay from 16 August 1814, he was admitted to the 1st Tirailleurs on 30 April 1815.

863 AN: LH 2624/59. See also: AN: LH 2624/60.

864 AN: LH 2688/5.

865 AN: LH 2701/93.

The 3rd Tirailleurs

In the fighting in Plancenoit, the table shows the losses of other ranks:[866]

3rd Tirailleurs					
	Wounded	Wounded & Prisoner	Prisoner of War	Killed	Missing
1st Battalion	7	0	13	0	266
2nd Battalion	3	0	0	1	172
Total	10	0	13	1	438

As with the 1st Tirailleurs, the regiment lost more men disappeared than killed or wounded. Again, it seems the regiment came under fire and then presumably retreated, with some men being made prisoner of war or running for their lives. It lost 462 men at Waterloo, representing 48 per cent of the regiment's effective strength. Between 20 and 26 June, a further 351 men were lost, or some 70 per cent of the regiment's remaining effective strength.

The 3rd Tirailleurs also suffered officers dead and wounded. Dieudonne Dieulin, born in Metz in 1789 had been admitted to the 3rd Tirailleurs on 13 April with the rank of lieutenant from the 59th Regiment of Line Infantry, in which he had served as a captain. He was wounded at Waterloo. Captain Claude Andre Adenis was wounded, and had joined the regiment on 1 June 1815, having been on half-pay since 15 September 1814 from the disbanded 14th Tirailleurs.[867] Also wounded were Captains Louis Beaudouin, Jean François Antoine Demonte (who was left for dead on the field of battle after suffering a canister shot to his right leg),[868] Jean François Hippolyte Dion (with a gunshot to the thigh),[869] and François Richard, with a gunshot to the pelvis.[870] Among the first-lieutenants, Vincent Bargigli, admitted from the Corsican Flanqueur, was wounded, as were Henry Pierre Bermond, Alexandre Bozio-Negroni, admitted from the Corsican Flanqueur, Victor Jean François Noel and Pierre Andre Plumart. Also wounded was the regiment's pay-officer, Adjutant-Sub-Officer Jean Baptiste

---

866 Compiled from SHDDT: GR 20 YC 18. See also: SHDDT: GR 20 YC 19.
867 AN: LH 8/6.
868 AN: LH 728/24.
869 AN: LH 779/21.
870 AN: LH 2320/25.

Adolphe Laforgue, who suffered a gunshot to the inner face of his left knee.[871] Killed in Plancenoit and commemorated by a plaque on the church was First-Lieutenant Medard Joseph Louis. Mortally wounded was Second-Lieutenant Henry Desire Gaudin. The officers leading their companies from the front appear to have been easy targets for the Prussian marksmen, and also show that the Young Guard as a whole, or perhaps just the 3rd Tirailleurs, came under artillery fire at some stage in the action.

1st Voltigeurs

The wounded and killed in the regiment among the other ranks is shown below:[872]

1st Voltigeurs					
	Wounded	Wounded & Prisoner	Prisoner of War	Killed	Missing
1st Battalion	87	0	136	25	116
2nd Battalion	64	0	73	26	220
Total	151	0	209	51	336

The 1st Voltigeurs lost far more men dead and wounded than the brigaded 1st Tirailleurs, so we suppose that either the voltigeurs formed the head of column or that the sector in which the regiment deployed in Plancenoit was far deadlier and far more bitter than where the 1st Tirailleurs stood; fifty-one men were lost at Ligny and 690 at Waterloo, representing 60 per cent of effective strength. Between 20 and 26 June, 565 men were lost, or 75 per cent of the remaining strength of the regiment. The retreat was far costlier in men than the actual battle.

Wounded among the officers in the 1st Voltigeurs was Captain Alexis Octave Delzons. He took a gunshot to the left thigh in Plancenoit, which rendered him incapable of continuing his service as an army officer.[873] First-Lieutenant François Nicolas Simon Eymard, born at Briançon on 22 February 1791, was wounded when a musket ball entered his left hip and exited through his right hip. Left for dead, he was taken prisoner

---

871 AN: LH 1437/75.
872 Compiled from SHDDT: GR 20 YC 55. See also: SHDDT: GR 20 YC 56.
873 AN: LH 723/16.

by the English and was released on 24 July 1815.[874] Also wounded was First-Lieutenant Marchandin, as well as Second-Lieutenant Jean François Victor Cordeviole, who had been admitted from the marines of the Imperial Guard in which he had served on Elba with the rank of sergeant. Other wounded officers were Second-Lieutenants du Tilliet, Duclos and Lorenzi. Killed was Captain Tavernier, whereas Second-Lieutenant Hollinger was mortally wounded and died on 10 July 1815.[875]

3rd Voltigeurs

The wounded and killed in the regiment among the other ranks is shown below:[876]

3rd Voltigeurs					
	Wounded	Wounded & Prisoner	Prisoner of War	Killed	Missing
1st Battalion	44	0	164	25	28
2nd Battalion	10	0	232	5	16
Total	54	0	396	30	44

At Waterloo, according to the regiment's muster list, 524 men were lost, or 58 per cent of effective strength. Between 20 and 26 June, 245 more were lost, representing losses of 66 per cent.

3rd Regiment of Voltigeurs of the Guard, 1 September 1815

Losses among the 3rd Regiment of Voltigeurs of the Imperial Guard were:

1st Battalion

1st Company: Captain Pailly died on the field of battle on 18 June.
2nd Company: Captain Laurent died on the battlefield on 18 June.
3rd Company: Sub-lieutenant Dormoy was made prisoner of war, and Sub-Lieutenant Jerier was wounded on 18 June.

---

874 AN: LH 917/7.
875 Author's collection.
876 Compiled from SHDDT: GR 20 YC 55. See also: SHDDT: GR 20 YC 56.

Company	Sergeant-Major	Sergeant	Fourrier	Caporal	Tambour	Soldat	Total	On leave	Wounded	Prisoner of War	Killed	Total	Grand Total
1st	1	2	2	2	0	8	15	0	9	25	6	40	55
2nd	1	4	2	2	0	7	16	0	16	47	8	71	87
3rd	1	4	1	1	1	6	14	0	6	37	0	43	57
4th	2	2	1	1	1	10	17	0	4	61	0	65	82
Total	5	12	6	6	2	31	62	0	35	170	14	219	281

2nd Battalion

1st Company: Sub-Lieutenant Humbert was wounded.
2nd Company: Sub-Lieutenant Bretet was wounded on 18 June.
4th Company: Captain Gaillot was wounded on 18 June.

Company	Sergeant-Major	Sergeant	Fourrier	Caporal	Tambour	Soldat	Total	On leave	Wounded	Prisoner of War	Killed	Total	Grand Total
1st	2	4	1	2	0	12	21	0	1	49	1	51	72
2nd	2	4	1	1	0	14	22	0	4	60	0	64	86
3rd	1	4	1	0	0	10	16	0	5	53	14	72	88
4th	1	4	1	3	0	14	23	0	8	62	15	85	108
Total	6	16	4	6	0	50	82	0	18	224	30	272	354

In total, the regiment had 144 men under arms at the time of disbandment. The situation report makes clear that fifty-three men were wounded in hospital (one man less than recorded in the regiment's muster list), 394 were prisoners of war (two less than the regiment's muster list), and forty-four had been killed for a total of 491 casualties. This is somewhat less than the 521 men recorded in the muster list. We assume, therefore, that the men listed as missing had returned to the regiment.

Among the wounded officers was Captain Jean Baptiste Gaillot. He had served as an officer in the 8th Company of the Battalion de

Montferme between 1791 and 1793 and as part of the ship's garrison of the *Le Censeur* in 1796, taking part in the Italian campaign of 1799, and in 1800 was named *Capitaine d'habillement* (clothing officer) of the 45th Regiment of Line Infantry. He was admitted to the 3rd Voltigeurs and wounded in the thigh in the defence of Plancenoit. Also wounded was Lieutenant-Adjutant-Major Million. First-Lieutenant Louis Joseph Gand, who had served with the Imperial Guard since entrance as a conscript to the fusilier-chasseurs on 3 October 1806, took a bayonet thrust that passed through his left buttock and into his left thigh.[877] Also wounded was Second-Lieutenant Charles Bretet, who had been a sergeant with the 1st Chasseurs à Pied of the Imperial Guard with the Elba Battalion. Second-Lieutenants Jean Alexandre Dormoy,[878] Humbert and Viesiez were wounded and Captains Laurent and Vailly were killed.

Summary

Total losses in both brigades were as follows:

1st Brigade					
	Wounded	Wounded & Prisoner	Prisoner of War	Killed	Missing
1st Tirailleurs	13	0	1	14	340
1st Voltigeurs	151	0	209	51	336
Total	164	0	210	65	676
2nd Brigade					
	Wounded	Wounded & Prisoner	Prisoner of War	Killed	Missing
3rd Tirailleurs	10	0	13	1	438
3rd Voltigeurs	54	0	396	30	44
Total	64		409	31	482

The 1st Brigade had a far higher number of men killed and wounded than the 2nd Brigade. The low number of wounded and the single man dead in the 3rd Tirailleurs could suggest, tallying with the high number of men missing, that the regiment broke under enemy fire. The

---

877 AN: LH 1066/62.
878 AN: LH 793/34.

first attack by the Imperial Guard in Plancenoit lasted for nearly two hours, the brunt of the fighting falling on the voltigeurs. The tirailleurs appear to have come under attack and, for whatever reason, pulled back or retreated from the Prussians, unlike the voltigeurs which, as we have seen, walled up in the churchyard, led a daring counter-attack, retook captured artillery pieces and decimated the Prussians before being forced to retreat. With the collapse of the tirailleurs and then the voltigeurs, two battalions of the Old Guard were fed into the fray.

In order to assess the battlefield performance of the 6th Corps at Waterloo, we turn to the total losses sustained: 142 cavalry, 1,065 in the 19th Division and 716 in the 20th Division, a total of 1,923 men lost. The 1st Young Guard Brigade lost 1,115 men, the 2nd Brigade 986 men, giving a total loss of 4,024 men.

The 19th and 20th Infantry Divisions were involved in action against the Prussian 13th and 15th Brigades. The 13th Brigade comprised the 1st Silesian Regiment, 2nd Neumark Landwehr Regiment and 3rd Neumark Landwehr Regiment. The 15th Brigade comprised the 18th Regiment, 3rd Silesian Landwehr Regiment and 4th Silesian Landwehr Regiment. Hiller's 16th Brigade, comprising the 15th Regiment and 1st and 2nd Silesian Landwehr Regiments, seems to have been kept as a reserve. The 13th Brigade lost 716 men, the 15th Brigade lost 1,631 men and the 16th Brigade some 1,645 men, a total of 3,992 men. The Prussians, if the French data is correct, lost slightly fewer men than the French. If the French data is a true record, it seems that Lobau was no easy pushover. Standing in prepared positions with artillery support, fighting on terrain of their choosing, Lobau in effect dictated the terms of the conflict with the Prussians. Defending troops clearly had the advantage here. So, we must ask, what caused the left wing of Lobau's 6th Corps, arguably the 107th Regiment of Line Infantry with the 10th Regiment of Line Infantry, to fall back.

After making a stand in front of the Paris Wood, between 19.30 to 20.00, Lobau's men had withdrawn back to Plancenoit, leaving the defence of the French right flank dangerously thin, as all that stood in the gaping void in the French right flank were the battered rumps of Donzelot, Marcognet and Durutte's single brigade, under the orders of General Brue. Such a gap in the French right wing seems to have been brutally exploited by the Prussian cavalry, which we are told were at La Haye Sainte at the climax of the battle when the Old Guard attacked.

Weight of numbers and the fear of being out-flanked had caused Lobau to withdraw. The choices he faced as field commander was to stand and fight an ever-increasing flood of Prussians, or to withdraw back to the main body of the Armée du Nord and get as many men as possible off the field of battle, seeing the battle was irrecoverably lost. Lobau, it seems, acted with caution and withdrew.

Chapter 18

The Old Guard Attack Plancenoit

Despite the failure of the initial wave of Prussian attacks, more of their troops were arriving and were now able to attack in overwhelming numbers. Buoyed by the sight of fresh troops, Pirch's 5th Brigade (commanded by Tipplskirch), Bülow was able to rally his men for another assault. The Prussians were now able to launch over 40,000 men against less than 15,000 French. On paper, the eventual outcome of an Allied victory here was almost guaranteed. Despite holding on against overwhelming odds, sheer weight of numbers finally overcame the French and they were slowly forced back.

Despite the efforts of their officers, many men of the Young Guard fled in disarray. The situation on Napoléon's right flank was now critical. Prussian cannonballs were by now landing on the Brussels road. It was vital that the French right wing was propped up. By 20.00 Lobau and Duhesme had withdrawn to Plancenoit, using the village as a defensive bastion to hold off the Prussians. The village was to remain in French hands for the next hour, during which Napoléon launched the remainder of his Imperial Guard against Wellington's army in an attempt to break the Allied lines in the centre.

No other troops were to hand other than the Old Guard, and three battalions were ordered to march to the village. Colonel Auguste Louis Pétiet, of the imperial staff, notes that:[879]

> About eight o'clock the Prussians forced our right and threatened the rear of the 6th Corps, four battalions of the Guard were sent by the emperor to Marshal Ney, to stop the enemy.

---

879 Pétiet, pp. 221-2.

General Pelet continues:[880]

> We were always in square, the grenadiers behind me; the 3rd and 4th Chasseurs were in front. I remember there was confusion about the order of the squares, and I do not know if the grenadiers were not then passing on the other side of the road. Finally, General Morand said 'go with your 1st Battalion to Plancenoit, for the Young Guard is all but beaten. Support them. Support this point, because it will only leave your 2nd Battalion, and the 1st Chasseurs for the last reserve'.

General Christiani notes that:[881]

> At five or six o'clock, maybe later, I received the order to send a battalion of the regiment into the village that was to the right, behind the position I occupied, to drive out the Prussians, they said that they were about to capture it. It was M. Golzio, head of the 1st Battalion of the regiment that went on this mission, I saw him that evening during the retreat. I do not remember if he had lost many men, but only that he told me he had done much harm to the enemy.

The two battalions of the Old Guard were noted by the Prussians:[882]

> Since Napoléon saw that the Prussians penetrated by force, the 2nd Regiments of Grenadiers and Chasseurs of the Old Guard were ordered to send a battalion each to Plancenoit, and these two battalions, which were led by General Morand, took back the village and pursued the Prussians up to their position behind the village. Their skirmishers came up to the Prussian batteries, but were chased away from them by the 2nd Squadron of the 1st Silesian Hussars Regiment. The French cavalry made a move to advance, and a regiment of lancers were repulsed by Major von Colomb with the 2nd Hussar Regiment; they, however, then came under the fire of a French infantry battalion formed in line and had to retreat back to their starting place, however, a French hussars regiment was repulsed by the Prussian infantry.

> Meanwhile, a battalion from the French 1st Grenadier Guard Regiment on the right of the road was placed at a height which

---

880 d'Avout, pp. 37-9.
881 ibid, pp. 111-3.
882 Wagner, p. 90.

dominates the road that leads from the highway to Plancenoit, the 2nd Battalion of this regiment stood together with six guns left of the road.

The hussars mentioned were surely Marbot's 7th Hussars. This clearly indicates the regiment had been pulled back from its advanced posts towards Saint-Lambert and was operating on the field of battle. Victor Dupuy, squadron-commander of the French 7th Hussars under Colonel Marbot, recalls that:[883]

> Until about four o'clock, we remained quiet spectators of the battle. In one moment, General Domon came to me when the fire of English was almost stopped, and he told me that the battle was won, the enemy was retreating, we were there to make junction with the troops of Grouchy and that we would be that evening in Brussels, he departed. A few moments later, instead of joining with the troops of Marshal Grouchy as we expected, we received an attack from a regiment of Prussian lancers. We repulsed him vigorously and gave chase, but we were forced to retreat by the fire of canister from six pieces of cannon, behind which the lancers retreated. Colonel Marbot was wounded by a lance thrust in the chest in the attack of the Prussians. They were attacked then by the infantry, we redeployed in the centre, slowly retreating. In our retrograde movement, we met Marshal Soult, general staff, which made us take post near a battery and give it support, the enemy's cannon made us no harm.

Second-in-command of the 1st Brigade of the Prussian 1st Army Corps under Ziethen was General Hoffmann. In this capacity, he witnessed much of the fighting at firsthand:[884]

> The brave Colonel Hiller had at about half-past six, with three columns, each of two battalions, stormed the two flanks and the centre of Plancenoit. The wing-columns took the outlying part and the cemetery, but had to yield to superior force, a second attack, supported by two battalions of the 15th Brigade had the same success, and both were followed by the French cavalry to the other side of the height. We had to wait for reinforcements.

---

883 Victor Dupuy, *Mémoires Militaire 1794-1816*, Librairie des deux Empirés, 2001.

884 Hoffmann, *Zur Geschichte des Feldzuges von 1815*, Berlin, 1851, pp. 108-9.

Napoléon had sent in just before this attack the two 2nd Battalions of the Old Guard of General Morand, and soon after that upon perceiving in the distance preparations of Blücher, two other battalions, under General Pelet, one of which to the right of Plancenoit was in nearby Chantelet Forest.

Hoffmann counted four French battalions. Two were clearly those that fought in the village, the one at Chantelet is surely that commanded by Battalion-Commander Duuring, the enigmatic 4th Battalion could well be that of the 1st Grenadiers, which was established at the junction of the Brussels road and the Plancenoit road acting as a reserve. Hoffmann also comments that in addition, Prussian Horse Battery No. 6 was posted on the high ground upon the right of the Virere Wood, and was principally occupied in diverting the fire from a battery of the Imperial Guard horse artillery, which had one-half of its guns above the hollow way formed by the road leading down into Plancenoit from La Maison du Roi, and the other half detached to an elevated spot in the south part of the village, whence it had a commanding view of a considerable portion of the advancing columns. The cavalry was clearly that of Domon or Subervie, but due to a lack of source material from the French and Prussians we are not able to elaborate on what occurred. General Petit narrates that:[885]

> The enemy, however, had made much progress on our right which was singularly overwhelmed. The Young Guard, who had been sent at two o'clock, and having been forced into a retrograde movement from the village of Plancenoit, the 2nd Regiment of Chasseurs and the 2nd Regiment of Grenadiers were ordered to detach a battalion and enter the village. The enemy was immediately chased out with great loss. We pursued them with bayonets up on the hill. The chasseurs and grenadiers marched right up to the Prussian batteries, which were for a time abandoned. The movement was effected at 6 p.m.
>
> During this movement, the 1st Grenadier Regiment was formed in two squares, one per battalion. The first was to the right of the roadway (facing the enemy) on an elevated position overlooking the small path that opens out into a highway and that leads to

---

885 J. Petit, 'General Petit's Account of the Waterloo Campaign' in *English Historical Review*, 1903.

Plancenoit. We sent some men with an adjutant-major to the far right of the village to observe the enemy that was there in force.

The adjutant-major sent with the 150 grenadiers was Charles Fare, who recounts:[886]

It was half-past six. The troops who were being extended to the right of the army were close to the woods whereby we expected Grouchy to arrive. Their appearance raised a cry of joy in the Old Guard, but soon the Prussian bullets hit their square and destroyed this brief illusion…Blücher's full attention was focused on Plancenoit, which was occupied by the 6th Corps and the Young Guard, and were in charge of opposing the march of the corps of Bülow. If they captured this village, the French army would be turned on his right and this movement would cause the enemy to fall on our flank and into the rear of our troops.

Pursuant to the orders of Blücher, Colonel Hiller soon formed three columns of attack, two battalions of the 15th Regiment, commanded by Major Wittich, right, two battalions of the 1st Silesian Landwehr, under the command of Major Fischer, centre, and Lieutenant-Colonel Blandowski, with two battalions of the 2nd Silesian Landwehr, left. The 14th Brigade, following in reserve, were detached the 1st Battalions of the 14th Line and 1st Pomeranian Landwehr to support the attacks.

The columns on the right and left entered the village through a pit of fire and captured a howitzer and two pieces and moved to the cemetery, but they cannot push back the Young Guard and the detachments of the 6th Corps from the houses and orchards where they are maintained during the first attack. At thirty yards began a most deadly fusillade which ended with the retreat of six Prussian battalions when their rear was threatened by a column of cavalry of General Domon. This cavalry wanted to engage, but was stopped by the fire of a battery that it charged. The Prussian battalions rallied, the 2nd Battalion of the 11th Line and the 1st Pomeranian Landwehr, of the 14th Brigade, joined them and they all moved forward, followed by the 15th Regiment. This second attack made with resolution by fourteen battalions succeeded. The Young Guard was forced to evacuate the village.

The Prussians strongly pushed forward, two battalions of the Old Guard were sent to aid the Young Guard, the 1st Battalion of the

---

886 John Franklin personal communication.

2nd Chasseurs and the 1st Battalion of the 2nd Grenadiers, between them a force of about 1,100 men and commanded by General Comte Morand, colonel of chasseurs, and under his command, General Pelet, of the same arm. The emperor was concerned with the movements of Bülow; he entered the square of the 2nd Grenadiers, and gave orders for the attack: Do not fire a single shot, come on them with the bayonet. The battalion immediately dispersed its square, moved to the right and came opposite to a hedge that separated them from the Prussians.

The charge was beaten, and in an instant the hedge was crossed by 530 grenadiers. A Prussian battalion was unmasked. He had no time to execute a volley. It was pushed back by the bayonet. In a fight lasting no more than a few minutes the battalion was annihilated. After having destroyed them, the grenadiers rushed to the Prussian masses that already crowded the ravines, orchards and streets of Plancenoit. Again, in this place, a dreadful slaughter was made. The enemy sought to escape the furious blows of the grenadiers with difficulty, and were desperate to win back the village. Nothing could stop them. They had promptly done the task that was asked of them by the emperor himself.

These few grenadiers were insufficient to halt the irresistible tide of the Prussians. General Pelet continues that:[887]

From then on, I went myself with the 1st Battalion and doubled with them to Plancenoit. It was then perhaps about six o'clock, maybe seven. I cannot recall how long I remained here, but it seemed to be a long time. I called Lieutenant Gourahel[888] to me and, finding Lepage[889] in the first houses of the village, I told him to move to the last houses of the village and to occupy them strongly.

Entering the village, I met poor General Duhesme, who was being carried on his horse, either dead or close to death. The voltigeurs were running away. Chartran[890] told me that he could do nothing

---

887 d'Avout, pp. 41-2.

888 Recorded on 1 June as serving in 1st Company of 1st Battalion. SHDDT: Xab 69 *Chasseurs à Pied (formation de 1815)*.

889 Recorded on 1 June as serving in 5th Company of 2nd Battalion. SHDDT: Xab 69.

890 Commanding 1st Brigade, comprising the 1st Tirailleurs and 1st Voltigeurs.

more. Colonel Hurel[891] said he had plenty of men, but they were all moving to the rear. I promised them I would stop the enemy, and urged them to rally behind me. Indeed, I got as far as the centre of the village and once there, seeing Lieutenant Lepage's men approaching and the Prussians that pursued them, I ordered Captain Peschot[892] to advance with the 1st Company and attack the enemy with the bayonet; the enemy were coming down the road opposite the one we were on. His sergeant, Cranges,[893] who was very keen, gave the order to the 1st Platoon and marched with it. He executed my order, but hardly had the enemy turned his back than the men began to skirmish and he lost control of them.

The enemy sent in new forces; Peschot was not able to concentrate his platoon and in consequence he was forced to fall back.

I called up another company, it insisted on opening fire; I led it forward myself and the enemy fled. But, this platoon dispersed and with each charge made the same thing happen. The men of my last company shouted 'en avant!' started firing and also dispersed.

I gave orders for some of my men to occupy the church. Here, I found myself face-to-face with the Prussians, who fired at me from point-blank range, but missed. Then, seeing how much resistance we were putting up, they began to lob a great shower of shells into the village and attempted to turn it by the valley of the Lasne and through the nearby woods.

I sent an officer there; I think it was Captain Angnis.[894]

In the course of our attacks, we had taken many enemy men prisoners; but our soldiers slaughtered them in a state of mad frenzy. I rushed to them to stop them doing this, and even as I ran I saw one of them die in front of my eyes (but they butchered and hung our own men in cold blood). I was revolted, overcome with fury, I took several under my protection, particularly an officer who

---

891 Commanding the 3rd Voltigeurs.

892 Recorded on 1 June as commanding 1st Company of 1st Battalion. SHDDT: Xab 69.

893 No such name could be found, but is likely to be MAT No. 1522 Joseph Crampes, born in 1777 and admitted to the 1st Chasseurs on 26 October 1811 and promoted to sergeant on 11 April 1813. SHDDT: GR 20 YC 44.

894 Recorded on 1 June as commanding 4th Company of 1st Battalion. SHDDT: Xab 69.

prostrated himself at my feet, telling me of his French friends and those of his family.

I put him behind my horse and then handed him over to my *sapeurs*, saying they would answer to me for his safety. I sent Captain Heuillette[895] to the left, to occupy and defend the church; to do so he advanced beyond the place, and advanced towards the wood opposite where the enemy was; from the rear came some men of the Young Guard who charged into the village.

However, the combat, having gone on for a long time, and in consequence all of my men had dispersed as skirmishers. I could not rally a single platoon, the enemy did not enter the village, but he deployed on all sides and, in each interval between the gardens, I saw muskets aiming at me from forty paces. I do not know why I was not struck down twenty times.

I went to and fro on Isabelle [his horse]; I had taken off my riding coat and yet our men did not seem to recognise me as a general officer. Certainly, I still held the village; I came, I went, I had the charge beaten, the rally, then the drum roll; nothing brought my men back together, not even a single platoon. Finally, at the moment when we were fully committed and sorely pressed as well as short of men, a company of grenadiers[896] arrived, sent by an unknown hand, for which I was extremely grateful. I ordered them to halt while I rallied to me some chasseurs. I sent them in with the bayonet, and off they went like a wall, and bowled all the Prussians over. I remained there in the middle of this hail of shells, lit up by the fire that had started to burn in a number of houses in a terrible and continuous fusillade; the Prussians surrounded us with numerous skirmishers. I didn't care, we held like demons; I could not form up my men, but they were all hidden away and laid down a murderous fire on the enemy that contained him; they were stopped despite the numbers that should have overwhelmed us.

While I came and went continually between the entry and the exit [of the village], animating and holding in place all those in the middle of this skirmishing, I encountered Colomban,[897] who appeared to me a little pale and I noticed this with regret, for perhaps he

---

895 Recorded on 1 June as commanding 3rd Company of 1st Battalion. SHDDT: Xab 69.
896 From the 1st Battalion of the 2nd Regiment.
897 Recorded on 1 June as commanding 1st Battalion of the 2nd Chasseurs. SHDDT: Xab 69.

was thinking the same of me, although I certainly felt as calm and tranquil as I had only a few times in my life, even in the middle of these enemies that I believed bore me a particular grudge.

In the attack, Captain Louis Crete, of the 1st Battalion 2nd Grenadiers, was shot in the heart by a Prussian sergeant and then cut down with a sabre cut to his right shoulder.[898] He was the only officer of the regiment killed. de Mauduit comments about this episode:[899]

> We dominated and guarded the by-road that went from Plancenoit to La Maison du Roi, by which the Prussians appeared to be advancing to cut off the army's retreat. Each of our four companies received the order to detach twenty-five grenadiers as skirmishers on the extreme right of the village to observe and contain the enemy, who was always looking to outflank the right of Duhesme's division.
>
> Hardly had these hundred grenadiers moved a few yards from us, then they found themselves face-to-face with the Prussian skirmishers hidden in the edge of the wood and in the meadows, that were on our right.
>
> There, several grenadiers, who were furthest forward, fell, after a vigorous struggle and covered in wounds, into the hands of the Prussians, as well as Adjutant-Major Fare, who tried to protect and rescue them. This officer's horse was shot and fell into a ditch. A platoon of Prussians rushed upon him and fired at point-blank range. By a miracle, he was struck by only one ball, but was so seriously wounded that the Prussians thought he was dead and did not take him. Unbelievably, he remained for six days on the battlefield without help, not being able to drag himself to the village, or even to the side of a road where the first person to pass would undoubtedly have helped him.
>
> Captain Crete was killed there, shot point-blank by a Prussian sergeant whose shoulder he had cut through with a sabre blow and who nevertheless still had the courage to aim at his heart. His musket ball struck the Cross [of the Legion of Honour] of this officer and knocked him down at the feet of Sergeant-Major Stonop.[900]

---

898 AN: LH 628/64.

899 de Mauduit, Vol. 2, pp. 445-6.

900 This man cannot be identified in the relevant muster lists for the four regiments of grenadiers à pied.

At the same instant, the Prussian sergeant was cut down by one of Captain Crete's grenadiers.

In this incredible struggle of one against seven, several Prussians asked for mercy and received it. One of them threw himself at the feet of my friend, Stonop, and begged for his life saying that his father was serving as a sergeant in the 3rd Hussars.

It is clear from de Mauduit's account that some Prussian troops were sent around the flanks of Plancenoit and these were engaged by the skirmishers sent out from his battalion.

To the south of Plancenoit stood Chantelet Wood; in an attempt to encircle the village, the light infantry battalion of the Prussian 25th Regiment was sent through it to cut it off. These troops were spotted by Chef-de-Battalion Duuring. Captain Heuillette, of the 2nd Chasseurs, remembers:[901]

> The regiment, commanded by General Pelet, and to which I belonged, was ordered to the village of Plancenoit, which the Prussians had just taken possession; the village was taken with the points of our bayonets. Comte Lobau, with the 6th Corps and the Young Guard, were there with us.

> We drove back the 30,000 men a half-mile from the village. The battle was in our favour again, but an hour later Blücher arrived with 30,000 men to reinforce the corps of Bülow, which brought the figure to 60,000. Our soldiers exhausted by a long combat then had to retreat in face of this number; we were cut off from the left flank.

The two battalions of the Old Guard and the battered rump of the Young Guard and Lobau's corps had recaptured Plancenoit. However, the counter-attack came at a cost: the French had taken major losses in the attack and, moreover, without any reserves to bolster the depleted French troops, the victory was a hollow one, as it could neither be exploited nor maintained. As the Prussians fled from Plancenoit, they were pursued by the cavalry of Domon and Subervie. Prussian sources tell us that Subervie's two lancer regiments charged the flanks of the fleeing Prussians, inflicting more casualties. Buoyed by this success, the French advanced beyond the confines of the village, and in doing so came under a heavy artillery barrage from the Prussian artillery, which

---

901 Captain Heuillette, of the 2nd Chasseurs. *Journal de Toulouse*, 24 October 1845, p. 2.

forced the French to withdraw back to the confines of the village. To cover the retreat, Subervie's lancers went in to action and forced the Prussian artillery to withdraw, and to abandon several batteries.[902] Plancenoit was once again in French hands after a tremendous counter-attack by the French Old Guard and whatever troops remained from 6th Corps, 1st Corps and the Young Guard. It was at about this time that the Prussian 2nd Corps, commanded by General Pirch, had arrived on the battlefield. As the situation deteriorated, de Mauduit recalls the following episode:[903]

> Lt-Col Golzio, commander of the 1st Battalion of the 2nd Grenadier Regiment, seeing no support arrive, and foreseeing only too clearly the inevitable disastrous outcome of the unequal struggle of his grenadiers, galloped up to inform General Christiani, major of those grenadiers, and met him alone in the middle of our square, for his regiment's 2nd Battalion had gone with the emperor beyond La Belle Alliance. The entreaties of Lt-Col Golzio were regrettably wasted; our battalion could not abandon the important post that it occupied, covering the exit from Plancenoit. Colonel Golzio returned to his grenadiers broken-hearted at not being able to bring these brave men even a hundred reinforcements.

In order to expel General Pelet from the bastion that was the churchyard, Prussian reinforcements were brought in. Like Masséna in the granary at Essling, General Pelet tenaciously clung on to the bastion. The churchyard was almost impossible to attack: from the east it was defended by a steep slope, and if the Prussians attempted to outflank the churchyard by advancing along the low, open space on its south they would become exposed to musket fire from its walls, as well as from the from the houses opposite which had also been occupied by the French.[904]

The Prussian high command decided to pound the French into submission. To do so, they deployed the No. 10 Foot Battery and No. 6 Horse Artillery Battery to open fire as close as possible to the churchyard. Under the cover of the barrage, the Prussians sent forward the fusilier battalion of the 25th Regiment and the 2nd Battalion of the 2nd Infantry Regiment from the 5th Brigade to capture the churchyard. At the same time, two Westphalian Landwehr battalions were ordered

---

902 John Franklin personal communication.
903 de Mauduit, Vol. 2, pp. 445-6.
904 Wagner, p. 94.

to attack the right side of the village. In support was the 1st Battalion 2nd Regiment. Every inch of ground, house, garden wall and hedge was bitterly contested. Withdrawn to comparative safety in the Paris Wood, the 11th Line and Pomeranian Landwehr Regiments, with the 1st Silesian Landwehr, were able to be rallied, and in consequence were sent back to the attack.[905]

The Prussians boldly attacked the churchyard and sent detachments to outflank the village. With the village now almost totally surrounded, the churchyard position was no longer tenable and the French had no option but to retreat. Wellington was now able to move troops from his left flank to protect his battered centre thanks to the arrival of Ziethen and Pirch. These troops were virtually unopposed by the French, as we shall see, and were able to sweep down onto the exposed and vulnerable French right wing and centre. The French were now surrounded.

Reille takes the offensive once more

The time was fast approaching 19.30. Napoléon was organising one last great effort to break through on their left flank. Despite his most recent offensive having been broken, Reille had been able to rally his divisions. On the right, d'Erlon hastily assembled what forces he could. The new attack would be supported by the Old Guard. Eight battalions of the Old Guard were ordered to attack, supported by whatever men Reille could muster from 2nd Corps, as well as Pégot's brigade from 1st Corps.

The fighting in the environs of Hougoumont lasted all day, with elements of the 2nd Corps being ordered to advance in support of the final attack of the Imperial Guard. It was not until around 18.00, according to General Trefcon, that the divisions of Foy and Bachelu were fully committed to the attack in the wake of the cavalry. The 2nd Corps was ordered forward once more.

At the front of Bachelu's column came the 2nd Regiment of Light Infantry. The carabinier company sporting tall bearskins made a number of Allied eyewitnesses think that this was the Imperial Guard.[906] The other troops on the French left wearing bearskins were the *sapeurs* of the 1st Regiment of Line Infantry.[907] But, it is unlikely that the presence of six men wearing bearskins could be mistaken for the Old Guard,

---

905 Wagner, p. 94.
906 SHDDT: Xb 567.
907 SHDDT: Xb 343 *1e de Ligne 1808-1815*. Dossier 1814.

whereas over 100 men at the front of the 2nd Regiment of Light Infantry could. The 2nd Regiment of Light Infantry was not unique in having its elite company in bearskins. Some of the grenadiers of the 11th Regiment of Line Infantry wore bearskins at Waterloo,[908] as did the grenadier company of 1st Battalion 10th Regiment of Line Infantry. Contrary to the Bardin regulations, they retained bearskins in 1813 and 1814.[909]

It was these bearskin-wearing troops of what in reality was the 2nd Regiment of Light Infantry that Major Friedrich Christian von Hammerstein, commanding the Salzfitter Landwehr Battalion, writes about on 24 June 1815:[910]

> Now finally it was necessary to conquer the wood and chateau, which throughout the day had been defended by a battalion of English guards, the 2nd Line Battalion and two battalions of Brunswickers, who had fought in vain. From these different battalions only small detachments remained in the wood; while on the enemy's side there were, the sharpshooters belonging to many different corps, especially those of the Imperial Guard, who seemed to threaten our flank, they being positioned on the left of the wood in strong close columns. This honourable duty was given to my battalion at around seven o'clock. The Osnabruck Battalion and the 95th English Regiment stood opposite the columns so that we covered each other. Upon our right were compact columns of the enemy's infantry and cavalry.

Lieutenant Augustus Winkler, of the same battalion, notes:[911]

> Our divisional general, Sir Henry Clinton, took us to the ridge, the highest I could see, to about two hundred paces from the enemy line, which consisted of grenadiers of the Imperial Guard.

Winkler places this event during the French cavalry charges, and makes numerous references to attacking cuirassiers close to the woods of Hougoumont, into which passed Scottish Highlanders and English sharpshooters. It is possible that he is seeing here the grenadiers à cheval of the Imperial Guard, or has confused line grenadiers with the Old Guard. Indeed, some Allied eyewitnesses like Friederich von Jeckeln, of the 28th Orange-Nassau Regiment, testifies to grenadiers of the Old

---

908 SHDDT: Xb 508 *92e de Ligne*. Dossier 1814.
909 SHDDT: Xb 364 *10e de Ligne 1791–1815*. Dossier 1814.
910 Franklin, Vol. 1, p. 50.
911 John Franklin personal communication.

Guard being at Quatre-Bras, which is clearly nonsense, so we cannot be sure what Winkler actually saw as opposed to what he thought he saw. He further notes his battalion captured a French general and two colours.

Ludwig van Dreves, with the Osnabruck Landwehr Battalion, notes that the battalion moved forward to the front of the Allied line, with its right flank resting on Hougoumont and were to the right of General Adams's brigade (the 52nd, 71st and 95th Rifles). Here, he notes they were, in a report of January 1825:[912]

> Face-to-face with our position stood very strong enemy columns; four of the battalions opposed to us were the French Imperial Guard, which attacked us in columns, and their sharpshooters approached within a very short distance.

This testimony is confused. In an earlier paragraph, he notes that the Imperial Guard attacked before his battalion had occupied its final position, and that he saw on his left English (Allied?) infantry advancing, but he could not see the direction in which it was advancing. This, it seems, was the advance of General Chasse, along with Nassau and Hanoverian troops, as will be discussed later. The quoted paragraph then comes after this passage about the English infantry driving back the Imperial Guard. Tellingly, Colonel Halket makes no mention of the troops his brigade attacked as being Imperial Guard, so we cannot be sure that these men were from the Imperial Guard.[913] Furthermore, according to William Richers, of the same battalion, albeit writing in 1854, the Osnabruck Battalion advanced as part of the general Allied advance and was not attacked by the Imperial Guard, contrary to Dreves and Hammerstein. He further notes that the battalion:[914]

> Once we crossed the hollow way and ascended the height opposite, we saw an enemy column some 300 to 400 paces from us. It was either a regiment or battalion of the Vielle Garde.

The Osnabrück Battalion only encountered the Imperial Guard during the latter's rearguard stand at La Belle Alliance, as opposed to them being attacked by the Imperial Guard. I do not doubt that the battalion did come into contact with the last squares of the Imperial Guard at

---

912 Franklin, Vol. 1, p. 52.
913 ibid, p. 48.
914 ibid, p. 52.

Waterloo, and on the balance of evidence, it seems more likely that they did so at the very end of the day. This scenario is as exactly noted by Carl Jacobi.[915]

These light infantry carabiniers wearing their towering bearskins were spotted by another officer, this time British:[916]

> The advance of the column of La Jeune Garde [in fact part of the 6th Corps] to cover the flight of the Moyenne Garde; the head of this column arrives on the face of the rise opening on their left, the space between the hedge of the garden of Hougoumont and the line of our original position, which space by this time is occupied by Maj.-Gen. Adams's brigade; then comes the charge of both brigades, taking an oblique direction to the left, across the plain towards the *chaussée* leading to Namur, leaving Hougoumont on our right, and increasing our distance from the line of its wood at every step.

To identify the body of troops as Young Guard and Old Guard, there must have been a mix of bearskins and shakos worn by the attacking French troops. As we said before, the leading company of the 2nd Regiment of Light Infantry wearing bearskins, supported by troops in shakos, coupled with the amount of powder smoke, could easily be seen as being the Imperial Guard supported by the Young Guard. Therefore, anything with a bearskin becomes 'Imperial Guard' or 'Imperial Old Guard', and by extension 'Imperial Old Guard' becomes 'grenadiers', irrespective if they have a bearskin plate or not (a minutiae of detail probably unknown to the observer and not apparent in battle). Any infantry grenadier of the line also seems to become Old Guard. The same is true of lancers. In Britain, they are invariably described as 'Polish', because the belief is that all lancers are Polish; a mistake that was even made in the Second Empire when one British observer described the Regiment des Lanciers de la Garde Impériale as the 'Polish lancers of the Guard', when they were not. Cuirassiers are always described as being Imperial Guard when they are not—this clouds and confuses descriptions of the action of the cavalry, as often the cavalry is referred to as cavalry of the Imperial Guard. Thus, it seems certain that the attacking force that ran against Halket and Adams was not the Imperial Guard, as argued by George Gawler, William Leeke and Nigel Sale in more recent years. Gawler relies on the identification of the troops which

---

915 ibid, p. 21.
916 'Waterloo' in The *United Service Magazine*, No. 62, January 1834, p. 113.

attacked the 52nd Regiment of Foot as being from the Imperial Guard, based solely on the French bulletin describing the Battle of Waterloo which fails to state that the troops of Reille in 2nd Corps advanced in support of the Guard, as opposed to personal recollections.[917] Indeed, Gawler's statement that the 52nd and 71st Regiments of Foot, with no support whatsoever from other regiments of the Allied army, solely defeated the Imperial Guard was treated with derision by other officers from Waterloo.[918] In later years, Gawler argued that the Imperial Guard was defeated, because they attacked the British and the British counter-attacked in line.[919] Gawler was refuted by Sir Hussey Vivian and an officer cited as 'Omega' in the *Dublin University Magazine*.[920]

Clearly, this eyewitness to the events states that the 52nd Regiment of Foot and Adams's brigade was attacked by French troops which were not the Old Guard. This officer's recollections then sparked a war of words in the British press, with officers from the regiment, primarily George Gawler, saying that it was their regiment which destroyed the Guard and, more importantly, the grenadiers.[921] However, the French bulletin notes that several regiments were near at hand to the attacking Guard infantry, a reference to the troops of 1st and 2nd Corps.

French writers clearly indicate that 2nd Corps attacked the Allied positions held by Halket and Adams. Allied writers mention this attack, but ascribe it to the Imperial Guard. As we have seen, these writers are confused in what they saw and when the attack happened. Therefore, we can be certain that such an attack took place, as it is mentioned in French, British and Hanoverian testimonies. It also seems certain that the attacking force was not the Imperial Guard, but the 2nd Regiment of Light Infantry. Through gun smoke, with the leading company wearing bearskins, it was an easy mistake to make. Perhaps this is why the British officer has a mixed force of Middle and Young Guard, the inference being a mix of bearskins and shakos, which to his mind could only be the Imperial Guard. In reality, many regiments of line had grenadiers in bearskins at Waterloo.

Foy's division had been involved in the attack on Hougoumont earlier in the day, and so was already reduced in terms of manpower and stamina. Bachelu's command had been in action an hour earlier.

---

917 The *United Service Magazine*, No. 63, February 1834, pp. 254-5.
918 The *United Service Magazine*, No. 58, October 1833, pp. 255-6.
919 The *Pall Mall Gazette*, 27 December 1872.
920 The *Dublin University Magazine*, Vol. 2, November 1833, p. 594.
921 The *United Service Magazine*, No. 63, February 1834, pp. 254-5.

Chapter 19

d'Erlon's Offensive

In support of Reille and the Old Guard, d'Erlon ordered whatever men he had at the centre to attack. This attack is not mentioned by French eyewitnesses, but it clearly took place, as a mass of Allied sources all mention it. Willem van Bijlandt, a former major-general commanding the 1st Brigade of the 2nd Netherlands Division, notes that 1st Corps was headed by the Young Guard and marched in close columns. This reinforces the point that observers did not know what they were looking at, and also to increase the prestige of their regiment in the defeat of the French and the Imperial Guard.

An officer in the Allied 5th Division makes a similar comment about an infantry assault prior to that of the Imperial Guard, which he observed from his position on the Allied left:[922]

> The French darted forwards out of the ravine and fired one-by-one, others behind them advanced some steps and fired also; his neighbour again preceded him, and so on till they came up to our advance (who had in like manner kept up a fire), and at last were almost muzzle-to-muzzle; neither party would recede: the contest was terrible, the British recoil a few paces! All is lost we thought, though we said nothing; highly excited and with beating hearts, as if we were watching a prize-fight—again the British rally! They push the French back step-by-step by dint of musquetry, and almost muzzle-to-muzzle, over the ravine or small breastwork in disorder.

---

922 Anon, 'Operations of the Fifth, or Thomas Picton's, Division in the Campaign of Waterloo' in *United Services Magazine*, Part 2, June 1841, p. 180.

Loud huzzahs, shaking the very welkin, proclaimed that this ground at last was our own; we shook hands with each other, we were mad with joy.

Captain Arendt Geradus von Bronkhorst, of the 7th Dutch Militia, narrates that:[923]

The French still manoeuvred, as they were the party who attacked. Following the first attack, we were not attacked for some hours, but yet we lost a great many men from the French artillery fire and that from the tirailleurs who advanced in great numbers.

An Allied eyewitness to the advance of 1st Corps in support of the Imperial Guard was Major F. Browne, of the 40th Regiment of Foot, who writes in 1835:[924]

At the moment when the French Imperial Guard advanced to attack the British position, the 40th Regiment, which had previously, and mostly throughout the day, been in square against cavalry, were formed in line, and thus quickly advanced to the brow of the hill, where there was a low and somewhat broken down hedge, short of which we halted and over which we fired. There were a few large trees here and there along the hedge, particularly on our side of it, the branches of which were much cut and lopped by cannon shot; but of what description the trees where I cannot now recollect.

A heavy column of French infantry was advancing, at the moment I observed them they were rather in front of the farmhouse of La Haye Sainte, by, I believe, the left of it as we faced the house; they having then crossed the road. The divisions of the column appeared to me to be at about quarter-distances.

The 40th was formed rather facing the house, the latter being a little to the right of the regiment, but more in front of us. There were several other similar columns advancing at the same time upon different points of our position, both to the right and left of the house; and much cavalry were congregating or re-forming in, or more properly speaking, that part of the enemy's position which artists would term the middle distance. In the extreme distance was the observatory, the key of the French position.

923 John Franklin personal communication, 2 July 2012.
924 Siborne, *Waterloo Letters*, No. 176.

Captain S. Stretton, also of the 40th Regiment of Foot, notes:[925]

> The formation of the 40th at the period when the French Imperial Guard advanced to attack the right of the British force was in line, having previously repulsed the enemy's cavalry in square.
>
> When the British line moved forward, the 40th drove the tirailleurs from the rising ground at its front and occupied it; at the same time the 27th with grenadiers of the 40th took possession of the farm of La Haye Sainte in which they made prisoners of a general officer and a part of the enemy.

This was likely to be the time that elements of the 8th Regiment of Line Infantry, as well as the 13th Regiment of Light Infantry and 17th Regiment of Line Infantry, were pushed back from La Haye Sainte. Major-General Sir John Lambert writes:[926]

> The great effort of the enemy in his last attack was on the right of the road leading from Brussels to Genappe. They advanced upon the left in line, but never came up to the crest of the position, as they had done in the two previous attacks. When they commenced retiring on the right an order arrived for the whole line to advance.

Lieutenant Leslie, of the 79th Regiment of Foot, narrates that:[927]

> This attack was late in the day and we had not long retained our position when at the period to which you allude to, the enemy in front of us seemed moving forward a fresh column of attack for a simultaneous attack to that on the right of our line.

John Lewis, of the 95th Rifles, in a letter to his parents dated 8 July 1815 narrates that this regiment was attacked by the Imperial Guard. It is not clear if he means the Guard cavalry, infantry or the line cuirassiers:[928]

> Seeing we had lost so many men and all our commanding officers, my heart began to fail, and Boney's Guards made another charge on as; but we made them retreat as before, and, while we was [sic] in square the second time, the Duke of Wellington and his staff came

---

925 Siborne, *Waterloo Letters*, No. 177.
926 Siborne, *Waterloo Letters*, No. 170.
927 Siborne, *Waterloo Letters*, No. 175.
928 Author's collection.

up to us in all the fire, and saw we had lost all our commanding officers; he, himself, gave the word of command; the words he said to our regiment were this '95th, unfix your swords, left face and extend yourselves once more, we shall soon have them over the other hill' and then he rode away on our right, and how he escaped being shot God only knows, for all that time the shot was flying like hailstones.

This was about four o'clock on 18 June, when Lord Wellington rode away from our regiment; and then we advanced like Britons, but we could not go five steps without walking over dead and wounded; and Boney's horses of the Imperial Guards, and the men that was [sic] not killed, was running loose about in all directions.

Brevet-Major Leach, of the 1st Battalion 95th Rifles, concurs with this statement that at the end of the day they were attacked again by the French:[929]

It consisted of one uninterrupted fire of musketry, the distance between the hostile lines I imagine to have been rather more than one hundred yards, between Kempt's and some of Lambert's regiments posted along the thorn hedge and the French infantry lining the knoll and the crest of the hill near it. Several times the French officers made desperate attempts to induce their men to charge Kempt's line, and I saw more than one party of the French in our front spring up from their kneeling position and advance some yards towards the thorn hedge, headed by their officers with vehement gestures, but our fire was so very hot and deadly that they almost instantly ran back behind the crest of the hill always leaving a great many killed or disabled behind themselves.

During this musketry contest, which I firmly believe was the closest and most protracted ever witnessed, some apprehension was entertained that the French would endeavour to advance along the *chaussée* and attack the rear of the troops lining the thorn hedge, and on a report of the kind being made to be by one of our officers, coupled with a suggestion that a part of the 95th Riflemen should be concentrated on the extreme right so as to fire into the road, my reply was the 27th Regiment is in square in our rear, having one of its faces looking directly into the road, and that regiment must protect our rear, for the French are gathering so fast and so thick in our front that we cannot spare a single man to detach to the right.

---

929 Siborne, *Waterloo Letters*, No. 170.

Clearly, it seems the 8th and 29th Regiments of Line Infantry, along with Donzelot's men were far from ineffective in their harassment of the Allied left. Therefore, we must envision the attack of the Imperial Guard as part of a general French advance. Both flanks of the double line of squares formed by battalion of the Imperial Guard were supported on each flank by attacking squares of line infantry from 1st and 2nd Corps. A French eyewitness writing in 1815 notes:[930]

> He formed, for this purpose, a fourth column, almost entirely composed of the Guards, and directed it at the *pas de charge* on Mont-Saint-Jean, after having dispatched instructions to every point that the movement, on which he thought victory to depend, might be seconded. The veterans marched up the hill with the intrepidity which might be expected of them.

General Michel leads the chasseurs to death and glory

Moving up with Reille and Pégot was the Old Guard. The spearhead of the attack was formed by the four battalions of the 3rd and 4th Chasseurs, led by General Michel. Marshal Ney led forward both battalions of the 4th Grenadiers and the 1st Battalion 3rd Grenadiers. An unknown French general, presumably of either 2nd Corps or a cavalry division, notes as follows about the attack:[931]

> Four battalions of the Guard who had not yet fought, advanced, dressing to the left of La Haye Sainte, commanded by the Prince of the Moskowa and by Generals Friant, Michel and Poret de Morvan. Eight other battalions arrived fifteen minutes later, and were also placed in line of battle. Meanwhile, General Reille, who had received orders to assemble his whole corps on their extreme left, and formed it into columns of attack, executed his orders, passed Hougoumont, and crossed the ravine. These are the reinforcements which went to join the Middle Guard, which was struggling against the masses deployed against it. The new columns were greeted by a terrible fire of musketry and grape. Marshal Ney was one of the first to fall from his horse, and several other generals were hit. General Michel, commander of the chasseurs, fell lifeless and a large number of the wounded spread out across the plain.

---

930 Anon, *Tales of War*, William Mark Clarke, London, 1836, pp. 260-1.
931 Marguerite, *Fastes militaires de la France*, Paris, 1836, pp. 260-2.

The wounding of General Michel caused not only a command and control vacuum with the chasseurs, but that his wounding caused a great deal of hesitation and perhaps panic among the men he had commanded. The panic is perhaps borne out in the casualty returns. His sudden death at the head of the attack spread panic through his troops, which it seems was only abated by the actions of General Poret de Morvan, as we shall see.[932]

Henry Frank, domestic servant of General Michel, in a letter dated 18 March 1845 to General Michel's son, notes:[933]

> Your father had deployed the battalion in square, composed of the 3rd Regiment of Chasseurs à Pied; we crossed the highway to take the left side of the road. We had to cross a ravine which was occupied by our cuirassiers. Upon reaching the plateau we were received with a discharge of shrapnel and musket fire from regiments there. Before us the fire stopped for a moment, during which time I heard your father exchange a few words with the enemy, but I could not really hear the response, because the smoke prevented me from seeing him and the sound of cannons and guns firing on the sides of our square prevented me from hearing or witnessing the summons.
>
> As soon as they stopped talking, General Michel, your father, who did not want to let the enemy see that he had no hope of success, turned to his chasseurs, raising his sword and he said 'now my friends, we must conquer or die!' I believe this was a supplement to the responses he made a moment before the summation of the enemy…Soon after, a rain of bullets, grapeshot and cannonballs began.
>
> General Michel, your father, took command of the right wing, and no sooner had he arrived then he received a mortal wound, and I quickly realised he could not remain mounted on his horse. I dismounted my horse, and went to the general to help him dismount, I cast away his feet from the stirrups.
>
> His aides, C and B, stood tranquilly by on their horses. When he was laid on the ground I un-buttoned his overcoat, during which time I saw that he had been shot in his left shoulder. I stood up, and I saw the horse of the general running away, I said therefore to the

---

932 Jean Baptiste Pierre Jullien de Courcelles, *Dictionnaire historique et biographique des généraux Francais* (Vol. 8), Paris, 1823, pp. 408-9.
933 *Le Monde Illustré*, 12 July 1862, pp. 18-19.

aides to stop the general's horse, and they ran across the field of action, and did not remain on the field of carnage.

I desperately hoped that they would come back. I went to unbutton his coat and removed his cravat, but when I got to the third button, a musket ball struck my left elbow, which fractured my arm and it also broke the Cross worn by the general. I picked myself up, and I lay there next to him, in the fervent hope that the aides C and B would return. I stayed, I think, a good twenty minutes in this attitude, but no one came.

This could have been between six and seven o'clock, because amidst this carnage and misfortune, there is no time to look at the watch as in a salon. Finally, as the day advanced, in hope not to be made a prisoner, I therefore made a last effort. I picked up the general's portfolio and placed it against the general, hoping the enemy would recognise him and respect his rank, I then had to try and retire in haste, I had been losing blood for about four hours: but while I was doing all these preparations, the enemy had gained ground, and in spite of my preparations I was taken prisoner.

Captain Guillaume Paul Berthelet des Verges, captain aide-de-camp to General Michel, narrates a rather different story:[934]

General Michel placed, as usual, a few steps behind the column, between his two aides, Chevreau and I, ascended the plateau without firing. We arrived on the plateau and at half a gunshot away from the English, who were still waiting for us, we were greeted by a terrible discharge they sent us. General Michel fell from his horse, crying, 'ah my God, I have a broken arm!' I rushed over to him and unbuttoned his coat to discover his injury. My general was dead for a bullet at the top of the left breast had pierced his body. The same discharge injured my comrades, Chevreau and Henry Franck, servant of the general.

The 3rd Chasseurs

The chasseurs had come against Halket's command, as well the 1st Foot Guards, and the men from 2nd Corps were enfiladed by fire from Adams's command. The chasseurs suffered huge losses as they advanced. Battalion-Commander Claud Cardinal, at the head of 1st

---

934 *Le Globe Illustré*, 7 April 1862.

Battalion 3rd Chasseurs, was killed in the attack. At the head of 2nd Battalion, Jean Baptiste Angelet fell wounded and would die on 5 July 1815. Captain-Adjutant-Major Noel suffered a gunshot wound to the right arm.[935] Captain Nicolas Blondon, who had served in the Imperial Guard since 1800, was wounded to the left leg by howitzer shell fragments, losing the use of the leg.[936] Captain Antoine Bonnel took a gunshot wound to the left arm and one to the right side of his abdomen. He was left for dead on the field of battle and made prisoner of war, returning to France on 3 May 1816.[937] Captain Antoine Felix, who had served in the Imperial Guard since 8 July 1800, suffered a gunshot wound to the head and two strong contusions.[938] Also wounded was Captain Jean Marie Lardinois, who suffered a gunshot to the left side of his chest.[939] At the head of the 4th Company of 2nd Battalion was Pierre Frederic Minal, who had an arm reportedly blown off by a canister shot.[940] Mortally wounded in 1st Battalion was Captain Avonde, and in 2nd Battalion were Captain Cabot, at the head of 1st Company, and Captain Sigismund Decouz, at the head of 2nd Company.[941]

Among the regiment's first-lieutenants and second-lieutenants, Angelet, Barbara, Dumont, Mathieu and Roussel were killed.[942] Wounded officers included Louis Marie Desire Landais, who suffered a gunshot to the left shoulder.[943] Charles Lorotte was wounded to the right leg,[944] Laurent Marie Marteville took a musket ball to the left thigh,[945] François Michaudon took a gunshot to the foot and suffered a serious bruise to the chest,[946] Joseph Marie Seguin also took a gunshot to the right leg[947] and Laurent Thirion suffered a musket ball pass through his

---

935 AN: LH 2006/51.
936 AN: LH 261/6.
937 AN: LH 286/11.
938 AN: LH 953/8.
939 AN: LH 1482/43.
940 AN: LH 1882/63.
941 Jean Marc Boisnard personal communication.
942 ibid.
943 AN: LH 1465/23.
944 AN: LH 1660/50.
945 AN: LH 1755/18.
946 AN: LH 1861/52.
947 AN: LH 2493/30.

left shoulder.[948] Pierre Antoine Andre was hit by a cannonball to the left thigh[949] and Pierre Deschamps took a musket ball to the left thigh and was left for dead, and was subsequently taken prisoner.[950]

Out of the eight captains and sixteen lieutenants of the regiment, only five officers were not wounded: Lieutenants Pierre François Beauvais, Antoine Joseph Plumatte Jean Ponsot, Jean Henri Hippolyte Tancoigne and Jean Joseph Vasset. With the battalion-commanders dead or wounded, Colonel-General-of-Brigade Pierre Malet mortally wounded with a gunshot to the left shoulder and with no company-commanders left standing, command and control devolved onto the sub-officers; men like Sergeant-Major Joseph Petit, who had joined the Imperial Guard on 9 February 1813. But, like the officers, he too was wounded by a canister shot to the left hip.[951] Little wonder, therefore, that the regiment, when attacked by the men of David Chasse and the Allied light cavalry, totally collapsed. The tables below show the known casualty returns:[952]

3rd Chasseurs à Pied					
	Wounded	Wounded & Prisoner	Prisoner of War	Killed	Missing
1st Battalion	23	0	0	0	380
2nd Battalion	21	0	0	0	401
Total	44	0	0	0	781

The missing men must include dead and wounded; in order for the regimental muster list to record such casualties, the event had to be verified by surviving soldiers. Therefore, we only have a very small percentage of men who remained in the ranks who could give a testimony of the fate of what happened to their comrades. This means we are aware of the fate of just forty-four men from the regiment. The 3rd Chasseurs lost a staggering 825 other ranks on 18 June, or 80 per cent of effective strength; it effectively ceased to exist. In total, the regiment lost one officer killed, eight mortally wounded and eighteen wounded;

---

948 AN: LH 2594/60.

949 AN: LH 35/60.

950 AN: LH 745/4.

951 AN: LH 2124/43.

952 Compiled from SHDDT: GR 20 YC 44. See also: SHDDT: GR 20 YC 45; SHDDT: GR 20 YC 46.

making a total loss of twenty-seven of the thirty-four officers present that day, or 79 per cent of all officers being out of action.

The 4th Chasseurs

In the 4th Chasseurs, we can only be certain of the fate of five men: one killed, four wounded. The regiment's paperwork lists just 158 men, of which the vast majority are listed as presumed prisoner (i.e. missing in action). Therefore, we cannot know the true fate of the 3rd and 4th Chasseurs beyond speculating that the two regiments were virtually destroyed. The regiment had 236 men on 23 June, therefore, we can suggest that the 3rd Chasseurs were the worst affected regiment at Waterloo, but, again, this is purely assumption based on the number of men remaining in ranks.

The 4th Chasseurs also suffered heavily under Allied firepower. During the attack, in the 1st Battalion: 1st Company lost Captain Decard with a canister shot to the left leg and First-Lieutenant Bues wounded; 2nd Company lost First-Lieutenant Denorroy and Second-Lieutenant Mazurier wounded; 3rd Company lost Captain Isselin and Second-Lieutenant Pavard di Pavare wounded; and 4th Company lost Captain Saisset and First-Lieutenant Mantigny wounded, leaving just Captain Goutenoive, First-Lieutenant Rousel and Second-Lieutenants Dunand and Marthier to command the battalion. In the 2nd Battalion: Battalion-Commander Agnes was killed; in 1st Company Captain Messagny was killed; 2nd Company lost no officers killed or wounded; 3rd Company lost First-Lieutenant Marteville wounded with a gunshot to the left thigh; and 4th Company lost First-Lieutenant Lambert and Second-Lieutenant Lauvergeon wounded with a gunshot to the left side of the body. This left Captains Arnoud, Ducros, and Renaud, as well as First-Lieutenants Mondrux and Joux and Second-Lieutenants Bony, Ponsot and Lepetre in command. It seems that 2nd Battalion suffered far fewer losses of officers than the 1st Battalion.[953]

In terms of other ranks lost, on 10 June the regiment mustered 1,048 other ranks. However, the paper archive for the regiment lists only 158 men, so we do not have the total numbers of dead, wounded, missing, deserted and prisoners of war.[954]

---

953 SHDDT: 15C20.
954 SHDDT: Xab 68 *Grenadiers à Pied (formation de 1815)*.

In total, four officers were mortally wounded and eleven wounded from the twenty-nine present on 10 June; losses of 52 per cent, leaving fourteen officers with the regiment on 20 June.

By 23 June, the regiment had just eight officers left, with six falling out from the ranks during the retreat. Between 10 and 23 June, 805 other ranks had been lost, and between 23 June and 30 June, a further 213 other ranks had disappeared. The regiment was disbanded on 1 July, when eight officers and thirty-two men were taken into the 3rd Chasseurs The tables below show the known casualty returns:[955]

4th Chasseurs à Pied					
	Wounded	Wounded & Prisoner	Prisoner of War	Killed	Missing
1st Battalion	1	0	80	1	0
2nd Battalion	3	0	43	0	0
Total	4	0	123	1	0

Of the 158 men, we have the names of thirty-three men who survived Waterloo. Thus, 79 per cent of the regiment's effective strength was lost based on these figures. Comparing the parade returns of 10 June and 23 June, we see that 77 per cent of effective strength was lost, with just 236 men out of the 1,070 in ranks on 10 June still being with the regiment. The men listed as prisoner must include dead and wounded men. It is clear, however, that the regiment did form two battalions at Waterloo, contrary to the suppositions of contemporary writers.

Comment

On 1 July, the remains of the 3rd and 4th Chasseurs were consolidated to form a new 3rd Regiment. It mustered, on 1 October 1815, six sergeant-majors, twenty-three sergeants, eight fourriers, thirty-four corporals, 148 privates and three drummers. In hospital that day were thirty-eight chasseurs and one drummer. In addition, nineteen chasseurs were listed as prisoners of war. Recorded missing were five sergeants, twelve corporals, 403 chasseurs and seven drummers; some 427 men missing, nineteen prisoners and thirty-nine wounded. This accounted for just 707 men from the 2,069 that had been under arms in both regiments

---

955 Compiled from SHDDT: GR 20 YC 44. See also: SHDDT: GR 20 YC 45; SHDDT: GR 20 YC 46.

on 1 June 1815; a loss of 1,362 men. With so few men listed as prisoner and wounded, and with 427 missing, the conclusion is the bulk of the men were killed or went missing (i.e. deserted) at Waterloo. The regiments must have come under intense artillery and musket fire, and must have left a pile of dead on the summit of the plateau, where the Lion Mound stands. The uncomfortable truth is that over 1,000 men of the two regiments were possibly killed. The Allied right wing must have been strewn in front of it, literally covering the ground with dead and wounded men and horses. There is no way a rapid Allied advance could be made across the battlefield with so many horse carcasses and dead and wounded men. When we consider the fate of the 3rd and 4th Chasseurs, the Guard had indeed not surrendered. But, as we shall see, the remainder of the Guard chose to flee or be taken prisoner rather than be killed.

Ney attacks with the grenadiers of the Old Guard

The most famous episode of the battle now took place. Immortalised in the Dino de Laurentis film and countless illustrations, the grenadiers of the Old Guard, with their drums beating the charge, Marshal Ney at their head flanked by General Friant, advanced up the slope to Wellington's line. With General Michel mortally wounded, the attack was starting to falter. The grenadiers, it was hoped, would soon turn the tide of the battle.

The leading element of the attack was the 1st Battalion of the 3rd Grenadiers. It was commanded by General Poret de Morvan. To the left and slightly behind came the conjoined battalions of the 4th Grenadiers. In the audacious attack, General Poret de Morvan:[956]

> Ascended the plateau, marching by La Haye Sainte at the head of the 3rd and 4th Regiments of Grenadiers of the Old Guard. Already in the first line of the Imperial Guard, the brave Generals Friant and Michel had been wounded, and the latter pierced by three shots, and Colonel Mallet was killed. Confusion began to set in among the ranks, when the appearance of the column, led by Poret de Morvan, who ascended the plateau to the *pas de charge* under a terrible fire, came to revive this first line. Poret deployed his column not twenty paces from the English line, lowered their bayonets and started a deadly charge, it forced the first English line to turn around and

---

956 de Courcelles, pp. 408-9.

flee: the struggle continues, however, and soon the carnage became appalling.

Guillemin, the officer commanding the 1st Battalion of the 3rd Grenadiers, notes:[957]

> To our left was a square of chasseurs of the Guard, commanded by General Michel, who was killed. A battery of the Guard was in front of us and to the left of this square. The emperor remained with us for a long time and only after many instances did he leave us. Shortly after, the battery dismounted the horses and gunners killed or knocked out.
>
> In the evening, we were ordered to march forward in column by battalion. We arrived on the plateau overlooking the battlefield, the brave General Poret de Morvan, who commanded us, ordered us to form square and to start firing by two ranks. We remained in position for a long time while losing a lot of people.
>
> Marshal Ney came to join the square and said to General Morvan 'we must die here!' We remained for some time, but the gunfire and shrapnel vomited death and in a moment, the general and my square were no more. We retired, the marshal, the general and joined the square of Old Grenadiers [actually the 2nd Battalion 1st Chasseurs] commanded by General Cambronne. Passing near a farm, we were assailed by a discharge of bullets by an enemy battery placed on the road and the shooting of several battalions.

About the attack, Second-Lieutenant Pierre Regne recalls:[958]

> I was wounded with two gunshots and two sabre cuts to the head and a sabre cut to my left thigh at the affair of Waterloo on 18 June 1815. I was made prisoner of war on 18 June and was returned from prison on 5 January 1816.

Grenadier Jacques Fauvergnier served in 2nd Company, 1st Battalion 3rd Grenadiers. He writes:[959]

> At Waterloo, I was wounded and left for dead in front of the square of the 3rd Grenadiers of the Imperial Guard. I spent two and a half

---

957 d'Avout, p. 114.
958 Author's collection.
959 Author's collection.

days abandoned on the field of battle. I was found by the English and made prisoner. I spent three years in captivity, and was released from the prisons in 1818. Due to my suffering, having had a leg removed, I was admitted to the Invalides on 16 April 1818.

Colonel Crabbe notes:[960]

I found the marshal in the middle of the 3rd Grenadiers on the plateau, on foot, bare-headed and his jacket torn, covered in dirt and mud, his bloody sword in his hand. At his side was General Friant, commander of the Guard infantry, and one of his old friends, Colonel Poret de Morvan. Followed by Besnard and reining back my horse to the pace of the *pas de charge* I gave the marshal the emperor's orders; but he replied to me 'my dear Crabbe, it is too late to change. It is here now that we must breakthrough or die, and there is no more I can do now'...at that moment, the grenadiers came into contact and descended unto hell. Two English batteries opened fire on us with grape shot and ball at one hundred paces, causing confusion in the ranks. My horse was shot as I endeavoured to leave the melee and return to the headquarters. The flank of the plateau was filled with a whirlwind of smoke and noise, the Prussians, the death heads of Brunswick and the redcoats of the English massacred the old-timers of the Old and the Middle Guard.

Surgeon-Major Pichot, attached to the artillery of the Imperial Guard, recalls the action thus:[961]

At Waterloo, 18 June, half of the 3rd Grenadiers had been killed. The colonel and the chief of the 1st Battalion were out of action, M. Hurault de Sorbee was charged with its command and formed in a square the rest of his grenadiers, who opposed like a giant barrier, the charges of British cavalry, but to this barrier, the canister fire was terrible and caused great gaps in the ranks, and M. Hurault de Sorbee received a shot which broke his jaw and knocked him down: the rout began: placed on his horse, he was bathed with his own blood, he wandered randomly, he crossed the ranks of the Prussians, he retraced his steps, and came to an isolated house.

---

960 Jean Louis Crabbe, *Jean-Louis Crabbe, Colonel d'Empire*, Editions du Cannonier, Nantes, 2006, p. 17.

961 *Biographie Le général Hurault de Sorbée par Amédée Pichot.*

Captain Antoine Nicolas Beraud, of the 4th Grenadiers, notes that the 4th Grenadiers and the 1st Battalion of the 3rd Grenadiers attacked in two columns. About the attack, he recalled that:[962]

> A new column of attack formed almost entirely by the Guard was to march against Mont-Saint-Jean; generals ran through the line to press forward with the attack, and the soldiers were filled with the hope of victory, which seemed to soon be fulfilled…But, fortune did not smile for a moment on the French, as she was to betray them with more cruelty.
>
> The Middle Guard marched forward, under the leadership of Marshal Ney, and supported by the emperor in person with the Old Guard.
>
> The attack was carried out in two columns. M. Gérard said that a fault, or rather a disadvantage particularly attached to the French army, was it marching to the sound of the drum and gave the English a warning to prepare to better receive us. The good people who have expressed this opinion have probably never seen a battle, they would not have known that when two or three hundred muskets are thundering fire from all sides, it is practically impossible for the same troops marching to the sound of the drum to hear it, let alone for the enemy to hear it also…the emperor (perhaps, indeed, with less force of genius than at Austerlitz, Wagram, and so many other days) has fulfilled the duties of a general; and at the end of the battle, he showed himself an intrepid soldier. In that fatal moment, we were fighting with him.
>
> We advanced at the *pas de charge* with our bayonets, but we were exposed to the fire of the English, whose fire wiped away a whole file: its effect was terrible. Ney was in a few minutes dismounted, he had three horses killed under him and several other generals were wounded. A large number of wounded, retiring then through the ranks, spread out on the plain and began to spread trouble and alarm…due to the nature of the difficult terrain it forced the two columns closer together, and merged into a single mass. The fault is this: the column, it is unclear by what order or what chance, stopped at a quarter of a gunshot from the enemy, without attacking.

---

962 Beraud, p. 279.

About Lieutenant Goyard's[963] actions in the 1815 campaign, General Poret de Morvan writes:[964]

> Plas de Mauberge 24 June 1831
>
> In response to the request by M. Goyan [Claude Urbain], Member of the Legion of Honour, captain in retirement, previously of the 3rd Regiment of Grenadiers à Pied of the Imperial Guard, who served under my command, I certify in all honesty that M. Goyard, at the Battle of Fleurus on 16 June 1815, he distinguished himself in the capture of the village of Ligny and in the square of the 1st Battn, in which the general was, during the charges of the Prussian cavalry, which made multiple attacks and pressed on the square, but it held firm for which the general demands the presentation of the Officer of the Legion of Honour dated to 17 June.
>
> The 18th, at Waterloo, he was notable by his good conduct during this unhappy affair. This good officer when the grenadiers had fired a volley, they moved forward, however the shooting of the enemy was very damaging to us, and he cried the order 'with the bayonet, with the bayonet'. It was at this moment the brave man received a mortal wound standing at my side. Overcome by fatigue from this, yet with a renewed force in his courage, he saw that the enemy line was too strong for his intrepid grenadiers and had been replaced with new forces. Recalling his energy, he contributed strongly to support the retreat...

Goyard himself writes:[965]

> General Poret de Morvan requested for my actions the Cross of the Legion of Honour when I was presented to the emperor during a

---

963 Claude Urbain Goyard, born on 22 January 1787 in the department of the Cote d'Or, was admitted to the army aged twenty on 12 February 1807, as a soldier in the fusilier-grenadiers. Due to his aptitude, he was swiftly promoted to fourrier on 13 July 1807, to sergeant-major of the 1st Tirailleurs on 20 April 1810 and to sergeant-major of the newly raised 2nd Grenadiers à Pied on 1 July 1811. Following the Russian campaign, he was promoted to second-lieutenant on 8 April 1813, to first-lieutenant on 22 January 1814 and to captain on 1 July 1814 in the Corps Royale de Grenadiers à Pied des France. He was admitted to 3rd Grenadiers on 1 April 1815.
964 Author's collection.
965 Author's collection.

review on 17 June 1815. Unfortunately, due to the unhappy events that took place on the following day, this was never realised.

During the fighting at Waterloo, Goyard was wounded with a musket ball that shattered his left clavicle and was left for dead on the field of battle. He was discharged from the army on 21 September 1815 on the orders of Surgeon-in-Chief Pierre Collas and Baron Larrey.

About the assault of the Guard, Macready, of the 30th Regiment of Foot, narrates:[966]

> A column of the Imperial Guard (Moyenne Garde, as I learned from the wounded and one unwounded man of them I subsequently spoke to), came over our ridge in splendid order. As they rose step-by-step before us, with their red epaulettes and cross belts put on over their blue great coats, and topped by their high, hairy caps, keeping time, and their officers looking to their alignment, they loomed most formidably, and when I thought of their character, and saw their noble bearing, I certainly thought we were in for very slashing work.
>
> I have heard that General Halkett spoke a few exciting and laudatory words to our men at this time, and that they cheered handsomely, but I cannot speak with confidence to this; but I know that we were called to silence, and told we were to fire one volley by word of command, and then to port our arms; and I have it swimming either in my memory or my imagination, that I still hear Sir Colin's own lips exclaiming at this moment, 'we have nothing for it but a charge!' Of what follows I am sure. They halted and fired—I think badly. We returned the volley, ported, and, giving a 'hurrah!' came to the charge.
>
> Our surprise was inexpressible when through the clearing smoke we saw the backs of the Imperials flying in a mass. We stared at each other as if mistrusting our eyesight. Some guns from the rear of our right poured in grape among them, and the slaughter was dreadful. Nowhere did I see carcasses so heaped upon each other. I never could account for their flight, nor did I ever hear an admissible reason assigned for it. Directly after they had fled there was an alarm of cavalry, and we hastily re-formed square, and again began to suffer from their artillery.

Rogers, of the 30th Regiment of Foot, says that:[967]

---

966 Macready, pp. 394-6.
967 John Franklin personal communication.

It was a column of the Imperial Guard, I know for two reasons: first, their dress, which was large, hairy caps, blue greatcoats, red epaulettes, their accoutrements over the greatcoat; second, sometime after, one of them crawled into our square. I had a flask with water, and gave him some—he blessed me for it. I asked him to what corps he belonged—he stroked his moustache, and said 'Garde Imperiale'.

This column came over the hill as if marching on a parade. I saw an officer a pace or two in front, as if regulating the time. I distinctly saw them carry arms as they halted, and then pour in their fire. We fired, cheered, and came to the charge—just at the time when I supposed we were closing with them, for we were on the ground they'd stood on, I was thunderstruck to hear our men damning their eyes for not waiting till they had their revenge for what the artillery had done.

Another officer from the regiment narrates that the Guard gave way only after a severe fire-fight, in contradiction of Rogers and Macready:[968]

On the 18th, the column with the bearskin caps which advanced on us late on that eventful evening was the leading column of the grenadiers of the Guard, and was stopped by ours and the 73rd, where we had pretty sharp practice, as you may well remember.

Officers from the 33rd and 69th Regiments of Foot also comment that they were attacked by the Guard and that the former received almost all of the Guard's fire. An officer of the 69th Regiment of Foot writes:[969]

We had scarcely recovered the confusion which this side movement had caused by the destruction which the grape-shot was making in our ranks, when we perceived directly in front of our skeleton brigade Buonaparte's Imperial Guard, advancing to the charge in a column of grand divisions.

Their appearance just then was most imposing; their high bearskin caps and tall, red feathers upon so stout and tall a body of men, caused them to look most formidable. The guns which covered their advance here filed off right and left, and exposed the column to our view.

968 Macready, p. 398.
969 *United Services Magazine*, 1845, p. 569.

George Barlow, captain in the 2nd Battalion 69th Regiment of Foot, narrates in a letter of 7 July 1815 that:[970]

> Eight o'clock came and found the battle yet undecided, for shortly afterwards four solid masses of Imperial Guard advanced, and made a most formidable attack. These fellows came up with carried arms to within seventy or eighty yards of the heights along which our infantry were posted, and opened a terrible fire; two pieces of cannon accompanied them and being placed opposite our brigade, which was then formed en masse, and raked it most severely with grape shot, this was indeed the crisis of the eventful day.

Despite the Allied musketry and artillery fire, the attack of the Old Guard had succeeded in pushing back the right centre of the Allied lines, as Sir Augustus Frazer notes in a letter dated 18 June 1815, timed at 23.00:[971]

> Napoléon at length pierced the left of our centre with the infantry of the Imperial Guard: the contest was severe beyond what I have seen, or could have fancied. I cannot describe the scene of carnage. The struggle lasted even by moonlight.

Wellington's right centre had given way, but the French were caught in a bottleneck trying to cross the sunken road behind La Haye Sainte. With troops unable to retreat or advance, the action developed into a fire-fight. The combined artillery and musket fire from the Allied lines whittled away the first three lines with devastating effect.

The brigade of General Pégot from 1st Corps, the 4th Grenadiers and the 1st Battalion 3rd Grenadiers seem to have come into contact with Ompteda's Hanoverians. Captain Carl Jacobi, of the Lüneburg Light Infantry Battalion standing immediately behind La Haye Sainte, notes:[972]

> Towards seven o'clock a last desperate encounter took place with the entire corps of the Imperial Guard, which was supported simultaneously by the advance of enemy formations which were already engaged at the battle. The enemy's main body of cavalry had

---

970 John Franklin personal communication.
971 Edward Sabine, *Letters of Colonel Sir Augustus Simon Frazer KCB*, Longman, Brown, Green, Longmans & Roberts, London, 1859, p. 547.
972 Franklin, Vol. 1, p. 20.

been positioned on their right wing at La Haye Sainte, and assembled in the hollow ground. They then advanced onto the heights with their infantry columns supported by light artillery on the left.

Carl von Scriba, of the Bremen Light Infantry, notes:[973]

> At this decisive moment, around half-past seven, a strong square of the French Imperial Guard advanced against us together with a number of cannon, which immediately began to fire violently. Our brave group could not withstand this violent attack for very long. At the beginning our men fired with great anger, but unfortunately the ammunition was exhausted.

The combination of limited ammunition supplies to the Allied troops caused by the continued and consistent pressure from the French cavalry all afternoon and the close co-ordination between some of the Guard infantry, cavalry and accompanying artillery allowed for local successes, as Wilhelm von Tschnitz, an officer with the Bremen Light Infantry, acknowledges:[974]

> We had hardly crossed the short distance when we had to stop to repel an attack by the enemy's cavalry, which attacked us impetuously for the fifth time. It was driven back again and now we had no doubts any more our inability to retain our former position until nightfall; at this moment, a square, comprised of the French Imperial Guard, which could be observed only now through the heavy smoke, advanced under a heavy cannonade to within fifty paces of us.

> Our ranks were so thin that we could not even call our formation a triangle anymore, because everyone just wanted to keep his neighbour close to him and everything was concentrated in the middle. Our ammunition had almost been expended during the fourth cavalry attack, and although an officer had been sent away earlier to get more ammunition, he could not fulfil his mission and the battalion, which was in deep trouble, received some rounds from the Verden Battalion so that every soldier had three or four cartridges.

> The soldiers continued to demand more ammunition and new muskets, because theirs had become so hot and dirty that they misfired frequently or did not function. In these critical

---

973 Franklin, Vol. 1, p. 117.
974 Franklin, Vol. 1, p. 125.

circumstances, several skirmishers who volunteered were thrown forward against the enemy's square, which advanced like a tempest. Captain von Bothmer ordered that 'the square should retire, about-turn march!' and this order was followed by a withdrawal.

The 4th Grenadiers and elements of Pégot's brigade ran into Kruse's Nassau troops. August von Kruse, commanding officer of the 1st Nassau Regiment, narrates:[975]

> The elite infantry, Napoléon's Imperial Guard, which advanced to capture the plateau, from which our infantry only withdrew a hundred paces. A violent fire with small arms commenced, during which the crown prince, who had commanded the plateau throughout the battle, and who showed as much courage and foresight, attempted to resolve with a bayonet charge. To this end, he called upon the Nassau troops. Thus, I ordered the 2nd Battalion to move forward, and I advanced with them in column; the remainder of the 1st Battalion joined with them.
>
> The attack took place with the utmost courage. I saw one side of a square of the Imperial Guard turn back, when, perhaps due to the fall of the crown prince, who was wounded, a wave of panic descended upon the young soldiers and at the moment of their greatest victory, the battalion became confused and fell back. The remaining battalions in the first line soon followed, so that the plateau was only held by small bodies of brave men, to which I added the landwehr and the remainder of the 2nd Battalion, but in such a way that the enemy fire could not have a great effect on them.
>
> While this event was occurring, the enemy's right flank had advanced, and occupied the rear of our centre.

Captain Friedrich Weiz, of the 1st Battalion 1st Nassau Regiment, narrates the events as he witnessed them as follows:[976]

> When the four battalions of the French Imperial Guard attacked, reinforcements were taken from the reserve and from the right wing of the army. The Guard and the whole of the French army were beaten. The Prussian army arrived in time.

---

975 Pflug-Hartig, *La Belle Alliance*, letter No. 72 dated 21 June 1815 by Major
      Kruse. Translated from the original German by the author.
976 John Franklin personal communication.

Are these the four battalions of chasseurs, or the four attacking regiments? We simply do not know what he actually witnessed, and could have been any of the three attacks made by the Old Guard. Captain Ludwig Wirths, of the 2nd Battalion 1st Nassau Regiment, writes about his battalion's action as follows:[977]

> I was faced by a line of artillery, which was covered by two batteries ready to shoot and a battalion of the Moyenne Garde. I operated here, half advancing, half driven back again, until I could place myself in a hollow way which protected my front and from where I advanced to drive the enemy back with a heavy fire, and I did not leave this position until the end. During this combat the company lost many men.

This hollow way mentioned must be the sunken road which is called 'difficult terrain' as noted by Captain Beraud, of the 4th Grenadiers. This topographical description nicely places both French and Allied troops in the same location, and verifies both accounts. The artillery is likely to be the Imperial Guard horse artillery under Duchand. One of these batteries, according to Guillemin (of the 3rd Grenadiers), was to his left beyond a battalion of chasseurs. A second battery, according to Gustave Pontécoulant (of the Imperial Guard horse artillery), was to the right of the 3rd Grenadiers. It seems that this is the battery mentioned by Wirths.

Heinrich von Gagern, also of the 2nd Battalion 1st Nassau Regiment, narrates in a letter of 26 July 1815 that:[978]

> The immense cannon fire was interrupted by several cavalry charges, which were always repulsed by the upright English cavalry and lasted from about midday until shortly before seven o'clock. Now our battalion was ordered to attack a battalion of French Guards with fixed bayonets. At that time the crisis had started, because the Prussians, who had long been expected, had still not arrived. Some of the Allied battalions were quite dispersed, and the French attacked with renewed courage.
>
> Our battalion, however, with the Landwehr Battalion on our left, and slightly behind, advanced while covered by the cavalry. One of the main mistakes was that our artillery had completely

977 ibid.
978 ibid.

run out of ammunition and no cannon were able to support us. We charged twice and were repulsed twice. The brave hereditary Prince of Orange rode alongside our square for the first time, and encouraged our soldiers, but was wounded beside our square too. Shortly after, I saw our gallant prince riding back past our square with his wound.

Clearly, it seems that the Nassau troops were no easy pushover for the Old Guard; he then notes that his regiment advanced, pushing the Old Guard down the slope and past La Haye Sainte. General Kielmansegge explained later that his brigade also had to retreat when von Kruse's men fell back. The Prince of Orange was wounded in the shoulder, but his officers had a difficult time persuading him to retire. He notes that:[979]

> At that very movement a very strong infantry column moved towards the square on the right. The two battalions which stood on the right advanced in square with some Nassau battalions, and they forced the enemy cavalry to retire. However, the violent canister and musket fire from the advancing column which met them caused the general commanding the 1st Corps and the remaining staff officers belonging to these two battalions to be wounded.

> The retreat of the two Nassau battalions made it completely impossible to maintain the ground we had won, and it was necessary to retire to a position further back. At this moment, another cavalry attack was repulsed, although the violent canister and musket fire had overpowered almost the entire flank of the square, which had become a triangle. The order to halt and reform was given, despite the fact that we were still within the enemy's range, and that the attack had disrupted all order. Our eagerness to regain the territory which had been lost as quickly as possible was great, and the battalions were led against the enemy once again.

> At this very moment, the enemy made his last and strongest attack; the fire from a strong column forced the battalion to retire once again, which this time was less orderly than the previous withdrawal, because of the heavy loss of officers and men.

Clearly in this narrative, we see that the attack was followed by, or supported with, the attack of the Guard cavalry, which will be described in a later chapter. Pégot's brigade advancing hard by La Haye Sainte

---

979 ibid.

was observed by Major F. Browne, of the 40th Regiment of Foot, who notes:[980]

> To the right of the house [La Haye Sainte] and near it was a bank or small hill, which was occupied by the head of a French column, halted, but not very regularly formed. I think they had been driven back from their attempt to ascend the hill, partly by our fire and partly by that of the troops on our right; but the cloud of smoke in which we were almost constantly enveloped prevented me from discovering their object there thus exposed, which they did in the most dauntless and daring manner; as fast as they fell, their places were supplied with French troops until the general advance of the British, when they retired.

---

980 Siborne, *Waterloo Letters*, No. 176.

Chapter 20

1st Battalion 3rd Grenadiers

The 3rd Grenadiers fought at Waterloo as two disparate battalions. The 1st Battalion, headed by General Poret de Morvan, attacked the Allied lines to the west of La Haye Sainte. The 2nd Battalion was established on a low rise in the ground where the fallen eagle monument stands, alongside of which was established a half-battery of 12-pounders from the Imperial Guard foot artillery. We look here at what befell the 1st Battalion as it attacked the Allied lines during the final French onslaught at Waterloo.

Among the vast amounts of archive paperwork in Vincennes for the Imperial Guard can be found the muster rolls for 1815. From these we find the casualty reports from the campaign, from which the table below is generated:[981]

1st Battalion 3rd Grenadiers à Pied						
	Wounded	Wounded & Prisoner	Prisoner of War	Killed	Deserted	Missing
1st Company	7	0	0	0	4	88
2nd Company	2	0	0	0	5	73
3rd Company	3	0	0	0	1	85
4th Company	0	0	0	1	0	80
Total	12	0	0	1	10	326

If we look at the nature of recorded wounds, we find that:[982]

---

981 Compiled from SHDDT: GR 20 YC 13. See also: SHDDT: GR 20 YC 14.
982 ibid.

- MAT No. 30 Ambroise Delamarr, born 25 April 1788. Conscripted to the fusilier-grenadiers on 28 May 1806 and admitted to the 2nd Grenadiers à Pied on 25 July 1812. Following the Russian campaign, he was promoted corporal in the 1st Grenadiers. Promotion to sergeant-major followed on 6 March 1814 in the Instruction Battalion. He was admitted to the Corps Royale des Grenadiers à Pied de France on 1 July 1814 and named as sergeant-major on the staff of the 3rd Grenadiers, before passing to 1st Company 2nd Battalion 4th Grenadiers and finally to 3rd Company 1st Battalion 3rd Grenadiers. Wounded with a gunshot to the right thigh at Waterloo,[983] he was discharged on 14 September 1815.
- MAT No 67 Corporal Jacques Petit, born 14 December 1775. Conscripted to the 30th Regiment of Line Infantry on 1 June 1793 and to the 1st Grenadiers on 19 February 1803, he was promoted to corporal on 8 April 1814 and dismissed from the regiment due to wounds in September 1815:

> At the Battle of Mont-Saint-Jean, he was wounded by a gunshot to the left arm; another to the left shoulder, another gunshot to the right shoulder, and a shell splinter across the eyes.

- MAT No. 475 Louis Alexis Balossier, born 28 March 1783. Admitted to the service of the 32nd Regiment of Line Infantry in 1803, promoted to corporal on 25 March 1808, to fourrier on 12 March 1809 and to sergeant on 19 May 1810. He was admitted to the 1st Grenadiers à Pied on 1 March 1813 and promoted to fourrier on 28 February 1814, to sergeant-major on 17 April 1814 and admitted to the Corps Royale des Grenadiers à Pied de France on 1 July 1814. He was finally admitted to 4th Company 1st Battalion 3rd Grenadiers on 1 April 1815:

> He was wounded with a gunshot, whereby a musket ball passed all the way through my right hip. I was left for dead, and made prisoner of war.

---

983 At Waterloo he either served with the 3rd or 4th Grenadiers, likely to be the 4th Grenadiers as that regiment was broken up into the 3rd Regiment on 1 July 1815.

- MAT No. 937 Denis Joseph Gahide, born at Lille on 13 September 1788. Admitted to the 60th Regiment of Line Infantry on 15 December 1806, he was quickly promoted to corporal on 21 June 1807 and to fourrier on 20 May 1809. He was then admitted to the 2nd Grenadiers à Pied on 15 January 1813, promoted once again to corporal on 30 February 1813, to fourrier on 2 December 1814 and to sergeant-major on 29 January 1814. He passed to the Corps Royale on 1 July 1813 and named as sergeant-major in 1st Company 1st Battalion 3rd Grenadiers à Pied on 1 April 1815:

  He was wounded with a gunshot to the head at the Battle of Mont-Saint-Jean on 18 June 1815.

- MAT No. 3295 Noel Bernard Joseph Foucard was born at Valenciennes on 6 November 1791. Admitted to the 48th Regiment of Line Infantry on 5 May 1809, he was made prisoner of War on 10 September 1812. Returned to France on 27 January 1815, he was admitted to the 22nd Regiment of Line Infantry, then to the 3rd Company 1st Battalion 3rd Grenadiers on 3 May 1815:

  He was wounded with fourteen lance thrusts on 10 September 1812, and he also suffered a wound from a canister shot to the right thigh at the Battle of Waterloo. He was made prisoner of war and was returned to France on 15 December 1815.

- MAT No. 3960 Jacques Barthelemy Fauvergnier, was born on 3 June 1790 at Dierney St Julian Aube. Admitted to the 62nd Regiment of Line Infantry on 19 May 1809 he took part in the campaign in Spain. Admitted to the Imperial Guard on 14 May 1815, he served in 2nd Company 1st Battalion 3rd Grenadiers. He writes:

  At Waterloo, I was wounded and left for dead in front of the square of the 3rd Grenadiers of the Imperial Guard. I spent two and a half days abandoned on the field of battle. Received by the English and made prisoner, I spent three years in captivity, and was released from the prisons in 1818. Due to my suffering, having had a leg from the thigh down removed, I was admitted to the Invalides on 16 April 1818.

- Jean Baptiste Vincent was born on 25 October 1773 at Viecourt in the Vosgers, the son of Nicolas and Catherine Vincent. He was admitted to the army aged twenty on 8 September 1793 and served in the 9th Regiment of Light Infantry. Promoted to corporal on 25 August 1801, to sergeant on 17 September 1806, he was admitted to the Old Guard on 10 July 1813 and served in the 1st Grenadiers. He was then admitted to the Corps Royale on 1 July 1814 and to the 3rd Grenadiers on 1 April 1815. At Waterloo, he was wounded with a lance thrust to the left thigh. This means at some stage Prussian cavalry overran or attacked the square of the battalion, or stragglers, during the retreat.

At least in the 1st Battalion, where wounds are recorded, artillery and musket fire occasioned the largest loss of manpower. It is easy to see how, advancing over the 1,000 metres of terrain, that the columns would have been an immense target for artillery and then musket fire. These men, having seen the cavalry defeated three or four times, and seen Reille's first major offensive checked, little wonder then, that when faced with a tremendous barrage of musket balls and canister shot the Old Guard did not hang around and turned to retreat out of harm's way to the relative security of the reserve squares of the Old Guard, drawn up near La Belle Alliance.

Perhaps also vital in understanding why the Old Guard fled was the lack of command and control. The 1st Battalion 3rd Grenadiers lost the following NCOs:[984]

1st Company

- Sergeant-Major Denis Joseph Gahide, born at Lille on 13 September 1788. Admitted to the 60th Regiment of Line Infantry on 15 December 1806, he was quickly promoted to corporal on 21 June 1807, to fourrier on 20 May 1809. He was admitted to the 2nd Grenadiers à Pied on 15 January 1813 and promoted once again to corporal on 30 February 1813, to fourrier on 2 December 1814 and to sergeant-major on 29 January 1814. He passed to the Corps Royale on 1 July 1813 and named as sergeant-major in 1st Company 1st Battalion 3rd Grenadiers à Pied on1 April 1815. He was wounded at Waterloo.
- Sergeant Jacques Sommer, born in 1776, was conscripted to the 5th Regiment of Line Infantry on 7 January 1811, promoted to corporal

---

984 Compiled from SHDDT: GR 20 YC 13. See also: SHDDT: GR 20 YC 14.

on 2 September 1811, demoted on 3 June 1812, again to corporal on 16 January 1813, to fourrier on1 April 1813 and to sergeant-major on 23 November 1814. Admitted to the grenadiers on 26 April 1815, he became a prisoner of war.

- Sergeant Jean Baptiste St Lechele was born in 1786 and conscripted to the 100th Regiment of Line Infantry in 1806, to the grenadiers in September 1812 and was promoted to sergeant on 1 January 1814. He was made a prisoner of war.
- Fourrier Claude Ordon, born in 1795, was conscripted into the fusilier-grenadiers on 15 December 1813, becoming a fourrier in the 1st Grenadiers on 21 April 1814. He was wounded and taken prisoner.
- Corporal Rene Guillbaux was born in 1780. Admitted to the 1st Grenadiers on 2 May 1812, he passed to the 3rd Grenadiers on 1 April 1815 and was taken as prisoner of war.
- Corporal Jean Pierre Keiffer, born in 1788, was conscripted to the fusilier-grenadiers on 7 July 1807. Promoted to corporal on 19 April 1814 and to grenadier on 1 July 1814, was became a prisoner of war at Waterloo.
- Corporal Pierre Adam, born in 1788, was conscripted to the fusilier-grenadiers in 1809, to the 1st Grenadiers on 1 January 1813 and promoted to corporal on 15 November 1813. He was taken prisoner.
- Corporal Charles Desmaret was born in 1783 and conscripted in 1804, becoming a grenadier on 21 February 1813 and corporal on 20 May 1814. He was also taken as a prisoner.
- Corporal Jacques Petit, born 14 December 1775, was conscripted into the 30th Regiment of Line Infantry on 1 June 1793, passed to the 1st Grenadiers on 19 February 1803 and promoted to corporal on 8 April 1814. He was wounded during the battle.

2nd Company

- Sergeant-Major Charles Antoine Nedey was born in 1795. He volunteered on 12 May 1812 with the 8th Tirailleurs, was promoted to fourrier on 21 April 1813, to sergeant-major in the 12th Tirailleurs on 21 May 1813 and to sergeant in the 2nd Grenadiers on 2 January 1814. He passed to the Corps Royale on 7 July 1814 and promoted to sergeant-major on 1 April 1815. He became a prisoner of war.

- Sergeant Vincent Duranton, born in 1789, was conscripted into the 4th Tirailleurs in 1810, to the fusilier-grenadiers in 1811, and promoted to corporal in 1813, to sergeant in 1813 and passed to the Grenadiers on 1 July 1814 with the rank of sergeant. He was made a prisoner of war.
- Sergeant Jacques Benneron, born in 1777, was conscripted in 1797, becoming a grenadier on 27 September 1806, a corporal on 28 August 1809 and a sergeant on 25 October 1813. Taken prisoner at Waterloo.
- Corporal George Etienne Boulanger, born on 20 February 1780, was conscripted to the 30th Regiment of Line Infantry in 1803, to the 1st Grenadiers on 1 June 1811 and was promoted to corporal on 8 April 1815. He was wounded at Waterloo.
- Corporal Roger, born in 1776, had been a soldier since 1798. He was promoted to grenadier on 1 May 1813 and to corporal on 23 April 1814. He was made a prisoner of war.
- Corporal Paul Reinlen was born in 1780 and conscripted in 1800, becoming a grenadier on 6 April 1813. He was taken prisoner on 18 June 1815.
- Corporal Denis D'huys, born 1787, was conscripted in 1807 and made a grenadier on 16 February 1813 and a corporal on 12 April 1814. He became a prisoner of war at Waterloo.
- Corporal Joseph Laubaies, born in 1775, joined the army in 1793, passing to the Garde Naples in 1806, to the Garde d'Espagne in 1808, to the 14th Tirailleurs on 1 February 1814 and to the grenadiers on 1 July 1814. He was taken prisoner at the battle.
- Corporal Bernard Volet was born in1780. He was conscripted in 1802, became a grenadier on 7 June 1811 and a corporal on 1 April 1814, becoming a prisoner of war.
- Drummer Pierre Carton, born 1795, was conscripted into the fusilier-grenadiers on 12 March 1812 and became a grenadier on 1 July 1814, before becoming a prisoner in 1815.

3rd Company

- Sergeant-Major Ambroise Delamarr was born on 25 April 1788. He was conscripted to the fusilier-grenadiers on 28 May 1806 and admitted to the 2nd Grenadiers à Pied on 25 July 1812. Named sergeant-major in 3rd Company 1st Battalion 3rd Grenadiers, he was wounded at Waterloo.

- Sergeant Augustin Adam, born in 1788, was conscripted into the fusilier-grenadiers on 6 November 1808 and to the 2nd Grenadiers on 1 August 1811, being promoted to corporal on 16 January 1812, to sergeant on 10 November 1813, on half-pay on 1 July 1814 and to grenadier on 13 December 1814. He was taken prisoner of war.
- Sergeant Jean Baptiste Kantillier, born in 1785, was conscripted into the fusilier-grenadiers on 11 October 1809, promoted to corporal on 1 March 1813, to sergeant on 1 November 1813 and to grenadier on 1 July 1814. He was also made prisoner at Waterloo.
- Sergeant Jean Baptiste Martin was born in 1778 and was conscripted in 1799, entering the Garde Naples in 1806, the Garde d'Espagne in 1808, the 14th Tirailleurs on 1 February 1814 and the grenadiers on 1 July 1814 before being made a prisoner of war in the battle.
- Sergeant Pierre Michel (born 1778) was conscripted in 1797 and admitted into the Garde Naples in 1806, the Garde d'Espagne in 1808, the 14th Tirailleurs on 1 February 1814 and the grenadiers on 1 July 1814. He was taken prisoner.
- Corporal Jean Carre, born 1781, had been a soldier since 1804. He entered the Garde Royale Naples on 1 April 1806, the Garde Royale d'Espagne on 17 July 1808, promoted to corporal on 19 March 1810, entered the 14th Tirailleurs on 1 February 1814 and the grenadiers on 1 July 1814. He was wounded with a gunshot wound to the left leg and was taken prisoner.
- Corporal Bernard Joseph Fassiau (born in 1787) was conscripted in 1808 and entered the 2nd Grenadiers on 1 March 1813, being made corporal on 1 July 1814 and becoming a prisoner of war at Waterloo.
- Corporal Claude Etienne Grou, born in 1787, was conscripted in 1806, entered the Garde d'Espagne in 1808, the 14th Tirailleurs on 1 February 1814 and the grenadiers on 1 July 1814. He was made prisoner.
- Drummer Pierre Branger was born in 1789 and was conscripted to the 1st Grenadiers as drummer on 18 May 1810, becoming a prisoner at Waterloo.
- Fifer Jacques Bauge (born 1795) was conscripted in 1814 to the flanqueur-chasseurs, being put on half-pay in July 1814. He was then admitted to the grenadiers on 28 April 1815 and became a prisoner of war at Waterloo.

4th Company

- Sergeant-Major Pierre Alexis Balossier was born in1783. He was conscripted in 1803, becoming a grenadier on 1 March 1813, fourrier on 28 February 1814 and sergeant-major on 17 April 1814. Wounded when a musket ball passed through right hip, he became a prisoner at Waterloo.
- Corporal Joseph Aubry, born in 1781 was conscripted in 1803 and became a grenadier in March 1813. He was taken as prisoner in 1815.
- Corporal Jacques Prosper Villermet was born in 1782 and conscripted in 1800, entering the grenadiers on 13 December 1812 and promoted to corporal on 16 January 1813. He was made prisoner on 18 June.
- Corporal Nicolas Mathieu, born in 1784, was conscripted in 1804, and entered the grenadiers on 20 February 1813, being made prisoner at Waterloo.
- Corporal Alexandre Cuvelle (born in 1789) entered the National Guardsmen in 24 February 1808 and the fusilier-grenadiers on 1 July 1810. He had been a prisoner of war between 10 December 1812 and 29 November 1814, entering the Grenadier Royale on 5 December 1814. He was made prisoner of war again at Waterloo.
- Drummer Gerard Heckul (born in 1797) was admitted to the regiment in 27 April 1815, having been in the National Guard since 1814.

In 1st Company, half of all NCOs were wounded or made prisoner. In 3rd Company, the sergeant-major and all four sergeants were missing from the ranks, along with three corporals. With the officers of the company knocked out as well, command devolved to the five remaining corporals.

Looking at the casualty returns, coupled with the numerous first-hand accounts of what occurred, we can start to see the three points of data corroborating each other. Colonel Crabbe and Ney speak of being fired at by musket volley and artillery, which is borne out by the wounds suffered by survivors of the actions. The missing are likely to be dead and wounded as well as prisoners of war. Crabbe says that the carnage was appalling, again borne out by the hard facts of the issue. The 1st Battalion lost 52 per cent of its effective strength. We can also see that at some point the battalion was attacked by cavalry, as the men wounded by lances tell us. This could have occurred north of La Belle Alliance, or of course much later in the day south of Rossomme.

The 4th Grenadiers

At the head of the 1st Battalion, Pierre Lafarge fell mortally wounded, and he died later that evening. Other wounded officers were Captains Pierre Amat,[985] Jean Baptiste Bertrand, Henri Prosper Angelique Legendre (died of wounds the same day), Charles Louis Eugene Lévesques (fell with a shattered left knee),[986] Gaetan Fortune, Eusebe François and Marie Benoit Viaris. Wounded first-lieutenants were François Belhomme, with a gunshot to the chest,[987] Jean Baptiste Prosper Berchet,[988] Claude Constant, Pierre Etienne Lefevre, Joseph de Lacoste, who was wounded at Ligny with a gunshot to the thigh and again at Waterloo,[989] and Jean Pierre Taurines (died the same day of wounds). Among the second-lieutenants wounded were Jean Baptiste Cuny, who served in the 2nd Battalion and took a musket ball to the right leg,[990] François Deliege, who was wounded with a canister shot to the head,[991] and Jean Baptiste Joseph Hansenuis took a musket ball to the left thigh.[992] Killed were Captains Paul Duhesme, Jean Nicolas Auguste Sommeilier and First-Lieutenant Fouquet. Captured was First-Lieutenant Claude Jean Duhesme. Out of the officers of the regiment, seven of the eight company-commanders were dead or wounded, all eight first-lieutenants were killed or wounded, and three of the eight second-lieutenants were killed or wounded. Thus, the command of the regiment devolved onto five second-lieutenants and the remaining sub-officers. Battalion-Commander Lafargue was mortally wounded. Unlike, it seems, the 3rd and 4th Chasseurs (who lost a similar proportion of officers), the 4th Grenadiers did not break and dissolve into a sea of fugitives who were captured almost to a man. It seems, perhaps, that the regiment

---

985 AN: LH 28/70.
986 AN: LH 1627/30.
987 AN: LH 168/15.
988 AN: LH 2777/39.
989 AN: LH 2210/50.
990 AN: LH 640/83.
991 AN: LH 713/13.
992 AN: LH 1265/91.

managed to retreat in good order and was able, along with the 1st and 2nd Grenadiers, to stand and fight at Genappe. The rout of the chasseurs à pied and 1st Battalion 3rd Grenadiers does not appear to have greatly impacted on the 4th Grenadiers, nor the neighbouring 2nd Battalion 2nd Grenadiers.

Among the rank and file, Sergeant Jean Baptiste Devaux, serving in 2nd Company of 2nd Battalion, had a musket ball pass through a shoulder[993] and Corporal Jacques Bille was also wounded.[994] Among the many hundreds of men taken prisoner from the regiment was Corporal Louis Joseph Brassart, who had served in the army since 1806 and had been admitted to the Imperial Guard in 1813. He had been a member of the Elba Battalion and joined the 4th Grenadiers on 19 May 1815.[995] Also made prisoners were Corporals Charles François Broglie,[996] François Buchet, Georges Enders (who was wounded to the right thigh with howitzer shell splinters)[997] and Jacques Louis Joseph Godard, who was also wounded as well as being made prisoner of war.[998]

For the 4th Grenadiers, the table below shows the loss of rank and file in the regiment on 18 June 1815:[999]

4th Grenadiers à Pied					
	Wounded	Wounded & Prisoner	Prisoner of War	Killed	Missing
1st Battalion	36	0	65	4	3
2nd Battalion	10	0	95	2	5
Total	46	0	160	6	8

The pattern observed in the 1st Battalion 3rd Grenadiers is repeated if we look at the 4th Grenadiers; we see a high number of company NCOs were lost. The 1st Company lost five of the eight corporals:[1000]

---

993 AN: LH 764/81.
994 AN: LH 240/1.
995 AN: LH 352/40.
996 AN: LH 371/21.
997 AN: LH 897/42.
998 AN: LH 1158/29.
999 Compiled from SHDDT: GR 20 YC 13. See also: SHDDT: GR 20 YC 14.
1000 ibid.

1st Company

- Sergeant-Major François Guenebeux, born in 1779, joined the army in 1793, entering the Garde Naples in 1806, the Garde d'Espagne in 1808, the 14th Tirailleurs on 1 February 1814 and the grenadiers on 1 July 1814. Promoted sergeant-major on 1 January 1815, he was killed at Waterloo.
- Sergeant-Major François Barthelemy Fourder was born in 1783 and was conscripted in 1804. He became a grenadier on 3 April 1813, fourrier on 23 November 1813, sergeant-major on 19 April 1814 and was wounded and taken prisoner at Waterloo.
- Sergeant Charles Louis Renard (born in 1776) was conscripted in 1798, entered the 1st Grenadiers on 27 July 1809, promoted to sergeant on 10 January 1811, and became a prisoner of war between 10 December 1812 and 15 December 1814. He became a grenadier on 25 December 1815 and was wounded and taken prisoner again at Waterloo.
- Sergeant Jean Jacqueline was born in 1779. He was conscripted in 1804 and admitted to the 1st Grenadiers on 1 March 1815. He was killed at Waterloo.
- Sergeant Simon Rene Tessier, born 1776, had been conscripted on 15 February 1807, admitted to the 1st Grenadiers on 8 July 1812, promoted to sergeant on 1 July 1814 and was killed at Waterloo.
- Fourrier Jean Lavigne (born in 1793), was conscripted into the Ouvriers d'Administration Imperial Guard on 6 April 1813, was promoted to corporal on 3 June 1813, to fourrier on 6 January 1814 and entered the fusilier-grenadiers on 7 January 1814, being placed on half-pay on 1 July 1814. He became a grenadier on 20 January 1815 and was taken prisoner.
- Corporal Antoine Felis was born in 1779 and conscripted in 1799, entering the Garde Royale Naples in 1806 and the grenadiers on 20 June 1814. He went missing at Waterloo.
- Corporal Michel Fedier, born in 1781, was conscripted in 1803, entered the Garde Naples in 1806, the Garde d'Espagne in 1808, the 14th Tirailleurs on 1 January 1814 and the grenadiers on 1 July 1814. He was wounded and taken prisoner.
- Corporal Denis Fendely (born 1773) joined the army on 20 September 1790, entering the Garde de Naples on 1806, the Garde d'Espagne on 1808, the 14th Tirailleurs on 1 February 1814 and the grenadiers on 1 July 1814. He, too, was wounded and taken prisoner at Waterloo.

- Corporal Louis Godard was born in 1772 and had joined the army in 1791. He entered the Garde Naples in 1806, the Garde d'Espagne in 1808, the 14th Tirailleurs on 1 February 1814 and became a grenadier on 1 July 1814, being made prisoner in 1815.
- Corporal Louis Joseph Brassard, born in1784, was admitted to the 23rd Regiment of Line Infantry on 6 Feb 1806, promoted to corporal on 1 June 1811, to sergeant on 21 Feb 1813 and passed to the 1st Grenadiers on 23 July 1813, serving with the Elba Battalion on 1 May 1814. He was promoted to corporal in the 4th Grenadiers on 8 April 1815 and made a prisoner of war at Waterloo.
- Corporal François Neue was born in 1782. He was conscripted into the 40th Regiment of Line Infantry in 1799, and admitted to the 1st Grenadiers on 1 April 1813. Promoted to corporal on 1 July 1814, he was wounded three times at Waterloo.

As well as loosing NCOs, the company-commander, Captain Lévesques, had his left knee shattered by a cannonball, and Second-Lieutenant Hansenuis took a musket ball to the left thigh, leaving the company commanded by Lieutenant Prugneaux. The same pattern is repeated in the 2nd, 3rd and 4th Companies:[1001]

2nd Company

- Corporal Charles Fevrier, born in 1783, was conscripted in 1805, entering the Garde de Naples in 1806, the 14th Tirailleurs on 1 January 1814, the grenadiers on 1 July 1814 and became a prisoner of war on 18 June 1815.
- Corporal Cheby (born in 1786) was conscripted in 1807, entering the grenadiers on 1 April 1813. He was made a prisoner at Waterloo.
- Corporal Jean Baptiste Amassiliere, born in 1783, was conscripted in 1804, entering the 2nd Grenadiers on 1 April 1813, promoted to sergeant in the 10th Tirailleurs on 12 May 1813, to corporal in the grenadiers on 16 August 1814 and was made prisoner on 18 June.
- Corporal Etienne Presial (born in 1783) had been conscripted to the fusilier-grenadiers on 5 February 1807, passing to the 2nd Grenadiers on 20 November 1812. He had been a prisoner of war

---

1001 Compiled from SHDDT: GR 20 YC 13. See also: SHDDT: GR 20 YC 14.

from 10 January 1814 to 9 August 1814 and entered the grenadiers on 20 December 1814, being promoted to corporal the same day. He became a prisoner for a second time at Waterloo.

- Corporal Fix Gaidon, born in 1781, was conscripted in 1805, serving in the Garde Naples in 1806, in the Garde d'Espagne in 1808, in the 14th Tirailleurs on 1 February 1814, and placed on half-pay in July 1814, before passing into the grenadiers on 31 January 1815. He was made prisoner of war during the battle.

3rd Company

- Sergeant-Major Jean Buchet was born in1789. He had been conscripted in 1803 and became a grenadier in 1813. At Waterloo, he was wounded and taken prisoner.
- Fourrier Edme Dumesgnil (born in 1794) was conscripted to the 8th Hussars on 22 February 1812, being promoted to corporal on 15 May 1812, to fourrier on 15 December 1812, to sergeant on 16 November 1813 and entered the grenadiers on 8 November 1814. Promoted to fourrier on 8 April 1815, he was also wounded and taken prisoner in the battle.
- Corporal Louis Haver was conscripted in 1803, passed to the 1st Grenadiers on 11 February 1813, promoted to sergeant in the 4th Tirailleurs on 21 August 1813, to corporal in the grenadiers on 1 July 1814 and was made prisoner of war in 1815.
- Corporal Noel Grocol, born in 1774, had been admitted to the army in 1793, serving in the grenadiers from 25 November 1806. Promotion to corporal came on 3 August 1814 and was wounded at Waterloo before deserting the army.
- Corporal Georges Enders was born in 1795 and was conscripted on 21 March 1806 to the 17th Regiment of Line Infantry. Sent to the Fontainebleau Battalion on 26 May 1813, he became a corporal on 10 September 1813 and was placed on half-pay in July 1814 before being admitted into the grenadiers à pied on 18 April 1815. He was wounded and made prisoner.

4th Company

- Fourrier Antoine François Decroux, born in 1789, was conscripted to the 3rd Regiment of Line Infantry in 1808 and admitted to the 4th

Grenadiers on 11 May 1815 with the rank of fourrier. He became a prisoner of war in the battle.[1002]

- Sergeant Alexis Huguet, born in 1788, had been conscripted into the fusilier-grenadiers in 1809 and promoted to sergeant-major on 26 January 1813. He passed to the 2nd Grenadiers on 20 February 1813 and to sergeant on 1 July 1814, before becoming a prisoner of war at Waterloo.

- Sergeant Pierre de Saint Omer was born in 1788 and conscripted in 1806, entering the 2nd Grenadiers in 1811. He was promoted to corporal on 9 July 1812, to sergeant on 25 January 1813 and was both wounded at Ligny and taken prisoner at Waterloo.

- Sergeant Germain Edme Ramez (born in 1779) had been conscripted in 1801, admitted to the 1st Grenadiers on 1 March 1812, promoted to corporal on 13 April 1812, to sergeant on 19 April 1813 and was wounded and made prisoner in the battle.

- Corporal Jean Gioles (born in 1790) was conscripted on 27 March 1809 into the fusilier-grenadiers. He became a grenadier on 1 July 1814 and was made a prisoner at Waterloo.

- Corporal Gabriel Alignes was born in 1784 and conscripted to the fusilier-grenadiers on 5 January 1806, promoted to corporal on 17 January 1814, and to grenadier on 1 July 1814. He was also taken prisoner of war.

- Corporal Hypolite Villaret, born in 1781, was conscripted in 1807, entering the 1st Grenadiers on 28 November 1808. He had been promoted to corporal on 1 December 1813 and was wounded and made prisoner in 1815.

- Corporal Anne Nicolas Gally (born in 1791) was conscripted to the fusilier-grenadiers on 1 February 1809, promoted to corporal on 1 October 1811, to sergeant on 26 December 1812, entered the 2nd Grenadiers on 24 September 1813, promoted to corporal

---

1002 SHDDT: GR 20 YC 14. MAT No. 3822 Antoine François Decroux, born 16 March 1789, was conscripted to the 3rd Regiment of Line Infantry on 30 November 1808, promoted to corporal on 16 August 1810, to fourrier on 1 January 1811, to sergeant-major on 1 June 1811 and admitted to the 4th Grenadiers on 11 May 1815. He became a prisoner of war at Waterloo. See also: SHDDT: Yj 11. Antoine François Decreux returned to France from prison in England in March 1816.

on 10 November 1813, placed on half-pay in July 1814 and was wounded at Waterloo.

- Sapeur Guillaume Baudin[1003] had been admitted to the regiment on 27 May from the 48th Regiment of Line Infantry, becoming a prisoner of war in the battle.

In the 2nd Company, as well as the 4th Company, all the officers were wounded, meaning command passed to the NCOs. When faced with a loss of officers and key NCOs, it is little wonder the command and control faltered and the Old Guard, or at least the 1st Battalion 3rd Grenadiers and the 4th Grenadiers, fell back, and in consequence the battalions were routed by the Allied cavalry. What also stands out is the very high ratio of men made prisoner from the former 14th Tirailleurs. These men were all veterans in terms of service, but in experience of campaigns and battles this was their first real exposure. Is it little wonder that many surrendered or allowed themselves to be herded up by the Allied cavalry? Were NCOs and drummers, as well as officers, highly conspicuous targets for Allied marksmen and for the Allied cavalry to round up?

The regiment lost 44 per cent of its effective strength on 18 June; some 214 other ranks. The 1st Battalion, at the head of the column, lost far more men dead and wounded than the 2nd Battalion, the latter losing more men as prisoners of war. If Beraud is correct that the regiment did not attack, we are certain it came under Allied artillery and musket fire. On balance of probability, it would be most surprising if the regiment did not fire any shots in anger at the Allied line. Compared to the data of the 1st Battalion 3rd Grenadiers and the 4th Grenadiers, when we look at the 1st Battalion 2nd Grenadiers at Plancenoit, we again do not see a marked degree of NCOs killed, wounded or made prisoner.[1004]

Clearly, something else was happening here. We do know that the battalion was not directly involved in the attack and seemingly only collapsed once it arrived at Genappe. Despite being obvious targets, NCOs were not taken out by Prussian snipers in Plancenoit.[1005]

1003 SHDDT: GR 20 YC 14. MAT No. 4553 Guillaume Baudin was admitted to the regiment on 27 May 1815, becoming a prisoner of war at Waterloo. See also: SHDDT: Yj 11. Guillaume Baudin returned to France from prison in England in March 1816.

1004 Compiled from SHDDT: GR 20 YC 13. See also: SHDDT: GR 20 YC 14.

1005 ibid.

For whatever reasons, the NCOs of 1st Company were clearly not as exposed to enemy fire as in the other three companies. The 3rd Company lost marginally higher NCOs than 2nd or 4th Companies, but it is very obvious that a different mechanism was in play for the 2nd Battalion 3rd Grenadiers, and the 2nd Grenadiers as a whole, compared to what happened to the 1st Battalion 3rd Grenadiers and the 4th Grenadiers. The difference is, I am sure, the arrival of Chasse's division and the Allied cavalry charge. The high ratio of NCOs made prisoner clearly shows that these men and their companies were gathered up by the Allied cavalry. The fate of the 2nd Battalion 3rd Grenadiers also demolishes the myth that it was this battalion which Adams's brigade took in the flank. If the battalion was as cut up by Allied infantry and hounded by the Allied cavalry, then one would expect the ratio of NCO loss to be comparable to regiments where we know this happened. Clearly, the battalion was not dispersed. The incidence of NCO loss is remarkably similar across the 1st Grenadiers, 2nd Grenadiers and 2nd Battalion 3rd Grenadiers. Clearly, whatever happened to the 1st Battalion 3rd Grenadiers and the 4th Grenadiers did not happen to these five other battalions, including the 1st Battalion 2nd Grenadiers, which was in Plancenoit. The fighting in which these three battalions faced was of a marked difference of intensity, as Crabbe states: 'they descended into hell'.

Comment

Did Friant attack in the wrong place? Two eyewitnesses to the attack of the Imperial Guard suggest that this first attack was in the wrong place, or at least not where Napoléon intended the attack to happen. With the 8th Regiment of Line Infantry holding La Haye Sainte, and the Allied centre worn thin at this point, it seems Napoléon's intention was to attack here with the Guard. The Guard, or at least the 3rd and 4th Regiments of Grenadiers and Chasseurs, had been standing behind La Haye Sainte in the positions occupied by 1st Corps from around 14.00 and may well have taken part in the attacks against La Haye Sainte and the Allied left. Marshal Soult wrote to Marshal Davout, the minister of war in Paris, from Philippeville on 19 June as follows:[1006]

1006 AN: AFIV 1939, pp. 54-5.

Monsieur the marshal, I have the honour to write to you for the first time since I wrote to you on the field of battle of Waterloo at half-past two o'clock when the battle was begun and we had experienced great success, however at seven o'clock a false movement was carried out with the orders of the emperor, all was changed. The combat continued until night fell and a retreat was effected, but it was in disorder.

The emperor rallied the army at Philippeville and Avesnes and began to organise the corps and to tend to their needs. You can well imagine that the disaster is immense.

For Soult, an event around 19.00 was the turning point on the battle. This false movement is either the attack of the Imperial Guard infantry on the French left, an attack on Plancenoit (though this has never been described as a false move), or the massed cavalry charges. If the latter, then Soult seems to be referring to the attack by the grenadiers à cheval and dragoons of the Imperial Guard, which Napoléon lists in his account of 20 June. The other candidate is that the first attack by the Imperial Guard was at the wrong place. Colonel Crabbe supports this hypothesis:[1007]

Towards 19.00 hours, Marshal Soult, the Duc de Dalmatie and the major-general summoned me. He told me that the emperor had confided his final reserve to Marshal Ney; all that remained of the Guard, to make a decisive attack on the English lines. He demanded an experienced officer of the headquarters to carry supplementary orders.

I reached the rise near the farm of La Belle Alliance, where the emperor was located. He was surrounded by a squadron of the chasseurs à cheval of the Imperial Guard, with the green coats and trousers trimmed with red, and *schabraques* of the same. Everyone wore their colpack bags unfurled, a sign of their escort duty.

From this position, one could see the whole battlefield which for six kilometres appeared like a furnace.

On the left, the chateau of Hougoumont was in flames and there was fighting throughout all the woods. Face-to-face with us was Mont-Saint-Jean, which the French columns ascended, and was crowned with smoke and the gunfire appeared like lightning

---

1007 Crabbe, pp. 18-19.

flashes. It seemed like a volcano whose sides were dotted with dead French and English and the cadavers of horses, testifying to the violence of fighting after the beginning of the afternoon to capture La Haye Sainte, then followed by the charges and counter-charges of French and Scottish cavalry at the top of the plateau. At the right extremity of the plateau, the fighting was fierce around the farms of La Haye and Papelotte, and the chateaux of Frischermont by the 6th Corps of General Mouton, Comte Lobau, who contained the Prussians of Bülow.

The emperor was on a chair in front of a table upon which some maps were laid out. This table stood on a pile of straw. General Comte Drouot and two aide-de-camps were at his side. He wore his usual grey greatcoat over his usual uniform of colonel of chasseurs, and on his head he wore his legendary hat. He was slumped in his chair, he appeared to me to seem exhausted and angry. One of the aide-de-camps informed him of my arrival. Without even turning to me, he said out of the blue 'Ney has acted stupidly again. He has cost us the day! He has destroyed my cavalry and is ready to destroy my Guard. He manoeuvres like a good for nothing. He attacks the plateau obliquely instead of assaulting the centre. Go at the best speed you can and order him to modify his march and to pierce the centre of the English in a compact mass. Our success depends on your journey'.

Removing Crabbe's overt bias against Marshal Ney, it does seem he is correct in where the first attack was located. Indeed, Friant attacked in the centre of the Allied right, as noted, where the Lion Mound now is. Friant, who nominally led the attack, was not either aware of where the attack was to take place nor that due to the nature of the terrain (i.e. the sunken road, which Napoléon does not seem to have been aware of) had to manoeuvre to avoid this obstacle and thus attacked in a different location to that prescribed by Napoléon. Certainly, the next attack, that of the 3rd and 4th Grenadiers, was hard by La Haye Sainte at the Allied centre just as mentioned by Crabbe. So, on balance it seems that this event is the false movement noted by Soult. It seems Napoléon was not aware of the sunken road, and thus his planned attack hard against La Haye Sainte had to move towards the centre of the Allied right.

For Baron Gourgaud, the second and third assaults by the Guard were the false move and not the first attack:[1008]

1008 The *Hull Packet*, 10 November 1818.

> The eight battalions of Guards, in among whom where were those of the Old Guard, instead of advancing to support the four battalions engaged, ought to have made a movement on the right to serve as a reserve and to rally the troops driven from La Haye—they would obstruct the whole of the field of battle by forming themselves into square by battalions.

So clearly, Marshal Soult, an aide-de-camp to Marshal Ney and Baron Gourgaud all felt that the attack of the Imperial Guard at some stage was wrong. Crabbe and Soult are writing in 1815, Soult the day after the battle, while Gourgaud is writing two years later, so on balance, the hypothesis presented by Crabbe seems more likely.

The arrival of David Chasse's fresh troops spelled the end for the Old Guard. General Petit, of the 1st Regiment of Grenadiers à Pied, narrates the assault thus:[1009]

> These troops went in as well as they could, but could not charge to beyond La Haye Sainte where they were vigorously assailed by everything the enemy had before them. They had the enemy in front of them and were greeted with a heavy fire of artillery and musketry.
>
> At this moment, General Friant, commander of the attack, was seriously wounded, General Michel, commander of the chasseurs, is killed. The latter's death occasioned a movement of excitation among his troops. They stopped their advance.

The Reserve of the Old Guard

Drawn up as a reserve were three battalions of Old Guard. In reserve for most of the Battle of Waterloo, deployed to the east of Hougoumont on a small hill where the fallen eagle monument stands, was the 2nd Battalion 3rd Grenadiers. Alongside them were the 2nd Battalions of the 1st and 2nd Chasseurs. General Petit confirms that the 2nd Battalion 3rd Grenadiers stood side-by-side with the 2nd Battalion 1st Chasseurs:[1010]

1009 J. Petit, 'General Petit's account of the Waterloo Campaign' in *English Historical Review*, 1903.

1010 ibid.

Forward on our left, the 2nd Battalion of the 3rd Grenadier Regiment was joined by the 2nd Battalion of the 1st Chasseurs (the 1st was seconded to headquarters), but the efforts of the enemy forced them to retire; General Cambronne was left for dead on the battlefield.

But, as we shall see later, this episode occurred a mile or so south of La Belle Alliance. General Friant confirms the general thrust of what General Petit says, in that the 2nd Battalion 1st Chasseurs had marched to the aid of the 2nd Battalion 3rd Grenadiers:[1011]

During all these misfortunes, the 2nd Battalion of the 3rd Grenadiers detached to the left and remained there, although he was heavily attacked, General Cambronne, a colonel of the 1st Chasseurs, came to his aid with the 2nd Battalion of his regiment, it was the most critical moment, the enemy redoubled his efforts in this regard along its entire line. General Cambronne was soon to be hurt, thrown from his horse, it is believed dead. Officers, chasseurs and grenadiers fell around him.

General Pelet writes, perhaps in 1821, based on testimonies of those involved:[1012]

General Roguet began to move a few moments, which according to General Cambronne, was with the 2nd Battalion of the 3rd Regiment of Grenadiers, which was commanded by Belcourt, and was placed on the left side of the road. The battalion had little more than 300 men. He moved forward, between La Belle Alliance and Haye Sainte, where the highway was higher than the fields by about three feet.

During his march, General Roguet met General Friant, who was wounded, and was returning on foot, as was wounded General Harlet, supported by grenadiers. The emperor came to this battalion and told General Roguet it was too close to that of Cambronne and had to move away a little.

The general himself replied that it would be too dangerous to perform this movement so close to the enemy. Indeed, there were more and more troops in front and the English had reoccupied La Haye Sainte. The emperor did not insist, and soon it fell back to La Belle Alliance. Soon after, General Roguet was attacked quite

---

1011 Friant, p. 391.
1012 d'Avout, pp. 48-9.

strongly by a considerable force, composed of Prussians and English, this small battalion could not offer more resistance than that of Cambronne, he fell back on Belle Alliance. The emperor had found the 2nd Battalion of the 1st Regiment of Grenadiers, commanded by M. Combes, and went with him on the road to retire to Genappe. The other battalion, commanded by General Petit, had followed the emperor in the same direction and by his orders.

de Mauduit, of the 1st Grenadiers stationed just south of La Belle Alliance, narrates that:[1013]

General Cambronne moved rapidly forward with the 1st Battalion of his regiment, the only one he had at his disposal, and he was followed by the 2nd Battalion of the 3rd Grenadiers and 2nd Battalion of the 2nd Chasseurs. With this small reinforcement the emperor would still try the offensive, but the excessive superiority of the enemy, overflowing on all sides, would not allow more: an orderly retreat was their last recourse.

The 2nd Battalion of the 3rd Regiment of Grenadiers, first posted on the left, where it was long maintained, but it began to give way under the weight of the English masses. General Cambronne, with the 1st Battalion of the 1st Chasseurs moved forward to join them in support and simultaneously cover the retreat of the battalions that descended from the plateau.

Formed in square, Cambronne's battalion soon became assailed on all four sides, but by his attitude and his manly courage, he was able to contain the enemy, while operating his retirement with great calm.

The 2nd Battalion 1st Chasseurs fought at Waterloo, under the orders of General Cambronne, in a vain attempt to stem the tide of Allied infantry and cavalry that surged down on the French left flank following the repulse of the 3rd and 4th Grenadiers and Chasseurs. General Pelet writes:[1014]

The 2nd Battalion of the 1st Chasseurs and 2nd Battalion 2nd Chasseurs were placed near La Belle Alliance, and formed the backbone of the movement. The 1st Battalion of the 1st Regiment

---

1013 de Mauduit, p. 436.
1014 d'Avout, 'L'infanterie de la garde a Waterloo' in *Carnet de la Sabretache*, Vol. 13, 1905, p. 40.

remained at the farm of La Caillou, charged to guard the imperial headquarters; the Prussians were already near the Chantelet Wood.

The centre was thus formed by the 2nd Battalion of the 2nd Regiment, who had formed on the crest under the orders of the emperor, then followed by the 2nd Battalion of the 1st, where General Cambronne was, and were behind the previous two regiments of grenadiers, 1st and 2nd, which had passed the other side of the road, still occupied the same height.

Lieutenant Bacheville, of the 2nd Battalion 1st Chasseurs à Pied, continues the narrative and details the stand of General Cambronne mentioned by General Petit as follows:[1015]

The four squares of the Old Grenadiers and chasseurs were intact, headed by Chief General Roguet and Morand, near them Generals Petit and Pelet, and they secured our retirement, and that of the whole army, despite attempts by the enemy, the square remained steadfast.

We continued our rout, firing on the enemy when he dared to approach us, but soon he stood at a respectful distance. We joined Napoléon.

Our square, commanded by General Cambronne, withdrew slowly and in good order, the terrain forced us to open ourselves for a moment and the British cavalry took the opportunity to enter our ranks, but it did not leave without asking if our chasseurs were injured by them, we turned and gave the English an internal fire.

Another eyewitness was MAT 1742 Jacques Raynal,[1016] who writes:[1017]

After the cavalry of the Imperial Guard and Kellermann's cuirassiers had been checked, Napoléon decided to carry out one

---

1015 Bacheville, pp. 42-8.
1016 Jacques Raynal, admitted to 2nd Company, 1st Battalion 2nd Chasseurs on 1 April 1815, deserted on 12 July 1815. If the memoir is to be believed, by the time of Waterloo he was in 2nd Battalion 1st Chasseurs, and his name, or at least *nom de geurre*, was Emile. No other Raynal served in the chasseurs à pied in 1815. SHDDT: GR 20 YC 44 *chasseurs à pied de la Garde, divers corps, 1814-1815*.
1017 Jean-Antoine Farges, *Recits de Temps Cruels*, Books on Demand, 2010. p. 244.

last attack against the centre of the English at Mont-Saint-Jean. What remained of the Guard—eight battalions—moved forward in the slow pace, at the rhythm of the drums, and under its unfurled flags. The grenadiers and chasseurs carried their arms, impassive, aligned like a parade with famous generals like Louis Friant and Colonel Mallet at their head. Impressed, the wounded stand up or rise to salute and shout 'long live the emperor!' The Guard advanced; the grenadiers corrected their dressing when one of them fell. We arrived at the summit of the slope when all at once there suddenly rose before us the red-coated regiments of the English infantry, which had been concealed behind the hedges and in the wheat. Their volley fire was terrible and murderous and at the same time we were furiously attacked by the Russian cavalry.

Surprised and rapidly decimated, the 'big hats' wavered. General Michel was killed. Friant and Mallet fell seriously wounded. Other French troops which stood with the battalions of the Guard cried 'the Guard retreats!'

The cavalry attack mentioned must be the same as that noted by Bacheville. The muster rolls of the Imperial Guard in 1815 details the casualty reports from the campaign, from which the table below is generated:[1018]

1st Chasseurs à Pied					
	Wounded	Wounded & Prisoner	Prisoner of War	Killed	Missing (presumed prisoner)
1st Company	0	0	0	1	150
2nd Company	2	0	0	4	103
3rd Company	3	0	0	5	82
4th Company	0	0	0	0	84
Total	5	0	0	10	419

The battalion under Cambronne lost a staggering 434 men. It mustered 635 men, of which 68 per cent were lost at Waterloo; only 201 men remained in ranks. Of note, 1st Company 2nd Battalion mustered 159 men, but nearly all of them were presumed prisoners of war. Does this mean they surrendered? The nature of the returns made by the regiment in 1815 relied upon men seeing what happened to their

---

1018 Compiled from SHDDT: GR 20 YC 44, SHDDT: GR 20 YC 45, SHDDT: GR 20 YC 46 chasseurs à pied de la Garde, divers corps, 1814-1815.

comrades. Therefore, we can only be certain of the fate of 204 men of the battalion. It is possible that with the Allied cavalry surging down the field towards the square, the square dissolved and entire companies were rounded up and made prisoner. This is possible, but it is likely that the missing includes dead and wounded men whose fate was not known, as no one remained in the regiment to say what happened to them. Certainly, the bulk of the 1st and 2nd Companies disappeared at Waterloo. In 1821 it was reported that the1st Division under Cambronne was destroyed by musket fire and artillery. If we follow this hypothesis, it seems possible that the 1st Division was the first two companies of the regiment, which do indeed seem to have been overthrown.[1019] Of course, it is not impossible that the battalion, seeing the fate of the 3rd and 4th Chasseurs, surrendered rather than be killed.

2nd Battalion 2nd Chasseurs

The 2nd Battalion of the 2nd Chasseurs also fought at Waterloo, and came under the orders of General Cambronne, in a vain attempt to stem the tide of Allied infantry and cavalry that surged down on the French left flank following the repulse of the 3rd and 4th Grenadiers and Chasseurs. Captain de Steurs, commanding officer of 6th Company of the 2nd Battalion 2nd Chasseurs, writes:[1020]

> Although we saw the progress of our left wing against the enemy, none of us had suspected the debacle that it was: we perceived that after the flight of the debris of the four battalions of the Middle Guard, and it was not possible to rally them behind the small reserve which we, the Imperial Guard, formed: but these battalions also took with them troops of the line from their positions before us, and also continued their retreat after they had passed us.

> The emperor, leaving the farm of La Belle Alliance, stood himself beside a square of the Guard in the hope that his presence would stop the retreat. I saw him very well: the chasseurs, upon seeing this, cried 'see the emperor! He desires to be killed!' Shortly after, a hail of bullets from the direction of Plancenoit rained down upon us: I lost sight of him, as the square of General Pelet, in which I commanded, had to make a retrograde movement, and I was busy going about by duties to close the ranks.

1019 d'Avout, pp. 48-9.
1020 Pawly and Courcelle, p. 34.

This made the rest of the march very bad indeed, because marching was extremely difficult on the water-logged ground; many fell over as we tried to traverse a rather slippery slope. A few minutes later my square was overthrown, as we had no warning of the approach of the English cavalry, which in the dark we had assumed to be other French fugitives who preceded them. A party of chasseurs grouped around the eagle and cried with great fearlessness 'save the eagle'. As for me, I was pushed over and trampled beneath the horses' hooves.

In the same episode, it seems Sub-Lieutenant Arnoux, who served in de Steurs's company, was wounded with a gunshot and made prisoner of war. Wounded by the cavalry which attacked the square of chasseurs was First-Lieutenant Felix Boquet with a sabre cut to the head. He seemingly had lost his headgear by this point, perhaps in the struggle against the cavalry.[1021]

The same episode with the eagle is reported by Bacheville, Pelet and Heuillette, and all reference the eagle of the 1st Chasseurs. Clearly at some point, the remaining chasseurs à pied had formed a composite regiment, under the orders of General Pelet.

MAT No. 1847 Corporal Pierre Salle, of the 2nd Chasseurs, narrates in a letter of 14 July 1862:[1022]

Before the start of the battle, he [General Cambronne] was in front of the 3rd Company, of which I was a part of, carrying out the functions of corporal-quartermaster. He then turned to us and said: 'my friends, in half an hour, the battle will be ours, as the enemy begins to retreat to Brussels'. His confidence was deceived by the arrival of an army corps of General Wellington, which established a battery on a plateau in front of the columns of the Guard, firing on the flank and behind the attacking columns, which spread terror along the whole line.

Our columns had already taken several positions of the enemy. The general gave orders to send out sharpshooters, who had to be good volunteers in order to bring to a fire against the enemy's skirmishers. We formed in square and could see the smoke from the village of Waterloo. This is where the action was at its most serious.

1021 Ian Smith personal communication, 17 August 2016.
1022 Author's collection.

From the casualty reports from the campaign, the battalion lost the following men:[1023]

2nd Chasseurs à Pied					
	Wounded	Wounded & Prisoner	Prisoner of War	Killed	Missing (presumed prisoner and deserters)
1st Company	2	0	0	0	30
2nd Company	1	0	0	0	36
3rd Company	0	0	0	0	37
4th Company	0	0	0	0	56
Total	3	0	0	0	159

Nearly all the men were presumed prisoners of war. Does this mean they surrendered? We know from de Steurs that the battalion was attacked by cavalry and then broke and fled. Therefore, it is possible that a lot of the men listed as missing were indeed prisoners or deserters, or perhaps wounded. The very low number of wounded, and no men dead, suggests that the 'missing' numbers cover up the true casualties.[1024]

1023 Compiled from SHDDT: GR 20 YC 44, SHDDT: GR 20 YC 45, SHDDT: GR 20 YC 46.
1024 d'Avout, pp. 48-9.

Chapter 21

2nd Battalion 2nd Grenadiers

The 2nd Battalion of the 2nd Grenadiers was held in reserve during the Battle of Waterloo; the 1st Battalion fought at Plancenoit. General Christiani, of the 2nd Regiment of Grenadiers, takes up the story about the 2nd Battalion:[1025]

> The 18th, a ray of sunshine appeared about nine o'clock in the morning. We received orders to clean our weapons and we were going to attack. Later, we took position behind the emperor, who was on a hill on the right of the road to Brussels.
>
> At five or six o'clock, maybe later I received the order to send a battalion of the regiment into the village that was to the right, behind the position I occupied, to drive out the Prussians; they said that they were about to capture it. It was M. Golzio, head of the 2nd [*sic*] Battalion of the regiment, that went on this mission. I saw him that evening during the retreat. I do not remember if he had lost many men, but only that he told me he had done much harm to the enemy.
>
> I do not remember the movements which were made by the other regiments of foot grenadiers, but I remember having received the order to move forward with the 2nd Regiment and take position to the right of the Brussels road. I had on my right a very deep ravine.
>
> I remained in this position throughout the march and I saw the debris of four regiments of foot guards, who had been sent under the command of General Friant to take and occupy the British position, which was defended by a deep ravine and by numerous entrenched artillery batteries.

1025 d'Avout, p. 113.

Finally, around seven to eight o'clock, I think, I went with the battalion of 2nd Grenadiers, which had remained with me, to go forward and join the emperor, who was on the left of the road a short distance from the position I had just quitted. He was on foot and had with him General Drouot. I made my battalion form square.

The emperor spent some time observing, I think, the retrograde motion carried out by the artillery of the army, which was deployed in the plain to the left of the road, and then mounted his horse to go. In that time, the enemy cavalry charged onto the highway and became mixed up with our cavalry and infantry, who retired in a mass. The English sharpshooters also emerged and began shooting. So, I made my retreat with my battalion in square. We received a few balls that occasioned confusion in the ranks.

It seems Christiani's sober impression of the action was felt rather differently by the men of the battalion. MAT No. 295 Antoine Deleau,[1026] a grenadier in the 1st Company of 2nd Battalion 2nd Grenadiers, notes in a letter of 30 June 1862 about the last stand of his battalion that:[1027]

I was at Waterloo in the square of the Old Guard, still only twenty-three years of age, placed in the front rank due to my height, but you know that the Young Guard had been called to fill the ranks of the Old Guard. The British artillery thundered upon us, and we answered each discharge by firing at them, though less and less each time…Between two discharges, the English general called 'grenadiers, go!' The square shook with our reply from our muskets. 'Grenadiers, go. You will be treated as the first soldiers of the world!' said a voice assigned to the English general…We suffered another discharge and we answered with our own. 'Go grenadiers, go!' cried all the English who surrounded us on all sides; Cambronne answered to the latter summons by an angry gesture accompanied

---

1026 MAT No. 295 Antoine Deleau was born on 2 April 1792, the son of Jean Deleau and Marie Catherine. A conscript of the class of 1812, he was admitted to the 9th Tirailleurs of the Imperial Guard on 15 January 1813. He was then admitted to 1st Grenadiers on 29 September 1813, passed to Corps Royale des Grenadiers à Pied de France on 1 July 1814, and served in 4th Company of 1st Battalion. On 1 April 1815 he passed to the 1st Company of 2nd Battalion 2nd Grenadiers. He was wounded and made prisoner at Waterloo. SHDDT: GR 20 YC 13.

1027 SHDDT: C 15 5. *Dossier 18 Juin*. This is the original document. For a published version of this document see also: Charles Deulin, *Histoires du Petite Ville*, Paris, 1875.

with words that I heard not. Now came a cannonball that took off my bearskin cap and threw me on a pile of corpses.

Another eyewitness was MAT No. 3182 François Lambert,[1028] who writes:[1029]

The Imperial Guard, which formed the reserve and which had remained under the hand of Napoléon, was then ordered to move forward, and Marshal Ney walked at the head of four battalions of this formidable corps to support our cuirassiers, which had remained masters of Mont-Saint-Jean. These soldiers, inflamed by the presence of the emperor and by the encouraging phrases of their generals, went forth with an admirable resolution under the terrible fire of the enemy batteries…A considerable body of Prussians took our army exhausted by six hours of a desperate battle in our flank. Our cavalry that had remained in position was pushed back by this body and retreated hastily, and carried with them chaos into the ranks of the infantry. Wellington took advantage of this deplorable circumstance, and ordered all his cavalry to charge. From that moment everything was lost, the army fled.

The table below shows the loss of rank and file in the battalion on 18 June 1815:[1030]

2nd Grenadiers à Pied					
	Wounded	Wounded & Prisoner	Prisoner of War	Killed	Missing
1st Company	5	0	29	0	4
2nd Company	4	0	26	0	1
3rd Company	9	0	35	2	4
4th Company	2	0	24	2	7
Total	20	0	114	4	16

1028 MAT No. 3182 François Lambert was admitted to the 2nd Company of 1st Battalion 2nd Grenadiers on 1 May 1815 from the 66th Regiment of Line Infantry. Wounded and made prisoner on 18 June 1815, arguably he was in Plancenoit, unless he was moved between battalions and that has not been recorded. It is likely, however, that he is reporting what he has been told rather than witnessed. SHDDT: GR 20 YC 14.

1029 Alexandre Barginet, *Le grenadier de l'île d'Elbe. Souvenirs de 1814 et 1815* (Vol. 2), Mame et Delaunay-Vallée, Paris, 1830, pp. 320-2.

1030 Compiled from SHDDT: GR 20 YC 13. See also: SHDDT: GR 20 YC 14.

For means of comparison, 1st Battalion lost 207 men (five dead, forty-four wounded) and 2nd Battalion lost 154 men (four dead, twenty wounded). It seems on balance the fighting for 1st Battalion was costlier than for the 2nd Battalion.[1031] This is to be expected, as the 1st Battalion was involved in heavy street-fighting, whereas the 2nd acted as a rearguard.

2nd Battalion 3rd Grenadiers

Deployed on the left of the French position was the 2nd Battalion 3rd Grenadiers, alongside the 2nd Battalions of the 1st and 2nd Chasseurs. An officer, presumably of the 3rd Chasseurs, notes that:[1032]

> Napoléon approached at the moment with the 2nd Battalion of the 3rd Grenadiers, and marched towards the enemy to support some platoons not yet committed. Generals Roguet and Christiani, majors of the grenadiers, advanced at that moment with the battalions of chasseurs and grenadiers and remained far in front of La Belle Alliance. Napoléon wanted to take the offensive with these reinforcements, but the vast superiority of the enemy would not allow it, it was necessary to continue the retrograde movement, but not without a fight; the veterans of the French army did not cease to meet the enemy.
>
> The 2nd Battalion of the 3rd Grenadiers detached on the left, had long maintained, but began to fall back. The 2nd Battalion of the 1st Chasseurs, commanded by General Cambronne, went on his part to support and cover the retreat and the flank of the other battalions of the Guard.

The table below shows the loss of rank and file in the battalion on 18 June 1815:[1033]

3rd Grenadiers à Pied					
	Wounded	Wounded & Prisoner	Prisoner of War	Killed	Missing
1st Company	3	0	8	6	4
2nd Company	2	0	76	0	0
3rd Company	2	0	70	0	1
4th Company	29	0	49	0	8
Total	36	0	203	6	13

1031 ibid.

1032 V. Duprez personal communication, 21 August 2011. Transcript of a letter from the ex-Rene Cochelin collection by V. Duprez.

1033 Compiled from SHDDT: GR 20 YC 13. See also: SHDDT: GR 20 YC 14.

On 10 June 1815, the regiment was 1,158 strong; the 2nd Battalion was 579 strong. In total, 258 men were lost on 18 June, representing a loss of 45 per cent of effective strength at Waterloo.

Jamin de Bermuy charges with the duty squadron

The attack of the Old Guard was stagnating and Napoléon had no more fresh troops to feed into the action. What remained as yet uncommitted were the five squadrons of Imperial Guard cavalry that formed his own immediate escort and bodyguard. General Guyot, with what remained of the grenadiers à cheval and Empress Dragoons, collected these fresh squadrons and set out on a last great charge to try and press home the French advantage, and turn the tide of the battle in favour of the French. Colonel Pétiet, of the imperial headquarters staff, notes that:[1034]

> The service squadrons charged furiously, but were overthrown by a division of cavalry, surrounded on all sides by superior forces, the disorder began in the ranks, they shouted treason, they no longer listened to the voices of leaders. The Anglo-Belgian and Prussian forces united.

Clearly, it seems that in order to give the squares of the Guard infantry some breathing space from the Allied assault, and to drive back the cavalry, the service squadrons of the Guard cavalry were sent forward in a final charge. Captain Beraud, of the 4th Grenadiers of the Imperial Guard, recalls that:[1035]

> The Old Guard, in square, endeavoured to stop the retrograde movement which was on all sides, the divisions were so shaken that the generals could not stop the disorder, and they were no longer heard. The two service squadrons endeavoured to move forward; they were to the rear of the Old Guard and were slowed by the crowd rushing to the rear, and finally, after a while they stopped the enemy, but became carried away by the general movement to the rear. Soon the army was no more than a confused mass, and the battle was irrevocably lost.

1034 Pétiet, pp. 221-2.
1035 Beraud, pp. 285-6.

The timing of this charge is not clear. Indeed, two charges could and seem to have taken place. Lieutenant Henckens, of the 6th Chasseurs à Cheval, writes:[1036]

> 18 June, in the evening the division of Piré remained at the same height as the Imperial Guard, which we supported as long as it was in our power to do so; there were several sword blows exchanged, but we did not let ourselves be cut off.

General Guyot says:[1037]

> As I prepared to execute a third charge, I received a musket ball in the chest and a shell splinter to the left elbow, the horse I rode was killed at the same instant. I then gave my command to General Jamin, major of the regiment. He executes the third charge I had prepared, and is immediately killed. My division then withdraws from the melee under the orders of a lieutenant-colonel of dragoons. I retired to the rear exhausted with fatigue and losing much blood.

General Jamin's aide-de-camp, Captain Valery de Siriaque, says about the death of Major Jamin on 30 June 1815:[1038]

> I, captain aide-de-camp to Monsieur Marshal-du-Camp Jamin (Auguste Marie), declare that the general-major of the grenadiers à cheval of the ex-Imperial Guard charged at the head of the regiment at the Battle of Waterloo on 18 June 1815. He fell at my side as we captured several English artillery pieces that had been abandoned. The shot, which threw him off his horse, came from a square of British infantry which was to our right and that we were no more than twenty paces from; I stayed close to his body for a quarter of an hour during which time he showed no signs of life, I would not have left him, but the gunners returned to their pieces and the regiment was therefore obliged to retreat.

de Mauduit, of the Imperial Guard foot grenadiers, notes that General Guyot[1039] led the four service squadrons in a desperate charge to defend

---

1036 Henckens.

1037 Guyot.

1038 Jean-Marc Largeaud, *Napoléon et Waterloo: la defaite glorieuse de 1815 a nos jours*, La Boutique de l'histoire, Paris, 2006, p. 364.

1039 This seems unlikely, as Guyot was wounded. It seems that de Mauduit was mistaken.

the square of the 2nd Regiment of Foot Grenadiers of the Imperial Guard, commanded by Lieutenant-Colonel Martenot. de Mauduit further noted that 400 cavalry of the Imperial Guard attacked the divisions of Generals Vandeleur and Vivian. These few remaining French cavalry faced down 2,500 Allied troops.[1040]

The charge of the grenadiers à cheval and accompanying Empress Dragoons was driven back by a counterattack. This was through the timely intervention of a heavy cavalry brigade of Dutch-Belgian General Trip, supported by the British 15th Hussars and 23rd Regiment of Light Dragoons. The troops of Dutch-Belgian General van Merlen (the 5th Light Dragoons and 6th Hussars) were in reserve behind the Dutch-Belgian infantry of Chassé. At some point during this movement they came into contact again with the grenadiers à cheval.[1041] Adrien Jacques Joseph Le Mayeur, a member of the Dutch-Belgian army, writes:[1042]

> Napoléon made a division of infantry of the Guard advance, with a great number of pieces of artillery of large calibre; the brigade was exposed to a terrible fire of grape-shot. At the same time there was a brisk fire of musketry; but our square battalions protected our brigade of carabiniers, who remained immoveable. The attempts of the enemy's cavalry, in several successive charges, not having succeeded in carrying this position, Napoléon made his grenadiers advance at the *pas de charge*, towards the division of Belgic infantry and National Militia, commanded by Lieutenant-General Chassé, and placed in the right of our line.
>
> The English batteries being in want of ammunition, our fire suddenly ceased. At this moment, the Imperial Guard advanced to charge with the bayonet, thinking our artillery abandoned. It was there that Lieutenant-General Chassé ordered a most admirable manoeuvre: he made the light battery, under the orders of Major Vandersmissen, advance, which poured a most terrible fire of grape into the ranks of the enemy's grenadiers.
>
> These latter did not give ground, but they were stopped. It is impossible to describe with what fury the battle raged along the whole line. The enemy had above one hundred pieces of artillery

---

1040 de Mauduit, Vol. 2, pp. 426-7. See also: de Mauduit, p. 443.

1041 Deleveot, p. 176. See also: Deleveot, p. 209.

1042 Adrien Jacques Joseph le Mayeur, *Ode sur la Bataille de Waterloo*, Brussels, 1816, pp. 72-8.

of large calibre, and his field-pieces spread death on all sides. At six o'clock the battle was still undecided.

At half-past six, the enemy's cavalry having obtained a slight advantage over the English dragoons, who were placed on our left, made an attempt to break our regiments. The square battalions of infantry remaining firm, the brigade of carabiniers immediately charged the French cuirassiers, and made a dreadful carnage of them. The brave Belgians being mingled pell-mell with their enemies did not cease to cut them down till they met with no more resistance.

The operations on our right wing not going on so well, it was necessary to rally again upon the same position. The enemy's grape-shot again rained upon our ranks. They remained firm. Our right wing soon repulsed the obstinate efforts of the enemy to carry its position. The carabiniers made a second charge, which succeeded very well. But, the French having masked batteries within reach of which they thought to draw our Belgians; the latter, being aware of the snare, pushed forward their squadrons only till the enemy's cavalry retreated, but, instead of pursuing them, returned to their position in the line. At seven o'clock, the Prince of Orange, our hero, who had made this charge with our Belgians, crossed his sabre on the breast of Colonel de Bruyn, commanding the 2nd Regiment of Carabiniers, crying: 'resume your positions brave carabiniers, you have done enough for today'. The prince seized the colonel's hand and pressed it in so affectionate a manner that this officer with difficulty suppressed his emotion. All the carabiniers eagerly cried: 'long live the king, long live our good prince!' at the same time clashing their sabres together in the air. Scarcely were our Belgians formed again in the line when the prince, having repaired to the division of Lieutenant-General Chassé, which was posted at the extremity of our right, made it advance, waving his hat.

At this moment, he was shot through the shoulder by a Biscayen: he did not perceive his wound till he fainted, and almost fell from his horse. He was held and conveyed to the rear. Rage seemed then to take possession of our army; all swore to conquer or die. Half an hour after, 15,000 Prussians, under General Bülow, debouched on the extreme right of the French. These Prussians had not time to reconnoitre all the positions. They only repulsed some squadrons of French light horse, which went to meet them in order to stop them. A general huzzah was ordered by the general-in-chief along the whole line; carabiniers, light cavalry, all advanced. This third charge was terrible and decisive.

With the French cavalry driven off, the scene was set for a dramatic fight back by the Allies. Without orders from Wellington, and acting upon his own initiative, Dutch-Belgian General Chassé ordered a counter-attack that was to seal the fate of the French. He writes as follows about his pivotal role in the battle:[1043]

> I have determined to tell you the reasons which caused me to advance without having received any orders and to attack the Imperial Guard at the *pas de charge*. When I saw the English artillery battery positioned on the left and forward of my division had stopped firing, I went to enquire the reason and learned that there was no ammunition. At the same time I saw the Imperial Guard advancing, while the English troops were leaving the plateau en masse and moving in the direction of Waterloo [these were probably the 33rd, 69th and 73rd Regiments of Foot]; the battle seemed lost.
>
> I immediately ordered the battery of horse artillery under the command of Major van der Smissen to advance and occupy the height, and to direct emphatic fire upon the enemy column. At this time I also ordered Major-General d'Aubreme to have the brigade he commanded form two squares in echelon and to form a reserve with the foot artillery.
>
> I positioned myself at the head of the 1st Brigade and advanced in closed columns at attack pace against the French (Lieutenant-Colonel Thiele was killed in this attack and was replaced by Captain Buhlmann). Having closed to within a few paces of the enemy I observed they made a rearward movement, and I pursued them on foot until the onset of darkness prevented us from continuing any further.

Carl van Delen, chief-of-staff of the 3rd Netherlands Infantry Division, concurs with what Chassé says, and notes in a letter of 19 June 1815:[1044]

> Towards the evening, General Baron Chassé noted that the English artillery in front of our position on a height had almost stopped firing, and had certainly diminished its fire, and he went forward with the utmost haste to know the reason for this; as he heard that they lacked ammunition and as he also saw the French Imperial Guard manoeuvre to attack this artillery, he did not lose a moment

---

1043 Franklin, Vol. 1, p 116.
1044 ibid, p.125.

to order our artillery, commanded by Major van der Smissen, to advance upon the height and commence a strong fire.

Meanwhile an English aide-de-camp came to Colonel Detmers and rode off quickly again, having ordered him to place himself with three battalions in the first line, whereupon the colonel marched with the 35th Jäger Battalion, the 2nd Line Battalion and the 4th National Militia Battalion in columns by division, marching up the slope of the height on which the English army had its position, in such a way that the battalions were partly covered from the musketry with bayonets fixed.

A Dutch infantryman belonging to General Chassé's division notes that:[1045]

The French made an about-turn and threw away their muskets, cartridge boxes, backpacks and even the caps from their heads, and our young men came forward with the bayonet to follow them. And our cavalry and that of the English came in between and hacked away at everything that came before them.

On the Allied right, Adams's brigade and the Foot Guards also played their own role in the defeat of the Imperial Guard. An officer in Adams's brigade, which comprised the 52nd, 71st and 95th Rifles, notes in 1815:[1046]

After the various hot, though desultory, attacks of the day, the last and most dreadful was made by the Old Imperial Guard, grown grey in an uninterrupted career of victory; in black massive solid columns, supported and covered by the fire of a numerous artillery, they advanced, in spite of the most desperate resistance. Lord Hill, who had foreseen the approaching storm, having formed General Adams's brigade a little *en potence* on the enemy's left, placed himself at its head, and advanced with dreadful regularity to the assistance of the Guards. General Adams's veterans of the Peninsula, after one terrible volley within a few yards of the Imperial Guard, cheered and charged; these gallant troops for the first time fled, although encouraged to the last by the conduct of the brave, but unfortunate, Ney. Lord Hill followed with his usual rapidity, the British guards supporting him, and at the same instant, our great duke ordered the general and decisive advance of the whole army; the enemy still rallied a few scattered hundreds here and there, but all combined resistance was at an end.

1045 John Franklin personal communication, 2 May 2012.
1046 ibid.

A Dutch writer notes that a combination of Chassé's Dutch-Belgians, Maitland's 1st Foot Guards and Adams's light division threw back the advance of the Imperial Guard and the 2nd Corps, and is probably a good summary of the events which took place:[1047]

> Napoléon placed himself in the Middle Guard and tried to pierce our centre, ordering the cuirassiers to attack by passing the big battery on the elevation of Mont-Saint-Jean. Believing was the only way to save this attack, he ordered Marshal Ney and General Friant at the head of the column, which, in narrow rows, and by a forced march with tremendous force, shouting 'long live the emperor!' walked through the valley in the centre of the English guards, commanded by General Maitland. Of the multitudes of the enemy, it is true, many were put down by our artillery, but the attack also continued undaunted and furiously.
>
> Our valiant hero, however, stood like a wall.
>
> The Duke of Wellington had anticipated this moment. The reserve and the brigade of General Adams advanced from Braine and the Leud descended the side of the French column. This resistance and the fire made them withdraw. The division of General Chassé also arrived, the brigade of Colonel Ditmar attacked with the bayonet and was supported with fire from a squad of the National Militia, Artillery Major van der Smissen also advanced the light cavalry under the orders of General Vivian to the left...Ney fell from his horse and General Friant was mortally wounded. This moment is no exception to Wellington. He ordered all the cavalry to attack. The Prince of Orange was wounded. At the same time he encouraged his triumphant troops. Now advanced the Dutch hussars, commanded by Colonel Boreel, and attacked the right wing of the enemy.

Under immense pressure, the grenadiers (and what remained of the French cavalry) retreated down the slope and reformed at the foot of the hill leading to La Haye Sainte in an attempt to draw the Dutch-Belgians against the French artillery and formed French infantry, which would have shot the cavalry to pieces.[1048]

About the role of the Netherlands troops in this tipping point of the battle, Brevet-Subaltern J. B. van Doren, of the 5th Light Dragoons,

---

1047 Everts Masskamp, *Description de la Bataille Glorieuse Waterloo*, 1818, pp. 12-14.
1048 Deleveot, p. 176. See also: Deleveot, p. 209.

confirming the pivotal role played by General Chassé in the battle, writes:[1049]

> Three regiments of French cuirassiers, together with a regiment of lancers, made several charges on these squares to enter them, but were fruitless, whereupon Napoléon had a division of infantry of his Guard with several heavy artillery pieces advance to attack both squares; but protected by the Netherlands carabiniers and cuirassiers they remained firm. As the attempt of the French cavalry, which made several charges to become in control of the position, were fruitless, Napoléon had his grenadiers march at *au pas de charge* towards the Netherlands division, under command of General Chassé, and which stood to the right of the Allied line. Here, a heavy fight took place and the Guard had to retreat, many were killed. It is impossible to describe with what tenacity one then fought along the entire line. The enemy had more than one hundred pieces of heavy artillery and the pieces of his field artillery made destruction on all points.

> Around six o'clock in the afternoon the battle was still uncertain, when the French cavalry gained a small advantage upon a regiment of English dragoons, which was on the left flank of the English line. As the squares of infantry remained firm, the Belgian carabiniers charged upon the French cuirassiers and caused a terrible bloodbath. The Belgians, mixed with the enemy, sabred until they found no more resistance. As the operations on the right wing of the English didn't go well, they had to return to the same position.

> At that time the enemy canister flew through the ranks on all points, but the Netherlands troops remained firm, while those on the right flank soon repelled the obstinate attempt to take their position. The Belgian carabiniers made a second charge with the Prince of Orange at their head, which went very well. The French, who had masked batteries in order to lure the carabiniers, had their hopes deceived, as this was discovered in time and the carabiniers didn't charge further than the point where the French seemingly retired. During the charge, the prince shouted to the carabiniers: '*allons mes camarades, sabrons les Français, la victoire est à nous*'. Afterwards he crossed his sabre on the chest of Colonel de Bruin, who commanded the regiment, and shouted to the carabiniers: '*reprenez vos positions, mes braves carabiniers: vous en avez assez fait aujourd'hui*'. He also shook the colonel's hand for which this officer was flattered, where

---

1049 J. B. J. van Doren.

upon the carabiniers again took their former position, under the calls of: *'vive le roi, vive notre bon prince'*.

The timely intervention of the heavy cavalry brigade of Dutch-Belgian General Trip, supported by the British 15th Hussars and 23rd Regiment of Light Dragoons as noted earlier, pushed back the French cavalry. With the troops of General Chassé having pushed back the attack of the Old Guard, the Prussians attacking and driving back Napoléon's right wing in a pincer movement, the light cavalry of Vandeleur and Vivian was launched at the Old Guard. This was to be the *coup de grâce* and cement the Allied victory over Napoléon. The appearance of these six British regiments, the 1st, 10th, 11th, 12th, 16th, and 18th, which had not yet been seriously involved in the action, greatly revived the spirits of the harassed troops. About this time two brigades of Prussian infantry and a brigade of cavalry, part of General Bülow's troops, had arrived at their intended position in a wood, on the right flank of the enemy. With the Imperial Guard cavalry being pushed back by the charge of the Dutch-Belgian cavalry in support of the Dutch-Belgian infantry of General David Chassé, General Vandeleur's brigade, with the assistance of what remained of Sir William Ponsonby's command and also the command of Sir Hussey Vivian, made a charge which changed the face of things, by putting the remaining French infantry and cavalry into confusion. From this time, and at the advance of the British line, these four brigades were of most vital and important service to Wellington in securing his victory. Confirming this event that the Allied cavalry scattered the Imperial Guard, a sergeant of the 1st Foot Guards writes about the attack and defeat of the Imperial Guard:[1050]

> We allowed our powerful opponents to come near enough so we might make short work of them, although one would have thought that their notion was that they had nothing to do but to run over us. When they came to about fifty yards or so from us, the duke cried 'now guardsmen, up and at them'. We poured one volley after another into them till the cry was given 'charge!' I noticed as the cloud of smoke took the air and when we passed over the ground they occupied I could have stepped off one part of man on to another for about a square acre—so great was the havoc we made among these giant-like men. I have mentioned that we had great difficulty in wading through the dead and wounded. Just at

---

1050 *Glasgow Herald*, 20 June 1866.

this moment a regiment of our light dragoons came dashing out, and as they passed cried out 'bravo guardsmen, you have lathered them, we will shave them'. I noticed at this time when looking up at the main body of the French army, that our quarry was beginning to melt away like snow before a bright sun. We chased them as far as La Belle Alliance. Then we took up our ground for the night. After we had piled our arms on the opposite side of the road from the farmhouse, the cry was raised that Wellington and Old Blücher had met.

The Allied cavalry now fell on the Old Guard, and whatever French infantry stood in their path. Sir Hussey Vivian describes what happened:[1051]

At this time, I heard infantry advancing and drums beating on my left, but the smoke was still so thick that I could see but little. When I had fully quitted the position, and was probably about midway to that of the enemy, it became clear, and several French columns of infantry were visible immediately in our front, with cavalry and guns formed on the flanks and between them. At this moment Sir Colin Campbell came to me from the Duke of Wellington, who was, so I understood, somewhere on the left, by his Grace's order, he having observed that we were more advanced of the infantry, and to desire me 'not to attack before the infantry arrived, unless I thought I could break the enemy's squares'. About the same moment, a severe fire of grape, by which several men in the leading squadron of the 10th were killed and wounded, was directed at us.

I observed to Sir Colin Campbell 'that as our infantry, in their anxiety to get on, were probably not in compact order, it might be dangerous should the French cavalry attack them; and that I thought it were better at once to drive off the latter, leaving the squares to be attacked by our infantry'. He agreed with me, and returned to the duke; and I continued my advance immediately afterwards, ordering the 10th and 18th into one line, and the 1st Hussars into the second.

It was while we were forming that the small body of the 23rd and Germans passed along our front at full speed, at about thirty yards from us; and I well recollect seeing one of the French hussars (several of whom were hovering in our front) in a most inhuman manner ride up, and with his pistol deliberately blow out the brains

---

1051 *Dublin University Magazine*, August 1833.

of one of those men whose horse had fallen, while he was struggling to disengage himself, and some of the soldiers felt so indignant at the time that there was a groan of execration, and an exclamation 'no quarter to them!'

Before the formation was quite completed, the right squadron of the 10th was attacked by the French cuirassiers and lost many men. The brigade was at that time so much in advance of all the other troops of the British army, that while the French were firing grape at us, shot and spherical case from our own guns fell among us.

So, clearly for Sir Hussey Vivian, the Imperial Guard was defeated by the Allied cavalry, no doubt assisted by the musketry of the 1st Foot Guards and also the other Allied infantry still formed on the Allied right wing.

Captain Taylor, of the 10th Hussars, remembers a charge against the French cavalry close to the end of the day. The red uniforms noted are either the Red Lancers of the Imperial Guard, or a French line lancer regiment, either the 1st or 2nd Regiment; the dragoons could either be the 2nd, 7th or those of the Imperial Guard, and the lancers in white could possibly be the Polish Lancers, as some officers did indeed wear white. Therefore, on balance these cavalry concerned are likely to be the Imperial Guard:[1052]

The last attack of the French being repulsed, we were ordered to advance in column right in front and to gallop. A staff officer met us (Colonel Harvey, I think) and said 'come along,' when I told him in passing that our right squadron was behind and begged him to rectify it. This I believe he did, or probably told Sir H. Vivian, for the right squadron came up at a great pace and took its situation at the head of the column. Before we passed the guns I remembered [saying] to Lord R. Manners that there was no squadron officer to the right squadron. Sir G. Quentin, having been wounded, Lord R. Manners took the command of the regiment, which vacated the squadron. I think he ordered Lieut Arnold to command it. I do not remember Major Howard changing from the left.

As we advanced at a gallop we saw the French army retiring in confusion up the hill, presenting a most picturesque sight of a mixture of all arms and uniforms. Some guns in their rear were firing, and there was also some musketry. At this time I conceive

---

1052 Siborne, *Waterloo Letters*, No. 75.

Lord Uxbridge was wounded near the left of our regiment. One of our officers told me he saw him fall. The Guards and other infantry were advancing in close columns on our left and cheered. I believe the Duke of Wellington was near them, observing our advance. There were some corps of French cavalry—one very conspicuous with red uniforms or red facings and red crests, also dragoons in green and French lancers white, formed to the right to protect the retreat. Sir H. Vivian led us towards these, bringing up the left shoulders rather and gave the order 'front, form line'. Each squadron formed, but the head was going so fast that we scarce got into line, rather *en echelon* of squadrons.

As we neared the enemy, a squadron, or half-squadron, of a light dragoon regiment with red facings, either the 23rd or some Germans, pushed rather in advance of our right rather obliquely. The lancers couched their lances and made a gallant charge down the hill and turned them.

Our right squadron came upon the lancers and sent them about; the dragoons in green charged to support the lancers, and the centre squadron came upon them, and the whole broke and fled, our men cutting in among them. Bringing up the right shoulders rather and passing over a hill we were halted and rallying. A square of French infantry was formed in a hollow under the road. Sir H. Vivian appeared to be preparing to attack them with the 18th. I do not know the result, as Lord R. Manners led us on in pursuit up the hill across the road, where we passed infantry, who surrendered and abandoned guns. Coming to the brow of the hill we found three or four companies about rallied and formed with cavalry close behind them. They commenced a fire; Lord R. Manners halted a minute to form and then charged. They turned and fled, and our men pursued to the brow of a hill with a steep dip beyond it on the opposite side. On a knoll another square of infantry was formed. Our men being much scattered I began to collect them and retired to join the rest of the regiment, which I found halted and forming, telling off, etc. and commenced collecting the squadron.

Before I left the last hill my horse was so knocked up he could hardly go, and I was going to change him for a French one. But, Sir H. Vivian coming up and expressing himself satisfied with the regiment, and that we should have no more to do that night, I desisted from changing my saddle. Just as I was coming back I saw about thirty of the 18th pass and dash down into the hollow and gallantly, though uselessly, charge the square on the hill, by which they were repulsed. It was now dusk and I remember several shells pitching at no great distance, whether thrown by friend or foe was difficult to say. In a little time we advanced and met many prisoners under the escort of light dragoons. We halted on rising ground. There was now fine moonlight.

Somewhere between La Haye Sainte and La Belle Alliance, Napoléon drew up the 1st Grenadiers and battalions from other regiments of the Old Guard to try and stem the Allied advance and flight of the French army. About what happened next, Louis-Etienne Saint-Denis, otherwise known as the Mameluck Ali, narrates that:[1053]

> Night began to cover the battlefield with its shadow when Marshal Blücher came on line against our right and brought disorder into some French regiments, and this disorder, spreading gradually became general soon after. It was necessary that the Guard should make a change of front and then it should be formed into squares, in one of which the emperor took refuge with his followers to escape the Prussian cavalry which flooded the battlefield.

We are often told that with the French Imperial Guard pushed back, Lord Wellington ordered a general advance of the Allied Line. However, this does not appear to have immediately followed the repulse of the Imperial Guard. British General Byng notes:[1054]

> The general movement forward did not commence until ten or twelve minutes after the Imperial Guard had been repulsed.

It seems impossible that the Allied infantry could advance until the sector of the battlefield was clear of the Allied light cavalry. Furthermore, it seems incredible that the 71st did not see any of the Allied cavalry. The term 'tirailleur' implies that the troops opposite the 71st were French sharpshooters as opposed to the Old Guard, further suggesting that the troops the 71st moved against were from the 2nd Corps. The French troops were pushed down the slopes of the plateau from the front and flank by an ever-increasing number of Allied infantry and cavalry. The retreat to the French starting positions took time, with the Guard and line losing men both to casualties and desertion, with men running for their lives.

1053 Ali.
1054 Siborne, *Waterloo Letters*, No. 261.

William Hay, of the 12th Light Dragoons, tells us that at 7 p.m. his regiment had moved to the British right flank, and were drawn up to the left of the 1st Foot Guards, and the right of Adams's brigade. Clearly, for Hay at least, like Vandeleur and others as cited in the previous chapter, it was the cavalry and not the infantry that won the day. The infantry checked the French attack, and thence the cavalry clinched the victory. The general advance of the Allied infantry then occurred behind the cavalry screen which swept all before it.[1055] By 22.00, the battle was lost and the French army was endeavouring to retreat (where regiments still had cohesion); others simply dissolved into a sea of fugitives.

1055 William Hay, *William Hay Reminiscences 1808-1815: under Wellington,* Simpkin, Marshall, Hamilton, Kent, & Co Ltd, London, 1901, pp 187-90.

Chapter 22

Defeat

By 20.30, the 2nd Grenadiers and chasseurs had pulled back out of Plancenoit, and were positioned at the crossroads behind La Haye Sainte, and thence at La Belle Alliance, as testified by Lambert de Steurs and General Pelet.[1056] A Prussian account graphically narrates the scene:[1057]

> Despite their great courage and stamina, the French Guards fighting in the village were beginning to show signs of wavering. The church was already on fire with columns of red flame coming out of the windows, aisles and doors. In the village itself was a scene of bitter hand-to-hand fighting; everything was burning, adding to the confusion.
>
> However, once Major von Winztleben's manoeuvre was accomplished the French Guards saw their flank and rear threatened, they began to withdraw. The Guard chasseurs, under General Pelet, formed the rearguard. The remnants of the Guard left in a great rush, leaving large numbers of artillery, equipment and ammunition wagons in the wake of their retreat. These spoils of war went to the victor. The evacuation of Plancenoit led to the loss of the position that was to be used to cover the withdrawal of the French army to Charleroi. The Guard fell back from Plancenoit in the direction of Maison du Roi and La Caillou.

Another Prussian eyewitness notes:[1058]

1056 Pawly and Courcelle, p. 34. See also: d'Avout, pp. 51-2.
1057 Ludwig Stawitzky, *Geschichte des Königlich Preussichen 25ten Infanterie-Regiments. Koblenz*, 1857, p. 106.
1058 Wagner, p. 94.

The French defended this position until the very end. Generals Duhesme and Barrois were wounded, General Pelet struck into the village, but all these efforts merely delayed the utter defeat of the French. They were all thrown out of the village and the Allied cavalry flooded the field. All the outputs of the village were taken by the fusilier battalion of the 2nd Regiment.

Grolman, one of Blücher's senior staff officers in the campaign, writes:[1059]

> General Pelet fought with unwavering courage in the middle of the village, but all these efforts could not inhibit the inexorable advance of the Prussian troops. The French were completely thrown out of the village and pursued by the Prussian cavalry.
>
> Colonel von Hiller, who led his brigade from the beginning of the action on the fight against Plancenoit, and later joined by the 14th, and was only later supported by the 5th Brigade, stormed completely trough Plancenoit, it was the decisive blow, and he is due the credit for the attack.
>
> From the French must be said, however, that they defended the village with the utmost resolution for half an hour, and that this distinguished especially the Old Imperial Guard, who were prepared to die to get their eagle bound with black crape from the village.

We should note here that Pelet did not take the eagle of the chasseurs into Plancenoit. Only much later did he come across the eagle of the 1st Chasseurs. At the entrance to the village, General Pelet rallied as many men as he could to prevent the Prussians flooding onto the Brussels road and blocking the line of retreat. As Plancenoit fell, Durutte's resistance at Frischermont and Papelotte collapsed:[1060]

> Around seven o'clock, we realised that our two wings faltered. That's when the emperor decided to make an effort on the centre, with part of the Guard which until then he had held in reserve.
>
> He observed advancing along the main road heading to the left onto the heights, where the enemy had numerous artillery batteries, the head of a column of grenadiers. The sinuosity of the land did not

---

1059 Karl von Damitz, *Geschichte des Feldzuges von 1815 in den Niederlanden und Frankreich* (Vol. 1), E. S. Mittler, Berlin, 1838, p. 312.

1060 *La Sentinelle de l'Armée*, 4th Year, No. 134, 8 March 1838.

permit General Durutte to see what was happening on this point. He was busy watching over a column of cavalry approaching on his right flank.

He sent several officers from his staff to notify the emperor. He then made his dispositions to cope with this approaching column that seemed to be very strong. All of a sudden, he saw on the road a lot of French soldiers who were retreating. Part approached the four 12-pounders that General d'Erlon had at its disposal: they communicated this terror to drivers and gunners of this battery.

He saw the battery flee at full gallop despite the efforts of the officers of his staff who could not stop it. He then marched with the brigade of Brue towards the main road to try to stop the fugitives, and to try and make them rally behind this brigade which was in perfect order and fairly calm. Their efforts were fruitless. He could see the corps on the left fall back quickly. As General Durutte was about the most advanced, he foresaw that he would soon be surrounded by the enemy if he did not begin a retrograde movement. He executed this movement with the intention of endeavouring to cross the road to try to rally with the brigade of General Pégot, who was on the other side, and which had, on arrival of the emperor, been prescribed to follow the movements of the Guard.

He met at this time General d'Erlon, who was alone with some officers of his staff, and General Garbe. General d'Erlon promised to stay with General Durutte and march with the brigade, which probably was the only company of his army corps which was in order at this moment: everything retreated in confusion.

The body of cavalry that General Durutte observed was Prussian. With Plancenoit lost, the Prussians flooded on the battlefield, cutting off any chance Napoléon had of covering his retreat and fighting a rearguard action. As Napoléon watched the Old Guard assail the Allied right, the Prussians broke through what remained of Lobau's line, and reached La Haye Sainte. The French army broke and fled in a sea of fugitives. Napoléon's last great gamble had failed. With no field commander for the French right wing to co-ordinate the defence against the Prussian onslaught, Generals Mouton and Pelet were left abandoned to their fate while Napoléon concentrated his efforts on the French left. Indeed, Napoléon seems to have been ignorant of the operations undertaken by Lobau on the French right. Only too late, when the Prussians broke through Lobau's meagre defences and attacked La Haye Sainte, did Napoléon perhaps realise that his last gamble had totally failed.

Sergeant-Major Jean Michel Chevalier, of the chasseurs à cheval of the Imperial Guard, confirms the sequence of events:[1061]

> Napoléon himself reformed the Guard and started at the head of four battalions of the Old Guard and marched in haste on to La Haye Sainte, where Marshal Ney was forced to retreat. He leaves his four battalions and ordered him to resume the main force of the plateau of Mont-Saint-Jean. The brave soldiers, despite the resistance, resume their first position. Marshal Ney, his horse killed under him, walked on foot at the head of the grenadiers.
>
> General Friant, with the other eight battalions of the Guard, falls on the enemy. The general was wounded, but the invincible battalions marching in close column, under a hail of bullets and shrapnel, and supported by their artillery, steadfast like walls and iron; they always marched forward knocking away everything in their path. Across the action the carnage is awful, for a moment victory is definitely with us and we 60,000 men had beaten 125,000.
>
> Everything is well. But, suddenly, a cry of alarm is heard. Blücher has possession of La Haye Sainte. This move cut our army in two.

Sergeant Caumartin, of the Old Guard foot artillery, provides an invaluable eyewitness account that confirms the narrative of Napoléon, Chevallier and Pontécoulant.[1062]

Caumartin was in command of the 2nd Half-Battery of 12-pounders of 3rd Company Old Guard Foot Artillery. He narrates in his account, written in the third person, that he recalls seeing the emperor in a nearby square, likely to be the 2nd Battalion 3rd Grenadiers, and that his half-battery was placed on a small rise in the ground. I think that this is very probably the position just south of the monument to the fallen eagle, where the field is about five feet above the main road and the little cobbled lane which runs along from the monument itself. This was probably the same battery deployed earlier in the day to support the 2nd Battalion 3rd Grenadiers.

In the defence of the last square, and to cover the retreating French army, Caumartin claims that he opened fire against the mass of British and Allied cavalry, and that it was one of his canister rounds that removed the leg of General Uxbridge, noting that he had never seen canister shot have such an effect as it did in this battle.

1061 Chevalier, p. 325.
1062 Ian Smith personal communication.

Caumartin, in his letter, says he endeavoured to fight his way back to the Brussels road, but was unsupported in this movement. It was here that the Prussians attacked the battery and in fifteen shots killed or wounded what remained of the gunners, drivers and horses of the battery. Caumartin's battery fired some of the last shots of the Battle of Waterloo.[1063] But, for the Prussians to be at, or close to, where the fallen eagle monument is today implies that the French right wing had totally collapsed during the attack of the Old Guard, and the Prussians were attacking the retreating Old Guard as it fled down the Brussels road. Colonel Gourgaud, attached to imperial headquarters, realising that all was lost comments:[1064]

> The attack of the Guard having failed, I judge the case to be lost, I try to get myself killed, I met Officer of Ordinance Amillet,[1065] and he stopped me from throwing myself in the midst of enemies.
>
> The disorder was around me in our ranks; cries of 'save us, we are cut off' can be heard. The attack of the Prussians on our right was again renewed with new fury during our general movement on the centre of the English. Mouton and Duhesme were crushed by their number and finally the army of Blücher fires their cannon on the road along which we were fleeing.

Caught up in the sea of fugitives and Allied troops at the end of the battle were the 2nd Battalion 3rd Grenadiers. Sergeant de Mauduit, of the 1st Grenadiers, narrates:[1066]

> The remaining battalions of the Guard maintained the retreat in square, disputing the ground inch-by-inch against the masses of all arms. Still, these *triaircs* of the French army, disorganised by the fugitives and wounded, driven by the multitude that swirls around them, crushed by the shock of a whole army, they succumb, some on the plateau others in the ravines that lead to La Belle Alliance, but there they die without being defeated. Allow us to give evidence here for the last moments of one of these battalions now immortal, and whose memory will bear more of a prodigy value!

1063 Anon, *Memoires pour servir a l'Histoire de France*, Richard Phillips & Co, London, 1820, p. 135.

1064 *Nouvelle Revue Retrospective*, Paris, January 1896, pp. 375-6.

1065 Chevalier Pierre Hippolyte Amillet, captain-ordinance-officer to Napoléon at Waterloo.

1066 de Mauduit, Vol.2, pp. 445-6.

The 2nd Battalion of the 3rd Grenadier Regiment, commanded by Lieutenant-Colonel Belcourt, was, we said, led by Napoléon himself, to Goumont, and left there like a sentinel lost, because it would have to bear almost alone, for beyond an hour, while the first shock of the cavalry and light artillery descended from the plateau of La Haye Sainte. The balls, shells and grapeshot fell on them, and they did experience significant losses.

Nevertheless, they did not move from the place, only tightened its ranks, losing men at each discharge, left hardly a quarter of the men and 150 grenadiers from the 550 were soon lying on the ground.

First-Lieutenant Bernelle, of the 2nd Battalion 3rd Grenadiers, notes how he played dead to prevent the Prussians murdering him. He noted he was:[1067]

One of the last to fall, musket in hand, the sword had become useless. Wounded at Ligny, seriously wounded at Waterloo, feigned death to avoid being killed, for he knew that the Prussians in the rage against us would sabre those that were left alive. For additional misfortune, his body was bruised by the feet of their horses.

At nightfall, he dressed his wounds as best he could, and walked over the ground soaked with the blood of his comrades and arrived at Genappe at midnight. The place was protected by troops who had kept a little order in their ranks. A hundred metres from this small town he saw some soldiers who deposited on the side of the road a mortally wounded colonel, leaving him to die under the stars and in the care of God.

This incident was probably one of many that took place on the night and early morning of 19 June 1815. MAT No. 1872 Edme Dumesgnil,[1068] fourrier of 3rd Company of 1st Battalion 4th Grenadiers, narrates that:[1069]

1067 Cornevin, *Les Marchands de vin de Paris*, Les Prinicpaux Libraries, Paris, 1869, pp. 64-5.

1068 SHDDT: GR 20 YC 13. MAT No. 1872 Edme Dumesgnil, born on 15 February 1794, was conscripted to the 8th Hussars on 28 February 1812, promoted to corporal on 15 May 1812, fourrier on 15 September 1812, to sergeant on 16 November 1812, admitted to the Royale Corps des Grenadiers à Pied de France on 8 November 1814, wounded and made prisoner of war on 18 June 1815. See also: AN: LH 1843/43. Edme du Mesgnil was born on 15 February 1794, promoted to sub-lieutenant in the 8th Regiment of Line Infantry in 1817, awarded the Legion of Honour in 1831, the Officer of the Legion of Honour in 1858 and died in 1873.

1069 de Mauduit, Vol. 2, pp. 450-5.

All that first night there was a constant rattle of men breathing their last! When the sun rose, this scene presented itself in all its horror: English, French and Brunswickers were all jumbled together. The dead, piled one upon another as they had fallen, the wounded and maimed more so, also extended such that the 1st had the fire knocked down. Those who had had the strength to drag himself had gathered and sought to console each other by talking of their families and their homeland that most, unfortunately, would no longer see. Here, there were more enemies, as they were also unfortunate.

Seven or eight hundred men, 200 grenadiers, approximately covering the surface of a hundred yards square, some rigid, others dying and mutilated at least sitting on their haunches, waiting for someone come to meet them.

Not far away, in a ravine, a creek was still fed by the rains of the night before. The less seriously injured were going to fetch water, they brought back in their helmets, their fur cap or shako, and then distributed, sometimes dragging himself on his knees, with their comrades in misfortune, without distinction of uniform, and had more so of a relief to a less cruel agony.

The language is different, one could not speak, but consoled himself and input helped him by signs.

Similar scenes took place at a hundred yards away, where the battalion had so bravely repulsed the first three charges.

Wounded were still dying long after the battle in British custody. Pierre Sanson, voltigeur of the 25th Regiment of Line Infantry, died on Bastille Day 1815 due to his wounds; he had been captured at Charleroi. Private Jean Paunstol, of the 22nd Regiment of Line Infantry, died on 18 August 1815 from an 'abscess of the brain caused by a fractured skull' and Martial Leroy, of the 28th Regiment of Line Infantry, died due to infected gunshot wounds on 23 August, as did Pierre Gerard, of the 73rd Regiment of Line Infantry, a few days later on 25 August. The same fate befell Claude Loraine, of the 4th Regiment of Light Infantry, captured at Quatre-Bras and who died of gangrene on 29 September 1815. Jean Pachet, a private with the 54th Regiment of Line Infantry, and captured at Quatre-Bras and died on 22 September due to a sabre wound to the skull which had become infected. He died on 16 September. Sergeant Etienne Laprelle, of the 6th Regiment of Foot Artillery, died aged thirty-four on 18 July 1815 from 'sabre wounds'. Captured at Genappe was Louis Delussier, who died after an above-the-knee amputation of the right leg. The same fate befell Claude Maubert, of the 100th Regiment of Line Infantry, who also died following amputation of a leg. Gangrene infection of a musket ball to the left hip was the cause of death of Jean Guianmaris, of the 13th Regiment of Light Infantry. He was captured at Waterloo and died on 1 September. Claude Rigole, of the 44th Regiment of Line Infantry, died on 23 October 1815 due to infection of the gunshot wound to the head; a musket ball passed through both cheeks. Jean Baptiste Morette, of the 54th Regiment of Line Infantry, was captured at Waterloo. He died on 17 November from an 'abscess of the brain after a gunshot wound to skull'. As well as wounds, men in captivity died from other ailments. Joseph Vambro, of the 26th Regiment of Line Infantry, died from dysentery on 14 July 1815, as did Jean Morain, also of the 26th Regiment of Line Infantry.[1070]

By now it was 22.30; the sun would set in half an hour. The battle had lasted nearly twelve hours as the French retreated to Genappe. The Prussians had re-taken Plancenoit, the assault of the Guard infantry had faltered and failed. As the infantry retreated, the Guard artillery was ordered to cover the retreat. Napoléon sought safety in the square of the 1st Regiment of Grenadiers à Pied of the Imperial Guard. What remained of the Guard cavalry endeavoured to cover the retreat of the French army.

The arrival of the Prussians on the battlefield, which had bled Napoléon's right flank dry from around 16.00, had robbed the French army of at least half its manpower, with what remained of 1st Corps, 6th Corps, the entire Young Guard and two battalions of the Old Guard being pinned down in a vicious struggle between Papelotte and Rossome. The Prussian attack on the French right was the vital tipping point of the battle. The collapse of the French right wing sealed the fate of Napoléon's army and secured victory. The defeat of the Imperial Guard was now a foregone conclusion. Because the story of Waterloo is primarily Anglo-phonic, the defeat of the Imperial Guard by the 'plucky band of redcoats' is seen as the great deciding moment of the day, thanks to Wellington's guiding genius. The truth is that the victory owed everything to Blücher, Zeithen and Bülow. The defeat of the Guard made the defeat far more total and hastened the end of the Armée du Nord.

The breakthrough of the Prussians broke the will and remaining resolve of the French army. Total chaos spread through the French ranks. Within minutes most of the French units were completely destroyed.

1070 National Archives, Kew: ADM 103. Report on dead prisoners of war 1796 to 1815.

Aide-de-camp to Marshal Ney, Octave Levavasseur, notes the panic that gripped the French army with the arrival of the Prussians, which in his narrative occurred before the Imperial Guard advanced:[1071]

> Shortly after arriving at the end of our line, cannon shots are heard in our rear. There came a great silence, amazement and worry about our enthusiasm to succeed. The plain is covered with our horse teams and the multitude of non-combatants who still follow the army; and the gunfire continues to approach. Officers and soldiers mingle, mingle with non-combatants. I went, overwhelmed, with the marshal, who prescribed me to go find the cause of this panic. I happened to General [name left blank by the author] who said: 'look! These are the Prussians!' I go looking for the marshal, but I cannot find him. Our army then formed but a shapeless mass, where all the regiments were combined. In that fatal moment, there is no command, each remains prohibited in the presence of a hazard that cannot be defined. Drouot exclaimed: 'Where is the Guard? Where is the Guard?' I showed him, he approaches it, shouting 'form square!' Then I see the emperor pass by me, followed by his officers. He arrived near his guard, placed in front of him, on the other side of the road. The 150 musicians came down ahead of the Guard, playing the triumphal marches of the carrousel. Soon, the road was covered with the Guard who marched by platoons past the emperor. Cannonball and canister shot thundered onto the left side of the road, which became littered with dead and wounded. A few more steps and Napoléon would have been alone at their head. Undoubtedly, the first resolution was to shut himself up in the square and wait for death, the second to die advancing. However, amidst the carnage, behind the square on the road, I saw a group of mounted officers: I think I recognised the emperor. I ran to this group, it was Napoléon indeed, that death had spared…our disorganised army, whose heads of column fled in great disorder on Genappe, filled the road. I followed some time the emperor and his staff, and each kept the most profound silence. However, thinking that I had to join the marshal, I retraced my steps and looked in vain, for it was then that was the danger from our rear.

The Prussian fusilier battalion of the 15th Regiment, and that of the 1st Silesian Landwehr, under Major Keller, as well as the men of the 25th Regiment, under Major Witzleben, pursued the defeated Imperial Guard in the direction of Maison du Roi and come into contact with the 1st Battalion 1st Chasseurs, which had advanced from La Caillou.[1072]

1071 Levavasseur, pp. 303-5.
1072 Wagner, pp. 94-6.

The 1st Battalion of the 1st Chasseurs had spent the day at La Caillou under the orders of Battalion-Commander Duuring.[1073] Duuring narrates the end of the battle as follows:[1074]

1073 Jan Coenraad Duuring was born on 13 January 1779 in Rotterdam. He began his military career on 15 February 1796 as a cadet in the 2nd Battalion of the Batavian army and participated in campaigns this year and the next. On 2 January 1798, he was transferred to the frigate *The Juno* and became a naval lieutenant on 2 January 1799 and was promoted to first-lieutenant on 20 March 1801. Appointed on 6 April 1802 to first-lieutenant in the 22nd Infantry Battalion, he was then stationed at the Cape of Good Hope, in the Dutch East Indies. In January 1806, after the capitulation of Cape Town and the surrender of the English Governor Janssens, he returned to The Netherlands with his battalion as a captain in the army of King Louis Napoléon of Holland on 12 December 1806. On 22 April 1809, he entered with the rank of captain into the regiment of Grenadiers of the Royal Guard of Holland. He participated in the siege of Stralsund and the capture of the Corps Franc Schill on 31 April 1809, and was wounded in this action. He was promoted to colonel on 11 June 1809 and received the Knight's Cross of the Order of the Union on 19 November 1809. In 1810, during the annexation of Holland to the empire, his regiment was incorporated into the Imperial Guard and he became battalion-commander of the 2nd Battalion of the 3rd Grenadiers of the Guard on 30 October 1810. He obtained the Cross Member of the Legion of Honour on 25 April 1812. Following the Russian campaign, he was transferred to the 2nd Grenadiers of the Guard and in April 1813 he was named commander of the 2nd Battalion of this regiment and distinguished himself in the campaign in Saxony. After the Battle of Bautzen, he was made an Officer of the Legion of Honour on 16 August 1813. He participated in the campaign of France in 1814 and is present at the farewell of the emperor at Fontainebleau on 20 April 1814, wishing to accompany him to Elba. This desire is not accepted; he remains in France for the First Restoration and wrote to his former commander, Tindal, for his assistance in obtaining employment in the Dutch army in the summer of 1814, which was not approved. Although a foreigner, he was confirmed with the rank of colonel in the Royal Corps of Chasseurs à Pied of France on 1 July 1814 and received the Cross of Knight of St. Louis on 25 July 1814. In August 1814, he joined the garrison at Nancy. He joined the emperor on his return from Elba, who appointed him commander of the 1st Battalion of the 1st Regiment of Chasseurs à Pied of the Guard on 13 April 1815. He was dismissed on 25 November 1815 and retired to Rotterdam with his brother.

1074 d'Avout, pp. 115-9.

I was informed by a post to my right that two columns could be seen leaving a wood, so I went to reconnoitre. Immediately I arrived I was convinced that they were enemy; each was of about eight hundred men [this would suggest that there were two battalions in two columns]. But, the rear was still in the wood and it was difficult to be sure of their exact strength.

I took my dispositions to receive this attack, putting two guns into battery loaded with canister and covered by a detachment of an officer and fifty men posted in a manner that it would be difficult to see them, giving them the order not to open fire without my order. My adjutant-major came to inform me that many stragglers were arriving; I placed two of my companies that I had kept back in the centre, with their bayonets crossed, on and either side of the main road with the order to let no one pass that was not wounded. I found among this number several officers, including a battalion-commander, who I forced to take command of an ad hoc battalion that I had assembled, with the threat of shooting him if he did not. I even found a marshal-du-camp [brigadier-general] whose name I do not know, who I forced to take command of another column.

The officer that I had detached to cover the two guns sent me word that the artillery officer that commanded them had decided to leave with his guns, saying that he was not under my command and that the enemy was approaching. I then begged some senior artillery officers to put other guns at my disposal but without effect.

Seeing myself about to be attacked by a superior force without any support, I decided to form into a battalion the 200 or so men that I had assembled, I put them in a position *en potence* a little behind and to my right to prevent me from being outflanked, I sent off the imperial treasure and equipages and then the guns without a single man as escort. I then attempted to repulse an attack that would have been very harmful to the army if the road behind us would have been cut. I reassembled my battalion with its back to the farm, detached a hundred men as skirmishers into the wood and a hundred others as a reserve. At the same time, the general (the provost marshal of the army) had the ad hoc battalion of infantry deploy to short range at the *pas de charge*, and also to deploy into the wood. This combination had a happy outcome: we suffered few casualties and the Prussians were repulsed. I had, at the same time, sent my adjutant-major to inform the emperor what had happened and that I had held the position.

Duuring further notes that his two centre companies blocked the road with advanced bayonets to try and stop the flood of routing French soldiers. Among those retreating men were several senior officers, one a battalion-commander who Duuring co-opted to command a company, as well as a general. An officer was appointed to command the two field guns, but he did nothing. About two hundred of the fugitives were made to stand with the chasseurs, which were formed in column to the right. Duuring knew he had to keep control of the road so that the enemy could not cut off the French army's line of retreat. A further hundred men were sent into the woods to act as sharpshooters. The stoic defence of the road by the Guard and a handful of line troops halted the advance of the Prussians, and Duuring sent his adjutant to inform Napoléon that the road and farm were still held. This was vital if the French were going to get to Genappe.

At some stage during the retreat the 1st Grenadiers were covered in their retreat by what remained of the French cavalry, as Flotard (of the 4th Line Lancers) narrates:[1075]

> Reduced from 600 to 250 riders at most, and combined with the foot grenadiers of the Guard, whose eagle-bearer, who had his left arm carried away, marched with a platoon of his comrades before our squadron retired, we stopped a few minutes under the fire of a British infantry division to give time to these grenadiers to rally around their flag.
>
> Our bravest soldiers paled seeing our ranks at every discharge were cleared away, and seemed about to disperse: 'my friends', said Captain Bertaux in an angry voice, that trembled with emotion, weeping bitterly, 'we are defeated but not disgraced! It remains for us to die as befits good people. Our post is here; death we will reach just as well elsewhere'. And more for the discouraged he cried: 'keep your dressing, keep your ranks aligned and march!

By 22.00, the battle was lost. Colonel Auguste Louis Pétiet, of the French imperial headquarters, recalls what followed:[1076]

> Almost all our generals were wounded, among the dead are Michel, Jamin and Depenne; the Generals Lobau, Cambronne, Duhesme, Durrieux, also injured, fell into the hands of the enemy. Lieutenant-

---

1075 Dulaure, p. 205, citing Armand Jean Flotard, of the 4th Lancers.
1076 Pétiet, pp. 222-3.

General Barrois, struck by a bullet, avoided this misfortune; his soldiers prevented him being captured.

The French army left their positions and rushed like a torrent, the troops of all arms are mixed and confused and we are on the road to Genappe, where some soldiers shouted that English riders have already overwhelmed the place, it was hoped that we would stop at this point to spend the night, but having seen some enemy squadrons, the rout was complete.

General Cambronne

If one man stands out from the French army as a key personality in the history of the battle it is General Cambronne. Immortalised in print by Hugo and Thiers and on film by Dino de Laurentis, the action of Cambronne is one of the most well-known, but least studied, episodes of the battle.

The myth tells us Cambronne was standing within the last square of the Old Guard at Waterloo, which when summoned to surrender, replied *'la garde meurt mais ne se rend pas'*. The square was then annihilated by Allied artillery and Cambronne was made prisoner by Colonel Halket. Halket himself states many times that it was he who captured Cambronne, and many eyewitnesses at Waterloo from the French army state they heard Cambronne utter his most famous words. Case closed? Not really, as none of the episode withstands critical evaluation.

Firstly, with Cambronne's words, we are dealing with false memory. The phrase was so famous that many participants honestly believed that the words were spoken, and so ardently believed in the glorious death of the Guard, rather than its flight in panic, that the story had to be true, despite Cambronne's own forceful denial.

In order to assess the myth, we look firstly at Cambronne's fate in the battle. Was he in the right place at the right time to be asked if the Guard was to surrender? Writing in 1815, Cambronne himself states that he was wounded to the head and left for dead. Writing to General Pelet about his actions at Waterloo, he states that he did not recall the last stand around the eagle of the chasseurs, so it is possible he was captured before this event took place.[1077] As we shall see, the rallying about the eagle took place south of Plancenoit.

1077 d'Avout, pp. 48-9.

In evidence given to the House of Peers in 1815, which put Cambronne, Drouot, Ney and other generals and marshals of France on trial for treason, General Cambronne's aide-de-camp states:[1078]

> General Cambronne, after being exposed to fire throughout the day, towards evening, at the head of a single battalion, that still kept off the attacks of the enemy, was then hit. He fell confused among the dead! What great and unhappy memories of courage that will always beat in the heart of French men.

So, for Cambronne's own aide to say he fell from his horse and was left for dead is rather different to what Colonel Halket states about pulling Cambronne off his horse. According to his own service records, Cambronne was wounded to the head with a gunshot wound to his left temple, removing part of the ear, which it seems rendered him unconscious, and he collapsed onto the ground from his horse.[1079]

The aide's own testimony is backed up by both Cambronne himself and General Petit, who notes that General Cambronne fell during the retreat, between the fields of La Belle Alliance and La Haye Sainte.[1080] It is of course possible that this is where Cambronne was found, and then picked off the battlefield. Carl Jacobi notes:[1081]

> In the hollow beyond [Hougoumont] they encountered an enemy square composed of troops of the Imperial Guard, which were completely destroyed with a bayonet charge. Colonel Halket personally captured General Cambronne. The enemy was driven back.

However, Ludwig von Dreves, captain with the Osnabrück Landwehr or 2nd Battalion Duke of York's Regiment, narrates that:[1082]

> During the retreat of the French Imperial Guard, who were completely disordered, a French general (whose name I believe was Cambronne), tried valiantly to get his battalions to resist and reassemble them, and he succeeded in this on a number of occasions;

1078 *Le Correspondent du Paris*, 1886, p. 74.
1079 AN: LH 413-66 service records of General Cambronne.
1080 J. Petit, 'General Petit's account of the Waterloo Campaign' in *English Historical Review*, 1903.
1081 Franklin, Vol. 1, p. 21.
1082 Franklin, Vol. 1, pp. 52-3.

however, because the battalions which pursued them advanced so swiftly, the French were compelled to retire again and again; this was noticed by our brigadier, Colonel Halket, and with an incomparable courage he rode through the line of French tirailleurs [skirmishers, not to be confused with the troops of the same name in the Young Guard], which were covering the withdrawing columns, to the position where the aforementioned general stood, and took him. The general resisted with all his might, but fortunately the line of tirailleurs were unable to prevent him from being taken prisoner.

The French Imperial Guard tried to reform on several occasions as they withdrew, following the capture of their general; they made every possible use of the terrain in an attempt to stop their pursuers with musket fire, but eventually they were forced to yield by our troops, who followed them as they dissolved into a disordered mess.

The story seems very credible, bar the episode about Cambronne. For hard, undeniable fact, Cambronne had a head wound and collapsed off his horse. Could he have been dragged off his horse? Perhaps, but with the major trauma to his head, and no doubt in shock, Cambronne could, we assume, have put up very little resistance indeed, so any struggle would have been minimal. On balance, whoever the officer was that Halket captured, if the episode took place in the manner frequently described by Allied eyewitnesses, it cannot have been Cambronne. Major Beaux, of the 1st Regiment of Line Infantry, notes in the immediate aftermath of the battle that:[1083]

> At six o'clock in the evening, everything was in our favour. The emperor and his staff were singularly exposed during the battle, Generals Cambronne and Michel, both of the Imperial Guard, were killed by his side.

Major Beaux is writing sometime before 27 June 1815. Therefore, in the immediate aftermath of the battle, Cambronne was considered killed in action by, we assume, the major head trauma he suffered that day.

On balance of evidence, Cambronne was wounded, fell from his horse and was picked off the battlefield rather than being captured. We need to ask another question: Waterloo myth places Cambronne with the Old Guard at the last stand, and it was here that he was wounded. The question is, was Cambronne at the last stand? Actually, no. A number

---

1083 *Journal de Rouen*, 27 June 1815, p. 4.

of eyewitnesses speak of the last stand of the Old Guard, both French and British, but the event did not take place on the field of Waterloo. It occurred south of Plancenoit and certainly south of Rossome and La Caillou.

At some stage on the Brussels road south of Plancenoit, battalions of the 1st Chasseurs, 2nd Chasseurs and the 2nd Grenadiers made a stand against the tide of fugitives and rallied around the eagle of the 1st Chasseurs. General Pelet recalls:[1084]

> Retaining about two hundred men around the eagle of the foot chasseurs of the Guard, we had been pursued strongly since leaving Plancenoit. The cannonballs fell among the group all the time, the cavalry sought to begin to remove the glorious trophy it contained: in a moment, the ranks were less tight and the platoon was surrounded by several bodies of cavalry and infantry, the eagle was compromised. General Pelet, taking advantage of a fold of land covering a little against the fire of grape shot, stopped the eagle-bearer, Lieutenant Martin,[1085] and cries out: 'to me, chasseurs! Save the eagle, or die around her.'
>
> As soon as Adjutant Gillet,[1086] Captains Langres,[1087] Baric,[1088] Amiot[1089] and all the chasseurs are formed tightly around him, they charged their bayonets. The charge of the cavalry is repulsed and many riders fall at the feet of the chasseurs, but the square then

1084 *Victoires, conquêtes, désastres, revers et guerres civiles des Francais de 1792-1815*, Vol. 21.

1085 Recorded on 1 June 1815 as second-lieutenant porte-aigle of the 1st Chasseurs. SHDDT: Xab 69.

1086 Recorded on 1 June 1815 as captain-adjutant-major on the staff of the 2nd Chasseurs. SHDDT: Xab 69.

1087 No officer of this name served in the 1st, 2nd or 3rd Chasseurs à Pied. The officer referred to is likely to be Captain Lancontre, who is recorded on 1 June 1815 as commanding the 7th Company of 2nd Battalion 2nd Chasseurs à Pied. SHDDT: Xab 69.

1088 No officer of this name served in the 1st Chasseurs. However, the officer in question is likely to be Captain Barret, commanding 8th Company of 2nd Battalion 1st Chasseurs. SHDDT: Xab 69.

1089 No captain called Amiot served in the 1st, 2nd or 3rd Chasseurs à Pied. The officer referred to is likely to be First-Lieutenant Amiot, who is recorded on 1 June 1815 as being lieutenant-adjutant-major of the 2nd Chasseurs à Pied. SHDDT: Xab 69.

received a blast of death in the middle of this sacrifice, dedication, and reap many of these noble victims. The ranks replied with a brisk fire which clears the ground in front of them, and the remains of this sacred cohort fill with despair, withdrew slowly, thus manage to save by the honour of the Guard and the flag.

General Pelet elaborates on the event in 1820 or 1821, based on his journal kept in 1815:[1090]

My major told me that that the enemy cavalry was at the entrance to the village [behind him], that we were outflanked on all sides and in particular by the wood [the Chantelet Wood] on the side of the Lasne.

I then gave the order to rally everyone who could be found. I ran around the whole village, where the enemy had entered on all sides.

I had the drums beat the rally and I retired with what remained of the battalion and the company of grenadiers, about half of my men, by the road that ran from Plancenoit to La Caillou Farm.

The entry [to Plancenoit] had already been blocked by the enemy. It was between 8.00 and 8.30. Beyond the village, I found myself in a terrible confusion of men saving themselves in rout while shouting 'stop! Stop! Halt! Halt!' It was those who shouted loudest that ran the fastest. These sounds were accompanied by cannon shots, which hastened even the slowest.

The enemy followed us with skirmishers, especially into the wood that stretched from Maransart, from where these rascals outflanked me. I had rallied all the men I could around me. I met the poor Langlois,[1091] the eagle bearer of the 1st Regiment, Baric, and recall that I embraced the eagle with great emotion in finding it and raising my hat shouted 'my friends, we must defend it to the death!' This animated and rallied the men.

About the 2nd Battalion 2nd Chasseurs, General Pelet adds:[1092]

The 2nd Battalion of the 2nd Regiment of Chasseurs, placed next to La Belle Alliance, where we remained after the departure of the

---

1090 d'Avout, p. 52.
1091 Recorded on 1 June 1815 as serving in 8th Company of 2nd Battalion. SHDDT: Xab 69.
1092 d'Avout, p. 50.

battalion of Cambronne. With the approach of the night, we had on our right regiments of cuirassiers and a regiment of chasseurs à cheval. The cavalry moved off, they say, without orders and without attacking.

Their commander, Mompez, assailed by the mob of men who left the battlefield, and without the support of the cavalry, began his retreat, and effected his movement along the road unmolested. This battalion, soon reduced to about thirty men, had received the eagle that Cambronne had guarded. Always marching in square, we could not long preserve the necessary order, and eventually dispersed. Soon, what remained of our bloody debris joined up with the 1st Battalion who had evacuated Plancenoit.

Duuring confirms that the eagle of the 1st Chasseurs was with Cambronne:[1093]

> The emperor ordered me roughly at seven o'clock the morning to stay with my battalion at the farm to guard his headquarters, the armies pay, etc. Several regiments of infantry and cavalry passed successively in front of the farm in line of battle, and then came the Old Guard, with the passage of the 1st Battalion, I handed the eagle to General Cambronne.

Clearly, for Pelet to be able to rally the chasseurs about the eagle, General Cambronne's square and the general himself must have retreated to the south of Plancenoit. It means that if the Old Guard made its heroic last stand as imagined in the film *Waterloo*, it must have been somewhere between Plancenoit and Genappe on the Brussels road.

Lieutenant Bacheville, of the 2nd Battalion 1st Chasseurs à Pied, remembers the same event as follows:[1094]

> Our square, commanded by General Cambronne, withdrew slowly and in good order, the terrain forced us to open ourselves for a moment and the British cavalry took the opportunity to enter our ranks, and without checking if any chasseurs were injured by them, we turned and gave the English an infernal fire and it is in that moment that an enemy general shouted 'go! Brave soldiers, you will not be done no wrong'. The eagle bearer then planted his eagle

---

1093 d'Avout, pp. 115-9.
1094 Bacheville, pp. 42-8.

on the ground, saying, 'come on form around me, comrades! Die at the foot of your eagle!'

Bacheville's event is very likely to be the same as the one Pelet recalls. Another eyewitness was Captain Gabriel Joseph Heuillette, of the 1st Battalion 2nd Chasseurs. He recalls this same incident as follows:[1095]

> The Old Guard, as you know, had formed several squares with one commanded by Cambronne, a second by Comte Michel, and the third which I was with, by General Pelet. We were all determined to die rather than surrender.
>
> The square commanded by General Pelet was attacked by a Prussian column six times greater in number. Despite this we continued with our retirement beyond the village of Plancenoit in the midst of a terrible fire of canister, it was not possible for us to respond. The situation became worse as an army corps of the English army arrived and cut our retirement. In this critical and desperate position, General Pelet grabbed the eagle, and raised it over the square and shouted 'chasseurs of the Old Guard! We have sworn, by receiving this flag, to defend it unto death! Swear to die here rather than abandon it to the enemy!' The soldiers, electrified by these noble words, cried 'long live the emperor! We swear!'
>
> The square continued its retreat in good order despite considerable losses keenly felt at every moment. Shortly after this episode, I was wounded in the leg, and I fell into the hands of the Prussians.

Given the last stand took place at least a mile south from where the traditional history places the episode, by which time Cambronne had been left on the field of battle, he can never have uttered his famous phrase. Neither can the other candidate, General Michel with the 3rd and 4th Chasseurs à Pied. Therefore, the episode cannot have happened the way we imagine it to have done. General Pelet rallied what he could of the debris of the Old Guard around the eagle of the chasseurs and was faced with Prussian cavalry and infantry, yet Waterloo myth states, or at least implies, that at the last stand of the Old Guard it was British troops that defeated them. The story of the battle is written largely in English by the victors to claim all the credit for the most famous episodes of the battle: the gallant soldiers at Hougoumont were like those poor souls at Rourke's Drift, the heroic British infantry mowed

---

1095 *Journal de Toulouse*, 24 October 1845, p. 2.

down the savage French cavalry; the British guards defeated the Old Guard, etc. Oft repeated nationalist, self-aggrandising jingoism, and yet honestly believed by many. Furthermore, the words uttered by General Pelet have been transformed into *'La Garde Meurt et ne se rend pas'* by the *Journal General de France* of 24 June 1815, and spoken by Cambronne.[1096] Cambronne refuted these words in 1818.[1097] Indeed Cambronne, when asked about this, commented that 'I am very sorry, but I did not say what you attribute to me.' Clearly, this most famous of incidents at Waterloo never took place in the form that the myth makers would have us believe.[1098] The words are also ascribed to General Michel, who was killed leading the 3rd and 4th Chasseurs to the attack on Wellington's right flank.

Thus, Cambronne was not dragged off his horse by General Halket, but merely recovered from the field of battle; the famous words attributed to him were never spoken on the day of the battle; the last stand of the Guard was between Plancenoit and Genappe, and this last bulwark was defeated by Prussians. Indeed, at Genappe General Roguet made another stand with the Guard, as we shall see in the next chapter.

1096 Author's collection.
1097 *Journal des debats*, 24 June 1815, p. 3.
1098 *Journal de Toulouse*, 24 October 1845, p. 2.

Chapter 23

Genappe to Paris

The scattered remains of the French army that had fought at Waterloo were fleeing along the various roads from Charleroi, moving towards Avesnes, Laon and Philippeville. Grouchy conducted his retreat so as to join the remnants of the army. An unknown French general, but probably Baron Albert Louis Emmanuel Fouler, Comte de Relinque (grand equerry to the emperor), wrote the following report to Marshal Davout, dated Avesnes 20 June 1815:[1099]

> On the 18th, the emperor attacked with the 2nd, 1st and 6th Corps without success. In the evening a Prussian corps presented itself on our right and eventually seized the village of Plancenoit, while the emperor, instead of evacuating the battlefield and taking position by withdrawing his right, threw all his Guard recklessly on the centre of the enemy in an operation which was unsuccessful and resulted in the rout being more complete, because there were no troops that had not been in action. The rout continued until Laon and some of the soldiers returned to their homes.
>
> The loss of our army in these four days is between 30,000 to 40,000 men and 200 guns. All the 2nd, 1st and 6th Corps, as well as the Guard, cannot present more than 6,000 men and twenty cannons, and the cavalry has barely 2,000 horses. There yet remains the 3rd and 4th Corps, but they have suffered greatly at Fleurus. We cannot say as usual that the consequences of this defeat are incalculable, but on the contrary they must lead to the loss of the emperor's throne and the annihilation of France.

1099 *'Lettre d'un Combattant de Waterloo'* in *Feuilles d'Histoire*, No. 6, 1911, pp. 441-5.

A French officer writing in 1815 notes the barricades and obstacles were placed by the French as opposed to an act of treason:[1100]

> The fugitives painfully pressed by an overwhelming force, ran rapidly over the two leagues which separate Genappe from the field of battle, and at length reached this small place, where the greatest number trusted that they should be able to pass the night. In order to oppose some obstacles to the enemy, they collected some carriages on the road and barricaded the entrance to the principal street. A few cannon were collected in the form of a battery; bivouacs were formed in the town and its environs, and the soldiers went into the houses for the purpose of finding an asylum and food; but scarcely were these dispositions made when the enemy appeared. The discharge of cannon on their part spread universal alarm among their downcast enemies. Everything fled again, and the retreat became more disorderly than ever.

The town of Genappe was crowded with fugitives, as de Mauduit, of the 1st Grenadiers, notes:[1101]

> Our march through many obstacles in the field, because we followed for some time the roadway parallel to the left, was painfully slow: the moon not having yet appeared on the horizon and the sky being responsible for thick clouds, the night was very dark. Also, we barely were able to walk without too much confusion for an hour. At every moment it became necessary to face the enemy when he pressed too closely, either to prevent him from rushing into the thousands of injured, the road and its two sides were crowded, either running away to allow time to clear the long parade of Genappe, because there accumulated every minute every embarrassment of the army: the wounded, the ambulances, parks, wagons and artillery, but in such a melee, that once fallen among it, he must give up the retreat.

General Roguet is noted to have:[1102]

> ...taken command of the Old Guard at Waterloo, after the wounding Comte de Friant, he remained till the end on the battlefield to

---

1100 The *Derby Mercury*, 16 November 1815.

1101 de Mauduit, Vol. 2, p. 471.

1102 *Notice nécrologique sur le lieutenant général Cte Roguet*, J. Dumain, Paris, 1847.

perform the last orders of Napoléon and the major-general with the last battalion, even when everything else had gone and there was no army, the English merely were the first to take their positions, while the Prussians sped down the right and the rear.

In one charge, and at the centre of his last square headed by the Prussian hussars, the general had his horse killed; an officer mounted him up on a horse taken from the artillery train.

Lieutenant-General Roguet did, from that moment, with the 2nd Battalion 1st Regiment of Foot Grenadiers of the Guard, commanded by Battalion-Chief Combes, retire from the army from the battlefield to Genappe: he, on arrival to this town, he took position on the road with about three hundred Grenadiers, where he was joined by the brave Brigadier-General Christiani. Roguet took this position to defend the entrance of the town and give time to those there to leave the place.

His little band long resisted the efforts of the conqueror, but finally, overwhelmed by their number and after having suffered considerable perils, General Roguet was forced to retire, it is then that the enemy entered Genappe: it was about eleven o'clock in the evening: it was not three leagues from Waterloo.

General Christiani and the few remaining men of the 2nd Grenadiers joined the stand of the 1st Grenadiers:[1103]

> The voice of the officers was ignored, and we come to the position that the 1st Regiment of Grenadiers occupied, my soldiers dispersed and it was impossible to rally them. I joined the road towards Genappe. General Roguet came there too. There we endeavoured to rally as many people as possible and to wait for the night, but we were abandoned. Nevertheless, General Roguet and I made our retirement until we heard the enemy advancing on the road to the sound of the fife. Then forced to withdraw, I lost sight of General Roguet in the tumult, and I took a path to the left of Genappe with the intention of gaining Charleroi, when I joined the men of General Petit.

1103 d'Avout, p. 113.

Clearly at Genappe, Christiani's few remaining 2nd Grenadiers met up with the 1st and 2nd Battalions of the 1st Grenadiers, under the command of Generals Petit and Roguet. General Petit narrates that:[1104]

> As the 1st Regiment arrived at Genappe, a panic seized the soldiers of the artillery train. They had cut the traces of their horses, leaving their pieces and their caissons as if to fire on us. The village and the roads were so crowded that we went around the village by turning to the left. The 1st Regiment marched through a field by various trails and pathways throughout the night.
>
> We arrived at the gates of Charleroi, we found the town so crowded that it took the 1st Regiment to defile man-by-man to cross. We reformed. A cannon fired from the other side of the Sombre.
>
> Around noon, they resumed their march to Beaumont. Here, General Roguet had command of everything that arrived at this point from the Guard, and he left the position in the evening, about a quarter-mile from the place. Such a sad debris of all regiments who had used this same road was seen.

The remains of the 4th Grenadiers also headed to Genappe under the orders of General Roguet, as Captain Beraud (of the 4th Grenadiers) narrates:[1105]

> We finally arrived in this city, where many thought they could stop for the night, there was a rush with the intention to oppose the enemy and created an obstacle by accumulating artillery caissons and wagons on the road and to barricade the entrance to the main street, and some cannon were even placed in battery; bivouacs were settled in and around the city, the soldiers spread out through the homes in order to seek asylum and bread. But, as those provisions were being taken, the enemy came, the camps were evacuated hastily and the disorderly retreat began again with the same confusion as before.
>
> At daybreak, the sad remnants of the army once so brilliant, coming, arrived at Charleroi, where they re-passed the Sambre.

Prussian General Gneisenau narrates:[1106]

1104 ibid, p. 110.
1105 Beraud, p. 296.
1106 John Franklin personal communication.

At Genappe, the enemy had entrenched himself with cannon and overturned carriages; at our approach, we suddenly heard in the town a great noise and a motion of carriages; at the entrance, we were exposed to a brisk fire of musketry; we replied by some cannon-shot, followed by a hurrah, and, in an instant after, the town was ours. It was here that, among many other equipages, the carriage of Napoléon was taken; he had just left it to mount on horseback, and, in his hurry, had forgotten his sword and hat. Thus, the affairs continued till break of day. About forty thousand men, in the most complete disorder, the remains of a whole army, have saved themselves retreating through Charleroi, partly without arms, and carrying with them only twenty-seven pieces of their numerous artillery.

The enemy, in his flight, has passed all his fortresses, the only defence of his frontiers, which are now passed by our armies.

At three o'clock, Napoléon had dispatched from the field of battle a courier to Paris, with the news that victory was no longer doubtful: a few hours after, he had no longer any army left. We have not yet an exact account of the enemy's loss; it is enough to know that two-thirds of the whole were killed, wounded, or prisoners: among the latter are Generals Mouton, Duhesme and Compans. Up to this time, about three hundred cannon and above five hundred caissons are in our hands.

Beyond Genappe, the wreck of the French army headed back to Charleroi and then ultimately onto Paris. In the evening of Waterloo, Blücher is said to have remarked 'tell your officers, now begins the pursuit of extermination'.[1107] No doubt he had in mind the French pursuit of the Prussians in 1806 which had completely destroyed her army.

Crucial to the success of the campaign was the Allies switching from defensive to offensive operations. The Prussians and their Allies in 1814 had learned crucial lessons. Napoléon had suffered setbacks in this campaign, but had been able to withdraw his troops, rally them and commit once more to the offensive. The Allies had learned that the success of the battle lay in the relentless pursuit and capture of enemy troops. Given breathing space, the French army could have rallied and fought a rearguard action while Napoléon gathered fresh resources to commit to the campaign, as he had so effectively done in 1813 and 1814, and dragging the campaign into a long struggle. As it was, in the

---

1107 Ollech, p. 253.

immediate aftermath of Waterloo the Prussians harassed the remains of the French army back into France.

According to Bellina Kupieski, a colonel attached to the imperial headquarters, in a dispatch to Marshal Davout dated 23 June 1815, the prince was originally at Beaumont and then moved to Avesnes:[1108]

> Prince Jérôme rallied at Beaumont bit-by-bit some 8,000 men, comprising infantry and cavalry and around twelve pieces of artillery. The major-general had rallied bit-by-bit around three thousand men at Philippeville, which left this place for Rocroi, where they arrived on the 20th where there already was 800 men of the Old Guard with two or three cannon. The same day, Prince Jérôme and his party at Beaumont moved to Avesnes, where he united a great number of soldiers of all arms and marched them to Vervins, where they arrived on the 21st. I estimate he had ten thousand men, the major part being cavalry.

With Napoléon leaving the field, it seems a good number of entourage and staff officers left. As Napoléon sped to Paris, Marshal Soult was left to try and save the wreckage of the army. Colonel Simon Hortode, chief-of-staff to 6th Division of 2nd Corps, wrote on 21 June 1815:[1109]

> I did not leave the battlefield until ten o'clock at night, along with the emperor and his brother [Jérôme], to whom I have consistently served as an aide throughout the day, and particularly during the last three hours when I was alone with him, as all the other officers of the staff had gone.

In the early hours of 19 June, Soult issued orders to General Reille in the name of the emperor:[1110]

> M. Lieutenant-General Reille, Comte the emperor gives you command of all corps from the Armée du Nord which are successively arriving on the glacis of Philippeville and it is of the utmost importance that we work on their rallying and reorganisation.

> To this end, we must take care to ensure each regiment is reformed, as are the brigades, regiments and companies. MM. general officers, staff officers, administrators, etc. should resume their duties and

---

1108 SHDDT: C15 5. Dossier 23 June 1815. Kupieski to Davout, 23 June 1815.
1109 *Revue Retrospective*, Paris, 1890.
1110 AN: AFIV 1939, pp. 55-7.

are immediately placed under your command. In this way, we reform our army promptly as well as its equipment, but this needs organisation.

The intention of the emperor is that you distribute during the day to every soldier food in the following proportion: two rations of bread, a water-of-life, meat and rice. There will also be distributed thirty cartridges to every infantryman, and ten to each cavalry trooper. The commander of Philippeville has been informed of your needs and has been ordered to aid you.

On 21 June, Wellington began his pursuit of the French towards Paris. The Prussians had a three day head start on the British troops. The same day, Napoléon was back in Paris and planned to form a new army and fight back against the Allies. However, the political situation soon overtook military considerations, just as they had done in April 1814. In Paris, the Chamber of Peers was openly hostile to the emperor, and had been since he had left Paris and declared itself in permanent session to avoid their dissolution by Napoléon.

Napoléon was ordered to resign the throne or be deposed on 22 June. He abdicated in favour of his son, the King of Rome, and he moved to Malmaison. A provisional government was formed. On 23 June, Marshal Davout was instructed to defend Paris by the provisional government. The following day, the new government began entreaties to the Allies about an armistice to end the war. A few days later, Marshal Grouchy assumed command of the entire army, with the resignation of Soult on 26 June.

On 30 June 1815, Davout had over 70,000 men available to defend Paris, and this number would continue to swell as mobilised National Guardsmen made their way to Paris and the command of General Lamraque returned from the Vendée. The army had in twelve days found a new sense of confidence and was ready and able to fight. If these men could inflict a major defeat on either Wellington or Blücher, just maybe the balance of power could shift back to the French and the defeat of Waterloo nullified under the walls of Paris. However, the political machinations of Fouche rendered these hopes null and void.

The capitulation of the French army and France herself was signed at 17.00 on 3 July. The armistice began at 8.00 on 4 July 1815, the French army was ordered to move behind the River Loire. Paris had fallen, the army had been vanquished and the emperor was in exile.[1111]

1111 Damitz, Vol. 2, pp. 314-6.

So, what did Waterloo achieve? We are often told Waterloo heralded one hundred years of peace in Europe. This is simply not true. Napoléon was once and for all removed from power, for good or ill. The Allies had achieved their objective: illegal regime change. In the short term, France was crippled economically and was in a virtual state of civil war for four years. Prussia gained massively territorially and fiscally. Germanic allies of Napoléon (Bavaria, Württemberg, and Saxony) were all absorbed into a greater Prussia. Peace was not secured. The Serb-Austrian War started soon after Waterloo, war in Spain erupted in 1823, the Belgian War of Independence in 1830, the French Revolution of 1830, the Vendée Revolt of 1832, the First Carlist War of 1833-39, the Prusso-Danish War, the Prusso-Austro War, the Franco-Austrian War, the Franco-Prussian War all marked a century of almost constant European fighting, but as it did not involve Britain, the traditional view is that Europe was peaceful. Was the freedom and independence of small states and nations a price worth paying for the stabilisation of Europe and the prevention of a major European war until the 1850s? Could the revolutionary ideas of the period really be put back in a box by the old monarchies of the continent? Was repression and persecution of religious minorities an acceptable price to pay? Britain did not go into the war united, nor did it emerge from the war united. The threat of Napoléon was not an invasion, but an intellectual revolution that threatened the unelected heads of state, that gave rights to all men and women. Napoléon and the French Revolution was a clear and present danger to kings and monarchies that sought to change the world, a world which the kings and princes sought to maintain. This they succeeded in for a few short years. The French Revolution of 1830 and the revolutions across Europe in 1848 and their suppression was the last gasp of kings and princes. Change would come to Europe, but not until after the First World War. We forget that in Napoléonic France democracy was far more developed than in Britain. France with Napoléon had freedom of religion, something Britain did not have. Freedom of thought, encapsulated by Thomas Pain and the rights of man, could not be suppressed forever.

Chapter 24

Waterloo Casualties

To summarise, Napoléon lost the campaign as his army was out-performed by the Allies. With hindsight we can see that some of the battlefield choices made by Napoléon were wrong, but at the time, to the French officers on the field, they made what they felt to be the correct judgement call. Only after the events do French officers begin to question what occurred and shift blame for the defeat onto others.

The data presented here is taken from the regimental muster rolls prepared in 1815, and annotated with the dead, wounded and prisoners of war, etc. between 15 and 30 June 1815. These, therefore, are the actual losses sustained by the French army at Waterloo, Genappe and men lost in the subsequent disintegration of the army. This data has never before appeared in print. It allows us to reconsider the events of 1815 with hard data.

The line and light infantry

What can the mass of recorded data tell us about Waterloo that we did not know already? Surprisingly, it can tell us a great deal. What follows is a corps-by-corps statement of losses and the implications the data has on our understanding of the battle.

1st Corps

The losses of the French army at Waterloo have, so far, never been used to understand the great battle. What follows is a detailed analysis of what this data tells us about the battle. We look firstly at 1st Corps:

1st Corps						
	Wounded	Wounded & Prisoner	Prisoner of War	Killed	Missing	Total
1st Division	150	113	1,721	52	96	2,132
2nd Division	117	437	43	104	1,466	2,167
3rd Division	158	263	1,209	19	857	2,506
4th Division	93	41	923	40	721	1,818
Total	518	854	3,896	215	3,140	8,623

The highest losses in 1st Corps was Marcognet's division, losing 2,535 men from the 3,735 present on 10 June, representing a loss of 68 per cent of the division. General Durutte's division lost the least, despite the 95th Regiment of Line Infantry being recorded as missing, losing 50 per cent of effective strength. Losses of 1st and 2nd Divisions were similar; 1st Division losing 55 per cent and 2nd Division 44 per cent, the lowest losses overall. In total, the division lost 8,694 men from the 16,140 men under arms on 10 June, or 54 per cent overall. The much higher rate of fatalities in the 2nd Division stands out. The division was not involved in the great attack by 1st Corps, and was not affected by the charge of the Union and Household Brigades. The heavy losses were occasioned by the division's assault of La Haye Sainte, which was far more deadly than the attack of the Allied cavalry. The Allied garrison had the fighting very much their own way here. Firing from prepared defensive positions, the French had to attack with no cover at all, and were constantly in the 'killing ground'. The French could not hope to inflict any casualties until the walls had been scaled or gates broken open. Thus, rank after rank of French infantry were mown down mercilessly by the garrison until it ran out of ammunition and the French could break into the farm unopposed.

2nd Corps

At Waterloo, only half of the Corps (six regiments) was involved in the fighting for Hougoumont; Jérôme›s division and half of Foy's. Even so, not all the battalions of the regiments committed to the attack were in action. Waterloo myth states all 2nd Corps was destroyed fighting at Hougoumont, which, as we have seen, is simply not true. Total corps losses are shown below:

2nd Corps							
	Wounded	Evacuated Wounded	Wounded & Prisoner	Prisoner of War	Killed	Missing	Total
5th Division	0	241	6	976	89	208	1,520
6th Division	639	267	58	293	218	201	1,676
9th Division	0	666	1	142	80	681	1,570
Total	639	1,174	65	1,411	387	1,090	4,766

Of interest, Jérôme's 6th Division only lost 106 more men than General Foy's 9th Division. On 10 June, the corps mustered 15,823 men. On 16 June 1,825 men were lost, giving 13,998 men on 18 June. Overall, the corps lost 34 per cent of its effective strength on 18 June, meaning over 9,300 men were still under arms with the corps on 19 June 1815. The vast majority of men were listed as missing or prisoner (some 2,501 men) or wounded (1,878 men), of which 62 per cent were evacuated to hospital. The mortality rate was 2.7 per cent overall in the corps. The losses in 2nd Corps were marginally higher than 6th Corps, a difference of 5 per cent. Given 6th Corps was far smaller than 2nd Corps, the fighting was comparable on both the French left and right wing in terms of intensity, which aligns well with the testimonies of Foy, Tissot and Trefcon concerning the two attacks the corps made on the Allied right later in the day when the fighting for Hougoumont was over. All the losses in 5th Division occurred after 18.00, whereas the losses for 6th Corps were in the period 15.00 to 20.00.

6th Corps

The total losses for 6th Corps were:

6th Corps							
	Wounded	Evacuated Wounded	Wounded & Prisoner	Prisoner of War	Killed	Missing	Total
19th Division	461	0	7	341	112	145	1,066
20th Division	85	0	7	141	18	111	849[1112]
Total							1,915

1112 The 5th Regiment of Light Infantry casualty data lists 487 men lost from 1 to 25 June 1815. This is added to the figure in the table.

It's interesting to note that 6th Corps lost significantly fewer men than 2nd Corps. Clearly, it seems the fighting on the French right wing was of less intensity, as well as a much shorter duration than the action that 2nd Corps was involved in. Does this mean 6th Corps withdrew from the fighting early? Where it was deployed, the position was easily outflanked, which we know the Prussians did. Did Lobau withdraw his corps to save being cut off from the army? A distinct possibility. Total loss was 1,915 men from the 6,625 men present on 10 June, or 29 per cent.

Artillery

On 25 June 1815, General Ruty reported to Marshal Soult that forty-six guns were with the Armée du Nord. Batteries, it seems, had been moved from one corps to another and reinforcements had arrived. The reserve mustered five gun crews, but had a single 12-pounder and a 6.4-pounder howitzer. The artillery train had suffered relatively few losses in terms of manpower and horses. Clearly, the guns were lost not through lack of horses. General Guyot, officer commanding the heavy cavalry brigade of the Imperial Guard, tells us that due to a bottleneck at Genappe, he had to abandon the guns of the horse artillery battery attached to the brigade. This then suggests that getting the guns through Genappe was a major stumbling block in getting the guns away from the field of battle. Some companies, primarily in 1st Corps, ceased to exist by the 25th. This implies that gunners and guns were lost at Waterloo. The status of the line artillery was as follows:[1113]

Auxiliary Artillery Young Guard

- 7th Foot Artillery, 11th Company, three officers, sixty men. Six 12-pounders, two 6.4-pounder howitzers.
- 7th Foot Artillery, 12th Company, five officers, seventy-eight men. Six 6-pounders, two 24-pounder howitzers.
- 6th Squadron Artillery Train, 9th Company, two officers, seventy-four men, 163 horses.
- 6th Squadron Artillery Train, 10th Company, two officers, seventy-eight men, 172 horses.

1113 SHDDT: C15 34.

1st Corps

- 8th (1st?) Company 8th Foot Artillery, three officers, sixty-four men. Six 6-pounders, one 24-pounder howitzer.
- 7th (1st?) Squadron Artillery Train, 7th Company, two officers, eighty-six men, 158 horses.

2nd Corps

- 2nd Foot Artillery, 2nd Company, four officers, sixty-four men. Five 6-pounders, one 24-pounder howitzer.
- 1st Squadron Artillery Train, 1st Company, two officers, seventy-nine men, 141 horses.
- 2nd Foot Artillery, 20th Company, four officers, one hundred men. Six 6-pounders, two 24-pounder howitzers (from the reserve park).
- 5th Squadron Artillery Train, 1st Company, three officers, ninety-three men, 176 horses.
- 7th Foot Artillery, 14th Company, three officers, eighty men. Six 6-pounders, two 24-pounder howitzers (latterly Auxiliary Artillery Young Guard).
- 6th Squadron Artillery Train, 11th Company, two officers, seventy-seven men, 172 horses.

Reserve Park Artillery

- 6th Foot Artillery, 9th Company, four officers, one hundred men (latterly 4th Infantry Division, 1st Corps).
- 3rd Company 1st Squadron Artillery Train, six officers, 342 men, 472 horses.
- 7th Foot Artillery, 4th Company, four officers, one hundred men (latterly Auxiliary Artillery Young Guard).
- 2nd Squadron Artillery Train, six officers, 157 men, 221 horses.
- 4th Company, 8th Foot Artillery, four officers, one hundred men. One 12-pounder, One 6.4-pounder howitzer (latterly 6th Corps reserve battery).
- Ouvriers, 9th Company, two officers, forty-two men.
- Pontonniers, 4th Company, four officers, eighty-two men.

- 2nd Horse Artillery, 2nd Company, four officers, eighty men (from 3rd Cavalry Corps).
- 5th Squadron Artillery Train, ten officers, 203 men, 361 horses.
- 3rd Horse Artillery, 3rd Company, four officers, eighty men (from 4th Corps).
- 6th Squadron Artillery Train, five officers, 124 men, 205 horses.

It seems 2nd and 6th Corps managed to evacuate some vestige of their artillery. Reille managed to evacuate the guns attached to Prince Jérôme's division. Lobau, with 6th Corps, extricated the 6-pounder battery attached to 19th Division and also two guns from its own reserve battery. 1st Corps got the gunners and horses attached to Durutte's 4th Infantry Division off the field. It also seems that the guns attached to the cavalry of 4th Corps and to the 2nd Brigade of 3rd Cavalry Corps were placed in the reserve. The Armée du Nord mustered, on 10 June, the following guns:[1114]

12-pounder	42
6-pounder	142
6.4-pounder howitzer	14
24-pounder howitzer	56
Total	254

Of these guns, the following were still with 1st, 2nd, 6th Corps and the reserve after Waterloo:[1115]

12-pounder	24
6-pounder	54
6.4-pounder howitzer	8
24-pounder howitzer	26
Total	112

Guns with the army on 25 June were:[1116]

12-pounder	7	17 lost
6-pounder	29	31 lost
6.4-pounder howitzer	3	5 lost
24-pounder howitzer	8	20 lost
Total	47	73 lost

1114 AN: AFIV 1939. Ruty to Soult, 10 June 1815.
1115 SHDDT: C15 34.
1116 ibid.

At Waterloo, the French lost seventy-three guns, or 58 per cent of artillery pieces from 1st, 2nd and 6th Corps. The Allies admit to the capture of 122 guns:[1117]

12-pounder	35
6-pounder	57
6.4-pounder howitzer	13
24-pounder howitzer	17
Total	122

Spare gun carriages:

12-pounder	6
6-pounder	6
Howitzer	8
Total	20

Caissons:

12-pounder	74
6-pounder	71
Howitzer	50
Total	195
Forge Wagons	20
Wagons	52
Total	72

We do not have the totals for guns lost with the Imperial Guard. Based on the English figures, 48 per cent of the French artillery's guns were lost at Waterloo; 122 guns lost out of a total of 254 guns, excluding the auxiliary batteries. Of these, sixty-five guns were lost with 1st, 2nd and 6th Corps, along with 3rd Cavalry Corps and the Auxiliary Guard Artillery. A further forty-seven were lost from the Imperial Guard, the cavalry divisions attached to 1st, 2nd and 6th Corps and 3rd Cavalry Corps. In terms of total losses, 132 guns remained with the army, of which we have details of just forty-six, leaving eighty-six guns with the Imperial Guard. The Guard foot artillery got all its guns off the field. The Auxiliary Guard artillery did leave some guns behind.

Looking at the engineers, every man of the ninety-one men from 2nd Battalion 1st Regiment of Engineers attached to 1st Corps, including officers, were made prisoners of war. Officers made prisoner were:[1118]

1117 Booth, Vol. 1, p. 39.
1118 Jean Marc Boisnard personal communication.

Staff

- Battalion-Commander Marie François Rousseau de Sibelle
- Battalion-Commander Joseph Victory Auduy, born on 9 May 1782 and was wounded at Waterloo
- Captain Aimont, wounded at Waterloo
- Captain Henry Jacques Bigot
- Lieutenant Henry Gregoire
- Lieutenant Gonbault
- Lieutenant Piere Sibelet

1st Corps

- Second-Captain Benjamin Aubert Ernest Vanechout, captured at the fall of La Haye Sainte
- Second-Captain Perpete Joseph Louis Urban had a leg carried away by a round shot in the assault on La Haye Sainte. Attached to 4th Division
- Second-Lieutenant Buquet, wounded during the attack on La Haye Sainte

2nd Corps

- Captain Jean Jules Jacquin de Cassieres, wounded in the fighting at Hougoumont
- Captain Louis Le Roux-Douville, wounded at Waterloo
- Second-Captain Jean Claudel, wounded with a sabre cut to the face at Waterloo
- First-Lieutenant Joseph Carrier, wounded with a gunshot at Waterloo
- Second-Captain Watrin, killed during the assault on La Haye Sainte
- Second-Captain Maignen, killed during the attack on La Haye Sainte

Overall, it seems the engineer troops suffered very heavily from being overrun. Were these men all captured when La Haye Sainte fell in the evening, or were they rounded up by the Allied cavalry when they attacked the farmhouse at the same moment when the infantry of 1st Corps was herded up by the cavalry? This seems a far more likely scenario, that the engineers of 1st Corps were virtually made prisoner to a man by the Allied cavalry.

Comment

Napoléon's line infantry at Waterloo lost the following casualties:

Line Infantry							
	Wounded	Evacuated Wounded	Wounded & Prisoner	Prisoner of War	Killed	Missing	Total
1st Corps	518	0	854	3,896	215	3,140	8,623 (54 per cent)
2nd Corps	639	1,174	65	1,411	387	1,090	4,766 (34 per cent)
6th Corps	546	0	14	482	130	256	1,915 (29 per cent)
Total	1,703	1,174	933	5,789	732	4,486	15,304 (38 per cent)

From the table, the huge losses in 1st Corps of men made prisoner or missing are very obvious. Also of note is the number of men killed; 732 men out of 15,355, or 4.7 per cent. The wounded account for some 3,810 men, or 25 per cent. Clearly, our ideas of heavy losses and the scale or mortality at Waterloo, and in early modern battles in general, has to be revised. The British army lost some 4,255 men dead or wounded; more than 10,000 less than the French.

The cavalry

The total losses for the 3rd and 5th Cavalry Divisions were as follows:

3rd and 5th Cavalry Divisions						
	Killed	Died of Wounds	Wounded	Prisoner of War	Missing	Total
3rd Division	14	0	13	17	46	90
5th Division	17	1	5	10	19	52
Total	31	1	18	27	65	142

From the table, it is clear the 3rd Cavalry Division lost far more men than the 5th. Due to a lack of data we cannot present any further details of losses for the light cavalry at Waterloo; however it does seem that the 5th Division were not as heavily engaged as the 3rd, though they had more men killed outright. Looking at all the recorded cavalry losses, we see:

Cavalry Corps							
	Killed	Died of Wounds	Wounded	Wounded & Missing	Prisoner of War	Missing	Total
3rd Cavalry Corps	67	0	36	89	99	388	679
4th Cavalry Corps	54	0	39	0	28	384	505
3rd and 5th Divisions	31	1	18	0	27	65	142
Total	152	1	93	89	154	837	1,326

The data for the 3rd and 5th Divisions is incomplete, plus, as noted earlier, the losses for the 1st Carabiniers and 2nd Dragoons, which combined could add another one hundred men lost. The data for 1st Division and 2nd Division is also massively incomplete, as is the 4th Division; losses only exist for one of the six lancer regiments present. Despite this, what is strikingly obvious from the data is that the 3rd and 5th Cavalry Divisions lost comparable numbers of men dead and wounded, and in terms of missing men, the 4th Corps far exceeded the light cavalry. The 3rd Corps had by far the highest number of dead. What it does show is that the fighting on the French right was as costly in the massed charges. As with the losses of the Young Guard, to be discussed below, the 3rd and 5th Cavalry Divisions fought as actively as Kellermann's and Milhaud's commands.

In comparison, the 3rd Chasseurs à Cheval (deployed on the right flank) lost just thirty-two men.[1119] The 6th Chasseurs, on the French left, lost sixty-two men.[1120] The notion that hundreds of men were mown down by Wellington's infantry is incorrect. With hindsight, the charges are seen as ineffective and doomed to failure, but on the day Napoléon only had the two cavalry reserves to hand with which to try and effect

---

1119 SHDDT: GR 24 YC 264.
1120 SHDDT: GR 24 YC 282.

a breakthrough without compromising the army and committing his reserves. Thus, the massed cavalry attacks were a logical attack, much as they were at Eylau, Aspern-Essling, Wagram and Borodino years before, simply because Napoléon had no other troops to use than the cavalry.

The Guard cavalry

Total losses for the Guard cavalry are shown below:

Guard Cavalry					
	Wounded	Wounded & Prisoner	Prisoner of War	Killed	Missing
Lancers	88	0	0	8	178
Chasseurs	17	0	11	29	2
Dragoons	24	0	2	16	96
Grenadiers	38	0	0	18	78
Total	167	0	13	71	354

The Guard cavalry lost in total some 605 NCOs and men. The Red Lancers had by far the highest losses of the day, with the heavy cavalry brigade having comparable numbers of losses. The relatively low losses of the chasseurs à cheval stands out, bar the very high number of dead, which is double that of other regiments. Clearly, whatever episode caused this high fatality was not experienced by the other regiments of the Guard; of course, the dead may well include mortally wounded who died later. But, when we look at the low ratio of missing and wounded, it seems that the regiment was clearly not involved in the same intensity of fighting as the rest of the Guard. Was it held back from more serious fighting at the close of the battle, to leave a strong body of cavalry as a direct escort to the emperor and his entourage? It seems very possible that this was the case. Compared to the line, the Guard suffered more losses than 3rd Corps, and its losses were overall on par with those of Milhaud's men. The cavalry of the Imperial Guard was reduced to a mere 1,937 men by 26 June 1815. Of the losses, some 924 officers, sub-officers and men had been killed in General Guyot's heavy cavalry division and 1,013 in the command of General Lefèbvre-Desnoëttes, which comprised the chasseurs à cheval and the regiment of light horse lancers. The grenadiers à cheval had the lowest attrition rate of any regiment of the Guard cavalry (387 officers, sub-officers and men), followed next by the Empress Dragoons with 416 casualties, the regiment of light horse lancers, which suffered the loss of 415 sub-officers and men, and lastly the chasseurs à cheval losing some 616 sub-officers and men. In addition, fifty-six sub-officers and men in the elite gendarmes of the Imperial Guard had been killed or wounded.

Comment

In order to assess combat effectiveness of the heavy cavalry at Waterloo, we can perhaps compare the charges to those of the cavalry reserve at Aspern-Essling:[1121]

	1st Heavy Cavalry Division	2nd Heavy Cavalry Division	3rd Heavy Cavalry Division
Horses lost to 20 May 1809	237	25	480
Horses present 20 May 1809	3,518	2,289	2,579
Horses lost to 5 June 1809	440	580	785
Total horses lost to 5 June 1809	677	605	1,265
Average horses lost per regiment	73	116	196

The total number of horse losses from 20 May to 5 June 1809 was 1,805 from twelve regiments of cavalry, an average of 150 horses per regiment. Where the data exists for Waterloo, 1,326 men were killed, wounded, deserted or taken prisoner. The deserted perhaps were mounted. It is hard to imagine how one could round up mounted cavalry to be made prisoner of war. The wounded were also likely dismounted, which gives a very basic ballpark figure of 1,326 horses lost, perhaps more based on Domon's figures from 17 June, which gives a figure of one man to every horse wounded or killed. The figure of horses lost was certainly around two thousand, if not much higher. This gives an average across twelve regiments as 166 horses, slightly higher than Aspern-Essling. In this context, the charges at Waterloo were on par with the great charges of the glory years of the empire. If Ney is blamed for destroying the cavalry at Waterloo, then Bessières, over the course of two days, is as culpable. But, that is the point. Aspern-Essling was fought over two

---

1121 AN: C2 472, situation report, 5 July 1809.

days; the cavalry at Waterloo were in action for a quarter of that time. The casualty rate was not unusual, but the rate in which the casualties occurred was. But, were these losses in 1809 and 1815 unique? How do they fit into other theatres of war? Losses for the campaign of September 1806 to 15 March 1807 were 13,100 horses.[1122] Of these, some 2,161 horses were lost at Eylau in the great cavalry charge.[1123] Thus, in this consideration, Waterloo (for the cavalry at least) was a replay of Eylau. In this context, Waterloo was not unique, yet it is often made out to be so. Perhaps because there were no redcoats at Aspern-Essling or Eylau, Waterloo takes on more importance due to the Anglo-phonic nature of the historiography of the campaign, and the performance of the French army is viewed from a misunderstanding of the army from the British experience of it in Spain and Walcheren. This totally misses the point about the nature of the French army away from these secondary theatres of conflict. When we place Waterloo into the context of the French army's operations since 1799, it is not unique.

We need to stress that unlike in previous years, the army Napoléon fielded in 1815 actually had less mounted troops than at the commencement of the 1814 campaign. On 25 January 1814, Napoléon had 35,000 riding horses with the cavalry and horse artillery, with 14,859 draught horses, making 49,859 horses, which reduced to 30,459 by the close of March 1814.[1124] In addition, 13,722 horses were still in Spain, and the army remount pool had 24,981 horses.[1125] Taking the horses still in Spain into consideration and the remounts held on 5 January 1814, the army had 88,562 horses, which reduced significantly by 25 March 1814 to 69,162. The total number of horses with France's armed forces in 1815 amounted to 59,600; 10,000 less than a year earlier and 27,000 less than he commenced the 1814 campaign with. On 20 March 1815, the army as a whole had 37,286 horses, a slight increase from the numbers in March 1814. Between 25 March 1814 and 20 March 1815, the horses with the army had been reduced by 31,876 horses.[1126]

In June 1815, Napoléon fielded 16,500 draught horses and 37,000 riding horses; some 53,500 horses. In real terms, Napoléon increased the horses with the army by 21,714. However, of this force, the troops

---

1122 AN: C2 470, Bourcier to Clarke, 14 March 1807.
1123 SHDDT: E 31, fol. 6.
1124 AN: AF IV 842 to 883, AF IV 1550-1580.
1125 ibid.
1126 ibid.

Napoléon fielded under his command in June 1815 amounted to only 15,489 riding horses with the cavalry supported by 286 guns. 80,350 infantry were also fielded. Ironically, Napoléon had less cavalry to hand at the start of the Waterloo campaign than he had at the Battle of Bautzen in 1813, when he had 16,867 cavalry, 200,000 infantry and 370 guns.[1127] Napoléon's spring campaign of 1813 has been traditionally one that was limited in success due to the lack of cavalry, as David Gates notes.[1128] In less than five months the cavalry arm had been regenerated from just over 4,000 men to a force of 36,252 men by 25 April 1813.[1129] This equates to a remount rate of 7,305 per month. In 1815, Napoléon managed to increase his cavalry by 10,000 in three months. Clearly, we must see the 1815 campaign as being one hampered by the lack of cavalry. To obtain horses for this campaign, Napoléon raided the remount service, corps purchase system and transferred horses from elsewhere into the army. The number of horses obtained during the campaign, 16,000 draught horses and 14,800 riding horses, were small by the large purchases of previous years. Napoléon's methods of late payment or partial payment for horses reduced the number of dealers willing to sell horses to the state, which hampered the remount operation. In 1813 and 1814, he had bled the gendarmes of their horses, who by 1815 had not been able to replace their mounts. Neither did society have large numbers of horses to give to the state. The 125,000 horses that had been volunteered to the state in 1813 were a finite resource which could not be easily replaced. Between 1812 and 1814, the Napoléonic state had used up the surplus of arms, equipment and horses created in the period 1801-1812. The actions of Napoléon in 1813-1814 in alienating the equine industry had serious repercussions in 1815. He was outnumbered and needed to use his available troops quickly to achieve numerical superiority over each Allied army in turn before they could unite. The haste in which the army was reformed and the lack of good officers and NCOs reduced the army's fighting abilities. Defeat in 1813 had not been inevitable, but it perhaps was in 1815. The Napoléonic regime lacked the economic strength of previous years. France had degenerated into the disarray that had hampered the last days of the Directory regime. With the

---

1127 SHDDT: C2. Bourcier to Clarke, 14 March 1813. See also: Napoléon to Eugene, 18 March 1813.
1128 David E. Gates, *The Napoleonic Wars 1803-1815*, Arnold, London, 1997, p. 233.
1129 Camille Rousset, *La Grande Armée de 1813*, Paris, 1871, pp. 17-18.

collapse of the wider empire, exhausted credit, being unable to raise taxes and unable to rely on requisitioning of goods and material, a successful defence of France relied on horses and muskets, neither of which Napoléon had in sufficient quantities. France was exhausted after twenty-five years of conflict.

The infantry of the Old Guard

No issue is more emotive to French and British writers than the fate of the Old Guard at Waterloo. The casualty data for the Old Guard provides vital clues in telling the real story of what happened. The table below gives total losses regiment-by-regiment for the grenadiers:[1130]

Division of Grenadiers à Pied							
Regiment	Battalion	Wounded	Evacuated Wounded	Wounded & Prisoner	Prisoner of War	Killed	Missing
1st	1st	1	0	0	3	1	52
	2nd	3	0	0	5	0	65
2nd	1st	44	0	0	132	5	26
	2nd	20	0	0	114	4	16
3rd	1st	12	0	0	326	1	10
	2nd	36	0	0	203	6	13
4th	1st	36	0	0	65	4	3
	2nd	10	0	0	93	2	5
Total		162	0	0	941	23	190

From the data, it is clear that as history suggests the 1st Grenadiers were kept in reserve and not committed to fighting. Even so, both battalions still lost men at Waterloo, no doubt in the retreat. The 3rd Grenadiers, with both battalions on the field of Waterloo, lost heavily, more so than any other regiment in the division. The heaviest losses were in the 1st Battalion 3rd Grenadiers, with over one hundred more men lost than the regiment's 2nd Battalion. It is this 2nd Battalion that has been described by some as attacked by Adams's brigade; in such a scenario surely the battalion would have lost far more men than the other battalions of the Guard? Clearly, based on the casualty data, the battalion lost heavily, but nothing like the massive losses sustained by the 2nd Battalion 1st

---

1130 Compiled from SHDDT: GR 20 YC 13. See also: SHDDT: GR 20 YC 14.

Chasseurs and 2nd Battalion 2nd Chasseurs, which history tells us stood close by the square of the 2nd Battalion 3rd Grenadiers. Losses for the chasseurs à pied were as follows:[1131]

Division of Chasseurs à Pied								
	Battalion	Wounded	Evacuated Wounded	Wounded & Prisoner	Prisoner of War	Killed	Missing	Total
1st	1st	0	0	0	37	2	1	40
	2nd	5	0	0	419	10	12	446
2nd	1st	19	0	0	144	6	17	186
	2nd	3	0	0	112	0	47	162
3rd	1st	23	0	0	520	0	0	543
	2nd	21	0	0	513	0	0	534
4th	No data available							805[1132]
Total								2,716

Of note, the 1st Battalion 1st Chasseurs was not involved in the action at Waterloo, as it was held in reserve. The 2nd Battalion of the regiment, under General Cambronne, was indeed at Waterloo, with the bulk of the battalion being made prisoner of war, also the case with the 3rd Chasseurs. This figure may also include dead, wounded and deserters. The chasseurs lost far more men than the grenadiers, explained by the 3rd and 4th Chasseurs ceasing to exist following Waterloo.

The largest loss to manpower of the Imperial Guard infantry was men made prisoner or who are recorded as deserting their regiments. This desertion rate is not surprising, given the collapse of the French army at the end of the battle. The prisoners would also include, as we noted earlier, incapacitated wounded men. Of interest, of the casualties recorded, some 2.2 per cent were mortalities, a similar number to the recorded deaths in 6th Corps, but far lower than in 1st or 2nd Corps. The number of wounded is also significantly lower than in the three corps of line infantry. The high number of prisoners matches with Allied accounts

---

1131 Compiled from SHDDT: GR 20 YC 44. See also: SHDDT: GR 20 YC 45; SHDDT: GR 20 YC 46.

1132 The *contrôle* of the regiment is incomplete. It lists just 158 out of 1,070 men under arms with the regiment on 10 June. Therefore, the only data is the difference between the two parade reports. This, however, will include losses on 16 June and after 19 June to 23 June.

The Old Guard as a whole had mustered 8,388 men in eight regiments formed into two divisions, and lost 4,061 men at Waterloo and the rearguard stand at Genappe on 19 June. This represents a loss of 48 per cent of effective strength at Waterloo. This is slightly lower than the Division of the Young Guard, which comprised four regiments. The losses of the Guard are noticeably higher than 2nd or 6th Corps, and close to that of 1st Corps. The 3rd Regiment of Chasseurs, shattered by the counter-attack of the Allied light cavalry and musketry of David Chassé's troops, broke and fled and were rounded up like sheep by the cavalry, the entire regiment being virtually captured on the field of battle.[1133] Neither the 3rd of 4th Chasseurs had been under fire as military formations before the attack at Waterloo, which may explain why when fired upon by the Allies, the regiments never made contact with the Allied lines before breaking and fleeing, the men being herded up by the cavalry. Allied reports from the 1st Foot Guards all make comment that the Imperial Guard was there one minute and then it disappeared—the striking sudden disappearance and routing of the regiment is borne out by archival paperwork from the regiments.

The 1st Battalion 3rd Grenadiers, shattered by the Allied musketry and artillery, according to Guillemin, broke and fled to seek safety in the square of the 2nd Battalion 1st Chasseurs, and it may well be the breaking of this square that resulted in large numbers of men from the 3rd Grenadiers being captured at the same time. The 2nd Battalion 3rd Grenadiers, contrary to de Mauduit's myth that the battalion was virtually annihilated, suffered the least men captured as prisoners of war, and appears to have made its way relatively unscathed to Genappe. Here, the 4th Company of the 2nd Battalion suffered twenty-seven men wounded and fifteen prisoners. The wounded men were subsequently captured. At Waterloo and Genappe, 154 men out of 520 were in the battalion, or 30 per cent. The 1st Battalion lost 207 men out of 518, or 40 per cent. The regiment as a whole lost 34 per cent of its manpower at Waterloo, but of great note is it lost a further 62 per cent after 20 June.[1134]

The 4th Grenadiers, said by Mark Adkin to have been annihilated at Waterloo, retreated in good order and took part in the stand of the

---

1133 Compiled from SHDDT: GR 20 YC 44. See also: SHDDT: GR 20 YC 45; SHDDT: GR 20 YC 46.

1134 Compiled from SHDDT: GR 20 YC 13. See also: SHDDT: GR 20 YC 14.

Guard at Genappe against the Prussians. At Waterloo, the regiment lost 364 men, but between 20 and 23 June a further 736 men were classed as deserted or prisoner of war. Clearly, the regiment was not destroyed at Waterloo, it fought well at Genappe and only disintegrated from 20 June onwards, spurred on, we are told, by the men desiring to be with Napoléon as opposed to remain with the army.[1135]

The 1st Grenadiers appear to have done very little in the battle. The 1st Company of 1st Battalion (sent to Plancenoit) lost two men made prisoner of war, one deserted, one killed and one wounded, whereas the remainder of the regiment lost nine men overall at Waterloo, but lost a staggering 600 men between 19 and 23 June. These men quit the army and headed off to Paris en masse. Mark Adkin lists all these men as dead, wounded or prisoners on the 18th, which is simply not true.[1136]

The ancillary and support services of the Imperial Guard also lost heavily in the battle. The Artillery Train of the Imperial Guard lost four men killed and forty-nine wounded. A further six were captured, 144 disappeared and 490 deserted;[1137] further proof that it was not battlefield attrition that destroyed the Old Guard, but the effective harassment of the French army afterwards and the vital role of the Allied cavalry and Prussians who executed this.

The Infantry of the Imperial Guard lost some 6,162 men from the 12,554 present on 15 June, a total loss of 49 per cent of effective strength. This means, as with 1st Corps, one in every two soldiers would be wounded or made prisoner at Waterloo. The Guard surrendered rather than died.

The Young Guard

The fighting in Plancenoit, in which the Young Guard was involved, was far costlier in men in a single division than all of 6th Corps losses combined. The Young Guard Division's losses, shown below, are also significantly higher than any division in 2nd Corps. Clearly, the fighting in Plancenoit was of a different level of intensity than experienced either by 2nd Corps or 6th Corps.

1135 ibid.

1136 ibid.

1137 SHDDT: GR 20 YC 197 *Registre matricule de d'Escadron du train d'artillerie de la Garde Impériale cree pat décret du 8 Avril 1815.*

Young Guard Division						
	Wounded	Evacuated Wounded	Wounded & Prisoner	Prisoner of War	Killed	Missing	Total
1st Brigade	164	0	0	210	65	676	1,115
2nd Brigade	64	0	0	409	31	482	986
Total	228	0	0	619	96	1,158	2,101

The Young Guard lost 2,101 men from a total of 4,166 present under arms on 15 June 1815. This represents a loss of 50 per cent of effective strength. Losses for the Guard infantry were as follows:

Imperial Guard Infantry						
	Wounded	Evacuated Wounded	Wounded & Prisoner	Prisoner of War	Killed	Missing	Total
Grenadiers à Pied	162	0	0	941	23	190	1316
Chasseurs à Pied	71	0	0	1,745	18	77	2,716
Young Guard	228	0	0	619	96	1,158	2,101
Total	461	0	0	3,305	137	1,425	6,133

Guard artillery and Allied troops

The Imperial Guard foot artillery lost two deserters, three wounded, six killed and seventy-four disappeared on 18 June and one wounded, one killed and fifty-six disappeared on 19 June. Furthermore, 129 men disappeared between 20 to 23 June.[1138] The losses of the horse artillery of the Guard were as follows:[1139]

1138 SHDDT: GR 20 YC 180 *1 avril 1815-7 novembre 1815 (matricules: 1 à 1 018).*

1139 SHDDT: GR 20 YC 187 *Artillerie à cheval de la garde impériale, 1er avril 1815-30 octobre 1815 (matricules: 1 à 472).*

Artillerie à Cheval de la Garde Imperiale					
	Wounded	Wounded & Prisoner	Prisoner of War	Killed	Missing
1st Company	1	0	1	6	4
2nd Company	0	0	0	2	1
3rd Company	0	0	0	0	4
4th Company	2	0	1	1	1
Total	3	0	2	9	10

The regiment lost 6 per cent of effective strength at Waterloo, some twenty-four men out of 354 present on 10 June 1815. A further ninety-eight men, some 66 per cent of the remaining effective strength of the regiment, were lost from 19 to 25 June 1815. In the 4th Company of Imperial Guard Horse Artillery, attached to the Empress Dragoons was Company-Commander Captain Antoine Marcel, who had two horses killed under him and was wounded.

Among the artillery train, Sergeant Jacques Martin Delacroix, of 2nd Company, took a gunshot wound to the right leg. Second-Lieutenant Pierre Fillon was hit by a cannonball, which killed his horse. He had his left leg amputated by the British after he had been taken prisoner. The artillery train of the Imperial Guard lost forty-five men deserted, forty-nine wounded, six prisoners of war and four killed on 18 June; a total loss of 104.[1140] Returned prisoners of war included:[1141]

- Claude Moussard, of 6th Company
- Pierre Benetre, of 2nd Company
- Jean Martin, of 2nd Company

Between 18 and 26 June, a further six men were captured, 144 disappeared and 490 deserted;[1142] further proof that it was not battlefield attrition that destroyed the Old Guard, but the effective harassment of the French army after the battle.

1140 SHDDT: GR 20 YC 197 *Escadron du train d'artillerie de la garde impériale, 8 avril 1815-1er décembre 1815 (matricules: 1 à 1 317).*

1141 SHDDT: Yj 11.

1142 SHDDT: GR 20 YC 197 *Registré matricule de l'escadron du train d'artillerie de la Garde Impériale crée pat décret du 8 Avril 1815.*

The equipment train of the Guard lost twenty-three men either deserted or prisoner of war.[1143] The company of sapeur-mineurs lost one man wounded on 15 June, one dead and one wounded on 16 June and eight deserted on 20 June. No losses were sustained on 18 or 19 June.[1144] The administration battalion recorded the following as prisoners:[1145]

- Andre Guillermain. Admitted to the equipment train of the Imperial Guard on 21 May 1815. Deserted from the 8th Voltigeurs then passed with the rank of corporal to the administration battalion on 26 May 1815. He disappeared on 18 June, presumed to be a prisoner of war.
- Louis François Boucher, born on 14 July 1792, was conscripted to the battalion on 24 January 1810 and placed on leave from 16 August 1814. Re-admitted to the battalion on 29 May 1815, he was promoted to corporal on 1 June 1815 and made a prisoner of war at Waterloo.
- Jean Louis Lelang was born on 30 December 1796. He enrolled on 25 May 1815 into the equipment train of the Imperial Guard and passed to the administration battalion on 26 May 1815. By profession he was a wagon driver and was made prisoner of war on 18 June 1815.

In total, twenty-four were made prisoners at Waterloo.[1146] In March 1816, five were returned from England.[1147] The marines of the Guard had three men returned from prison in England in 1816. No further details of losses for the company are known.[1148]

1143 SHDDT: GR 20 YC 209 *Bataillons du train des équipages militaires de la garde impériale, 8 avril 1815-1er octobre 1815 (matricules: 1 à 807). Créés par décret du 8 avril 1815.*

1144 SHDDT: GR 20 YC 204 *Sapeurs mineurs 1815.*

1145 SHDDT: GR 20 YC 211 *Compagnies d'ouvriers d'administration, 26 mai 1815-1er octobre 1815 (matricules: 1 à 475).*

1146 SHDDT: GR 20 YC 211.

1147 ibid.

1148 SHDDT: Yj 11.

Chapter 25

The Analysis

What does this mass of data tell us about Waterloo, if anything? Firstly, it is worth comparing this data to the losses for the army as a whole:

	Wounded	Evacuated Wounded	Wounded & Prisoner of War	Prisoner of War	Killed	Missing	Total
Grenadiers à Pied	162	0	0	940	23	190	1,316
Chasseurs à Pied	71	0	0	1,745	18	77	2,745
Young Guard	228	0	0	619	96	1,158	2,101
Sub-Total	461	0	0	3,304	137	1,425	6,162
1st Corps	518	0	854	4,819	215	3,140	8,694
2nd Corps	639	1,174	65	1,411	387	1,090	4,749
6th Corps	546	0	14	482	130	256	1,912
Sub-Total	1,703	1,174	933	6,712	732	4,486	15,355
Overall Total	2,164	1,174	933	10,016	869	5,911	21,517

Looking at the data, by far the highest losses were in 1st Corps, as one would expect. What is interesting is that the Young Guard in Plancenoit, just four regiments, lost more men than all of 6th Corps, some seven regiments. As will be discussed below, the disparity in losses strongly suggests that the fighting that 6th Corps was involved in was not as costly in terms of dead and wounded, and moreover that 6th Corps was perhaps not in action as long as the Young Guard. The Young Guard's losses were lower than the Corps of Chasseurs à Pied, a comparable formation of four regiments, the bulk coming from the 3rd and 4th Chasseurs, which shows just how deadly the Allied attack against General Michel and these two latter regiments was. The Old Guard as a whole lost in reality some 700 men less than 2nd Corps. Clearly, the fighting that 2nd Corps was involved with throughout the day of 18 June was of less intensity than the Old Guard's hour or so in combat. The 2nd Corps lost 33 per cent effective strength and 6th Corps 28 per cent; this figure does not seem greatly different, but the 5 per cent difference equates to 2,000 men. The 6th Corps, based on the known recorded data, was involved in a different intensity of fighting when compared to the Old Guard, the Young Guard, as well as 1st and 2nd Corps. Did Lobau retreat early to save his corps from becoming trapped? Occupying the terrain between Frischermont and Plancenoit in a shallow valley, with ridges to each side, the Prussians debouched at La Haye Sainte and Smohain and, it seems, Plancenoit at the same time. The main Prussian force did eventually arrive down the road to the Paris Wood, but by this time it seems Lobau, for fear of being out-flanked and cut off from the army, retreated.

Total French infantry losses were 21,517 men, of which just 874 men were killed. This means just 4 per cent of all recorded casualties at Waterloo were fatalities. Some 4,271 men were wounded, representing 19 per cent of casualties. This means 10,000 men were made prisoners, including 933 men who were wounded and made prisoner of war, so this figure is included also in the wounded and prisoner totals. Some 5,911 men, or 27 per cent of all casualties among the infantry, were men who ran away as deserters. This means that the bulk of the infantry of Napoléon's last army were made prisoners of war by the Allies at Waterloo. When we factor in the 1,120 recorded losses for the cavalry, with a possible 900 men lost in the artillery and train, the total French loss would be 24,000 to 25,000 men.

The highest factor in the French losses were men made prisoner of war. Indeed, Allied accounts, as we have seen, speak of the Old Guard being rounded up and made prisoner. This does indeed tally with the recorded casualty data.

For example, the recorded casualty data shows that the 3rd and 4th Chasseurs disappeared almost to a man at Waterloo. The overwhelming majority of the men are listed as missing. For the 3rd Chasseurs, we have the fate of forty-four men at Waterloo and 159 men were still under arms, thus we have the whereabouts of 203 of the 1,028 men that had been under arms on 1 June 1815. The 3rd Chasseurs lost a staggering 825 other ranks on 18 June.

The missing men must include dead and wounded. On 23 June, six officers and 159 men were in ranks. We are only aware of the fate of forty-four men from the regiment among the casualties at Waterloo. The regiment effectively ceased to exist. The 4th Chasseurs lost 805 other ranks, but we can only be certain of the fate of five men: one killed, four wounded. The regiment's paperwork lists just 158 men, of which the vast majority are listed as presumed prisoner, i.e. missing in action. Therefore, we cannot know the true fate of the 3rd and 4th Chasseurs beyond speculation that the two regiments were virtually destroyed.[1149] The regiment's two battalions seem to have been shattered by the 1st Foot Guards and the men rounded up by the cavalry.

On 1 July, some 427 men are listed as missing from the combined 3rd and 4th Chasseurs, with a further nineteen men known to be prisoner of war and thirty-nine wounded still in hospital. The 3rd Chasseurs contributed 159 men and the 4th 236 men; a total of 395 men under arms. Thus, of the 2,069 men on 1 June, we know the fate of 880, meaning the whereabouts of 1,189 men is not known. The question is: what was the fate of these missing men?

In the other regiments of chasseurs, huge numbers of men were listed as prisoner of war or missing. Indeed, the 2nd Battalion of the 1st Chasseurs, in which General Cambronne is said to have uttered the famous words 'the Guard dies! It does not surrender!' was nearly entirely captured. Only nine men from the 1st Company escaped being made prisoner of war. The battalion lost 446 other ranks out of 635 men, or 70 per cent of the total, of which 419 (65 per cent) were prisoners of war.[1150] The 2nd Battalion 2nd Chasseurs, compared to the huge losses of the 2nd Battalion 1st Chasseurs or the 3rd Chasseurs, seem to have suffered far fewer casualties: three men wounded, twenty deserted and 112 taken prisoner. The battalion seems to have held together against the attack of the Allied cavalry and infantry.[1151]

What occasioned the large losses in Cambronne's battalion? For Bacheville, the battalion dissolved during an attack by the Allied cavalry. This is confirmed by Chasseur Claude Jacquot, also of the 2nd

---

1149 SHDDT: Xab 68 *Grenadiers à Pied (formation de 1815)*.
1150 Compiled from SHDDT: GR 20 YC 44. See also: SHDDT: GR 20 YC 45; SHDDT: GR 20 YC 46.
1151 ibid.

Battalion 1st Chasseurs, who in a letter of 28 November 1832 recalls that:[1152]

> I was with the 1st Chasseurs à Pied of the Old Guard, along with MM. Desplange and Walters. The square was on the plateau overlooking the two valleys, at the confluence of three roads near to where General Michel was killed. We were assailed by German hussars and artillery in our left flank.

When we look at the fate of the 1st Battalion 3rd Grenadiers and the 4th Grenadiers, which we know were also charged by the Allied cavalry, the losses, though heavier, are comparable. With a square broken open by cavalry, many hundreds of men were easy prey to the cavalry to either be killed or captured. Clearly, what happened to the 2nd Battalion 1st Chasseurs was of a totally different scale to what affected the 2nd Battalion 3rd Grenadiers and 2nd Battalion 2nd Chasseurs when we look at the data, and here we have an answer to why the battalion suffered catastrophic losses in manpower.

However, the regimental muster lists recorded that the bulk of the Old Guard was missing at Waterloo, so we cannot therefore ultimately know the fate of all the men at Waterloo by using this data alone, as these figures will include dead and wounded men. Furthermore, the figures were obtained by the regimental roll being called, and the adjutant asking the survivors about the fate of the men not on parade. If no one witnessed the fate of the missing men, it was only natural for the adjutant to write down these men were presumably missing or prisoners. Thus, we know the number of men missing, but not what happened to them. However, we are able to resolve this issue to some extent.

From the muster list we know that thousands of men were listed as prisoner of war. What happened to these prisoners? The vast majority were transported to England. Thanks to the level of bureaucracy in the French army we know what happened to perhaps 90 per cent of the prisoners taken at Waterloo. As well as preserving the regimental muster lists at the Army Archives at Vincennes, the collection also houses another vast resource about Waterloo.

When the prisoners of war were taken by the British army on 18 June, and on the immediate days after (at Charleroi and other field

---

1152 Author's collection.

hospitals which were captured wholesale), these men were transported to the Dutch coast for transport to England. Many hundreds of the prisoners were no doubt wounded and would die before ever reaching England and a good number would die in England. But, of great importance to our study in endeavouring to define the fate of the Old Guard at Waterloo, for all those prisoners who remained in England and were subsequently shipped back to France in 1816, the Army Archives preserves lists of the men returned to France. The French War Ministry, in order to keep a track on the men being returned, recorded the name, rank, number and regiment of all the men shipped back. This then provides details of thousands of men who were presumably listed as missing or prisoner of war at Waterloo. The data is shown below:[1153]

Imperial Guard Infantry				
	Prisoners of War registered at Dartmoor	Prisoners of War registered a Fleet Prison, Plymouth	Prisoners of War returned to France	Comment
1st Grenadiers	7	5	21	
2nd Grenadiers	26	2	14	
3rd Grenadiers	22	3	57	
4th Grenadiers	3	2	22	
Sub-Total	58	12	114	
1st Chasseurs	3	4	51	
2nd Chasseurs	10	2	19	
3rd Chasseurs	1	5	66	
4th Chasseurs	2	4	68	
Sub-Total	16	15	204	

1153 SHDDT: Yj11, SHDDT: Yj 12, SHDDT: Yj 13. See also: The National Archives, Kew: ADM 103/513; ADM 103/99; ADM 103/311; ADM 103/595.

Old Guard no regiment given	347	0	204	
1st Tirailleurs	28	2	67	
3rd Tirailleurs	18	0	1	
Sub-Total	46	2	68	
1st Voltigeurs	69	2	118	
3rd Voltigeurs	34	3	65	
Sub-Total	103	5	183	
Young Guard no regiment given	66	5	12	
Total Prisoners of War	636	39	785	

Imperial Guard Cavalry

	Prisoners of War registered at Dartmoor	Prisoners of War registers at Fleet Prison, Plymouth	Prisoners of War returned to France	Comment
Grenadiers	1	0	1	
Dragoons	7	0	12	one officer
Chasseurs	5	1	2	one mamluke at Fleet Prison
Red Lancers	6	3	2	one officer
Polish Squadron	0	0	5	
Gendarmes	0	0	3	
Total Prisoners of War	19	4	25	

Imperial Guard Artillery

	Prisoners of War registered in England	Prisoners of War registers at Fleet Prison, Plymouth	Prisoners of War returned to France	Comment
Artillerie à Pied	4	0	14	
Artillerie à Cheval	0	0	3	one officer
Train d'artillerie	0	0	0	
Train des Equipage	1	0	1	
Sapeur du Genie	0	0	0	
Marines	1	0	3	
Ouvriers d'Administration	1	0	5	
Total Prisoners of War	7	0	26	

Cavalry

	Prisoners of War registered at Dartmoor	Prisoners of War registered at Fleet Prison, Plymouth	Prisoners of War returned to France	Comment
1st Carabiniers	9	0	6	one adjutant-sous-officer
2nd Carabiniers	3	0.	1	
Sub-Total	12	0	7	
1st Cuirassiers	30	2	21	two officers
2nd Cuirassiers	11	2	5	
3rd Cuirassiers	6	0	8	
4th Cuirassiers	15	1	5	
5th Cuirassiers	12	0	10	one officer
6th Cuirassiers	2	0	3	
7th Cuirassiers	0	0	4	
8th Cuirassiers	7	0	10	
9th Cuirassiers	4	0	9	
10th Cuirassiers	5	1	7	
11th Cuirassiers	3	2	5	
12th Cuirassiers	9	1	16	
Sub-Total	104	9	103	
1st Chasseurs	40	0	9	one officer

3rd Chasseurs	24	0	2	
4th Chasseurs	37	1	7	
6th Chasseurs	15	0	22	
9th Chasseurs	0	1	3	
11th Chasseurs	3	0	2	two officers
12th Chasseurs	4	0	3	two officers
Sub-Total	123	2	48	
1st Lancers	7	0	5	
2nd Lancers	7	1	1	
3rd Lancers	14	2	4	three officers
4th Lancers	8	0	7	one officer
5th Lancers	4	1	3	
6th Lancers	0	0	0	
Sub-Total	40	4	20	
2nd Dragoons	10	0	7	one officer
7th Dragoons	5	3	7	
Sub-Total	15	3	14	
1st Hussars	2	0	4	
4th Hussars	1	0	1	
6th Hussars	0	0	2	
7th Hussars	7	0	6	
9th Hussar	1	0	0	
Sub-Total	11	0	13	
Total Prisoners of War	305	18	205	

Line Artillery and Engineers

	Prisoners of War registered at Dartmoor	Prisoners of War registered at Fleet Prison, Plymouth	Prisoners of War returned to France	Comment
1st Foot Artillery	30	1	0	
2nd Foot Artillery	5	1	0	
6th Foot Artillery	25	1	0	
7th Foot Artillery	9	0	0	
8th Foot Artillery	16	8	0	
9th Foot Artillery	1	0	0	
No Regimental Affiliation	0	0	41	one officer

3rd Horse Artillery	8	1	0	
5th Horse Artillery	9	1	0	
No Regimental Affiliation	0	0	14	
Train d'artillerie	3	1	21	one officer
Train des Equipage	1	0	3	
Genie	212	11	103	five officers
Pontonniers	0	0	2	
Total Prisoners of War	319	25	184	

1st Corps

Regiment	Prisoners of War registered at Dartmoor	Prisoners of War registered at Fleet Prison, Plymouth	Prisoners of War returned to France	Comment
54th Line	79	7	77	one officer
55th Line	82	12	91	one officer
28th Line	191	11	85	one officer
105th Line	210	13	241	5 officers
Sub-Total	562	43	494	
13th Light	104	8	142	
17th Line	87	8	81	three officers
19th Line	56	5	70	five officers
51st Line	57	4	71	
Sub-Total	304	25	364	
25th Line	369	21	256	twelve officers
46th Line	164	8	100	nine officers
21st Line	213	9	142	five officers
45th Line	355	13	175	eleven officers.
Sub-Total	1101	51	673	
8th Line	84	3	84	
29th Line	163	7	161	four officers
85th Line	67	8	61	
95th Line	142	2	118	two officers
Sub-Total	456	20	424	
Total Prisoners of War	2,423	139	1,955	

2nd Corps				
Regiment	Prisoners of War registered at Dartmoor	Prisoners of War registered at Fleet Prison, Plymouth	Prisoners of War returned to France	Comment
2nd Light	24	14	134	
61st Line	38	4	51	two officers
72nd Line	61	2	57	four officers
108th Line	77	8	59	two officers
Sub-Total	200	28	301	
1st Light	3	4	79	
3rd Line	147	16	60	three officers
1st Line	276	5	59	one officer
2nd Line	197	12	83	three officers
Sub-Total	623	37	281	
11th Light	1	0	2	
82nd Line	12	0	6	
12th Light	11	1	3	
4th Line	40	0	0	
Sub-Total	64	1	11	
92nd Line	29	4	40	
93rd Line	61	7	58	
4th Light	55	16	107	
100th Line	60	15	70	
Sub-Total	205	42	275	
Total Prisoners of War	1,092	108	868	

3rd Corps				
Regiment	Prisoners of War registered at Dartmoor	Prisoners of War registered at Fleet Prison, Plymouth	Prisoners of War returned to France	Comment
15th Light	40	0	15	
23rd Line	7	2	8	
37th Line	2	1	2	

64th Line	7	0	6	
Sub-Total	56	3	31	
34th Line	6	1	10	
88th Line	4	0	6	two officers
22nd Line	9	1	5	
70th Line	6	1	2	
Swiss	25	0	13	
Sub-Total	50	3	36	
12th Line	11	2	4	
56th Line	3	0	4	
33rd Line	1	0	1	
86th Line	0	0	2	one officer
Sub-Total	15	2	11	
Total Prisoners of War	121	8	78	

4th Corps

Regiment	Prisoners of War registered at Dartmoor	Prisoners of War registered at Fleet Prison, Plymouth	Prisoners of War returned to France	Comment
30th Line	14	1	14	
96th Line	2	1	4	
6th Light	2	0	4	
63rd Line	0	0	1	
Sub-Total	18	2	23	
59th Line	3	1	3	
76th Line	2	0	2	
48th Line	0	1	2	
69th Line	0	0	0	
Sub-Total	5	2	7	
9th Light	5	0	3	
111th Line	3	0	2	
44th Line	9	1	1	
50th Line	9	3	13	
Sub-Total	26	4	19	

479

Total Prisoners of War	49	8	49	

6th Corps

Regiment	Prisoners of War registered at Dartmoor	Prisoners of War registered at Fleet Prison, Plymouth	Prisoners of War returned to France	Comment
5th Line	109	9	63	
10th Line	38	1	2	
27th Line	48	3	46	
84th Line	63	9	68	
Sub-Total	258	22	179	
5th Light	10	7	63	
11th Line	43	8	40	
107th Line	37	1	47	two officers
Sub-Total	90	16	150	
Total Prisoners of War	348	38	329	

Regiments not assigned to the Armée du Nord, but likely incorporated into it

	Prisoners of War registered at Dartmoor	Prisoners of War registered at Fleet Prison, Plymouth	Prisoners of War returned to France	Comment
6th Line	1	0	0	
7th Line	19	0	0	
18th Line	4	0	0	
20th Line	1	0	0	
24th Line	2	1	0	
30th Line	1	0	0	
36th Line	3	0	0	
37th Line	1	1	0	
41st Line	1	0	0	
42nd Line	3	0	0	
47th Line	5	0	0	

48th Line	0	1	0	
53rd Line	1	0	0	
56th Line	1	0	0	
57th Line	1	0	0	
59th Line	0	1	0	
62nd Line	1	0	0	
63rd Line	1	0	0	
64th Line	6	0	0	
65th Line	3	0	0	6th Corps, 21st Division
70th Line	6	1	0	
75th Line	1	0	0	6th Corps, 21st Division
77th Line	1	0	0	
83rd Line	5	1	0	
97th Line	1	0	0	
101st Line	4	0	0	
102nd Line	1	0	0	
113th Line	1	0	0	
Total Prisoners of War	75	6	0	

The data summary for the above tables is shown below for the other ranks:

	Prisoners of War registered at Dartmoor	Prisoners of War registered at Fleet Prison, Plymouth	Prisoners of War returned to France
Guard Infantry	636	39	785
Guard Cavalry	19	4	25
Guard Artillery	7	0	26
Line Cavalry	305	18	205
Line Artillery	319	25	184
1st Corps	2,423	139	1,955
2nd Corps	1,092	108	868
3rd Corps	121	8	78

4th Corps	49	8	49
6th Corps	348	38	329
Unassigned	75	6	0
Total Prisoners of War	5,394	393	4,504

Dartmoor Prison held a total of 6,542 French prisoners of war, including the entire 26th Regiment of Line Infantry. From the table, it is very apparent that not all of the prisoner of war records survive. We have the records of 5,787 men taken off Waterloo battlefield in prison in England and for 4,504 men returned to France, some 10,291 men in total. When we try and cross-check both lists, it becomes apparent that the two lists don't record the same men. Analysis of the paperwork lists reveals that of the 5,787 men in England, only around 700 names can be found on the returned lists, therefore we are dealing with a very incomplete data set indeed. Clearly a vast amount of paperwork is missing in England and France. Furthermore, given in some cases the number of men registered in England and returned to France for the same regiment do not tally in the majority of cases, paperwork for registered prisoners in England returned to France no longer exist, therefore we cannot generate an accurate total for the actual number of prisoners of war taken at Waterloo. It is very likely indeed, however, that the total would be close to the 10,500 or so recorded as sent to England. We are missing records for 50 per cent of all the prisoners of war recorded by the French. Even with the missing data, it is very obvious that dismounted cavalry troopers had fled the battlefield long before the rout occurred. The other scenario being the men trapped under a fallen horse, or when falling from their horse, died of wounds on the field of battle. Indeed, both are likely to have occurred. Allied eyewitness accounts that speak of rounding up hundreds of dismounted cuirassiers is, it seems, very much an over-exaggeration. With absolutely no prisoners from the 6th Lancers recorded in England or as returned to France, we do wonder why. Were dismounted men quickly off the field of battle, or was the regiment not heavily committed to action? Without the regiment's muster list, we cannot answer this question.

From this list of returned men, we can cross-reference the names recorded of prisoners of war in England and returned to France with their regimental muster list to check the accuracy of the records. When we look at the 3rd Grenadiers à Pied, we do find that men listed as prisoner of war were actually prisoners in England, and were returned to France in spring 1816:[1154]

- MAT No. 2462 Joseph Docre, born 1790. Admitted to the 3rd Company of 2nd Battalion 3rd Grenadiers on 25 February 1815. Recorded as a prisoner of war at Waterloo. Returned March 1816, but listed as in the 4th Grenadiers.
- MAT No. 3391 Jean Charraux, born 1788. Admitted to the 4th Company of 2nd Battalion 3rd Grenadiers on 4 May 1815 from the 25th Regiment of Line Infantry. Recorded as a prisoner of war at Waterloo. Returned March 1816, the record indicating he had the rank of sergeant.
- MAT No. 3549 Louis Barreau. Admitted to the 3rd Company of 1st Battalion 3rd Grenadiers on 7 May 1815 from the 41st Regiment of Line Infantry. Recorded as a prisoner of war at Waterloo. Returned March 1816.
- MAT No. 3567 Jean Claude Baudon, born 1787. Admitted to the 4th Company of 1st Battalion 3rd Grenadiers on 7 May 1815 from the 9th Regiment of Light Infantry. Recorded as deserted and as a prisoner of war in England.
- MAT No. 3565 Pierre Marechal, born 1789. Admitted to the 4th Company of 1st Battalion 3rd Grenadiers. Recorded as a prisoner of war at Waterloo and in England.
- MAT No. 3579 Nicolas Vivier, born 1790. Admitted to the 1st Company of 2nd Battalion 3rd Grenadiers on 7 May 1815. Recorded as missing at Waterloo. Returned as a prisoner of war in March 1816.
- MAT No. 3594 Pierre Escoffie. Admitted to the 3rd Company of 2nd Battalion 3rd Grenadiers on 7 May 1815 from the 90th Regiment of Line Infantry. Recorded as a prisoner of war at Waterloo. Returned March 1816.
- MAT No. 3907 Alexandre Jehan, born 1790. Admitted to the 3rd Company of 2nd Battalion 3rd Grenadiers on 13 May 1815 from the 18th Regiment of Line Infantry. Recorded as a prisoner of war at Waterloo. Returned March 1816, but listed in 4th Grenadiers.
- MAT No. 3992 Pierre François Simon, born 1786. Admitted to the 3rd Company of 1st Battalion 3rd Grenadiers on 14 May 1815 from

---

1154 Compiled from SHDDT: GR 20 YC 13. See also: SHDDT: GR 20 YC 14; SHDDT: Yj 11; SHDDT: Yj 12; SHDDT: Yj 13.

the 20th Regiment of Line Infantry. Recorded as a prisoner of war at Waterloo. Returned March 1816 in the 4th Grenadiers.

- MAT No. 4002 Thomas Benoit, born 1789. Admitted to the 4th Company of 1st Battalion 3rd Grenadiers on 14 May from the 20th Regiment of Line Infantry. Recorded as a prisoner of war at Waterloo. Returned March 1816.
- MAT No. 4308 Augustin Russier, born 1788. Conscripted to the 47th Regiment of Line Infantry in 1807, admitted to the 4th Company of 1st Battalion 3rd Grenadiers on 21 May 1815. Recorded as a prisoner of war at Waterloo. Returned March 1816, but listed as in the 4th Grenadiers.

Does this mean that where the muster list records men as prisoners, that this was indeed the case? It does appear to be so. We can double check this by looking at other muster lists. If we look at the 4th Grenadiers, we find that twenty-two men were returned in spring 1816. Some of the names given in the returnee lists are not found in the pages of the muster list. However, the original records made when the ships carrying the prisoners of war docked have been written up into 'best copy' and in the process some names have been changed. The following men were identified in regimental musters and the list of returnee prisoners of war for the 4th Grenadiers:[1155]

- MAT No. 1601 Louis Godard, born on 8 March 1772. Admitted to the 78th Regiment of Line Infantry in 1798. Admitted to the Corps Royale des Grenadiers à Pied de France on 18 August 1814. Admitted to the 1st Company of 1st Battalion 4th Grenadiers on 8 April 1815 with the rank of corporal. Recorded as a prisoner of war at Waterloo. Returned March 1816.
- MAT No. 3822 Antoine François Decroux, born on 16 March 1789. Conscripted to the 3rd Regiment of Line Infantry on 30 November 1808, promoted to corporal on 16 August 1810, to fourrier on 1 January 1811, to sergeant-major on 1 June 1811. Admitted to the 4th Grenadiers on 11 May 1815. Recorded as a prisoner of war at Waterloo. Returned March 1816.
- MAT No. 4108 Pierre Jean Nicolas. Admitted to the 1st Company of 1st Battalion 4th Grenadiers on 16 May from the 31st Regiment of

---

1155 ibid.

Line Infantry. Wounded at Ligny. Recorded as a prisoner of war at Waterloo. Returned March 1816.

- MAT No. 4175 Pierre Breissiel. Admitted to the 2nd Company of 1st Battalion 4th Grenadiers on 18 May 1815 from the 78th Regiment of Line Infantry. Recorded as missing at Waterloo. Returned as a prisoner of war in March 1816.

- MAT No. 4177 Michel Haetelle. Admitted to the 1st Company of 2nd Battalion 4th Grenadiers on 18 May 1815 from the 78th Regiment of Line Infantry. Recorded as missing at Waterloo. Returned as a prisoner of war in March 1816.

- MAT No. 4222 Gabriel Detraz, born 1788. Admitted to the 1st Company of 2nd Battalion 4th Grenadiers on 18 May 1815 from the 5th Regiment of Line Infantry. Recorded as a prisoner of war at Waterloo. Returned March 1816.

- MAT No. 4339 Joseph Doucet, born on 5 April 1797. Passed to the 4th Company of 1st Battalion 4th Grenadiers on 22 May 1815. Recorded as a prisoner of war at Waterloo. Retuned March 1816.

- MAT No. 4447 Claude Compagnon, born 1782. Admitted to the 3rd Company of 2nd Battalion 4th Grenadiers on 25 May 1815 from the 2nd Regiment of Marine Artillery. Recorded as a prisoner of war at Waterloo. Returned March 1816.

- MAT No. 4481 Jean Pierre Delaigne. Admitted to the 4th Company of 1st Battalion 4th Grenadiers on 26 May 1815 from the 14th Regiment of Light Infantry. Recorded as a prisoner of war at Waterloo. Returned March 1816.

- MAT No. 4522 Antoine Ferdinance Coulon, born on 20 October 1788. Admitted to the 4th Company of 1st Battalion 4th Grenadiers on 27 May 1815 from the 82nd Regiment of Line Infantry. Recorded as a prisoner of war at Waterloo. Returned March 1816.

- MAT No. 4542 Honore Simon. Admitted to the 2nd Company of 2nd Battalion 4th Grenadiers on 27 May 1815 from the 48th Regiment of Line Infantry. Recorded as a prisoner of war at Waterloo. Returned March 1816.

- MAT No. 4553 Guillaume Boudin. Admitted to the 3rd Company of 2nd Battalion 4th Grenadiers on 27 May 1815 from the 48th Regiment of Line Infantry. Recorded as a prisoner of war at Waterloo. Returned March 1816.

- MAT No. 455 Henry Joseph Hypolite Lami, born 1789. Admitted to the 4th Grenadiers on 27 May 1815 from the 48th Regiment of Line

Infantry, which he had served with since 22 May 1808. Served in the 4th Company of 2nd Battalion 4th Grenadiers. Was made a prisoner of war at Waterloo. Returned March 1816.

- MAT No. 4564 Jean Heitz, born on 1 September 1790. Conscripted to the 4th Voltigeurs on 14 March 1809. Discharged on 1 August 1814 and recalled to the 3rd Tirailleurs on 21 May 1815, passing to the 2nd Company of 1st Battalion 4th Grenadiers on 27 May 1815. Recorded as a prisoner of war at Waterloo. Returned March 1816.
- MAT No. 4574 Louis Guilleau. Admitted to the 3rd Company of 1st Battalion 4th Grenadiers on 27 May 1815 from the 79th Regiment of Line Infantry. Recorded as a prisoner of war at Waterloo. Returned March 1816.
- MAT No. 4768 Jean Perrone. Admitted to the 2nd Company of 2nd Battalion 4th Grenadiers on 2 June 1815 from the 39th Regiment of Line Infantry. Recorded as a prisoner of war at Waterloo and as returned on 21 January 1816.
- MAT No. 4724 Jean Galibert, born on 30 June 1786. Admitted to the 2nd Company of 2nd Battalion 4th Grenadiers on 30 March from the disbanded fusilier-chasseurs in which he had served since 1806. Recorded as a prisoner of war at Waterloo. Returned March 1816.
- MAT No. 4554 Adrien Segare. Admitted to the 4th Company of 2nd Battalion 4th Grenadiers on 27 May 1815 from the 48th Regiment of Line Infantry. Recorded as a prisoner of war at Waterloo and in England.
- MAT No. 4220 Pierre Rocher. Admitted to the 1st Company of 1st Battalion 4th Grenadiers on 18 May 1815 from the 79th Regiment of Line Infantry. Wounded and made prisoner of war at Ligny. Recorded as a prisoner of war in England as Pierre Rochez.

Therefore, we can start to nail down what happened to the 3rd and 4th Grenadiers, as well as the 3rd and 4th Chasseurs. It does seem that in the case of the 4th Grenadiers 'prisoner of war' does in fact mean 'prisoner of war'. Therefore, it really does seem that the 3rd and 4th Grenadiers panicked, broke and the men rounded up like sheep, presumably by the Allied cavalry. To corroborate this, we turn to look at non-Imperial Guard regiments. A very quick, cursory and non-exhaustive study of the records for the cuirassiers reveals the same pattern: men listed as 'prisoners of war' were in reality 'prisoners of war'. The 4th Cuirassiers regimental muster list and the retuned prisoner of war list tally:[1156]

- MAT No. 53 Jean Michel Zorn, born 1787. Admitted to the regiment on 5 April 1807. Listed as missing at Waterloo. Returned as a prisoner of war in March 1816.
- MAT No. 238 Mathieu Pedron, born 1785. Admitted to the regiment on 10 April 1813. Listed as missing at Waterloo. Returned as a prisoner of war in March 1816.
- MAT No. 281 Pierre Duchesne, born 1793. Admitted to the regiment on 10 December 1813. Listed as missing at Waterloo. Returned as a prisoner of war in March 1816.

In the 7th Cuirassiers:[1157]

- MAT No. 70 Jean Couchou, born 1787. Admitted to the regiment on 10 April 1813. Recorded as lost at Waterloo. Returned as a prisoner of war in March 1816.
- MAT No. 168 Antoine Thomas Jacques, born 1793. Admitted to the regiment on 1 July 1813. Recorded as a prisoner of war at Waterloo. Returned March 1816.
- MAT No. 423 Alexis Vacq, born 1789. Admitted to the regiment on 22 September 1814. Recorded as a prisoner of war at Waterloo. Returned March 1816.
- MAT No. 538 Aubin Reiss (known as Senatour), born 1793. Admitted to the regiment in 1814. Recorded as a prisoner of war at Waterloo. Returned March 1816.

Thus, we do seem to be able to say that where a regimental muster list records men as missing or prisoner of war, they really were prisoners of war. It does seem that Cambronne's company was indeed made prisoner along with the general.

No doubt a good number of men listed as prisoner were in fact dead, or had deserted. Furthermore, we don't have the data of the men who died as prisoners before embarking in The Netherlands and those who died in England. Discount these two unknown factors, we still have the details of over 5,500 men from the Armée du Nord. The vast majority of

---

1156 SHDDT: GR 24 YC 24. See also: SHDDT: Yj 11; SHDDT: Yj 12; SHDDT: Yj 13.

1157 ibid.

these documents have not been consulted since the nineteenth century, and indeed the vast majority of the documents were sewn closed in spring 1816 and were only opened for the first time in December 2016, allowing the wealth of material found within the pages to be consulted.

The data discussed has been extracted from the lists of men made prisoner of war in the immediate aftermath of Waterloo. It is clear that the field hospital of 3rd and 4th Corps was overrun and the wounded made prisoner. It records 4,119 other ranks who returned to France in spring 1816 who survived their evacuation. Furthermore, what we are seeing in the regimental muster rolls is what the company adjutants were told, and thought, had happened when the company roll was called. No doubt many men had gone home after the battle and were listed as prisoners of war. We are, moreover, not seeing the French wounded who were evacuated to Charleroi, Soissons, Philippeville, Laon, etc. who were no doubt made prisoners of war by the Allied armies and were never heard of again by their parent regiment. We are dealing with a very fragmentary dataset, but despite these major issues, it provides objective data from which we can start to interpret the true events of the day of 18 June 1815, by being able to compare casualty data from all armed forces present. But, as we commented earlier, of the 4,119 men listed, all are recorded in their regimental muster lists as either missing or prisoners of war. Thus, it does seem, unless evidence can be found to the contrary, that the French army at Waterloo, and in particular the Old Guard, ran away from the battle.

When we compare the muster list of prisoners in England and the list of returnees, we find that around 75 per cent of the men on the returnee list are not recorded in England. Clearly therefore, both datasets are grossly incomplete, but combined they provide a mutually compatible dataset which allows us to fill in blanks where regimental muster rolls are not able to be consulted.

Men would also have died in England from infection contracted as prisoners, from starvation and other factors external to men coming from France already wounded. A total of 10,019 Frenchmen were recorded prisoners of war by the French at Waterloo. The difference between the two figures will include men who died in the immediate aftermath of the battle from shock, blood loss, gangrene and other factors. The march to Ostend would have killed some men, and we know some were taken to hospital in The Netherlands, which could easily equate for the difference in numbers.

However, what we are seeing with the data is those men who, if wounded, did not die immediately after the battle; the men who survived evacuation to Brussels and then survived transportation to Ostend, and thence onwards to England. The journey would no doubt have killed many wounded men. The heat and warm weather in the days after the battle would have made wounds become rapidly infected, allowing blood poisoning and gangrene to set in. Seriously wounded prisoners of war were treated at Saint Elisabeth's Hospital in Brussels; these men are not listed in the returns of men from England. These were the more serious cases involving multiple flesh wounds, broken limbs or amputations. Any form of major surgery had an incredibly high mortality rate.

If the wounded among the prisoners of war survived the journey to England, they still had to survive for a further nine months before being shipped back to France. We know that over one hundred badly wounded prisoners of war were disembarked at La Havre and Calais to military hospital. Many of the returnees died on the voyage, or very soon after landing in France.

The prisoner of war returnee lists number up to 118, but only lists 111 to 118 exist. Where are the missing lists? How many men were on these now lost documents? A very simple comparison of returnees and men listed in the regimental muster lists gives us a major shortfall in men. In simple terms, these men, by summer 1816, were dead, victims of the battle who died of wounds later, were killed on the day of battle and not recorded properly, or had scarpered never to be seen again. Some prisoners managed to escape before being shipped to England. Fellow comrade in arms, MAT No. 987 Chasseur Jean Baptiste Seraphin Jacques,[1158] of the 2nd Battalion 1st Chasseurs, says:[1159]

> I was nominated for the brevet of the Legion of Honour in April 1815. I was made a prisoner at the Battle of Waterloo on 18 June 1815. The enemy came and worked me over and took away my effects and papers from my haversack, I was left with just my shirt and trousers. I was captured and conducted to Brussels. After two

1158 Jean Baptiste Jacques was born at Saint-Amand, Ligny, on 30 November 1771 and was admitted to the 1st Regiment of Marines on 20 March 1795 and to the 1st Chasseurs on 29 May 1807. He is recorded as missing on 5 July 1815. SHDDT: GR 20 YC 44.
1159 Author's collection.

days, I escaped in the middle of the night and made my way back
with six of my comrades.

He goes on to explain that in prison he met others from the Guard:
Cesar Desmouttiers, Michel Chotteau (former sergeant-major of the
Empress Dragoons), Marcelline Desplangue (of the 1st Grenadiers) and
Ferdinand Wallier (also of the 1st Chasseurs). Wounded prisoners of
war were discharged from the hospitals directly back to civilian life, as
MAT No. 4423 Corporal Pierre Alexander Toussaint LeCats,[1160] of 3rd
Company 2nd battalion 3rd Chasseurs, writes about, and notes how the
Allies robbed him of his possessions:[1161]

> I joined the colours as a conscript on 18 March 1809 and was taken
> into the departmental company under the name Lecat Pierre
> Toussaint. In the year 1810 I was taken into the Young Guard and
> was sent to Spain and soon after was placed in the Regiment of
> Fusilier-Chasseurs of the Old Guard. I remained with this regiment
> for two years in Spain and with the same regiment I took part in the
> campaign of Russia. In the year 1813 I was with the army and the
> same regiment. In the next year, I passed to the 2nd Regiment of
> Foot Chasseurs of the Imperial Guard and with this regiment took
> part in the campaign of 1814.
>
> With the return of King Louis I was placed in the Royal Chasseurs,
> 1st Regiment of France, as a corporal. I was placed with the return
> of Napoléon from the Island of Elba into the 3rd Regiment of
> Chasseurs of the Imperial Guard, with the rank of corporal. On
> 1 May 1815 I was awarded the Cross of the Legion of Honour.
>
> I, with my regiment, crossed the frontier into Belgium; I took part
> in the battles which I recorded in my pay book. I was seriously
> wounded at Waterloo and I was left on the field of battle. I was
> worked over and in consequence all my papers and belongings
> were stolen. I was taken to hospital and then allowed to convalesce
> in a hostel, then allowed home on leave and released from the
> service.

1160 Toussaints Lecats, born on 12 July 1789, was conscripted on 29 April
    1808, admitted to the 2nd Chasseurs on 10 February 1813, promoted to
    corporal on 1 July 1814 and recorded as a presumed prisoner of war at
    Waterloo. SHDDT: GR 20 YC 45.
1161 Author's collection.

We have no data at all concerning the fate of the men taken to Saint Elisabeth Hospital, or the other military hospitals in France, the number of men sent to the hospitals and, importantly, those that survived.

A vital point is that the prisoner of war records at Kew are totally useless without having the original French muster lists to cross-check the regiment and rank they gave the English authorities. For example, Claude Chardonnet gives his rank to the English as 'colonel' when in fact he was a trooper.[1162] Clearly, he was trying to 'milk the system' for better food and accommodation. But, without being able to cross-check his entry in the 2nd Cuirassiers, researchers not aware of the French archive material would state that the colonel of the 2nd Cuirassiers was made prisoner at Waterloo. Furthermore, the overwhelming number of names in the Kew archives cannot be reconciled with the regiment's muster list in which they claim they served. The men either gave false names or false regiments. Therefore, without the vital cross-reference of the French prisoner of war material concerning men returned to France, and cross-checked with the regimental muster lists, the material at Kew seen and used as a standalone archive is, in my view, totally worthless.

In returning to the analysis of the battle, what the data does do is to start to give us an idea about what could have happened, as long as we acknowledge the unknown factors involved in the data. Furthermore, we do not know if a lot of prisoners of war were released soon after the battle, or had been taken into custody in The Netherlands rather than being shipped to England. We are dealing, therefore, with a dataset that is grossly incomplete, and could be used to support the notion that 1st Corps was almost killed to man, along with the Old Guard. Where regiments have a very high number of prisoners of war returning to other regiments, when we look at the men recorded as 'presumably prisoner of war' or as 'prisoner of war' at Waterloo, perhaps we are seeing where regiments were less affected by musket and artillery fire and from cavalry attacks. The basic presumption is the higher the number of returnees compared to recorded prisoners of war, the more men simply gave themselves up rather than being killed or made prisoner once wounded. No doubt during the rout at Waterloo a vast number of wounded were left for dead. Trampled underfoot by Allied infantry and cavalry, these men, without proper treatment, would have died of their wounds.

1162 SHDDT: GR 24 YC 21.

The very low ratio of cavalrymen as prisoners of war is perhaps due to a number of different reasons. When riding a horse and the horse is killed, and you fall along with the horse onto your sabre, saddle, etc. bones will be broken, internal haemorrhages will occur and with major bruising. Coupled with a broken bone, or being trapped in the midst of artillery and musket fire, with other horses galloping close by, or indeed over you, the chance of survival is very minimal indeed. As a horseman and cavalry living historian, I have had a number of instances of severe trauma inflicted falling from a horse onto a sabre or ammunition box. Dazed, winded, bruised and not sure of what is going on, it is little wonder that many horsemen whose horse had been killed under them would be killed by being trapped in the immediate killing zone in front of Allied artillery and infantry squares. Struggling in stiff riding boots and burdened down by a heavy cuirass, a slow-moving cuirassier struggling between piles of dead and dying horses, slithering back to the French lines, would have been a very easy target for Allied marksmen. But, the casualty data does not present this scenario. For the Old Guard, the data can be manipulated to show it was destroyed to a man, by assuming men made prisoner of war or missing were killed.

The only problem with this kind of sensationalising history is that it does not stand up to much academic scrutiny. We need to acknowledge the limitation of the data and couple it with firsthand eyewitness commentary. The data shows that the 1st Company of 2nd Battalion 1st Chasseurs, in which General Cambronne stood with the eagle of the corps at the end of the battle, had lost over 140 men, but we do not know the cause. The bulk are recorded as prisoners of war, be they wounded or otherwise. The difference between the number of men listed in the regimental muster list and those who returned to France could be used to say his entire company was killed by the Allies on the attack on the ridge overlooking Hougoumont. But French eyewitnesses like Barthelemy Bacheville, Lambert de Steurs, Captain Heuillette and General Pelet all indicate that the square of the battalion in question retreated in good order, and due to the terrain encountered the square had to disperse to cross undulating ground, a situation which was ruthlessly exploited by the pursuing Allied cavalry. With the square broken open by cavalry somewhere south of Plancenoit, it then becomes more realistic to understand that the battalion lost heavily due to it being broken by cavalry rather than by artillery and musket fire. The uncomfortable truth is that the French version of the day's events is very much at odds to what the Waterloo myth-making machine tells us. What we cannot say without further research is that of the 10,019 prisoners of war from Waterloo, all bar 4,119 were actually dead or wounded, and thus the true human cost of Waterloo was potentially far higher. It is very likely that the paperwork for the shipment of a lot of the prisoners of war back to France has not actually survived.

Thus, until we can find archive material for the treatment of French prisoners of war in England in 1815 and 1816 can we say that 4,000 prisoners of war were mortally wounded at Waterloo, and that indeed the army had not run away. We have to rely upon the regimental muster lists, which can be padded out with the data from the returnees. Given that of the 10,019 prisoners of war, some 8,000 had arrived at Ostend, the men who were close to death had already died by this point. Thus, if 4,000 had died, infection and disease in England may have been a bigger killer than Waterloo had been for the French. Clearly, 80 per cent of the French Waterloo prisoners of war made it alive to Ostend, the other 2,000 may well have died from wounds at Saint Elisabeth Hospital, were unfit to travel, or had escaped.

In getting back to our narrative on Waterloo, the British army lost some 4,255 men dead or wounded; more than 20,000 less than the French. There appears to be a huge disparity between the two figures. However, when one realises the French losses include huge numbers of prisoners and missing, and instead compare the two tallies of dead and wounded, we get a total of 5,140. When we factor out losses against the Prussians (6th Corps and the Young Guard) we get 3,420 wounded and 637 dead; a total of 4,057, which equates to roughly one British soldier killed or wounded for one French soldier killed or wounded. The ratio is, of course, very basic, as it is missing the casualty data for the non-British contingents. Based on these basic numbers, Wellington and Napoléon were evenly matched, perhaps with Napoléon's men having the advantage by a small margin. The battle was lost through men fleeing or made prisoners of war, rather than by the number of men killed and wounded. The arrival of the Prussians and the lie about Grouchy's arrival being cruelly exposed for what it was, the undeniable truth is that the army panicked and ran away.

Many commentators on 1815 point out that the army Napoléon fielded was one of his best ever. John Elting states that:[1163]

1163 John Robert Elting, *Swords Around a Throne*, Phoenix Giant, 1996, p. 653.

> The Armée du Nord was one of the most formidable Napoléon had ever commanded. Officers and men were mostly veterans, skilled, hardened and eager to fight, determined to win.

However, reality was somewhat different to this view. The bulk of the men were the conscripts of 1814, with a few veteran sub-officers and officers. Many regiments, particularly the infantry and cavalry, were new formations, with little time to build a sense of *esprit des corps* or cohesion. The army Napoléon fielded in 1815 actually had less mounted troops than at the commencement of the 1814 campaign. The cavalry lacked horses and men and was poorly equipped.

Crucial to the success of any military formation was the experience and capability of the officers. Unlike the troopers, no officers or sub-officers in the regiments studied were admitted fresh from the military schools. When we analysed the regimental musters to create the casualty data, we also recorded the average age and length of service of the men in the Armée du Nord. The result of this analysis is, depending on your viewpoint, shocking, though not unexpected. On average, 85 per cent of the men at Waterloo were fairly inexperienced. On average, cavalry troopers had seen three years two months' active service, almost a year longer than their infantry counterparts, who had served for two years three months. This should not be a major shock, as the French army had lost thousands of men in the 1813 campaign. However, given the poor training of the army in 1813 and 1814, and the rapid way in which it was re-generated in winter 1813 to 1814, one supposes that, contrary to the myth peddled by Elting and others, these men were far from being the well-drilled, battle hardened veterans many believe the army to have been. In the 4th Regiment of Line Infantry, of the 1,312 men, only seventy-eight had served before 1813. A similar picture is true of the 42nd Regiment of Line Infantry: of 1,372 men, 212 had served with the army since 1782, thirty-one from 1803, twenty-nine from 1805, fifty-two from 1806 and 1,067 from 1813, representing some 78 per cent of the regiment. In the 57th Regiment of Line Infantry, 141 men had served since 1792, thirty-four since 1805 and the remainder (958 men), or 84 per cent, had been admitted since 1813.

In the light infantry, a similar story emerges. In the 7th Regiment of Light Infantry, 159 men had served since 1795, and similar numbers from 1803, 1804 and 1805, with 676 men serving since 1813, making 49 per cent of the regiment long-serving veterans. In the 8th Regiment of Light Infantry, only 141 men had served since 1795, eighty-four since

1805 and 1,087 since 1813. Those who had served from 1813 represented 83 per cent of the regiment, which mustered 1,312 men.

In terms of unit cohesion, some regiments were better than others. As we have seen, the bulk of the 2nd Regiment of Line Infantry had served together either from 1813 or 1814 and experienced little in the way of expansion in 1815. The 50th Regiment of Line Infantry, moreover, had very few men brought into the regiment in 1814. Of the 1,051 men present under arms on 27 September 1814, 769 men were from the former 50th Regiment of Line Infantry, supplemented with 157 from the former 144th Regiment of Line Infantry, sixty-nine men from the 18th Regiment of Line Infantry, forty-three men from the 4th Regiment of Line Infantry, six men from the 11th Voltigeurs of the Imperial Guard, four men from the 81st Regiment of Line Infantry, two men from the 15th Regiment of Line Infantry and one man from the 16th Regiment of Line Infantry. By 21 March 1815, the regiment mustered 953 men and undertook little or no expansion for form six battalions in 1815,[1164] therefore the regiment was fairly cohesive and had not been filled up with *federes*, or reservists, which as we have seen earlier did occur in some regiments. In the mounted arm, the average age of a trooper of the French line cavalry at Waterloo was twenty-five. On average, 50 per cent of the British army were aged twenty-five to thirty-five years of age, and 26 per cent were aged eighteen to twenty-four.[1165] Conversely, 48 per cent of the French line cavalry at Waterloo were aged eighteen to twenty-four. This is not surprising, as the average age at enlistment in the French army was twenty-one years four months. The French cavalry soldiers on average had served for two years nine months, and thus had less experience than their British counterparts in regiments that had served in Spain by an average of almost 75 per cent. In 1815, about 30 per cent of the line cavalry had joined in 1815 to bring the weak royalist regiments up to strength. These men could barely ride and wield a sabre, yet fared better than the British Union and Household Brigades.

1164 Anon, *50e Regiment d'Infanterie de Ligne Historique 1803-1815*, ancestramil, available at http://www.ancestramil.fr/uploads/01_doc/terre/ infanterie/1789-1815/50_ri_historique_1803-1816.pdf [accessed 11 February 2013].

1165 Kevin B. Linch, *The recruitment of the British Army 1807-1815 Ph.D. Thesis*, University of Leeds, 2001, pp. 194-8, citing The National Archives, Kew: WO 27.

The regiments of infantry at Waterloo, despite consisting of some veterans and experienced men, belied a number of defects at command level. The purges, organisational changes and reinstatements of senior and junior officers (as well as sub-officers to a limited extent), during the Hundred Days campaign meant that many officers had only been recently appointed prior to the commencement of the campaign and had not had the time or opportunity to build the vital bonds of confidence and loyalty essential for exerting their authority.

Despite poor equipment and clothing, and far from cohesive regiments, the army Napoléon fielded in 1815 achieved some remarkable successes. Ligny, although doubtful if it was a French victory, demonstrated that the French army in 1815 could fight and that the corps commanders could cooperate with each other and deploy all arms to push back the Prussians. Ligny also demonstrates excellently the great weakness of the army. When the French were winning, the soldiers fought well, but when checked or losing, the French soldiers simply fled and ran; the 70th Regiment of Line Infantry and Lefol's brigade being a case in point. It was not just the infantry that was shaky in 1815. The cavalry was also far from a strong, committed and cohesive formation; the fact that Kellermann's cuirassiers broke and fled at Quatre-Bras being another case in point.

Arguably, Napoléon's infantry was at its best in 1805 to 1807. The hard core of veterans from the Revolutionary Wars, mixed with new conscripts, had been welded into a cohesive and superb fighting force at the camps of Boulogne. The losses of the 1807 campaign in Poland, in Austria in 1809 and Russia in 1812 destroyed the French army. The veteran soldiers of 1815 were those men lucky enough not to have been killed in the Peninsular War, and a few men who had not frozen to death in Russia. Waterloo, as at Wagram, and more significantly Borodino, where Ney formed his infantry into huge attacking columns which seem to be the direct inspiration for those at Waterloo, saw the French infantry no longer manoeuvre; instead it was used as a crude hammer to strike at the enemy, which was softened up by artillery fire. MacDonald's grand eloquent attack at Wagram perhaps is what Napoléon and d'Erlon had in mind for 1st Corps that morning at Waterloo. MacDonald's crude sledgehammer, supported by cavalry, was eviscerated by Austrian firepower, but did succeed, albeit at a very high price in manpower. d'Erlon's attack faced similar obstacles, and had every chance of succeeding.

What d'Erlon and Napoléon did not know was the number and type of troops being concealed behind the Allied ridge. The Allied cavalry was on 1st Corps before the battalion-commanders knew what was happening, and were totally unprepared for what happened. Donzelot was able to form his division into square, as did Charlet and Durutte, while the cavalry appears to have paralysed Marcognet's division. Marshal Soult and other field commanders, especially General Foy, had learned how Wellington fought in the Peninsular War; their master had not, and had yet to learn how to overcome Wellington. Waterloo was not as Wellington put it: the French coming on in the same old style and defeated in the same old style.

d'Erlon and others had learned how to fight Wellington after years of defeats and checks. They knew that they had to fight in line. They also, perhaps over-confidently, knew - based on experience in Spain - that the English cavalry was relatively weak numerically and at times no match for the French. The French in no way came on in the same old style as Wellington put it, but came on in a new style. If d'Erlon's attack had worked he would no doubt have been assailed as a great innovator in tactics; alas, it was not to be. What the French underestimated was the Allied cavalry. The English light and heavy cavalry, the King's German Legion and the Dutch-Belgian cavalry combined was one of, if not the, largest cavalry force Wellington had commanded, and it was used ruthlessly to crush two French initiatives.

The French army in 1815 was not the army of 1813 and it was certainly not one of the best armies Napoléon had ever commanded. It was short of cavalry and lacked the bonds of trust vital in forming a group of men into a cohesive fighting formation from the marshalate down to the privates. In conclusion, despite having veterans in the ranks, the men were little more than boys with at most two years of soldiering behind them, and were poorly dressed and fed.

To put the French army data in context, we can compare the French average soldier's service with the Allied contingents. The average age of a French private at Waterloo was twenty-five. Thanks to the ground-breaking work of Dr K. B. Linch, of the University of Leeds, he deduced that for the British army in the Hundred Days campaign, the average age of a private was twenty-nine years six months; these men having served on average for eight years six months, which was in some cases comparable to the best of Napoléon's army: the Imperial Guard. Moreover, the British army, in terms of experience of battle, was far superior to the bulk of the line cavalry, and in other cases considerably higher than other French regiments in terms of age. Only the Imperial Guard had the highest number of veterans with comparable service to the average British private.

Of the 1,292 men of the regiment present on 10 June 1815, 11 per cent (144 men) were from the Elba Battalion, 10 per cent (132 men) were recalled from the former 1st Grenadiers, 2 per cent (thirty men) came from the line and 1.4 per cent (nineteen men) from other Guard regiments, making a total of 333 new entrants. Thus, by the start of the campaign, some 25 per cent of the men had been with the regiment since 19 April 1815, making the regiment far from cohesive. Some 967 men of the regiment came from the former Royal Corps of Grenadiers à Pied, of which 70 per cent (663 men) were from the former 1st Grenadiers and 30 per cent (304 men) came from the former 2nd Grenadiers.[1166] The average age at disbandment was a little over twenty-six, the average length of service again being six years. In real terms, one hundred or so men in the grenadiers in 1815 had enlisted in 1799-1803; over 80 per cent of the regiment's men had joined in 1813.

This lack of experience, even in the senior regiment of the Guard, was noted upon at the time, one officer remarking that the only similarity between the Guard of 1815 and that of previous years was the name, the men on the whole having nothing in common with guardsmen of earlier years and they lacked the devotion to both Napoléon and the Guard, and the self-assurance this had given the Guard in the past.[1167] Thus in 1815, the 1st Regiment of Grenadiers of the Old Guard was a collection of conscripts, who on the whole had been in the regiment for less than two years. The grenadiers of 1815 were no longer the crack troops or the elite of the army.

In general terms, the average age of members of the Old Guard, when we look at the grenadiers and chasseurs, was twenty-nine years three months. They had served for an average of six years four months, perhaps unsurprisingly some three years five months more than the line. The Imperial Guard had served for the same length of time as their British counterparts. Thus, the Imperial Guard was marginally more experienced on average than the British line, and the only French troops equivalent to the British army when we look at broad generalisations. The British army was superior to the French on paper. French veterans of the Imperial Guard at Waterloo were comparable in age and experience, whereas the French line infantry

---

1166 SHDDT: GR 20 YC 14 *registre matricules corps des grenadiers de La Garde Imperial lors des Cent-Jours 30 Avril à 24 Septembre.*

1167 d'Avout, *'L'infanterie de la garde à Waterloo'* in *Carnet de la Sabretache*, Vol. 13, 1905, p. 51.

was vastly inferior to the British in terms of experience. Thus, it is hardly surprising that the French Imperial Guard had a higher percentage of veterans than the line, even in the most junior regiments of the Old Guard. The 1st Grenadiers of the Imperial Guard were on average some fifteen years the senior of the men in the 2nd Regiment of Line Infantry.

The line, however, had one clear advantage compared to the Imperial Guard in that the cadre, and at least 50 per cent of the men and sub-officers, had served together since July 1814. A group of experienced soldiers serving together does not make an experienced unit. Only experience as a unit can make the unit effective in its responses. However, the rapid changes of senior officers in 1815 would have undermined the bond of trust between the senior officers of a regiment.

We cannot solely rely on the age of the men to give an idea of the manpower of the regiments' relative experience based on ages under arms in this instance. Overall, regiments with a high percentage of reservists and former National Guardsmen need to be seen as inexperienced and fragile regiments, easily checked and liable to rout. Therefore, the average age of the soldiers is negated by the men's experience. Length of service and therefore age does not always equate to combat experience. However, the data for the British overlies in its generalities divergence from the average. Not all of Wellington's redcoat regiments were veterans that were battle-hardened in the Peninsular War. Some regiments in the British army were no better than their Allied counterparts in terms of experience and age. It is hardly surprising that the 69th Regiment of Foot fared badly, as like many in the French, Hanoverian, Prussian and Dutch-Belgian armies, the men had little experience of fighting. The 2nd Battalion 69th (South Lincolnshire) Regiment of Foot was one such inexperienced battalion. It had not served in the Peninsular War and had no recent combat experience. In most British battalions we could expect that there would be a small number of men, perhaps no more than a dozen or so, who had joined the ranks underage, that is under eighteen. However, in the 2nd Battalion, the relative low level of underage recruits was a staggering 159. Why this is so is perhaps reflected by unemployment in the battalion' recruiting area, as well as NCOs and officers willing to turn a blind eye to bring the battalion up to strength, no questions asked. These teenagers comprised nearly 30 per cent of the other ranks. In general terms for the battalion, the average length of service among the privates was only three and a half years, far less, almost 50 per cent less, than any other British regiment at Waterloo. Indeed, the battalion had only twenty men who had served for over ten years, and we note that 44 per cent of all privates had joined in 1813 or later. The average age was twenty-one years old, with over a quarter of the men aged fifteen to nineteen. This cumulative inexperience probably proved fatal to a great number of these young men and the fighting capacity of the battalion. Did the battalion suffer so badly at Quatre-Bras because of this lack of combat experience of officers and men? Perhaps so.[1168]

Details for the demographics of the Dutch-Belgian army are scarce. However, a study of the 8th Militia Battalion provides some information. The regiment mustered 561 other ranks with twenty-two officers. Of the men, some 286 were aged twenty years or less, 388 men were aged twenty-one to thirty, 163 were between the ages of thirty-one and forty, forty men were aged forty-one to fifty and a single man was aged over fifty. The average age was twenty-five years eight months, slightly older than the average French infantryman; 61 per cent of the men had joined as recruits from June 1814, 39 per cent (218 men) had served in the French army from 1812.[1169] Thus on paper, the French army was inferior to the British army, and even inferior to the Dutch-Belgians which are so badly maligned by Anglo-phonic studies of the battle. The French army, based on its demographics, was on par with the Dutch-Belgians and Prussian Landwehr, and greatly inferior to Wellington's redcoats. Why did Napoléon lose Waterloo? Simply because the Armée du Nord was inferior to the Allies. That coupled with superior generalship by Blücher and Wellington and a genuine mistrust of officers by the French rank and file made the outcome of the campaign all rather predictable. Compared to armies with almost like-for-like combat experience, the French army performed with sufficient degree of superiority to win battles, or at least make bloody stalemates, but when faced with the vastly superior British army, the French army was outclassed.

1168 Martin Aaron, *2nd Battalion 69th (South Lincolnshire) Foot during the Waterloo Campaign*, The Napoleon Series, October 2007, available at http://www.napoleon-series.org/military/organization/Britain/Infantry/c_2-69Waterloo.html [accessed22 August 2012].

1169 Marco Bijl, *History and Organisation of the Dutch 8th Militia Battalion*, The Napoleon Series, June 2008, available at http://www.napoleon-series.org/military/organization/Dutch/8thMilitia/c_8thMilitia1.html [accessed 4 January 2012].

The army of 1815 was a shaky formation with little trust between men and sub-officers and their officers. There is little wonder that when checked, due to the lack of command and control, lack of inspirational leaders and stopped by terrain, that the Guard, like the army as a whole, broke and fled. As we have seen, French eyewitnesses who stated that many regiments included a high percentage of young soldiers who had never been under fire were correct. Of the several battalions of Young Guard that were in the Vendée, General Lamarque complained that they were filled with recruits and deserters who neither knew how to manoeuvre nor shoot. Captain Duthlitt thought the soldiers who had suffered the defeats of the emperor's recent campaigns and the returned prisoners of war from Russia had lost a great deal of their enthusiasm. To summarise, the Old Guard failed at Waterloo and the army collapsed due to:

1. Poor generalship on the part of Napoléon and lack of co-ordination resulted in failure and the collapse of the French offensive;

2. The Guard failed at Waterloo due to lack of leadership and the poor choice of attacking terrain. The sunken road stopped the advance of the grenadiers in the first assault. The lack of forward movement is noted by Captain Beraud, of the 4th Grenadiers, who claims that the 4th and 3rd Grenadiers merged into a single force due to poor marching discipline. This poor marching discipline, if Beraud is accurate in his summary of events, would no doubt slow down the rate of progress of General Friant's command, and would also have affected the combat performance of the two battalions. It is possible that the grenadiers merged with the chasseurs in order to pass the sunken road to the north and north-west of La Haye Sainte, which Beraud alludes to. However, Battalion-Commander Guillemin makes no mention of this in his narration, so we cannot be sure that the grenadiers were slower in their advance, which may have been due to poor marching discipline. It is clear that Pelet decries the grenadiers for not attacking at the same time, and also bemoans Michel for allowing his attack to be piecemeal, and that the four battalions did not attack together, but rather one battalion followed another at different points on the Allied lines;

3. The army felt betrayed when Grouchy's promised troops turned out to be Prussians. The desertion of a dozen or so officers

undermined morale. General Trochu then dwells on the necessity of the existence of the most absolute confidence between officers and soldiers, and of the award of proper recompenses to those who deserve them. In 1815, the Imperial Guard and the army as a whole lacked this absolute trust and confidence between the officers, sub-officers and men. Trochu notes that the real character of men is revealed in war; in all armies there exist braggarts and bullies. Boastful men and loud-talkers, theoretically brave, but apt to become silent and disconcerted at the approach of a combat. Some unable to conquer their feelings practise that part of valour which is considered to be the most discreet, and disappear. Others, a prey to a painful agitation, restrain its appearance by force of character, but are incapable to lead or to be led. A certain number of a cool, calm, and apparently mild temperament suddenly and unexpectedly become the bravest of the brave, and exercise, by the force of their example, an irresistible influence over the masses;

4. Once one French regiment began to panic, as General Trochu notes, panic becomes infectious, rendering the bulk of the army useless for further offensive or defensive actions. Joachim Ambert, later a general and baron of France, writing in 1837 stressed that the French soldier was unsuited to standing in lines on the defensive like the Prussians and British. Either they were attacking, or if the attack was checked, ran away. He noted that the French soldier was timid and had to be coaxed and inspired by a charismatic leader before they would stand steadily under fire. The lack of such a leader would, in his thought, precipitate defeat, and so it was at Waterloo. The battalions of the Old Guard which performed markedly better at Waterloo were those headed by inspiring, and perhaps charismatic, generals like Morand, Pelet, Roguet or those who the men trusted like Christiani, Petit and Cambronne due to their long association with the Guard. General Poret de Morvan, and later Marshal Ney, by the sheer force of their personality could not motivate the first two attacking waves to move beyond the sunken road. The moment of hesitation caused by the wounding of Friant, Michel and Mallet resulted in the 3rd and 4th Chasseurs being exposed to enemy fire without a figurehead to lead them to the assault. Ambert notes that the act of making an attack would raise morale, whereas standing under fire would obviously not. However, the

success of the attack, Ambert commented, depended on who 'blinked first', i.e. who fired first. The initiative belongs to those who shouted and lowered their bayonets menacingly at the last moment, they would overcome their fears and be carried away on a crowd of mass hysteria. It seems that the Allied line fired first. General Poret de Morvan endeavoured to deploy both the first and second assaults under a hail of close-range enemy musketry and artillery fire. The French lost the initiative and therefore the combat;

5. The overwhelming numbers of the Allied counter-attack. Attacked in front by General Chassé's commanded and rallied Nassau troops, bombarded by artillery from the front and flank, attacked by cavalry and attacked partially in the flank, it is little wonder that the Imperial Guard broke and fled. Napoléon had badly underestimated the strength and stamina of the Allies and their commitment to battle, and the importance of Wellington and other field commanders in making their men fight on until the Prussians arrived; and

6. The 6th Corps of General Lobau was used to plug the gap in the French right wing between the troops of 1st Corps and Plancenoit. It is likely, therefore, that when the Prussians started to move into Plancenoit, Lobau and Duhesme withdrew their respective corps to prevent them being encircled. Moving Quiot's division to Plancenoit and Pégot's brigade to the centre with Donzelot's division left the wreck of Marcognet's division and Brue's brigade from Durutte's division standing in the way of 30,000 Prussians commanded by Pirch and Ziethen, and Wellington's left flank. Napoléon ordered this shift of manpower, leaving the gap between La Haye Sainte and Papelotte extremely vulnerable. Thus, no large body of French troops filled the line between La Haye Sainte and Plancenoit. In the gap where 6th Corps was meant to be, the Prussians flooded the battlefield and became intermingled with the Old Guard south of La Haye Sainte. Seeing the arrival of the Prussians, which had been reported as being Grouchy, the army panicked and collapsed.

These are the six key reasons why Napoléon lost Waterloo. No secret treason of Soult, no blundering by Ney or Grouchy. Napoléon lost because of command and control decisions he made.

Bibliography

Archive Material

The National Archives, Kew, London:

ADM 103/99 Dartmoor. French prisoners of war, 1815
ADM 103/102 Dartmoor. French prisoners of war, 1815
ADM 103/311 Plymouth. French prisoners of war, 1815
ADM 103/513 Alphabetical List of prisoners of war, Dartmoor, 1755-1831
ADM 103/595 Register of French POWs Released on parole, Okehampton and Oswestry, 1815

British Library, London:
ADD MS 34706 FO 480

Oldham Local Studies and Archives, Oldham:
2006-046

Archives Nationales, Paris:
82 AP 5 Fonds Bro de Commerce

AF IV 842-883 & 1550-1580
AF IV 1939 Registre d'Ordres du Major General 13 Juin au 26 Juin 1815
AF IV 1940

C2 470 & 472

LH 5/65, 8/6, 24/25, 28/70, 35/60, 38/37, 41/53, 41/109, 45/36, 64/3, 95/50, 99/30, 108/8/10, 120/86, 131/17, 168/15, 172/56, 194/21, 219/79, 228/72, 231/27, 232/74, 240/1, 241/62, 243/78, 246/42, 261/6, 268/41, 276/60, 286/11, 299/20, 299/37, 307/70, 319/12, 325/27, 325/44, 329/82, 352/40, 368/77, 371/21, 373/38, 376/26, 392/54, 404/17, 407/2, 412/35, 413/66, 419/92, 424/79, 427/5, 429/26, 432/6, 444/25, 458/41, 462/81, 480/8, 481/29, 491/91, 504/70, 547/37, 560/22, 565/14, 566/35, 571/69, 582/26, 590/78, 611/45, 621/26, 622/12, 628/64, 640/78, 640/83, 644/3, 663/5, 674/40, 703/88, 707/79, 708/24, 710/13, 713/13, 714/58, 723/16, 728/24, 738/25, 745/4, 750/58, 757/1, 758/71, 760/47, 764/81, 779/21, 793/34, 795/75, 799/70, 812/42, 819/72, 829/70, 837/30, 840/35, 851/64, 863/74, 864/38, 871/25, 892/2, 897/42, 917/7, 934/30, 941/34, 953/8, 976/29, 1012/42, 1018/38, 1031/41, 1032/75, 1034/42, 1053/29, 1062/20, 1063/05, 1066/62, 1113/30, 1113/34, 1118/72, 1150/28, 1152/41, 1158/29, 1190/22, 1199/10, 1206/63, 1211/54, 1245/18, 1256/59, 1257/65, 1263/65, 1265/91, 1271/67, 1273/73, 1291/25, 1300/58, 1301/5, 1308/67, 1312/45, 1329/54, 1349/68, 1351/35, 1367/9, 1378/52, 1387/57, 1395/52, 1426/83, 1437/16, 1437/75, 1445/40, 1465/23, 1474/9, 1480/20, 1482/43, 1505/43, 1515/9, 1517/6, 1537/27, 1537/181, 1548/79, 1552/76, 1556/18, 1559/50, 1565/75, 1575/13, 1592/47, 1593/39, 1593/74, 1623/35, 1627/30, 1646/24, 1660/50, 1666/5, 1675/22, 1677/23, 1690/12, 1712/37, 1715/56, 1722/27, 1746/67, 1750/51, 1755/18, 1772/3, 1788/9, 1806/47, 1809/18, 1820/13, 1843/43, 1861/52, 1881/58, 1882/63, 1891/29, 1897/8, 1919/71, 1923/45, 1935/17, 1949/72, 1958/37, 1958/46, 2002/42, 2006/51, 2012/12, 2014/56, 2020/22, 2024/35, 2046/70, 2048/6, 2060/34, 2068/38, 2094/42, 2096/76, 2101/33, 2117/35, 2124/43, 2135/8, 2138/25, 2138/62, 2210/28, 2210/50, 2218/13, 2222/55, 2293/60, 2296/12, 2300/55, 2309/35, 2312/270, 2316/60, 2320/25, 2337/21, 2339/9, 2351/17, 2351/67, 2356/28, 2372/17, 2407/25, 2460/50, 2464/38, 2476/74, 2493/30, 2529/28, 2531/70, 2594/60, 2616/53, 2617/76, 2624/59, 2624/60, 2625/62, 2670/44, 2688/5, 2688/27, 2696/68, 2701/93, 2704/91, 2724/27, 2777/39, 8058/43.

Service Historique Armée du Terre, Paris:

15C20

2 Yb 208 Contrôle Nominatif Officier 28e regiment d'infanterie de ligne 18 Octobre 1808 a 23 Juin 1815

2 Yb 641-05 & 644

C2 & C3

C15 Registre d'Ordres et de correspondance du major-general à partir du 13 Juin jusqu'au 26 Juin au Maréchal Grouchy

C15 5 Correspondance Armée du Nord 11 Juin au 21 Juin 1815

C15 6 Correspondance Armée du Nord 22 Juin au 3 Juillet 1815

C15 34 Situations Garde Impériale 1815

C15 35 Situations Armée du Nord 1815 Rapport Vialla 1 Juillet 1815

C15 39 Décrets Cent-Jours 1815 Deriot Ordre du Jour, 4 Juin 1815

C16 Correspondence 1815

Dossier Charles Nicolas Thurot

E 31

GD 2 1135

GR 2 YB 87 2e regiment de chevau-legers lancers de la Garde Impériale

GR 18 YC 9 2e Regiment de Carabiniers (Monsieur) officiers 1814-1815

GR 20 YC 13

GR 20 YC 14 registre matricules corps des grenadiers de La Garde Imperial lors des Cent-Jours 30 Avril à 24 Septembre

GR 20 YC 18 & 19

GR 20 YC 44 chasseurs à pied de la Garde, divers corps, 1814-1815

GR 20 YC 45, 46, 55, 56, 137, 143, 144

GR 20 YC 154 registre matricule Dragons Garde Impériale

GR 20 YC 166 Régiment de chevau-légers lanciers, crée par décret du 8 avril 1815 et formé de l'ex-corps royal des lanciers de France, 8 avril 1815-22 décembre 1815 (matricules: 1 à 1,608)

GR 20 YC 180 1 avril 1815-7 novembre 1815 (matricules: 1 à 1 018)

GR 20 YC 187 Artillerie à cheval de la garde impériale, 1er avril 1815-30 octobre 1815 (matricules: 1 à 472)

GR 20 YC 197 Registré matricule de l'escadron du train d'artillerie de la Garde Impériale crée pat décret du 8 Avril 1815

GR 20 YC 204 Sapeurs mineurs 1815

GR 20 YC 209 Bataillons du train des équipages militaires de la garde impériale, 8 avril 1815-1er octobre 1815 (matricules: 1 à 807) Créés par décret du 8 avril 1815

GR 20 YC 211 Compagnies d'ouvriers d'administration, 26 mai 1815-1er octobre 1815 (matricules: 1 à 475)

GR 21 YC 8 1er régiment d'infanterie de ligne dit régiment du Roi, 1 mai 1814-6 décembre 1814 (matricules 1 à 3,000)

GR 21 YC 9 1er régiment d'infanterie de ligne dit régiment du Roi, 6 décembre 1814-3 juillet 1815 (matricules 3,001 à 4,386)

GR 21 YC 19 2e régiment d'infanterie de ligne dit régiment de la Reine, 20 mai 1814-21 août 1814 (matricules 1 à 2,997)

GR 21 YC 20 2e régiment d'infanterie de ligne dit régiment de la Reine, 9 septembre 1814-6 juin 1815 (matricules 3,000 à 4,723)

GR 21 YC 31 3e régiment d'infanterie de ligne dit régiment du Dauphin, 16 Juillet 1814-17 Décembre 1814 (matricules 1 à 1,800)

GR 21 YC 32 3e régiment d'infanterie de ligne dit régiment du Dauphin, 17 décembre 1814-1 Juillet 1815 (matricules 1,801 à 2,135)

GR 21 YC 49 5e régiment d'infanterie de ligne dit régiment d'Angoulême, 6 septembre 1814-23 décembre 1814 (matricules 1 à 1,800)

GR 21 YC 50 5e régiment d'infanterie de ligne dit régiment d'Angoulême, 23 décembre 1814-25 août 1815 (matricules 1,800 à 2,208)

GR 21 YC 74 8e régiment d'infanterie de Ligne dit régiment de Condé, 30 août 1814-11 mai 1815 (matricules 1 à 1,800)

GR 21 YC 75 8e régiment d'infanterie de ligne dit régiment de Condé, 14 mai 1815-10 juillet 1815 (matricules 1,801 à 2,379)

GR 21 YC 92 10e régiment d'infanterie de ligne dit régiment Colonel-Général, 1 septembre 1814-6 mai 1815 (matricules 1 à 1,800)

GR 21 YC 93 10e régiment d'infanterie de ligne dit régiment Colonel-Général, 6 mai 1815-22 juillet 1815 (matricules 1,801 à 1,943)

GR 21 YC 100 11e régiment d'infanterie de ligne, 9 septembre 1814-4 février 1815 (matricules 1 à 1,800)

GR 21 YC 101 11e régiment d'infanterie de ligne, 4 février 1815-23 août 1815 (matricules 1,801 à 2,690)

GR 21 YC 116 13er régiment d'infanterie Legere 1806 à 1815

GR 21 YC 158 17e régiment d'infanterie de ligne, Octobre 1814-22 juin 1815 (matricules 1 à 2,593)

GR 21 YC 178 19e régiment d'infanterie de ligne, 18 août 1814-26 avril 1815 (matricules 1 à 1,800)

GR 21 YC 179 19e régiment d'infanterie de ligne, 26 avril 1815-16 juillet 1815 (matricules 1,801 à 2,598)

GR 21 YC 197 21e régiment d'infanterie de ligne, 18-20 mai 1815 (matricules 1 à 1,800)

GR 21 YC 198 21e régiment d'infanterie de ligne, 29 avril 1815-16 juin 1815 (matricules 1,801 à 1,817)

GR 21 YC 238 25e régiment d'infanterie de ligne, 1er août 1814-20 janvier 1815 (matricules 1 à 1 800)

GR 21 YC 255 27e régiment d'infanterie de ligne, 1 août 1814 (matricules 1 à 1,800)

GR 21 YC 256 27e régiment d'infanterie de ligne, 1 juillet 1814-19 juillet 1815 (matricules 1,801 à 2,778)

GR 21 YC 264 28e régiment d'infanterie de ligne, 6 juillet 1808-23 juin 1815 (matricules 1 à 1,762)

GR 21 YC 271 29e régiment d'infanterie de ligne, 21 juillet 1814-24 décembre 1814 (matricules 1 à 1,800)

GR 21 YC 272 29e régiment d'infanterie de ligne, 24 décembre 1814-21 juillet 1815 (matricules 1,801 à 2,226)

GR 21 YC 391 42e régiment d'infanterie de ligne (ex 45e régiment d'infanterie de ligne), 1 août 1814-4 juin 1815 (matricules 1 à 1,800)

GR 21 YC 400 43e régiment d'infanterie de ligne (ex 46e régiment d'infanterie de ligne), 1 août 1814-31 mai 1815 (matricules 1 à 1,800)

GR 21 YC 401 43e régiment d'infanterie de ligne (ex 46e régiment d'infanterie de ligne), 31 mai 1815-30 juillet 1815 (matricules 1,801 à 2,075)

GR 21 YC 433 47e régiment d'infanterie de ligne (ex 51e régiment d'infanterie de ligne), 6 août 1814-15 mars 1815 (matricules 1 à 1 800)

GR 21 YC 434 47e régiment d'infanterie de ligne (ex 51e régiment d'infanterie de ligne), 20 mars 1815-13 septembre 1815 (matricules 1 801 à 2 627)

GR 21 YC 456 50e régiment d'infanterie de ligne (ex 54e régiment d'infanterie de ligne), 21 juillet 1814-10 mai 1815 (matricules 1 à 1,660)

GR 21 YC 463 51e régiment d'infanterie de ligne (ex 55e régiment d'infanterie de ligne), 1 août 1814-3 août 1815 (matricules 1 à 2,049)

GR 21 YC 516 57e régiment d'infanterie de ligne (ex 61e régiment d'infanterie de ligne), 1 août 1814-14 juin 1815 (matricules 1 à 1,800)

GR 21 YC 599 66e régiment d'infanterie de ligne (ex 72e régiment d'infanterie de ligne), 11 août 1814-27 février 1815 (matricules 1 à 1,800)

GR 21 YC 600 66e régiment d'infanterie de ligne (ex 72e régiment d'infanterie de ligne), 21 février 1815-4 août 1815 (matricules 1,801 à 2,092)

GR 21 YC 653 72e régiment d'infanterie de ligne (ex 84e régiment d'infanterie de ligne), 1 août 1814-4 février 1815 (matricules 1 à 1,800)

GR 21 YC 655 72e régiment d'infanterie de ligne (ex 84e régiment d'infanterie de ligne), 20 janvier 1815-24 juillet 1815 (matricules 1,801 à 2,756)

GR 21 YC 690 76e régiment d'infanterie de ligne (ex 92e régiment d'infanterie de ligne), 4 septembre 1814-28 mars 1815 (matricules 1 à 1 512)

GR 21 YC 691 76e régiment d'infanterie de ligne (ex 92e régiment d'infanterie de ligne), 25 avril 1815-27 juin 1815 (matricules 1 513 à 1 728)

GR 21 YC 701 77e régiment d'infanterie de ligne (ex 93e régiment d'infanterie de ligne), 13 août 1814-22 décembre 1814 (matricules 1 à 1 800)

GR 21 YC 702 77e régiment d'infanterie de ligne (ex 93e régiment d'infanterie de ligne), 22 décembre 1814-8 août 1815 (matricules 1 801 à 3 108)

GR 21 YC 717 79e régiment d'infanterie de ligne (ex 95e régiment d'infanterie de ligne), 26 août 1814-25 mai 1815 (matricules 1 à 1,800)

GR 21 YC 734 81e régiment d'infanterie de ligne (ex 100e régiment d'infanterie de ligne), 24 septembre 1814-1er mai 1815 (matricules 1 à 1,800)

GR 21 YC 735 100e régiment d'infanterie de ligne, 1 mai 1815-16 août 1815 (matricules 1,801 à 2,248)

GR 21 YC 771 86e régiment d'infanterie de ligne (ex 105e régiment d'infanterie de ligne), 13 août 1814-21 février 1815 (matricules 1 à 1,800)

GR 21 YC 772 86e régiment d'infanterie de ligne (ex 105e régiment d'infanterie de ligne), 24 février 1815-10 août 1815 (matricules 1,801 à 1,881)

GR 21 YC 781 88e régiment d'infanterie de ligne (ex 107e régiment d'infanterie de ligne), 21 juillet 1814-6 juillet 1815 (matricules 1 à 1,396)

GR 21 YC 790 89e régiment d'infanterie de ligne (ex 108e régiment d'infanterie de ligne), 9 septembre 1814-7 juin 1815 (matricules 1 à 1,800)

GR 22 YC 19 2er régiment d'infanterie Légère 1814 à 1815

GR 22 YC 40 4er régiment d'infanterie Légère 1814 à 1815

GR 22 YC 47 & 48

GR 22 YC 116 13er régiment d'infanterie Légère 1806 à 1815
GR 24 YC 9 Contrôle Nominatif, Troupe 1814-1815
GR 24 YC 21 Régiment de Reine organisation 1814-29 Juillet 1815
GR 24 YC 24
GR 24 YC 26 Régiment du Dauphin organisation 1814-Juin 1815
GR 24 YC 41
GR 24 YC 46 Contrôle Nominatif Troupe 7e Cuirassiers 9 Aout 1814-6 Aout 1815
GR 24 YC 50 & 55
GR 24 YC 60 Contrôle Nominatif Troupe 10e Cuirassiers 15 Avril 1815 a 27 Juillet 1815 organisation 1814
GR 24 YC 64, 96, 158, 254, YC 264, 274, YC 282, 299, 309
GR 25 YC 14 1e Artillerie à Cheval
GR 25 YC 21 2e Artillerie à Pied 1814–1815
GR 25 YC 40 3e Artillerie à Cheval
GR 29 YC 422 Contrôle Nominatif Troupe 7e Hussards 9 Septembre 1814 à 12 Aout 1815
GR 30 YC 61

IM 1962 Correspondence au ministre de guerre-Infanterie

M291

MR 717 letter du Chef d'Escadron l'Etang
MR 718 Observations sur la campagne de 1815
MR 7178 Observations sur la Campagne du 1815

Xab 68 Grenadiers à Pied (formation de 1815)
Xab 69 Chasseurs à Pied (formation de 1815)
Xab 73 Dragons et Chevau-léger (formation de 1815)
Xab 74 Artillerie à Pied (formation de 1815)

Xb 343 1e de Ligne 1808-1815
Xb 348 3e de Ligne 1808-1815
Xb 364 10e de Ligne 1791–1815
Xb 453 54e de Ligne 1813-1815
Xb 455 55e de Ligne 1791-1815
Xb 508 92e de Ligne
Xb 561 1er régiment d'infanterie Legere 1814 a 1815
Xb 565 1e Légère
Xb 567 2e Légère

Xc 93 2e Carabiniers
Xc 99 3e Cuirassiers
Xc 103 5e régiment de Cuirassiers
Xc 110 9e Cuirassiers
Xc 135 2e Dragons
Xc 182 3e et 4e Chevau-légers
Xc 183 5e et 6e Chevau-légers, pertes officiers depuis 18 Juin 1815
Xc 192 4e Chasseurs à Cheval
Xc 206 11e Chasseurs à Cheval
Xc 249 7e Hussard 1791-1815

Xd 360 Artillerie Armée du Nord 1815

Yj 11-13 Etat nominatif des militaires prisonniers de Guerre français
arrivés d'Angleterre

Printed Works

Books:

Winand Aerts, *Waterloo, opérations de l'armée prussienne du Bas-Rhin
pendant la campagne de Belgique en 1815, depuis, la bataille de Ligny
jusqu'a l'entrée en France des troupes prussiennes*, Spineux, Brussels,
1908

Maurice Girod de l'Ain, *Vie militaire du Géneral* Foy, E. Plon, Nourrit et
Cie, Paris, 1900

de Ainslie, Historical *record of the First or the Royal Regiment of Dragoons*,
London, Chapman and Hall, 1887

Mameluck Ali, *Souvenirs sur l'empereur Napoléon*, Ed. Christophe
Bourachot, Arléa, Paris, 2000

Anon, *Biographie du Gal Rogé* Impr, De Julien, Lanier et Cie, Le Mans,
1849

Anon, *Memoires pour servir a l'Histoire de France*, Richard Phillips & Co,
London, 1820

Anon, *Notice nécrologique sur le lieutenant général Cte Roguet*, J. Dumain,
Paris, 1847

Anon, *Tales of War*, William Mark Clarke, London, 1836

Anon, *The Journal of the Three Days of the Battle of Waterloo*, T. Chaplin,
London, 1816

Thomas Joseph Aubry, *Mémoires d'un capitaine de chasseurs à cheval*, Jourdan, Paris, 2011

Paul Avers, *Historique du 82e Régiment d'Infanterie de Ligne et du 7e Régiment d'Infanterie Légère, 1684-1876*, Lahure, Paris, 1876

Jean-Pierre Babelon and Suzanne d'Huart, *Napoléon's Last Will and Testament*, Paddington Press, New York, 1977

Alexandre Barginet, *Le grenadier de l'Ile d'Elbe: souvenirs de 1814 et 1815* (two volumes), Mame et Delaunay-Vallée, Paris, 1830

C. R. B. Barrett, *The History of the XIIIth Hussars*, London, 1911

Robert Batty, *An Historical Account of the Campaign of Waterloo*, Rodwell and Martin and Co, London, 1820

Marie Élli Guillaume de Baudus, *Études sur Napoléon* (two volumes), Debecourt, Paris, 1841

Charles Paris Nicholas Beauvais, *Victoires, conquêtes, désastres, revers et guerres civils des Français, de 1792 à 1815*, C. L. F. Panckoucke, Paris, 1821

Pierre Berthezène, *Souvenirs militaires de la republique et de l'empire*, J. Dumaine, Paris, 1855

John Booth, *The Battle of Waterloo*, Booth, Egerton, London, 1816

General Bro, *Mémoires, 1796-1844*, Librairie des deux Empires, 2001

Pierre Bruyere, *Historique du 2e regiment des Dragons*, de Garnier, Chartres, 1885

P. Brye, *Historique du 6e regiment de Cuirassiers*, 1893

Albert Burow, *Geschichte des Könglich Preussischen 18 Infanterie-Regiments von 1813 bis 1847* ed. Rudolph von Wedell, Posen, 1848

Louis Canler, *Mémoires de Canler* (Vol. 1), Roy, Paris, 1882

Lieutenant Chevalier, *Souvenirs des Guerres Napoleoniennes* ed. Jean Mistler and Helene Michaud, Hachette, Paris, 1970

Silvain Larreguy de Civrieux, *Souvenirs d'un cadet, 1813-1823*, Hachette, Paris, 1912

John Coates, *The Hour Between Dog and Wolf*, Fourth Estate, London, 2012

Jean-Roch Coignet, *The Narrative of Captain Coignet Soldier of the Empire, 1776-1850*, Chatto & Windus, London, 1897

Combes-Brassard, *Notice sur la bataille de Mont-Saint-Jean* in *Souvenirs et Correspondance sur la bataille de Waterloo*, Librairie historique Teissèdre, Paris, 2000

Emile von Conrady, *Geschichte des Könglich preussischen sechsten Infaterie-regiments*, Glogau, 1857

Cornevin, *Les Marchands de vin de Paris*, Les Prinicpaux Libraries, Paris, 1869

Rene Marie Timoleon de Cosse-Brissac, *Historique du 7e regiment de dragons*. Lerory, Paris, 1909

Edward Cotton, *A Voice from Waterloo*, Mont-St-Jean, Belgium, 1877

Jean Baptiste Pierre Jullien de Courcelles, *Dictionnaire historique et biographique des généraux Francais* (Vol. 8), Paris, 1823

Jean Louis Crabbe, *Jean-Louis Crabbe, Colonel d'Empire*, Editions du Cannonier, Nantes, 2006

Charles Dalton, *The Waterloo Roll Call*, Eyre and Spottiswood, London, 1904

Karl von Damitz, *Geschichte des Feldzuges von 1815 in den Niederlanden und Frankreich* (Vol. 1), E. S. Mittler, Berlin, 1838

François-Thomas Delbare, *Relation circonstanciée de la dernière campagne de Buonaparte, terminée par le bataille de Mont-Saint-Jean, dite de Waterloo ou de la Belle-Alliance*, J. G. Dentu, Paris, 1816

Henri Martial Edmond Manceaux Demiau, *Historique du 5e régiment d'infanterie de ligne (1569-1890): rédigé conformément aux ordres de MM. les colonels Livet et Guasco*, E. Brulfert, Caen, 1890

Charles Deulin, Histoires du Petite Ville, Paris, 1875

J. B. J. van Doren, *Strategisch verhaal van de veldslagen tusschen het Fransche leger en dat der Geallieerden op 15, 16, 17 en 18 Junij 1815, Mont-Saint-Jean*, Amsterdam, 1865

Jean-Baptiste Drouët, *Le maréchal Drouet, comte d'Erlon: Vie militaire écrit par lui même*, Guvatve, Paris, 1844

Jacques-Antoine Dulaure, *1814-1830 Historie des Cent-jours*, Paris, 1834

Victor Dupuy, *Mémoires Militaire 1794-1816*, Librairie des deux Empirés, 2001

Pierre Duthlit, *Les Mémoires du Capitaine Duthlit*, Lille, 1909

John Robert Elting, *Swords Around a Throne*, Phoenix Giant, 1996

Louis Florimond Fantin des Odoards, *Journal du général Fantin des Odoards*, E. Plon, Nourrit et Cie, Paris, 1895

Jean-Antoine Farges, *Recits de Temps Cruels*, Books on Demand, 2010

Théo Fleischmen, *L'Armée impériale racontée par la Grande Armée*, Librairie Académique Perrin, Paris, 1964

Fernand Fleuret, *Description des passages de Dominique Fleuret*, Firmin-Didot et Cie, Paris, 1929

Maurice Fleury, *Les prisonniers de Cabrera; souvenirs d'un caporal de grenadiers (1808-1809) publiés par le comte Fleury*, E. Paul, Paris, 1902

Maurice Fleury, *Souvenirs anecdotiques et militaires du colonel Biot*, Henri Vivien, Paris, 1901

John Franklin, *Waterloo Hanoverian Correspondence*, 1815 Limited, 2010

Paul Fussell, *The Great War and Modern Memory*, Oxford University Press, Oxford, 1975

David E. Gates, *The Napoleonic Wars 1803-1815*, Arnold, London, 1997

Gaspard Gourgaud, *La campagne de 1815*, P. Mongie, Paris, 1818

Anna Green, Kathleen Troup, *The Houses of History*, Manchester University Press, 1999

Emmanuel Grouchy, George Grouchy, *Mémoires du maréchal de Grouchy*, E. Dentu, 1873

Emmanuel Grouchy, *Relation de la campagne de 1815*, n.d.

Emmanuel Grouchy, *Relation succincte de la campagne de 1815 en Belgique*, Delanchy, Paris, 1843

Aron Guverich, *The French Historical Revolution: The Annales School*, in Hodder et al, *Interpreting Archaeology*, Routledge, London, 1995

Guyot, *Carnets de la Campagne du General Comte Guyot 1792-1815*, Tessedire, 1999

William Hay, *William Hay Reminiscences 1808-1815: under Wellington*, Simpkin, Marshall, Hamilton, Kent, & Co Ltd, London, 1901

J. L. Henckens, *Mémoires se rapportant à son service militaire au 6e régiment de chasseurs à cheval français de février 1803 à août 1816*, M. Nijhoff, La Haie, 1910

Émile Herbillon, *Quelques pages d'un vieux cahier: souvenirs du Général Herbillon (1794-1866)*, Berger-Levrault, Paris, 1928

Colonel Heymès, *Relation de la campagne de 1815, dite de Waterloo*, Gaultier-Laguionie, Paris, 1829

Hoffmann, *Zur Geschichte des Feldzuges von 1815*, Berlin, 1851

Peter Hofschroer, *Waterloo 1815 Quatre Bras and Ligny*, Pen & Sword, Barnsley, 2006

James Hope, *Letters from Portugal, Spain, and France, during the memorable campaigns of 1811, 1812 and 1813 and from Belgium and France in the year 1815*, Michael Anderson, Edinburgh, 1819

Henry Houssaye, *1815 Waterloo*, Paris, 1903

François Hue, *Jean-Louis de Crabbé, colonel d'empire*, Canonnier, Nantes, 2006

E. F. Janin, *Campagne de Waterloo*, Chaumerot Jeune, Paris, 1820

Georges Guimet de Juzancourt, *Historique de 10e regiment de Cuirassiers (1643-1891)*, Paris, Berger-Levrault, 1893

Christopher Kelly, *A Full and Circumstantial Account Of The Memorable Battle of Waterloo*, London, 1836

Henry Lachouque, *Le General Tommelin*, Tournai, n.d.

Jean-Marc Largeaud, *Napoléon et Waterloo: la defaite glorieuse de 1815 a nos jours*, La Boutique de l'histoire, Paris, 2006

Jonathan Leach, *Rough Sketches of the life of an Old Soldier*, London, Brown and Green, London, 1831

Lefol, *Souvenirs sur le prytanée de Saint-Cyr sur la campagne de 1814, le retour de l'empereur Napoléon de l'île d'Elbe, et la campagne de 1815, pendant les Cent-jours*, Montalant-Bougleux, Versailles, 1854

Jean Baptiste Lemonnier-Delafosse, *Campagnes de 1810 à 1815: souvenirs militaires faisant suite a ceux première et deuxième campagnes se St-Domingue de 1801 a 1809*, Alph. Lemale, Havre, 1850

Octave Levavasseur, *Souvenirs militaires 1800-1815*, Librairie des Deux Empirés, 2001

Kevin B. Linch, *The recruitment of the British Army 1807-1815 Ph.D. Thesis*, University of Leeds, 2001

Henri Lot, *Les deux généraux Ordener*, R. Roger et F. Chernoviz, Paris, 1910

Edmund Charles Constant Louvat, *Historique du 7e Hussards*, Pirault, Paris, 1889

Mackenzie MacBride, *With Napoleon at Waterloo*, J. B. Lippincott & Co, Philadelphia, 1911

Raymond-Balthasard Maiseau, *Vie du Maréchal Ney*, Pillet, Paris, 1816

Jarry de Mancy, *Portraits et Histoire des Hommes Utiles*, Imprime Chez Paul Renouard, Paris, 1833

Marguerite, *Fastes militaires de la France*, Paris, 1836

Jacques François Martin, *Souvenirs d'un ex-officier 1812-1815*, Paris, 1867

Everts Masskamp, *Description de la Bataille Glorieuse Waterloo*, 1818

Hippolyte de Mauduit, *Les derniers jours de la Grande Armée* (Vol. 2), Paris, 1848

William Hamilton Maxwell, *Stories of Waterloo*, Henry Colburn and Richard Bentley, London, 1833

Adrien Jacques Joseph le Mayeur, *Ode sur la Bataille de Waterloo*, Brussels, 1816

Hubert Miot-Putigny, *Putigny, grognard d'empire*, Gallimard, Paris, 1950

Molieres and Plainville, *Dictionnaire des Braves des Napoléon* (Vol. 2), Paris, Livre Chez Vous, 2004

Thomas Morris, *Recollections of Military Service in 1813, 1814 and 1815*, James Madden & Co, London, 1845

Charles Mullié, *Biographie des célébrités militaires des armées de terre et de mer de 1789 à 1850*, 1852

Wilhelm Neff, *Geschichte des Infanterie-Regiments von Goeben (2. Rheinischen) Nr. 28*, Ernst Siegfried Mittler und Sohn, Berlin, 1890

Michel Louis Felix Ney, *Documents inédits sur la campagne de 1815*, Anselin, Paris, 1840

Jean-Nicolas-Auguste Noël, *Souvenirs Militaires d'un officier du Premier Empire*, Librairie des Deux Empires, 1999

Antoine Noguès, André Maricourt, *Mémoires du général Noguès (1777-1853) sur les guerres de l'Empire*, A. Lemerre, Paris, 1922

Ollech, *Geschichte des Feldzuges von 1815 nach archivalischen quellen Berlin*, 1876

Ronald Pawly, *Napoléon's Mounted Chasseurs of the Imperial Guard*, Osprey, Oxford, 2008

Auguste-Louis Pétiet, *Souvenirs militaires de l'histoire contemporaine*, Dumaine, Paris, 1844

Julius von Pflugk-Harttung, *Vorgeschichte der Schlacht bei Belle-Alliance, Wellington*, R. Schröder, Berlin, 1903

Amédée Pichot, *Biographie Le général Hurault de Sorbée*, H. Simon Dautreville, Paris, 1850

Rene Louis Gustave de Place, *Historique de 12e Cuirassiers (1688 to 1888)*, Paris, A. Lahure, 1889

Thomas Pockoke, *Journal of a soldier of the 71st or Glasgow regiment, Highland Light Infantry 1806-1815*, William and Charles Taite, Edinburgh, 1819

Gustave de Pontécoulant, *Mémoires*, Paris, 1866

Colonel du Génie Répécaud, *Napoléon à Ligny et le Maréchal Ney à Quatre-Bras*, Degeorge, Arras, 1847

Rigau, *Souvenirs des Guerres de l'Empire,* Garniere Freres, Paris, 1846

Pierre Robinaux, Gustave Léon Schlumberger, *Journal de route du Capitaine Robinaux 1803-1832,* Plon-Nourrit, Paris, 1908

Moulins de Rochefort, *Histoire de 4e regiment de Cuirassiers,* Paris, A Lahure, 1897

Antoine Ernest Rothwiller, *Histoire du deuxième régiment de cuirassiers, ancien Royal de cavalerie, 1635-1876, d'après les archives du corps, celles du dépôt de la guerre et autres documents originaux,* E. Plon, Paris, 1877

Camille Rousset, *La Grande Armée de 1813,* Paris, 1871

Edward Sabine, *Letters of Colonel Sir Augustus Simon Frazer KCB,* Longman, Brown, Green, Longmans & Roberts, London, 1859

Germain Sarrut, *Biographie des Hommes du Jour* (Vol. 4), Pluout, Paris, 1838

Gustave Schlumberger, *Lettres du commandant Coudreux, à son frère, 1804-1815 : soldats de Napoléon,* Plon, Nourrit et Cie, Paris, 1908

Sénécal, *General le Sénécal campagne de Waterloo,* Philadelphia, 1818

C. W. Serjeant, Joseph Butterworth, *Some particulars of the battle at Waterloo,* J & T Clarke, London, 1816

Michael Shanks, Ian Hodder, *Processual, postprocessual and interpretive archaeologies* in Hodder et al, *Interpreting Archaeology,* Routledge, London, 1995

William Siborne, *The Waterloo Campaign 1815,* A. Constable, 1900

William Siborne, *Waterloo Letters* ed. H. T. Siborne, Greenhill Books, 1993

Ludwig Stawitzky, *Geschichte des Königlich Preussichen 25ten Infanterie-Regiments. Koblenz,* 1857

Gaston Steigler, *Le Maréchal Oudinot,* Plon, Paris, 1894

E. de Stein, *Notice biographique sur M. le chevalier Jacquot (Claude), lieutenant-colonel,* Panthéon Universel, Paris, 1856

Eugene Tattet, *Lettres inédits du Maréchal Bugeaud, duc d'Isly (1808-1849) colligées et annotés par M. le Capitaine Tattet et publiées par Mademoiselle Féray-Bugeaud d'Isly,* Paris, Emile-Paul Freres, 1922

Pierre François Tissot, *Histoire de Napoléon, rédigée d'après les papiers d'État, les documents officiels, les mémoires et les notes secrètes de ses contemporains, suivie d'un précis sur la famille Bonaparte* (Vol. 2), Delange-Taffin, Paris, 1833

William Tomkinson, James Tomkinson, *The Diary of a Cavalry Officer in the Peninsular and Waterloo Campaigns 1809-1815*, S. Sonnenschein, London, 1894

Jean-Phillipe Tondeur, Patrice Courcelle, Jean Jacques Patyn, Paul Megnak, *Carnets de la Campagne No. 1—Hougoumont*, Tondeur Diffusion, Brussels, 1999

Jean-Phillipe Tondeur, Patrice Courcelle, Jean Jacques Patyn, Paul Megnak, *Carnets de la Campagne No. 10*—Editions de La Belle Alliance, 2007

Toussaint-Jean Trefcon, *Carnet de la campagne du colonel Trefcon, 1793-1815*, E. Dubois, Paris, 1914

Frédéric François Guillaume Vaudoncourt, *Histoire des campagnes de 11814 et 1815, en France*, Chez A. de Gastel, Paris, 1826

Achille de Vaulabelle, *Campagne et bataille de Waterloo*, Perrotin, Paris, 1845

J. B. du Vergier, *Collection complète des lois, décrets, ordonnances, réglements, et avis du Conseil d'Etat*, Guyot et Scribe, Paris, 1827

August Wagner, *Plane der Schlachten und Treffen, welche von der Preussischen Armee in den Feldzügen der Jahre 1813, 14 und 15 geliefert worden* (Vol. 4), Reimer, Berlin, 1825

Hans Wellmann, *Geschichte des Infanterie-Regiments von Horn (3-tes Rheinisches) N. 29*, Lintzcher Verlag, Trier, 1894

Periodicals:

Braunschweig Magazin
Bulletin des Lois
Caledonian Mercury
Carnet de la Sabretache
Correspondent du Paris
Derby Mercury
Dublin University Magazine
English Historical Review
Feuilles d'Histoire
Glasgow Herald
Globe Illustré
Hereford Times

Historiche Beilage
Hull Packet
Journal de l'Empire
Journal de Paris
Journal de Rouen
Journal de Toulouse
Journal des débats politiques et littéraires
Journal Militaire
Leeds Mercury
Middleton Albion
Monde Illustré
Moniteur de l'Armée
Napoléon
Nieuwe Militaire Spectator
Nottinghamshire Guardian
Nouvelle Revue Retrospective
Pall Mall Gazette
Revue de l'Empire
Revue de Paris
Revue Etudes Napoléoniennes
Revue Hebdomadaire
Revue historique des Armées
Sentinalle de l'armée
Souvenir Napoléonien
The Times
Traditions Magazine
United Service Magazine

Websites:

15th or King's Light Dragoons (Hussars) Historial Re-enactment Group, *Battle of Waterloo 1815*, XVLD, 2014, available at http://www.xvld.org/waterloo-1815.html [accessed 1 November 2011].

Martin Aaron, *2nd Battalion 69th (South Lincolnshire) Foot during the Waterloo Campaign*, The Napoleon Series, October 2007, available at

519

http://www.napoleon-series.org/military/organization/Britain/Infantry/c_2-69Waterloo.html [accessed 22 August 2012].

Anon, *50e Regiment d'Infanterie de Ligne Historique 1803-1815*, ancestramil, available at http://www.ancestramil.fr/uploads/01_doc/terre/infanterie/1789-1815/50_ri_historique_1803-1816.pdf [accessed 11 February 2013].

Marco Bijl, *History and Organisation of the Dutch 8th Militia Battalion*, The Napoleon Series, June 2008, available at http://www.napoleon-series.org/military/organization/Dutch/8thMilitia/c_8thMilitia1.html [accessed 4 January 2012].

Paul L. Dawson, *Memoires: Fact or Fiction? The Campaign of 1814*, The Napoleon Series, December 2013, available at http://www.napoleon-series.org/research/eyewitness/c_memoires.html [accessed 28 February 2017]

Project Hougoumont, *Defence of Hougoumont*, Project Hougoumont, 2016, available at https://projecthougoumont.com/defence-of-hougoumont/ [accessed 11 February 2017].

Index

Subervie, 163–64, 166, 252, 321, 339, 345
Sub-Lieutenant Achille Carimantrand, 287
Sub-Lieutenant Ambroise Sault, 263
Sub-Lieutenant Anselme Felix Paul Normand, 77
Sub-Lieutenant Antoine Faustin Renaud, 172
Sub-Lieutenant Antoine Florentin Moutardier, 287
Sub-Lieutenant Arnoux, 400
Sub-Lieutenant Augustin Louis Pierre Perardel, 172
Sub-Lieutenant Bretet, 332
Sub-Lieutenant Charles Benjamin Robinot, 170
Sub-Lieutenant Charles Louis Urbain Acier, 287
Sub-Lieutenant Combescue, 38
Sub-Lieutenant Corneille Joseph Frankard, 200
Sub-Lieutenant Degueus, 86
Sub-Lieutenant Delale, 260
Sub-Lieutenant Desereinnes and Lieutenant Macrez, 189
Sub-Lieutenant Detchemendy, 54
Sub-Lieutenant Dominique Botte, 39
Sub-lieutenant Dormoy, 331
Sub-Lieutenant Dumoulin, 38
Sub-Lieutenant Etienne Cronnier, 40
Sub-Lieutenant Fleury Brossette, 229
Sub-Lieutenant François Celu, 40
Sub-Lieutenant François Fitu, 86
Sub-Lieutenant Gervais Hanin, 191

Sub-Lieutenant Gorget, 40
Sub-Lieutenant Gouvoine, 37
Sub-Lieutenant Guillaume Dessaux, 128
Sub-Lieutenant Guillemin, 37
Sub-Lieutenant Henri Fleurus Olivier, 276
Sub-Lieutenant Henry Joseph Mathieu, 175
Sub-Lieutenant Herbillon, 292–93
Sub-Lieutenant Humbert, 332
Sub-lieutenant Jacob, 38
Sub-Lieutenant Jacques Griou, 260
Sub-Lieutenant Jacques Louis Levacher, 102
Sub-Lieutenant Jean Antoine Azaret Scevola Anthouard, 266
Sub-Lieutenant Jean Baptiste Barre, 99
Sub-Lieutenant Jean Baptiste Millet, 40
Sub-Lieutenant Jean Baptiste Peres, 85
Sub-Lieutenant Jean Bezian, 291
Sub-Lieutenant Jean Claude Xavier LeRoy, 85
Sub-Lieutenant Jean Fleury, 125
Sub-Lieutenant Jean François, 128
Sub-Lieutenant Jean Laurent, 259
Sub-Lieutenant Jean Laurent Martin Simon Litti, 255, 262
Sub-Lieutenant Jean Louis Mayeux, 102
Sub-Lieutenant Jeanne Marie Verrand, 123
Sub-Lieutenant Jean Pierre Moutard, 170